D1561034

George P. Davis'

Massachusetts Conveyancers' Handbook with Forms

FOURTH EDITION

By
EDWARD C. MENDLER
of the Boston Bar

THOMSON

WEST

For Customer Assistance Call 1-800-328-4880

This publication was created to provide you with accurate and authoritative information concerning the subject matter covered; however, this publication was not necessarily prepared by persons licensed to practice law in a particular jurisdiction. The publisher is not engaged in rendering legal or other professional advice and this publication is not a substitute for the advice of an attorney. If you require legal or other expert advice, you should seek the services of a competent attorney or other professional.

ISBN # 978-0-314-98857-7

PREFACE

This Fourth Edition of the Massachusetts Conveyancers' Handbook came into being for a number of reasons. In the first place, the Cumulative Supplement to the Third Edition had reached an unwieldy thickness of nearly half an inch. Besides the physical constraints, the contents of that Supplement had extensively supplemented, revised, and in some respects even changed or overruled, the contents of the volume itself. It is, of course, the purpose and function of such a supplement to keep a law book abreast of developments and changes, but there are practical limits.

The developments and changes in law and the practice thereof—in Massachusetts and elsewhere—have been substantial and significant since 1984 when the Third Edition was published, and real estate law and practice have not been immune from the phenomena. Nevertheless, most of the fundamentals of real estate law are of hoary origin, and they are not forgotten in this volume, but are restated in light of the changes in law and practice that have occurred.

In bringing the Massachusetts Conveyancers' Handbook up to date, I have sought not only to incorporate the changes effected in the past 25 years by statutes and judicial decisions, as well as to recognize the changes wrought by the hectic pace of today's practice and the prevalence of electronic aids, but also to improve the presentation of the materials.

In this Fourth Edition, the organization of chapters and sections and of the subjects therein has been rationalized to associate related matters to each other, with many cross-references. There are entirely new or greatly expanded chapters and sections on many subjects, including possessory titles and prescription, servitudes, comprising easements and restrictions, Land Court jurisdiction, the new forms of title insurance policies, various types of governmental regulations affecting real estate transactions, historic preservation, and homeowners associations and time-shares, as well as cooperatives and condominiums. The chapters on zoning, subdivision control and environmental controls continue to grow—for reasons familiar to all real estate practitioners.

The text of the book has been rewritten throughout, and I have endeavored to make it "readable" to the extent that is possible in an expository law book. My aim has been to make the book more usable and useful as a learning and teaching resource for lawyers—and others in various fields of real estate business or governmental regulation—who seek to gain or expand a general knowledge of real estate law and practice.

At the same time, the other purpose of the book—as a reference to particular points and to the statutory and judicial sources of principles and precepts of real estate law and practice—has not been forgotten or ignored. Actually, an attempt has been made to reduce and "modernize" the case citations themselves. In some instances, the asserted propositions are now so well established that case citation is no longer necessary. In other instances, a cited case of recent years will itself refer to the earlier cases. Also, detailed citation of statutory sections has been eliminated for the simple reason that there is no substitute for reading the statute itself—and no excuse not to! Recognizing the importance of the Land Court in interpreting and applying principles of real estate law, and often contributing new developments thereto, I continue to cite many Land Court cases, using the Land Court Reporter (L.C.R.) system published by LandLaw, Inc. 675 VFW Parkway #354, Chestnut Hill, MA 02467.

Finally, the forms in the appendices have themselves been modernized, replacing old forms with new ones.

Notwithstanding all the "modernization," this Fourth Edition remains a "conveyancers" book, aimed at preserving the art of conveyancing among real estate lawyers, some of whom nowadays focus exclusively on the business aspects of real estate practice and pay too little attention to "conveyancing." While it is our clients' personal or business goals that we are engaged to serve, it is this author's opinion that carelessness or inattention to the details of proper conveyancing often frustrate the fulfillment of those goals. In reviewing cases for the annual supplements for so many years since 1984, I have always noted the great number of law suits that arose from poor drafting of instruments and inattention to possible or likely consequences of carelessly drafted provisions. It is, of course, not the archaic arts of "conveyancing" as such that I seek to promote, but rather the recognition by real estate lawyers that the drafting of instruments related in any way to the transfer of title to or interests in real estate needs to be done with care and a full understanding of the applicable laws, statutory and common, that govern such transfers. In order to achieve the client's goal, you have to know *how* to achieve it.

In adhering to that principle, I honor the memory of George P. Davis, who originated the concept of the Massachusetts Conveyancers' Handbook in the First Edition of 1956 and Second Edition of 1967. While most of George Davis' actual words, as well as a good deal of mine in the Third Edition, have now disappeared, it remains true that this book would not exist without his having led the way. I must also mention that Robert A. Fishman was the author of the chapter on Environmental Controls in the Third Edition, and without that I would not have been able to write the chapter on that subject in the present volume. However, this Fourth Edition is entirely my work, and I take full responsibility for any errors that may exist.

The research and review of law necessary for this book was conducted by me largely through the electronic marvels of access to the data bases of the Massachusetts Social Law Library, for which I am very grateful. When the occasion arose for me to place my hands on an actual law book, I did so in the Boston law library of Nutter, McClennen & Fish, LLP, and I am grateful to my former partners for that opportunity also. My gratitude is also due and given to Jenny Mockenhaupt, Principal Attorney Editor at Thomson-West, who encouraged me to produce this Fourth Edition and abided with my hesitations and delays, and to Kathy O'Dell, Principal Attorney Editor, and Susan Campean, Senior Publishing Specialist at Thomson-West, who saw the project through its final stages to actual production of the book.

Forms and information for the text and the appendices were kindly furnished by:

1. The Greater Boston Real Estate Board (GBREB), whose copyrighted forms may be obtained from it at www.gbreb.com or 11 Beacon Street, Boston, MA 02108. Appendices A, B, C and D are GBREB forms, subject to its copyrights, kindly provided by it.

2. The American Land Title Association (ALTA), whose copyrighted forms may be obtained from it at www.alta.org or 1828 L Street, Washington, D.C. 20036-5104. Appendices G, H, I, J and K are ALTA forms, subject to its copyrights, kindly provided by it.

3. The Real Estate Bar Association for Massachusetts (REBA), whose copyrighted Title Standards, Practice Standards, Ethical Standards and Forms are available to members of REBA, may be contacted at www.reba.net or 50 Congress Street, Suite 600, Boston, MA 02109-4075.

REBA kindly provided me with electronic copies of its materials, and there are many references throughout this book to Title Standards, Practice Standards, Ethical Standards and Forms promulgated by REBA.

Although I am now substantially retired from the practice of law, my hope and expectation is that I will provide annual supplements for this new Fourth Edition for many years into the future. As a postscript, let me note that by Chapter 19 of the Acts of 2007 the Massachusetts legislature reorganized and renamed several executive offices and departments of the Massachusetts government. Since most of this book was written before that Act became available for review, the changes are not reflected herein. Insofar as such changes prove to be significant to the subjects of this book, recognizing them will become task no. 1 for the first supplement, which will cover developments since May 2007 when the research for this volume was completed.

EDWARD C. MENDLER
Wayland, Massachusetts
April 2008

I Think that I shall Never see
  A Leasehold lovely as a Fee;

A Fee to Have, a Fee to Hold,
  Devised by Noble Men of Old;

A Fee in Tenure of the Crown,
  Which Lords did give Condign Reknown;

A Fee Estate, one held in Tail,
  As Holy as the Holy Grail;

A Fee conditioned on an Act,
  By Right of Entry firmly backed;

A Fee so long as Ye take care,
  And then Revert to Grantor's Heir;

A Fee in Simple Absolute,
  Beyond Cavil, beyond Dispute.

Ah, once a Man has been Enfeoffed,
  What Treasure still could Life have left?

ecm 12/27/1961

WESTLAW ELECTRONIC RESEARCH GUIDE

Westlaw—Expanding the Reach of Your Library

Westlaw is West's online legal research service. With Westlaw, you experience the same quality and integrity that you have come to expect from West books, plus quick, easy access to West's vast collection of statutes, case law materials, public records, and other legal resources, in addition to current news articles and business information. For the most current and comprehensive legal research, combine the strengths of West books and Westlaw.

When you research with westlaw.com you get the convenience of the Internet combined with comprehensive and accurate Westlaw content, including exclusive editorial enhancements, plus features found only in westlaw.com such as ResultsPlus™ or StatutesPlus™.

Accessing Databases Using the Westlaw Directory

The Westlaw Directory lists all databases on Westlaw and contains links to detailed information relating to the content of each database. Click Directory on the westlaw.com toolbar. There are several ways to access a database even when you don't know the database identifier. Browse a directory view. Scan the directory. Type all or part of a database name in the Search these Databases box. The Find a Database Wizard can help you select relevant databases for your search. You can access up to ten databases at one time for user-defined multibase searching.

Retrieving a Specific Document

To retrieve a specific document by citation or title on westlaw.com click **Find** on the toolbar to display the Find a Document page. If you are unsure of the correct citation format, type the publication abbreviation, e.g., **xx st** (where xx is a state's two-letter postal abbreviation), in the Enter Citation box and click **Go** to display a fill-in-the-blank template. To retrieve a specific case when you know one or more parties' names, click **Find by Title**.

KeyCite®

KeyCite, the citation research service on Westlaw, makes it easy to trace the history of your case, statute, administrative decision or regulation to determine if there are recent updates, and to find other documents that cite your document. KeyCite will also find pending legislation relating to federal or state statutes. Access the powerful features of KeyCite from the westlaw.com toolbar, the **Links** tab, or KeyCite flags in a document display. KeyCite's red and yellow warning flags tell you at a glance whether your document has negative history. Depth-of-treatment stars help you focus on the most important citing references. KeyCite Alert allows you to monitor the status of your case, statute or rule, and automatically sends you updates at the frequency you specify.

ResultsPlus™

ResultsPlus is a Westlaw technology that automatically suggests additional information related to your search. The suggested materials are accessible by a set of links that appear to the right of your westlaw.com search results:

- Go directly to relevant ALR® articles and Am Jur® annotations.

- Find on-point resources by key number.

- See information from related treatises and law reviews.

StatutesPlus™

When you access a statutes database in westlaw.com you are brought to a powerful Search Center which collects, on one toolbar, the tools that are most useful for fast, efficient retrieval of statutes documents:

- Have a few key terms? Click **Index**.

- Know the common name? Click **Popular Name Table**.

- Familiar with the subject matter? Click **Table of Contents**.

- Have a citation or section number? Click **Find by Citation**.

- Or, simply search with **Natural Language** or **Terms and Connectors**.

When you access a statutes section, click on the **Links** tab for all relevant links for the current document that will also include a

KeyCite section with a description of the KeyCite status flag. Depending on your document, links may also include administrative, bill text, and other sources that were previously only available by accessing and searching other databases.

Additional Information

Westlaw is available on the Web at www.westlaw.com.

For search assistance, call the West Reference Attorneys at 1-800-REF-ATTY (1-800-733-2889).

For technical assistance, call West Customer Technical Support at 1-800-WESTLAW (1-800-937-8529).

RELATED PRODUCTS FROM WEST

STATUTES AND COURT RULES

Massachusetts General Laws Annotated
Massachusetts Court Rules—State, Local and Federal
United States Code Annotated

CASE LAW, REPORTERS, DIGESTS, ATTORNEY GENERAL OPINIONS

Massachusetts Digest
Massachusetts Law Finder
Northeastern Reporter

GENERAL LEGAL REFERENCES

Corpus Juris Secundum

MASSACHUSETTS DATABASES ON WESTLAW

Cases, General & Topical
Statutes and Index
Legislative Service
Legislative History & Bill Tracking
Administrative & Executive Materials
Court Rules
Jury Instructions & Jury Verdicts
Trial Court Filings
BNA Corporate Practice Portfolios
Workers' Compensation Materials Combined

Westlaw State Bulletins
West Legal Directory
Massachusetts Practice Series

CD-ROM

Massachusetts General Laws Annotated
Massachusetts Decisions
Massachusetts Digest CD-ROM Edition
Massachusetts Practice Series Premise CD-ROM
United States Code Annotated
West's Supreme Court Reporter
Federal Reporter, 1st, 2d, and 3d Series
Federal Supplement
Federal Rules Decisions
Wright & Miller, Federal Practice and Procedure
Topical CD-ROM Libraries

PRACTICE AND PROCEDURE

Talty, Talty and Braunstein, Methods of Practice with Forms
Smith and Zobel, Rules Practice
Nolan and Henry, Civil Practice
Rodman, Procedural Forms Annotated
Randall and Franklin, Municipal Law and Practice
Savery, Corso and Harrington, Federal Civil Practice
Lauriat, McChesney, Gordon and Rainer, Discovery
Alperin, Summary of Basic Law
Bishop, Prima Facie Case—Proof and Defense
Swartz, Trial Handbook for Massachusetts Lawyers

CRIMINAL LAW AND PRACTICE

Smith, Criminal Practice and Procedure
Nolan and Sartorio, Criminal Law
Nadel and Witkin, Criminal Defense Motions
Lauriat, McChesney, Gordon and Rainer, Discovery
Bishop, Prima Facie Case—Proof and Defense
Jones, Drunk Driving Defense

TRIAL AND APPELLATE PRACTICE

Nolan and Caldeira, Appellate Procedure
Flanagan, Trial Practice
Swartz, Trial Handbook for Massachusetts Lawyers

DAMAGES AND REMEDIES

Nolan and Sartorio, Equitable Remedies
Alperin and Chase, Consumer Law
Shapiro, Perlin and Connors, Collection Law

ADMINISTRATIVE LAW

Cella, Administrative Law and Practice

MUNICIPAL LAW

Randall and Franklin, Municipal Law and Practice

DOMESTIC RELATIONS

Kindregan and Inker, Family Law and Practice with Forms

PERSONAL INJURY

Nolan and Sartorio, Tort Law

HEALTH LAW

Minehan and Kantrowitz, Mental Health Law

PROBATE AND JUVENILE LAW

Dunphy, Probate Law and Practice with Forms

Annino, Estate Planning with Forms

Ireland, Juvenile Law

Belknap, Newhall's Settlement of Estates and Fiduciary Law in Massachusetts

BUSINESS ORGANIZATIONS

Polubinski, Business Corporations with Forms

Lemelman, Manual on Uniform Commercial Code

Lemelman, Uniform Commercial Code Forms Annotated

Shapiro, Perlin and Connors, Collection Law

Gilleran, The Law of Chapter 93A

EVIDENCE

Young, Pollets and Poreda, Evidence

Young, Pollets and Poreda, Evidentiary Standards

REAL ESTATE

Eno and Hovey, Real Estate Law with Forms

Daher and Chopp, Landlord and Tenant Law with Forms

Mendler, Massachusetts Conveyancers' Handbook with Forms

LEGAL FORMS

West's Legal Forms, 2d

Hovey and Koenig, Legal Forms

Rodman, Procedural Forms Annotated

Doniger and Truesdell, Massachusetts Litigation Forms and Analysis

MOTOR VEHICLES

Kenny and Farris, Motor Vehicle Law and Practice with Forms

Jones, Drunk Driving Defense

TAXATION

Bailey and Van Dorn, Taxation

EMPLOYMENT AND LABOR LAW

Moriearty, Adkins, Rubin and Jackson, Employment Law

Adkins, Rodriques, Rubin and Harrison, Employment Law Statutes and Regulations

Nason, Koziol and Wall, Workers' Compensation

Finn and McCarthy, Mediation and Arbitration

CONSUMER LAW

Alperin and Chase, Consumer Law

Gilleran, The Law of Chapter 93A

PROFESSIONAL MALPRACTICE

Jacobs and Laurence, Professional Malpractice

If you would like to inquire about these West publications or place an order, please call 1–800–344–5009.

West
610 Opperman Drive
Eagan, MN 55123

Visit West on the Internet:
http://west.thomson.com

Table of Contents

PART III. DETERMINING THE STATUS OF USABILITY

CHAPTER 11. ZONING 207

Index

Part I

MAKING AND ENFORCING AN AGREEMENT AFFECTING REAL ESTATE

Chapter 1

Purchase and Sale Agreement

TOPIC A: FORMS OF AGREEMENT

TOPIC B: PARTIES

TOPIC C: PROPERTY DESCRIPTION

TOPIC D: FORM OF DEED

TOPIC E: ENCUMBRANCES

KeyCite®: Cases and other legal materials listed in KeyCite Scope can be researched through the KeyCite service on Westlaw®. Use KeyCite to check citations for form, parallel references, prior and later history, and comprehensive citator information, including citations to other decisions and secondary materials.

TOPIC A: FORMS OF AGREEMENT

§ 1:1 Residence

For simple residential transactions printed forms of

purchase and sale agreement are often used, including primarily that published by the Greater Boston Real Estate Board (GBREB).[1] The standard clauses (or boiler plate) in that form are well established as the Massachusetts norm, and are usually found in other printed forms and in the word processing forms now widely used by many law firms.

§ 1:2 Condominium unit

GBREB publishes a form intended for use in condominium unit sales, containing provisions adapted for condominium requirements, but lawyers often use standard forms and include their own adaptations. Other aspects of condominium unit sales, including provisions for a purchase and sale agreement, are discussed in § **17:17**.

§ 1:3 Massachusetts custom

The customary approach in Massachusetts has long been for all requirements essential to consummation of the transaction to be set forth as conditions of the buyer's obligation, but not as affirmative obligations or warranties of the seller to fulfill. The buyer makes his own investigations and determinations as to sufficiency of the title, compliance with zoning laws, building code, environmental regulations, etc., and if the premises do not conform to the conditions of the agreement, the buyer may cancel and have his deposit refunded, but the seller is not liable to cure or correct any deficiencies. The form of purchase and sale agreement promulgated by REBA (Form 21) differs in some respects, but sets forth provisions and procedures which are acceptable to many Massachusetts attorneys.

§ 1:4 Commercial and complex

For commercial transactions, as well as for residential or land deals involving complexities (which are not at all uncommon), purchase and sale agreements often arise as the products of a word processing form used by the Seller's attorney as his office norm. In most cases these follow the Massachusetts approach as described above, but the provisions in such agreements are as a rule heavily negotiated, and there is an increasing tendency to include representations and affirmative obligations of the seller. That approach is

---

[Section 1:1]

[1]See **Appendix A, GBREB Standard Form of Purchase and** **Sale Agreement**. Copyright by GBREB.

customary in New York and elsewhere, and there are of course many circumstances in which seller representations and obligations are warranted, especially when the seller or seller's attorney has knowledge of prior permitting, environmental testing, and the like, which would be burdensome for a buyer to duplicate independently. The GBREB form of Commercial Purchase and Sale Agreement incorporates a number of such seller warranties.

It should be noted that an agreement can arise from or be comprised in several separate documents.[1]

§ 1:5 Due diligence

It is always important, however, for the lawyers on both sides of the transaction to be clear about the distinction between conditions of performance and actionable obligations. And especially in light of the demise of *caveat emptor* as a governing rule of law, a buyer's attorney should never regard a seller's representations, however detailed and firmly stated, as a substitute for thorough "due diligence" investigation.

§ 1:6 Exchange

A special circumstance that sometimes arises is the desire of a seller to affect a tax free exchange under § 1031 of the Internal Revenue Code. In that case the purchase and sale agreement should contain an express reference thereto and provision that the conveyance of the property shall be made through a Qualified Intermediary and in accordance with applicable IRS regulations. The buyer may request, and is ordinarily entitled to, a provision to the effect that the seller will indemnify and hold the buyer harmless against and from any liability arising out of the exchange. The Seller needs also of course to enter into a "like kind exchange agreement" with a qualified intermediary of seller's choice, assigning the purchase and sale agreement to the intermediary and making provision for selection of the exchange property and application of proceeds of the basic sale to the purchase

---

[Section 1:4]
[1]Imper Realty Corp. v. Riss,   358 Mass. 529, 265 N.E.2d 594 (1970).

thereof, all in compliance with the IRS rules.

TOPIC B: PARTIES

§ 1:7   Names; nominees

Sellers' names should be given as they appear in the instrument by which they acquired title, reciting such changes as may be appropriate, including change of an individual's name by marriage or legal action, or amendment of a corporate or other business name. Agreements have been held enforceable when signed by a husband acting as agent for his wife,[1] and when signed by a "straw" acting for a principal.[2] A signature by an individual "dba" a named business was held binding on him and not the corporation of that name of which he was president and treasurer.[3] In light of the Uniform Electronic Transactions Act, M.G.L.A. c. 110G, care should be taken in formulating a purchase and sale agreement by e-mail.

A buyer's name should ordinarily be specified in the form in which the buyer intends to take title. The named buyer is the party to whom the seller may look for payment of the purchase price or for damages in the event of breach, and it is obviously an error to name the buyer as "John Jones or nominee."

However, a nominee clause permitting the contractual buyer to designate another party to take title in his stead is sometimes important to a buyer and acceptable to seller. If there is to be purchase money financing, the seller will ordinarily require the buyer to be the maker or guarantor of the note, while the mortgage securing it will be executed by the nominee. Provisions to that effect should be clearly set forth in the agreement.[4] If these parties are corporations, there may be problems of authority, and these should also be carefully considered and dealt with when the agreement is drafted. A seller may also wish to eliminate or limit a nominee clause in circumstances where the seller retains a repurchase option, first refusal or other continuing interest in the premises being sold, or in adjoining properties such as

---

[Section 1:7]

[1]Campbell v. Olender, 27 Mass. App. Ct. 1197, 543 N.E.2d 708 (1989).

[2]Kelly v. Cucchiella, 26 Mass. App. Ct. 983, 529 N.E.2d 411 (1988).

[3]Pedersen v. Leahy, 397 Mass. 689, 493 N.E.2d 486 (1986).

[4]Lee v. Ravanis, 349 Mass. 742, 212 N.E.2d 480 (1965).

lots in a subdivision or condominium units.

§ 1:8   Corporation (as to which and other business entities, see Chapter 16, Topic B)

Corporate names may be found in a state publication of "Massachusetts Corporations and Foreign Corporations Subject to an Excise." For the correct name of a charitable corporation it may be necessary to consult records of the Division of Public Charities. The correct name of a corporation misstated in an agreement may in some circumstances be shown by extrinsic evidence.[1] An agreement of a corporation to sell land of its subsidiary, parent or affiliate is not acceptable.[2] The fact of incorporation may be evidenced by a Certificate of Legal Existence from the Office of the Secretary of State.

Under M.G.L.A. c. 156D, § 8.46 and c. 180, § 10C, a purchase and sale agreement (as well as a deed) of a corporation is binding if signed by the president or vice president and the treasurer or an assistant treasurer, who may be one and the same person. This applies to foreign corporations qualified to do business in Massachusetts as well as to domestic corporations organized under M.G.L.A. c. 155, c. 156A, c. 156B or c. 180, but not to corporations organized under other Massachusetts statutes or special acts. Nevertheless it is advisable as a matter of procedure for the signatory officers to be in fact authorized to act by vote of their board of directors, and buyers' lawyers often insist upon obtaining a certificate of such a vote.

When a corporation sells a major fraction of its assets, a vote adopted by the holders of at least two-thirds of its voting stock is necessary.[3] The statute refers to a sale or mortgage of "all or substantially all its property and assets, including its good will," but the cases make it clear that the requirements of the statute apply to sale or mortgage of less than all of the assets, providing that a substantial or vitally important portion of the assets is involved.[4] While a deed executed by the president or a vice president and the treasurer or an assistant treasurer may be effective to convey even

---

[Section 1:8]

[1]Simpionbato v. Royal Ins. Co., 253 Mass. 606, 149 N.E. 666 (1925); Coken Co., Inc. v. Department of Public Works, 9 Mass. App. Ct. 586, 402 N.E.2d 1110 (1980).

[2]Elm Farm Foods Co. v. Cifrino, 328 Mass. 549, 105 N.E.2d 366 (1952).

[3]M.G.L.A. c. 156D, § 12.02.

[4]Susser v. Cambria Chocolate Co., 300 Mass. 1, 13 N.E.2d 609 (1938); McDonald v. First Nat. Bank, 70 F.2d 69 (C.C.A. 1st Cir. 1934).

substantially all the corporate assets without such a stockholder vote, it will not convey the premises free of the corporate excise tax lien imposed by M.G.L.A. c. 62C, § 51. Consequently, the prudent conveyancer will generally make investigation of the corporate assets, and applying a practical test, if more than half of the Massachusetts real estate of the corporation is to be conveyed, will require a stockholder vote and a waiver of the corporate excise tax lien, usually to be provided by the selling corporation's attorney.

In substantial transactions, it is always advisable for the buyer's counsel to obtain true copies of the seller's corporate charter, articles of organization and by-laws, certification of the identity of the incumbent officers and certificates of the clerk or secretary of the corporation of any votes of the stockholders, board of directors or executive committee authorizing the transaction. The by-laws should be reviewed to determine that the votes have been adopted at the proper level and that any special requirements have been met.

§ 1:9 LLC

If the seller is a limited liability company, the buyer's attorney should obtain a certificate of good standing and review the certificate of organization. If these documents name persons authorized to execute document affecting real estate, that may be relied upon, but if not, specific action by the managers or members may be needed.[1]

§ 1:10 Partnership

A partnership may be identified by its own distinctive name or by the names of its general partners, designated as such. If two or more persons are identified as "doing business as" (dba) a named "company" or named "associates", that ordinarily imports a partnership. The statutory rules for determining the existence of a partnership are quite explicit. The term "joint venture" usually refers to a partnership formed for a particular purpose or venture. In order to be sure that a partnership is bound, one may generally rely upon the common law principles of mutual agency and apparent authority, but the specific provisions of M.G.L.A. c. 108A, § 10 must be carefully considered, and one would not be remiss to seek an opinion of the partnership's counsel as to its existence and the authority of the signing partner.

[Section 1:9]

[1]See REBA Title Standard 59.

Where the partnership is a seller, the deed by which it acquired title may be examined to confirm its name and those of its partners, and then inquiry of the selling parties may be made as to any changes.[1]

A limited partnership is a statutory, rather than a common law entity. In dealing with a limited partnership the conveyancer will usually need to consider both the partnership agreement and the certificate of limited partnership filed with the office of the secretary of state, as well as the statutory provisions. A foreign limited partnership may act in Massachusetts, provided that it is duly qualified to do business and has met related requirements.

A limited liability partnership (LLP) is also a statutory creature, and as with respect to an LLC, a buyer's attorney should examine the filings with the Secretary of State and determine who is authorized to execute instruments affecting real estate.[2]

§ 1:11   Fiduciaries

Fiduciaries come in several types, and there are different considerations for different types.

§ 1:12   Power of sale

Executors under a will which confers upon them a general power to sell real estate may do so without a court license, and their deed will convey to a bona fide purchaser for value a title free from claims of general creditors of the testator and of legatees and devisees under the will, as stated in REBA Title Standard 10. If there is any doubt about such things as the scope of the power of sale, the "arms-length" status of the buyer or the adequacy of the price, a license should be required.

§ 1:13   Court license

For sales by executors which cannot meet the foregoing tests, and any sale by an administrator, guardian or conservator, a license should be required, and buyer's counsel is well advised to review the appointments and the applicable provisions of M.G.L.A. c. 201 and c. 202 before the purchase and sale agreement is finalized. When a license is needed, the buyer should seek a provision requiring diligent efforts to obtain it, and seller will wish to make it clear that it has

---

[Section 1:10]

[1]See REBA Title Standards

37 and 44.

[2]See REBA Title Standard 60.

no obligation other than return of the deposit if the license is not granted. See § **6:33**.

§ 1:14 Trustees

The rules for trustees under a will are like those for executors. For trustees under a written instrument it is also important to review the terms of the instrument as to their powers. Unless otherwise provided, all of the trustees must sign, and it should be determined that there are no vacancies in the office which the will or instrument requires to be filled. In certain circumstances courts have allowed deviations from these strict rules, but that does not warrant any laxity in drafting an agreement.

The rule that a foreign trustee has no authority to convey land in another state except where permitted by statute has been softened by statute in Massachusetts.[1]

If the trust instrument (or any amendments) have not been recorded, the original trust instrument and all amendments should be examined; and the agreement should provide that the original trust instrument and amendments will be recorded at or prior to the time of passing papers. It is preferable that such recording be in the registry of deeds where the land lies; but, in the case of lengthy trust instruments intended to be used in several counties, it may be acceptable if the original trust instrument and all amendments are recorded in a registry of deeds in Massachusetts with an appropriate cross-reference thereto being made in the agreement and deed. However, that practice may not be acceptable with respect to registered land.

If the trust is established by a declaration or deed of trust, care should be exercised to see that the trust is described by reference to the date of the instrument creating it and the recording data. If the trust is described only by name it may well be the case that the trustees are not protected from individual liability, and also that the buyer is not entitled to specific performance. Designation of a person as "trustee" without setting forth the terms of the trust or specifying the place in the public records where the instrument which sets forth such terms is recorded constitutes an "indefinite reference" against which a purchaser who is not subject to or on notice of such terms is afforded statutory protection. Many trusts contain provision that third parties dealing with the

---

[Section 1:14]

[1]M.G.L.A. c. 202, §§ 32, 33; Assessors of Everett v. Albert N. Parlin House, Inc., 331 Mass. 359, 118 N.E.2d 861 (1954).

trustees may rely without inquiry on acts of the trustees or certification of their own authority, and generally these provisions may be honored.

The "curative" provisions of M.G.L.A. c. 184, §§ 24, 25 and 34, discussed in § **10:22**, may sometimes serve to patch up or save a transaction, but again that is no warrant for laxity in diligence and careful drafting.

A Massachusetts Business Trust is in many respects like a corporation (as discussed in § **16:13**), but title to its property resides in the trustees, not the entity, and it must be dealt with as a trust. A Nominee Trust (also discussed in § **16:15**) is sometimes also held out as if it were an entity, but specific authorization by the beneficiaries for actions by the trustees is necessary. It is customary to require a Trustees' Certificate to be recorded, backed up by a Beneficiaries' Certificate which is not recorded.[2] Reliance on a "bootstrap" clause is not a good idea.

With respect to an agreement by a Trust constituting the organization of unit owners of a Condominium, there are special statutory requirements, discussed in **Topic C of Chapter 17**.

§ 1:15 Body politic

Cities, towns, the Commonwealth of Massachusetts acting through various departments, commissions or agencies, and other governmental bodies are encountered as sellers or grantors and as purchasers with rather surprising frequency. This subject is discussed further in **Chapter 2**.

TOPIC C: PROPERTY DESCRIPTION

§ 1:16 Land and buildings

A binding agreement may be made without a detailed description of the premises if they are adequately identified by street address, common or characteristic name which could not refer to any other land. For simple transactions such minimal identification is often used and may be regarded as sufficient, at least if accompanied by an adequate title reference, specifying the Book and Page of the seller's deed. If the premises are shown on a fairly modern survey plan of rec-

---

[2]See REBA Forms 20a through   20h.

ord, then a reference thereto, specifying the caption, date, surveyor's name, lot number, and the Book and Page of recording will generally suffice. In fact, if there is such a plan and if the seller's title-source deed sets forth a proper description based thereon, it is probably preferable that that description not be set forth in the agreement for the simple reason that each transcription of a complex metes and bounds description is a new occasion for possible error.

When the purchase and sale agreement describes the premises by reference to plan and seller's title-source deed, the buyer generally still expects to, and does, receive a deed setting forth a full metes and bounds description. That results, however, from customary practice and comity among conveyancers, rather than from any principle of law. It is, therefore, desirable to provide expressly in the agreement that the deed will be so cast, or that it will be in a form reasonably satisfactory to buyer's counsel. If the agreement does set forth a detailed description, buyer's counsel should, by the same token, be sure that it is a proper one.

When no adequate description presents itself at the time of agreement, provision should be made for a new survey and for the deed to the buyer to be based thereon. The identification of the land may often be augmented by examination of and reference to municipal atlases or assessors' maps, which are now available for all or most of the urban areas of Massachusetts.

In addition to being adequate to meet contract and deed requirements, the buyer needs a description sufficient for determining compliance of the premises with applicable zoning provisions. The area and frontage of the lot, and the public or private status of the abutting way, are of course pertinent, and a plot plan showing building locations is often also needed. If the area, frontage or other pertinent dimensions are not certainly known at the time of the agreement, it may be important to the buyer to provide that he will not be bound to close unless specified sizes are met, as determined by survey. It is also very important to a seller to make the fact of uncertainty clear, since an overstatement of lot area, although not constituting a misrepresentation, did afford a basis of recovery to a buyer after closing under M.G.L.A. c. 93A relating to unfair trade practices.[1]

With respect to abutting ways, it is also important to make

[Section 1:16]

[1]Anzalone v. Strand, 14 Mass. App. Ct. 45, 436 N.E.2d 960 (1982).

clear whether or not the fee title therein goes with the land. Absent express exclusion, the fee title in an abutting way to the centerline will pass with a conveyance of the adjoining land. The same rule applies to abutting watercourses, stone fences and the like, and sometimes to railroad rights of way. (See § **15:4**)

Finally, it should not go unsaid that a contract description, however detailed and accurate in itself, is seriously defective if it does not describe the premises which the buyer thinks he is buying. The buyer's concept of the premises being purchased is often purely visual, and the words of metes and bounds may have little meaning to him. It is the task—a sometimes difficult one—of the conveyancer to be sure that the words and the mental picture do coincide.

§ 1:17   Condominium unit

The description of a condominium unit and references to the condominium documents in a purchase and sale agreement should track all of the requirements with respect to a deed of a condominium unit required by the statute, as discussed in § **17:18**. REBA has a form of Condominium Rider.[1]

§ 1:18   Appurtenances

If the property being sold has rights or easements appurtenant thereto, they will ordinarily remain appurtenant and pass with the land even if not mentioned in the agreement or the deed. Nevertheless, one acts at his peril in eschewing specific mention of appurtenances. If the land is described as fronting on Main Street, one might readily assume, but should not, that that is a public street. And if it is not, the existence of private rights therein appurtenant to the locus is a matter of primary importance to the buyer. Since the buyer will usually not have had the title examined at the time of agreement, he will wish to specify such an essential appurtenance as part of the property which the seller is obligated to convey. The seller will, of course, not wish to make the bargain contingent on his conveying more than he has, but the seller presumably has some knowledge of what the existing appurtenances are.

In addition to primary access easements, there are many other possible matters of interest as to appurtenances. Is

---

[Section 1:17]

[1]See REBA Form 21a.

there a secondary access? What other parcels share rights in appurtenant private easements, and are there limitations on the exercise thereof? Does locus have rights as a dominant estate of enforcement of restrictions on an adjacent servient estate? Are there easements of view or of light and air? Where do utilities enter the premises?

The circumstances of the transaction will establish the extent to which it is important to specify and define such appurtenances. In some instances there are valuable licenses, leases or contractual rights related to the locus which are not appurtenances running with the land and may be lost unless specifically covered by the purchase and sale agreement and assigned to the buyer.

§ 1:19 Fixtures; personal property

The distinction between fixtures and personal property is, as every law student learns, not always clear. Consequently, a broadly written clause is often advisable, "including without limitation" a long list of items, however prolix and redundant it may sound to the client. Items which are particularly included or excluded should be carefully specified.

In residential transactions sellers many times intend to retain and remove such items as certain lighting fixtures, sconces, wall mirrors or drapery hardware, which are fixtures and will pass with the real estate unless excluded by the agreement. Buyers on the other hand sometimes expect a refrigerator or other non-fixture to be included.

In a transaction involving commercial property one should consider also the inclusion or exclusion of maintenance equipment, cleaning machines, janitorial supplies and the like. In selling a tenanted building the distinction between tenant fixtures and landlord or building fixtures is important. The seller must take care not to purport to sell property belonging to his tenants. The buyer will wish to know whether such items as partitions, special heating, air-conditioning or lighting facilities or other improvements belong to the tenants or are to pass with the real estate.

An allocation of the purchase price among land, buildings, other depreciable property and personal property may be desirable for business, financing or tax reasons. This involves, of course, questions of reasonableness for negotiation between the parties and may involve questions of propriety of concern of the attorneys.[1]

TOPIC D: FORM OF DEED

§ 1:20   Quitclaim; warranty; fiduciary; release

The purchase and sale agreement should specify whether the deed to be delivered is to be a quitclaim deed, warranty deed, fiduciary deed, or release deed. The meanings of these terms, largely defined by statute, are set forth in § **19:2**. The most usual form is the statutory quitclaim deed. A warranty deed may be called for in special circumstances, but is now fairly rare in Massachusetts.

Sometimes it is useful or important to pre-draft the deed and provide in the agreement for delivery of a deed substantially in the form attached. That is particularly true when the property description is not well established on the record or when there are new provisions to be carried forward, such as restrictions, first refusal, etc.

If the seller is an executor, administrator, trustee, guardian or conservator, a "fiduciary deed without covenants" (which is in essence a release deed) is often preferred since executors, administrators and conservators do not hold title and their deeds convey the title of the decedent or ward, arguably making covenants by such fiduciaries inapt. Trustees and guardians, however, do hold title and may well make encumbrances thereon. Some trusts in fact are business entities, and there is no evident reason for their deeds to be without covenants. Indeed, statutory quitclaim deeds from trusts are the norm.

Aside from fiduciaries, when a seller proposes to give only a release deed, instead of a quitclaim deed, that often indicates some doubt on the seller's part as to how good and clear his title is.

For land registered under the land registration law the same forms of deed are used as referred to above. The description must contain correct references to the land court plan and certificate of title numbers and book and page of registration, and under that law a deed takes effect only upon acceptance thereof for registration. It is consequently customary for a purchase and sale agreement to require a

---

[Section 1:19]

[1]See REBA Ethical Standard
1.

14

deed in form sufficient to entitle the buyer to a new certificate of title.

TOPIC E: ENCUMBRANCES

§ 1:21 Introduction

A purchase and sale agreement will ordinarily provide for the seller to convey "a good and clear record and marketable title" which is "free from encumbrances" except such as are specifically referred to. The specific reference to existing encumbrances is most important to both parties. Title examination should turn up no surprises because when that happens it often leads to delays, extensions, further negotiations and sometimes compromises which annoy both the parties and their lawyers. The matters commonly encountered and dealt with as encumbrances which may continue to affect the buyer's title after closing are as follows:

§ 1:22 Real estate taxes

Real estate taxes are assessed for a fiscal year beginning July 1, and are payable in up to four installments. The assessment date is the previous January 1, but the actual assessments and the tax rate are often not available in many cities and towns until late summer. The installments for "preliminary tax," provided for in M.G.L.A. c. 59, § 57C, are due on August 1 and November 1, both deferred to the latter date if bills were not sent before August 1. The regular due dates are February 1 and May 1, and become delinquent and go on interest from the due dates if not paid within a month after those dates, provided that the delinquency dates are tolled to thirty days after mailing of the tax bills if they are sent out late. A seller will wish to require the buyer to "assume and agree to pay" taxes not yet payable, because these taxes are a personal liability of the property owner on the assessment date.

Special provision may be required with respect to land subject to a tax classification which involves a "conveyance tax" or a "rollback tax." See § 14:4, with respect to M.G.L.A. c. 61, 61A and 61B.

§ 1:23 Betterment assessments

A betterment assessment arises from an order for municipal improvements and a lien arises upon recording of the order. It is usual to provide that a buyer will take subject to liens for betterments assessed after the date of the agreement. However, a bill for the assessment will not be issued until the work is completed, and the assessment may then be added to the real estate tax bill on the affected premises. The owner at the time of assessment has the right to require the assessment to be billed in installments over a period of up to fifteen years. If a seller has not fully taken into account in the purchase price the value added to the premises by a municipal betterment, then he may deem it fair to pass along to the buyer the obligation to pay the assessment even though it arose before the sale. That is particularly so when a seller has exercised the election to pay the assessments in installments. Absent a specially negotiated clause, it might well come as a shock to the seller at closing that the deferred payments were then in effect due in full as a credit to the buyer. It is, of course, incumbent on seller's counsel to make inquiry about possible betterments prior to negotiating the agreement to avoid such an untoward situation.

§ 1:24   Water and other liens

Water rates, sewer use charges, and in some cases electric charges, generally become a lien if not paid when due. Buyers and sellers ordinarily contemplate the payment at or before closing of any such which have become due, and consequently it is not appropriate to make exception in a purchase and sale agreement for such liens. There are occasions on which such liens do exist and either the seller is to pay them off out of purchase money or the buyer is to take subject to them and to dispose of them himself, in which case the agreement should make express provision with respect thereto.

§ 1:25   Laws; regulations; orders

Although laws and regulations affecting the use or development of land, enacted or promulgated pursuant to the police power, do not constitute encumbrances as such on the affected land, they have a somewhat similar effect and are commonly dealt with in purchase and sale agreements in much the same manner as are continuing encumbrances. Zoning laws and building codes are of nearly universal application, and the agreement will usually provide that the buyer is not obligated to close unless the premises comply with such laws. This is particularly important because in many instances sufficient investigation of that matter will not have been made at the time of agreement. However, some prior review of the laws is essential if the buyer is to accept the usual clause stating that he is to take title subject to such laws as they exist at the time of agreement. Preferably, from the buyer's standpoint, the agreement will provide that the buyer's obligation to close is contingent upon a specified use's being permitted, and it may be desirable to state that such use is permitted as a matter of right and not by virtue of variance, special permit or pre-existing status. The seller, of course, will not wish to agree to a contingency with which the premises may not comply, and will often be unwilling to represent the zoning status of the premises. Faced with such conflicting positions, counsel to seller and buyer will of course negotiate vigorously, but will both be well served by devoting some of their efforts to a review of the applicable law and investigation of the status of the premises.

The status of many parcels, and particularly their rights of access to public ways, depends on compliance and performance under the subdivision control law, and consequently that is also a subject for at least preliminary investigation by a prospective buyer.

The wetland protection law and other environmental laws are now also of universal application and primary importance. Printed forms of purchase and sale agreement may not mention environmental laws specifically, and it is incumbent on counsel to insert properly drafted clauses. It should be noted that the procedure under the wetland protection law leads to the issuance of an order by a local conservation commission which is to be recorded. This does constitute an encumbrance, and the seller should make specific exception for it.

Two items are worthy of particular note. Whenever the property is served by an on-site sewage disposal system, a condition of compliance with requirements of Title 5 (§ **13:20**) should be included; **Appendix B** being the GBREB form. And in any situation where there is a risk or possibility of the presence of oil or hazardous substance (§ **13:18**), an inspection condition should be included; **Appendix C** being the GBREB form.

A number of other potentially applicable laws are discussed in **Chapter 14**, and a prudent buyer's attorney will review all of them.

§ 1:26 Easements (as to which, see Chapter 15, Topic B)

As to easements, a seller will wish to make his sale subject to rights of the public and to private rights of others in streets and ways abutting the premises, and the buyer will wish to specify that these are only rights to use the same "for purposes for which streets and ways are customarily used" in the community or for the purpose to which the property is devoted. This includes at least vehicular travel and installation of utilities. If the seller is a subdivider or owner of other premises to be served by the same private ways as those abutting the land being sold, it is most important to the seller that he expressly reserve such rights as appurtenant to his remaining land. At the same time, the seller will wish to negate the creation of any rights of way by implication or by necessity over the remaining land.

With respect to utility easements, the buyer is also well advised to make careful inquiry and to require specific provision in the agreement. Are the electric and telephone lines overhead or underground? Does the granted easement specify the exact location, does it permit installation of additional lines, is it part of a major trunk line, does it provide for restoration of any damage done by future maintenance or repair, etc? A clause which provides that the premises are to be conveyed subject to "easements of record" is sometimes seen, but is obviously undesirable and of high risk to a buyer.

Party wall rights are sometimes established by recorded agreement, but may also exist as a matter of law. When a building on the property being sold abuts a building on adjoining property, inquiry and a clause in the agreement are called for.

§ 1:27   Restrictions (as to which, see Topics C and D of Chapter 15)

Restrictions are fairly common. In Boston the so-called Back Bay restrictions were an early example of residential building control, and the practice of achieving such controls by means of private restrictions is fairly wide-spread in residential subdivisions in Massachusetts. In the Back Bay section of Boston these restrictions established the prevailing residential use, limited height, made a standard setback from the street, and allowed for the front bay window to fill a trapezoidal area, although that shape was originally defined to accommodate the rounded Bullfinch front.

In the suburbs the modern equivalent often specify residential use, require prior approval of building plans by the developer or a designated committee, prohibit outside storage of vehicles, limit cutting of trees, etc. These are generally considered beneficial, and consequently it became fairly common for purchase and sale agreements to take exception for "restrictions of record; if any, insofar as now in force and applicable." However, a buyer who accepts that—like the buyer who is subject to "easements of record"—is buying a pig in a poke. Such uncertainty should at the very least be mitigated by the added clause: "provided that such restrictions (or easements) do not prevent or interfere with the use of the premises for ordinary and customary residential purposes." Such a provision, variously phrased, is sometimes still used, but it leaves large areas of uncertainty and is rejected by most real estate lawyers. As with easements, the only proper solution is to require the seller to specify exactly what the restrictions are or where they may be found of record. The buyer's attorney should read them and describe their import to his client before he signs the agreement.

Aside from the substance of the restrictive provisions, the buyer may be concerned with such related matters as: whether or not there is a "common scheme" of restrictions applicable to all lots in a subdivision; what standards and criteria have been or are likely to be applied to prior approval of building plans; the means of enforcement of the restrictions, whether by a developer or by lot purchasers; and the period of time in which the restrictions will remain in force.

Non-residential properties are, of course, also sometimes subjected to restrictions. Although the purposes may be quite different, and there may be other questions of applicability and enforceability, the basic concern at the level of a purchase and sale agreement is the same: clarity and certainty.

Whenever an agreement provides that the buyer is to take title subject to restrictions, there should also be a provision which in effect absolves the buyer of his obligation to purchase if there is a violation or non-compliance with the restrictions existing at the time for closing. This may be a simple affirmative statement that at the time for delivery of the deed the premises shall be then "in compliance with the provisions" of any such restrictive instruments, such a statement being generally accepted as setting forth an essential condition of the contract.

§ 1:28   Tenancies

A lease which appears of record, in full or by statutory Notice of Lease (see § 3:5), is an encumbrance on title, and should be referred to as such in a purchase and sale agreement. This is a matter of record title which should not be confused with the matter of possession and occupancy of the premises. Often in a multi-tenanted building there will be some tenants who have recorded their leases, or notices thereof, and some who have not. The buyer will want a full tenant roster and pertinent data as to each. It is acceptable for the seller to take exception to title to any leases or notices thereof appearing of record with respect to tenancies referred to on the listing thereof provided by the seller; it is not unusual for a seller to be ignorant of which tenants have in fact recorded.

§ 1:29   Mortgages (See Chapter 20)

Because of the prevalence of due-on-sale clauses in mortgages, strictly enforced in Massachusetts, conveyance of property subject to an existing mortgage is fairly rare. In some circumstances a lender will consent to a buyer's taking over an existing mortgage, usually with a novation by which the buyer becomes a promissor or guarantor of the secured debt, and with higher interest or other modified terms. The seller should seek to provide in the purchase and sale agreement that the buyer will enter such a novation and that the lender will release the seller from liability, as a condition of the agreement, and that if that condition is not met, then the buyer will pay the full purchase price in cash, so that the seller may pay off the mortgage.

If there is no due-on-sale clause or the lender consents without requiring a novation, the seller will wish to provide for sale subject to the specified mortgage "which the buyer shall assume and agree to pay." Even then the seller remains at substantial risk because he is still liable on his note to the lender, and subject to deficiency judgment if the mortgage is later foreclosed. A seller can afford himself some further protection by taking a second mortgage securing the buyer's obligation to pay the first mortgage. Then if the buyer defaults on the first mortgage, the seller is in a position to recover his equity and reinstate or pay off the first mortgage. A somewhat stronger position might possibly be afforded by a wrap-around mortgage under which the seller collects from the buyer periodic payments sufficient to enable the seller to continue to make the first mortgage payments himself.

Sometimes it is the seller who wishes the existing mortgage to remain outstanding, to avoid a prepayment penalty, for instance. In that case the buyer's bargaining position might be substantially improved, and he might avoid assuming and agreeing to pay the existing debt,[1] although the seller might still expect some indemnity against a default by the buyer.[2] When the mortgage to be kept in effect is a non-recourse one, then the buyer would, of course, neither assume nor indemnify.

In any case, the agreement should identify the mortgage, state the principal terms of the debt, provide that no breach or default shall exist at the time of closing, and require that such facts be confirmed by estoppel certificates from the seller-mortgagor and, if possible, the mortgagee.

Even when, as is usually the case, the existing mortgage is to be paid off out of sale proceeds upon closing, there are concerns of interest to a buyer. Some of these are closing concerns, discussed in **Chapter 21**, but some need to be addressed at the time of the purchase and sale agreement. For instance, if the existing loan allows for further advances, such as a construction loan or a home equity loan, agreement should be obtained from the seller and the lender that further advances will be barred, or capped at a specified amount. It is also important to a buyer to be sure that he is authorized to disburse sale proceeds at closing directly to the lender, and that the amount of net sale proceeds is sufficient to pay off the existing debt, as well as any other outstanding liens.

TOPIC F: PAYMENT TERMS

§ 1:30 Purchase price; payment; deposit

Beginning with the deposit, the rule of thumb sets the amount at ten percent of the purchase price, but of course that is subject to bargaining in many cases. In complex deals there is sometimes provision for a series of deposits to be made at intervals and depending on achievement of permitting or other touchstones. It is customary to provide for deposits to be held in escrow and "duly accounted for" at closing. The escrowee may be the broker, seller's attorney or even the buyer's attorney. An escrowee should require a formal agreement spelling out his obligations and exculpations, including ultimately a way out, possibly by submission to arbitration or some sort of interpleader, if the parties can-

---

[Section 1:29]

[1]Flynn v. Kenrick, 285 Mass. 446, 189 N.E. 207 (1934).

[2]Brown v. Kaplan, 302 Mass. 510, 19 N.E.2d 913 (1939).

not themselves come to agreement.

The purchase price is usually stated in a fixed amount, but provision may be made for computing it by a formula, based on land area to be determined by survey, the number of lots or dwelling units permitted, or on some other pertinent factor. If the sale is to be made subject to an existing mortgage, the considerations referred to in § **1:29**, should be taken into account. If the purchase price is to be paid in part by a purchase money note and mortgage, the terms thereof should be specified in detail in the agreement. It is preferable to draft the note itself and attach it as an exhibit to the agreement, and either to do the same with the mortgage or at least specify that it is to be "in statutory form" and set forth any additional covenants to be included in it.

The purchase price, or the balance due at closing in addition to any mortgage amount involved, is specified in the GBREB form to be payable "in cash, or by certified, cashier's, treasurer's or bank check." It is exceedingly rare for payment to be made in cash, and preferably the option of cash should be omitted. Certified or bank cashier's checks are a proper equivalent to cash, and it is often desirable to add that the checks must be "drawn on a bank having an office in the city of closing, or at least in Massachusetts," and must be "payable to seller without intervening endorsement except of buyer." It must be observed that the phrase "cashier's, treasurer's or bank check" is somewhat lacking in clarity and should be replaced with "bank cashier's or treasurer's check."

Payment by wire transfer is now often made. If provided for in the agreement, it is desirable to specify that it be of "federal funds," and to set forth the pertinent account numbers and Bank ABA numbers.

It is customary to provide that the seller may use purchase money to pay off encumbrances which must be disposed of in order for him to convey title as agreed, provided that the instruments so clearing the title are procured at the closing. Without that clause a buyer may escape unless the seller is able to pay off the mortgage out of his own funds.[1] In practice, at the seller's request the buyer often provides part of the purchase money in a separate check in the exact amount needed to pay off the seller's mortgage or other

---

[Section 1:30]

[1]Greenberg v. Lannigan, 263 Mass. 594, 161 N.E. 882 (1928).

encumbrance to be disposed of. Such checks should be made payable to the seller and endorsed by him to his mortgagee. In the case of wire transfer directly to seller's lender, buyer should obtain specific written authorization.

Other considerations with respect to payments at closing are discussed in **Chapter 21**, and it is worth reviewing them when one is drafting a purchase and sale agreement.

TOPIC G: CLOSING PROVISIONS

§ 1:31 Time

The agreement should specify a fixed hour and date for closing. Provision for closing "on or before" a specified date is undesirable. If it is desired to give the buyer the election of moving up the closing date, then the agreement should provide for performance at a specified date "or such earlier date as the buyer shall specify by notice in writing to the seller given at least seven days before the date so specified." By similar language this election could be given to the seller, or the right to defer the closing given to either party.

When the premises are being newly developed, or there are permitting or other conditions to be met, it may not be possible to set a fixed date. In such cases a formula or set of criteria may be used to determine the closing date, but it is always desirable to have some backstop end-date specified.

It is customary and advisable to provide that time is of the essence of the agreement. If not so provided, time will not be of the essence and the parties may require performance within a reasonable time.[1]

Extensions of the time for performance should be in writing, although deferral of the hour specified for closing, or even deferral of a day or two, are frequently made by oral undertakings between buyer's and seller's counsel. Oral agreements, some of which are considered in **Chapter 4**, more often lead to litigation than do properly drafted written agreements, which should be the norm.

§ 1:32 Place

In the GBREB form and other printed forms it is provided

[Section 1:31]

[1]Porter v. Harrington, 262 Mass. 203, 159 N.E. 530 (1928); Preferred Underwriters v. New York, N.H. & H.R. Co., 243 Mass. 457, 137 N.E. 590 (1923).

for the closing to be at the registry of deeds where the deed is to be recorded, but in fact most closings are conducted at banks and lawyers' offices, and most lawyers' word-processing forms so provide. In prior years when a lawsuit could be commenced by attachment without prior notice, it was essential to close at the registry or to escrow the purchase money until the deed was recorded—with no attachment appearing of record. Now that attachments cannot be placed on property without prior judicial action, the risks of closing elsewhere than the registry of deeds are reduced, but not wholly eliminated. Most of the registries are now pretty hectic places to conduct a closing.

Lawyers drafting agreements often provide, understandably, for closing at their own office. As a rule of thumb, one goes where the money is: i.e., the office of the buyer's attorney, or the buyer's bank or its attorney. However, if something goes wrong and one party or the other wishes to make a tender, there may be a problem if the specified place of closing is "enemy territory." Cautious lawyers may develop clauses to deal with this, possibly by providing for tender by mail or at the registry within 24 hours after the specified closing date.

§ 1:33   Possession

The agreement will ordinarily provide that simultaneously with the delivery of the deed the seller will deliver to the buyer full possession of the premises free of all tenants and occupants except such as are specified. If there are tenants, it is of course important to the buyer, as stated in § **1:28**, to have a complete and accurate tenant roster, copies of all leases and related amendments or supplemental agreements, and adequate evidence of the status of each lease and tenant as to payment of rent and as to any claims of breach by landlord or tenant. In large buildings that is a complex and extensive package of data and documents, and often even experienced property owners fail to keep adequate records enabling them to provide what is needed by a buyer. Consequently, this may be a major and time-consuming element of negotiation of a purchase and sale agreement. Missing data or uncertainties can often be resolved by estoppel certificates from tenants, but obtaining them is likely to be a task, and usually sellers are unwilling to seek them until they have a binding agreement of sale.

A matter of particular interest to a buyer are any options of extension or renewal of leases, or purchase options set forth therein, because the buyer will ordinarily take title subject to such options.[1]

A buyer does not have any right to possession prior to closing unless there is agreement to that effect.[2] When the buyer is given possession before closing, the seller will usually wish to have provisions in the agreement that the buyer accepts the status of title and condition of the premises at the time of his possession, waiving subsequent changes, assumes the carrying costs as of his possession, takes possession only as a licensee and agrees to vacate if the closing does not occur, and agrees to indemnify the seller against loss occurring as a result of buyer's possession.

If, on the other hand, there is need for the seller to remain in possession after closing, the buyer will want provision in the agreement for escrowing a substantial portion of the purchase price until the seller vacates the premises, and also provision that the seller remains as a licensee and not a tenant, shall pay a use and occupancy charge covering at least the carrying charges on the property, and agrees to indemnify the buyer against loss occurring as a result of seller's occupancy.

§ 1:34 Condition of premises; risk of loss

Purchase and sale agreements usually provide that upon delivery of the deed the premises will be "in the same condition as they now are" with certain specified exceptions. The exceptions make all the difference. The exception of "reasonable use and wear" should not be of concern to a buyer, but an exception of "damage by fire or unavoidable casualty" is another story. It effectively shifts the risk of loss to the buyer upon signing of the agreement: if the building burns down thereafter, the buyer must still take title and pay the purchase price. There are, of course, circumstances in which a buyer is willing to do that—and protect himself with adequate insurance. But note that reference to "unavoidable casualty," which conceivably could be an uninsured, possibly uninsurable, casualty. Even a buyer who is willing to accept risk of loss will usually want "unavoidable" changed to "insured" in that clause. Even when the buyer wants the land, free of an existing building, he should consider the cost and liabilities of accepting and removing a partially burnt-out structure.

[Section 1:33]

[1]Bickford v. Dillon, 321 Mass. 82, 71 N.E.2d 611 (1947); Judkins v. Charette, 255 Mass. 76, 151 N.E. 81, 45 A.L.R. 1 (1926).

[2]Barrell v. Britton, 252 Mass. 504, 148 N.E. 134 (1925).

On the other hand, some purchase and sale agreement forms contain no casualty loss exception.[1] A seller's attorney might regard that as too lax, since it would enable a buyer to use a very minor change in condition as an excuse to cancel the transaction. Consequently, one sometimes sees a clause inserted making exception for "damage by fire or other insured casualty to an extent of not more than $ [a specified amount]."

In larger commercial transactions, one will see clauses specifying that the "risk of loss," using that term, is on seller or buyer, or stating that the premises are sold "as is." These clauses are generally imports from other states (or law seminars) and while there is nothing inherently wrong with them, great care should be taken in mixing them willy-nilly with customary Massachusetts clauses.

Agreements usually require the seller to carry insurance until closing, and this is so even where the risk of loss remains on the seller. In that case buyers sometimes accept a clause which does not specify the amount, and require only that the seller keep the premises insured "as now insured." However, adequate insurance is usually important to a buyer even when the risk of loss remains on the seller until closing, and if the seller's coverage is not sufficient, the buyer should consider obtaining his own, which he may do as a contract vendee.

The risks covered, as well as the amount, should be carefully considered. It is common to require so-called extended coverage, and the circumstances may also call for flood, boiler, elevator or other special coverages.

Other aspects of the condition of the premises are also important, and it is usually provided that a buyer may have inspections of the premises made as to the condition of the structure, equipment and appliances, or the presence of termites, etc., or hazardous substances. On the purchase of a residence it is advisable to provide for inspection by a home inspector licensed under M.G.L.A. c. 112, §§ 201 to 206.

With respect to newly built structures, often incomplete when the purchase and sale agreement is signed, it is necessary to specify the proposed completed condition, and warranties are often set forth. An implied warranty of habitability is applicable in certain cases, as discussed in § 5:5.

[Section 1:34]

[1]Bissonnette v. Keyes, 319 Mass. 134, 64 N.E.2d 926 (1946); Schanberg v. Automobile Ins. Co. of Hartford, Conn., 285 Mass. 316, 189 N.E. 105 (1934).

§ 1:35   Adjustments

Provision is ordinarily made for adjustment of ongoing charges which are or could become a lien on the title or which may directly affect possessory rights or the condition of the premises. These include: real estate taxes, water and sewer use charges, electric service charges of certain municipal lighting plants (discussed in § 1:24); insurance premiums if the buyer is taking over the seller's existing insurance, and contracts for elevator maintenance, security services, janitorial services and other operating expenses if the buyer is taking them over; the cost of fuel stored on the premises; and rents. That is, of course, quite a mixed bag, and on larger transactions it is usually desirable to break it down into components and to provide specifically for the means of computation and adjustment of each item or category.[1]

With respect to real estate taxes it is customary to provide for apportionment on the basis of the taxes for the preceding year if the current rate or assessment has not yet been set, and for reapportionment when the actual tax amount is determined. However, there are many situations when that provision is inapt or insufficient, and special allocation, apportionment, and escrow for payment clauses often need to be drafted. As to rents, specifically drafted clauses are also often necessary, particularly where there are percentage rents or tax or other escalator payments. If there are any substantial unpaid, overdue rents, a provision would be in order other than merely calling for apportionment "if and when collected by either party."

§ 1:36   Brokerage

Printed forms of purchase and sale agreement often have their origin with brokers' organizations and consequently usually contain a provision which in effect entitles the broker to a commission. Sellers' lawyers usually insist on a provision that the broker is entitled to a commission only if and when the transaction is in fact closed by delivery and acceptance of the deed and payment of the purchase price. It is sometimes regarded as fair, in the event of a defaulted deposit, to split it between seller and broker. The *Tristram's Landing* case, discussed in § 3:4, is pertinent on this point.

The subject of entitlement to brokerage fee or commission

[Section 1:35]

[1]See REBA Practice Standards 1, 5, 7 and 15.

has had the attention of the courts, and a review of § **3:4** would be worthwhile for one drafting a listing agreement or a brokerage clause in a purchase and sale agreement.

Often sellers list property for sale with many brokers, and buyers consult many brokers. The agreement should of course identify the particular broker or brokers to or among whom a commission is to be paid or shared, and the seller is entitled to some representation from the buyer as to the brokers with whom the buyer dealt, in order that the seller is not exposed to multiple claims for commission. A seller may seek to have the buyer indemnify him against any commission other than the specified one, but the buyer cannot be faulted for resisting that, and is certainly entitled to exclude from his indemnity any claim arising from the seller's own acts.

The broker should join in the agreement to acknowledge and agree to its terms, and therein represent his being duly licensed to act as broker.

TOPIC H: FAILURE TO PERFORM

§ 1:37   Seller

The essence of the Massachusetts custom, as referred to in § **1:3**, is that "if the seller shall be unable to give title or to make conveyance," as usually provided, the seller is not bound by his agreement to sell, and may simply refund the deposit. Leaving aside other clauses, discussed below, as to a seller's election or obligation to remove a defect or a buyer's right to take title despite a defect, the frame of this clause, turning on the word "unable," is, one must admit, somewhat peculiar from an ordinary contract law standpoint. Lawyers from other states—and many in Massachusetts—often raise quizzical brows at this clause. However, the clause does have real substance: a seller cannot take refuge in a defect or encumbrance caused by his own act, and he would ordinarily have a duty of reasonable diligence to enable himself to perform.[1]

Recognizing this, the common "escape clause" goes on to say that when the seller is unable to give title as specified, the deposit shall be refunded and the agreement terminated

---

[Section 1:37]

[1]LaFond v. Frame, 327 Mass. 364, 99 N.E.2d 51 (1951); Oberg v. Burke, 345 Mass. 596, 188 N.E.2d 566 (1963); Everets v. Webster, 4 L.C.R. 612 (2006).

unless "the seller elects to use reasonable effort to remove any defects in title." That is, any duty of the seller to enable himself to perform is expressly negated. This is at the root of the traditional Massachusetts approach to land sale transactions: the buyer is not bound to take anything other than a good title, but the seller is not liable for failure to have one. Nevertheless, it is almost universal for buyer's counsel to seek a change of that clause from a seller's election to seller's obligation to use reasonable efforts to cure. Aside from economic bargaining power, the considerations involved in arriving at one clause or another include such things as the ready availability of detailed title information, the likelihood of there being defects, the nature of any likely defects, and the relative effect on buyer and seller of the delay which might be involved in the process of curing defects. A seller who accedes to an obligation to cure defects will often add a proviso that he is not obligated to spend more than a specified amount for such curing.

If the buyer does not succeed in reversing the usual seller election provisions, all is not lost. The agreement should still include a provision allowing the buyer to waive any defect and accept such title as the seller can convey. This clause ordinarily requires the buyer to pay the full purchase price and it is rarely applied literally. It should, however, always be included because it tends to foster a negotiated solution, fairly balanced between buyer and seller, when there is a relatively minor, curable defect. Even without an express clause, the buyer will have a right to waive defects.[2]

§ 1:38   Buyer

Prevalent forms of purchase and sale agreement provide in effect that if the buyer fails to perform, the seller shall retain the deposit as liquidated damages unless within thirty days after the time for performance the seller "otherwise notifies" the buyer in writing. When a seller so "otherwise notifies" the buyer, it indicates an intention to hold the buyer for actual damages, and such notice would ordinarily be given in conjunction with suit for breach seeking full contract damages for loss of the bargain. Before taking that course, a seller should carefully assess his chances of proving actual damages in excess of the deposit and also should consider his duty to mitigate. Rather than face such considerations, sellers are often well advised to obtain a ten percent deposit

---

[2]Margolis v. Tarutz, 265 Mass. 540, 164 N.E. 451 (1929); Brookings v. Cooper, 256 Mass. 121, 152 N.E. 243, 46 A.L.R. 745 (1926).

and to limit their claim for buyer's default to that deposit as liquidated damages.

Upon negotiation of an agreement it is in fact quite common for buyers to propose and sellers to agree that the above referred to "unless" clause be stricken out and a clause inserted that the buyer shall have no further obligation [other than loss of the deposit] in law or in equity. It is curious, but undeniable, that buyers' attorneys often demand the liquidated damages limitation even when there is little practical likelihood that actual damages would reach ten percent. If the property is a "bargain" for which there is strong market demand, a buyer might better seek a clause limiting the seller to actual damages, since there will be little or none if the seller quickly finds another buyer at an equal or higher price.

The provision for liquidated damages payable to a seller in the case of a buyer's default does not by itself bar an action for specific performance by the seller against the buyer, but it is often followed by the statement that it "shall be the sole and exclusive remedy" or that "the seller shall have no other or further remedy at law or in equity." Even less specific phrases may be construed as evincing an intent of the parties to preclude specific performance.[1] See § 5:1 and § 5:2.

§ 1:39   Conditions

Sometimes purchase and sale agreements set forth special conditions on the obligation of a buyer or seller to perform. As to a seller, the condition might be such as waiver of a first approval right granted to another party, or subdivision approval of a plan showing the lot to be sold. The seller is certainly entitled to the protection of such conditions as these, but he should be willing to agree to use reasonable efforts to fulfill them. On the buyer's side, the most common condition is one of mortgage financing, which does not render the agreement any less binding.[1] The precise terms of such a condition are of considerable importance to both parties, and careful drafting is necessary, particularly in light of the variety and complexity of modern lending practices.[2] If a seller accepts such a condition, he is entitled to an agreement of

---

[Section 1:38]

[1]Rigs v. Sokol, 318 Mass. 337, 61 N.E.2d 538 (1945); De Blois v. Boylston & Tremont Corp., 281 Mass. 498, 183 N.E. 823 (1933); see Perroncello v. Donahue, 448 Mass. 199, 859 N.E.2d 827 (2007).

[Section 1:39]

[1]Geoffrion v. Lucier, 336 Mass. 532, 146 N.E.2d 654 (1957).

[2]Alfeo v. Dinsmore, 68 Mass. App. Ct. 249, 861 N.E.2d 491 (2007).

the buyer to use at least reasonable efforts to fulfill it, which may be the buyer's obligation even without such express provision.[3] Sometimes sellers call for the buyer to use diligent efforts, or even retain the right to find a loan commitment for the buyer and require the buyer to accept it.

Other conditions on buyer's obligation often relate to subdivision, zoning, environmental and other governmental permits and approvals. With respect to these it is much more difficult to determine what may constitute reasonable or diligent efforts to fulfill, and any provision with respect thereto should be cautiously negotiated and carefully drafted.

TOPIC I: LEGAL EFFECT; RECORDING; ASSIGNABILITY

§ 1:40 Legal effect

As with respect to any contract, a purchase and sale agreement of real estate must meet basic contractual tests, including that of fair dealing, and such fundamentals as meeting of the minds, i.e. adequate expression of the terms of the deal to indicate the parties mutual intent, and of course, the statute of frauds, discussed in **Chapter 4**. The agreement should contain provisions to the effect that (i) it is to be construed pursuant to and governed by the laws of Massachusetts, (ii) it sets forth the entire contract, (iii) it is binding upon the parties and their respective heirs, devisees, legal representatives, successors and assigns, and (iv) it may be cancelled or amended only by written instrument signed by both parties. Such provisions will take effect and be enforceable in accordance with general principles of contract law.

In Massachusetts, contrary to the majority view, the interest of a vendor of real estate subject to a purchase and sale agreement is not regarded as having been equitably converted into personalty upon execution of the agreement;[1] such conversion taking place only upon payment of the purchase price. It has been held that: (i) a purchase and sale

---

[3]Stabile v. McCarthy, 336 Mass. 399, 145 N.E.2d 821 (1957); Sechrest v. Safiol, 383 Mass. 568, 419 N.E.2d 1384 (1981).

[Section 1:40]

[1]Sondheim v. Fenton, 326 Mass. 28, 92 N.E.2d 587 (1950).

agreement constitutes the seller a trustee for the buyer;[2] (ii) the buyer, as well as the seller, has an insurable interest in the property.[3]

In order to give effect to notices called for in a purchase and sale agreement, a specific notice clause should be included, such as the one in paragraph 15 in the form in **Appendix E**.

§ 1:41   Recording

The requirements for and effect of recording of a purchase and sale agreement are governed by statute.[1] In order to be recordable, the agreement must be acknowledged by the seller, or at least one of co-sellers. Even within the statutory limitations sellers generally are unwilling to encumber their titles of record with the claims of a contract vendee, and both parties are usually loath to make such public disclosure of the financial or other terms of the transaction. However, if the deposit is large, the closing date remote, the ability of the seller to give good title or possession dubious—and a secure escrow of the deposit cannot be arranged—the buyer's only protection may lie in some record claim on the premises. One technique sometimes used in lieu of recording the agreement is for the seller to give the buyer a mortgage on the premises securing the performance of the seller's obligation to refund the deposit if it should become refundable pursuant to the terms of the agreement. A provision to the effect that the agreement shall become voidable by the seller if it is recorded by or at the instance of the buyer may be advisable.

§ 1:42   Assignability

In accordance with general contract principles a real estate purchase and sale agreement will be assignable unless it expressly provides otherwise. If there are any special or ongoing relationships between seller and buyer, such as purchase money financing, repurchase option, leaseback, ownership of other nearby premises, etc., a seller may wish to prohibit assignment by a buyer. If the seller is marketing lots in a subdivision, units in a condominium or other real estate which he deems to be competitive with the premises

---

[2]J.J. Newberry Co. v. Shannon, 268 Mass. 116, 167 N.E. 292, 63 A.L.R. 133 (1929).

[3]Shumway v. Home Fire &

Marine Ins. Co. of California, 301 Mass. 391, 17 N.E.2d 212 (1938).

[Section 1:41]

[1]M.G.L.A. c. 184, § 17A.

being sold, he may wish to prohibit assignment of the agreement by the buyer in order to deter speculation and resale. Any prohibition of assignability should be coordinated with elimination or limitation of a nominee clause, as discussed in § **1:7**.

As to assignment of the agreement by a seller, that would, of course, involve conveyance of the premises to another party who would become the selling grantor at the closing. Such a change in the maker of the deed covenants may not be of any great moment, and the buyer would not be otherwise concerned unless there are in fact on-going relationships with the original contract seller. If it is important to the buyer, the agreement should expressly provide that the deed is to be one "by the Seller."

Chapter 2

Purchase and Sale by a Governmental Agency

TOPIC A: SOURCES OF AUTHORITY

TOPIC B: PROCEDURAL REQUIREMENTS

> **KeyCite®:** Cases and other legal materials listed in KeyCite Scope can be researched through the KeyCite service on Westlaw®. Use KeyCite to check citations for form, parallel references, prior and later history, and comprehensive citator information, including citations to other decisions and secondary materials.

TOPIC A: SOURCES OF AUTHORITY

§ 2:1   Introduction

As noted in § **1:15** the Commonwealth of Massachusetts acting through various departments, commissions or agencies, and other governmental bodies are often encountered in real estate transactions. They are both buyers and sellers of real estate, and private practitioners will need to deal with attorneys representing the government agency involved. The authority of such entities to act in the particular transaction will generally arise from a specific statutory provision, which may be either in the General Laws or in a Special Act of the legislature. It is essential for the private practitioner to analyze the law to determine the scope of authority thereunder, and that will often require a substantial research job. Reliance should not be placed solely on proffers of assurance from representatives of the governmental body, and in fact it sometimes takes some digging to identify the incumbent officials who are empowered to act.

One of the means of acquisition of real estate by a governmental agency is of course taking by eminent domain, but that subject is beyond the scope of this volume.

§ 2:2   State agencies

Agencies of the Commonwealth derive their powers with respect to real estate from the Constitution and provisions of the general laws relating thereto. Chapter 7 of the General Laws relates to the Executive Office of Administration and Finance. The key provisions are found in Chapter 7, as follows: § 4A creates a Division of Capital Asset Management and Maintenance, with a Commissioner, herein referred to as CAMM. Pertinent definitions are set forth in § 39A. The general responsibility of CAMM for "acquisition, allocation and disposition of real property" is provided in § 39B, and its jurisdiction over projects of other state agencies is set forth in § 40A. Section 40E contains an important and useful listing of other pertinent statutes, and provides that real estate held in the name of any state agency is the property of the Commonwealth. Sections 40F and 40F 1/2 define the responsibility of CAMM for acquisition and disposal of real estate, and the somewhat complicated procedures for determination of what is "surplus." These sections are again referred to in § 2:7.

§ 2:3   Counties

The status of counties in Massachusetts is, to put it mildly, a peculiar mess. There were 14 counties, but laws in the late 1990s, now constituting M.G.L.A. c. 34B, abolished Middlesex, Hampden, Worcester, Hampshire, Essex and Berkshire Counties, with various effective dates up to July 1, 2000. Under M.G.L.A. c. 34B, § 6, all real and personal property of abolished counties was vested in the Commonwealth and made subject to the jurisdiction of CAMM under M.G.L.A. c. 7, with a few specific exceptions relating to properties of Hampshire County in Northampton.

As to the still extant counties, there are provisions for acquisition and sale of real property in M.G.L.A. c. 34, §§ 14 and 25, and limited powers with respect thereto in M.G.L.A. c. 34A. For purchase of real estate from a non-abolished county, a special act would seem to be called for. The interests of abolished counties in county roads were transferred to their "successor council of governments."[1]

§ 2:4 Cities and towns

The power of municipalities to deal with real estate is set forth in M.G.L.A. c. 40. Section 1 of that chapter provides that "except as otherwise expressly provided, cities shall have all the powers of towns and such additional powers as are granted to them by their charters or by general or special law, and all laws relative to towns shall apply to cities." Section 3 of that chapter provides that a town may convey real estate "by a deed of its selectmen thereto duly authorized, or by a deed of a committee or agent thereto duly authorized," and also provides that "All real estate or personal property of the town, not by law or by vote of the town placed in the charge of any particular board, officer or department shall be under the control of the selectmen, except as otherwise provided in this section or section nine." The statute also provides for leasing of municipal property to others, including an express provision with respect to surplus space in a school building.

When property held by a town for any municipal purpose is to be sold, it must first be transferred for the purpose of sale, by a two-thirds vote of town meeting under M.G.L.A. c. 40, § 15A, before the power of the selectmen under § 3 may be exercised.[1]

M.G.L.A. c. 40, § 3A, provides that "Any recordable instrument purporting to affect an interest in real estate, title to which is held by a city, town, district or regional school district, executed by an appropriate officer," shall be binding on the city, town, district or regional school district in favor of a purchaser or other person relying in good faith on such instrument notwithstanding inconsistent provisions of general or special law, the city or town charter, by-laws, resolutions or votes."

Section 15 of M.G.L.A. c. 40 deals with disposition of any

[Section 2:3]

[1]Chapter 336, Acts of 2006.

[Section 2:4]

[1]Harris v. Town of Wayland, 392 Mass. 237, 466 N.E.2d 822, 19

Ed. Law Rep. 358 (1984).

land or interest therein which is no longer needed for public purposes and was acquired by eminent domain. This requires a two-thirds vote of a city council or town meeting authorizing the conveyance and specifying the minimum sale price. It is also therein provided that when a municipality wishes to dispose of land it owns in another city or town, the land must first be offered at the specified minimum price to the city or town in which it is located. These requirements do not apply to land not acquired by eminent domain,[2] and may not apply if the taking was made only to perfect a title otherwise acquired.[3] Acting under this section a municipality is not obliged in all circumstances to sell the property to the highest bidder.[4]

Under M.G.L.A. c. 44, § 63A, cities and towns are required, as a condition precedent to power to deliver a deed, to collect from the grantee a payment in lieu of real estate taxes for the portion of the current tax year then remaining. A recital of compliance in the deed is conclusive.

§ 2:5   Tax titles

Title to real estate is sometimes acquired by a city or town as a "tax title" arising under M.G.L.A. c. 60, §§ 37 et seq., by taking or sale at public auction by the local Collector of Taxes for non-payment of real estate taxes. A lien arises upon assessment of the tax, as of January 1 in the year of assessment. In order to collect, the collector must first make demand for payment, including demand on a mortgagee who has given notice, and if payment is not made within 14 days, may proceed to collection "in the manner provided by law." In addition to collection by action, and arrest in certain cases, the collector may make a taking of the premises or a sale thereof by public auction. The collector's deed "shall contain a warranty that the sale has in all particulars been conducted according to law," conveys the property "subject to the right of redemption," "shall not be valid unless recorded within sixty days after the sale," and does not give the purchaser "any right to possession of the land until the right of redemption is foreclosed." If no one bids at the auction, the collector conveys to the town.

When either a sale or taking has been made, the previously taxed owner has an equity of redemption, and may

---

[2]Muir v. City of Leominster, 2 Mass. App. Ct. 587, 317 N.E.2d 212 (1974).

[3]Oliver v. Town of Mattapoisett, 17 Mass. App. Ct. 286, 457 N.E.2d 679 (1983).

[4]Gennari v. City of Revere, 23 Mass. App. Ct. 979, 503 N.E.2d 1331 (1987).

redeem at any time prior to foreclosure by paying the back taxes, interest, costs and subsequently accrued taxes. Such owner then receives, and should record, a certificate of redemption. If the title is not redeemed, the collector may proceed to foreclose the equity of redemption by action in the Land Court. Such proceeding may not be commenced until the expiration of six months after the tax taking or sale, or sooner if the owner consents or if buildings on the premises are abandoned.

A decree of foreclosure bars all right of redemption, and M.G.L.A. c. 60, § 69A, provides that: "No petition to vacate a decree of foreclosure . . . and no proceeding at law or in equity for reversing or modifying such a decree shall be commenced by any person other than the petitioner except within one year after the final entry of the decree."

The courts have generally affirmed the concept that "there is an interest in the stability of tax titles."[1] Voiding of tax titles or vacating of decrees of foreclosure has been allowed only when there are apparent strong due process grounds, and the one year limit has usually prevailed. However, the Appeals Court has said that "a substantial due process claim trumps § 69A."[2] Insufficient notice or other irregularities in procedure have been held to bar foreclosure or to permit late redemption after the one year period.[3] However, some procedural errors have passed muster, and long delay in seeking redemption has been rejected.[4] Unusual circumstances have also sometimes been considered.[5]

Under M.G.L.A. c. 60, §§ 79 et seq., there are simplified

[Section 2:5]

[1]Devine v. Town of Nantucket, 16 Mass. App. Ct. 548, 452 N.E.2d 1167 (1983).

[2]Town of Andover v. State Financial Services, Inc., 48 Mass. App. Ct. 536, 723 N.E.2d 531 (2000), rev'd, 432 Mass. 571, 736 N.E.2d 837 (2000).

[3]Scott v. Commonwealth (Land Court, Reg. Case No. 40742, 1987); City of Boston v. James, 26 Mass. App. Ct. 625, 530 N.E.2d 1254 (1988); City of Boston v. Bethlehem Healing Temple, Inc., 3 L.C.R. 240 (1995); Town of North Reading v. Welch, 46 Mass. App. Ct. 818, 711 N.E.2d 603 (1999).

[4]Town of Brewster v. Sherwood Forest Realty, Inc., 7 L.C.R. 141 (1999), aff'd 56 Mass.App. Ct. 905, 778 N.E.2d 924 (2002); McCormack & Zatzman Ltd. v. Saint John (City), 1975 WL 184381 (N.B. L.C.B. 1975); Woodworth v. Poor, 11 L.C.R. 141 (2003); Town of Orange v. Cook Court Limited Partnership, 11 L.C.R. 174 (2003); Town of Norwell v. Owners Unknown, 12 L.C.R. 101 (2004).

[5]Ch. 334, Acts of 1990, made provisions for clearing up old Nantucket tax titles, and was upheld in Opinion of the Justices to the House of Representatives, 408 Mass. 1215, 563 N.E.2d 203 (1990). In Town of Wareham v. Onset Bay Corporation, 10 L.C.R. 131 (2002), the town was required to respect the alloca-

procedures for the disposition by a town of tax title properties of "low value." It is interesting to note that the original "low value" figure of $1,000 prevailed from the 1930s to 1968, then went to $2,500, up to $5,000 in 1985 and to $15,000 in 2002. The pertinent low-value facts are certified by recorded affidavit of the commissioner of taxation, after which a tax sale may be made on short notice, including notice by registered mail to persons interested in the equity, who will be barred if they do not redeem prior to the public auction sale. The purchaser of the tax title may thereafter bring a proceeding in the Land Court under M.G.L.A. c. 60, § 80B, in which persons interested in the equity must assert their claims or be barred. As above, the statute prohibits vacating the decree or other attack after one year. In addition, M.G.L.A. c. 60, § 80C, enacted in 1986, provides in effect that after 20 years the sale of a low value tax title cannot be contested regardless of procedural defects. In any event the Land Court has usually rejected challenges to low value tax titles after the expiration of the one year period, and been upheld on appeal.[6]

When one is purchasing a tax title from a city or town, or from another holder thereof, it is important to review the pertinent provisions in M.G.L.A. c. 60, of which the foregoing are only a small part, and to satisfy oneself that they and the requirements of due process have been complied with.

§ 2:6   Redevelopment authorities

Redevelopment Authorities, established pursuant to M.G.L.A. c. 121B, usually acquire title to real estate by taking. Their sales to redevelopers are usually effected through a "land disposition agreement" which sets forth not only the usual terms of a purchase and sale agreement, but also a description of the project, timing requirements, enforcement and compliance provisions, and rights of reacquisition. Some aspects of such provisions have been considered by the courts.[1]

TOPIC B: PROCEDURAL REQUIREMENTS

---

tion of payments made by the defendant to different tax accounts.

In Chicopee v. Hallahan, 5 L.C.R. 156 (1994), the tax taking of land

§ 2:7 State acquisition and disposition

As referred to in § 2:2, the controlling provisions are set forth in M.G.L.A., c. 7. Sections 40E and others, particularly §§ 40 H, I and J, are parts of the so-called Ward Commission legislation, enacted in 1980 as remedial measures concerning the letting of architectural, engineering, and construction contracts by state, county and other public officials and substantially affecting also the leasing, sale and conveyance of, and the granting of easements or other interests in real estate by public officials and agencies. The principal requirements of the act as to disposition of public lands are (1) advertisement and invitation to bid, (2) notice to local governmental bodies, and public hearing, and (3) disclosure of beneficial interests.

The requirement of advertisement and invitation to bid applies to any rental or sale of real property, of any kind or size, "used by state agencies." The definition of "state agencies" excludes counties and municipalities. The duty so to advertise is imposed on CAMM, originally on "the Deputy Commissioner of Capital Planning and Operations." Section 40H still contains a reference to DCPO, an earlier name of CAMM, which may be a useful historical reference for

---

owned by the town was construed as a taking of the leasehold it had granted to the defendant.

[6]Lamontagne v. Knightly, 30 Mass. App. Ct. 647, 572 N.E.2d 1375 (1991); Homer v. Town of Yarmouth, 40 Mass. App. Ct. 916, 662 N.E.2d 1056 (1996).

[Section 2:6]

[1]Electronics Corp. of America v. City Council of Cambridge, 348 Mass. 563, 204 N.E.2d 707 (1965); Moskow v. Boston Redevelopment Authority, 349 Mass. 553, 210 N.E.2d 699 (1965); Charbonnier v. Amico, 367 Mass. 146, 324 N.E.2d 895 (1975); Reid v. Acting Com'r of Dept. of Community Affairs, 362 Mass. 136, 284 N.E.2d 245 (1972); Commissioner of Dept. of Community Affairs v. Boston Redevelopment Authority, 362 Mass. 602, 289 N.E.2d 867 (1972); Trager v. Peabody Redevelopment Authority, 367 F. Supp. 1000 (D. Mass. 1973); Bronstein v. Prudential Ins. Co. of America, 390 Mass. 701, 459 N.E.2d 772 (1984); Charles River Park, Inc. v. Boston Redevelopment Authority, 28 Mass. App. Ct. 795, 557 N.E.2d 20 (1990); St. Botolph Citizens Committee, Inc. v. Boston Redevelopment Authority, 429 Mass. 1, 705 N.E.2d 617 (1999); Russell v. Zoning Bd. of Appeals of Brookline, 349 Mass. 532, 209 N.E.2d 337 (1965); Com. v. Boston Redevelopment Authority, 418 Mass. 29, 633 N.E.2d 1043 (1994); Gloucester Landing Associates Ltd. Partnership v. Gloucester Redevelopment Authority, 60 Mass. App. Ct. 403, 802 N.E.2d 1046 (2004); LeBeau v. Board of Selectmen of East Brookfield, 13 Mass. App. Ct. 942, 431 N.E.2d 257 (1982); Gardner v. Governor Apartments Associates, 396 Mass. 661, 488 N.E.2d 3 (1986); Christensen v. Boston Redevelopment Authority, 60 Mass. App. Ct. 615, 804 N.E.2d 947 (2004); Anderson Street Associates v. City Of Boston, 442 Mass. 812, 817 N.E.2d 759 (2004).

lawyers examining titles involving an earlier conveyance by a Commonwealth agency. The advertisement by CAMM must appear in the state register at least 30 days before a proposal for purchase or rental of such real property by a private party is accepted. The 30 day period may be shortened or waived upon certification of an emergency. If the property contains over 2500 square feet, the advertisement must also be published for four consecutive weeks in a newspaper. Compliance is "a condition precedent to the validity of any deed or rental agreement executed by or on behalf of the commonwealth."

The requirements of notice to local governmental bodies and public hearing do not apply in all cases, but only when the real property in question contains 2 acres or more. In that case 60 days notice must be given to officials of any city or town, or regional planning agency, where the property is located, and public hearing must be held at least 30 days before the sale or other disposition is effected. The notice of hearing must state the present use, reason for the proposed action, and proposed use of the property.

The final requirement, that of disclosure of beneficial interests, applies to disposition of realty by any public agency—state, county, regional or local. The disclosure must be made by written statement under the penalties of perjury, executed by the private party proposing to lease from or to, or to purchase from or sell to, the governmental agency, "giving the true names and addresses of all persons who have or will have a direct or indirect beneficial interest in said property," excluding any holder of less than 10 percent of the voting stock in a corporation with publicly listed shares. Although the language is somewhat less explicit than that of § 40H quoted above, § 40J of M.G.L.A. c. 7 also says that "no agreement . . . shall be valid . . ." unless those requirements are met.

§ 2:8 Uniform Procurement Act

M.G.L.A. c. 30B, the Uniform Procurement Act, established procedures and requirements for the procurement of supplies, services or real property or for disposing of supplies or real property by cities, towns, counties and other governmental agencies which are not state agencies. When a price of $10,000 or more is involved, the basic requirement is for competitive sealed bids, responding to a duly published invitation, with award made to the lowest responsible and responsive bidder. Alternatively, the procurement officer may solicit proposals, separating price and non-price criteria, select on the basis of an evaluation, and negotiate final terms. There are also provisions for sole source and emergency procurements. With respect to disposition of real estate the first requirement is a determination that the property is no longer needed and declaration of its surplus status. Section 16 of the Act provides for determination of value by a recognized procedure, publication of a request for proposals, notice in the central register, public opening of bids, and in the event of sale for less than the determined value, publication in the central register of an explanation of the reasons and the price differential. The guidelines published by the Inspector General do recognize that there are sometimes non-price goals and criteria, and in particular that a redevelopment authority may have a variety of development objectives to accomplish through real property dispositions. The act has been upheld and applied.[1]

§ 2:9   Cities and towns

Massachusetts law provides for a variety of forms of municipal government for cities and towns under M.G.L.A. c. 39, and consequently their governmental procedures vary in some respects, but are uniformly governed in important respects by M.G.L.A. c. 30A, the Administrative Procedures Act. With respect to the acquisition and disposition of real estate these elements are essentially common to all under M.G.L.A. c. 40, as referred to in § 2:4. Rules with respect to takings by eminent domain are set forth in M.G.L.A. c. 79, and some municipal agencies have special powers with respect to real estate, such as those of conservation commissions under M.G.L.A. c. 40, § 8C.

§ 2:10   Park, conservation and natural resources lands

Article XCVII of the Articles of Amendment to the Massachusetts Constitution, adopted in 1972, provides a fundamental protection of "the conservation, development and utilization of the agricultural, mineral, forest, water, air and other natural resources" of the commonwealth. There-

---

[Section 2:8]

[1]Edwards v. City of Boston, 408 Mass. 643, 562 N.E.2d 834, 63 Ed. Law Rep. 998 (1990). In Mangano v. Town of Wilmington, 51 Mass. App. Ct. 857, 748 N.E.2d 1052 (2001), plaintiff was highest bidder on the Town's RFP for sale of land, but before bids were opened, the Board of Selectmen voted to refrain from sale of the parcel. The Court held that the absence in **c. 30B** of provision for rejection of all bids did not bar the Town's withdrawal.

under "lands and easements" acquired for such purposes may not be used for other purposes or otherwise disposed of "except by laws enacted by a two-thirds vote, taken by yeas and nays, of each branch of the general court."

This constitutional provision has been the subject of two opinions of the attorney general. In Op. Atty Gen. June 6, 1973, p. 139, in response to questions of the legislature, the Attorney General expressed the opinion that the provisions of Article XCVII applied to (1) land acquired prior to the adoption of the Article, (2) land held for park purposes, (3) broadly defined categories of natural resources, and (4) strictly defined limits of "other purposes" and disposition. With respect to land held for park purposes, there was prior case law which generally established strict limits on the diversion thereof to other uses, including an Opinion of Justices to Senate.[1] These constraints apply to all Massachusetts governmental agencies, including cities and towns. The Ward Commission legislation, discussed in § 2:7, makes specific reference to this constitutional provision. The SJC has given consideration to the subject.[2]

[Section 2:10]

[1]Opinion of the Justices to the Senate, 369 Mass. 979, 338 N.E.2d 806 (1975).

[2]Cranberry Growers Service, Inc. v. Town of Duxbury, 415 Mass. 354, 613 N.E.2d 105 (1993).

Chapter 3

Other Agreements

TOPIC A: OFFER AND ACCEPTANCE

TOPIC B: OPTION

TOPIC C: FIRST REFUSAL

TOPIC D: BROKERAGE

TOPIC E: TENANCY; OCCUPANCY

TOPIC F: BOUNDARY

TOPIC G: OTHER

KeyCite®: Cases and other legal materials listed in KeyCite Scope can be researched through the KeyCite service on Westlaw®. Use KeyCite to check citations for form, parallel references, prior and later history, and comprehensive citator information, including citations to other decisions and secondary materials.

TOPIC A: OFFER AND ACCEPTANCE

§ 3:1   Form and substance

In an understandable desire to bind the bargain, brokers often propose the execution of a form of Offer and Acceptance. The usual form[1] identifies the parties, the property, a preliminary deposit, the price, the type of deed, the closing date, a date by which the offer must be accepted, and a date by which the parties shall execute a purchase and sale agreement, usually a specified "standard" form, and that "time is of the essence." The printed forms have a blank space for "riders" or "additional terms and conditions," and quite often mortgage or occupancy conditions or others are written in. In short, this looks like a contract and contains all the elements required by contract law for formation of a contract, but is still, at most, a contract to make a contract, and lacks the "boiler plate" detail of a purchase and sale agreement. And, most significantly, it leaves open the intent of the parties: was there or was there not a meeting of the minds, or an intention to make a binding contract.

The courts have been called upon repeatedly, continuing from year to year, to struggle with those issues. In the great majority of the cases specific performance has been denied, often on the ground that a meeting of the minds was not evinced by the writing.[2]

In the leading case of *Goren v. Royal Investments Inc.*,[3] Justice Kass reviewed prior decisions, particularly *Rosenfield v. U.S. Trust Co.*[4] and its progeny, holding that "language looking to execution of a final written agreement justifies a strong inference that significant items on the agenda of the transaction are still open and, hence, that the parties do not intend to be bound." In *Goren*, however, the trial court's findings showed that all material terms had been heavily negotiated and agreed to, and that the defendant seller had then failed to act in good faith, motivated by a better offer. In those circumstances the court ordered specific performance.

In the immediately following decision, *Blomendale v. Imbrescia*,[5] Justice Kass found the written offer "crude," lacking in important detail, and thus rejected as a binding contract under the rule of *Rosenfield*. Similar results were

[Section 3:1]

[1]**Appendix D, GBREB Offer to Purchase Real Estate**. Copyright by GBREB.

[2]Coldwell Banker/Hunneman v. Shostack, 62 Mass. App. Ct. 635, 818 N.E.2d 1079 (2004) affords a good example and review of prior cases.

[3]Goren v. Royal Investments Inc., 25 Mass. App. Ct. 137, 516 N.E.2d 173 (1987).

[4]Rosenfield v. U. S. Trust Co., 290 Mass. 210, 195 N.E. 323, 122 A.L.R. 1210 (1935).

[5]Blomendale v. Imbrescia, 25 Mass. App. Ct. 144, 516 N.E.2d 177 (1987).

reached in later cases.[6]

In *Goren*, Justice Kass pointed out that "parties to a preliminary agreement" may provide that "they do not intend to be bound," observing that: "There is commercial utility to allowing persons to hug before they marry." Such a provision should, he said, speak plainly, e.g., "The purpose of this document is to memorialize certain business points. The parties mutually acknowledge that their agreement is qualified and that they, therefore, contemplate the drafting and execution of a more detailed agreement. They intend to be bound only by the execution of such an agreement and not by this preliminary document."

If a provision of that kind were included in every offer and acceptance, it would eliminate a lot of costly and wasteful litigation. It would also reduce the instrument to a sort of Letter of Intent or Term Sheet, devices frequently used to initiate the proposed sale of a business, an office building or a commercial or industrial property. The owner therein sets forth the terms and conditions on which it might consider sale, and prospective buyers usually respond with modifications. The provisions of Letters of Intent or Term Sheets responding to them are thus often heavily negotiated, always with the statement therein that neither party is bound and reserves the right to propose different terms and conditions and to withdraw at any time. Only when the provisions of a Term Sheet come to a point at which they seem satisfactory to both sides does either deem it worthwhile to draw up a formal purchase and sale agreement, and neither party is bound until that document is signed.[7]

When a purchase and sale agreement called for in an offer to purchase had actually been signed and was escrowed solely for fulfillment of a readily fulfillable condition, the court held that the buyer was entitled to specific performance, saying further that in those circumstances the buyer

---

[6]Trifiro v. New York Life Ins. Co., 845 F.2d 30 (1st Cir. 1988); Pappas Indus. Parks, Inc. v. Psarros, 24 Mass. App. Ct. 596, 511 N.E.2d 621 (1987); Nelsen v. Rebello, 26 Mass. App. Ct. 270, 526 N.E.2d 262 (1988), opinion amended and superseded, 26 Mass. App. Ct. 270, 530 N.E.2d 798 (1988); Hamad v. Manuel, 26 Mass. App. Ct. 966, 527 N.E.2d 242 (1988); Vickery v. Walton, 26 Mass. App. Ct. 1030, 533 N.E.2d 1381 (1989); Levenson v. L.M.I. Realty Corp., 31 Mass. App. Ct. 127, 575 N.E.2d 370 (1991); Germagian v. Berrini, 60 Mass. App. Ct. 456, 803 N.E.2d 354 (2004); but see McCarthy v. Tobin, 429 Mass. 84, 706 N.E.2d 629 (1999); Howard v. Wee, 61 Mass. App. Ct. 912, 811 N.E.2d 1050 (2004).

[7]See Schwanbeck v. Federal-Mogul Corp., 412 Mass. 703, 592 N.E.2d 1289 (1992).

"would be entitled to specific performance of the final OTP even if, hypothetically, the execution of a purchase and sale agreement were a condition to the enforceability of the final OTP."[8]

TOPIC B: OPTION*

*Appendix E, Option Agreement, containing provisions of the types usually important in such agreements.

§ 3:2 Purposes and types

A buyer may wish to have an option to purchase real estate in order to gain control of the parcel and the price before making substantial expenditures to determine if the land is suitable for his intended use or development and if such development is feasible. A seller may accede to grant an option if he receives a satisfactory option payment, or if the premises are not otherwise likely to be sold at a price commensurate with that offered by the option buyer. An option agreement has been held to create an equitable servitude.[1] When the option property was subject to a ground lease to the Boston Redevelopment Authority, a purchase option was enforced, but subject to the lease which remained in force.[2]

An option should specify the period and the manner in which it may be exercised by the buyer, and should contain, or incorporate a separate agreement containing, all of the same provisions as are appropriate to a purchase and sale agreement. Under the statutory rule against perpetuities (§ **10:23**) the time for exercise of an option is limited to thirty years.

Options are sometimes used when a tract of land requires rezoning, zoning permits or variances, subdivision approval, environmental approvals or other governmental action in order to be used or developed, or when extensive studies of physical conditions of the land, marketing prospects, financing arrangements or other prerequisites are involved. The buyer will usually need a substantial period of time in which to meet all of his conditions, and generally will incur substantial planning expenses. In return for holding the

---

[8]Kurker v. Shoestring Properties Ltd. Partnership, 68 Mass. App. Ct. 644, 864 N.E.2d 24 (2007).

[Section 3:2]

[1]Clark v. Mead Realty Group, Inc., 67 Mass. App. Ct. 491, 854 N.E.2d 972 (2006).

[2]Franklin Square Apartments, Inc. v. Boston Redevelopment Authority, 14 L.C.R. 236 (2006).

property off the market during this time the seller may wish to have all of the plans, studies and data turned over to him if the option is not exercised, and will wish to have the land returned to its former condition if excavations have been made. In those circumstances a seller may wish to provide that the buyer shall use diligent efforts to cause his essential conditions to be met, and that if they are in fact met, the seller may then require the buyer to purchase. That is, in effect, a put option in the seller. An option agreement so cast is in effect little different than a purchase and sale agreement subject to conditions, and indeed sometimes the bargaining for a purchase and sale agreement or an option comes down to matters of form, style and psychology. There is, as the saying goes, more than one way to skin a cat.

Options are often granted in leases, allowing the tenant to purchase the premises upon termination of the lease or occurrence of some other event. It is usually the lessee who requests such provisions, and presumably lessee's attorney who drafts them. When they are litigated, lessees seem to prevail more often than lessors[3] but there are limits,[4] and the need for careful drafting is always evident.

TOPIC C: FIRST REFUSAL*

*Appendix F, Agreement of First Refusal, contains provisions often pertinent.

§ 3:3 Types and consequences

The term first refusal may be applied to any instrument by which A agrees with B that A will not sell a specified parcel of land without first giving B the opportunity to buy it. Various permutations and the enforceability thereof have been considered by the courts.[1] There are several manners of determining the price and other terms on which B may

---

[3]Blum v. Kenyon, 29 Mass. App. Ct. 417, 560 N.E.2d 742 (1990); Amerada Hess Corp. v. Garabedian, 416 Mass. 149, 617 N.E.2d 630 (1993); Nissan Automobiles Of Marlborough, Inc. v. Glick, 62 Mass. App. Ct. 302, 816 N.E.2d 161 (2004); Turner v. Community Homeowner's Ass'n, Inc., 62 Mass. App. Ct. 319, 816 N.E.2d 537 (2004).

[4]Stone v. W.E. Aubuchon Co., Inc., 29 Mass. App. Ct. 523, 562

N.E.2d 852 (1990); Mullett v. Peltier, 31 Mass. App. Ct. 445, 579 N.E.2d 174 (1991); Hawthorne's, Inc. v. Warrenton Realty, Inc., 414 Mass. 200, 606 N.E.2d 908 (1993).

[Section 3:3]

[1]Fisher v. Fisher, 23 Mass. App. Ct. 205, 500 N.E.2d 821 (1986); Reef v. Bernstein, 23 Mass. App. Ct. 599, 504 N.E.2d 374 (1987); Roy v. George W. Greene, Inc., 404 Mass. 67, 533 N.E.2d 1323 (1989); Schwanbeck v. Federal-

purchase, the most common being the matching of a bona fide offer for the premises made by a third party. The term bona fide offer may itself need some definition.[2] Another is appraisal, made on the instance of either party. Sometimes there is a fixed price, or a formula resting on a base price to be adjusted according to the passage of time and a cost of living or other index.

A pre-emptive right to purchase at a fixed price, which was far below market value at the time of the purported exercise, was held unenforceable as a restraint on alienation not meeting the tests of reasonableness.[3] However, an agreement between a seller and buyer, who continued to be abutting owners, setting forth reciprocal restrictions and reciprocal first refusals, based in part on formula prices, was upheld as meeting the tests set forth in the Restatement of Property.[4]

A leading case involving a first refusal in a commercial context is *UNO Restaurants, Inc. v. Boston Kenmore Realty Corp.*[5] Plaintiff was lessee of a condominium unit on which it also held a right of first refusal, in a building owned by defendant as owner of all of the units. Unsolicited by the defendant, a third party offered to purchase all of the units, specifying separate prices for plaintiff's unit and the balance of the building. Defendant notified plaintiff and offered to sell plaintiff's unit to it at the so specified price. Believing the price distorted upward for its unit and downward for the balance, plaintiff purported to exercise the first refusal and specified a price based on the ratio of assessed values to the total offered by the third party. In its suit to enforce its first refusal plaintiff asserted breach of the implied covenant of good faith and fair dealing, but the court held for the defendant, saying that even if the third party's purpose was to defeat plaintiff's first refusal, there was no collusion by defendant, which had no duty except to give plaintiff the opportunity to match the offer it received.

Since a first refusal if exercised will lead to conveyance of real estate, the instrument granting it should contain provi-

---

Mogul Corp., 412 Mass. 703, 592 N.E.2d 1289 (1992).

[2]Mucci v. Brockton Bocce Club, Inc., 19 Mass. App. Ct. 155, 472 N.E.2d 966 (1985).

[3]Coleman v. Tenney, 1 L.C.R. 179 (1993); see also Sher v. Cohen, 9 L.C.R. 416 (2001).

[4]Johnson v. Cohan, (Middlesex Superior Ct., C.A. No. 96-07352, Decision Feb. 3, 1999), citing Franklin v. Spadafora, 388 Mass. 764, 447 N.E.2d 1244, 39 A.L.R.4th 77 (1983).

[5]Uno Restaurants, Inc. v. Boston Kenmore Realty Corp., 441 Mass. 376, 805 N.E.2d 957 (2004).

sions as to conveyance of good title, delivery of possession, condition of the premises, insurance, adjustments and other appropriate provisions of the type used in purchase and sale agreements.[6] The statutory rule against perpetuities (§ **10:23**) sets a thirty year limit for a first refusal in gross, but possibly an appurtenant first refusal could be extended to ninety years.

An owner who grants a first refusal will not wish to hinder or delay any sale of his property more than is necessary in order to fulfill the purpose of his having granted the first refusal. To protect that interest, the procedure for offering the property to the holder of the first refusal and for his accepting it, or deciding not to purchase, are important and the requirements of notice and the applicable time periods should be carefully spelled out. Furthermore, an owner who grants a first refusal may wish to be free to mortgage the property, convey to members of his family or an estate plan trust, or to make a gift of the property to a charity.[7] In some instances the first refusal may be made to apply to and bind grantees, including even a purchaser at a mortgage foreclosure sale, but the grantor of the first refusal may be unwilling to go that far, and mortgage lenders might balk at it.

If an instrument designated as a first refusal gives the holder thereof the right in any manner to initiate the sale of the premises by the owner, then the instrument is really more in the nature of an option. If, on the other hand, the owner may to any extent require the holder of the first refusal to purchase, then it resembles a put option. All of the permutations of these instruments have their place, but of course that should be determined with deliberation.

TOPIC D: BROKERAGE

§ 3:4 Fair deals

In residential transactions would-be sellers usually start by engaging a real estate broker and signing the broker's listing agreement. This is usually a multiple listing agree-

---

[6]See Knott v. Racicot, 442 Mass. 314, 812 N.E.2d 1207 (2004), in which the SJC accepted a recital of consideration as controlling, and disposed of the old "common law fiction" that seal imports consideration.

[7]See Douglas-Hamilton v. Batchelder, 10 L.C.R. 32 (2002), in which the grant of a conservation and preservation restriction (§ **15:21**) was held not to be a "transfer" requiring notice under a first refusal.

ment pursuant to which the property is listed for sale with all members of the realtors organization, and the commission may ultimately be shared between the "listing broker" and the "selling broker" who procures a buyer. This is a perfectly sensible approach so long as the seller confirms that the broker is duly licensed and bonded.[1] Brokerage firms and their organizations are generally professional entities which comply with the required Professional Standards of Practice.[2]

When a developer is preparing to market subdivision lots or condominium units, or in the case of a substantial commercial transaction, it is more likely that the seller will seek the assistance of a lawyer in negotiating a brokerage agreement. The essential elements may be found in a form proffered by the prospective broker, but there are many possible variants of clauses with respect to duration of the agreement, exclusivity, asking prices and optional elements, respective roles and duties of the seller and broker, marketing practices, and of course the terms and times of payment of commissions. As to marketing practices, some developers and even a few lawyers regard themselves as skilled in the field. The drafting of a "presentation" for a new subdivision or condominium project is at least in part a lawyer's job since there are indeed legal issues involved.

The issues that are most frequently litigated are understandably those related to the terms and conditions under which a commission becomes payable. The leading case, often cited, is *Tristram's Landing, Inc. v. Wait*.[3] In that case the broker had procured a buyer, who signed a purchase and sale agreement, paid a ten percent deposit, and then failed to close. The broker sued for the customary five percent commission (half of the defaulted deposit, which the seller had retained), and probably expected to win the case, did so at trial, but lost on appeal. Reviewing prior cases, the court conceded that on their rules the plaintiff broker might have won, but the time had come for a new rule, reflecting the reality that a seller's ordinary "expectation is that the money for the payment of commission will come out of the proceeds of the sale." That quotation, culled from a New Jersey decision, came from "the opinion of Lord Justice Denning, in

---

[Section 3:4]

[1]M.G.L.A. c. 112, §§ 87RR, 87SS, 87TT; 254 CMR 2.00.

[2]254 CMR 3.00. Standards as to escrow accounts and dual agency,

effective in April 2005, are of particular interest.

[3]Tristram's Landing, Inc. v. Wait, 367 Mass. 622, 327 N.E.2d 727 (1975).

Dennis Reed, Ltd. v. Goody, [1950] 2 K.B. 277." Noting that not only New Jersey but quite a few other states had adopted the new rule, the SJC held that "under a brokerage agreement hereafter made," a broker is entitled to a commission only if (again quoting from Lord Justice Denning via the New Jersey decision): "(a) he produces a purchaser ready, willing and able to buy on the terms fixed by the owner, (b) the purchaser enters into a binding contract with the owner to do so, and (c) the purchaser completes the transaction by closing the title in accordance with the provisions of the contract." The quotation continues to provide, however, that "if the failure of completion of the contract results from the wrongful act or interference of the seller, the broker's claim is valid and must be paid." Beyond that, the court in *Tristram* conceded that its new rule "could be easily circumvented by language to the contrary in purchase and sale agreements or in agreements between sellers and brokers."

The strict application of the *Tristram's Landing* rules is indicated in a number of subsequent cases.[4] In *Hillis v. Lake*, the court held that seller's failure to perform (with respect an agreement that did not close because of hazardous materials on the property) was "innocent" and thus did not constitute a "wrongful act." Referring to *Bennett v. McCabe*,[5] in which the U.S. District Court opined that the *Tristram's Landing* rule would allow payment of a commission where a seller prevented closing, even if innocently, the SJC said "The Bennett decision does not state Massachusetts law correctly."

TOPIC E: TENANCY; OCCUPANCY

§ 3:5 Statutory notice and effect

From the conveyancer's standpoint, it is always important to remember that a lease is both a contract and a conveyance. The contractual aspects and the general law of landlord and tenant are, of course, subjects of law of enormous scope,

---

[4]Notably Hillis v. Lake, 38 Mass. App. Ct. 221, 646 N.E.2d 1081 (1995), aff'd, 421 Mass. 537, 658 N.E.2d 687 (1995); Sparks v. Fidelity Nat. Title Ins. Co., 294 F.3d 259 (1st Cir. 2002); Coldwell Banker/Hunneman v. Shostack, 62 Mass. App. Ct. 635, 818 N.E.2d 1079 (2004); Lewis v. Emerson, 391 Mass. 517, 462 N.E.2d 295 (1984); Turnpike Motors, Inc. v. Newbury Group, Inc., 413 Mass. 119, 596 N.E.2d 989 (1992); Currier v. Kosinski, 24 Mass. App. Ct. 106, 506 N.E.2d 895 (1987).

[5]Bennett v. McCabe, 808 F.2d 178 (1st Cir. 1987).

not to be dealt with here. When dealing with matters of conveyance by deed or mortgage, the conveyancer should keep in mind that a term of years under a lease is an interest in land which encumbers a title. If that term is shorter than the period which requires recording in order to be effective, as hereinafter referred to, then the conveyancer will learn of such interest in the land only if the parties advise him of it or if he makes or has made an inspection of the premises.

Under M.G.L.A. c. 183, § 4, a lease for a term of seven years or more is not valid against persons other than the lessor, his heirs, devisees, and persons having actual notice of it, unless the lease or a notice of lease meeting statutory requirements is recorded. A notice of lease, defined in that § 4, must be executed by the parties to the lease and contain the date of execution, a description of the leased premises "in the form contained in such lease", the term of such lease with the date of commencement of the term, and all rights of extension or renewal. M.G.L.A. c. 185, § 71, applies the same to registered land. Rights of extension and renewal pursuant to which the term could last for more than seven years make the lease subject to the statute. An option to purchase in a lease is not required to be referred to in a notice of lease, but it is certainly the better practice to do so.

It may be noted that the statute prescribes the contents of a notice of lease, but not the form, and sometimes one encounters instruments styled as "short form" or "declaration" of lease. It is also noteworthy that the financial terms of the lease need not be disclosed of record.

In negotiating a lease, a tenant taking for a term which extends or may extend for more than 7 years will wish to require the landlord to execute and deliver a notice of lease in order that the tenant may record it and protect his leasehold. It may also be desirable from the landlord's standpoint to require that a notice of lease, or some other form indicating the existence of a tenancy, be executed and recorded, even if the term is less than seven years, in order that the term of encumbrance of the landlord's title by the tenancy be made clear of record.

With respect to pre-closing occupancy by a buyer or holdover occupancy by a seller, see § 1:33.

TOPIC F: BOUNDARY

§ 3:6 Location; cross-conveyance

A boundary agreement is a means by which abutting owners may establish the location of a boundary between their lands which was previously indeterminate or in dispute, or to adjust a known or assumed boundary to an agreed and defined location. Usually a plan will be prepared, to be referred to in the boundary agreement, showing the parcels of both owners, or at least the line between them, with adequate monumentation to locate it with respect to their parcels and other known points. Such an agreement should identify the parcels of the two abutting owners, at least by street address and title reference, if not full description, declare the purpose of establishing the boundary between their parcels and set forth (a) their agreement for themselves and their heirs, successors and assigns that the new boundary, shown on the referenced plan, shall henceforth constitute the boundary between their respective parcels, and also (b) a cross-conveyance whereby each owner grants to the other all his right, title and interest in and to the land lying on the specified opposite side of the defined line. Such cross-conveyance should be carefully drawn, usually in two parts, A to B, and B to A, and is an essential element of such an agreement. Thereafter the title source of each party will be in part the back title of the other, and consequently, each party will be concerned with the other's having a good title to convey, and should have it examined as a prerequisite to entering the boundary agreement.

It may be observed that a boundary agreement of this type will in some circumstances be all that is needed, and the apt remedy, for a title which is flawed only by a poor description susceptible to correction or clarification by anchoring one or more of the boundaries.

TOPIC G: OTHER

§ 3:7 References

There are of course a great variety of other types of agreements affecting the title and use of real estate. Primary among them are agreements creating or granting easements or restrictions, or modifying or terminating them, or interpreting and providing for exercise or enforcement thereof (as to which, see **Chapter 15**). There are also the documents governing the organization and conduct of condominiums, and phasing thereof (see **Chapter 17**), and Cooperatives, homeowners' associations and time-share arrangements (see **Chapter 18**). Agreements relating to and affecting financing and mortgages come in various forms, as referred to in **Chapter 20**. And beyond those the variety of agreements one may encounter is limited only by the imagination and ingenuity of lawyers.

Chapter 4

Statute of Frauds

KeyCite®: Cases and other legal materials listed in KeyCite Scope can be researched through the KeyCite service on Westlaw®. Use KeyCite to check citations for form, parallel references, prior and later history, and comprehensive citator information, including citations to other decisions and secondary materials.

TOPIC A: THE STATUTE

§ 4:1 Terms

The Massachusetts statute of frauds is set forth in M.G.L.A. c. 259, § 1, and provides that:

> No action shall be brought:

> First, To charge an executor or administrator, or an assignee under an insolvent law of the commonwealth, upon a special promise to answer damages out of his own estate;

> Second, To charge a person upon a special promise to answer for the debt, default or misdoings of another;

> Third, Upon an agreement made upon consideration of

marriage;

Fourth, Upon a contract for the sale of lands, tenements or hereditaments or of any interest in or concerning them; or,

Fifth, Upon an agreement that is not to be performed within one year from the making thereof;

Unless the promise, contract or agreement upon which such action is brought, or some memorandum or note thereof, is in writing and signed by the party to be charged therewith or by some person thereunto by him lawfully authorized.

Clause Fourth is of course the most important to a real estate lawyer, but the other clauses and other provisions of Chapter 259 have application in some real estate transactions.

M.G.L.A. c. 259, § 2 provides that: "The consideration of such promise, contract or agreement need not be set forth or expressed in the writing signed by the party to be charged therewith, but may be proved by any legal evidence."

And M.G.L.A. c. 259, § 7 provides that:

Any agreement to pay compensation for service as a broker or finder or for service rendered in negotiating a loan or in negotiating the purchase, sale or exchange of a business, its good will, inventory, fixtures, or an interest therein, including a majority of voting interest in a corporation, shall be void and unenforceable unless such agreement is in writing, signed by the party to be charged therewith, or by some other person authorized. For the purpose of this section, the term "negotiating" shall include identifying prospective parties, providing information concerning prospective parties, procuring an introduction to a party to the transaction or assisting in the negotiation or consummation of the transaction. The provisions of this section shall apply to a contract implied in fact or in law to pay reasonable compensation but shall not apply to a contract to pay compensation for professional services of an attorney-at-law or a licensed real estate broker or real estate salesman acting in their professional capacity.

Besides the basic statute, one must consider M.G.L.A. c. 183, § 3, which provides that:

An estate or interest in land created without an instrument in writing signed by the grantor or by his attorney shall have the force and effect of an estate at will only, and no estate or interest in land shall be assigned, granted or surrendered unless by such writing or by operation of law.

and also M.G.L.A. c. 203, § 1, which provides that:

No trust concerning land, except such as may arise or result by implication of law, shall be created or declared unless by a written instrument signed by the party creating or declaring the trust or by his attorney.

§ 4:2 Legal import

It is most important to observe that M.G.L.A. c. 259, § 1, does not invalidate an oral contract, but operates only to prevent the bringing of an action to enforce such a contract. Furthermore, "some memorandum or note thereof" is all it takes to make an oral contract actionable, and, as will appear below, the requirements for such a memorandum are pretty skimpy.

TOPIC B: INSTRUMENTS AFFECTED

§ 4:3 Those that need to comply

The statute refers to "a contract for the sale of lands . . ." or of "any interest in or concerning them." Such contracts, and such interests and concerns, come in many varieties, and over the years almost every type has been tested by the courts and found to be subject to the statute of frauds. Instead of listing the cases for each permutation, the aim herein is to indicate general groupings of types of agreements subject to the statute and to cite only a few leading cases and more current cases, from which one might by appropriate research be led to the full panoply of judicial decisions. The areas touched upon include the following:

- Ordinary contracts for the sale of land, in various forms;[1]
- Agreements relating to financing and mortgages;[2]
- Agreements relating to partition or restricting construction;[3]
- Agreements concerning equitable interests;[4]
- Leases and tenancies, as affected also by M.G.L.A. c.

[Section 4:3]

[1]Epdee Corp. v. Richmond, 321 Mass. 673, 75 N.E.2d 238 (1947); Watkins v. Briggs, 314 Mass. 282, 50 N.E.2d 64 (1943); Ravosa v. Zais, 40 Mass. App. Ct. 47, 661 N.E.2d 111 (1996).

[2]Duff v. U. S. Trust Co., 327 Mass. 17, 97 N.E.2d 189 (1951); Montuori v. Bailen, 290 Mass. 72, 194 N.E. 714, 97 A.L.R. 789 (1935); Metropolitan Credit Union v. Matthes, 46 Mass. App. Ct. 326, 706 N.E.2d 296 (1999).

[3]Bendetson v. Coolidge, 7 Mass. App. Ct. 798, 390 N.E.2d 1124 (1979); Alexander v. Snell, 12 Mass. App. Ct. 323, 424 N.E.2d 262 (1981).

[4]Town of Belmont v. Massachusetts Amusement Corp., 333 Mass. 565, 132 N.E.2d 172 (1956).

183, § 3;[5]
- Agreements relating to easements;[6] and
- Agreements relating to brokerage commissions, as affected by M.G.L.A. c. 259, § 7;[7] and also as affected by Clause Fifth of M.G.L.A. c. 259, § 1.[8]

§ 4:4   Those that need not comply

The penchant to make oral deals being as prevalent as it is, there are also a great number of cases in which the validity thereof has been tested, and upheld. Again the approach here will be to group them into types and to cite only a few leading cases and more current cases. The types of oral agreements which are exempt from the statute of frauds may be categorized as follows:

- Amendments of a contract which *is* subject to the statute of frauds, provided that the amended terms themselves do not fall within the requirements of the statute;[1]
- Agreements that are in the nature of licenses and do not affect *interests* in land, as recognized in common law or by statute, including such things as hotel lodgings, access rights, timbering agreements, a broker's agreement to find a buyer, and construction contracts;[2]
- Agreements for payments, including payments of a mortgage debt, taxes, divisions of sale or rental proceeds, or support.[3]

It should be emphasized, however, that the listing of these categories is not gospel, and there are likely to be many close calls on possible enforcement of the requirement of a

---

[5]First Nat. Bank of Boston v. Fairhaven Amusement Co., 347 Mass. 243, 197 N.E.2d 607 (1964).

[6]Baseball Pub. Co. v. Bruton, 302 Mass. 54, 18 N.E.2d 362, 119 A.L.R. 1518 (1938); Silverleib v. Hebshie, 33 Mass. App. Ct. 911, 596 N.E.2d 401 (1992).

[7]Alexander v. Berman, 29 Mass. App. Ct. 458, 560 N.E.2d 1295 (1990).

[8]Richard Tucker Associates, Inc. v. Smith, 395 Mass. 648, 481 N.E.2d 489 (1985).

[Section 4:4]

[1]Levin v. Rose, 302 Mass. 378, 19 N.E.2d 297 (1939); Wesley v. Marsman, 393 Mass. 1003, 471 N.E.2d 51 (1984); McKinley Investments, Inc. v. Middleborough Land, LLC., 62 Mass. App. Ct. 616, 818 N.E.2d 627 (2004).

[2]Montuori v. Bailen, 290 Mass. 72, 194 N.E. 714, 97 A.L.R. 789 (1935); Bushkin Associates, Inc. v. Raytheon Co., 393 Mass. 622, 473 N.E.2d 662 (1985); Novel Iron Works, Inc. v. Wexler Const. Co., Inc., 26 Mass. App. Ct. 401, 528 N.E.2d 142 (1988).

[3]Sokol v. Nathanson, 317 Mass. 325, 58 N.E.2d 126 (1944); Reum v. Brazeau, 1 Mass. App. Ct. 549, 303 N.E.2d 119 (1973); First Pennsylvania Mortg. Trust v. Dorchester Sav. Bank, 395 Mass. 614, 481 N.E.2d 1132 (1985).

writing.

TOPIC C: THE WRITING

§ 4:5   Memorandum

As noted in § **4:2**, an oral contract may become enforceable by virtue of a "memorandum or note" thereof, the requirements for which are not very strict. A mere identification of the parties and the land may in some circumstances suffice, even without specification of the price. In such cases the court may imply requirements of conveyance of good title free of encumbrances, within a reasonable time, and at a fair and reasonable price.[1] Of course it is not always so easy or so risky, and the courts do require proof of the existence of an oral contract, and do reject some proffered memoranda as insufficient, either in themselves or as evidence of an oral contract.[2] With respect to the requirements for a memorandum sufficient to evidence an oral contract and to meet the requirements of the statute of frauds, it may be noted that:

(1) The form is not important; it need not have a purpose of being such a memorandum; it may be pieced together from separate writings; separate writings and "shorthand" expressions, initials, property references, etc. may be elucidated by parole evidence.[3] Under M.G.L.A. c. 110G, an electronic record would surely now suffice.

(2) Such things as notations on a check, letters, informal memos, or official records may suffice.[4]

(3) The "essential elements" of the contract must be identified, but that includes only (i) the parties, who need

---

[Section 4:5]

[1]Epdee Corp. v. Richmond, 321 Mass. 673, 75 N.E.2d 238 (1947); Shayeb v. Holland, 321 Mass. 429, 73 N.E.2d 731 (1947); M.G.L.A. c. 259, § 2.

[2]Epdee Corp. v. Richmond, 321 Mass. 673, 75 N.E.2d 238 (1947); Bouvier v. L'Eveque, 324 Mass. 476, 86 N.E.2d 915 (1949); Ucello v. Cosentino, 354 Mass. 48, 235 N.E.2d 44 (1968); Tull v. Mister Donut Development Corp., 7 Mass. App. Ct. 626, 389 N.E.2d 447 (1979).

[3]Cousbelis v. Alexander, 315 Mass. 729, 54 N.E.2d 47, 153 A.L.R. 1108 (1944); Des Brisay v. Foss, 264 Mass. 102, 162 N.E. 4 (1928); Nickerson v. Bridges, 216 Mass. 416, 103 N.E. 939 (1914); Nickerson v. Weld, 204 Mass. 346, 90 N.E. 589 (1910); Michelson v. Sherman, 310 Mass. 774, 39 N.E.2d 633, 139 A.L.R. 960 (1942).

[4]Cousbelis v. Alexander, 315 Mass. 729, 54 N.E.2d 47, 153 A.L.R. 1108 (1944); A. B. C. Auto Parts, Inc. v. Moran, 359 Mass. 327, 268 N.E.2d 844 (1971); McManus v. City of Boston, 171 Mass. 152, 50 N.E. 607 (1898); Technical Economist Corporation v. Moors, 255 Mass. 591, 152 N.E. 83 (1926).

not be formally named if they can be identified to the exclusion of others, (ii) the property, which need not be specifically described if it can be identified to the exclusion of other properties, and (iii) some indication of the nature or the transaction, i.e., whether sale, lease, easement, or other.[5]

The message for real estate lawyers, the principal audience for this book, is of course to avoid, and educate your clients to avoid, oral contracts and any writings which conceivably could identify oral dealings as constituting a contract.

§ 4:6 Signature

The statute requires a signature of "the party to be charged . . . or by some person . . . by him lawfully authorized." In the case of a memorandum evidencing an oral contract, the signature may appear anywhere therein. Any party so signing is bound, and it is not necessary for both parties to be bound. The signature may be by an agent, and the authority of the agent may be proved by parole evidence.[1] An auctioneer's signature may bind both parties to an auction sale.[2]

A signature may consist of initials or in a printed, stamped or typed form if it can be determined that the person charged meant to authenticate the document as his own act.[3] Both a telegram[4] and an e-mail[5] have been held sufficient, and M.G.L.A. c. 110G, the Uniform Electronic Transactions Act, confirms the validity of an electronically recorded or

---

[5]Young v. Young, 251 Mass. 218, 146 N.E. 574 (1925); Sands v. Arruda, 359 Mass. 591, 270 N.E.2d 826 (1971); Sanjean v. Miller, 248 Mass. 288, 142 N.E. 799 (1924); Andre v. Ellison, 324 Mass. 665, 88 N.E.2d 340 (1949); Michelson v. Sherman, 310 Mass. 774, 39 N.E.2d 633, 139 A.L.R. 960 (1942).

[Section 4:6]

[1]Des Brisay v. Foss, 264 Mass. 102, 162 N.E. 4 (1928); Freeman v. Fishman, 245 Mass. 222, 139 N.E. 846 (1923) (overruled in part by,

Morad v. Silva, 331 Mass. 94, 117 N.E.2d 290 (1954)).

[2]Rix v. Dooley, 322 Mass. 303, 77 N.E.2d 233 (1948).

[3]Irving v. Goodimate Co., 320 Mass. 454, 70 N.E.2d 414, 171 A.L.R. 326 (1946).

[4]Providence Granite Co., Inc. v. Joseph Rugo, Inc., 362 Mass. 888, 291 N.E.2d 159 (1972).

[5]Shattuck v. Klotzbach, Plymouth Superior Court, C.A. No. 01-1109A (Dec. 11, 2001).

transmitted signature.

TOPIC D: PART PERFORMANCE EXCEPTION

§ 4:7 Required elements

The exception to the statute of frauds based on partial performance arises from equitable considerations, particularly those related to change of position in reliance on a promise. The courts have evaluated such reliance in terms of justification, nature and extent, and in terms of whether the change of position in reliance was sufficient to work an estoppel on the party asserting the statute of frauds as a defense.[1]

Payment of the purchase price in whole or in part is not enough, nor is possession of the land, although that is a pertinent factor.[2] The giving up of other business deals has been deemed sufficient.[3] The making of improvements by a buyer in possession of the land certainly indicates reliance, but has not always been deemed sufficient.[4] The modern trend has been toward liberalization. In *Hickey v. Green*,[5] the appeals court remanded to permit an order for specific performance where there had been a change in position in reliance on the oral promise, but no payment, possession or improvements, and recognized that its decision "may well go somewhat beyond the circumstances considered in" prior cases. In *Sullivan v. Rooney*,[6] the SJC declined to decide the issue of estoppel, but did find a constructive trust, and said that "the circumstances that demonstrate a constructive trust in this case are remarkably similar to circumstances that would deny the defendant the right to rely on the Statute of Frauds on principles of estoppel." The appeals court accepted failure of consideration and partial performance as

---

[Section 4:7]

[1]Fisher v. MacDonald, 332 Mass. 727, 127 N.E.2d 484 (1955); Winstanley v. Chapman, 325 Mass. 130, 89 N.E.2d 506 (1949).

[2]Chase v. Aetna Rubber Co., 321 Mass. 721, 75 N.E.2d 637 (1947); Andrews v. Charon, 289 Mass. 1, 193 N.E. 737 (1935).

[3]Chase v. Aetna Rubber Co., 321 Mass. 721, 75 N.E.2d 637 (1947); Des Brisay v. Foss, 264 Mass. 102, 162 N.E. 4 (1928).

[4]Fisher v. MacDonald, 332 Mass. 727, 127 N.E.2d 484 (1955); Winstanley v. Chapman, 325 Mass. 130, 89 N.E.2d 506 (1949); Bruni v. Andre, 339 Mass. 708, 162 N.E.2d 52 (1959).

[5]Hickey v. Green, 14 Mass. App. Ct. 671, 442 N.E.2d 37 (1982).

[6]Sullivan v. Rooney, 404 Mass. 160, 533 N.E.2d 1372 (1989).

the basis for enforcing oral promises of life tenancy.[7] The Housing Court upheld an executory oral agreement to grant a tenancy at will, noting that payment and acceptance of the first month's rent arguably took the case out of the statute of frauds.[8] But the land court found an alleged oral agreement of the FDIC not to have been proved, nor reliance thereon sufficient to take it out of the statute of frauds.[9]

The provisions of §§ 13 and 14 of M.G.L.A. c. 260, are pertinent, as follows:

Section 13. No acknowledgment or promise shall be evidence of a new or continuing contract whereby to take an action of contract out of the operation of this chapter or to deprive a party of the benefit thereof, unless such acknowledgment or promise has been made by, or is contained in, a writing signed by the party chargeable thereby.

Section 14. The preceding section shall not alter or impair the effect of a payment of principal or interest made by any person; but no endorsement or memorandum of any such payment, written or made upon a promissory note, bill of exchange or other writing by or on behalf of the party to whom such payment has been or purports to have been made, shall be sufficient proof of the payment to take the case out of the provisions of this chapter.

---

[7]Mulvanity v. Pelletier, 40 Mass. App. Ct. 106, 661 N.E.2d 952 (1996).

[8]Carolan v. Imperial Real Estate, (Housing Court, No. 92-CV-0081, 1992).

[9]Halsing v. Atlantic National Trust, LLC, 6 L.C.R. 205 (1998).

Chapter 5

Remedies for Breach

TOPIC A: THE REMEDIES

TOPIC B: UNFAIR TRADE PRACTICES

TOPIC C: WARRANTY

TOPIC D: LIMITATIONS OF ACTIONS

KeyCite®: Cases and other legal materials listed in KeyCite Scope can be researched through the KeyCite service on Westlaw®. Use KeyCite to check citations for form, parallel references, prior and later history, and comprehensive citator information, including citations to other decisions and secondary materials.

TOPIC A: THE REMEDIES

§ 5:1   Specific performance

The basis for "specific" performance of a contract for the conveyance of real estate lies in the "uniqueness" of every piece of real estate. While real estate is surely not a fungible commodity, the uniqueness of, say one lot in a subdivision over another, or one unit in a condominium over another, may be subject to philosophical debate. Nevertheless, the legal concept, deriving in part from the importance of "location," is firmly embedded and here to stay. Long ago the SJC said that the fact that a plaintiff "had an action at law to recover damages for breach of agreement does not deprive equity of its jurisdiction to compel specific performance of the contract," and also that "It is not necessary in a bill to compel specific performance of a contract to convey real estate to set forth any specific reason why the plaintiff is entitled to relief in equity."[1]

The uniqueness of land works both ways, and a seller is also entitled to specific performance, that is, to compel a buyer to accept a conveyance and pay the agreed price. In the cited case of *Olszewski v. Sardynski*,[2] the court said, in words which may well be pondered by all owners of real estate:

> The fact that the plaintiff is the vendor and that performance by the vendee would consist entirely or primarily of the payment of money have never prevented specific performance. Commonly, the remedy at law of a vendor is not adequate. Every piece of real estate has some unique disadvantage as well as advantage. The eagerness of buyers to acquire some properties is matched by the joy with which sellers part with others. Ownership of real estate is burdensome even when profitable. It hampers mobility. Years may be required to find a buyer. When at last a buyer is found, and a contract made which is broken by the buyer, the owner, with the real estate still on his hands, finds that at law he can recover only the excess, if any, of the price over the value as judicially appraised. [Citations omitted] For these reasons, to say nothing of more technical ones . . . a vendor is regularly granted specific performance unless some ground for denying it exists in the particular case.

There are cases in which a seller was unable to convey all that he had contracted to sell and the buyer still wished to take what could be conveyed with an appropriate reduction in the purchase price to compensate for the deficiency. Such partial specific performance with price reduction has in appropriate circumstances been granted as a proper equitable remedy.[3] The application of this concept has a relationship to the meaning in a purchase and sale agreement of a clause referring to the seller's "inability" to convey,[4] referred to in **§ 1:37**.

While the granting of specific performance is fairly common, it is a discretionary equitable remedy, and consequently

---

[Section 5:1]

[1]Noyes v. Bragg, 220 Mass. 106, 107 N.E. 669 (1915); see also Grant v. Pizzano, 264 Mass. 475, 163 N.E. 162 (1928).

[2]Olszewski v. Sardynski, 316 Mass. 715, 56 N.E.2d 607 (1944); Rix v. Dooley, 322 Mass. 303, 77 N.E.2d 233 (1948).

[3]Margolis v. Tarutz, 265 Mass. 540, 164 N.E. 451 (1929); Radley v. Johnson, 25 Mass. App. Ct. 969, 519 N.E.2d 788 (1988).

[4]Margolis v. Tarutz, 265 Mass. 540, 164 N.E. 451 (1929).

depends on the court's evaluation of the circumstances.[5] The pertinent considerations include the intent of the parties, or abandonment of or unreasonable delay in pursuing the remedy.[6] As noted in § 1:38, the intent of the parties is sometimes indicated by a clause in the purchase and sale agreement providing for liquidated damages as the sole remedy for breach.

Since 2002 the Land Court has had concurrent jurisdiction with the Superior Court in suits for specific performance.[7]

§ 5:2 Damages

As in the case of any breach of contract, a suit for damages may be brought upon breach by either party to an agreement for the purchase and sale of real estate. The measure of damages is ordinarily the value of the loss of the bargain, in whatever way that may be established or proved.

As noted in § 1:38, purchase and sale agreements often provide that upon breach by a buyer the seller may retain the deposit as liquidated damages. Such a provision is enforced "Where actual damages are difficult to ascertain and where the sum agreed upon by the parties at the time of the execution of the contract represents a reasonable estimate of the actual damages. . . . But where the actual damages are easily ascertainable and the stipulated sum is unreasonably and grossly disproportionate to the real damages from a breach, or is unconscionably excessive, the court will award the aggrieved party no more than his actual

---

[5]Exchange Realty Co. v. Bines, 302 Mass. 93, 18 N.E.2d 425 (1939) (overruled on other grounds by, Nalbandian v. Hanson Restaurant & Lounge, Inc., 369 Mass. 150, 338 N.E.2d 335 (1975)); Linse v. O'Meara, 338 Mass. 338, 155 N.E.2d 448 (1959); Kline v. Gutzler, 18 Mass. App. Ct. 915, 464 N.E.2d 399 (1984); Hunt v. Rice, 25 Mass. App. Ct. 622, 521 N.E.2d 751 (1988); Carrigg v. Cordeiro, 26 Mass. App. Ct. 611, 530 N.E.2d 809 (1988); Rex Lumber Co. v. Acton Block Co., Inc., 29 Mass. App. Ct. 510, 562 N.E.2d 845 (1990); Blum v. Kenyon, 29 Mass. App. Ct. 417, 560 N.E.2d 742 (1990); Hawthorne's, Inc. v. Warrenton Realty, Inc., 414 Mass. 200, 606 N.E.2d 908 (1993); Pierce v. Clark,

66 Mass. App. Ct. 912, 851 N.E.2d 450 (2006); Everets v. Webster, 14 L.C.R. 612 (2006); Berajawala v. Mureithi, 14 L.C.R. 594 (2006); Normandin v. Eastland Partners, Inc., 68 Mass. App. Ct. 377, 862 N.E.2d 402 (2007).

[6]Rigs v. Sokol, 318 Mass. 337, 61 N.E.2d 538 (1945); Simpson v. Vasiliou, 29 Mass. App. Ct. 699, 564 N.E.2d 607 (1991); Amerada Hess Corp. v. Garabedian, 416 Mass. 149, 617 N.E.2d 630 (1993); Oliver v. Poulos, 312 Mass. 188, 44 N.E.2d 1, 142 A.L.R. 1094 (1942); Merry v. A.W. Perry, Inc., 18 Mass. App. Ct. 628, 469 N.E.2d 73 (1984).

[7]Ch. 393, Acts of 2002, amending M.G.L.A. c. 185, § 1(k).

damages."[1]

Accordingly, a liquidated damage clause is rejected when the court finds the specified amount to be so disproportionate or excessive as to constitute a penalty.[2] But enforcement remains the usual rule, and the alternate approach of "second guess" had only a mistaken and brief fling in Massachusetts.[3]

When it comes to determination of actual damages, the "usual rule" is the difference between the contract price and the market value of the property. However, that is not a "rigid rule," but is "only a variation on the theme of the dominant principle, that the injured party should be as well off as if the transaction had gone through—but not better off."[4]

The grant of specific performance, or even the pursuit and abandonment of that equitable remedy, has a significant effect on the possibility or amount of an award of damages. When specific performance was granted, damages were limited or barred.[5] When specific performance was sought and denied, that had an effect on the measure of damages.[6] The SJC has ruled that when specific performance is granted, damages cannot then be granted also.[7]

§ 5:3 Rescission

The remedy of rescission of an executory contract is available with respect to purchase and sale agreements and other contracts having to do with real estate. To warrant rescission there must be one or more of (i) mutual mistake of a fact that is material to the transaction, (ii) misrepresentation of such a fact, (iii) a total failure of consideration, (iv)

[Section 5:2]

[1] A-Z Servicenter, Inc. v. Segall, 334 Mass. 672, 138 N.E.2d 266 (1956).

[2] A-Z Servicenter, Inc. v. Segall, 334 Mass. 672, 138 N.E.2d 266 (1956); Schrenko v. Regnante, 27 Mass. App. Ct. 282, 537 N.E.2d 1261 (1989); Security Safety Corp. v. Kuznicki, 350 Mass. 157, 213 N.E.2d 866 (1966).

[3] Lynch v. Andrew, 20 Mass. App. Ct. 623, 481 N.E.2d 1383 (1985); Kelly v. Marx, 44 Mass. App. Ct. 825, 694 N.E.2d 869 (1998), rev'd, 428 Mass. 877, 705 N.E.2d 1114 (1999); cf. Clean Harbors, Inc.

v. John Hancock Life Ins. Co., 64 Mass. App. Ct. 347, 833 N.E.2d 611 (2005), review denied, 445 Mass. 1105, 836 N.E.2d 1095 (2005).

[4] Foster v. Bartolomeo, 31 Mass. App. Ct. 592, 581 N.E.2d 1033 (1991).

[5] Foster v. Bartolomeo, 31 Mass. App. Ct. 592, 581 N.E.2d 1033 (1991); Rix v. Dooley, 322 Mass. 303, 77 N.E.2d 233 (1948).

[6] Normandin v. Eastland Partners, Inc., 68 Mass. App. Ct. 377, 862 N.E.2d 402 (2007).

[7] Perroncello v. Donahue, 448 Mass. 199, 859 N.E.2d 827 (2007).

duress, or (v) something very much like one or more of the foregoing. Other prerequisites to the remedy are reliance on the wrongful act and the materiality thereof. Contracts afflicted by such wrongs are ordinarily not void, but voidable, and the party seeking rescission may need to be able to put the wrongdoer back in the position he was in before the contract was made, particularly if there has been partial performance.

When one is faced with such issues, a full review of the case law is called for, and only a few clues to a start are cited here.[1]

TOPIC B: UNFAIR TRADE PRACTICES

§ 5:4   The statute and its application

M.G.L.A. c. 93A, enacted in 1967, declares unlawful and makes actionable "unfair methods of competition and unfair or deceptive acts or practices in the conduct of any trade or commerce." The Act looks for guidance to the Federal Trade Commission Act and the FTC and the federal courts in interpreting it, and authorizes the attorney general of Massachusetts to make rules and regulations,[1] but it does not itself define unfair trade practices. In addition to rule-making power, the attorney general has direct enforcement rights, and must be given notice of every civil action under the statute.

The Act exempts (a) transactions or actions otherwise permitted under laws as administered by a Massachusetts or federal regulatory body, and (b) trade or commerce of persons with 20% or more of their gross revenue from interstate commerce, except as to transactions which "occur primarily and substantially within the commonwealth" or when the FTC does not within fourteen days of notice object to ac-

---

[Section 5:3]

[1]Cherry v. Crispin, 346 Mass. 89, 190 N.E.2d 93 (1963); Levy v. Bendetson, 6 Mass. App. Ct. 558, 379 N.E.2d 1121 (1978); Maloney v. Sargisson, 18 Mass. App. Ct. 341, 465 N.E.2d 296 (1984); Solomon v. Birger, 19 Mass. App. Ct. 634, 477 N.E.2d 137 (1985); Zimmerman v. Kent, 31 Mass. App. Ct. 72, 575 N.E.2d 70 (1991); Waste Management of Massachusetts, Inc. v. Carver, 37 Mass. App. Ct. 694, 642 N.E.2d 1058 (1994); Scattaretico v. Puglisi, 60 Mass. App. Ct. 138, 799 N.E.2d 1258 (2003).

[Section 5:4]

[1]940 CMR 3.16.

tion at the state level.[2] The statute does permit class actions.[3]

Civil remedies are provided under §§ 9 and 11. Under § 11 a remedy (the businessman's remedy) is given to "Any person who engages in the conduct of any trade or commerce and who suffers any loss of money or property, real or personal, as a result of the use or employment by another person who engages in any trade or commerce of an unfair method of competition or an unfair or deceptive act . . . " Under § 9 a remedy (the consumer's remedy) is given to "Any person, other than a person entitled to bring action under section eleven of this chapter, who has been injured by another person's use or employment of any method, act or practice declared to be unlawful . . . "

One of the requirements of § 9 is that a written demand for relief, identifying the claimant and reasonably describing the unfair or deceptive act or practice complained of and the injury suffered, must be sent to the prospective respondent at least 30 days prior to the filing of an action thereunder.[4] If the person receiving such a demand shall within 30 days make a written tender of settlement which is rejected by the claimant, the amount of recovery will thereafter be limited to the tendered settlement if the court finds that it was reasonable in relation to the injury actually suffered by the claimant.[5] Otherwise the recovery shall be the amount of actual damages, but double to treble actual damages may be awarded if the court finds that the act or practice complained of was a willful or knowing violation of the statute or that the refusal to grant relief upon demand was made in bad faith, and the court may also award reasonable attorney's fees and costs, or frame equitable relief.[6]

Such demand requirements do not apply if the claim is as-

---

[2]Dodd v. Commercial Union Ins. Co., 373 Mass. 72, 365 N.E.2d 802 (1977); Bushkin Associates, Inc. v. Raytheon Co., 393 Mass. 622, 473 N.E.2d 662 (1985).

[3]Fletcher v. Cape Cod Gas Co., 394 Mass. 595, 477 N.E.2d 116 (1985).

[4]Carter v. Empire Mut. Ins. Co., 6 Mass. App. Ct. 114, 374 N.E.2d 585 (1978); Cassano v. Gogos, 20 Mass. App. Ct. 348, 480 N.E.2d 649 (1985).

[5]Russell v. Denton, 14 Mass. App. Ct. 936, 437 N.E.2d 238 (1982).

[6]Bachman v. Parkin, 19 Mass. App. Ct. 908, 471 N.E.2d 759 (1984); Charles River Const. Co., Inc. v. Kirksey, 20 Mass. App. Ct. 333, 480 N.E.2d 315 (1985); Greenstein v. Flatley, 19 Mass. App. Ct. 351, 474 N.E.2d 1130 (1985); Leardi v. Brown, 394 Mass. 151, 474 N.E.2d 1094 (1985); Rousseau v. Gelinas, 24 Mass. App. Ct. 154, 507 N.E.2d 265 (1987); Rex Lumber Co. v. Acton Block Co., Inc., 29 Mass. App. Ct. 510, 562 N.E.2d 845 (1990); Schwartz v. Rose, 418 Mass. 41, 634 N.E.2d 105 (1994); Tufankjian v. Rockland Trust Co., 57 Mass. App. Ct. 173, 782 N.E.2d 1 (2003).

serted as a counterclaim or cross-claim or if the respondent has no place of business or assets in Massachusetts, but even then respondents may protect themselves against the risk of multiple damages "by making a written offer of relief and paying the rejected tender into court as soon as practicable after receiving notice of an action commenced under this section."

The gravamen of many complaints under Chapter 93A is non-disclosure. As provided in the Attorney General's regulations (n. 1), an actionable unfair trade practice may lie in the mere non-disclosure of "any fact, the disclosure of which may have influenced the buyer or prospective buyer not to enter into the transaction." That regulation has certainly promoted and broadened the beneficial practice by those engaged in selling real estate of (usually) making disclosure of all conceivably pertinent facts.[7]

Nevertheless, claims persist, all too often warranted, and sometimes by disgruntled or dissatisfied parties who perceive some form of alleged unfair trade practice to assert in fortification of their actual complaints which may or may not in themselves be actionable. Claims under Chapter 93A are usually coupled with other claims and counts of misrepresentation or breach of contract, but can stand alone.[8] The isolated sale of a private home was held not to constitute conduct of a trade or business, and thus not subject to a Chapter 93A claim.[9] A broker involved in such a transaction is, however, conducting a trade or business, and may be

---

[7]Nei v. Burley, 388 Mass. 307, 446 N.E.2d 674 (1983); Nei v. Boston Survey Consultants, Inc., 388 Mass. 320, 446 N.E.2d 681 (1983); Glickman v. Brown, 21 Mass. App. Ct. 229, 486 N.E.2d 737 (1985) (abrogated by, Cigal v. Leader Development Corp., 408 Mass. 212, 557 N.E.2d 1119 (1990)); Pelletier v. Chicopee Sav. Bank, 23 Mass. App. Ct. 708, 505 N.E.2d 543 (1987); Greenery Rehabilitation Group, Inc. v. Antaramian, 36 Mass. App. Ct. 73, 628 N.E.2d 1291 (1994).

[8]Heller v. Silverbranch Const. Corp., 376 Mass. 621, 382 N.E.2d 1065 (1978); Ditommaso v. Laliberte, 9 Mass. App. Ct. 890, 402 N.E.2d 1079 (1980); Nolan v. Parker,

15 Mass. App. Ct. 475, 446 N.E.2d 722 (1983); Cassano v. Gogos, 20 Mass. App. Ct. 348, 480 N.E.2d 649 (1985); American Mechanical Corp. v. Union Mach. Co. of Lynn, Inc., 21 Mass. App. Ct. 97, 485 N.E.2d 680 (1985); Doliner v. Brown, 21 Mass. App. Ct. 692, 489 N.E.2d 1036 (1986); Hartford Nat. Bank and Trust Co. v. United Truck Leasing Corp., 24 Mass. App. Ct. 626, 511 N.E.2d 637 (1987); Danusis v. Longo, 48 Mass. App. Ct. 254, 720 N.E.2d 470 (1999); Diamond Crystal Brands, Inc. v. Backleaf, LLC, 60 Mass. App. Ct. 502, 803 N.E.2d 744 (2004).

[9]Lantner v. Carson, 374 Mass. 606, 373 N.E.2d 973 (1978).

subject to a Chapter 93A claim.[10] The distinction of applicability is, however, dependent on the facts and may turn on levels of sophistication and involvement of the parties in the transaction and whether they were motivated by business or personal reasons.[11]

Not every unlawful act is automatically an unfair or deceptive one under Chapter 93A. The applicability to various aspects of mortgage loan transactions has continued to develop from early cases, some arising before a 1979 amendment of § 9, and in light of the exemption, cited above, of transactions affected by a "regulatory body."[12]

In the well-known *Anthony's Pier Four* decision, the court said that "the rule is clear in Massachusetts that every contract is subject to an implied covenant of good faith and fair dealing," and that principle is widely recognized in many Chapter 93A cases.[13]

TOPIC C: WARRANTY

§ 5:5   Habitability; other

In 2002 the Supreme Judicial Court expressly abandoned the common law rule of *caveat emptor* and adopted a rule of implied warranty of habitability to newly built dwellings.[1] Such a rule had previously been applied to rental housing,[2]

---

[10]Mongeau v. Boutelle, 10 Mass. App. Ct. 246, 407 N.E.2d 352 (1980).

[11]Bullard v. Chase, 8 Mass. App. Ct. 926, 396 N.E.2d 722 (1979); Begelfer v. Najarian, 381 Mass. 177, 409 N.E.2d 167 (1980); Nei v. Burley, 388 Mass. 307, 446 N.E.2d 674 (1983); Harris v. Doyle, 14 Mass. App. Ct. 1037, 442 N.E.2d 741 (1982); Discover Realty Corp. v. David, 49 Mass. App. Ct. 535, 731 N.E.2d 79 (2000).

[12]Mechanics Nat. Bank of Worcester v. Killeen, 377 Mass. 100, 384 N.E.2d 1231, 25 U.C.C. Rep. Serv. 891 (1979); Murphy v. Charlestown Sav. Bank, 380 Mass. 738, 405 N.E.2d 954 (1980); Danca v. Taunton Sav. Bank, 385 Mass. 1, 429 N.E.2d 1129 (1982); Cambridgeport Sav. Bank v. Boersner, 413 Mass. 432, 597 N.E.2d 1017 (1992); Williams v. Resolution GGF OY, 417 Mass. 377, 630 N.E.2d 581 (1994); Kattar v. Demoulas, 433 Mass. 1, 739 N.E.2d 246 (2000); Tufankjian v. Rockland Trust Co., 57 Mass. App. Ct. 173, 782 N.E.2d 1 (2003).

[13]Anthony's Pier Four, Inc. v. HBC Associates, 411 Mass. 451, 583 N.E.2d 806 (1991); Schwanbeck v. Federal-Mogul Corp., 412 Mass. 703, 592 N.E.2d 1289 (1992); Tufankjian v. Rockland Trust Co., 57 Mass. App. Ct. 173, 782 N.E.2d 1 (2003).

[Section 5:5]

[1]Albrecht v. Clifford, 436 Mass. 706, 767 N.E.2d 42 (2002).

[2]Boston Housing Authority v. Hemingway, 363 Mass. 184, 293 N.E.2d 831 (1973).

and it is now applicable with respect to the sale of newly built dwellings, including condominium units.[3]

In the cited *Albrecht* case, the defects were in fireplaces that the house purchaser had not used or inspected until long after acceptance of the deed and expiration of express warranties. The SJC held that a claim on those defects was not tolled by the discovery rule because they were not inherently unknowable and would have been disclosed by reasonable diligence which the plaintiff had not exercised. The claim rested, therefore, solely on an implied warranty of habitability, which the court adopted.

Citing M.G.L.A. c. 260, § 2B, referred to in the following § 5:6, the court said that any claim based on an implied warranty of habitability would have to be brought within the three-year statute of limitations and the six-year statute of repose thereunder. The court also set forth a list of limitations on the implied warranty, as follows: (1) The rule applies only to a newly built residence, purchased from the builder-vendor; (2) The rule applies only when the dwelling contains a latent defect; (3) The defect was manifested only after closing of the purchase; (4) The defect was caused by builder's improper design, materials or workmanship; and (5) The defect created a substantial question of safety or made the residence unfit for human habitation. Furthermore, the court said that a claim on such grounds cannot be waived; and the court expressly left open the question of assertion of such a claim by a subsequent purchaser.

The issue of warranty of habitability has been raised primarily in cases involving tenancy.[4]

As referred to in § 17:17, developers of new condominium units often provide written warranties.

TOPIC D: LIMITATIONS OF ACTIONS

§ 5:6 The statutes

Chapter 260 of the General Laws, entitled Limitation of Actions, is the source of most Massachusetts laws on the

---

[3]Berish v. Bornstein, 437 Mass. 252, 770 N.E.2d 961 (2002).

[4]Jablonski v. Clemons, 60 Mass. App. Ct. 473, 803 N.E.2d 730 (2004); Abdeljaber v. Gaddoura, 60 Mass. App. Ct. 294, 801 N.E.2d 290 (2004); Fletcher v. Littleton, 68 Mass. App. Ct. 22, 859 N.E.2d 882 (2007), review denied, 448 Mass. 1106, 862 N.E.2d 380 (2007).

subject. Section 1 provides a limitation of twenty years after the cause of action accrues on (1) contracts under seal, (2) bills, notes or other evidence of indebtedness issued by a bank, (3) witnessed promissory notes, if the action is brought by the original payee or his executor, (4) contracts not limited by § 2 or any other law, and (5) one other category relating to support of jail inmates.

Section 2 sets a six-year limitation on contracts, except those under § 1 and a few specified others. In drafting instruments real estate lawyers ordinarily provide that they are "under seal," shooting for applicability of § 1. This is at least a bit anomalous in light of M.G.L.A. c. 183, § 1A, which disposes of a requirement of seal on any instrument affecting an interest in land. In any case, many claims relating to real estate transactions arise in tort, not contract, or upon a statutory claim, and as to those, there are other limitations.

M.G.L.A. c. 260, § 2A, sets a limitation of three years on torts (of the kind ordinarily pertinent to real estate matters) and on replevin, and § 2B confirms that with respect to "any deficiency or neglect in the design, planning, construction or general administration of an improvement to real property." In addition to setting the three year limit from the time when the cause of action accrues, § 2B adds a limitation of six years after "substantial completion," or other specified equivalents.

Those limitations apply to equitable remedies as well as to common law contract actions.[1] The cause of action has been held to accrue at the time of discovery of the wrong or when it reasonably should have been discovered, but M.G.L.A. c. 260, § 12, provides that fraudulent concealment will toll the period.[2] The twenty-year period has been found applicable in some circumstances, but not others,[3] as has also the three-year provision of § 2B.[4]

M.G.L.A. c. 260, § 5A, provides for a limitation of four

[Section 5:6]

[1]Ballentine v. Eaton, 297 Mass. 389, 8 N.E.2d 808 (1937); Falk v. Levine, 66 F. Supp. 700 (D. Mass. 1946).

[2]Hendrickson v. Sears, 365 Mass. 83, 310 N.E.2d 131 (1974); Friedman v. Jablonski, 371 Mass. 482, 358 N.E.2d 994 (1976); Solomon v. Birger, 19 Mass. App. Ct. 634, 477 N.E.2d 137 (1985); Moretti v. Deveau, (U.S. Dist. Ct. Mass., C.A. 85-3930); but see Graveline v. Baybank Valley Trust Co., 19 Mass. App. Ct. 253, 473 N.E.2d 700 (1985).

[3]Nutter v. Mroczka, 303 Mass. 343, 21 N.E.2d 979 (1939); D'Annolfo v. D'Annolfo Const. Co., Inc., 39 Mass. App. Ct. 189, 654 N.E.2d 82, 27 U.C.C. Rep. Serv. 2d 493 (1995); Barber v. Fox, 36 Mass. App. Ct. 525, 632 N.E.2d 1246 (1994).

[4]Milligan v. Tibbetts Engineering Corp., 391 Mass. 364, 461 N.E.2d 808 (1984); Melrose

years from the accrual of the cause of action on actions under M.G.L.A. c. 93A or any other laws "intended for the protection of consumers," of which there is a listing in § 5A.

Among other provisions in Chapter 260 which may at times become pertinent in real estate matters are (i) those in § 11 relating to contracts or "acts done" by executors, trustees, guardians or conservators; (ii) provisions in §§ 13, 14, 33, 34 and 35 relating to mortgages (discussed in § **10:5**, § **10:12**, an **Chapter 20**), and (iii) limitation on rights of entry and reverters (discussed in § **10:16**).

Also worth noting is the provision in M.G.L.A. c. 184, § 17A, referred to in § **1:41**, limiting the effective time and extension of a recorded purchase and sale agreement.

Housing Authority v. New Hampshire Ins. Co., 402 Mass. 27, 520 N.E.2d 493 (1988); Libman v. Zuckerman, 33 Mass. App. Ct. 341, 599 N.E.2d 642 (1992).

Part II

DETERMINING THE STATUS OF TITLE

Chapter 6

Title Examination and Abstract

TOPIC D: DOCUMENTS RELATING TO COURT ACTIONS

TOPIC E: DOCUMENTS RELATING TO GOVERNMENTAL ACTIONS

TOPIC F: PROBATE COURT INSTRUMENTS

TOPIC G: USING THE ABSTRACT

KeyCite®: Cases and other legal materials listed in KeyCite Scope can be researched through the KeyCite service on Westlaw®. Use KeyCite to check citations for form, parallel references, prior and later history, and comprehensive citator information, including citations to other decisions and secondary materials.

TOPIC A: THE BASICS

§ 6:1 Introduction

The focus of this chapter is on the examination of record

title to real estate and review of an abstract of such an examination. That process inevitably and necessarily involves consideration of many points of substantive real estate law. To read and review an abstract of title with competence, one needs to have a broad understanding of the whole field of real estate law. Many of the pertinent points are discussed to the extent necessary as they arise herein. Nevertheless, in this volume many of the substantive considerations that are pertinent to the practice of law in the real estate field are dealt with in more depth in other chapters, particularized as to subject. Consequently, in order to make this chapter more readable and useful, there are often abbreviations of substantive points and references to those other chapters. Such abbreviation should not to any extent be taken as a derogation of their importance. Whenever a lawyer reviewing a title abstract encounters a point with which he is not fully familiar, he should bone up on it—by review of the pertinent chapter herein or otherwise.

§ 6:2 Sources of information

The principal sources of information for examination of title to real estate are, of course, to be found in the registries of deeds, established and regulated under M.G.L.A. c. 36. Massachusetts has fourteen "counties," of which nine have a single registry for the entire county, three (Middlesex, Essex and Worcester) have two registry districts each, and two (Bristol and Berkshire) have three registry districts each, making a total of 21 registries. As noted in § 2:3, some of these counties have been abolished as governmental entities, and their registries are now administered directly by the Commonwealth. With respect to registries of deeds, "sources" is deliberately in the plural, as will appear below.

A second major source of title information lies in the registries of probate, also organized on a county basis. Title to real estate may be passed by a will or by intestate succession, evidenced by appropriate proceedings in the probate court, without any instrument, or even notice of the owner's death, appearing in the registry of deeds. Furthermore, during the life of an owner, title to real estate could be affected by other proceedings in the probate court, including conservatorship, guardianship, divorce, adoption, change of name, partition and certain actions relating to inter vivos trusts.

A third source of information which is involved in practically every title search is the local tax collector's office in the city or town where the land in question lies.

In addition, a real estate title search often leads an

examiner to seek information from one or more of (a) the offices of the secretary of state of the commonwealth and city and town clerks, in relation to filings under the Uniform Commercial Code, (b) the corporation division of the office of the secretary of state, in relation to matters of corporate organization, standing and officers, (c) the department of revenue in relation to waivers of corporate excise tax liens and other tax matters, (d) the vital statistics offices in Massachusetts and other states, in relation to matters of intestate succession not determinable from probate records, (e) genealogical and historical records of private organizations, (f) city and town clerks and clerks of Planning Boards and Boards of Appeal, in relation to subdivision control and zoning matters, (g) building departments and health departments, in relation to permits and other matters, and (h) conservation commissions, historic district commissions, county commissioners and other public bodies.

§ 6:3 Indices; record books

The books in which instruments are "recorded in the registry of deeds" are known as Record Books. The importance of the quoted phrase arises from M.G.L.A. c. 183, § 4, which provides that:

> A conveyance of an estate in fee simple, fee tail or for life, or a lease for a term of seven years, or an assignment of rents or profits from an estate or lease, shall not be valid as against any person, except the grantor or lessor, his heirs and devisees and persons having actual notice of it, unless it, or an office copy as provided in section thirteen of chapter thirty-six, or, with respect to such a lease, or an assignment of rents or profits, a notice of lease or a notice of assignment of rents or profits, as hereinafter defined, is recorded in the registry of deeds for the county or district in which the land to which it relates lies.

Record Books are numbered sequentially, and instruments are copied into them in essentially chronological order. Recorded instruments are thus identified by their Book and Page numbers.

The other basic books in a registry of deeds are the indices: the Grantor Index and the Grantee Index. These are tools of search by which pertinent instruments may be found in the Record Books.

The process of recording is in brief as follows: When an instrument is presented for recording in a Registry of Deeds, it is first examined by clerks who stamp it with the date, hour and minute of receipt and an instrument number. They make basic determinations as to how it is to be indexed; the names of the "grantors" in the Grantor Index and those of the "grantees" in the Grantee Index. Some instruments may call for both, or several, parties to be indexed both ways. The Registries generally prepare lists or "daily sheets" of instruments received in chronological order, with each instrument being noted thereon immediately upon receipt at the counter, naming the grantor and grantee. Within a few hours to a few days (depending on the volume of transactions the particular Registry handles) the instruments are assigned book and page numbers and noted in the grantor and grantee indices. Generally, all parties who appear in the instruments as acting or moving parties are entered as grantors. In the case of a mutual agreement, both parties may appear as both grantor and grantee. A lawyer (or a paralegal assistant) can sometimes influence the mode of indexing by identification of parties in the instrument and by specific requests to Registry personnel.

The date and time of recording of an instrument, and the book and page number thus assigned to it, are noted on the instrument itself, and the instrument is then photocopied into the Record Book. In most registries these processes are now controlled by or conducted with the aid of computer programs. The original of the recorded instrument is then returned to the person who recorded it and provided a name and address for such return.

Since Massachusetts has an active system of Title Registration (see **Chapter 8**), each registry of deeds has a "registered land department" which keeps a separate set of grantor and grantee indices, and a separate set of books in which the certificates of title of registered lands are kept.

In addition, registries commonly have separate Plan Books and Plan Files, an index of federal bankruptcy filings, an index of city and town subdivision regulations adopted by local planning boards (see § **12:10**) and sometimes an index of conservation plans (see § **15:23**).

§ 6:4 Mechanics of title search and abstract

The examination of real estate titles is a special discipline which is taught as such in schools for paralegal training and in classes conducted by experienced examiners. There are many free-lance practitioners of the art and some abstract companies, generally available at the registries, and law firms with substantial conveyancing practice often employ title examiners.

Although it is not very common for lawyers regularly to examine titles, every neophyte real estate lawyer might be well advised to learn to do so. The ability of a lawyer to read and pass on an abstract of title (or a title insurance policy) with competence and assurance might be questioned if he is ignorant of the process by which it was written.

The goal and scope of this section is not to elucidate the entire process of preparing an abstract, which has been well covered elsewhere,[1] but rather to describe in brief the essential elements, particularly with a view to the role of the conveyancer in guiding his examiner to accomplishment of the goal with certainty and efficiency.

The first step is to provide a starting point. Most commonly that is a reference to the last deed; i.e., the deed by which the seller or mortgagor in the transaction acquired title, identified by names of grantor and grantee, date, and record book and page numbers. If the seller cannot provide the book and page numbers, the parties names and at least an approximate date will enable the examiner to find the book and page numbers by searching the grantor or grantee index. If only the seller's name is known, then the examiner will need to run that name in the grantee index backward from the current date until a deed to the seller of the specified property is found.

With respect to names, keep in mind that the Registries use conventions for the ordering of individual and complex corporate names. Permutations of spelling may be pertinent, as well as local pronunciation: in Boston such names as Horton and Haughton may be deemed to be homophones!

If the prospective seller or mortgagor (here referred to as the grantor) acquired the property by inheritance or devise, the search of the grantee index will be fruitless, and the grantor should be called upon to identify the decedent, the estate administration, which may have been in another county than the real estate, and the decedent's source of title. If such information is not available, the examiner must resort to more random searches. An atlas or assessor's map available at the registry may give the name of some former owner who can then be searched for in the grantor and grantee indices. Other sources are assessors' and tax collectors' records, and local histories. If all else fails, it may be necessary to examine title to adjoining land in order to find reference therein to reputed owners of the locus being

----

[Section 6:4]

[1]See the article by Richard B. Johnson entitled "Mechanics of Title Examination in Massachu-setts," in Crocker's Notes on Common Forms, carried forward in the 8th Edition, published by MCLE in 1995.

examined.

Assuming that one has reference to the deed by which the current grantor acquired title, then the standard method of title examination calls for chaining back through the grantee index; that is, searching the grantee index under the current owner's name backwards in time until a source deed is found, then that grantor's name backwards as a grantee to his source deed, and so forth until a satisfactory deed is found, long enough ago to serve as a starting point. In practice the chaining back is more often accomplished in the record books themselves, by means of references in each deed to the book and page of the prior deed, and in many cases little or no reference to the grantee index is necessary. Well written deeds also refer to probate docket numbers and deed sources of decedents, but when these are lacking, the examiner will need to employ other search techniques referred to above.

Once an apparently satisfactory source deed is found, the examiner turns to the grantor index. Beginning with the source deed and running forward in time, the examiner must run each owner in the grantor index from the date of the deed (or probate source of title) to that grantor through the date of recording of the deed by which that grantor conveyed to the next person in the chain. The "grantor schedule" prepared by the examiner should show all instruments appearing in the grantor index during that period, for several reasons: (1) The recording statute requires that the index identify the town where the land lies,[2] but street addresses or other descriptions are unofficial and may not be relied upon; (2) a deed may contain a catch-all conveyance of land in other towns than the location of a described parcel; (3) the schedule may later be used for other purposes and could be misleading if anything is left out; and (4) in any event it should be the responsibility of the lawyer passing on the title, not the preparer of the abstract, to decide what, if any, potentially pertinent information may be skipped.

As mentioned, the schedule for each grantor should begin with the date of his acquisition of title, i.e., the date of the deed to him even though substantially earlier than its recording, or the date of death of a decedent source of title, not the date of probate. In addition to a complete schedule through the date of recording of the deed to the grantor's successor, the grantor index should be run, but not necessarily copied, for four years thereafter in search for tax takings (but any other pertinent instrument which appears should

---

[2]M.G.L.A. c. 36, § 14.

also be noted).[3] As referred to above, similar surnames are grouped together in the indices, and this may lead to scheduling of persons who are not in fact grantors in the title chain being examined. Furthermore, common names, such as John Jones and William Sullivan, can cause considerable problems of identification, and it is risky to rely on middle initials.

Generally, it is better to err on the side of over-inclusion of grantor schedules. It is only from these schedules that a person reading an abstract can determine whether or not it is complete. Sometimes, however, the scheduling must be curtailed as a practical matter because of pressure of time or cost, and whenever that is done, the examiner should clearly label the schedule as incomplete or selective and briefly specify the criteria on which choices of inclusion or exclusion were based.

It may be noted that a search conducted as above described will not necessarily guard against the risk of "estoppel by deed" which has been recognized as in effect in Massachusetts,[4] and the practical protection may lie in title insurance.

Once a complete set of grantor schedules has been assembled, the examiner is ready to turn to the record books. If the chaining back was accomplished from title references in instruments in the record books, the examiner probably abstracted every apparently pertinent instrument which came to eye when the heavy books were in hand. From this collection a nearly complete abstract may be compiled.

The correct procedure requires, however, that the examiner look at every instrument on every grantor schedule in the chain. Having read an instrument and determined that it contains nothing which could conceivably affect the premises being examined, the examiner may refrain from abstracting it and simply mark it "not locus" on the grantor schedule. That is the most crucial judgment an examiner will make, and if an examiner designates an item as "not locus" without having read it in full, that fact and the grounds for making that judgment should be noted. When there is an owner with an unusually extensive schedule, such as a town, railroad or

---

[3]See Morse v. Curtis, 140 Mass. 112, 2 N.E. 929 (1885); Hughes v. Williams, 218 Mass. 448, 105 N.E. 1056 (1914).

[4]Mt. Washington Co-op. Bank v. Benard, 289 Mass. 498, 194 N.E.

839 (1935); Zayka v. Giambro, 32 Mass. App. Ct. 748, 594 N.E.2d 894 (1992); Dallessio v. Baggia, 8 L.C.R. 319 (2000), aff'd, 57 Mass.App.Ct. 468, 783 N.E.2d 890 (2003).

a corporation with active real estate dealings, it may be acceptable for the examiner to mark items on the grantor schedules as "assumed not locus" without having read them. Nevertheless, the conveyancer reading the abstract should not shy away from asking his examiner to return to the registry to abstract the instrument if he has any doubt as to its possibly affecting locus.

A completed title report should contain an abstract or copy of every instrument which affects locus. As to mortgages which have been discharged, easements which have been released, restrictions which have expired, and the like, the better practice is to abstract them, but the abstracts may be abbreviated. Generally abstracts are preferable to full copies because they show that the examiner has read the instrument and because brevity is itself a virtue. A full copy is warranted when the instrument contains complex provisions which do not lend themselves to abstracting, and it is usually advisable for a purchaser's attorney to review a full copy of each instrument establishing an easement, restriction or encumbrance which is to survive the closing. Copies of record plans should also be included, and if there are none, then atlas plans and assessors plans are important. Modern copy machines have made examiners' tracings of plans rather old-fashioned, but where a title involves multiple parcels, boundary changes, overlaid easements or dimensional discrepancies, there is nothing to match a well-prepared examiner's sketch as an analytical tool.

Forms of abstract blanks are commonly used. The data called for on customary abstract forms may serve as a useful checklist, but of course filling in the blanks should not be accepted as a substitute for examination itself.

§ 6:5 Period covered

The Suffolk County Registry of Deeds has archives containing records of the Town of Boston dating from 1630. The historic interest of these is great, but happily for those who bear the costs of title examination, it is extremely rare that a search anywhere near that far back is needed. It should be remembered, however, that in origin and theory the title to real estate is not allodial, but tenurial, and it is essentially true that the *record* is the title (livery of seisin and feudal incidents being long gone). The period of search must be sufficient to establish a record which appears to preclude contradictory record claimants, and there is always an element of judgment as to what that period is.

The rules of thumb evolving from "60 years from a warranty deed" to "50 years from a warranty, quitclaim, or duly authorized or empowered fiduciary's deed which on its face does not suggest any defects,"[1] are perfectly good ones, but should not be applied blindly. Any title chain which in such a period contains very few conveyances, depends primarily on estate transfers, contains broad references to unspecified easements or other encumbrances, involves descriptions which are undimensioned, not precisely locatable or erroneous, or is otherwise vague or flawed, is certainly a candidate for further search. As specified in the cited REBA standard, reference in the starting deed to a mortgage, an easement, an agreement, a restriction or another encumbrance which might still be in existence and applicable, calls for further examination.

The twenty-year period for adverse possession and the twenty-year statute of limitations in M.G.L.A. c. 260, § 21, may have some pertinence to a title search, but they certainly do not warrant limitation of search to that period. Curative statutes and other limitations considered in **Topic C of Chapter 10** may dispose of old encumbrances or defects, but their applicability in the particular circumstances must be carefully considered, and they are no substitute for adequate title examination. It is unfortunate that some mortgage lenders, and evidently their title insurers, seem to be inclined to rely on abbreviated title searches.

TOPIC B: EXECUTION OF INSTRUMENTS FOR RECORDING

§ 6:6   Signature

The signature of a grantor should match his name as given at the beginning of the instrument, which should match his name as given in his deed or probate source title. Any discrepancies or recitals of aliases should be noted.

§ 6:7   Address

M.G.L.A. c. 183, § 6, as to deeds, and § 28 as to mortgages and assignments thereof, require the address of the grantee, mortgagee or assignee to be set forth in the instrument, and provide that registers shall not accept those lacking it, but if

---

[Section 6:5]

[1]As provided in REBA, Title Standard 1.

recorded, the lack does not void the instrument.

§ 6:8 Seal

The common law rule required an instrument purporting to convey real estate to be under seal in order to be effective, and a real seal was necessary. In 1929 a mere recital of seal, without actual seal, became sufficient by statute. In 1956 another statute made the absence of seal, even by recital, not pertinent ten years after the recording of an instrument. And in 1977, the requirement of a seal or recital thereof was eliminated by statute.[1] This applies to corporate as well as to individual seals. Nevertheless it is still the practice to recite seal, and title examiners may continue to flag its absence.

§ 6:9 Acknowledgment

Under M.G.L.A. c. 183, § 29, a deed must be acknowledged in order to be validly recorded.[1] Deeds recorded without proper acknowledgment have been held to be valid against the grantor, but otherwise a nullity.[2] The acknowledgment may be made by any one of several co-grantors, or by an attorney-in-fact who executed the instrument, subject to requirements as to the power of attorney itself.[3] An acknowledgment may be valid even if dated before, or long after, the date of the instrument.[4]

On December 19, 2003, by Executive Order of the Governor in 2003, a new form of acknowledgment was prescribed. See **§ 19:11**.

§ 6:10 Business authorization

As noted in **§ 1:8**, a deed (or other instrument affecting real estate) of a business or non-profit corporation is effective if signed by the president or vice president and the treasurer or assistant treasurer, who may be one and the same

[Section 6:8]

[1]M.G.L.A. c. 183, § 1A.

[Section 6:9]

[1]Gordon v. Gordon, 8 Mass. App. Ct. 860, 398 N.E.2d 497 (1979).

[2]Dole v. Thurlow, 53 Mass. 157, 12 Met. 157, 1846 WL 4099 (1846); Blood v. Blood, 40 Mass. 80, 23 Pick. 80, 1839 WL 3019 (1839); Pidge v. Tyler, 4 Mass. 541, 1808 WL 1173 (1808).

[3]M.G.L.A. c. 183, §§ 30, 32.

[4]McOuatt v. McOuatt, 320 Mass. 410, 69 N.E.2d 806 (1946); Ashkenazy v. R.M. Bradley & Co., 328 Mass. 242, 103 N.E.2d 251 (1952); REBA Title Standard 16.

person.[1] An important proviso is that the person relying on the instrument must be doing so in good faith. If that test is met, contrary provisions of the corporate charter, by-laws or even specific resolutions, and requirements of corporate seal, may be disregarded. If the instrument is not so executed, or there is any ground to doubt good faith reliance, the examiner should search for and abstract a certificate of corporate vote or resolution. Corporations having frequent real estate transactions often adopt standing votes and provide them to the pertinent registries, which sometimes keep these in a separate file, not appearing in the grantor index or record books.

With respect to institutional lenders holding mortgages, execution of instruments is governed by M.G.L.A. c. 183, § 54B, quoted in § 20:30.

As to acceptable signatures on behalf of an LLC, a general partnership, a limited partnership or an LLP, the tests are the same as for execution of a purchase and sale agreement as discussed in § 1:9 and § 1:10, and in **Topic B of Chapter 16**.

§ 6:11 Power of attorney

Under M.G.L.A. c. 201B, the Uniform Durable Power of Attorney Act, a power of attorney which contains the recital that "This power of attorney shall not be affected by subsequent disability or incapacity of the principal" remains effective despite the disability or incapacity of the principal. It may be revoked by a conservator or guardian of the principal, but the appointment of such a fiduciary does not by itself revoke the power. The statute also provides that a power of attorney, even if not durable in accordance with the statutory definition, shall not be revoked by the death, disability or incapacity of the principal with respect to action taken by the attorney-in-fact in good faith and without actual knowledge of his principal's death, disability or incapacity. Whenever an instrument to be recorded affecting real estate is executed by an attorney-in-fact, the power of attorney should also be recorded. An affidavit by the attorney-in-fact, relied upon in good faith, is conclusive as to facts pertinent to the power's remaining in effect, and such affidavit should

---

[Section 6:10]

[1]M.G.L.A. c. 155, § 8, c. 156A, § 4, c. 156B, § 115, c. 156D, § 8.46, c. 180, § 10C; Fields v. Revolution Trust Corporation, 6 L.C.R. 250 (1998); see REBA Title Standard 11.

also be recorded.[1]

The form of signature on a deed executed under a power of attorney is important. A deed of X as attorney for Y was long ago held invalid as the deed of Y. It must be written as a deed of Y "by his attorney" X.

Signature of a grantor's name by a third party at the grantor's request and in his presence has also been held valid. The person so signing for another (e.g., a blind person) should recite: "I, X, have signed the name of Y at his request and in his presence," and the notary should so confirm in the acknowledgement.

§ 6:12   Alterations

All alterations on a deed noted by the register of deeds as he copied the instrument into the record book and all alterations that are found in the photographic copies of the more recent deeds should be noted carefully by the examiner. Although there has been some disagreement in the cases as to the effect of changing the name of the grantee on the face of the deed after execution but before recording, the better view seems to be to rely on the record and to hold title to be in the owner of record, the substituted grantee, provided, of course, that the original grantee and grantor agreed to the substitution, there being a complete absence of fraud.[1] The general rule is that alterations made prior to execution and delivery are effective and do not affect the instrument's overall validity. The best evidence that an alteration was prior to execution is a note to that effect in the attestation clause of the deed. If there is no such note and there are obvious and important changes in the deed, the burden of proof is on the grantee to show that he did not alter the deed subsequent to execution.[2] Subsequent unauthorized changes by a grantee may deprive him of rights under the covenants of the deed, but do not necessarily to divest him of title.[3]

<hr>

[Section 6:11]

[1]M.G.L.A. c. 201B, § 5; Gagnon v. Coombs, 39 Mass. App. Ct. 144, 654 N.E.2d 54 (1995); see REBA Title Standard 34.

[Section 6:12]

[1]Long v. Lowrey, 243 Mass. 414, 137 N.E. 634 (1923).

[2]New England Grape Co. v. Fidelity & Deposit Co. of Maryland, 268 Mass. 298, 167 N.E. 646 (1929).

[3]Carr v. Frye, 225 Mass. 531, 114 N.E. 745 (1917); Lima v. Lima, 30 Mass. App. Ct. 479, 570 N.E.2d 158 (1991); Graves v. Hutchinson, 39 Mass. App. Ct. 634, 659 N.E.2d 1212 (1996) (abrogated by, Cleary v. Cleary, 427 Mass. 286, 692 N.E.2d 955 (1998)); Massidda v. Lurvey, 12 L.C.R. 95 (2004).

§ 6:13   Recording fees

Recording fees are set by statute and are uniform throughout the Commonwealth. Occasionally some differences may arise from interpretation, such as: Does a single instrument that, say, assigns four mortgages, owe one recording fee or four? If a grantee signs a deed in token of acceptance of, say, restrictive covenants, does he then need to be indexed as a grantor? Since recording fees have increased substantially in recent decades, the cautious lawyer may need to explain such nuances to his clients.

§ 6:14   Deed excise taxes

Federal conveyance taxes were repealed as of January 1, 1968, but a title examiner will find federal revenue stamps on deeds before then. At the rate of $1.10 per $1,000 of consideration, they may give a clue to prices paid at a time before recital of the amount of consideration was required in a deed. Massachusetts has imposed a deed excise tax since 1952, under M.G.L.A. c. 64D, currently (2007) providing a rate of $2 for each $500 of consideration, except in Barnstable County where the rate is $1.50 for each $500. The tax is not applicable to mortgages, nor to conveyances to or from the federal government, the Commonwealth, a city or town in Massachusetts, or any of their agencies.

The tax applies to the consideration for the property "exclusive of the value of any lien or encumbrance remaining thereon at the time of sale." It is, of course, not proper to deduct for a mortgage or other lien which the grantee is forthwith paying off as part of the purchase transaction.[1] When the consideration for a deed is not in money but in other property, the value thereof is the amount upon which the tax is measured. In the case of an exchange of real estate, deed tax stamps are required on both deeds.

The tax stamps are sold at the registries through meters, and the registry personnel are usually quite astute in not accepting deeds for recording without proper stamps. The statute provides a penalty for signing and delivering, or for leaving for recording, any deed which does not have the required stamps affixed. Because of that, it behooves a seller's attorney to be certain that he has a firm commitment of the buyer's attorney to purchase and affix the stamps.

[Section 6:14]

1. [1]See REBA Ethical Standard

§ 6:15 Land bank fees

The Nantucket Islands Land Bank and the Dukes County Land Bank were established in the mid 1980s.[1] Section 10 of each Act imposes a fee of 2% of the purchase price on the transfer of an interest in real property. In Nantucket it is applicable throughout the county, coterminous with the town, and in Dukes County it is applicable to the six towns on Martha's Vineyard, but not to the town of Gosnold on the Elizabeth Islands. The fee is payable by the purchaser to the commission established by the act, accompanied by affidavit on forms provided by the respective commissions, which then issue a certificate of payment or exemption, requisite for recording of a deed (but not a mortgage).

Section 11 of each Act provides a window of seven days after issuance of a certificate of payment in which a purchaser can obtain a refund upon affidavit that the transaction has not been consummated.

Section 12 of each Act sets forth exemptions, including transfers to governmental entities, confirmatory transfers, gifts, certain contributions to and distributions from trusts and corporations, certain transfers to charitable and religious organizations, mortgage foreclosure or deed in lieu, certain marital transfers, multi-county property transfers and finally, partial exemption of first-time residence purchases. The requirements for and limitations on many of these exemptions are such that careful review of the statutory details is well advised for planning of any possibly exempt transaction. The Acts provide for interest on unpaid fees and penalties for fraud.

The funds thus collected by the land bank commissions may be expended by them, pursuant to specified procedures, for acquisitions of lands for specified environmental protection and recreational purposes.

TOPIC C: RECORDED INSTRUMENTS

§ 6:16 Deeds and elements thereof

The things one needs to look for and consider when review-

[Section 6:15]

[1]See § 14:13; Ch. 669, Acts of 1983; Ch. 736, Acts of 1985. Note that the proposal under Ch. 144, Acts of 1997, for a Land Bank for Cape Cod failed of adoption by referendum.

ing an abstract of title begin with the following elements of deeds (discussed further in **Chapter 19**):

• **Identities.** Names and addresses of grantors, as referred to in **§ 6:6**, and specification of the capacity, individual or other, in which the grantors act. Then the names and addresses of grantees, as referred to in **§ 6:7**, and the manner in which they take title, the forms of ownership (including declarations of homestead) as discussed in **Topic A of Chapter 16**, **Chapter 17**, and **Chapter 18**.

• **Consideration.** The amount thereof is almost always of interest for practical or business reasons. As noted in **§ 19:4**, failure to comply with the statutory requirement of recital of consideration will usually bar recording, but does not void the deed.

• **Grant, Covenants, Habendum.** Most deeds use the word "grant" to evince a transfer of title, but "release" or "convey" will suffice. Warranty deeds are now rare in Massachusetts, and quitclaim deeds are the norm, definitions being set forth in **§ 19:2**. It is worth noting here that the Massachusetts statutory quitclaim deed is not a simple release, but is equivalent to what is elsewhere called a "limited warranty." It is sometimes useful, however, to note that "give, grant, bargain, sell and convey" are the old terms of a warranty deed, and "remise, release, and forever quitclaim" are the old terms of a quitclaim deed. Almost all deeds are in statutory "short form," for which no habendum is required. But when a deed does contain a habendum, it is most important to determine that it runs to "the grantee and his heirs and assigns to his and their own use and behoof forever." As referred to in **§ 19:5**, sometimes a habendum clause is deliberately included in a modern deed to create a fee simple determinable, fee simple subject to a condition subsequent, a life estate, a conveyance to uses, or simply to spell out or clarify shares of tenants in common. While occasionally useful, such a device should be used cautiously because it is likely to confuse registry personnel and even some lawyers. The Statute of Uses is alive in Massachusetts, and a deed of A to B to the use of C, whether so expressed in the granting clause or in a habendum, vests title in C, but the registry will usually index both B and C as grantees.[1]

• **Description.** In abstracting the description of the premises, the examiner may abbreviate words, but should

---

[Section 6:16]

[1]See Hillman v. Roman Catholic Bishop of Fall River, 24 Mass. App. Ct. 241, 508 N.E.2d 118, 39 Ed. Law Rep. 776 (1987).

not omit any words or abbreviate or paraphrase the description itself. When all or part of a description remains identical through a series of deeds, the examiner need not copy it in full on each sheet, but may identify the description in one deed as "Same as X to Y in Bk ____ Page ____ on Sheet ____," and then note any variations or additional provisions.

Sometimes a description will remain substantially the same through a series of deeds, but in one or more instances contain a reversed bearing, a missing or misstated dimension, or other flaw which seems on the face of it to have been a scrivener's error. These should be noted, and can usually be passed, particularly if each deed contains a "being the same premises" title reference or an adequate "meaning and intending" clause. However, there is a world of difference between an essentially sound and consistent description affected by occasional discrepancies and a description which lacks clarity, cohesiveness and definition. The latter poses a definite title problem.

In fact the problem of poor description is all too often ignored or passed over lightly. A title chain may be flawless in all other respects, and may establish good title to a parcel which meets the street address or other generalized definition of the locus, but what is the locus? Unless the conveyancer can define precisely, and relate precisely to identifiable locations on the ground, the premises on which he is reporting to his client, then he has a defect to report. The absence in the record title of such precision of definition and location is itself a defect. It may be a defect which the client is willing to accept, but it remains the conveyancer's job to make clear to the client exactly how great the uncertainties are and what the implications may be in terms of marketability or potential adverse claims.

Obviously that rather strict test cannot be met without adequate survey. It cannot be gainsaid that survey, monumentation, plan and metes, bounds and bearings are in fact essential elements of a good title to real estate and that the absence of, or error in, any of them, is a deficiency which should always be reported. It follows that a conveyancer must know how to read a plan, to use a protractor, and to perform at least rudimentary trigonometric computations.

The most common style of description used in Massachusetts is the bounding description, but running descriptions are also used and must be understood by examiner and conveyancer. Examples of bounding and running descriptions are given in § 19:7.

An examiner will surely encounter some seriously flawed

descriptions, bounding, running or a combination of both. There may be flip-flops between bounding and running descriptions, reversed bearings, 90 degree transposition of bearings, absence of dimensions, reference to non-existent monuments, etc. With persistence there is usually a way to struggle through and produce a title chain on any given parcel, which may then be cured or perfected by some means. When a deed contains two inconsistent descriptions, the more specific will govern. If the problem is a discrepancy between stated bearings or courses and distances and the actual locations of physical boundary markers and monuments, the general rules of construction are that bounds or monuments (including abutting land of another owner) govern over running courses and bearings, and the latter govern over stated distances and area.[2]

A description of a parcel must be capable of referring to only one parcel; a description of part of a tract must specify its location within the tract.[3] When a deed contains two inconsistent descriptions, the more specific will govern.[4] Erroneous or ambiguous descriptions may be cured by reference to a specific lot on a recorded plan or to a deed containing an adequate description.[5] A consistent specific description is not affected by an inconsistent general reference.[6] With respect to some uncertainties of description, extrinsic evidence may be considered to clarify the parties' intent or to clear up ambiguities.[7]

Nowadays one would rarely examine far enough back to

---

[2]Ellis v. Wingate, 338 Mass. 481, 155 N.E.2d 783 (1959); Ryan v. Stavros, 348 Mass. 251, 203 N.E.2d 85 (1964); Sheppard Envelope Co. v. Arcade Malleable Iron Co., 335 Mass. 180, 138 N.E.2d 777 (1956). The principles are recited and applied to variants in many Land Court cases, including those reported in: 1 L.C.R. 44; 2 L.C.R. 65; 6 L.C.R.293; 7 L.C.R. 61; 9 L.C.R. 232, aff'd in part and rev'd in part in Town of Blackstone v. Town of Millville, 59 Mass. App. Ct. 565, 797 N.E.2d 390 (2003); 11 L.C.R. 183, aff'd in Paull v. Kelly, 62 Mass. App. Ct. 673, 819 N.E.2d 963 (2004); 14 L.C.R. 245 (2006). See also REBA Title Standard 27.

[3]McHale v. Treworgy, 325 Mass. 381, 90 N.E.2d 908 (1950); Stenmark Realty Trust v. Finn, 1 L.C.R. 163 (1993).

[4]Ellis v. Wingate, 338 Mass. 481, 155 N.E.2d 783 (1959); Bellingham Venture Limited Partnership v. Dexter, 10 L.C.R. 23 (2002); Lesiak v. Hinault, 10 L.C.R. 81 (2002).

[5]Ide v. Bowden, 342 Mass. 22, 172 N.E.2d 88 (1961).

[6]Morse v. Chase, 305 Mass. 504, 26 N.E.2d 326, 127 A.L.R. 1037 (1940).

[7]Bernard v. Nantucket Boys' Club, Inc., 391 Mass. 823, 465 N.E.2d 236 (1984); Suga v. Maum, 29 Mass. App. Ct. 733, 565 N.E.2d 793 (1991); Buk Lhu v. Dignoti, 431 Mass. 292, 727 N.E.2d 73 (2000). The Land Court has applied this principle in various circumstances in cases reported in: 1 L.C.R. 40,

encounter an old description with dimensions in rods, poles or perches, or chains and links. For the record, equivalent distances in feet are as follows: A rod, pole or perch is 16.5 feet; and a chain is four rods or 66 feet, comprised of 100 links each 7.92 inches in length. A square chain is 16 square rods or 1/10th of an acre. A square rod is 272.25 square feet and there are 160 square rods in an acre, containing 43,560 square feet. The word rood is sometimes used to mean rod, but it also means 40 square rods, or 1/4th of an acre.

• **Title Reference.** A proper title reference may overcome deficiencies in description of the premises. If a prior deed contains an adequate description, then a later deed referring to it by the expression "Being the same premises conveyed by . . ." or "Meaning and intending to convey and hereby conveying the same premises conveyed by . . ." will suffice to convey the parcel despite some errors in the description in the later deed. The title expression "For grantor's title, see . . ." could refer to a deed of a larger tract out of which the parcel being conveyed was subdivided, but if that does not appear to be the case, then that expression may be accepted as equivalent to "Being the same premises."

§ 6:17 Mortgages; related instruments; foreclosure documents

This section focuses on instruments commonly found of record upon an examination of title and the basic criteria involved in evaluating their effect on the title. One passing on a title should of course have a broad understanding of the substantive law relating to all such instruments, and consequently this section should be read in conjunction with **Chapter 20**.

• **Mortgages.** Most mortgages in Massachusetts use or are based on the statutory short form, although there are a great variety of printed forms, proprietary to banks and other lending institutions. The key recitals to take advantage of the statutory provisions are that the mortgage is granted with "mortgage covenants," is upon the "mortgage conditions" and includes the statutory "power of sale." If any of those is missing from an extant mortgage, the examiner should certainly make note of it, and thoroughly abstract or copy all the provisions that do appear in the mortgage.

As to mortgages in the title chain that have been dis-

97, 168, 204 and 207 (1993); 2 L.C.R. 65 (1994); 5 L.C.R. 213 (1997); 6 L.C.R. 275 (1998); 9 L.C.R. 30, 184 and 397 (2001); and 10 L.C.R. 89 (2002).

charged, only enough data needs to be abstracted to enable a reader of the abstract to determine that the mortgage was properly discharged. It is preferable for the examiner to have found and read the discharge itself, and not to rely merely on a marginal reference noted on the mortgage in the record book.

As to extant mortgages, the examiner should make note of the amount secured. Besides securing a debt, almost all mortgages also secure compliance with and performance of a variety of conditions, statutory and otherwise. If the client for whom the title is being examined contemplates taking title subject to the mortgage, then all of those provisions are of course important to him. That is particularly so because most lenders' forms provide expressly that the debt is "due on sale" and "due on encumbrance."

• **Related Documents.** Often recorded with a mortgage on a commercial property are financing statements under the Uniform Commercial Code, and additional security instruments such as a collateral assignment of leases and rents. Those need to be abstracted with respect to an extant mortgage because they will also need to be dealt with or disposed of. Other instruments found of record include assignments, partial releases, and subordinations, each of which may have an important effect on the status of the mortgage in question. The registries commonly refer to such instruments by a notation to their book and page numbers on the margin of the record of the mortgage affected, but one cannot always rely on such notations. In some circumstances it may be advisable for the title examiner to run a grantor schedule on the mortgagee, though that is obviously burdensome with respect to an institutional lender.

M.G.L.A. c. 183, § 28, requires mortgages and assignments thereof to contain the address of the mortgagee or assignee, but failure to comply does not invalidate the instrument.

• **Foreclosure Documents.** The procedure for foreclosure of a mortgage in Massachusetts is briefly described in **Topic H of Chapter 20**. Ordinarily it involves a sale at public auction, followed by a statutorily required Affidavit.[1] The affidavit, usually appended to the foreclosure deed, should be carefully reviewed to show that it recites (i) a breach or default under the mortgage, (ii) publication in accordance with the statute (and includes a full copy of the advertised notice), (iii) that sale took place at the time and place specified in

----

[Section 6:17]

    [1]M.G.L.A. c. 244, § 15.

the notice or pursuant to specified adjournments, and (iv) that sale was made by public auction by a licensed auctioneer to a named highest bidder in a specified amount.

The foreclosure deed itself is fairly simple, as described in § **20:37**. The description may simply be "the premises conveyed by said mortgage", but the examiner should look for clauses that (i) exclude parcels which had previously been partially released from the mortgage, (ii) refer to easements or other rights subsequently granted and to which the mortgage had been subordinated, or (iii) refer to a new plan, description, title reference or other corrective or supplementary data.

A Certificate of Possession is almost always also recorded, either with the foreclosure deed and affidavit or prior thereto. This is important because possession continued peaceably for three years from the recording of the certificate effects foreclosure.[2] Foreclosure by this means alone is rare, but such entry is regularly made and a certificate recorded so that foreclosure will be effected in three years even if there were defects in the sale procedures.

§ 6:18 Easements

Whether set forth in a deed, granted by a separate instrument, implied, established by a taking (see § **6:29**), or by prescription (see § **7:18**), easements which either burden or are appurtenant to a parcel of land are of prime importance. They certainly warrant more than a deed reference to "easements and restrictions of record, insofar as now in force and applicable," a protective phrase favored by grantors, which should be taken with caution by grantees.

Easements are common law interests in land and are not terminated by mere non-use,[1] but may only be terminated by a proper recorded instrument, by abandonment, or by sufficient adverse action, as discussed in § **7:20**. Whenever easements are found of record burdening or serving the property being examined, there are various aspects thereof that are all pertinent to a proper report on the title, all discussed in **Topic B of Chapter 15**.

§ 6:19 Restrictions

A parcel of land may be subject to restrictions or may have

---

[2]M.G.L.A. c. 244, § 1.

[Section 6:18]

[1]See § **15:10**.

an appurtenant right to enforce restrictions on other land. The substantive law governing the creation, effectiveness and enforcement of restrictions is dealt with in **Topics C and D in Chapter 15**. The important points for one examining title include the exact provisions of the restrictions, the identity of persons who have the right to enforce them, and their duration. One cannot safely ignore all restrictions created more than 30 years ago, because they may be effective for a longer period, or may be renewable, or may have been renewed or extended.

In residential subdivisions there are often "common scheme" restrictions, imposing controls and prior approval requirements on such things as size and style of houses that may be built, types of ancillary structures, fences, vehicles, etc. In condominium developments, discussed in **Chapter 17**, there are usually restrictions governing use of common areas and facilities, and often affecting some interior aspects of units.

Conservation, historic preservation and agricultural preservation restrictions are also discussed in **Topic D of Chapter 15**, as well as environmental restrictions and "activity and use limitation" instruments.

§ 6:20   Leases and tenancies

Under M.G.L.A. c. 183, § 4, quoted in § **6:3**, a lease for a term of seven years or more is protected only if the lease, or an "office copy" or a notice of lease is recorded. The statute then states that:

> "notice of lease", as used in this section, shall mean an instrument in writing executed by all persons who are parties to the lease of which notice is given and shall contain the following information with respect to such lease: the date of execution thereof and a description, in the form contained in such lease, of the premises demised, and the term of such lease, with the date of commencement of such term and all rights of extension or renewal.

Options of extension and renewal pursuant to which the term could last for more than seven years make the lease subject to the statute,[1] but a lease for one year and thereafter from year to year does not require recording.[2]

The recording of a notice of lease has the same effect as recording of the entire lease, since either serves as actual

---

[Section 6:20]

[1]Leominster Gaslight Co. v. Hillery, 197 Mass. 267, 83 N.E. 870 (1908).

[2]Fanger v. Leeder, 327 Mass. 501, 99 N.E.2d 533 (1951).

notice.[3] Absent recording, the requisite actual notice would need to include notice that the lease is for a term of more than seven years.[4] While it is not required that an option to purchase in a lease be referred to in a notice of lease, it is certainly the better practice to do so.[5]

The statute specifies the required contents of a notice of lease, but not the form, and a variety of forms are used, including some styled "short form of lease" or "declaration of lease." The statute does not preclude the recording of leases, notices of lease, tenancy at will agreements and other occupancy agreements providing for terms of less than seven years, and these should all be abstracted as part of the record title.

The record alone does not tell the whole story about tenants' rights. Careful review of actual possession of the premises is always advisable.

§ 6:21 Plans

Plans are an integral and essential part of any abstract. They are not only the basis for a proper description of the land, they are required by the subdivision control law and often necessary for determination of compliance with zoning laws. A chain of title may include a plan of a large tract and later plans of subdivisions thereof leading eventually to a plan of the parcel being examined. The land may also be affected by plans of easements and street layouts.

Since the Boston environs and much of the rest of Massachusetts were populated so long ago, there was a good deal of subdivision done before modern survey standards were developed, and many old descriptions have been carried forward and survive of record. In urban and suburban areas there are often modern subdivision plans, but the tracts from which they were derived may be shown only on very sketchy plans, if any, and more rural areas away from cities are even less likely to be covered by adequate plans. The old descriptions usually recite compass bearings with respect to magnetic north of the time, and the variation therefrom to true north has changed substantially over the years. Atlas plans, assessors' plans, and even road and street maps are a useful adjunct to an abstract, as are also aerial photographs.

---

[3]Mister Donut of America, Inc. v. Kemp, 368 Mass. 220, 330 N.E.2d 810, 89 A.L.R.3d 896 (1975).

[4]South St. Inn v. Muehsam, 323 Mass. 310, 81 N.E.2d 821 (1948).

[5]Mister Donut of America, Inc. v. Kemp, 368 Mass. 220, 330 N.E.2d 810, 89 A.L.R.3d 896 (1975).

Plans usually bear a statement of scale. If a bar scale is lacking, it is advisable to draw one on the original copy at full size so that later facsimile-reduced copies may be used for scale measurements and will not be misread because of the stated scale. A conveyancer should have some familiarity with the requirements as to surveying set forth in M.G.L.A. c. 97. The size and form of plans are subject to regulation by the registers of deeds,[1] who are often quite fussy about compliance. Requirements for approval of plans are referred to in § **6:27**, § **12:3**, and § **12:7**.

§ 6:22   Mechanics liens

M.G.L.A. c. 254 was extensively amended in 1966.[1] Under M.G.L.A. c. 254, § 1, a workman may establish a lien on real estate on which he has performed work for 30 days of labor performed within 90 days prior to his recording of a notice of lien. It applies to work done by agreement with or upon consent of the owner of the property or "a person having authority from or rightfully acting for such owner."

Under M.G.L.A. c. 254, § 2, a contractor or supplier of materials may acquire a lien by recording a notice of contract. It must be recorded no later than the earliest of (i) 60 days after recording of a notice of substantial completion, (ii) 90 days after recording of a notice of termination, or (iii) 90 days after the contractor or any person claiming by, through or under it [such as a subcontractor] last performed or furnished labor and/or materials. A notice of substantial completion, to be executed by the owner and contractor, and recorded, is provided for in § 2A, and a possible notice of termination by the owner prior to substantial completion is provided for in § 2B, in both cases with requirements of notice to other contracting parties.

[Section 6:21]

[1]M.G.L.A. c. 36, §§ 13A, 13B.

[Section 6:22]

[1]Ch. 364, Acts of 1996. Pertinent cases on the subject since then include: Ng Brothers Const., Inc. v. Cranney, 436 Mass. 638, 766 N.E.2d 864 (2002); Tremont Tower Condominium, LLC v. George B.H. Macomber Co., 436 Mass. 677, 767 N.E.2d 20 (2002); National Lumber Co. v. United Cas. and Sur. Ins. Co., Inc., 440 Mass. 723, 802 N.E.2d 82 (2004); National Lumber Co. v. LeFrancois Const. Corp., 430 Mass. 663, 723 N.E.2d 10 (2000); Golden v. General Builders Supply LLC, 441 Mass. 652, 807 N.E.2d 822 (2004); National Lumber Co. v. Lombardi, 64 Mass. App. Ct. 490, 834 N.E.2d 267 (2005); Interstate Electrical Services Corp. v. Cummings Properties, LLC, 63 Mass. App. Ct. 295, 825 N.E.2d 1059 (2005); Chicago Title Ins. Co. v. Sherred Village Associates, 708 F.2d 804 (1st Cir. 1983); Johnson Lumber Co., Inc. v. Woodscape Homes, Inc., 51 Mass. App. Ct. 323, 746 N.E.2d 533 (2001).

M.G.L.A. c. 254, § 4, provides for notice of contract by subcontractors, including any subordinate tier of contract. The time of recording, duration of effectiveness and manner of disposition are substantially the same as those for § 2 notices. The statutory form of notice of contract with respect to a subcontract calls for listing of contract price, agreed change orders, pending change orders, disputed claims and payments received, all as asserted by the sub giving notice, who is, however, obliged to give "actual notice to the owner of such filing," whereupon the sub acquires a lien for payment of all labor and materials which he "is to furnish or has furnished," "regardless of the amount stated in the notice of contract." It is provided, however, that "such lien shall not exceed the amount due or to become due under the original contract as of the date notice of the filing of the subcontract is given by the subcontractor to the owner." Also, a contractor who "has no direct contractual relationship with the original contractor" is limited to "the amount due or to become due under the subcontract between the original contractor and the subcontractor whose work includes the work of the person claiming the lien as of the date such person files his notice of contract," but that limitation can be eliminated by the giving of a statutory notice of identification to "the original contractor." The latter term is not defined, but in the quoted context appears to mean the contracting party two tiers up.

Under § 7 of the statute a pre-recorded mortgage is given priority not only "to the extent of amounts actually advanced or unconditionally committed" prior to recording of the notice of contract, but also to amounts advanced after the notice of contract and within 25 days after a date specified in a partial waiver and subordination of lien, a statutory form in which the contractor lists contract amount, change orders, amount completed to date, retainage, previous payments, pending change orders and disputed claims. While a construction lender may thus retain priority of lien, it may not, under § 33, withhold loan advances because of the recording of a notice of lien under §§ 1 or 2. This provision (referred to as "forced funding") does not apply to loans on one to four dwelling units, nor require funding over § 4 liens if the loan documents so provide, nor require funding if there is "failure of the owner to comply with" other loan conditions.

Nevertheless, construction lenders as well as owners may find it desirable to opt out of the strictures and complexities of the statute by use of the lien bond provisions of § 12. After the recording of such a bond, contractors and workmen look to the bond and cannot obtain a lien on the property. Under

§ 32 the principal of a lien bond, usually the general contractor, may waive its own right to lien. That and the statutory partial waiver are the only exceptions to the provisions of § 33 voiding any agreement purporting to bar the filing or enforcement of a lien under c. 254.

Any lien under the statute will dissolve unless a statement of account, meeting requirements of § 8, is recorded within the time therein provided and a suit to enforce it is commenced within 90 days after the recording of the statement.

§ 6:23 Other

The "other" instruments one may expect to find of record in a registry of deeds include of course many of those referred to in the following **Topics D, E, and F in this Chapter**. Beyond that, there are instruments referred to in **Chapter 10**, some documents referred to in **Chapter 13**, organizational documents referred to in **Chapter 17**, and **Chapter 18**, and a variety of affidavits, court orders, agreements and other concoctions deemed to be pertinent to the title, use, occupancy or financing of some item of real estate.

TOPIC D: DOCUMENTS RELATING TO COURT ACTIONS

§ 6:24 Attachment; execution

Although not expressly provided in M.G.L.A. c. 223, judicial action is required under the rules of civil procedure for issuance of a writ of attachment.[1] To be effective, an attachment must state the name and last known residence of each defendant, and be recorded in the registry where the attached land lies.[2] If a defendant holds title as a trustee, the attachment must so specify to be effective against him.[3] An attachment remains in effect for six years if not carried forward or earlier dissolved by judicial action or otherwise.[4] When an attachment is found outstanding of record, the abstract thereof should show parties, dates, court in which the suit is filed, nature of the claim and amount of

---

[Section 6:24]

[1] See Bay State Harness Horse Racing & Breeding Ass'n, Inc. v. PPG Industries, Inc., 365 F. Supp. 1299 (D. Mass. 1973).

[2] M.G.L.A. c. 223, § 62.

[3] M.G.L.A. c. 223, § 67.

[4] M.G.L.A. c. 223, §§ 114A, 115, 115A, 116, 120, 130 and 132.

attachment. The attorney reviewing the title will ordinarily wish to have an examination made of the court records themselves in order to determine the status of the suit.

A recorded seizure on execution requires similar abstracting and review, and it also expires in six years if not enforced or brought forward in accordance with the statute.[5] Levy of execution by sale requires: giving of notice in accordance with the statute, sale by public auction to the highest bidder, an officer's return, a sheriff's deed recorded within six years after the levy and within three months after the sale if the debtor's estate was conveyed in the interim.[6]

§ 6:25   Lis pendens

While the purpose of an attachment is to secure an asset for payment of a prospectively successful plaintiff, the purpose of recording of a memorandum of lis pendens is to give notice to persons who might otherwise suffer the "harsh effects" of a common law rule of constructive notice.[1] To that end M.G.L.A. c. 184, § 15, provides that any "proceeding that affects the title to real property or the use and occupation thereof or the buildings thereon, shall not have any effect except against the parties thereto, their heirs and devisees and persons having actual non-record notice thereof, until a memorandum containing the names of the parties to the proceeding, the court in which it is pending, the date of the writ or other commencement thereof, the name of the town where the real property liable to be affected thereby lies and a description of the real property sufficiently accurate for identification is recorded in the registry of deed for the county or district where the real property lies."

To be recorded a memorandum of lis pendens must bear endorsement by the court, based on required findings, which are subject to contest and further review. The statute expressly provides that no affidavit under M.G.L.A. c. 183, § 5B (see § **10:10**) or any other recorded document shall constitute notice, constructive or actual, thus protecting persons without actual non-record notice unless a properly issued memorandum of lis pendens is recorded. When such a memorandum is found of record, it is therefore important to make careful examination of the court records.

---

[5]M.G.L.A. c. 236, § 49A.   (1982).

[6]M.G.L.A. c. 236, §§ 26 to 30.

[Section 6:25]

[1]True v. Wisniowski, 13 Mass. App. Ct. 501, 434 N.E.2d 686

The statute excludes actions relating to zoning and wetland regulations from the category of those that "affect title to real property or the use and occupation thereof or the buildings thereon," and the scope of that category has received judicial attention.[2]

§ 6:26   Bankruptcy

Notices of filings in bankruptcy should appear in each registry of deeds except in Boston, the situs of the bankruptcy court for Massachusetts. These notices may be kept by various registries in a separate bankruptcy index or file card box. When such a filing is found, there are several points pertinent to the title examination. When an owner in the chain of title is found to have been in bankruptcy, the conveyance of title may then come from a trustee, receiver, or the bankrupt as debtor in possession, accompanied in any case by a certified copy of the bankruptcy judge's order either approving the bond of the trustee or receiver or approving the debtor as in possession, and certified copies of the judge's orders authorizing and confirming the conveyance, including copies of the application for such authority, all of which should be recorded with the deed. The conveyance may be free of prior encumbrances as and to the extent specified in the orders of the bankruptcy court. If fewer than 20 years have passed since the bankruptcy filing, the records of the bankruptcy court should be reviewed to determine that any applicable appeal periods have expired and that no appeals are pending, and that creditors were given due notice and opportunity to be heard. If property of a bankrupt has not been conveyed within 20 years after filing, it may be deemed abandoned, and thereafter conveyed by the bankrupt or his heirs or devisees. Within such 20 year period one should examine the bankruptcy records for a discharge of the bankrupt and for specific evidence of abandonment of the premises to him.[1]

TOPIC E: DOCUMENTS RELATING TO GOVERNMENTAL ACTIONS

---

[2]Sutherland v. Aolean Development Corp., 399 Mass. 36, 502 N.E.2d 528 (1987); Maglione v. BancBoston Mortg. Corp., 29 Mass. App. Ct. 88, 557 N.E.2d 756 (1990); McCarthy v. Hurley, 24 Mass. App.

§ 6:27   Zoning; subdivision control

Under M.G.L.A. c. 40A, § 11, a variance or special permit (see **§ 11:19** and **§ 11:21**) does not take effect until a copy of the decision granting it, bearing required certifications of the city or town clerk, is recorded in the registry of deeds and indexed in the grantor index under the name of the owner of record of the land affected. Extensions and amendments of variances and special permits should be similarly recorded.

With respect to actions under the subdivision control law (see **Chapter 12**) there are several things to look for in the registry of deeds, beginning with two documents which every planning board is required to certify to the registry of deeds: (1) the names of the members entitled to act for the planning board, and (2) the rules and regulations adopted by the board governing subdivision. Actions of planning boards and signatures of such members are often endorsed on the face of recorded plans, including both "approval not required" and approval under the subdivision control law. Sometimes one finds other provisions set forth on the face of plans, including conditions of approval, waiver of particular regulations, or even covenants of enforcement. Those matters should preferably be set forth in a separate recorded instrument.

The performance of the construction requirements in connection with subdivision approval are secured either by a covenant of the owner with the planning board, which is recorded, or by bond, which is usually not recorded. There is a standard form for such a covenant, but there are often adaptations and special provisions which need to be carefully abstracted. Releases of lots from the covenant may be recorded as the work progresses, and eventually a certificate of completion should be recorded.

§ 6:28   Environmental controls

Instruments found of record relating to environmental controls include the following: (1) Orders of Condition by local conservation commissions (**§ 13:9**). These are often not very instructive as to the work to be done, and it is usually necessary to obtain a copy of the applicant's Notice of Intent. Sometimes there are superseding Orders from DEP, and

Ct. 533, 510 N.E.2d 779 (1987); Heller v. Turner Bros. Const., Inc., 40 Mass. App. Ct. 363, 663 N.E.2d 1243 (1996); Wolfe v. Gormally, 440 Mass. 699, 802 N.E.2d 64 (2004).

[Section 6:26]

[1]See REBA Title Standards 30, 31 and 32.

extensions and certificates of compliance are also recorded. A determination of non-applicability of the statute may also be recorded. A state-issued wetland control order (or mountain region order in Berkshire County) may also be recorded (§ **13:11**, § **13:22**), requiring review to determine the scope in relation to the site being examined.

Licenses for alteration, filling or erection of structures affecting tidal waters, great ponds and certain rivers and streams (§ **13:12**) also must be recorded, usually accompanied by detailed plans.

In relation to environmental cleanup an instrument of Activity and Use Limitations (§ **13:18**) may be recorded.

Beside instruments arising from state law there are others that may arise from federal law, and in any event one surely cannot learn about the environmental status of a parcel of land from record search alone, but must become familiar with the broad panoply of environmental protection laws, as discussed in **Chapter 13**.

§ 6:29 Takings

Takings for street layouts and for water and sewer lines are very common and affect most land titles. They are usually accompanied by plans and are often very lengthy and prolix in style. A skilled examiner may be permitted to condense the abstract, but it should always include the name of the taking authority, the law under which it purports to act, the stated purpose of the taking, and any statement of whether the taking is in fee or of an easement. Sometimes temporary construction easements are also taken, and the time periods and locations thereof should be noted. Takings often affect multiple owners, and the name of the party in the chain of title being examined should be flagged in the list of affected parties, and the location of locus within the taking description and on the taking plan should be marked. The award for damages is not directly pertinent to title, but it is usually of interest and should be noted.

It is a long-standing principle of law that a taking is limited to the interests needed for its purpose to be fulfilled.[1] Consequently, a taking for a street layout (as for water and

------

[Section 6:29]

[1]Inhabitants of Town of Lexington v. Suburban Land Co., 235 Mass. 108, 126 N.E. 360 (1920); Leroy v. Worcester St. Ry. Co., 287 Mass. 1, 191 N.E. 39 (1934);

Anderson v. Healy, 36 Mass. App. Ct. 131, 629 N.E.2d 312 (1994); Martin v. Building Inspector of Freetown, 38 Mass. App. Ct. 509, 649 N.E.2d 779 (1995).

sewer lines) establishes only an easement for highway purposes unless a taking in fee is expressly made. Most local street takings, and many county and state highway takings, are of easements, not fees. Some municipalities do seem to have adopted in some eras a policy of making fee takings for streets, and this practice may lead to complications when there is need for relocation or discontinuance. The process of discontinuance is similar to that of taking, and instruments of discontinuance are of course of great interest to the underlying fee owner.[2]

In the case of major highway layouts, on the other hand, taking in fee does make sense, and that is the practice of the Massachusetts Department of Highways. Such takings often provide for "limited access," that is, prohibition of access to the highway from abutting lands; the highway being accessible only at planned interchanges. That feature of a taking is, of course, of vital importance to an abutter, and such provisions must be carefully abstracted.

§ 6:30 Municipal liens and other liens

The recording of a certificate of municipal liens issued under M.G.L.A. c. 60, § 23, is a means of barring prior liens for taxes, assessments, water rates and other municipal charges.[1] The statute provides that such a certificate, recorded within 150 days after its date, "shall operate to discharge the parcel of real estate specified from the liens for all taxes, assessments, or portions thereof, rates and charges which do not appear by said certificate to constitute liens thereon, except taxes, assessments, or portions thereof, rates and charges with respect to which there has been filed for record or registration evidence of a taking or a sale by the municipality or concerning which a statement or order creating or continuing such lien has been so filed under any provision of law, if said lien can be discharged by the recording or registration of an instrument other than a certificate under this section; but a certificate issued under this section shall not affect the obligation of any person liable for the payment of any tax, assessment, rate, or charge by reason of being the assessed owner of such parcel of real estate at the time any such lien became effective."

---

[2]M.G.L.A. c. 82, § 32A.

[Section 6:30]

[1]Including: betterment assessments, M.G.L.A. c. 80, § 12; old age assistance liens, M.G.L.A. c. 118A, § 4; veterans assistance liens, M.G.L.A. c. 115, § 5A; and rates and charges of a municipal lighting plant, M.G.L.A. c. 164, §§ 58B to 58E.

While the fees for such certificates range from $25 to $150, depending on the size and use of the property, and the recording fee is $50, purchasers and mortgagees regularly require them to be obtained and recorded.

Absent a tax taking or sale, or recording of a statement continuing the lien pursuant to M.G.L.A. c. 60, § 37A, the lien for unpaid real estate taxes is terminated, as provided in M.G.L.A. c. 60, § 37, (and except as provided in § 61) "at the expiration of three years and six months from the end of the fiscal year for which such taxes were assessed, if in the meantime the estate has been alienated and the instrument alienating the same has been recorded, otherwise it shall continue until a recorded alienation thereof, ..."

At the state level, the corporate excise tax lien is, in the absence of a waiver (as referred to in § 1:8), barred three years after the corporate sale or transfer of all or substantially all of its assets in Massachusetts. Liens relating to employment security laws or other state tax laws may also sometimes be found of record.

Federal liens (other than those related to estates, referred to in § 6:34) may arise in relation to income, withholding, gift or other taxes. The question of priorities among federal tax liens, state and municipal tax liens and mortgages is one that has engaged the attention of the courts and Congress over the years.[2] When faced with any complex question of lien priority, there is no substitute for a careful study of the applicable statutes and an ad hoc analysis of their application to the particular factual situation.

TOPIC F: PROBATE COURT INSTRUMENTS

§ 6:31   Testate estate—General review

Whenever title to real estate passes through a decedent's estate, the probate court records are fundamental elements of the title chain. In abstracting the probate it is well to start with the docket, which may serve as a check list and also disclose any will contest or other unusual proceeding. A

---

[2]U.S. v. City of New Britain, Conn., 347 U.S. 81, 74 S. Ct. 367, 98 L. Ed. 520 (1954); U.S. v. Boyd, 246 F.2d 477 (5th Cir. 1957); U.S. v. Brosnan, 363 U.S. 237, 80 S. Ct. 1108, 4 L. Ed. 2d 1192 (1960); Milton Sav. Bank v. U.S., 345 Mass. 302, 187 N.E.2d 379 (1963); U. S. v. Rahar's Inn, Inc., 243 F. Supp. 459 (D. Mass. 1965); Zuroff v. First Wisconsin Trust Co., 41 Mass. App. Ct. 491, 671 N.E.2d 982 (1996).

surviving spouse may waive the will and claim a statutory share, as discussed below. The petition for probate should be abstracted, showing the deceased's name, place of residence at death and date of death. It should recite that he left a will and specify the codicils, if any, giving names, addresses and relationships of surviving spouse and heirs, and pray that petitioner be appointed executor. If the spouse and heirs have assented, that should also be noted. If one or more of the persons named in the will to be executor has declined to serve, the petition should so recite and written declinations, or evidence of the death or incapacity of such persons, should be on file with the probate papers. When the person appointed to administer the will was not named therein to be an executor, then he is properly styled an administrator with the will annexed (*cum testamento annexo*).

Other points which it may be important to note include the publication requirements and return date of the citation, the filing of the return, the entry of the decree, the filing of bond and the approval thereof, which may be without sureties if the will so provides; the issuance of "letters testamentary" and giving of notice of such appointment; the filing of an inventory (and the inclusion of the locus therein); the filing of inheritance and estate tax receipts or waivers, the payment of legacies, and the allowance of accounts. Some of these matters are discussed further below.

The examiner must of course also abstract the will. Wills are often lengthy documents, and a skilled examiner may be relied upon to summarize provisions which do not appear to have a direct bearing on the title being examined. The minimum essentials include: identification of the acting fiduciary; disposition of the real estate in question either by specific devise or as part of the residuary estate; the names and addresses or other identification of the devisees and the precise terms of the devise; the existence of pecuniary legacies or other obligations which may be charges on the real estate; and the existence and terms of any power of sale.

Pecuniary legacies are chargeable against the residuary estate, and consequently when the locus has not been specifically devised as an identifiable parcel, it is important to determine that the legacies have been paid. Legacy receipts may be on file, or the payment thereof may be shown in an account. If the account has been filed, but not yet allowed, one relies on it at peril. Legacies may be asserted for 20 years, but there is a 6–year limitation on sale of real estate for that purpose.

If there is delay in allowance of a will and appointment of

the executor, a special administrator may be appointed, and may be licensed to convey real estate. Once the will is allowed, property may be devised thereunder to a testamentary trustee who will also be appointed by the probate court and may be authorized to sell real estate. All such proceedings need to be abstracted.

§ 6:32 Testate estate—Spousal share

Under M.G.L.A. c. 191, § 15, a surviving husband or wife may waive the provisions of the will within six months after probate of the will and take a statutory share as follows: (1) if there are issue—one-third of the real and personal property up to $25,000 and the income for life of the excess of such one-third over $25,000; (2) if there are kindred but no issue—the first $25,000 of real and personal property plus the income for life of one-half the remainder; or (3) if there are neither issue nor kindred—the first $25,000 plus half the remainder outright. The assets which are subject to the surviving spouse's claim may include not only probate assets, but those in trusts over which the decedent spouse had power of revocation or disposition.[1]

§ 6:33 Sale under power or license or by devisee

When the will confers a power of sale on the executor, a deed of the executor will convey to a purchaser for value a title free from the claims of general creditors of the testator and of legatees and devisees under the will.[1]

Even if there is a power of sale (and the will does not *require* sale by the executor), a devisee of the property may convey it and his deed will convey title free of all debts, legacies, expenses of administration and applicable death taxes if a final account has been allowed showing payment thereof, or if claims for such charges are barred.[2]

When there is no power of sale in the will, sale may be authorized by license of the probate court. Issuance of a license may be occasioned by insufficiency of the personalty in the estate to pay debts, legacies and charges of administration,[3] or simply by the desire of the executor to sell in order to ef-

---

[Section 6:32]

[1]Sullivan v. Burkin, 390 Mass. 864, 460 N.E.2d 572 (1984).

[Section 6:33]

[1]See REBA Title Standard 10, derived from correspondence in 1912 between George A. Sawyer and John C. Gray, published in Issue No. 1 of Volume 36 of the Massachusetts Law Quarterly.

[2]See REBA Title Standard 40.

[3]M.G.L.A. c. 202, § 1.

fect the orderly liquidation of the estate.[4] The petition for license, assents thereto, notice ordered and given, and the decree authorizing sale should all be abstracted in detail. The decree usually authorizes sale at a private sale at a specified price or at public auction at a higher price. The stated price, represented to the court in the petition, is usually one established by a purchase and sale agreement which has been entered by the executor or administrator. It is important for the abstract to show the concordance of the consideration figures in the petition, decree and deed given pursuant to the license. The property description should also be consistent. Often the petition and decree descriptions are somewhat skimpy, and after setting it forth verbatim in the deed, one may go on to add a full and proper description.

Sales made by a fiduciary pursuant to a license are protected by statutes which prohibit their being voided for certain procedural defects or attacked more than five years after the sale by persons claiming under the decedent.[5]

§ 6:34 Debts; tax liens

Claims of creditors of a decedent can be asserted as charges on the estate, but there is a one-year statute of limitations, running from the date of death.[1] Generally, a purchaser in good faith from a court-appointed fiduciary or from a devisee or heir may rely on the decree appointing the fiduciary or allowing the will as being final and conclusive one year after its date.

The federal estate tax lien arises automatically without notice on estates of taxable size, and since non-probate assets are included in the taxable estate, probate inventory valuations are not a reliable guide to taxability. The statute of limitations on the lien is 10 years from date of death,[2] but there are exceptions. In abstracting an estate more than 10 years back, it is reassuring if the probate records show payment of the tax, and on estates within the limitation period it is essential to have proof of payment of the amount shown as due by the estate tax closing letter or a release of lien on file.[3]

The Massachusetts estate tax—a so-called "sponge tax"— imposes a lien with a statute of limitations of 10 years from

---

[4]M.G.L.A. c. 202, § 19.

[5]M.G.L.A. c. 202, § 2 and § 38.

[Section 6:34]

[1]M.G.L.A. c. 197, § 9.

[2]I.R.C. § 6324(a).

[3]The closing letter alone will not suffice; U.S. v. Vohland, 675 F.2d 1071 (9th Cir. 1982).

date of death.[4] It also applies to non-probate assets, so a probate inventory may not be relied upon. As a practical matter conveyancers do sometimes rely on a recordable affidavit of the executor or administrator, but it is always advisable to obtain a release of the lien.

§ 6:35   Self-dealing

When a fiduciary conveys to himself, the fact should be noted in the abstract and data should also be included to show either that the will or other instrument authorized self-dealing, or that a court of competent jurisdiction authorized the sale. Absent either of those, it may be sufficient to show consent by competent beneficiaries or the long (30 years) passage of time without adverse claim,[1] but otherwise the fiduciary may be compelled to reconvey or provide restitution.[2]

§ 6:36   Intestate estate—General review

The review of an intestate estate involves many of the same considerations as referred to in the preceding paragraph A, leading to the appointment of an administrator of the estate, and including matters as to debts and tax liens. The identity of the heirs is in this case of even greater importance. Although judicial decisions do not establish the list of heirs as conclusive, lawyers generally rely on the recital in the petition unless other data in the title render it subject to doubts.[1]

When the administration of an estate is not completed by the person first appointed, a successor may be appointed as administrator of "goods not yet administered" (de bonis non).

Administrators of an intestate estate may be licensed by the Probate Court to sell real estate in the same manner as discussed above for executors.

§ 6:37   Intestate estate—Spousal share

Under M.G.L.A. c. 190, § 1, the surviving spouse of an

---

[4]M.G.L.A. c. 65C, § 14.

[Section 6:35]

[1]See REBA Title Standard 23.

[2]Gunther v. Gove, 275 Mass. 235, 175 N.E. 464 (1931).

[Section 6:36]

[1]Cassidy v. Truscott, 287 Mass. 515, 192 N.E. 164 (1934);

Behan v. Treasurer and Receiver General, 276 Mass. 502, 177 N.E. 654 (1931); see REBA Title Standard 41.

intestate decedent is entitled to take distribution as follows: (i) If the decedent left kindred but no issue—$200,000 and one-half of the rest of the estate, with provision for raising the $200,000 minimum by sale or mortgage of real estate; (ii) If the decedent left issue—one-half of the estate; and (iii) If the decedent left no issue and no kindred—the whole estate.

§ 6:38 Descent and distribution

Subject to the spousal share, the estate of an intestate decedent passes pursuant to M.G.L.A. c. 190, § 3, as follows:

(i) In equal shares to decedent's children and to issue of any deceased child by right of representation, or if there are no surviving children but more remote issue, to them, equally if all are of the same degree of kindred (i.e., level of descent), or otherwise by right of representation;

(ii) If decedent left no issue, to his father and mother, in equal shares, or to the survivor of them;

(iii) If decedent left no issue and no father or mother, to his brothers and sisters and issue of brothers and sisters by right of representation, and if only issue of siblings to them equally if all are of the same degree of kindred, or otherwise by right of representation;

(iv) If decedent left none of the foregoing, to his next of kin in equal degree, the degrees of kinship being defined in the statute, and there being a preference for those claiming through the nearest ancestor; and

(v) If decedent left no spouse or kin, the estate escheats to the Commonwealth, or in some cases to a Soldiers' Home.

The laws of descent and distribution have changed and evolved over the ages, and occasionally a title may turn on intestate succession under earlier law. While the rarity of need to search back that far no longer warrants setting forth the prior laws herein, it is worth noting that a review of prior laws is set forth in § 5:10.04 of the Third Edition of this volume.

§ 6:39 Missing probates

In a title chain one may occasionally find a deed into a person from whom neither a deed out nor a probate proceeding can be found, but there are deeds of the locus from the putative heirs of such decedent. A sensible rule is that such a title shall not be deemed defective (a) if the decedent died more than 25 years ago, his date of death and then place of residence are shown by recorded affidavit or death certificate, and a recorded affidavit names his heirs and states that he died intestate, or (b) if the decedent died more than 50 years ago and any recorded instruments in the chain of title identify his heirs.[1] The appropriate forms of such affidavits would be those provided for in M.G.L.A. c. 183, §§ 5A and 5B, referred to in § **10:10**.

§ 6:40   Guardianship; conservatorship

Guardians and conservators appointed pursuant to provisions of M.G.L.A. c. 201 may also be licensed to sell real estate of a ward, in a manner similar to and subject to the same or similar requirements as are applicable to sales by executors and administrators. Provision for sale of real estate where personalty is insufficient to pay debts of the ward is made in M.G.L.A. c. 202, § 5, and provision for sale for purposes of increasing the ward's income or for his general benefit is made in § 21. Petitions for license under §§ 7 and 22, respectively, are similar to those for sale by executors and administrators.

Provision is also made in Chapter 202 for: sale of property of a minor for investment by a guardian or friend (§ 25); transfer to a foreign custodian of property of a ward who moves out of state (§ 27); mortgage of property by an executor or administrator (§ 28) or a guardian or conservator (§ 29); leasing of property of a ward (§ 31); authorization of sale of Massachusetts real estate by a foreign executor or administrator (§ 32) or foreign guardian or conservator (§ 33); and for sale of the entire estate (§ 32) or foreign guardian or conservator (§ 33); and for sale of the entire estate where the ward is a tenant by the entirety and the other tenant consents (§ 36).

§ 6:41   Partition

Historically, exclusive jurisdiction for partition was in the Probate Courts, but concurrent jurisdiction was vested in the Land Court, effective January 1, 2003.[1] Under M.G.L.A. c. 241, partition may be sought by any owner of an undivided interest (except a tenant by the entirety) in a fee title, life estate or term of years. The petition for partition must set forth the share of each co-tenant, describe the land sufficiently for identification, reference the source of title, and pray in the alternative for division of the land or for sale, ei-

---

[Section 6:39]
[1]See REBA Title Standard 14.

[Section 6:41]
[1]Ch. 393, Acts of 2002.

ther public or private, and if private, the minimum sale amount. All other owners are necessary parties, but mortgagees and other lienors are not, but must be named and notified, and may be allowed to intervene. A notice of the petition must be recorded in the registry of deeds. Commissioners appointed by the court recommend a division or a sale, which the court may accept or reject. If physical division is made, but the parcels are not equal in value, payments may be required for equalization. If the land "cannot be divided advantageously," the court may order the commissioners to sell it, on terms the court may specify, and distribute the proceeds as the court orders. The final decree must be recorded in the registry of deeds and is conclusive.

§ 6:42 Other

As mentioned in § **6:2**, the jurisdiction of the Probate Courts under M.G.L.A. c. 215, § 3 includes other matters which often have a bearing on a record title, including divorce, adoption, and change of name, decrees with respect to which may appear in the registry of deeds or may need to be sought out of probate court records. Also, the Probate Courts have general equity jurisdiction which includes jurisdiction over real estate involved in estates and also inter vivos trusts.

TOPIC G: USING THE ABSTRACT

§ 6:43 The reading

Assuming a basically chronological organization of the completed abstract, the first reading may be "backwards," that is, from the deed into the present owner backward step by step through the chain of prior owners. A reason for this approach is that recent documents often tell one all there is to know about the current description and status of encumbrances, and the earlier part of the abstract serves only to verify that there is an adequate chain and to exclude the existence of defects or unanticipated encumbrances. Also, the locus being examined is always (if you go back far enough) a part of a previously larger tract, and reading backward will most quickly locate the point at which the current parcel was first divided out of the tract. In many cases nowadays that point may be further back than the starting point of the abstract.

Having read the abstract backwards, then read it forward, this time analyzing each grantor schedule and each instrument with particular care. Keep in mind that every item on every grantor schedule must be considered. The title examiner will have prepared a summary report sheet noting all outstanding encumbrances and indicating any title defects. Preferably these should be flagged (by red pencil or otherwise) on the summary sheet and on the sheets in the abstract at which they appear. A careful lawyer reading the abstract will always make his own judgments as to peculiarities or defects, and as to the adequacy or accuracy of the description of the property, or the terms of easements, restrictions and other encumbrances. Based upon his conclusions, a talk with the examiner and perhaps another trip to the registry will be in order.

In addition to a summary report sheet, many conveyancers find that a diagram of the chain of title is an invaluable tool. This is particularly true if the locus is composed of multiple parcels, or the devolution of title is complex, branching into multiple chains or with probates involving ramified family trees. Such a diagram may make it possible to comprehend a title which could otherwise not be grasped as an integrated whole, and by relating every sheet in the abstract to its proper place in the chain, it may be crucial in avoiding errors and oversights. Aside from that, it certainly would be a great aid to any other lawyer subsequently reading the abstract.

An example of such a diagram might appear as shown below. This indicates a hypothetical search of title to Lots 13 and 14 on Branch Lane, made on behalf of a prospective purchaser of that property from Mr. and Mrs. Ohner. Such a diagram would of course usually be entirely handwritten. The page or sheet numbers in the abstract are circled. In this case the plans and Grantor Schedules were placed at the end. Items indicating possible problems or matters of continuing interest are here underlined, while in an actual diagram they might be marked with a red pencil.

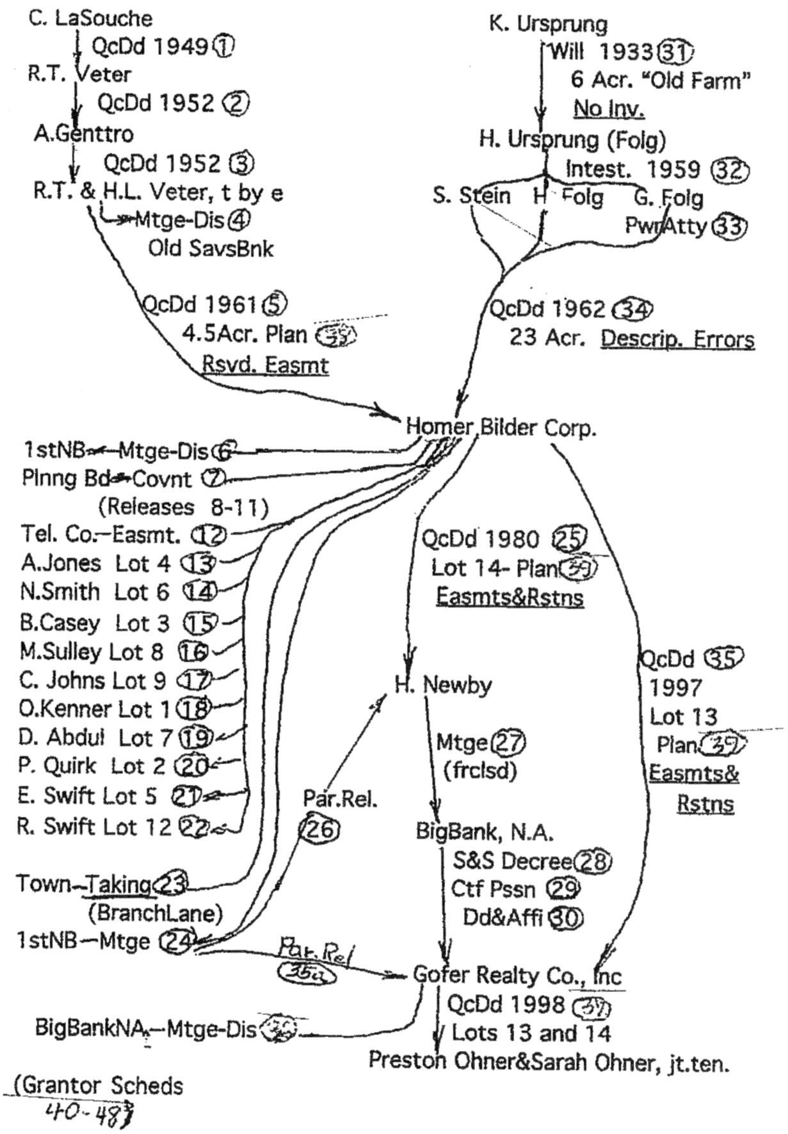
C. LaSouche
QcDd 1949 ①
R.T. Veter
QcDd 1952 ②
A.Genttro
QcDd 1952 ③
R.T. & H.L. Veter, t by e
Mtge-Dis ④
Old SavsBnk
QcDd 1961 ⑤
4.5Acr. Plan 39
Rsvd. Easmt
K. Ursprung
Will 1933 31
6 Acr. "Old Farm"
No Inv.
H. Ursprung (Folg)
Intest. 1959 32
S. Stein
H Folg
G. Folg
PwrAtty 33
QcDd 1962 34
23 Acr. Descrip. Errors
Homer Bilder Corp.
1stNB—Mtge-Dis 6
Plnng Bd—Covnt 7
(Releases 8-11)
Tel. Co.—Easmt. 12
A.Jones Lot 4 13
N.Smith Lot 6 14
B.Casey Lot 3 15
M.Sulley Lot 8 16
C. Johns Lot 9 17
O.Kenner Lot 1 18
D. Abdul Lot 7 19
P. Quirk Lot 2 20
E. Swift Lot 5 21
R. Swift Lot 12 22
Town—Taking 23
(BranchLane)
1stNB—Mtge 24
QcDd 1980 25
Lot 14- Plan 39
Easmts&Rstns
H. Newby
Par.Rel.
26
Mtge 27
(frclsd)
BigBank, N.A.
S&S Decree 28
Ctf Pssn 29
Dd&Affi 30
QcDd 35
1997
Lot 13
Plan 39
Easmts&
Rstns
Par. Rel
35a
Gofer Realty Co., Inc
QcDd 1998 37
Lots 13 and 14
BigBankNA—Mtge-Dis 36
Preston Ohner&Sarah Ohner, jt.ten.
(Grantor Scheds
40-48)

§ 6:44   Passing on the title

When all of the examination and all of the reading is done, the conveyancer must make his decision on the title. Is it or is it not sufficient and satisfactory for his client's purposes? What defects, doubts or questions need to be cited? Are they such that title insurance may protect against them or will curative instruments or procedures be required? In answering these questions a useful technique, and a step toward fulfillment of the conveyancer's obligation, is the preparation of a draft of a title opinion letter or a report on title to a title insurance company. The success of the transaction being handled will ordinarily depend on the determination that the title is satisfactory, and consequently the conveyancer should always seek to find a way to make it so. He must, however, report all outstanding encumbrances and defects, for he will be subject to action for errors in his opinion, running from the date of discovery thereof.

Since title insurance is now nearly universal, it must be acknowledged that some real estate lawyers seldom read and pass on title abstracts, but instead review only title insurance commitments or specimen policies. This author, an old conveyancer, regards that as an unfortunate lapse in professional standards. Without at all denigrating title insurance as a valuable tool in modern real estate practice, the goal in Massachusetts has always been to discern and cure defects in title, and not to ignore or "insure over" them. Upon request, title insurers are generally willing to provide a copy of the abstract on which their policy is to be based, and at the very least should provide full copies of every title source document and every instrument referred to as an "exception" to the coverage. Without reading at least those, understanding their relation to and effect on the locus, and relating that information to his client in intelligible form, a real estate lawyer cannot properly serve his client.

§ 6:45   Organizing the file

A logical and often used system for organizing title files is as follows: Arrange all grantor schedules in chronological order, and if a grantee schedule was run on any owner, place it immediately before his grantor schedule. Start the abstract with a report sheet numbered 1, and follow it with the collection of grantor and grantee schedules, numbered consecutively. Then proceed with the abstracts of instruments, essentially in chronological order. As an exception to strict chronological order, place partial releases, assignments and discharges of mortgages immediately following the mortgage abstracted, and other discharge instruments after the encumbrances to which they relate. If there are multiple parcels, designate them as, say, Parcels A, B and C, group together the whole chain on Parcel A, follow it with the whole chain on Parcel B and then the whole chain on Parcel C. Plans may be included in the abstract in chronological order together with the particular instrument to which they relate, such as an easement plan with the grant of easement, a taking plan with the instrument of taking, etc. However, tract plans which relate to the title chain generally or to major parts of it may better be placed at the end of the abstract or kept separately. In either case notation thereof should be inserted at the proper chronological places of such plans in the abstract. At the end, place the notes and title chain diagram prepared in the course of reading the abstract, and following that place copies of any explanatory or curative instruments which were obtained, and a copy of the opinion on title which was rendered. Then all sheets should be consecutively numbered, and the appropriate sheet numbers inserted on the face of the report sheet in reference to outstanding encumbrances, plans, descriptions and other special features. The file number for that abstract should be written on each sheet and on every other document kept in the file, so that if any of them become separated, it will be possible to return them to their proper place.

Later occasions may arise for continued examination of the same title. All subsequent grantor schedules, abstracts and copies of instruments may be added at the end of the existing file, or organized in a separate clip designated part 2, with the original abstract then designated part 1. A properly kept abstract is a valuable tool which may be used many times by successive attorneys.

Chapter 7

Possessory Title

TOPIC A: ADVERSE POSSESSION

§ 7:1 Fundamentals

Possession has always been an important element of the ownership of real estate. It was essential to "seisin," a feudal term which now means (if anything) little more than possession of a freehold estate. The correlative "disseisin" is defined as "a usurpation of the right of seisin and possession, and an exercise of such powers and privileges of ownership as to keep out or displace him to whom those rightfully belong."[1] That is close to a definition of "adverse possession," and in fact it is said that a basic test of effective adverse possession is "disseisin."[2]

The legal concept of adverse possession has of course evolved since feudal times, and the rules and tests have been developed and articulated by judicial decisions and statutes. The rules and tests are not the same in all jurisdictions, sometimes differing markedly. For instance, in Massachusetts the period required for possession is twenty years, said to be derived from common law, but some states have reduced that by statute to as little as seven years.

In Massachusetts (and elsewhere) the basic requirements are described in brief as possession which is open and notorious, adverse, and continuous for the requisite period. Each of those terms is considered separately in the following sections of this chapter in light of Massachusetts judicial decisions. The courts have consistently held that whether or not adverse possession has been effected is always a question of fact.[3] But physical situations and the actions of persons seeking or claiming possessory rights come in great

---

[Section 7:1]

[1]Black's Law Dictionary, Third Edition, West Publishing Company.

[2]See Leavitt v. Elkin, 314 Mass. 396, 49 N.E.2d 1020 (1943); Rothery v. MacDonald, 329 Mass. 238, 107 N.E.2d 432 (1952);

Kershaw v. Zecchini, 342 Mass. 318, 173 N.E.2d 624 (1961).

[3]Inhabitants of Nantucket v. Mitchell, 271 Mass. 62, 170 N.E. 807 (1930); Kershaw v. Zecchini, 342 Mass. 318, 173 N.E.2d 624 (1961); Mendonca v. Cities Service Oil Co. of Pa., 354 Mass. 323, 237

variety, and the application of the fundamental concepts does not always appear in "bright lines." That is hardly surprising when one considers that a tract of land, with or without buildings thereon, is hardly susceptible to "possession" in the same way as is a tangible chattel. There is a big difference between manual custody of a chattel and the "possession," evidenced by use and control, of real estate.

The days of "squatters" and land-stealers are bygone, and the assertion of adverse possession nowadays arises largely from or in relation to flaws in record title. When descriptions of the boundaries of land are unclear or overlap with respect to adjoining parcels, or when there are areas of "shared" use, arising either from unclear documents or by practice, or simply when a record title is uncertain for any reason, the assertion and proof of adverse possession may afford a solution. Similarly, the assertion of easements by prescription is often related to uncertainty as to the scope of a grant or implication of an easement. Cases involving such issues often arise in the Land Court, and some of them involving adverse possession are discussed in **Chapter 8**.

§ 7:2 Basic requirements

In order to succeed in a claim of title acquired by adverse possession, all of the necessary elements must be proved, and the burden of proof is on the claimant.[1] In addition to the rubrics of paragraphs A, B, C and D of this section, the courts often include in the listing of essential elements the words "actual," "exclusive," "dominion," "ouster," "claim of right," "hostile," "non-permissive," "color of title," and various permutations thereof. For the sake of compactness and clarity of exposition these terms are subsumed under one or more of the following rubrics. Because all elements are necessary, almost every judicial decision considers all of them. The citations herein consequently involve some culling of points deemed to be pertinent to the particular matter under discussion, but of course the several elements are interrelated.

§ 7:3 Period of possession

As stated in § 7:1, the period required for adverse posses-

N.E.2d 16 (1968).

[Section 7:2]

[1]Gadreault v. Hillman, 317 Mass. 656, 59 N.E.2d 477 (1945); Holmes v. Johnson, 324 Mass. 450, 86 N.E.2d 924 (1949); Mendonca v.

Cities Service Oil Co. of Pa., 354 Mass. 323, 237 N.E.2d 16 (1968); Boothroyd v. Bogartz, 68 Mass. App. Ct. 40, 859 N.E.2d 876 (2007), review denied, 448 Mass. 1107, 864 N.E.2d 22 (2007).

sion is twenty years. That is confirmed by two statutes. M.G.L.A. c. 260, § 21, provides that: "An action for the recovery of land shall be commenced, or an entry made thereon, only within twenty years after the right of action or of entry first accrued, or within twenty years after the demandant or the person making the entry, or those under whom they claim, have been seized or possessed of the premises; provided, however, that this section shall not bar an action by or on behalf of a nonprofit land conservation corporation or trust for the recovery of land or interests in land held for conservation, parks, recreation, water protection or wildlife protection purposes." And M.G.L.A. c. 187, § 2, provides that: "No person shall acquire by adverse use or enjoyment a right or privilege of way or other easement from, in, upon or over the land of another, unless such use or enjoyment is continued uninterruptedly for twenty years."

§ 7:4   General tests of possession

As suggested in § **7:1**, possession of land is a matter of use and control, sometimes referred to as "possession and enjoyment."[1] The acts evidencing use and control are called acts of dominion. In order to be effective, the claimant must perform the acts, not just propose or contemplate them; they must be "actual."[2] The acts performed must be such that, when taken all together, they substantially exclude use and control of the property by others, including the record owner, and thereby constitute an ouster or disseisin.[3] It is sometimes said that such acts give rise to a presumption of a "lost grant," the term being more suggestive than explanatory.

§ 7:5   Types of dominion

It was held long ago that "a title by adverse possession cannot be shown to wild or woodland that has always been open and unenclosed."[1] The principle that fencing or cultivation of such land is a necessary action has subsequently been cited and relied upon to bar title by adverse posses-

---

[Section 7:4]

[1]The appealing term for which in French is "jouissance."

[2]See McLaughlin v. Town of Marblehead, 68 Mass. App. Ct. 490, 863 N.E.2d 61 (2007).

[3]Inhabitants of Nantucket v. Mitchell, 271 Mass. 62, 170 N.E. 807 (1930); Ottavia v. Savarese, 338 Mass. 330, 155 N.E.2d 432, 2 A.L.R.3d 997 (1959); Kershaw v. Zecchini, 342 Mass. 318, 173 N.E.2d 624 (1961).

[Section 7:5]

[1]Dow v. Dow, 243 Mass. 587, 137 N.E. 746 (1923), citing earlier cases.

sion,[2] but it should not be considered to be a fixed rule of law, but rather an evidentiary test.[3] In the cited *Dow v. Dow* case the court upheld adverse possession, finding that the seven acres of woodland was "substantially enclosed" by fences not constructed by the claimant, and that his cutting wood and paying taxes sufficed. Possessory title has also been upheld on other unfenced parcels when there were substantial acts of dominion, such as: (i) clearing brush and trees, putting in boundary markers, performing circus stunts, and later erection of a wall and a house,[4] and (ii) making a vegetable garden, selling Christmas trees, setting up a children's playhouse, and later clearing and grading a driveway and erecting signs.[5] When the act of dominion was clearing brush and the brush grew back, the court said that such natural revegetation "does not itself determine that the area was wild and uncultivated."[6]

In other cases upholding title by adverse possession the acts of dominion have included such things as (i) installing a lawn and rock garden extending from claimant's adjoining residence,[7] (ii) building a house, enclosed by a hedge,[8] (iii) successive use of parts of the site as driveway, parking area, lawn, chicken coop area and fencing,[9] (iv) maintaining a cranberry bog,[10] and (v) brush, lawn and compost activities, and construction of a seawall and play equipment.[11] Paying real estate taxes, as an adverse possessor may do under M.G.L.A. c. 60, § 60, is an act of dominion, but surely not sufficient in itself.

As indicated, the uses may be diverse. In *Shaw v. Solari*, the court pointed out that the claimants "used various portions of the strip for various purposes, all as they chose, and their possession of the whole strip was exclusive and indicative of a claim by them of ownership of the entire locus."

---

[2]Cowden v. Cutting, 339 Mass. 164, 158 N.E.2d 324 (1959); Senn v. Western Massachusetts Elec. Co., 18 Mass. App. Ct. 992, 471 N.E.2d 131 (1984).

[3]See La Chance v. Rubashe, 301 Mass. 488, 17 N.E.2d 685 (1938).

[4]Kershaw v. Zecchini, 342 Mass. 318, 173 N.E.2d 624 (1961).

[5]Masa Builders, Inc. v. Hanson, 30 Mass. App. Ct. 930, 568 N.E.2d 636 (1991).

[6]Sea Pines Condominium III Ass'n v. Steffens, 61 Mass. App. Ct. 838, 814 N.E.2d 752 (2004).

[7]Lyon v. Parkinson, 330 Mass. 374, 113 N.E.2d 861 (1953).

[8]Shoer v. Daffe, 337 Mass. 420, 149 N.E.2d 625 (1958).

[9]Shaw v. Solari, 8 Mass. App. Ct. 151, 392 N.E.2d 853 (1979).

[10]Macallister v. DeStefano, 18 Mass. App. Ct. 39, 463 N.E.2d 346 (1984).

[11]Lebel v. Nelson, 29 Mass. App. Ct. 300, 560 N.E.2d 135 (1990).

§ 7:6 Color of title

The meaning and significance of "color of title" was explained by Justice Kass as follows: "Color of title, in the context of an adverse possession claim, is an assertion of a claim of ownership based on an instrument of title, such as a deed or lease, even though that instrument does not pass a valid title.[1] The advantage which a person may gain from that doctrine is that the activities relied upon to establish adverse possession reach not only the part of the premises actually occupied, but the entire premises described in a deed to the claimant.[2] For example, if the act of adverse possession were cultivating a half acre parcel of land, but the claimant held an invalid deed describing three acres, the claimant would have constructive possession of the three acres for the reason that it is the presumed intention of the grantee of the deed to assert such possession."[3]

That principle was applied to vest the area surrounding a cranberry bog in a claimant who established adverse possession of the bog.[4] It may not be applied to non-contiguous parcels, or stretched from one area to another.[5]

§ 7:7 Open and notorious

Quoting from a treatise, the SJC endorsed as the "true rule" that:

> To be open the use must be made without attempted concealment. To be notorious it must be known to some who might reasonably be expected to communicate their knowledge to the owner if he maintained a reasonable degree of supervision over his premises. It is not necessary that the use be actually known to the owner for it to meet the test of being notorious.[1]

Applying that rule in the cited case, the court upheld a sewer easement established by prescription, saying that it

---

[Section 7:6]

[1]Norton v. West, 8 Mass. App. Ct. 348, 394 N.E.2d 1125, 1127–28 (1979).

[2]Dow v. Dow, 243 Mass. 587, 137 N.E. 746 (1923).

[3]Norton v. West, 8 Mass. App. Ct. 348, 394 N.E.2d 1125 (1979); Inhabitants of Nantucket v. Mitchell, 271 Mass. 62, 170 N.E. 807 (1930).

[4]Macallister v. DeStefano, 18 Mass. App. Ct. 39, 463 N.E.2d 346 (1984).

[5]Dow v. Dow, 243 Mass. 587, 137 N.E. 746 (1923); Conte v. Marine Lumber Co., Inc., 66 Mass. App. Ct. 505, 848 N.E.2d 1246 (2006), review denied, 447 Mass. 1109, 853 N.E.2d 1060 (2006).

[Section 7:7]

[1]Foot v. Bauman, 333 Mass. 214, 129 N.E.2d 916, 55 A.L.R.2d 1139 (1955).

was not necessary for the servient owner to have "actual knowledge" of it, and that the sewer was unconcealed, being discernable by manhole covers and periodic maintenance activities. The ignorance of a town that it had a record title claim to property did not protect or insulate the town from actions of an adverse possessor of the property.[2]

§ 7:8 Adverse

The requisite degree and nature of adverseness has been a touchy subject. Many old cases established a rule that "a claim of right" was essential, evincing an intention of the adverse possessor to hold the property "as owner, and to the exclusion, rightfully or wrongfully, of everyone else."[1] In the cited *Ottavia* case the SJC acknowledge that "This rule has been severely criticized," and does not comport with conclusions set forth in the American Law of Property. The authors of that treatise found adequate "hostility" in the use and enjoyment of the property without the consent of the true owner, regardless of the possessor's actual state of mind or intent. This view puts emphasis on the element of the openness and notoriousness of the possessor's actions, giving notice to the true owner of acts which are by their nature hostile to the owner's interests. In the *Ottavia* case the SJC accepted these views and upheld defendant's prescriptive right to maintain roof girders set into and supported by plaintiff's abutting brick wall, even though defendant did not know that his roof beams extended into the wall and did know that the wall belonged to plaintiff, and did not claim to own it or deprive plaintiff of any part of it.

Before the *Ottavia* decision adverse possession had been upheld with respect to a strip of land in which the claimant already had an easement.[2] The rejection of "claim of right" as a necessary element was later further strengthened. A prescriptive right based upon automobile travel over a strip of land was upheld in favor of a woman who said that "she didn't do it deliberately," the court holding that "her actual use . . . without permission of the true owner constitutes a claim of right," citing an earlier case in which the claimant

---

[2]Lawrence v. Town Of Concord, 439 Mass. 416, 788 N.E.2d 546 (2003).

[Section 7:8]

[1]Ottavia v. Savarese, 338 Mass. 330, 155 N.E.2d 432, 2 A.L.R.3d 997 (1959), citing earlier cases.

[2]Lyon v. Parkinson, 330 Mass. 374, 113 N.E.2d 861 (1953).

had said "I do not want anything not belonging to me."[3] Where there was a misunderstanding by both plaintiff and defendant as to the location of the boundary line between their properties, defendant's possessory claim was upheld though his only claim of right, as well as plaintiff's putative acquiescence, rested solely on that misunderstanding.[4] It has been reaffirmed that a mutual mistake as to a boundary line does not import consent or permission as to use by an adverse claimant.[5] The irrelevance of the claimant's state of mind has been firmly reasserted.[6]

It should be noted that the courts have not expressly disposed of the requirement of a claim of right; they have just made it clear that it need not be expressed or formed as a subjective intent, but may be implied from acts. It has also been made fairly clear that if the acts relied upon do not afford an objective indication of intent to acquire fee title, they will at most support prescriptive rights, short of fee title.[7]

The acts which suffice to establish adverseness to the owner need not provoke open hostility. An adverse claimant's discussion with the owner as to management of a way did not bar his acquisition of a prescriptive easement,[8] nor did the "forbearance" of an owner who "tacitly agreed" to accept the adverse action bar a prescriptive easment.[9] An offer to buy the disputed parcel from the record owner did not bar an acquisition of title by adverse possession.[10] Countering an owner's allegation of permission, the court observed that the adverse possessor made "no recognition" of the owner's authority to prevent or permit continuance of the use, and that: "It is the nonrecognition of such authority at the time a use is made which determines whether it is adverse; and permissive use is inconsistent with adverse use."[11]

---

[3]Flynn v. Korsack, 343 Mass. 15, 175 N.E.2d 397 (1961); Van Allen v. Sweet, 239 Mass. 571, 132 N.E. 348 (1921).

[4]Boutin v. Perreault, 343 Mass. 329, 178 N.E.2d 482 (1961).

[5]Kendall v. Selvaggio, 413 Mass. 619, 602 N.E.2d 206 (1992).

[6]Totman v. Malloy, 431 Mass. 143, 725 N.E.2d 1045 (2000).

[7]Holmes v. Johnson, 324 Mass. 450, 86 N.E.2d 924 (1949); Ottavia v. Savarese, 338 Mass. 330, 155 N.E.2d 432, 2 A.L.R.3d 997 (1959); Foot v. Bauman, 333 Mass. 214,

129 N.E.2d 916, 55 A.L.R.2d 1139 (1955).

[8]Ryan v. Stavros, 348 Mass. 251, 203 N.E.2d 85 (1964).

[9]Ivons-Nispel, Inc. v. Lowe, 347 Mass. 760, 200 N.E.2d 282 (1964).

[10]Lebel v. Nelson, 29 Mass. App. Ct. 300, 560 N.E.2d 135 (1990).

[11]Ryan v. Stavros, 348 Mass. 251, 203 N.E.2d 85 (1964); see Begg v. Ganson, 34 Mass. App. Ct. 217, 609 N.E.2d 1225 (1993).

§ 7:9 Continuous

In the dictionary "continuous" means incessant or without break or interruption, but human activities are never ceaseless or free of breaks and interruptions. The courts must therefore define the types and extent of interruptions that are acceptable in reference to the requirement of continuous possession. As indicated in paragraph A of this section, acts of dominion come in considerable variety, and a series of different acts at different times may be sufficient to constitute possession, and seasonal uses may suffice.[1]

As to interruptions, the SJC said that "Not every act by the owner on the land interrupts actual and adverse possession," citing a number of cases, and held that the filing of a notice to prevent easement under M.G.L.A. c. 187, § 3, was not relevant to and did not interrupt possession intended to establish fee title.[2] When the adverse claimant was a circus performer and "the continuity of his actual presence on the locus was disrupted by circus trips," his possession was not found to be "occasional or intermittent."[3] The placing of saw horses in a way by the owner did not interrupt the acquisition of a prescriptive easement.[4] The collapse of a wooden fence, leaving only base remnants for a year or two during the period of possession was held not to constitute an interruption.[5]

Acts that are sporadic, insubstantial or equivocal will not in any event suffice.[6] When the claimant of title by adverse possession to a strip of land adjoining his house, rented the house to a tenant for several years during the asserted 20–year period of possession, that was held to constitute an interruption because the tenant "claimed neither a title nor right to possession of the disputed strip."[7] On the other hand, when the property subject to the claim of adverse possession was for part of the 20–year period owned by a foreclosing mortgagee, the mortgagee was held to recognize the adverse claim and itself to claim title, so that the period of its claim

[Section 7:9]

[1]Shaw v. Solari, 8 Mass. App. Ct. 151, 392 N.E.2d 853 (1979); Lebel v. Nelson, 29 Mass. App. Ct. 300, 560 N.E.2d 135 (1990).

[2]Rothery v. MacDonald, 329 Mass. 238, 107 N.E.2d 432 (1952).

[3]Kershaw v. Zecchini, 342 Mass. 318, 173 N.E.2d 624 (1961).

[4]Ryan v. Stavros, 348 Mass. 251, 203 N.E.2d 85 (1964).

[5]MacDonald v. McGillvary, 35 Mass. App. Ct. 902, 616 N.E.2d 138 (1993).

[6]Gadreault v. Hillman, 317 Mass. 656, 59 N.E.2d 477 (1945); Cowden v. Cutting, 339 Mass. 164, 158 N.E.2d 324 (1959); Norton v. West, 8 Mass. App. Ct. 348, 394 N.E.2d 1125 (1979).

[7]Holmes v. Johnson, 324 Mass. 450, 86 N.E.2d 924 (1949).

could be tacked with that of the mortgagor claimant.[8] In a case in which there was otherwise rather clear adverse possession for twenty years of a strip of land, fenced in by the claimant, the claim of title failed because of an interruption for a few weeks during the period by the true owner, an abutter, who removed the fences and used the site for storage of building materials while he remodeled his property.[9]

Other situations in which interruption of the 20–year period was found to have occurred involved: (i) building a house on one of the several contested parcels,[10] (ii) a resulting trust situation,[11] and (iii) the taking and foreclosure of a tax title, which the court held as a matter of public policy interrupted the running of adverse possession.[12]

Aside from interruption, a question may arise as to when adverse possession may begin. When holders of a remainder interest claimed adverse possession against life tenants who had not claimed or occupied the premises for over twenty years, it was held that the writ of entry was premature while the life tenants were still living.[13] When a contract vendee under a sale that did not close occupied the premises for over twenty years and asserted adverse possession, he was denied relief in essence because his contract rights deprived him of a claim of right sufficient to effect a disseisin.[14]

TOPIC B: CLAIMS AND DEFENSES

§ 7:10 Permissive use—Specific or implied

When a person who is not the owner occupies or uses property with the permission of the owner, that person's possession of the property is not adverse to the owner. Permission for full and exclusive occupancy is properly and ordinarily evidenced by a lease or tenancy agreement, and permission for particular uses by a grant of easement or license. With respect to claims of acquisition of title or rights by adverse

---

[8]Shoer v. Daffe, 337 Mass. 420, 149 N.E.2d 625 (1958).

[9]Mendonca v. Cities Service Oil Co. of Pa., 354 Mass. 323, 237 N.E.2d 16 (1968).

[10]Rothery v. MacDonald, 329 Mass. 238, 107 N.E.2d 432 (1952).

[11]Bodman v. Martha's Vineyard Nat. Bank of Tisbury, 330 Mass. 125, 111 N.E.2d 670 (1953).

[12]Town of Sandwich v. Quirk, 409 Mass. 380, 566 N.E.2d 614 (1991).

[13]Daley v. Daley, 308 Mass. 293, 32 N.E.2d 286 (1941).

[14]Leavitt v. Elkin, 314 Mass. 396, 49 N.E.2d 1020 (1943).

possession, the assertion of permission usually relies on less salient acts, almost always unwritten and often non-verbal. Permission may be implied from acts of the true owner, but the courts are not easily convinced. As noted in paragraph C above, permission is not implied from tacit acquiescence or forbearance, nor from ignorance or mistake with respect to location of a boundary.

When an adverse claimant held a deed to the property containing a condition that it was subject to a prior deed of the same property to the Proprietors upon trusts, the acts and "nature of the occupation" by the claimant were held to be "consistent" with the trusts under the prior deed and done pursuant to an "inference of permission" by the Proprietors.[1]

When the claimant of a prescriptive easement to use a parking lot had used it with the permission of a long-term tenant of the land under a lease which granted the tenant the right to give such permission, a prescriptive easement was denied, on the ground that the use was not "notorious" so as to put the landlord on notice of such use being adverse to his title.[2]

As a practical matter, granting permission is surely a simple and direct means of barring the acquisition of title or easements by adverse possession or use. But oral permission is always risky and subject to doubts. If a lawyer's client wants to be a "good neighbor" and let the people next door use part of his land, the lawyer should advise him to get the neighbor's acknowledgement of permissive use in writing. In commercial settings such written acknowledgement is even more important.

§ 7:11 Presumptive permission

Extensive acts of dominion conducted for over 40 years on a neighbor's land, the neighbors being father and son, were held by the Land Court not to be "sufficiently hostile to overcome the inference of permissive use grounded in the close family relationship," the principle of such an inference being set forth in Corpus Juris Secundum, but the SJC reversed, saying that: "we decline to create a presumption of

[Section 7:10]

[1]Inhabitants of Nantucket v. Mitchell, 271 Mass. 62, 170 N.E. 807 (1930).

[2]Boston Seaman's Friend Soc., Inc. v. Rifkin Management, Inc., 19 Mass. App. Ct. 248, 473 N.E.2d 702 (1985).

inference of permissive use among "close" family members."[1] There was no dispute until the servient one of the houses was sold to persons not in the family. The court acknowledged that family relationships were pertinent to the determination, citing prior cases from Massachusetts and other states, but emphasized that that was only one of many diverse circumstances. Besides seeing such a presumption as an encouragement to family strife, the court rejected it as at odds with the principles of possessory title claims developed in *Ottavia v. Savarese, Kendall v. Selvaggio, Flynn v. Korsack*, and other cases, all cited herein.

§ 7:12   Insufficiency of claim

As noted above, all of the requisite elements must be proved, the burden is on the claimant of adverse possession, the evidence must add up to a disseisin (or a clear prescriptive easement), and the courts are inclined to make careful review of the evidentiary details and to apply a complete analysis thereto. Prior inconsistent statements by an adverse claimant may effect an "equitable estoppel" of his claim.[1] Without here listing the great number of cases considered by the Land Court in the last few decades, let it be said that claims of adverse possession more often fail than succeed.

TOPIC C: EXEMPT AND SUBJECT LAND

§ 7:13   Protective actions

The exemptions of land from adverse possession and prescription are statutory and come in several categories. M.G.L.A. c. 185, § 53, provides that:

> No title to registered land, or easement or other right therein, in derogation of the title of the registered owner, shall be acquired by prescription or adverse possession. Nor shall a right of way by necessity be implied under a conveyance of registered land.

The provisions of this statute take effect upon the recording

---

[Section 7:11]

[1]Totman v. Malloy, 431 Mass. 143, 725 N.E.2d 1045 (2000).

[Section 7:12]

[1]Moran v. Gala, 66 Mass. App. Ct. 135, 845 N.E.2d 1170 (2006),

review denied, 447 Mass. 1103, 848 N.E.2d 1212 (2006).

of a notice of Complaint to Register.[1]

M.G.L.A. c. 187, § 3, provides that:

If a person apprehends that a right of way or other easement in or over his land may be acquired by custom, use or otherwise by any person or class of persons, he may give public notice of his intention to prevent the acquisition of such easement, by causing a copy of such notice to be posted in a conspicuous place upon the premises for six successive days, and such posting shall prevent the acquiring of such easement by use for any length of time thereafter; or he may prevent a particular person or persons from acquiring such easement by causing a copy of such notice to be served upon him or them as provided by law for the service of an original summons in a civil action. Such notice from the agent, guardian or conservator of the owner of land shall have the same effect as a notice from the owner himself. A certificate, by an officer qualified to serve civil process, that such copy has been served or posted by him as above provided, if made upon the original notice and recorded with it, within three months after the service or posting, in the registry of deeds for the county or district in which the land lies, shall be conclusive evidence of such service or posting.

Once such a notice to prevent easement is so posted, served and recorded, it is effective forever. Nevertheless, prudence or caution sometimes leads to reposting after, say, twenty years or so. Another caution, often ignored, is that persistent occupation of a way even after the posting of a statutory notice, could constitute an ouster leading to establishment of title by adverse possession. As the SJC pointed out: "In the face of the written notice continued actual possession by petitioners is all the more open and defiant. It contains the essence of a disseizin."[2]

§ 7:14 Railroad lands

M.G.L.A. c. 160, § 88, provides that: "No length of possession or occupancy of land, which belongs to a railroad corporation, by an owner or occupier of adjoining land shall create in him or in a person claiming under him a right to such land of the corporation." And M.G.L.A. c. 160, § 114 provides that: "No right of way across any railroad track or location which is in use for railroad purposes shall be acquired by prescription. This section shall not apply to rights of way which existed on June fifth, eighteen hundred

[Section 7:13]

[1]Snow v. E. L. Dauphinais, Inc., 13 Mass. App. Ct. 330, 432 N.E.2d 730 (1982).

[2]Rothery v. MacDonald, 329 Mass. 238, 107 N.E.2d 432 (1952).

and ninety-two." The extent of applicability of those statutes has been brought into question.[1]

§ 7:15   Telecommunication lines

M.G.L.A. c. 166, § 37, provides that:

> No enjoyment, for the purposes specified in section twenty-one, [telecommunications] for any length of time of the privi-lege of having or maintaining poles, wires or apparatus in, upon, over or attached to any building or land of other persons shall give a legal right to the continued enjoyment of such easement or raise any presumption of a grant thereof.

§ 7:16   State lands

The common law rule is that the sovereign is exempt from suit, but the Commonwealth has given limited consent to claims of adverse possession against it and its political subdivisions, including cities and towns. M.G.L.A. c. 260, § 31, referred to by the SJC as stating "a general rule that the Commonwealth and its political subdivisions may lose rights to land through twenty years of adverse possession,"[1] provides that:

> No action for the recovery of land shall be commenced by or in behalf of the commonwealth, except within twenty years after its right or title thereto first accrued, or within twenty years after it or those under whom it claims have been seized or pos-sessed of the premises; but this section shall not apply to the province lands in the town of Provincetown lying north and west of the line fixed by section twenty-five of chapter ninety-one, to the Back Bay lands, so called, in Boston, or to any property, right, title or interest of the commonwealth below high water mark or in the great ponds; provided, further, that this section shall not bar any action by or on behalf of the commonwealth, or any political subdivision thereof, for the recovery of land or interests in land held for conservation, open space, parks, recreation, water protection, wildlife protec-tion or other public purpose.

The concluding phrase, protecting from possessory claim land held for "other public purpose," may have a broad ap-plication since there is little reason for a government to hold any land except for public purposes. Land held for urban re-

---

[Section 7:14]

[1]Weiner v. Southampton Holdings, LLC, 14 L.C.R. 568 (2006).

[Section 7:16]

[1]Town of Sandwich v. Quirk, 409 Mass. 380, 566 N.E.2d 614 (1991).

newal was found to be held for a "public purpose."[2] Furthermore, it is provided in M.G.L.A. c. 7, § 40E, that: "Notwithstanding any general or special law to the contrary, no person shall acquire any rights by prescription or adverse possession in any lands or rights in lands held in the name of the commonwealth," preceded by the provision that "Real property, record title to which is held in the name of a state agency or the board of trustees of a state agency or similar board of a state agency, shall be deemed to be real property of the commonwealth." A similar provision with respect to land of the Commonwealth held by the Department of Environmental Management was set forth in M.G.L.A. c. 132, § 36A, repealed in 2003.

There are specific exceptions with respect to state highways and other public ways. M.G.L.A. c. 81, § 22, provides that:

> No length of possession, or occupancy of land within the limits of a state highway by an owner or occupant of adjoining land shall give him any title thereto, and any fences, buildings or other objects encroaching upon a state highway shall, upon written notice by the department, be removed within fourteen days by the owner or occupant of adjoining land, and if not so removed, the department may either remove the same to such adjoining land or such encroaching objects, other than a building used for residential purposes, may be removed by the department forces and shall be placed in the nearest maintenance area of the department. Notice by certified mail, return receipt requested shall be given to the owner stating where such encroaching object is located and further stating that if not claimed within three weeks said object may be destroyed.

And M.G.L.A. c. 86, § 3, provides that:

> If the boundaries of a public way are known or can be made certain by records or monuments, no length of possession, or occupancy of land within the limits thereof, by the owner or occupant of adjoining land shall give him any title thereto, unless it has been acquired prior to May twenty-sixth, nineteen hundred and seventeen, and any fences, buildings or other obstructions encroaching upon such way shall, upon written notice from the county commissioners or board or officer having authority over ways in towns, be forthwith removed by the owner or occupant of adjoining land, and if not so removed said commissioners, board or officer may cause the same to be removed upon said adjoining land.

§ 7:17   Federal lands

The United States has also given a limited consent to

[2]Aaron v. Boston Redevelopment Authority, 66 Mass. App. Ct. 804, 850 N.E.2d 1105 (2006).

adverse possession against it. 43 U.S.C.A. § 1068 provides that:

> The Secretary of the Interior (a) shall, whenever it shall be shown to his satisfaction that a tract of public land has been held in good faith and in peaceful, adverse, possession by a claimant, his ancestors or grantors, under claim or color of title for more than twenty years, and that valuable improvements have been placed on such land or some part thereof has been reduced to cultivation, or (b) may, in his discretion, whenever it shall be shown to his satisfaction that a tract of public land has been held in good faith and in peaceful, adverse, possession by a claimant, his ancestors or grantors, under claim or color of title for the period commencing not later than January 1, 1901, to the date of application during which time they have paid taxes levied on the land by State and local governmental units, issue a patent for not to exceed one hundred and sixty acres of such land upon the payment of not less than $1.25 per acre: Provided, That where the area so held is in excess of one hundred and sixty acres the Secretary may determine what particular subdivisions, not exceeding one hundred and sixty acres, may be patented hereunder: Provided further, That coal and all other minerals contained therein are reserved to the United States; that said coal and other minerals shall be subject to sale or disposal by the United States under applicable leasing and mineral land laws, and permittees, lessees, or grantees of the United States shall have the right to enter upon said lands for the purpose of prospecting for and mining such deposits: And provided further, That no patent shall issue under the provisions of this chapter for any tract to which there is a conflicting claim adverse to that of the applicant, unless and until such claim shall have been finally adjudicated in favor of such applicant.

TOPIC D: PRESCRIPTIVE EASEMENTS

§ 7:18   Acquisition

The acquisition of an easement by prescription requires proof of substantially the same elements as are involved in acquisition of title by adverse possession, but with significant exceptions and additional requirements. The principal exception is of course a demonstration of ouster or disseisin. As referred to in § 15:2, an easement is a right of use that is not inconsistent with or wholly exclusive of the use of the property by the servient owner. A prescriptive easement likewise does not oust the record owner, who may in fact use the same easement for his own purposes, as may also others than the claimant asserting a prescriptive easement, "exclusivity" not being a requirement.[1]

In order to establish an easement by prescription, the use or exercise of the easement must be "actual," open and notorious, adverse to the fee owner and continuous for twenty years, as provided in M.G.L.A. c. 187, § 2, quoted in § **7:3**. The requirements as to notice (being open and notorious) are as stated in § **7:7**. It is not necessary that the claimant know the identity of the fee owner,[2] or that the fee owner have actual knowledge of the use.[3] It is necessary that the use "be sufficiently pronounced so as to be made known, directly or indirectly, to the landowner if he or she maintained a reasonable degree or supervision over the property," and the application of that test "varies with the character of the land."[4] The requirements as to adverseness are as referred to in § **7:8**, measured by the nature and extent of the acts, the subjective intent of the claimant being irrelevant. The acts must be "continuous" and not "interrupted," as indicated in decisions cited in § **7:9**. Intermittent and disjointed acts will not suffice.[5]

A prescriptive easement of an abutter to a way, owning title to the center line, was upheld when the opposite abutter, owning to the center line on the other side, sought to block the way with a fence down the center line, more than twenty years after the owners had released granted rights in the way to each other.[6] A prescriptive easement was established in a way after discontinuance of the former public way.[7]

Another requirement for the establishment of a prescriptive easement is that the location thereof must be shown as fixed; that is, "substantially confined to a regular and particularized route." The court pointed out that when granted easements are not definitely located, a court may fix the location of the way on the servient premises, and explained why that is not appropriate with respect to

---

[Section 7:18]

[1]Labounty v. Vickers, 352 Mass. 337, 225 N.E.2d 333 (1967); Bills v. Nunno, 4 Mass. App. Ct. 279, 346 N.E.2d 718 (1976).

[2]Bills v. Nunno, 4 Mass. App. Ct. 279, 346 N.E.2d 718 (1976).

[3]Foot v. Bauman, 333 Mass. 214, 129 N.E.2d 916, 55 A.L.R.2d 1139 (1955).

[4]Boothroyd v. Bogartz, 68 Mass. App. Ct. 40, 859 N.E.2d 876 (2007), review denied, 448 Mass.

1107, 864 N.E.2d 22 (2007).

[5]Gadreault v. Hillman, 317 Mass. 656, 59 N.E.2d 477 (1945); Boothroyd v. Bogartz, 68 Mass. App. Ct. 40, 859 N.E.2d 876 (2007), review denied, 448 Mass. 1107, 864 N.E.2d 22 (2007).

[6]Tucker v. Poch, 321 Mass. 321, 73 N.E.2d 595 (1947).

[7]Stone v. Perkins, 59 Mass. App. Ct. 265, 795 N.E.2d 583 (2003).

prescriptive easements.

The barring of prescription by the posting of a statutory notice to prevent easement, and the cautions with respect thereto, are described in **§ 7:13**.

§ 7:19 Scope; improvement

The persons entitled to use a prescriptive easement are only those who created it by their acts, or are successors in title to premises to which such acts made the easement appurtenant. That principle was applied to beach easements, and the court found that "persons of the local community" and the "general public" were too broad a group to acquire an easement by prescription.[1]

The scope of a prescriptive easement is also determined by the actual use that created it, but subject to some change, though "the variations in use cannot be substantial; they must be consistent with the general pattern formed by the adverse use."[2] Citing that proposition and the principle that once an easement is created, every right necessary for its enjoyment is included by implication,[3] the court in *Glenn v. Poole*[4] affirmed approval of substantial improvements to a prescriptive way and significantly increased usage, saying, however, that "the limits of the Pooles' easement have been closely approached, if not reached," and that "additional expansion of the uses and width of the easement would probably be over those limits." The users of an access way were held to have a prescriptive easement therein, and entitled to allow its use by "social and business invitees," but the change from "occasional use . . . by a relatively few persons" to "frequent in-and-out trips . . . and trips by ten wheelers hauling gravel" was held to be an overload of the easement.[5] The same principle applies to the quantity of water that may be flowed through a prescriptively established easement to flow water onto land of another owner.[6]

[Section 7:19]

[1]Ivons-Nispel, Inc. v. Lowe, 347 Mass. 760, 200 N.E.2d 282 (1964); Labounty v. Vickers, 352 Mass. 337, 225 N.E.2d 333 (1967).

[2]Lawless v. Trumbull, 343 Mass. 561, 180 N.E.2d 80, 5 A.L.R.3d 434 (1962).

[3]Hodgkins v. Bianchini, 323 Mass. 169, 80 N.E.2d 464 (1948).

[4]Glenn v. Poole, 12 Mass. App. Ct. 292, 423 N.E.2d 1030 (1981).

[5]Carmel v. Baillargeon, 21 Mass. App. Ct. 426, 487 N.E.2d 867 (1986).

[6]Trenz v. Town of Norwell, 68 Mass. App. Ct. 271, 861 N.E.2d 777 (2007); Fortier v. H.P. Hood & Sons, 307 Mass. 292, 30 N.E.2d 253 (1940).

§ 7:20   Barring an easement

An easement established by grant or implication may be barred or terminated by possessory acts which are inconsistent with the continued existence or use of the easement.[1] In order to have that effect, the possessory acts must meet the other tests described above. Maintenance of a fence across a way, blocking use, for over 20 years, was held to extinguish the right of way.[2] But when gates in a fence across a way were left open in the daytime, the easement was not extinguished,[3] nor when the easement location was confused by a mistaken "stake line."[4] The extensive use of a shared easement by one owner was held not to be irreconcilable with the rights of the other owner and thus not to extinguish those rights.[5]

[Section 7:20]

[1]New England Home for Deaf Mutes v. Leader Filling Stations Corporation, 276 Mass. 153, 177 N.E. 97 (1931).

[2]Yagjian v. O'Brien, 19 Mass. App. Ct. 733, 477 N.E.2d 202 (1985).

[3]Lemieux v. Rex Leather Finishing Corp., 7 Mass. App. Ct. 417, 388 N.E.2d 1195 (1979).

[4]Pappas v. Maxwell, 337 Mass. 552, 150 N.E.2d 521 (1958).

[5]Patterson v. Simonds, 324 Mass. 344, 86 N.E.2d 630 (1949).

Chapter 8

The Land Court and Title Registration

> **KeyCite®:** Cases and other legal materials listed in KeyCite Scope can be researched through the KeyCite service on Westlaw®. Use KeyCite to check citations for form, parallel references, prior and later history, and comprehensive citator information, including citations to other decisions and secondary materials.

TOPIC A: INTRODUCTION

§ 8:1 Origins of title registration and the Land Court

Land title registration, based on the Torrens System first adopted in Australia in 1858, has been in effect in Massachusetts since 1898. The Land Court was established to implement it.[1] While implementation and management of the registered land system is in the exclusive jurisdiction of the Land Court and remains an important part of its activities, the Land Court has over the years acquired a reputation for knowledge, skill and sensitivity in real estate matters, and consequently it has been endowed with a considerable number of other functions and several areas of concurrent jurisdiction with the Superior Courts and the SJC, and with the Probate Courts.

§ 8:2 Land Court jurisdiction

The jurisdiction of the Land Court is set forth in M.G.L.A. c. 185, § 1.[1] The Land Court presently has six justices. Traditionally it sat in Boston for all counties, but occasionally sat in other counties. Pursuant to amendment, effective in August 2006, the Land Court now sits in Boston, Fall River and Worcester, as well as "other places as public convenience may require."[2] Sessions in Fall River and Worcester are to be held "as the caseload requires but not less than once per quarter."

The Land Court does not conduct jury trials, and in cases where jury issues are properly framed, such issues will be referred to the Superior Court for trial and report back to the Land Court.

Besides registration and confirmation, and dealing with

[Section 8:1]

[1]Ch. 562, Acts of 1898. The Land Court was known until 1904 as the Court of Land Registration. The Land Court's web site includes an interesting article on its history.

[Section 8:2]

[1]As amended by Ch. 393, Acts of 2002.

[2]Chapter 205, § 14, Acts of 2006.

registered land, the Land Court's exclusive jurisdiction includes: tax title matters (§ **2:5**); matters under M.G.L.A. c. 240, including various curative proceedings (**Topic B of Chapter 10**); some writ of entry and execution matters under M.G.L.A. c. 236 and c. 237; and some fraudulent conveyance matters. The Land Court has concurrent jurisdiction with the Superior Courts and the SJC with respect to: equity matters relating to real estate, including specific performance (§ **5:1**); trespass; zoning appeals (§ **11:22** and § **11:24**); and subdivision appeals (§ **12:15**). And the Land Court has concurrent jurisdiction with the Probate Courts with respect to partition (§ **6:41**).

In addition to the foregoing, a new § 3A was added to M.G.L.A. c. 185, § 1, by an Act in 2006 "Relative to Streamlining and Expediting the Permitting Process in the Commonwealth,"[3] establishing a separate "permit session" in the Land Court, to be held "in Suffolk, Middlesex, Essex, Norfolk, Plymouth, Worcester and Hampden counties, and other counties as the chief justice of the land court department shall from time to time designate." Section 3A goes on to provide that:

The permit session shall have original jurisdiction, concurrently with the superior court department, over civil actions in whole or part: (a) based on or arising out of the appeal of any municipal, regional or state permit, order, certificate or approval, or the denial thereof, concerning the use or development of real property, including without limitation appeals of such permits, orders, certificates or approvals, or denials thereof, arising under or based on or relating to [M.G.L.A. chapters 21, §§ 61 to 62H, chapters 40R, 41, 43D, 91, 131, 131A, 249, §§ 4 and 5]; or chapter 665 of the acts of 1956; or any local bylaw or ordinance; (b) seeking equitable or declaratory relief (i) designed to secure or protect the issuance of any municipal, regional or state permit or approval concerning the use or development of real property or (ii) challenging the interpretation or application of any municipal, regional or state rules, regulations, statutes, laws, bylaws, ordinances concerning any permit or approval; (c) claims under section 6F of chapter 231, or for malicious prosecution, abuse of process, intentional or negligent interference with advantageous relations or intentional or negligent interference with contractual relations arising out of or based upon or relating to the appeal of any municipal, regional, state permit or approval concerning the use or development of real property; and (d) any other claims between persons holding any right, title or interest in land and any municipal, regional or state board, authority, commission or public official based on or arising out of any ac-

---

[3]Chapter 205, § 15, Acts of 2006.

tion taken with respect to any permit or approval concerning the use or development of real property but in all such cases of claims (a) to (d), inclusive, only if the underlying project or development involves either 25 or more dwelling units or the construction or alteration of 25,000 square feet or more of gross floor area or both.

Section 3A provides also for a system of "Tracks," contemplating periods of 6, 9 or 12 months to trial, and disposition after the filing of a trial transcript or the taking under advisement of a motion for summary judgment, in 2, 3 or 4 months. It is provided that:

> The chief justice of the land court shall report to the chief justice for administration and management, the clerks of the house and senate, and the chairs of the judiciary committee of the general court on an annual basis, with: (1) the number of cases handled under this session; (2) the timelines achieved in cases pursuant to this session; (3) any additional resources required by the land court to meet its goals for this session; and (4) the number of cases before the land court according to the county from which they originate. To the extent that the chief justice of the land court does not have sufficient resources to maintain the timeframes mentioned above, then the chief justice for administration and management shall assign judges with land use and environmental expertise from other departments of the trial court to sit as justices of the permit session. In making such appointments, the chief justice for administration shall make reasonable efforts to select justices who, by reason of their past experience in private practice or practice with public agencies or as jurists have particular skills related to environmental and land use permitting and disputes concerning the same.

Expediting the permitting process is surely a long-sought and desirable goal, and we may expect members of the real estate community and their litigation colleagues to give every assistance to the Court in fulfilling this ambitious project.

§ 8:3   The essence of title registration

In Massachusetts the system of title registration has fared well, and it has well served, and continues to serve well, the interests of landowners and real estate lawyers, albeit not without some objections and cavil. The land title registration system involves a document of title on which all transfers of ownership and all encumbrances are noted, and a registry in which such documentation is filed and in which the title may be examined. The essence lies in the fact that once the particular parcel is identified and its basic title document is found in the registry, then the search (subject to certain exceptions considered in this Chapter) is over: everything to be known about the title to that parcel (subject to such exceptions) is to be found in that document or other documents specifically referred to therein. That is to say, the organization of documents in the registry is based upon identity of the parcels to which they relate, that is, tract indexed, whereas the organization in a traditional registry is based upon grantor-grantee indexing, regardless of the identity of the parcels conveyed. Needless to say, that is an oversimplification, but the tract-oriented organization of the land records is one of the fundamental characteristics of the land title registration system.

As noted in § **6:3**, each registry of deeds has a "registered land department," more accurately called a registry district, and under M.G.L.A. c. 185, § 10, each register of deeds is an assistant recorder of the Land Court, charged with maintenance of a separate set of record books in which certificates of title are entered, as further referred to below.

The other fundamental characteristic of the system, as it is structured in Massachusetts, is judicial determination of the status of title. Registration is accomplished by a judicial proceeding, and a judgment of registration establishes the title in rem. The matters judicially determined include the identity of the owner, the precise description of the land and its location with respect to established monuments, and the identity of all matters encumbering or affecting the title, subject to statutory exceptions, as follows:

M.G.L.A. c. 185, § 46, provides that every person to whom an original certificate of title is issued, and every purchaser taking a certificate of title for value and in good faith, shall hold it "free from all encumbrances" except those noted on the certificate and any which may be existing of the following: (1) liens, claims or rights arising or existing under the laws or constitution of the United States (including the bankruptcy laws) or the statutes of the commonwealth which are not by law required to appear of record in the registry of deeds in order to be valid against subsequent purchasers or encumbrances of record; (2) real estate taxes within three years after they have been committed to the collector; (3) any highway, town way or any private way laid out under M.G.L.A. c. 82, § 21, if the certificate of title does not state that the boundary of such way has been determined; (4) any lease for a term not exceeding seven years; (5) betterment assessments and similar liens; (6) federal tax liens; and (7) liens in favor of the commonwealth for unpaid taxes arising or existing under the laws of the commonwealth.

As stated in M.G.L.A. c. 185, § 45, the effect of a judgment of registration is that it "shall bind the land and quiet the title thereto," subject to the § 46 exceptions referred to above, and:

> It shall be conclusive upon and against all persons, including the commonwealth, whether mentioned by name in the complaint, notice or citation, or included in the general description 'to all whom it may concern.' Such judgment shall not be opened by reason of the absence, infancy, or other disability of any person affected thereby, nor by any proceeding at law or in equity for reversing judgments or decrees

subject to a specified exception. That sole exception permits a person who has been deprived of land or an interest therein by a judgment of registration "obtained by fraud" to file a complaint for review within one year after entry of judgment. Even that review is limited by the proviso that "no innocent purchaser for value has acquired an interest," and that if there is such a purchaser, then "the judgment of registration shall not be opened but shall remain in full force and effect forever." A person aggrieved retains, as the statute specifies, a remedy in tort for fraud in procuring the judgment.

The constitutionality of the registration statute was upheld,[1] and the statute has generally been strictly applied,[2] including holdings that registration is conclusive upon everyone; that the provision for review provided by § 45 is exclusive of all other remedies; that an easement established by registration is binding and easements not recognized in the decree of registration are unenforceable; and that in order to obtain review, a petitioner must show not only that the decree of registration was obtained by fraud but that the petitioner was thereby deprived of land or an estate or interest therein.

Notwithstanding all that, there have been a few situations in which the integrity or finality of registration has been

---

[Section 8:3]

[1]Tyler v. Judges of the Court of Registration, 175 Mass. 71, 55 N.E. 812 (1900).

[2]Wood v. Wilson, 260 Mass. 412, 157 N.E. 592 (1927); Levenson v. Ciampa, 251 Mass. 379, 146 N.E. 681 (1925); City of Boston v. Jenney, 282 Mass. 168, 184 N.E. 464 (1933); McMullen v. Porch, 286 Mass. 383, 190 N.E. 835 (1934); Bell v. Eames, 310 Mass. 642, 39 N.E.2d 582 (1942); Wareham Sav. Bank v. Partridge, 317 Mass. 83, 56 N.E.2d 867 (1944); Goldstein v. Beal, 317 Mass. 750, 59 N.E.2d 712 (1945); Marshall v. Francis, 327 Mass. 702, 100 N.E.2d 840 (1951); Otis Power Co. v. Wolin, 340 Mass. 391, 164 N.E.2d 306 (1960); Cerel v. Town of Framingham, 342 Mass. 17, 171 N.E.2d 840 (1961); Butler v. Haley Greystone Corp., 347 Mass. 478, 198 N.E.2d 635 (1964); McDonnell v. Quirk, 22 Mass. App. Ct. 126, 491 N.E.2d 646 (1986); Lasell College v. Leonard, 32 Mass. App. Ct. 383, 589 N.E.2d 342 (1992); Rizzo v. Johnson, 14 L.C.R. 139 (2006).

called into question. In the notable *Kozdras* case a Superior Court order for conveying land contrary to a decree of registration was upheld on the basis that a factually untrue statement or the non-disclosure thereof constituted "constructive fraud."[3]

Other cases involve easements asserted to affect registered land although not noted or imperfectly noted on registration certificates. In special, limited circumstances an easement may affect registered land even though not excepted in the original judgment of registration, such as a de minimis right to drain water from a highway, when the commonwealth had not received notice of the registration because the land being drained was not identified as a state road.[4] More significantly, the owner of a servient estate who acquired title with actual knowledge of the easement has been held to be subject to it even though the easement was not noted on his certificate of title.[5] Conversely, an easement shown on a Land Court Plan and referred to in registration certificates was rejected by the SJC as not expressly granted and not meeting the tests by which a purchaser might take subject to an easement not expressly described, namely that (1) facts described on the certificate prompted further investigation or (2) he had actual knowledge of it.[6]

The registration statute specifically bans the acquisition of any title, easement or other right in registered land by adverse possession or prescription, and also bans implication of a right of way by necessity in registered land.[7] There is no exception to this rule, and no period of any possessory claim will be of any avail after the filing of a complaint for registration.[8]

TOPIC B: ORIGINAL REGISTRATION OR CONFIRMATION

---

[3]Kozdras v. Land/Vest Properties, Inc., 382 Mass. 34, 413 N.E.2d 1105 (1980).

[4]Triangle Center, Inc. v. Department of Public Works, 386 Mass. 858, 438 N.E.2d 798 (1982).

[5]Feldman v. Souza, 27 Mass. App. Ct. 1142, 538 N.E.2d 64 (1989); Killam v. March, 316 Mass. 646, 55 N.E.2d 945 (1944), involving an unrecorded lease; Wild v. Constantini, 415 Mass. 663, 615 N.E.2d 557 (1993).

[6]Jackson v. Knott, 418 Mass. 704, 640 N.E.2d 109 (1994); see also Johnson v. Knott, 7 L.C.R. 339

§ 8:4   Complaint; plan; notice; examination of title

Registration is initiated by a sworn complaint[1] of the land-owner on a form prescribed by the Land Court, filed with the court at its office in Boston. The complaint sets forth a simple bounding description of the land based on a new survey plan prepared in accordance with Land Court engineering specifications and filed with the complaint, the names and addresses of plaintiff and abutting owners and occupants, any claim of plaintiff to fee title within an abutting way, any claim of appurtenant rights, a statement of plaintiff's source of title and reference to any mortgage recognized by the plaintiff as outstanding. The required plan must conform with the strict requirements established by the Land Court's Engineering department, including a tie-in to the state grid and tie-in to existing nearby registrations.[2]

The form of complaint also contains an election of plaintiff to proceed in the event of an adverse report on his title, which election may be withdrawn by timely notice. The statute provides that the plaintiff shall file "all original muniments of title within his control,"[3] but this is generally not done except upon request of the court or upon motion of a defendant party. Forthwith upon filing of the complaint, the plaintiff is required to record a notice thereof in the registry of deeds.

The court then refers the complaint to an official examiner. Many experienced conveyancers have been appointed as

---

(1999); Richmond v. Yacino, 3 L.C.R. 145 (1995); Commonwealth Elec. Co. v. MacCardell, 66 Mass. App. Ct. 646, 849 N.E.2d 910 (2006), review granted, 447 Mass. 1110, 854 N.E.2d 441 (2006) and aff'd, 450 Mass. 48, 876 N.E.2d 405 (2007).

[7]M.G.L.A. c. 185, § 53.

[8]Snow v. E. L. Dauphinais, Inc., 13 Mass. App. Ct. 330, 432 N.E.2d 730 (1982); Tetrault v. Bruscoe, 398 Mass. 454, 497 N.E.2d 275 (1986); Bruggeman v. McMullen, 26 Mass. App. Ct. 963, 526 N.E.2d 1338 (1988); but see Capodilupo v. Vozzella, 46 Mass. App. Ct. 224, 704 N.E.2d 534 (1999), involving de minimis encroachment; Gifford v. Otis, 14 L.C.R. 197 (2006).

[Section 8:4]

[1]M.G.L.A. c. 185, §§ 26, 27, 28. If by a corporation, it must be approved by vote of the directors. Until 1981 it was called a "petition," and that terminology persists in some sections of the statute. In Bernard v. Nantucket Boys' Club, Inc., 391 Mass. 823, 465 N.E.2d 236 (1984), the court referred to the duty to disclose all adverse claims, however dubious.

[2]The requirements are set forth in a 53–page Manual of Instructions for the Survey of Lands and Preparation of Plans, promulgated by the Court, effective January 2, 2006.

[3]M.G.L.A. c. 185, § 33.

Land Court Examiners,[4] and the interests of efficiency and economy, as well as the assurance of a proper report on title, are served by cooperation between the plaintiff's counsel and the examiner.[5] An abstract of title and a certificate of opinion are prepared by the examiner and filed in the court. If the examiner reports his opinion that the plaintiff does not have sufficient record title for registration, then the plaintiff may withdraw, and if he does not do so, he will be called upon to perfect his record title or prove a title by adverse possession, which may be sufficient to entitle him to a judgment of registration.

Registration of a title established by adverse possession has been upheld a number of times,[6] sometimes simply by Land Court action.[7] Registration has succeeded against claims of adverse possession by respondants,[8] but an assertion of adverse possession may block registration.[9]

After the examiner reports a citation is issued for notice of the complaint to be given by newspaper publication, by mail to abutters and persons having adverse interests, and by posting on the land. Notice may also be given to the city or town where the land lies, the county commissioners, the attorney general or others as the court may determine.

Any persons claiming an interest, whether named in the notice or not, may answer, stating their claim or objections. If none, the court may allow a motion for general default and to take the complaint as confessed, and enter a judgment of registration. The court is not bound by the examiner's report, but may require other or further proof.[10] The court often does require further information or explanation from the examiner or the plaintiff's counsel, and when the

---

[4]M.G.L.A. c. 185, § 37.

[5]Subject to the limitation referred to in Marshall v. Francis, 327 Mass. 702, 100 N.E.2d 840 (1951).

[6]Rothery v. MacDonald, 329 Mass. 238, 107 N.E.2d 432 (1952); Lyon v. Parkinson, 330 Mass. 374, 113 N.E.2d 861 (1953); Dugan v. Wellock, 348 Mass. 778, 202 N.E.2d 921 (1964); Nordblom v. Moss, 351 Mass. 172, 218 N.E.2d 87 (1966); see Macallister v. DeStefano, 18 Mass. App. Ct. 39, 463 N.E.2d 346 (1984); Senn v. Western Massachusetts Elec. Co., 18 Mass. App. Ct. 992, 471 N.E.2d 131 (1984); McCarthy v. Town of Oak

Bluffs, 419 Mass. 227, 643 N.E.2d 1015 (1994).

[7]Jackson, Reg.Case No. 43108, 13 L.C.R. 613 (2005).

[8]Inhabitants of Nantucket v. Mitchell, 271 Mass. 62, 170 N.E. 807 (1930); Cerel v. Town of Framingham, 342 Mass. 17, 171 N.E.2d 840 (1961); McLaughlin v. Town of Marblehead, 68 Mass. App. Ct. 490, 863 N.E.2d 61 (2007), review denied, 449 Mass. 1103, 865 N.E.2d 1141 (2007).

[9]Snow v. E. L. Dauphinais, Inc., 13 Mass. App. Ct. 330, 432 N.E.2d 730 (1982).

[10]M.G.L.A. c. 185, § 42.

examiner's report is adverse, at least two substantial affidavits of adverse possession supporting the plaintiff's title will ordinarily be required, and sometimes testimony or other documentation.

If an answer to the complaint is filed asserting interests contrary or adverse to the plaintiff's claims, the court will hear the case, or may refer it to an examiner to act as a master. After hearing the court may dismiss the complaint,[11] permit the plaintiff to withdraw with or without prejudice, or make a finding of proper title and enter a judgment of registration.

Before entering a judgment of registration the court ordinarily issues a memorandum for judgment and affords plaintiff's counsel an opportunity to review it. Since the wording of the judgment itself will become the original certificate of title, a careful review at this point is well worthwhile. It has been held that a judgment of registration is "a reasonably self-contained document" and that the petition (complaint) is not comprised in it and may not be looked to in order to determine the scope of an easement set forth in the judgment only in general terms.[12] It is also to be noted that the statute does not provide for registration of easements appurtenant to the registered locus,[13] but reference to them may certainly be included in the description of the property.

If title is conveyed during the pendency of a complaint, the new owner may be substituted as plaintiff upon motion. The holder of any mortgage outstanding upon judgment will be requested to submit his mortgage for registration. If he does not, the mortgage will be referred to in the judgment, but it will not be registered, and if it is subsequently foreclosed, it may terminate the registration.

§ 8:5　Judgment of registration; Land Court plan

When a judgment of registration is entered, the Land Court engineers prepare a plan, based on the plan filed by the plaintiff with the complaint, and incorporating any pertinent data from the court's order. The plan so prepared becomes the official Land Court Plan and is designated by the case docket number followed by the letter A. If there is more than one lot shown, they are numbered consecutively.

---

[11]See Gagne v. City of Chicopee, 278 Mass. 121, 179 N.E. 680 (1932).

[12]Butler v. Haley Greystone Corp., 347 Mass. 478, 198 N.E.2d 635 (1964).

[13]Dubinsky v. Cama, 261 Mass. 47, 158 N.E. 321 (1927).

When completed, that plan is sent to the pertinent registry district.

The judgment of registration is cast in the form of a certificate of title, and pursuant to M.G.L.A. c. 185, § 48, a certified copy thereof is sent to the registry district and there entered into a record book as the original certificate of title of the land thereby registered. The land description, based on the new Land Court Plan, is set forth in the judgment and will thereafter continue to be the proper official description of the property. There are provisions for continuation of title examination from the closing date of the examiner's report to the actual entry of the original certificate of title. In addition to the owner's name and a description of the property the certificate sets forth "in such manner as to show their relative priority, all particular estates, mortgage, easements, liens, attachments and other encumbrances . . . to which the land or the owner's estate is subject." While abutters are usually named on land court plans, that is not an adjudication.[1]

Sometimes some of such items, such as easements, are included in the property description on the face of the certificate, but a mortgage or any other encumbrance set forth in a separate instrument should be filed with the registry district, assigned a document number, and noted on the "encumbrance page" of the certificate. Until 1997 an "owner's duplicate certificate" was also issued and required to be presented with every instrument thereafter recorded, but that cumbersome procedure has been wholly eliminated.[2]

It is provided in M.G.L.A. c. 185, § 52, that "a judgment of registration and the entry of a certificate of title shall be regarded as an agreement running with the land and binding upon the plaintiff and his successors in title that the land shall be and forever remain registered land and subject to this chapter and all acts in amendment thereof, unless withdrawn . . ." in one of the modes of withdrawal discussed in § 8:16.

§ 8:6 Judgment of confirmation

The procedure for confirmation without registration is the same as for registration, and a judgment of confirmation has

[Section 8:5]
[1]Hutchinson v. Emmerton, 14 L.C.R. 74 (2006).

[2]Ch. 481, Acts of 1996, effective April 9, 1997.

the same legal effect as of the date of its entry.[1] The difference is that a judgment of confirmation is recorded in the registry of deeds in the same manner as any other document (not in the Land Court registry district), and the land thereafter continues to be dealt with in the general recording system. That is, confirmation establishes title as of the date of judgment, but does not put the land into a tract indexing system or continue judicial determination of the subsequent title chain. In examining a title one need not go behind a judgment of confirmation, but all documents affecting that title thereafter must be searched for in the usual grantor-grantee fashion.

TOPIC C: DEALING WITH REGISTERED LAND

§ 8:7 Conveyance of fee title

An owner of registered land may convey, mortgage, lease, or otherwise deal with it in the same manner, and using the same forms, statutory or other, including voluntary ad hoc forms, as for unregistered land. However, such instruments operate only as "a contract between the parties, and as evidence of authority to the recorder or assistant recorder to make registration." And it is "the act of registration only" that is "operative to convey or affect the land."[1] In view of that it is important to be sure that any instrument filed for registration meets the standards set forth in the Guidelines on Registered Land promulgated by the Court on May 1, 2000, comprising some 114 pages. When registered, an instrument has the same effect as it would if recorded with respect to unregistered land. A forged deed and any certificate issued pursuant thereto are wholly invalid under M.G.L.A. c. 185, § 62.

Upon conveyance in fee of a registered owner's estate, the deed is noted as a document on the memoranda sheet of the grantor's certificate of title, which is then marked canceled, with a reference thereon to the number and book and page

---

[Section 8:6]

[1]M.G.L.A. c. 185, § 56A.

[Section 8:7]

[1]M.G.L.A. c. 185, § 57; M.G.L.A. c. 185, §§ 77 et seq.

of the new certificate of title to be issued to the grantee.[2] Such transfer certificate of title has the same conclusive effect as the original certificate.[3] Encumbrances noted on the grantor's certificate which have been, or are at the time of conveyance, discharged, will not appear on the grantee's new certificate of title, but all other matters and instruments appearing on the grantor's certificate of title will be carried forward to the grantee's new certificate. Sometimes this results in complications and confusion, as discussed in § 8:11.

When a deed conveys only part of the land registered under a certificate of title, e.g., a lot in a subdivision, the deed is noted on the memoranda sheet, the lot and subdivision plan on which it is shown are there noted, and it is there stated that the certificate is canceled as to the lot; and the grantor's certificate remains in effect for the balance of the land. An owner holding a certificate covering several parcels may surrender it and obtain separate certificates for each parcel, and an owner holding separate certificates for several parcels may surrender them for consolidation into a single certificate. When there are several owners, as tenants in common or otherwise, one certificate covers all of their interest, but they may obtain separate owner's duplicate certificates for their undivided shares. The holder of a long term leasehold estate which is deemed to be a fee pursuant to provisions of M.G.L.A. c. 186, § 1, may register that title only jointly with the registration of the ownership of the reversionary estate.

§ 8:8 Encumbrances

When a mortgage, grant of easement or any other instrument which does not divest the registered owner's fee title is registered, it is assigned a document number and noted on the certificate of title. Such notations are set forth chronologically on addenda to the certificate, known as memoranda or encumbrance sheets. The notation includes the document number, names of parties, brief characterization of the nature of the instrument, dates of execution and registration and verification of the recorder. When a discharge of a mortgage or other lien instrument is registered, a notation thereof is generally made at the same place as the notation of the mortgage or lien instrument. Instruments affecting registered land are appropriately identified by Document No. and Certificate of Title No., rather than by Book and

---

[2]M.G.L.A. c. 185, § 64.

[3]Michaelson v. Silver Beach Imp. Ass'n, Inc., 342 Mass. 251, 173 N.E.2d 273, 91 A.L.R.2d 846 (1961).

Page.

§ 8:9   Involuntary instruments; trusts; other

When an involuntary instrument of encumbrance, such as an attachment, mechanic's lien, lis pendens, easement, taking, etc., is presented for registration, it must contain specific reference to the certificate of title number and book and page thereof. Federal tax liens are registerable without specific reference to the certificate and its book and page numbers. There are further particular requirements for attachments, and provisions with respect to the enforcement thereof and of mechanic's liens and other liens.[1]

An involuntary transfer of title may be effected by a fee taking. An instrument of fee taking will upon registration be noted on the memoranda sheet as an "adverse claim," but the certificate will not thereby be canceled. The taking statute, M.G.L.A. c. 79, § 4, requires issuance of a new certificate, but without reference to M.G.L.A. c. 185, § 112.[2] A taking by an order that was not registered was held to be ineffective as to registered easements.[3] Only when the taking authority obtains an order of the court will the old certificate be canceled and a new one issued to it.

Other pertinent subjects governed by specific provisions of the statute include: foreclosure of a mortgage; sale on execution or for enforcement of a lien; partition; various types of judgments and executions; bankruptcy; reverter; trusts in registered land; and also transfer by descent and devise, discussed in § 8:12.

With respect to trusts, it is provided that the terms of the trust are not to be set forth in the certificate of title, but the certificate is to specify that the registered owner holds "in trust" and to specify the trust instrument, usually registered as a document noted on the certificate. When the trust instrument confers a power to sell, mortgage or otherwise deal with the land in certain matters, the certificate of title will so state by such words as "with power to sell and mortgage" or other apt words following the name of the owner in trust. An instrument affecting registered land which is in trust will not be accepted for registration unless the power authorizing the instrument is expressly conferred by the trust instrument or by a decree of a court of competent

---

[Section 8:9]

[1]M.G.L.A. c. 185, § 112.
[2]Ch. 528, Acts of 1989.

[3]DDRC Gateway, LLC v. Massachusetts Bay Transportation Authority, 8 L.C.R. 177 (2000).

jurisdiction, in which case the decree must be registered also. An implied or constructive trust may be imposed on registered land. Any claim thereof must be set forth in writing and registered as a document, which will be entered on the memoranda sheet of the affected certificate of title as an adverse claim, and such claim will have no effect on a purchaser for value and in good faith before its registration. An adverse claim so registered is, of course, not self-effectuating, and would ordinarily be accompanied by a proceeding in the land court to establish the constructive trust and its terms. Such a proceeding is not deemed to be a complaint for review under § 45 of the statute, and is not limited to one year after the judgment of registration.[4]

§ 8:10 Condominiums

The applicability of title registration to condominiums has evolved over the years. When the condominium statute (M.G.L.A. c. 183A; see **Chapter 17**) was adopted in 1963, § 16 thereof provided simply that owners who wish to establish a condominium may petition the Land Court for removal of the land from Chapter 185, and for a number of years such petitions were granted. Later the Land Court developed means of dealing with condominiums of registered land, and M.G.L.A. c. 183A, § 16, was amended in 1973 to provide either (i) for registration of a master deed, or (ii) that if a portion of the condominium land, but not all, was registered, the recording (on the unregistered side of the registry) of the master deed "shall be a sufficient ground for withdrawal of the registered land" from Chapter 185.[1]

The current Land Court regulations refer to two "classes" of condominiums, consisting of Class I, where the Master Deed was reviewed, approved and "allowed for filing" prior to September 15, 1986 (of which few remain), as to which the "Survey Division" (Land Court Engineers) will continue to prepare modification plans for filing at the local Registry of Deeds for changes to Class I plans; and Class II, where the Master Deed was reviewed, approved and "allowed for filing" on or after September 15, 1986, as to which the Survey Division will not prepare modification plans for changes to

---

[4]State St. Bank & Trust Co. v. Beale, 353 Mass. 103, 227 N.E.2d 924 (1967).

[Section 8:10]

[1]The Land Court may not regard that provision as mandatory.

Class II plans.[2]

The term "modification plans" has particular reference to the original site plan of a condominium and plans of subsequent phases or parts of a condominium developed in stages. The distinction between Class I and Class II has been important to condominium developers, who are regularly faced with pressures to get each phase on the market as quickly as possible, and are loath to face the delays involved in preparation of new formal Land Court Plans by the Survey Division. Since over twenty years have passed since Class II was established, the problem, one hopes, is now also in the past.

The regulations referred to are part of the Land Court's Manual of Instructions for the Survey of Lands and Preparation of Plans.[3] That Manual does spell out requirements for condominium plans, and a careful compliance with them is the route to expeditious approval by the Survey Division. The Manual also contains substantive provisions as to the review of condominium documents by the "Land Court Legal Division." It is stated that: "The Land Court examines and approves all documents and plans for condominiums on registered land. The site plan, together with the floor plans and condominium documents, are reviewed by the Land Court Legal Division. After the condominium has been allowed by a Judge of the Court (evidenced by the judge's signature on the face page of the Master Deed), the condominium and plans may be filed at the proper registry."[4] The Court also provides a "Condominium Checklist" which lists the documents required to be submitted, requirements of contents of the Master Deed, condominium trust or association and by-laws, and two specific items: (1) "The Court requires that all trust documents contain a clause which provides for the "takeover event", that is, the point at which the trustee appointed by the declarant must resign in favor of those elected by owners other than the declarant." (2) "The Court has taken the position that rules and regulation may govern only use of the common areas, not use or conduct in the units themselves. (Johnson v. Keith, 368 Mass. 316, 331 N.E.2d 879 (1975).)"[5]

When a condominium of registered land is filed with the registry district, a Master Condominium Certificate of Title

---

[2]Manual of Instructions, § 2.4.2, discussed below.

[3]See note 2 to § 8:4.

[4]Manual of Instructions,

§ 2.4.1.

[5]Land Court Condominium Checklist, ¶¶ III, C and IV.

is entered in the record book. When Units in the condominium are conveyed, the grantees do not obtain a new Certificate of Title, but rather a Memorandum of Unit Ownership. With respect to Unit deeds and other subsequent recordings there are further pertinent Land Court provisions, set forth in a monograph entitled "Land Court Guidelines on Registered Land," dated May 1, 2000, containing 114 pages. Section 9 thereof provides a form of Unit Deed which the registry districts are authorized to accept, but if any other form is used, it must first be approved at the Land Court office. Sections 8, 10 and 11 set forth provisions to guide the registry districts (and lawyers) with respect to various other actions, including enforcement of liens for unpaid common expenses, and procedures for dealing with mortgages, and a mortgagees consent to the condominium and release of units. Section 12 makes it clear that any amendment of the Master Deed, including a phasing amendment, requires approval of a judge of the court.

There is no doubt that these requirements in sum cause a registered land condominium to involve quite a bit more "lawyering" than an unregistered condominium.

§ 8:11 Subdivisions

The procedure for subdivision of registered land begins with the filing of a subdivision plan with the Land Court Survey Division. The plan must of course have met the requirements of the subdivision control law (see **Chapter 12**) and bear any necessary planning board endorsement. The Land Court engineering staff checks each subdivision plan for consistency with prior plans and proper monumentation. When a lot is carved out of a larger tract the balance of the tract must also be closed and shown as a lot on a plan. If that were not done, then one could wind up with a certificate of title which defined a tract in part by an "excepting and excluding" clause. The Court formerly permitted exception deeds in very limited circumstances where no new bound was created, but that is no longer done.

The Manual of Instructions referred to above sets forth extensive requirements in Section 2.3 for "Subsequent Divisions of Registered Land." A copy of the extant certificate of title must be presented to the Survey Division, and also: any instrument by which a planning board imposed conditions on a subdivision approval, evidence of the authority of planning board signatories, city or town clerk's certification, a municipal lien certificate, as required by M.G.L.A. c. 60, § 23, (preferably identifying the land by Land Court case and lot numbers), and in Boston, evidence of payment of the so-called Tregor tax.

There are detailed requirements as to prior plans, abutting plans, monuments, ways, easements, cart paths, watercourses, etc. Once shown on a Land Court Plan, a way, watercourse or other easement must be carried forward onto new plans unless relocated or eliminated by order of the Court pursuant to an S-Petition (§ 8:13). If it is intended by the subdivider or required by the town to retain fee title in any new way, the way itself must be shown, dimensioned and numbered as one or more lots. In any case, new streets must be adequately monumented.

If there are discrepancies between field measurements and record data, then Section 3.2 of the Manual of Instructions becomes pertinent. It is recognized in Section 3.2.3 that "Some of the earlier plans prepared by the Court . . . do not show the actual property lines . . ." and "Many times walls, monuments, ditches, pipes, and other physical monuments are shown but not dimensioned." Following Sections of the Manual refer to situations in which: as to stone walls "the record math does not fit the wall"; "discrepancy exists between the record math and record monuments"; and "record monuments have been disturbed or destroyed." It is then provided that any plan that "differs from record" must be presented to a judge for review, and an S-Petition may be required. It is unfortunately true that even if the problem arose from errors or deficiencies in earlier Land Court Plans, the costs of correction fall upon the current applicant.

When the Survey division issues a new plan of a subdivision, it is given the same number (the case docket number) as the original plan (the "A plan"), followed by a letter, in alphabetic order. The lots are also numbered consecutively. There is often quite a spell between the date of approval of a subdivision plan and the actual preparation of the new Land Court Plan and its transmission to the registry district, and in that meanwhile it may be necessary to have each instrument approved for registration by the Survey Department before it will be accepted at the registry.

As noted in § 8:7, all provisions set forth on the face of a certificate of title and all items on the memoranda sheets (except liens discharged by registered documents) will be carried forward to every subsequent certificate of title derived therefrom unless and until removed by order of the land court. When a large tract has been registered and subdivided into many parcels and the certificate of the owner-subdivider has had numerous instruments noted on the memoranda sheets, such as grants of easements, planning board covenants, mortgages, deeds, restrictive instruments, etc., it is often difficult to sort out which instruments do and which do not affect title to a particular lot being conveyed. In the first instance it is the responsibility of the conveyancers involved to make all instruments clear and specific in that respect; a deed of a lot should specify by document number which ones of the prior encumbrances apply to it. However, that alone may not be sufficient, because the registry personnel are not authorized to omit anything which is prima facie outstanding and possibly applicable.

For example, a tract of, say, 100 acres may be subdivided into 60 lots, and an easement noted on the original certificate of title may affect 5 of these lots. But that easement will be noted on the certificates of all 60 lots, and will continue to appear on subsequent certificates thereof forever, until ordered removed by the Land Court. Ideally, the owner-subdivider who first filed the 60 lot plan should thereupon petition the Land Court to amend his certificate of title on the tract to specify precisely which 5 of the lots are affected by that easement, and to free the rest of the lots from having reference thereto brought forward on their certificates.

Another example is that of a restriction noted in a judgment of registration in, say, 1975, as then outstanding. If unlimited as to time, that restriction expired by law no later than 2005, but it will still be carried forward on certificates issued thereafter unless the court orders it expunged. If the original judgment of registration had expressly stated that the restriction expired in 2005, then presumably the registry would be able to omit reference to it from a certificate issued thereafter without any new order of the court.

The procedure for correcting such problems is discussed in § 8:13, but again the costs thereof are borne by the current owner seeking correction.

§ 8:12 Proceedings on death of owner

The Land Court Guidelines on Registered Land, referred to above, describe the several possible situations on death of a registered owner and the means of dealing with them. If there were several registered owners holding as joint tenants (with right of survivorship), the death of any one (except the last survivor) calls only for the filing of a certificate of death as a document noted on the memorandum page of the extant certificate of title. If the joint owners were tenants by the entirety, an "affidavit of no divorce" should also be filed.

On the death of the sole (including a last survivor)

registered owner or of one of several tenants in common, his heirs or devisees may obtain a new certificate of title. Once the probate of the will or appointment of the administrator is final, and a year has passed from date of death barring claims of creditors, the heirs or devisees entitled to the registered land may file with the land court a petition (LCP-2), including a statement signed by the executor or administrator and notarized, accompanied by an attested copy of the decedent's certificate of title and adequate evidence of the pertinent facts showing that the applicants are entitled to a new certificate. This may consist of certified copies of probate documents, including the petition, decree of the probate court and the will, if any, or it may consist of an abstract of all pertinent probate documents and a report thereon prepared and signed by a land court examiner. In the case of a tenant in common, the consent of the surviving co-tenants must also be provided. The Guidelines also provide that: (1) "Unless there is a specific devise of the real property, if a will directs the payment of legacies, the Land Court requires evidence of their payment unless six years have elapsed from the date of death." (2) "If property is devised to the trustees of a testamentary trust, attested copies of the trustees' appointment and bond must be included with the probate papers." (3) "If real property is devised to the trustees of an inter vivos trust which is not on record, the original trust instrument and any amendment(s) thereto must be presented at the Land Court. The Court Order will issue to the trustees, and the trust will be registered and noted on the new certificate issued."

With those requirements met, an Order of the Land Court is sent to the registry for issuance of a new certificate. Since Massachusetts tax liens apply without registration (as noted in § 8:3), they need not be referred to.

As an alternative to issuance of a new certificate to the heirs or devisees, the land may be sold by the executor or administrator, pursuant to license or power of sale. The required filings include the executed deed effecting the sale, referring specifically to the license and its terms or to the power of sale. There must also be filed with the court attested copies of the decedent's certificate of title, the Probate Court docket, the license decree or a "Probate Court copy of the will" with the power of sale clause marked, and the executor's appointment. If the license decree does not describe the property, the Land Court will want to see the petition for it also. And if the grantee is the fiduciary, the license decree must so permit. When these documents are in order, the Court will endorse the deed as approved for registration, and the registry district will issue a new certificate of title to the grantee pursuant to the deed.

§ 8:13 Corrective proceedings

M.G.L.A. c. 185, § 114, provides that: "No erasure, alteration or amendment shall be made upon the registration book after the entry of a certificate of title . . . except by order of the court," and that "A registered owner or other person in interest may apply by motion to the court" upon various specified grounds . . . "or upon any other reasonable ground; and the court may hear and determine the motion after notice to all parties in interest, and may order the entry of a new certificate, the entry or cancellation of a memorandum upon a certificate, or grant any other relief upon such terms, requiring security if necessary, as it may consider proper." It is then further provided that: "this section shall not authorize the court to open the original judgment of registration, and nothing shall be done or ordered by the court which shall impair the title or other interest of a purchaser holding a certificate for value and in good faith, or his heirs or assigns, without his or their written consent."

Notwithstanding the 1981 amendment introducing the word "motion," action under that section was always called and is still called an "S-Petition," the S meaning supplemental, in the original land court case. And notwithstanding the prohibition on alteration of a certificate of title, in some registry districts certificates have sometimes been substantially altered by notations by registry officials on the face thereof.

The cases involving S-Petitions under § 114 are varied and understandably fact-dependent, often involving easements.[1] Some of them arise from egregious registry errors.[2] In the cited *Doyle* case the SJC voided an improperly issued certificate of title and held that: "The statute's near absolute protection afforded to purchasers in good faith is no bar to the judge here exercising his authority here," because the er-

---

[Section 8:13]

[1]Green v. Hayes, 3 L.C.R. 148 (1995); McConville v. Skol, 12 L.C.R. 157 (2004); JE & T Construction, LLC v. Jann, 12 L.C.R. 310 (2004); One-O-Six Realty, Inc. v. Quinn, 12 L.C.R. 336 (2004), revsd. 66 Mass.App.Ct. 149 (2006); Rauseo v. Commonwealth, 12 L.C.R. 278 (2004), affmd. 65 Mass.App.Ct. 219 (2005); Commonwealth Electric Co. v. MacCardle, 13 L.C.R. 256 (2005), affmd. 66 Mass. App. Ct. 646 (2006).

[2]South Registry District of Essex County v. Gilbride, 7 L.C.R. 109 (1999); Powers v. Orr, 10 L.C.R. 137 (2002); Doyle v. Commonwealth, 11 L.C.R. 234 (2003), 444 Mass. 686, 830 N.E.2d 1074 (2005); JE & T Construction, LLC v. Jann, 12 L.C.R. 310 (2004).

ror in the certificate appeared on its face.[3] In the cited *JE & T* case the Court conceded that defendant Jann was a purchaser in good faith without knowledge of the easement, but held that she lost that status by sharing title with her husband.

As mentioned in § 8:9, an "adverse claim" may be registered as a document noted on a certificate of title. The requirements for doing so are set forth in M.G.L.A. c. 185, § 112, which provides further that "the court, upon the motion of any party in interest, shall grant a speedy hearing upon the validity of such adverse claim, and shall enter such judgment thereon as justice and equity may require." If the claim is adjudged to be invalid, the registration thereof shall be cancelled, and if the court finds such a claim to be frivolous or vexatious, it may tax the adverse claimant double costs.

§ 8:14   Title examination

In examining a registered land title it is not necessary to establish a title chain or to run grantor schedules on any owners prior to the registered owner under the extant certificate of title. Usually the search includes only copies of the currently outstanding certificate of title, the land court plan showing the locus being examined, and copies or abstracts of all instruments referred to on the face of that certificate and on the memoranda sheets thereof, plus examination, as referred to below, with respect to encumbrances statutorily excepted from the effect of a judgment of registration, as described in § 8:3.

The registry districts generally make notation of newly registered documents on the memoranda sheets of certificates of title within a few days after registration, and a grantor schedule of the current owner need be made only from that date of posting onward. Usually that means it is not necessary to consult a grantor index book at all, but only a few daily sheets on the registry counter.

As to instruments noted on the face of the certificate of title being examined or on the memoranda sheets thereof, the considerations are the same as for such documents found in a title on the unregistered side. In some cases instruments noted on the face of a certificate of title, transcribed

---

[3]Citing Jackson v. Knott, 418 Mass. 704, 640 N.E.2d 109 (1994); Killam v. March, 316 Mass. 646, 55 N.E.2d 945 (1944); Wild v. Constantini, 415 Mass. 663, 615 N.E.2d 557 (1993); and Kozdras v. Land/Vest Properties, Inc., 382 Mass. 34, 413 N.E.2d 1105 (1980).

from the judgment of registration, will be referred to by original book and page numbers thereof as recorded on the unregistered side of the registry, and it will be necessary to look them up in the registry of deeds. Those instruments which are noted as registered documents will be found on file, generally in the original, in the office of the registry district. Those are not copied into books, and it is necessary to ask the registry clerk to provide the document itself for examination.

Examination with respect to the statutorily excepted encumbrances does involve chaining back prior registered owners to the original decree of registration. Each certificate of title bears a notation of the prior certificate from which it was issued, so it is quite easy to determine the names of prior registered owners and their periods of ownership. Once determined, each such owner should be run during the period of his ownership in the indices of bankruptcies and federal tax liens. Finding Massachusetts tax liens may require more search. Of course a certificate of municipal liens should also be obtained and it may be advisable to check the offices of the city or town street department, the county commissioners and the state department of public works for highway layouts if the certificate does not determine the line of an abutting way.

Furthermore, in light of the principles discussed in § 8:3, upon which the inviolability of a certificate of title may be questioned,[1] one should examine the certificate and instruments noted thereon with care to determine whether they raise any doubts or may be deemed to put one on notice of a need for further search. Even risks of forgery may be reduced by examination of signatures of the same parties on earlier recorded instruments.

When a title has been confirmed but not registered, title examination need not go behind the recorded judgment of confirmation, the terms and encumbrances of which may be considered in the same manner as a certificate of title. From the date of the judgment of confirmation forward, the exami-

---

[Section 8:14]

[1]See in particular Tyler v. Judges of the Court of Registration, 175 Mass. 71, 55 N.E. 812 (1900); Kozdras v. Land/Vest Properties, Inc., 382 Mass. 34, 413 N.E.2d 1105 (1980); Triangle Center, Inc. v. Department of Public Works, 386 Mass. 858, 438 N.E.2d 798 (1982).

nation is the same as for unregistered land.

TOPIC D: REMEDIES AND PROBLEMS

§ 8:15 Remedies; assurance fund

As mentioned to in § **8:3**, M.G.L.A. c. 185, § 45, provides for a complaint for review of an original judgment of registration within one year after it is entered. It says that: "Such judgment shall not be opened by . . . any proceeding at law or in equity for reversing judgments or decrees"; and goes on to provide in effect that a person deprived of property by a judgment of registration obtained by fraud may sue within one year after the entry of the judgment, but the remedy available is only in tort for fraud, and it may not impair the registered title of an innocent purchaser for value.

With respect to title issues arising after the original judgment of registration there are the procedures available under §§ 112 and 114 of Chapter 185, discussed in § **8:13**.

Then M.G.L.A. c. 185, § 101, provides that: "A person who, without negligence on his part, sustains loss or damage by reason of any error, omission, mistake or misdescription in any certificate of title or in any entry or memorandum in a registration book, or a person who, without negligence on his part, is deprived of land or of any estate or interest therein, by the registration of another person as owner of such land or of any estate or interest therein, through fraud or in consequence of any error, omission, mistake or misdescription in any certificate of title or in any entry or memorandum in a registration book may institute an action in contract in the superior court for compensation from the assurance fund for such loss, damage or deprivation; but a person so deprived of land or of any estate or interest therein, having a right of action or other remedy for the recovery of such land, estate or interest, shall exhaust such remedy before resorting to the action of contract herein provided."

Such compensation may be sought by action of contract in the superior court against the state treasurer, alone if only registry personnel are at fault, or jointly with other persons alleged to be at fault. Under § 99 an assurance fund is created by assessment upon each original registration of 0.1% of the assessed value of the land, but if the fund is insufficient to pay a claim, it may be charged against general funds of the Commonwealth. There is a six-year statute of limitations, limits to the amount of recovery and subrogation provisions.

Attempts to recover from the assurance fund have been few and far between and have enjoyed scant success. In fact, only one successful case is reported at the appellate level, involving a registration in which a boundary measuring about 300 feet was erroneously certified as about 900 feet.[1] Other claimants failed to recover; one was a contract vendee who was not "deprived of land" that he didn't own, and the other did not show any Land Court or registry error and did not meet the test of being "without negligence."[2]

§ 8:16 Deregistration

As noted in § 8:5, M.G.L.A. c. 185, § 52, provides that a judgment of registration is binding forever unless the land is duly withdrawn. One basis of withdrawal, referred to in § 8:10, is establishment of a condominium of partly registered and partly unregistered land. The Land Court provides an Outline for Withdrawal from Registration with respect to action under M.G.L.A. c. 183A, § 16. It is also provided in § 52 that if registered land is acquired by the commonwealth or any agency, etc. thereof, or any political subdivision thereof, the land may be withdrawn from registration upon application to the Land Court by the public entity for withdrawal.

Responding to concerns within the real estate community, including lawyers, about perceived problems with the land registration system, relating primarily to costs and delays, the legislature amended § 52 in 2000[1] to provide for "voluntary withdrawal." This applies, however, in limited circumstances, and is subject to various hurdles. In the first place, a "notice of voluntary withdrawal," setting forth specified title references and description, must be signed by all owners of the registered land, and filed with the Land Court with a complaint for withdrawal, accompanied by deposit of "a sum sufficient to cover costs of the proceeding." The Land Court prescribes forms for both the Notice of Voluntary Withdrawal and Complaint for Voluntary Withdrawal. The Court then appoints an examiner to report on record owners, mortgagees and lessees, who are given notice.

[Section 8:15]

[1]Overly v. Treasurer and Receiver General, 344 Mass. 188, 181 N.E.2d 660 (1962).

[2]Briggs v. Stevens, 224 Mass. 46, 112 N.E. 487 (1916); Putignano v. Treasurer and Receiver General, 55 Mass. App. Ct. 828, 774 N.E.2d 1157 (2002).

[Section 8:16]

[1]Chapter 413, Acts of 2000.

The Court is then to endorse its approval of the notice of voluntary withdrawal if one of certain tests are met, as follows: (1) The land sought to be deregistered is less than 50% in area of a tract in common ownership; (2) The land sought to be deregistered is less that 10% in area upon original registration of a tract then in common ownership and the balance has since then been conveyed; (3) The land sought to be deregistered has been submitted to a Chapter 183A (condominium) or 183B (time share) regime, or (4) "the court finds that the owners of the registered land have demonstrated other good cause for withdrawal under this section, including but not limited to, economic hardship by reason of the land being registered." If a mortgagee or lessee files objection, the court may still grant withdrawal unless it finds that there is good cause for the objection. As to the fourth category, the forms provided by the Land Court call for the "good cause" for deregistration to be specified with particularity, but otherwise there are no guidelines. As to the third category, it is notoriously difficult in any condominium of more than a very few units to obtain unanimous consent to anything.

Once endorsed by the Court, the notice of voluntary withdrawal is to be noted on the memorandum of encumbrances of the certificate of title, and the land then becomes unregistered land with title thereto established "as though a judgment of confirmation without registration had been recorded under section 56A."

Chapter 9

Title Insurance

TOPIC A: INTRODUCTION
§ 9:1   The Massachusetts style

TOPIC B: POLICY FORMS
§ 9:2   Owner's, mortgagee's, other
§ 9:3   Commitments; binders

TOPIC C: COVERAGES; EXCLUSIONS
§ 9:4   Owner's policy
§ 9:5   Mortgagee's policy

TOPIC D: EXCEPTIONS
§ 9:6   Persons in possession
§ 9:7   Taxes and assessments
§ 9:8   Mechanics' liens
§ 9:9   Survey
§ 9:10   Itemized
§ 9:11   Riparian and littoral rights
§ 9:12   Indian claims
§ 9:13   Condominium law
§ 9:14   Partner's loan
§ 9:15   Other

TOPIC E: SUPPLEMENTAL COVERAGE
§ 9:16   Amendments
§ 9:17   Endorsements
§ 9:18   Affirmative insurance

TOPIC F: RECOVERY; REMEDIES
§ 9:19   General
§ 9:20   Reinsurance

TOPIC A: INTRODUCTION

§ 9:1 The Massachusetts style

Title insurance is required by purchasers and lenders in almost all purchase and loan transactions, excepting only minor or non-commercial transactions.

The title insurance companies do not, however, maintain so-called "title plants" in Massachusetts, and in many cases do not do their own title examination. The common system is for private attorneys to have titles examined and abstracts prepared by title examiners or abstract companies, to read the abstracts and pass on the titles, and based thereon to submit reports on title to the title insurers who then issue binders or commitments in accordance with such reports. The title insurance companies generally accept such reports on title from a number of qualified and experienced conveyancers whom they have approved for that purpose. The title insurance companies may require any submitting attorney to accompany his report on title with an abstract supporting the report, but that requirement is often waived when the reporting attorney is one whose reliability and practice of preserving a library of his abstracts is well known to the title insurers.

Alternatively, an attorney whose client is in need of title insurance may apply to a title insurer which will itself engage, or have on its staff, an attorney who will examine the title and prepare the abstract.

Some private attorneys become designated as an "agent" for a title insurance company, and undertake to issue or to commit for the issuance of policies on behalf of the insurer. That approach is said to reduce the cost of title insurance to the agent-attorney's clients, but it obviously poses issues of divided interest or loyalty.[1]

[Section 9:1]

[1]See Private Lending & Purchasing, Inc. v. First American Title Ins. Co., 54 Mass. App. Ct. 532, 766 N.E.2d 532 (2002); Somerset Sav. Bank v. Chicago Title Ins. Co., 420 Mass. 422, 649 N.E.2d 1123 (1995).

The closing of most real estate transactions in Massachusetts remains in the hands of private attorneys. A representative of the title insurer may attend the closing in order to sign off on the sufficiency of documents presented to meet insurance commitment requirements, but it is the attorney conducting the closing who usually attends to having a final rundown of title made and having the documents recorded. When that is accomplished, a final report is made to the title insurer so that the policy may be issued.

So-called escrow closings, common in other states, are sometimes conducted in Massachusetts. In that mode, the escrow agent, usually a title insurance company, receives all of the documents and funds, determines compliance with all contract requirements, continues examination of title, records the documents and disburses the funds.

These procedures and alternatives work well to preserve the traditionally high quality of conveyancing in Massachusetts. The policy and practice of an active conveyancing bar of curing and correcting title defects, drafting errors, inadequate descriptions, etc., tends to be maintained. The title insurance companies, on their part, also maintain high standards of professionalism among their staff personnel, since their underwriting decisions are necessarily based in substantial part on the title reports submitted to them and on negotiation of particular policy provisions with attorneys acting for the insureds.

TOPIC B: POLICY FORMS

§ 9:2   Owner's, mortgagee's, other

In 2006 the American Land Title Association (ALTA) promulgated new forms of title insurance policies (06-17-06 forms). The widely used prior forms, dating from 1992 (10-17-92 forms) and from 1970 (10-17-70 forms), may still be available, but the aim is surely to promote the use of the new forms. When the new forms appeared, the American Bar Association and other organizations offered seminars to explain the new forms and the differences from the old forms. ALTA itself has documents of comparisons of 1992 and 2006 forms, available to subscribers. While those analyses are surely of value, the descriptions of the forms and their contents set forth herein are based simply on the author's own reading and understanding of the terms of the new forms themselves. ALTA forms have evolved over the years. The 1992 versions were more detailed and clear than the

1970 forms, and the new 2006 forms are surely aimed at being more "user-friendly" and making clear to the insured exactly what is covered. As indicated in the following sections of this chapter, that may often still depend on the wording of the property description and of the specified exceptions, and on endorsements attached.

The basic forms are an Owner's Policy and a Loan Policy. The format of these policies comprises: (a) a statement of "Covered Risks," (b) a statement of "Exclusions from Coverage," (c) Schedule A, in which are specified the amount of insurance, date of policy, name of insured, estate insured, title owner, property description, and listing of endorsements, (d) Schedule B, in which Exceptions from Coverage are listed, sometimes in two "parts," and (e) "Conditions," setting forth definitions of terms, requirements and procedures for assertion of loss and recovery, and limitations thereon.

An **Owner's Policy**[1] is intended obviously to cover an owner of real estate; that is, a person having record title to a recognized interest in real estate. The insured under such a policy includes certain successors, specified in the definition of "insured," such as (i) heirs, devisees, survivors of a joint tenancy, (ii) a grantee without consideration which is still effectively owned by the named insured, and (iii) in the case of a corporate insured, a successor by merger or other type of reorganization. The fundamental item insured is the validity of the owner's record title.

A **Loan Policy**[2] is intended to cover a mortgagee, and is often referred to as a "mortgagee's policy." The definition of "mortgage" includes "deed of trust, trust deed, or other security instrument, including one evidenced by electronic means authorized by law." The fundamental items insured are the validity of the mortgagor's record title and the validity of the mortgagee's lien thereon.

Since most real estate transactions involve mortgage financing, the Loan Policy is the most frequently issued. An Owner's Policy is often issued "simultaneously" (construed broadly) therewith, and the premium therefore is reduced on such a packaged basis.

Other. In addition to the standard owner's and mortgagee's policies, ALTA provides "short" forms for one-to-four family dwellings. They are called the Homeowner's Policy of Title Insurance For A One-To-Four Family Residence (is-

---

[Section 9:2]

[1]Appendix G, ALTA Owner's Policy, 6/17/06.

[2]Appendix H, ALTA Loan Policy, 6/17/06.

sued 10-22-03) and a Short Form Residential Loan Policy—
One-To-Four Family (issued 10-21-00). Besides those, there
are other forms available, including one designed for
construction loans, and several types of residential policies.
Some residential policies afford "inflation protection" by
increasing the coverage automatically without additional
premium.

Insurance commissioners in various states need to pass on
these forms, and some states have their own particular
requirements. In Massachusetts and in most if not all other
states the new 2006 forms are likely to become widely used.

§ 9:3 Commitments; binders

A Commitment is a formal undertaking by an insurer to
issue a specified policy. It contains substantially all of the
contents and terms of the policy itself which is to be issued,
and also sets forth the requirements (or "calls") which must
be fulfilled for the policy to be issued, including recording of
the proposed deed and mortgage, recording of instruments
disposing of existing encumbrances, payment of taxes, and
the like. ALTA provides three forms: Commitment Form (06-
17-06), Plain Language Commitment Form (06-17-06) and
Short Form Commitment (01-17-04). In complex deals where
a number of specialized policy endorsements are appropriate, it is often advisable to obtain a Commitment so that any
issues can be worked out in advance and there are no
surprises at or after a closing.

A so-called "Binder" is simply an acceptance by an
insurer's agent of a submitted title report as being in a form
generally acceptable for issuance of title insurance.

In between a commitment and a binder is a "specimen
policy" which an insurer may be willing to provide when the
terms are certain and there are no complexities of title clearing in the offing. This is a useful device for a prospective
insured, particularly in order to establish the exact wording
of policy exceptions.

TOPIC C: COVERAGES;
EXCLUSIONS

§ 9:4 Owner's policy

● **Coverages.** ALTA Owner's Policy (6-17-06) provides
that "Subject to the Exclusions from coverage, the Exceptions from coverage contained in Schedule B, and the Condi-

tions," the insurer insures against loss or damage by reason of: (1) title being vested other than as stated in Schedule A; (2) any defect in or lien or encumbrance on the title [followed by a list of examples, but not limited to them]; (3) unmarketable title; (4) no right of access to and from the land; (5) and (6) violation or enforcement of various laws and regulations if (a notable "if") a notice of the violation or of enforcement action has been recorded; (7) and (8) exercise of the right of eminent domain if a notice thereof has been recorded or if it is effective even though the insured owner had no knowledge thereof; (9) title being defective because of judicial action or conflict with bankruptcy or creditors' rights rules; and (10) defects or encumbrances occurring between the policy date and recording of the deed to the insured owner.

• **Exclusions.** The Exclusions from Coverage are as follows: (1) zoning, subdivision and environmental laws and regulations; (2) eminent domain; (3) defects and encumbrances (a) "created, suffered, assumed, or agreed to by the Insured Claimant," (b) not recorded or known to the insurer, but known to the insured and not disclosed, (c) resulting in no loss, (d) arising after the policy date, or (e) that would not cause loss if the insured had "paid value for the Title;" (4) fraudulent conveyance or preferential transfer under bankruptcy laws; and (5) real estate taxes or assessments after the policy date. With respect to several of these Exclusions the policy form states specifically that they do not "modify or limit" a coverage in a related area.

From these abbreviated listings of inclusions and exclusions it is apparent that (a) a detailed title report is essential, (b) full disclosure by the insured is important, (c) an evaluation of risks particular to the circumstances is needed, (d) in all events there are some close calls, and (e) the option of special endorsements should be carefully considered. Also salient is the importance of an accurate description in Schedule A of the estate and interests therein to be covered, whether fee simple, leasehold or other, and including essential appurtenances. While lack of a right of access is a general coverage item, it is usually advisable to include specific reference to access ways and easements in the property description so that the specific appurtenances are insured.

§ 9:5 Mortgagee's policy

The coverages and exclusions in a loan policy include in substance all and the same as in an owner's policy, stated when appropriate as applicable to the mortgage lien; and others are added relating specifically to the insured mortgage lien.

• **Coverages.** The added coverages include loss or damage because of (1) invalidity or unenforceability of the mortgage due to "forgery, fraud, undue influence, duress, incompetency, incapacity, or impersonation; lack of authorization, faulty execution, electronic or otherwise, faulty power of attorney; improper recording, or defective judicial or administrative proceeding"; (2) lack of priority over other liens or encumbrances, including "assessments for street improvements," and in some circumstances with respect to future advances over mechanics' liens; and (3) invalidity or unenforceability of an assignment specified in Schedule A of the insured mortgage.

• **Exclusions.** The added exclusions include unenforceability of the lien of the mortgage due to failure to comply with "doing-business" laws, usury laws, consumer protection laws or truth in lending laws.

The same points made above with respect to an owner's policy are of course equally pertinent with respect to a loan policy. The particular special endorsements desirable with respect to a loan policy may not be the same as for an owner's policy and are likely to be greater, as referred to in § **9:17**.

TOPIC D: EXCEPTIONS

§ **9:6** Persons in possession

The 2006 ALTA forms do not set forth any "standard" exceptions, but simply provide parenthetically that the "Policy may include regional exceptions if so desired by the issuing Company." In Massachusetts title insurers generally include standard exceptions for matters that may encumber a title without first appearing of record, such as those referred to in this section and the following § **9:7** to § **9:9**.

A tenant under a lease for less than seven years, an ousted tenant-in-common, or a person claiming rights by adverse possession or prescription, for instance, may have valid claims that do not appear of record. An exception from insurance coverage against such claims may ordinarily be eliminated by an affidavit of the insured owner specifying the persons who are actually in occupancy, including a list of any tenants, which would then be incorporated in the policy terms.

§ **9:7** Taxes and assessments

Real estate taxes are assessed as of January 1 each year

for a fiscal year beginning the following July 1, billed there-after, and are a lien without recording of notice. In light of that, a policy issued in, say, March 2008, might make exception for: "Taxes assessed as of January 1, 2007, for the tax year beginning July 1, 2007, and taxes assessed as of January 1, 2008, for the tax year beginning July 1, 2008, and taxes assessed for subsequent years." In that example the policy might also note that it is affirmatively insured that taxes due and payable before March 2008 have been paid. There are various ways of phrasing all this, but it is important both to the insurer and the insured to cover all the points. The insurer will ordinarily require that a Certificate of Municipal Liens (see **§ 6:30**) be obtained and recorded.

§ 9:8 Mechanics' liens

Under M.G.L.A. c. 254, § 1, a lien for up to 30 days of wages may be established by subsequent recording of a notice of lien for work performed within 90 days prior to the recording. (See **§ 6:22**.) A policy exception therefore may be eliminated upon proper affidavit that no work for which such a lien could be established has been performed on the premises during such 90-day period prior to the effective date of the policy. Even if work has been performed within that period, title insurers are often willing to omit any exception therefore upon being furnished by a responsible owner of the premises with a simple agreement of indemnity against loss on account of any such liens.

§ 9:9 Survey

A common standard exception is for "such state of facts as an accurate survey and examination of the premises might disclose," or words to that effect. Under such an exception, if a survey should later show that the Schedule A description, however detailed, was incorrect, the insurer would not be liable for losses due to the earlier error. Some such errors, involving encroachments, for example, could be quite costly to correct.

The solution is to have a survey certified to the insurer. In 2006 ALTA promulgated its "2005 Minimum Standard Detail Requirements forALTA/ACSM Land Title Surveys."[1] It is not always necessary to have a new survey made; a surveyor may certify a prior survey plan of record on which the prop-

---

[Section 9:9]

[1]Appendix I, ALTA Minimum Standard Detail Requirements for ALTA/ACSM Land Title Surveys.

erty description in Schedule A is based, making a current examination in the field to verify controlling monuments or other survey points, but not the entire traverse. Based on a survey certification on the ALTA form or on the insurer's own form, title insurance companies will eliminate the "survey exception" or replace it in effect with an affirmative insurance of the validity of the certified survey. When a survey is so certified to the insurer, then Schedule B will specifically refer thereto and to matters particularly disclosed thereby. Both the substance and the wording of such a "survey reading" require careful attention, and it is essential that the description in Schedule A does in fact comply with it.

§ 9:10 Itemized

Instruments referred to in a report on title which have any continuing effect on the premises will be referred to as Exceptions in Schedule B (sometimes Part 2 thereof.) These may include mortgages which are not to be discharged, grants of rights and easements, restrictive agreements, covenants, agreements, deeds containing grants or reservations, leases and notices of lease, orders of taking by eminent domain, orders establishing building lines, orders of specific public improvements, subdivision covenants with planning boards, decisions of boards of appeals granting variances or special permits, conservation restrictions, orders of conditions issued by conservation commissions, and so forth. They may be listed chronologically or grouped according to subject matter. The manner in which any such instrument is referred to or characterized may be of substantial importance. Each instrument should be identified by parties, date and book and page of recording, or document number and certificate of title with respect to registered land.

A mortgage encumbering the entire insured property may be identified only by parties, date and recording data, and by designation as a mortgage. If, however, it encumbers only one of several parcels included in the insured's premises, the mortgaged parcel should be specifically identified.

As to easements, it is even more important to identify the nature and scope of the easement and its location. An exception, for instance, for an easement granted to Boston Edison Company et al., may refer to a local electric service connection or to a high voltage cross-country transmission line. The line may be underground or overhead, or the easement may permit either. The location may be within the street adjoining the insured locus, or it may run across locus or include

175

poles, guys or transformer pads or vaults on locus. The "et al." may refer to New England Telephone and Telegraph Company, and the easements granted to it may in terms confer rights to handle all communication of intelligence by electricity, which may include computer data transfer.

As to restrictions, it is important to identify the dominant estate and the term. For takings of streets, water main and sewer easements and the like, it is important to determine the location with respect to the insured premises. And for agreements, covenants, orders, decisions, and other such instruments, reference to them solely by such a generic label may often be insufficient to afford the insured the protection to which he is entitled.

In preparing or accepting a policy for an insured, counsel must always study not only the policy, but every instrument referred to therein. Having done so, he will be able to give his opinion to his client on the import and effect thereof. But his client is buying title insurance and should be able to look to the insurer if he suffers loss, and should not have to look to the attorney or rely on his interpretation of the exception instruments. For example, suppose there is a grant of easement which could be interpreted to be "wild," i.e., to affect the entire locus, but there is data of record sufficient to support an opinion that the exercise of the easement is limited to a defined strip across locus. In such a case adequate certification should be made so that the policy itself specifically insures that the exercise of the easement is confined to the defined strip. A situation of that type and other locational matters, such as easements, street lines, utility easement takings, conservation restriction areas, building setback lines, etc., are best handled by having a certified survey which is referred to in the policy. Then all specific exceptions referring to documents establishing such matters can be specifically defined by and limited to locations shown and identified on the certified survey plan.

For matters which are not locational, but involve interpretation of complex provisions, the task of properly framing the wording of exceptions, and affirmative insurance clauses as referred to in § 9:18, is considerably greater, but it is a task well worth doing in order to afford one's client with fully effective title insurance coverage.

§ 9:11 Riparian and littoral rights

Specific exception is made in appropriate circumstances for certain matters which arise at law, but are not set forth in specific instruments. Examples include those referred to in this section and in the following § **9:12** to § **9:15**. For rivers, brooks and streams, the exception may be for "rights of upper and lower riparian owners in and to waters of [the specified stream] and the natural flow thereof." For the ocean and great ponds, the exception may be for "rights of the public and the commonwealth in and to the portions of the premises lying below mean high tide," or "within the limits of Lake X, a great pond."

§ 9:12 Indian claims

In the areas where Indian claims are pending the title insurers may in some cases affirmatively insure against dispossession of occupied property, but ordinarily not as to marketability, nor with respect to vacant land. Most Indian claims in Massachusetts have now been resolved.

§ 9:13 Condominium law

Exception is sometimes taken in policies on condominium units for "limitations on title created by M.G.L.A. Chapter 183A," but it is now much more common simply to include a "condominium endorsement."[1]

§ 9:14 Partner's loan

When a loan policy is issued to a mortgagee who is a partner or joint venturer in the mortgagor entity, an exception is ordinarily taken on account thereof because of the fact that by law a third-party creditor of the partnership or joint venture may have priority over such mortgage lien.

§ 9:15 Other

There are of course many other possible examples. Most of the issues of this type are now dealt with by special policy endorsements, as discussed in § **9:17**.

TOPIC E: SUPPLEMENTAL COVERAGE

§ 9:16 Amendments

Once issued, a policy may be amended and supplemented

[Section 9:13]

[1]Appendix J, ALTA Condominium Endorsement 4.1-06.

by separate documents issued by the insurer, generally referred to as endorsements. An owner's policy may be endorsed to reflect such things as a revised description based on a new survey, or newly recorded appurtenances or encumbrances. A mortgagee's policy may be endorsed in those respects, and also to reflect further loan advances, or "pending disbursements," or assignment of a construction loan mortgage to a permanent lender. A mortgagee's policy may be so assigned with the insured mortgage, but an owner's policy is not assignable to a subsequent owner.

§ 9:17   Endorsements

As noted in the preceding paragraph, amendment of an existing policy is made by endorsement. Also, when a policy is first being issued, there are often endorsements attached. Endorsements are available in considerable number and variety, there being more than 80 forms of endorsement listed by ALTA. In Schedule A of the 2006 loan policy form itself there is a listing of endorsements which may commonly be appropriate for loan policies, including endorsements relating to: condominium, planned unit development, variable rate, environmental protection lien,[1] restrictions, encroachments, minerals, leasehold loan, future advances, and location of improvements.

Other endorsements that may be pertinent to a loan policy deal with: truth in lending, "date down" (relating to loan advances), mortgage modification, non-imputation (of the knowledge of one partner to another), mezzanine financing, and revolving credit.

Some of the forms mentioned are also pertinent to an owner's policy, and there are many others. These include endorsements with respect to: condominium units, manufactured housing units, environmental protection, restrictions, encroachments, access, contiguity of multiple parcels, street assessments, and finally, but by no means least, zoning. With respect to zoning insurance, it is always worth considering, but it is never a substitute for a thorough zoning analysis by an owner's attorney and a detailed opinion with respect thereto.

§ 9:18   Affirmative insurance

Whenever an instrument appears of record to have an ef-

[Section 9:17]
[1]Appendix K, ALTA En- dorsemental Protection Lien 8.1-06.

fect on the property being insured, the policy will refer to it in Schedule B. Sometimes, however, the import thereof or the risk taken by the insured because of the existence thereof may not be clear or certain, and in that event the coverage of the insurance may be modified and clarified. Sometimes such modification may be accomplished by means of an available form of endorsement, but in some situations it is necessary to negotiate an "affirmative insurance" provision in the policy. While most of the provisions of a title insurance policy are not susceptible to change, the terms of the description in Schedule A and the Exceptions in Schedule B are not set in stone and the wording thereof may be negotiated.

Among common affirmative insurance provisions are those which: (a) specifically include appurtenant rights and easements in the insured premises, (b) specify partial payment of taxes for a particular tax year, (c) insure that particular restrictions for which exception has been taken have not been violated and that any future violation will not cause a forfeiture or reversion of title, or (d) locate easements or other rights for the area in which they may be exercised.

One example of a title situation in which special provisions are useful is one in which the parcel to be insured was taken as part of an urban renewal project and then sold pursuant to a so-called land disposition agreement, under which there was a deed of conveyance and later a certificate of completion. The record title will include all these instruments, containing extensive and complex provisions and broad references to the original urban renewal plan. Once the new construction is completed, as evidenced by the certificate of completion, the provisions of these instruments are almost entirely outmoded and no longer applicable, excepting only certain identifiable nondiscrimination covenants and others which remain in effect. A title policy which simply takes as exception the rights, easements, restrictions, reservations, covenants, agreements and other provisions of all of the specified instruments will be correct in the sense that it reflects the record, but it will be in fact misleading as to the state of the title. The solution, insofar as title insurance is involved, is to include in the policy a special provision which specifies and affirmatively insures that the only provisions of said instruments which remain in effect are the specified covenants, which have specified terms, which have been complied with, and which if violated in the future will not cause a forfeiture or reversion of the title.

It should be observed that when an exception is taken for a particular instrument, and then affirmative insurance is given against loss because of assertion of that instrument, that does not per se insure marketability despite the existence of that instrument of record. That is, if a contract of sale is made without that instrument taken therein as an exception, and the buyer asserts that the title is unmarketable because of the existence of that instrument, the title insurer of the seller will not be liable. The insurer has by affirmative insurance insured the seller only against loss because of assertion of the instrument itself, not its existence or the possibility of its assertion. In order to obtain marketability coverage, it would be necessary either to eliminate reference to the encumbrance instrument completely from Schedule B of the policy, or to have the affirmative insurance clause expressly include coverage of marketability.

TOPIC F: RECOVERY; REMEDIES

§ 9:19   General

As noted in § 9:2, the conditions of a policy set forth definitions of terms, and the requirements and procedures for assertion of loss and recovery.

A title insurance policy is in essence a contract of indemnity. The insured pays a single premium for the policy; there are no annual or other renewal payments, although additional premium may be payable for additional coverage. An owner's policy does not run with the land and is not assignable to a subsequent owner. However, the insured owner continues to be covered after he has sold the property with respect to (a) his deed covenants and (b) a purchase money mortgage. A loan policy continues to cover a mortgagee after it has taken possession, and after its acquisition of title by purchase at its own foreclosure sale or by deed in lieu of foreclosure, and with respect to liabilities on its deed covenants when it conveys to a third party.

With respect to enforcement of and recovery under a title insurance policy the following points are pertinent: Prompt notice of loss or of a claim that might result in loss is required, and recovery may be reduced to the extent the insurer is prejudiced by failure to give such notice. A proof of loss may be required. When notified of litigation involving an alleged defect, lien or encumbrance contrary to the policy, the insurer may pay off the claim or may, if the insured so requests, defend the claim with counsel of its own choice, or may institute its own action to clear or establish the title as insured. In any such litigation the insured is required to cooperate with and assist the insurer in all reasonable respects. If an action involves "causes of action that allege matters not insured by this policy," the insurer will not pay costs incurred by the insured in defense thereof.

The extent of the insurer's liability is the lesser of the policy amount or "the difference between the value of the Title as insured and the value of the Title subject to the risk insured against by this policy." However, it is provided that if the insurer undertakes its own action to clear the title and fails, the amount of insurance is increased by 10%, and the insured has an option of having the loss determined as of the date of claim or date of settlement. Payment is to be made within 30 days after liability is determined.

When the insurer makes a payment in settlement of a claim, the amount of insurance coverage is reduced by the amount paid, and the insurer is subrogated to the insured's rights to that extent, but is to defer assertion of its subrogated rights until the insured has completed its claim for loss.

On policies of $2 million or less, either party may require arbitration. The law of the situs of the insured property applies.

§ 9:20 Reinsurance

Reinsurance is a procedure under which the original insurer is primarily liable for the entire coverage, and lays off portions thereof to other insurers in specified amounts. The lead insurer retains a portion, usually the largest portion, of the risk to itself, and the reinsurers are reached only if a claim exceeds that primary amount. On large loan transactions institutional lenders often specify a maximum dollar amount which they are willing to have insured by any specified title insurers, and reinsurance must be arranged for accordingly.

ALTA's forms issued in 2006 include a Facultative Reinsurance Agreement, a Tertiary Facultative Reinsurance Agreement and a Quaternary Facultative Reinsurance Agreement. The appropriate forms should be executed by the original insurer and the reinsurers. The right of the insured to reach a reinsurer directly may be obtained by amendment, but that change may not be worth the cost.

Chapter 10

Marketability; Curative Procedures; Curative Statutes

TOPIC A: MARKETABILITY

TOPIC B: CURATIVE PROCEDURES

TOPIC C: CURATIVE STATUTES

TOPIC A: MARKETABILITY

§ 10:1 General principles

Purchase and sale agreements now almost always require "a good and clear record title and a marketable title," and the two concepts need to be considered in tandem.

The Court stated long ago that: "The general rule is well settled, that, in order to maintain a bill for specific performance of a purchase of land, the plaintiff must show that the title tendered by him is good beyond reasonable doubt. But a doubt must be reasonable, and such as would cause a prudent man to pause and hesitate before investing his money. It would be seldom that a case could occur where some state of facts might not be imagined which, if it existed, would defeat a title. When questions as to the validity of a title are settled beyond reasonable doubt, although there may be still the possibility of a defect, such mere possibility will not exempt one from his liability to complete the purchase he has made."[1]

Although that rule makes no distinction between "good title" and "marketable title," the court did articulate such distinctions, stating that:

A good and clear record title free from all incumbrances means a title which on the record itself can be again sold as free from obvious defects, and substantial doubts. [citations omitted] The distinction is plain between the obligation of the defendant under the wording of the agreement, and that which would have attached if the language had been 'conveying a good and clear title free from all incumbrances' as pointed out in [citations omitted] A 'good marketable title' also is not the same as 'a good and clear record title'. The first embraces an actual title which may rest on disseisin for twenty years or more, and is established by evidence independently of the record. The second rests on the record alone, which must show

---

[Section 10:1]

[1]Foster, Hall & Adams Co. v. Sayles, 213 Mass. 319, 100 N.E. 644 (1913), quoting from First African M. E. Church v. Brown, 147 Mass. 296, 17 N.E. 549 (1888).

an indefeasible unencumbered estate. [citations omitted][2]

The distinctions therein made may serve at least as guidelines to drafting of purchase and sale agreements, and the language used therein will be of some effect. Nevertheless, both earlier and later decisions seemed to ignore any refined distinctions and generally to apply a "reasonable doubt" test in all cases, regardless of the agreement language.[3]

In general, a title is unmarketable when record title is deficient and one cannot adduce enough facts to warrant a finding of title by adverse possession.

§ 10:2 Marketability and record defects

In the cases (beyond enumeration here) in which title to real estate has been held to be unacceptable, the grounds specified usually rest upon and emphasize record defects and not lack of marketability. The situations in which marketability per se looms into importance are often those in which the title rests on adverse possession. If title by adverse possession is easily shown, then the title may be "good and marketable" despite record defects, but when establishing adverse possession depends on a long and difficult investigation and proof of facts, a seller cannot force specific performance.[1]

The likelihood of a buyer's becoming involved in litigation relating to the premises and other matters may also be asserted (not always successfully) as defects of the marketability type.[2]

TOPIC B: CURATIVE PROCEDURES

---

[2]O'Meara v. Gleason, 246 Mass. 136, 140 N.E. 426 (1923).

[3]Morse v. Stober, 233 Mass. 223, 123 N.E. 780, 9 A.L.R. 78 (1919); Sullivan v. F.E. Atteaux & Co., 284 Mass. 515, 187 N.E. 906 (1933); Ryder v. Garden Estates, 329 Mass. 10, 105 N.E.2d 854 (1952); Guleserian v. Pilgrim Trust Co., 331 Mass. 431, 120 N.E.2d 193 (1954).

[Section 10:2]

[1]Aroian v. Fairbanks, 216 Mass. 215, 103 N.E. 629 (1913); Conley v. Finn, 171 Mass. 70, 50 N.E. 460 (1898); Noyes v. Johnson, 139 Mass. 436, 31 N.E. 767 (1885).

[2]Institution for Savings in Newburyport and Its Vicinity v. Puffer, 201 Mass. 41, 87 N.E. 562 (1909); Daniel v. Shaw, 166 Mass. 582, 44 N.E. 991 (1896); Smith v.

§ 10:3   Registration or confirmation

As set forth in § **8:3**, registration or confirmation of title under M.G.L.A. c. 185 constitutes judicial determination of the status of title, and a judgment of registration is expressly stated to "bind the land and quiet the title." Despite that phrase, registration was not conceived as a curative procedure in itself, and in fact it has been held with respect to Chapter 185 that "The general purpose of that statute is to empower the Land Court to determine the actual state of the title to the land described in the petition, and not to clear the land of encumbrances manifestly existing of record."[1] The Torrens System has not prospered in some other states, perhaps because of strict application of that concept. In Massachusetts, however, registration of title long ago became and continues to be the most powerful curative tool, and the one most often used to establish a title which has a fundamental flaw in the title chain or the description of the premises, or multiple defects.

The registration process involves all of the elements and procedures which have been deemed by the courts to be requisite to meet constitutional due process requirements in relation to curative statutes dealing with specific matters.[2] Furthermore, the Land Court has broad powers in equity with respect to land title matters, and has exclusive or concurrent jurisdiction under those statutes providing for the curing of particular defects.[3] Consequently, judicial economy and the orderly administration of justice, as well as of a land title system, are well served by the use and application by the Land Court of title registration as a curative tool of broad scope.

That is not to say, however, that registration is a universal substitute for all other curative procedures, or that they may be subsumed into a registration proceeding. There are sometimes circumstances in which it may be necessary to ac-

---

Allmon, 17 Mass. App. Ct. 712, 461 N.E.2d 1237 (1984); Mucci v. Brockton Bocce Club, Inc., 19 Mass. App. Ct. 155, 472 N.E.2d 966 (1985); Coons v. Carstensen, 15 Mass. App. Ct. 431, 446 N.E.2d 114 (1983); Chicago Title Ins. Co. v. Kumar, 24 Mass. App. Ct. 53, 506 N.E.2d 154 (1987).

[2]See Selectmen of Town of Nahant v. U.S., 293 F. Supp. 1076 (D. Mass. 1968); Town of Brookline v. Carey, 355 Mass. 424, 245 N.E.2d 446 (1969).

[3]For example, see M.G.L.A. c. 240, §§ 16 and 17, as to restrictions, discussed in § **10:6**.

[Section 10:3]

[1]Sederquist v. Brown, 225 Mass. 217, 114 N.E. 365 (1916).

company or precede a complaint for registration with a specific curative procedure. In doubtful cases, inquiry may be made of a judge or other official of the Land Court before proceeding.

It is unfortunately true that in some circumstances *withdrawal* from registration may be deemed to be a curative procedure.

§ 10:4 Clearing a cloud on title

M.G.L.A. c. 240 provides two methods of clearing a cloud on title. The first method, under §§ 1 to 5, referred to in M.G.L.A. c. 185, § 1(d), is little used, and attempts to use it have often been frustrated. This is a petition in the Land Court by an owner of a freehold estate or an unexpired term of 10 years or more, to require a person having an adverse claim to bring an action to try such claim. That is, if the petition succeeds, the adverse claimant will then be obliged to bring a new action, which may possibly lie in a Superior Court, Probate Court or the Supreme Judicial Court, as well as the Land Court. This is clearly a two-step procedure: the Land Court is not to adjudicate the title upon the original petition unless the respondent defaults. Such multiplicity of action has little appeal to parties who must bear the legal costs, nor does it comport with modern notions of judicial economy.

This remedy is strictly construed and does not supersede any remedy in equity or limit the general authority of courts in equity. Furthermore, plaintiffs' efforts to assert it have been rejected time and again.[1] In one case the respondent to a Chapter 240, § 1, suit then filed under M.G.L.A. c. 185 to register the disputed land—and succeeded—which the original Chapter 240, § 1, petitioner might have regarded as a Pyrrhic victory for that statutory procedure.[2] That this remedy leads to complexity and multiplicity of suits continues to

---

[Section 10:4]

[1]Gilman v. Gilman, 171 Mass. 46, 50 N.E. 452 (1898); Arnold v. Reed, 162 Mass. 438, 38 N.E. 1132 (1894); Proprietors of India Wharf v. Central Wharf & Wet Dock Corp., 117 Mass. 504, 1875 WL 9098 (1875); Leary v. Duff, 137 Mass. 147, 1884 WL 10560 (1884); Boston Mfg. Co. v. Burgin, 114 Mass. 340, 1874 WL 9418 (1874); May v. New England R. Co., 171 Mass. 367, 50 N.E. 652 (1898); Tisdale v. Brabrook, 102 Mass. 374, 1869 WL 5754 (1869); Dewey v. Bulkley, 67 Mass. 416, 1 Gray 416, 1854 WL 4957 (1854).

[2]Marshall v. Francis, 327 Mass. 702, 100 N.E.2d 840 (1951).

be illustrated.[3] The Commonwealth is expressly excepted from this statute.[4]

The other method of clearing a cloud on title is much preferable and more widely used: that is, a civil action in equity, under §§ 6 to 10 of M.G.L.A. c. 240, to "quiet or establish" title or to "remove a cloud" from the title. This action lies in the Supreme Judicial Court, the Superior Court or the Land Court, and involves the general equitable jurisdiction of the court. The defendants need not have a claim of record or under a written instrument which they could release. The statute provides that it suffices if the defendants "claim or may claim by purchase, descent or otherwise, some right, title, interest or estate in the land which is the subject of the action and that their claim depends upon the construction of a written instrument or cannot be met by the plaintiffs without the production of evidence."[5]

The statute expressly provides that where there are potential claimants who are persons unascertained, not in being, unknown, out of the commonwealth or otherwise not amenable to service and personal jurisdiction of the court, they may be made defendants, and if necessary described generally as heirs or legal representatives. When actual service is not made, the court may order notice of the action by posting on the land or by publication in a newspaper, which shall then constitute constructive service. Provision is made for the appointment of a guardian ad litem to represent any defendants who were not actually served in the commonwealth and have not appeared in the proceeding.

It is provided in § 10 of the statute that, notice having been given as previously described and a guardian ad litem appointed, if the court does so, then the court may proceed "as though all defendants have been actually served with process," and the action "shall be a proceeding in rem against the land, and a judgment establishing or declaring the validity, nature or extent of the plaintiff's title may be entered, and shall operate directly on the land and have the force of a release made by or on behalf of all defendants of all claims inconsistent with the title established or declared thereby." It is also provided, however, that the court may exercise ju-

---

[3]Goulding v. Cook, 38 Mass. App. Ct. 92, 645 N.E.2d 54 (1995), vacated, 422 Mass. 276, 661 N.E.2d 1322 (1996); Schair v. Duquet, 38 Mass. App. Ct. 970, 650 N.E.2d 809 (1995); Conloin v. Jensen, 6 L.C.R. 119 (1998).

[4]M.G.L.A. c. 240, § 5; Greene v. Commonwealth, 6 L.C.R. 95 (1998).

[5]M.G.L.A. c. 240, § 6; Adams v. Peterson, 35 Mass. App. Ct. 782, 625 N.E.2d 575 (1994).

risdiction in personam against defendants served and amenable to its jurisdiction. The constitutionality of this statute has been upheld and it is clearly the most powerful curative procedure available other than registration itself.

§ 10:5 Disposing of old mortgages

Section 15 of M.G.L.A. c. 240, referred to in M.G.L.A. c. 185, § 1(f), deals specifically with the discharge of an old mortgage. The statute refers to an "undischarged mortgage or a mortgage not properly or legally discharged of record." The statute was amended in 2006 to add reference to neglect or refusal to provide a discharge in accordance with M.G.L.A. c. 183, § 55 (discussed in § **20:30**).[1] The court has said that this applies where there is no controversy, but the statute gives no jurisdiction to determine the validity or invalidity of a disputed mortgage.[2] The action lies in the land court or, if the land is not registered, the superior court, and may be brought by the mortgagor, or his successors in title, or any freeholder of the affected land, person who conveyed the title with covenants, or holder of an easement thereon. If the plaintiff does not have "actual or direct evidence of full payment or satisfaction of the mortgage," the action may be sustained by showing of title or possession for 20 years with no payment or recognition of the mortgage.[3] The statute specifies the 20-year period as being either (a) "after the recording of a deed from the mortgagor or his heirs or devisees to a bona fide purchaser," not referring to the mortgage, (b) "after the expiration of the time limited in the mortgage for the full performance of the condition thereof," or (c) "after the date of a mortgage not given to secure the payment of money or a debt but to secure the mortgagee against a contingent liability which has so ceased to exist that no person will be prejudiced by the discharge thereof." Recognition of the mortgage by the petitioner bars relief,[4] but in the case of a mortgage securing a contingent liability, the court may determine whether the liability has ceased to exist.[5]

The decree of the court, setting forth the facts and its finding that the mortgage ought to be discharged, when recorded in the registry of deeds, bars the enforcement of any title under the mortgage.

[Section 10:5]

[1]Wojtkowski v. Vetrano, 14 L.C.R. 278 (2006).

[2]McMahan v. McMahan, 205 Mass. 99, 91 N.E. 298 (1910).

[3]Mitchell v. Bickford, 192 Mass. 244, 78 N.E. 453 (1906).

[4]Brintnall v. Graves, 168 Mass. 384, 47 N.E. 119 (1897).

[5]Lewis v. Crowell, 205 Mass. 497, 91 N.E. 910 (1910).

§ 10:6   Disposing of restrictions

Restrictions imposed more than 30 years before the filing of a petition under M.G.L.A. c. 240, § 11, are among the matters which may be dealt with thereunder by the Land Court. A suit thereunder may be brought by a freeholder "to determine the validity, or define the nature and extent" of such a restriction.

Under M.G.L.A. c. 240, § 10C the Superior Court and the Land Court have concurrent jurisdiction with respect to restrictions to which M.G.L.A. c. 184, § 26 (see § 15:14) is applicable, whenever they were imposed. A suit thereunder may be brought by a freeholder or a tenant with an unexpired term of 10 years or more, and the court may determine "whether and in what manner and to what extent and for the benefit of what land the restriction is then enforceable, whether or not a violation has occurred or is threatened."

The complaint must identify the owners of the subject land and the benefited land and any other persons benefited. The complaint must be accompanied by (1) a certified copy of the instrument imposing the restriction or "a representative instrument if there are many and the complaint includes a summary of the remainder," which might apply in the case of a common scheme appearing from deeds of lots in a subdivision containing identical or similar restrictive provisions, and (2) "a plan or sketch showing the approximate locations of the parcels as to which the determination is sought, and the other parcel or parcels, if any, which may have the benefit of the restriction, and the ways, public or open to public use, upon which the respective parcels abut or nearest thereto, and the street numbers, if any, of such parcels."

The notice to be given of such a complaint is to be prescribed by the court after consideration of the complaint and the accompanying documents, and "such further documents or evidence as it may require." It is provided in § 10C that a determination by the court shall be "in rem and operate directly upon the subject land, and be binding upon all persons entitled to enforce the restriction thereon." Such determination may be that the restriction is enforceable, is not enforceable, or is enforceable "only in a certain manner or to a certain extent or for the benefit of certain land." Or the court may make an award of money damages and declare the land free from the restriction. This statute has been applied in several cases.[1]

With respect to registered land or land pending registration, jurisdiction is specifically conferred upon the Land Court under M.G.L.A. c. 240, § 16, referred to in M.G.L.A. c. 185, § 1(i), to determine whether or not equitable restrictions "limiting or restraining the use or the manner of using land are enforceable in whole or in part." Despite the emphasis on "use," this is presumably applicable to dimensional and procedural restrictions because they also effect the "manner of using land." M.G.L.A. c. 240, § 17, empowers the Land Court to register titles free from restriction if "the enforcement . . . would be injurious to the public interest." Although this statute was enacted in 1915 and on its face confers a jurisdiction and sets a standard separate and to some extent different from that of M.G.L.A. c. 240, § 10A, and M.G.L.A. c. 184, §§ 26 to 30, it is likely that the court would only apply it in a manner consistent with the application of those statutes as to unregistered land since there is no evident reason for treating registered land differently.

There are also practical and legal reasons for the Land Court to limit the application of M.G.L.A. c. 240, §§ 16 to 18. If the court determines that certain restrictions "ought not to be enforced" even though they are "valid and have not become inoperative," then it must determine whether any persons may be damaged by the non-enforcement thereof, and the case must be referred to the Superior Court for the assessment of such damages. The amount of damages so assessed must be paid into the Superior Court and payment certified to the Land Court before the restrictions may be voided. An appeal is provided for in M.G.L.A. c. 240, § 18. In considering the application of these provisions the Supreme Judicial Court has expressed doubts about their constitutionality or that of particular applications.[2]

§ 10:7 Disposing of other encumbrances

Sections 11 to 14A of M.G.L.A c. 240 authorizes the Court to determine the validity, or to define the nature and extent, of a "condition, restriction, reservation, stipulation or agree-

---

[Section 10:6]

[1]Walker v. Sanderson, 348 Mass. 409, 204 N.E.2d 108 (1965); Walker v. Gross, 362 Mass. 703, 290 N.E.2d 543 (1972); Garland v. Rosenschein, 2 L.C.R. 52 (1994).

[2]Riverbank Improvement Co. v. Chadwick, 228 Mass. 242, 117 N.E. 244 (1917); Peters v. Archambault, 361 Mass. 91 278 N.E.2d 729 (1972); and see Blakeley v. Gorin, 365 Mass. 590, 313 N.E.2d 903 (1974).

ment made or imposed more than thirty years prior to the commencement of the proceedings." As referred to in the preceding paragraph B, the petition may be brought by anyone having a freehold estate, or part thereof, whether vested or contingent, in possession or in reversion or remainder; or it may be brought by a former owner who conveyed with covenants of title or warranty. The defendant is "any person who might be entitled in any event to enforce [the particular encumbrance] or avail himself thereof."

The statute provides that if there are unknown respondents or classes of respondents whom it is "impracticable and unnecessary" to name and serve individually, they may be described generally. It also provides for the court to prescribe the notice to be given to such respondents, and that if there are respondents to be affected by the decree who have not had actual notice, the court shall appoint "a disinterested person to act for them." This language, which has not been changed since 1889, may be compared with that in §§ 6, 7 and 8 of M.G.L.A. c. 240, and would probably be construed so as to be consistent therewith.

This statute has been upheld as constitutional.[1] The court said in 1899 that a proceeding under it was "rather equitable than legal,"[2] and in 1904 that it was "at law"[3] and in 1915 that it did not deprive the superior court of its jurisdiction in equity to remove clouds on title.[4]

This statute applies only to an encumbrance which "appears of record" and it does not apply to claims of adverse possession or prescriptive rights.[5] A record easement is within the meaning of the section, although not specifically mentioned.[6]

§ 10:8 Testing the validity and extent of zoning provisions

Under M.G.L.A. c. 240, § 14A, referred to in M.G.L.A. c. 185, § 1(j1/2), the Land Court has exclusive jurisdiction, as it

[Section 10:7]

[1]Whiteside v. Merchants' Nat. Bank of Boston, 284 Mass. 165, 187 N.E. 706 (1933); Crocker v. Cotting, 173 Mass. 68, 53 N.E. 158 (1899).

[2]Crocker v. Cotting, 173 Mass. 68, 53 N.E. 158 (1899).

[3]American Unitarian Ass'n v. Minot, 185 Mass. 589, 71 N.E. 551 (1904).

[4]McArthur v. Hood Rubber Co., 221 Mass. 372, 109 N.E. 162 (1915).

[5]New England Home for Deaf Mutes v. Leader Filling Stations Corporation, 276 Mass. 153, 177 N.E. 97 (1931); Crocker v. Cotting, 173 Mass. 68, 53 N.E. 158 (1899).

[6]Levenson v. Ciampa, 251 Mass. 379, 146 N.E. 681 (1925).

has had since 1934, to render a judgment on the validity of a zoning ordinance or by-law and the extent to which it affects the land of a petitioner. The adoption in 1975 of a new zoning act under M.G.L.A. c. 40A, which conferred enforcement jurisdiction on the Superior Court (subsequently shared with the Land Court), did not alter or impede the application of the statute or the Land Court's exclusive and broad jurisdiction, emphasized by the Supreme Judicial Court.[1]

In order to maintain this action, the petitioner must own a freehold estate in possession in land of which the use, enjoyment, improvement or development is affected by the zoning law in question. Suits by former owners have been rejected,[2] but the holder of an unforeclosed right of redemption in a tax title was held to have standing.[3] The remedy applies to an "ordinance, by-law or regulation" or "any special law relating to zoning." It is not clear what is meant in this context by a "regulation" but the jurisdiction does not extend to subdivision regulations or to historic district regulations.[4] However, the reference to a "special law relating to zoning" does make the statute applicable to Boston as well as to other cities and towns. The respondent in such an action is the city or town in which the affected land is located. The statute is broadly construed.[5]

The statute provides that for this remedy there is no prerequisite of any controversy,[6] or of application for any permit or license, or preparation of plans of any proposed improvements. The Land Court has, however, shown some reluctance to decide on application of a zoning provision to a verbally described project without presentation of some

---

[Section 10:8]

[1]Harrison v. Town of Braintree, 355 Mass. 651, 247 N.E.2d 356 (1969); Sisters of Holy Cross of Mass. v. Town of Brookline, 347 Mass. 486, 198 N.E.2d 624 (1964).

[2]Lewis v. Town of Leverett, 5 L.C.R. 116 (1997); Tara Leigh Development Corporation v. Town of North Andover, 7 L.C.R. 254 (1999).

[3]Hanna v. Town of Framingham, 60 Mass. App. Ct. 420, 802 N.E.2d 1061 (2004).

[4]Ranieri v. Planning Board, 2 L.C.R. 73 (1994); Lasell College v. City of Newton, 13 L.C.R. 331 (2005).

[5]Harrison v. Town of Braintree, 355 Mass. 651, 247 N.E.2d 356 (1969); Mantoni v. Board of Appeals of Harwich, 34 Mass. App. Ct. 273, 609 N.E.2d 502 (1993), in which the court held that constitutional issues could be raised under the statute without notice to the attorney general; but see Rattigan v. Wile, 3 L.C.R. 99 (1995), 445 Mass. 850 (2006), in which the court rejected a "pre-emptive attack" by an abutter.

[6]Harrison v. Town of Braintree, 355 Mass. 651, 247 N.E.2d 356 (1969); Woods v. City of Newton, 349 Mass. 373, 208 N.E.2d 508 (1965); Radcliffe College v. City of Cambridge, 350 Mass. 613, 215 N.E.2d 892 (1966).

plans.[7]

Even where the petitioner's land itself is not subject to the zoning law which he seeks to have determined, it has been held that he may maintain an action under this statute if that zoning law applies to neighboring land in a manner which could affect the "use, enjoyment, improvement or development" of the petitioner's land.[8] This principle could apply in proper circumstances even when the land directly affected by the zoning regulation does not abut the petitioner's land. However, the proper remedy for declaratory relief by one landowner to determine the validity of a zoning by-law as applied to land of another landowner lies in the superior court under M.G.L.A. c. 231A.[9] If there is in fact a justiciable controversy, the Land Court proceeding under M.G.L.A. c. 240, § 14A, may be deemed inappropriate.[10] However, the question of whether there is or is not a controversy may often depend on the court's determination of the validity or applicability of the zoning provision in question, and it certainly is desirable to avoid multiplicity of actions on the same subject. Consequently, it would seem desirable and sensible for the Land Court to exercise its powers within their proper scope to permit the joinder of parties, other than the city or town, who are potentially affected landowners.

Once a petition is pending under this statute, it may be amended to present facts arising after it was filed such as subsequently adopted zoning provisions.[11] When a petitioner seeks to have a zoning law declared invalid, the burden is on him to show the invalidity.[12]

Some of the leading cases brought under this statute have led to important points of substantive zoning law, and they are consequently discussed in **Chapter 11**.

---

[7]Trustees of Tufts College v. City of Medford, 33 Mass. App. Ct. 580, 602 N.E.2d 1105, 78 Ed. Law Rep. 493 (1992), aff'd, 415 Mass. 753, 616 N.E.2d 433, 84 Ed. Law Rep. 430 (1993).

[8]Harrison v. Town of Braintree, 355 Mass. 651, 247 N.E.2d 356 (1969); Hansen & Donahue, Inc. v. Town of Norwood, 61 Mass. App. Ct. 292, 809 N.E.2d 1079 (2004).

[9]Noonan v. Moulton, 348 Mass. 633, 204 N.E.2d 897 (1965).

[10]Woods v. City of Newton, 349 Mass. 373, 208 N.E.2d 508 (1965); but see Clark & Clark Hotel Corp. v. Building Inspector of Falmouth, 20 Mass. App. Ct. 206, 479 N.E.2d 699 (1985).

[11]Schertzer v. City of Somerville, 345 Mass. 747, 189 N.E.2d 555 (1963).

[12]Anderson v. Town of Wilmington, 347 Mass. 302, 197 N.E.2d 682 (1964); see Mahoney v. City of Chelsea, 20 Mass. App. Ct. 91, 478 N.E.2d 160 (1985).

§ 10:9 Other curative proceedings

• **Flats**. M.G.L.A. c. 240, §§ 19 to 26, referred to in M.G.L.A. c. 185, § 1(h), contains provision for determination of the lines and boundaries of ownership of land or flats adjacent to or covered by high water." This action lies in the Land Court, which may but is not required to, appoint commissioners to hear and report on the subject. The determination of the court is final, but does not affect any right or title of the commonwealth to any flat unless it consents to become a party to the proceeding. Costs are to be apportioned among the parties according to the value, not the area, of their respective interests.

• **Fiduciary Acts**. Under M.G.L.A. c. 240, §§ 27 and 28, referred to in M.G.L.A. c. 185, § 1(g), the Land Court may, upon petition of a person purporting to have power or authority created by a written instrument "in a representative or fiduciary capacity or otherwise" to sell, convey, mortgage or otherwise transfer any interest in real estate, determine the existence and extent of power or authority to do the acts proposed by the petitioner. The Probate Courts have similar powers, as referred to in § **6:33**.

• **Other**. M.G.L.A. c. 185, § 1 contains references to other matters with respect to which the Land Court has jurisdiction, either exclusive or concurrent, including: procedures for foreclosure of or redemption from tax titles under M.G.L.A. c. 60, discussed in § **2:5**; writs of entry under M.G.L.A. c. 237; petitions to determine county and municipal boundaries under M.G.L.A. c. 42, § 12; and suits in equity under certain provisions of M.G.L.A. c. 214, § 3, or M.G.L.A. c. 109A, § 9, or otherwise "where any right, title or interest in land is involved, and suits in equity for specific performance."

Furthermore, certain probate court proceedings often have the purpose or effect of being curative of a land title problem. Partition, discussed in § **6:41**, is among these. With respect to out-of-state decedent landowners, ancillary administration may be a necessary curative step. And the application of cy-pres to a charitable trust may also be regarded in some instances as a curative procedure.[1]

§ 10:10 Curative instruments

Sometimes title defects can be cleared or outmoded or inapplicable encumbrances can be disposed of by voluntary

---

[Section 10:9]
[1]Cohen v. City of Lynn, 33 Mass. App. Ct. 271, 598 N.E.2d 682 (1992).

instruments without judicial proceedings. Recognizing that most title defects arise from lack of carefulness or foresight in the first place, it is often worthwhile to try to patch things up first. If the holder of an old mortgage or other encumbrance can be tracked down, he may upon request give a discharge or release. If there are problems of description or location, abutting landowners may join in preparation and recording of a plan and boundary agreement. Where there are restrictions of uncertain applicability or doubtful benefit, the persons putatively entitled to enforce them may agree to waive them or give approval for a particular use or structure. And when a way is of doubtful status as to its origins by grant, implication, prescription or necessity, the parties affected may give it the status of a granted easement by appropriate instrument of record.

If one begins his quest to cure or correct a title by seeking voluntary instruments, and fails, he may, of course, still have his day in court. Since the judicial proceeding will always involve notice, one rarely needs to worry, in seeking voluntary instruments, about needlessly disturbing sleeping dogs or yielding a tactical advantage.

If the instruments obtained do not themselves adequately relate to or tie in with the chain of title sought to be cured or corrected, an affidavit under M.G.L.A. c. 183, § 5A or § 5B will often solve that problem. Section 5A provides for a sworn statement with respect to a person's marital status, kinship or date of birth or death relating to a land title, and § 5B provides for an affidavit of any facts made by any person having knowledge, which facts are certified by an attorney to be relevant to a land title and of benefit and assistance in clarifying the title chain. As noted in § **6:25**, such an affidavit may not be used as a stealth lis pendens, an obvious abuse which led to a statute barring it.

TOPIC C: CURATIVE STATUTES

§ 10:11   Retrospective

When driving along a smooth, straight highway, one may not recall, or ever have known, that it was formerly a windy, bumpy gravel road. The paving done decades before is no longer recognized as a significant improvement in the transportation system. In the same way, statutes adopted in past decades may not still be recognized as curative of snags and snarls in conveyancing practice. As we navigate today, we understandably complain about the current impediments—such as heavy traffic and high tolls—and take for granted the facility of the present highway—or the present conveyancing systems.

Nevertheless, it is worth reviewing the curative statutes of past decades. An awareness of the issues and problems that have been dealt with or overcome may contribute to our understanding of the nature of the conveyancing art, and may help us design further improvements for the future.

§ 10:12 Outdated mortgages

M.G.L.A. c. 260, §§ 33 to 35,[1] provide that after the expiration of 35 years from the recording of a mortgage "in which no term of the mortgage is stated," or 5 years from a stated maturity, it may no longer be foreclosed, by sale or possession unless within such period an extension, or an acknowledgment or affidavit of non-satisfaction of the mortgage, is recorded in the registry of deeds. The recording of such an acknowledgment or affidavit effects continuation of the mortgage claim for 5 years, which may be renewed for successive 5-year periods by further recordings.

Extensions and acknowledgments of nonsatisfaction are effective only if signed by a current record owner of the affected real estate, identify the record of the mortgage and state that the property is subject to the unsatisfied mortgage. An affidavit of nonsatisfaction must be executed by the holder of the mortgage, contain similar identification thereof and of the current record owner, and state the amount believed to be unpaid. The periods are not extended by nonresidence or disability of any person interested in the mortgage or the real estate, by a partial payment, or by any other action not meeting the specific requirements of the statute.

The statute provides that: "Upon the expiration of the period provided herein, the mortgage shall be considered discharged for all purposes without the necessity of further action by the owner of the equity of redemption or any other persons having an interest in the mortgaged property and, in the case of registered land, upon the payment of the fee for the recording of a discharge, the mortgage shall be marked as discharged on the relevant memorandum of encumbrances in the same manner as for any other mortgage duly discharged."

[Section 10:12]

[1]As amended by Chapter 63, § 6, Acts of 2006.

Other aspects of discharge of mortgages are discussed in § **20:30**.

§ 10:13 Long-term leases

Under M.G.L.A. c. 186, § 1, a statute first enacted in 1834, a lease for a term of 100 years or more, so long as 50 years thereof remains unexpired, is regarded as a fee simple for various specified purposes, and the holder thereof is to be regarded as a freeholder.[1] Under M.G.L.A. c. 184, § 19, as amended in 1956, a reversion under such a lease created before January 2, 1956, is barred, unless a person holding the right of reversion recorded a sworn statement prior to January 1, 1966, specifying the land, the instrument creating the reversion, and the current owner, and in the case of registered land, the certificate of title number. The statute expressly applies even to rights held by a government or persons under disability. It expressly excludes leases with less than 50 years of the term unexpired, and any lease under M.G.L.A. c. 186, § 1, on which rent has been paid or tendered to the reversionary owner within twenty years prior to January 1, 1957.

§ 10:14 Limits on restrictions

Since 1887 Massachusetts law, now embodied in M.G.L.A. c. 184, § 23, has limited to 30 years the enforcement of restrictions which are "unlimited as to time" by the terms thereof. The modern statutes, considered generally in **Chapter 15**, contain many complex provisions, and it is here noted only that (a) pre-1962 restrictions are now subject to an overall 50 year limitation unless extended by a recorded notice, and (b) since 1965 there has been a 6 year statute of limitations on actions under restrictions to compel removal, alteration or relocation of any structure, all as described in more detail in **Chapter 15**.

§ 10:15 Limits on attachments and levies

Under M.G.L.A. c. 223, § 114A, attachments expire in six years from the date made unless brought forward, and under M.G.L.A. c. 236, § 49A, levies expire in six years from the date made unless brought forward or completed. A recording to bring an attachment or levy forward is indexed under the

---

[Section 10:13]

[1]In 1834 only freeholders had the vote.

name of the debtor, not the record owner of the affected real estate at the time of the recording. Under M.G.L.A. c. 223, § 115A, attachments are dissolved if no service is made on the defendant, unless notice is given as the court may order within 60 days after entry of the action.

The Massachusetts statutes providing for prejudgment attachment of real estate without notice or hearing in a judicial proceeding[1] were declared in 1973 to be an unconstitutional violation of the due process clause.[2] The legislature has not changed the statutes, but the issuance of attachments in judicial proceedings is now governed by a rule of civil procedure.

§ 10:16 Limits on right of entry and possibility of reverter

M.G.L.A. c. 184A, § 3, as enacted in 1954, limited to 30 years the period in which a right of entry or possibility of reverter created after January 1, 1955 might be asserted. That principle was carried forward in the new statutory rule against perpetuities adopted in 1989, providing in § 7 of the new Chapter 184A that: "A fee simple determinable in land or a fee simple in land subject to a right of entry for condition broken shall become a fee simple absolute if the specified contingency does not occur within thirty years from the date when such fee simple determinable or such fee simple subject to a right of entry becomes possessory. If such contingency occurs within said 30 years the succeeding interest, which may be an interest in a person other than the person creating the interest or his heirs,[1] shall become possessory or the right of entry exercisable notwithstanding the rule against perpetuities." By § 9 of the present Chapter 184A the first sentence of the quoted provision is made applicable to pre-1955 limitations as well as those subsequently created.

M.G.L.A. c. 260, § 31A, enacted in 1956, barred rights of entry and possibilities of reverter created prior to January 2, 1955, unless prior to January 1, 1964, the holder of such interest either took possession pursuant thereto or recorded a notice in the registry of deeds, indexed in the name of the

---

[Section 10:15]

[1]M.G.L.A. c. 223, §§ 42, 62 to 66.

[2]Bay State Harness Horse Racing & Breeding Ass'n, Inc. v. PPG Industries, Inc., 365 F. Supp. 1299 (D. Mass. 1973).

[Section 10:16]

[1]This reverses the common law rule prohibiting assignment rights of entry for condition broken. Walorz v. Town of Braintree, 2 L.C.R. 53 (1994).

current record owner, describing the affected land and the nature of the right claimed, and specifying the instrument creating it and place of record thereof. The statute provides that it does not apply to a reversionary interest owned by the commonwealth.

These statutes have been construed and applied in several contexts.[2]

In addition, M.G.L.A. c. 184, § 23B, renders void any right of entry or possibility of reverter which "directly or indirectly limits the use or occupancy of real property" on proscribed discriminatory bases.

§ 10:17   Limits on zoning enforcement

M.G.L.A. c. 40A, § 7, sets forth a 6-year statute of limitations barring suit on account of zoning requirements to compel the abandonment, limitation or modification of a use allowed by a building permit issued by a person duly authorized to issue such permits, and a 10-year statute of limitations barring suit to compel removal, alteration, or relocation of any structure by reason of any zoning violation, whether arising under the statute, a zoning by-law or ordinance, or a variance or special permit. It has been held that structures are protected by the 10-year provision, but not use.[1] A sign was not protected by the 6-year statute because it was not erected pursuant to a building permit, nor by the 10-year statute because it was not a structure.[2] These limitations are sometimes interrelated with "grandfather" provisions, as discussed in **Chapter 11**.[3]

---

[2]Boston Waterfront Development Corp. v. Com., 378 Mass. 629, 393 N.E.2d 356 (1979); Oak's Oil Service, Inc. v. Massachusetts Bay Transp. Authority, 15 Mass. App. Ct. 593, 447 N.E.2d 27 (1983); Harrison v. Marcus, 396 Mass. 424, 486 N.E.2d 710 (1985); Howson v. Crombie Street Congregational Church, 412 Mass. 526, 590 N.E.2d 687 (1992); Carlson v. Czerpik, 3 L.C.R. 58 (1995).

[Section 10:17]

[1]Lord v. Zoning Bd. of Appeals of Somerset, 30 Mass. App. Ct. 226,

567 N.E.2d 954 (1991); Lynch v. Zoning Board of Appeals of Waltham, 2 L.C.R. 93 (1993); Flynn v. Barnstable Zoning Board of Appeals, 6 L.C.R. 215 (1998); Feuer v. Stoneham Board of Appeals, 9 L.C.R. 326 (2001).

[2]Wagner v. Bd. of Appeals of Acton, 2 L.C.R. 141 (1994).

[3]Moreis v. Oak Bluffs Bd. of Appeals, 62 Mass. App. Ct. 53, 814 N.E.2d 1132 (2004); Bruno v. Board of Appeals of Wrentham, 62 Mass. App. Ct. 527, 818 N.E.2d 199 (2004).

§ 10:18 Elimination of dower and curtesy, and worthier title; limitation of claims of pretermitted issue

Since January 1, 1966, dower (by statute including curtesy) have been limited to property owned by a husband or wife at death. While both spouses are living, either one who holds title separately may convey such title free of any claim of dower without any joinder or release by the other spouse. Under M.G.L.A. c. 189, § 1, encumbrances existing at the time of death have precedence over dower. Furthermore, an election of dower must be filed in the registry of probate within 6 months after the approval of the executor's or administrator's bond.

In 1973 M.G.L.A. c. 184, §§ 33A and 33B, abolished the ancient doctrine of worthier title. Pursuant thereto a limitation to heirs or next of kin of a grantor or testator takes effect according to its purport; they take as "purchasers" and are not subject to having their interests revoked by the grantor or by contrary interests created by the testator.[1]

Under M.G.L.A. c. 191, § 20, pretermitted issue may not take any share in real estate of the testator unless a claim of pretermission is filed in the registry of probate within one year after the approval of the executor's bond.[2]

§ 10:19 Limitation of claims of creditors, legatees, expenses, tax liens

M.G.L.A. c. 197, § 9, limits the time period for action by a creditor of a decedent to one year from date of death, and requires notice of the action to be filed in the registry of probate within that period.

Under M.G.L.A. c. 197, § 19, real estate of a deceased testator may not be sold for payment of a legacy unless a bill in equity for authority to do so is filed in the Probate Court within six years after the testator's death.

Under M.G.L.A. c. 202, § 20A, real estate of a deceased which is conveyed or mortgaged of record for value and in good faith is thereby protected against being taken on execution or sold to raise funds for payment of expenses of administration after six years from the giving of bond by the

---

[Section 10:18]

[1]See National Shawmut Bank of Boston v. Joy, 315 Mass. 457, 53 N.E.2d 113 (1944). The Rule in Shelley's Case was abolished long ago; M.G.L.A. c. 184, § 5; Knight v. Travell, 13 Mass. App. Ct. 1008, 433 N.E.2d 464 (1982).

[2]See REBA Title Standard 50.

executor or administrator, unless a license for sale is issued by the Probate Court pursuant to petition filed therefore within the six-year period.

As referred to in **§ 6:34**, M.G.L.A. c. 65, § 9, limits the Massachusetts inheritance tax lien to 10 years after the date of decedent's death, or with respect to a future interest, 10 years after accrual of the right of possession or enjoyment, unless within that period the commissioner commences enforcement action and gives notice thereof.

§ 10:20   Disposing of formal defects

M.G.L.A. c. 184, § 24, bars actions ten years after the recording of an instrument purporting to convey or affect a land title (excluding registered titles) on account of defects, irregularities or omissions with respect to seals, whether corporate or individual, acknowledgment, witnesses, attestations, proof of execution, time of execution, recital of consideration, residence address, or date, or authority of a person purporting to be president or treasurer of a corporation. This statute not only bars action unless it is brought within ten years and notice thereof is recorded, indexed and marginally noted on the instrument referred to, it also provides affirmatively that in the absence of such attack "such instrument and the record thereof shall notwithstanding any or all of such defects, irregularities and omissions, be effective for all purposes to the same extent as though the instrument and the record thereof had originally not been subject to the defect, irregularity or omission."[1]

While curing old defects affords assurance to land titles, ten years is a long time, and this statute provides no excuse for carelessness in drafting instruments today.

§ 10:21   Disposing of indefinite references

M.G.L.A. c. 184, § 25, defines an indefinite reference as "(1) a recital indicating directly or by implication that real estate may be subject to restrictions, easements, mortgages, encumbrances or other interests not created by instruments recorded in due course, (2) a recital or indication affecting a description of real estate which by excluding generally real estate previously conveyed or by being in general terms of a person's right, title or interest, or for any other reason, can

---

[Section 10:20]

[1]In Howson v. Crombie Street Congregational Church, 412 Mass. 526, 590 N.E.2d 687 (1992), the use of an acknowledgment in place of a statutorily prescribed jurat was held to be cured by this statute.

be construed to refer in a manner limiting the real estate described to any interest not created by instruments recorded in due course, (3) a description of a person as trustee or an indication that a person is acting as trustee, unless the instrument containing the description or indication either sets forth the terms of the trust or specifies a recorded instrument which sets forth its terms and the place in the public records where such instrument is recorded, and (4) any other reference to any interest in real estate, unless the instrument containing the reference either creates the interest referred to or specifies a recorded instrument by which the interest is created and the place in the public records where such instrument is recorded."

The statute further specifies that "recorded in due course" shall mean, in effect, recorded in the appropriate registry and indexed under the name of the owner of record of the affected real estate at the time of recording.

The operative words and effect of the statute, then, are simply to provide that no indefinite reference shall subject anyone not a party thereto to any interest in real estate, or put such person on inquiry, or constitute a cloud on title. The statute ends with the somewhat cryptic saving clause: "This section shall not apply to a reference to an instrument in a notice or statement permitted by law to be recorded instead of such instrument, nor to a reference to the secured obligation in a mortgage or other instrument appearing of record to be given as security, nor in any proceeding for enforcement of any warranty of title." It might also be noted that indefinite references are an indicia of carelessness in conveyancing practice.

Prior to this statute an indefinite reference may or may not have rendered a title unmarketable, depending on the circumstances, but the statute disposes of marketability doubts.[1] This statute does not impinge upon the implication of an easement which may arise from a recorded plan or from bounding of a parcel on a way, nor impair the creation of an easement by reservation in a recorded deed.[2]

M.G.L.A. c. 184, § 35, enacted in 2002, excludes from § 25 certain certificates of trustees of non-testamentary trusts. While aimed at facilitating conveyance of real estate held by such trusts, it may be seen to enshrine a type of indefinite reference arising out of less than careful conveyancing prac-

---

[Section 10:21]

[1]Mishara v. Albion, 341 Mass. 652, 171 N.E.2d 478 (1961).

[2]Labounty v. Vickers, 352 Mass. 337, 225 N.E.2d 333 (1967).

tices, and its effect on M.G.L.A. c. 184, § 34, discussed in the following paragraph 3, is unclear.

§ 10:22　Protecting against unrecorded trust instruments

When an instrument of conveyance (deed, mortgage, etc.) is recorded and was executed by a person or persons appearing of record to be a trustee or trustees (expressly excluding testamentary trustees), but the trust instrument itself or amendment instruments changing trustees or the like are not on record, M.G.L.A. c. 184, § 34, makes the instrument of conveyance effective and binding on the trust in favor of a purchaser or other person relying thereon in good faith, notwithstanding inconsistent provisions of the unrecorded trust or of unrecorded amendments, changes of trustees or other matters affecting the trust.[1] Furthermore, even if the trust is recorded, amendments, changes of trustees, etc., will have no effect on such a relying party unless they also are recorded and marginally noted on the trust. Finally, this statute protects a person relying in good faith against "any inadequacy in the consideration recited." It may be observed that many situations to which this statute would apply also involve an indefinite reference as defined in M.G.L.A. c. 184, § 25, but this statute possibly covers some circumstances which would not be protected by the indefinite reference statute.

The absence from the record of a trust instrument or related document is almost always the result of careless conveyancing, and it is worth noting that the Land Court does not tolerate it on registered land.

§ 10:23　Statutory Rule Against Perpetuities

The rule against perpetuities is governed in Massachusetts by M.G.L.A. c. 184A, first enacted in 1954 and extensively amended in 1989.[1] This is the Statutory Rule Against Perpetuities, a uniform law which entirely supersedes the common law rule against perpetuities. The basic concept remains that "A nonvested property interest is invalid unless when the interest is created, it is certain to vest or terminate no later than twenty-one years after the death of an individual

---

[Section 10:22]

[1] Cf. Plunkett v. First Federal Sav. and Loan Ass'n of Boston, 18 Mass. App. Ct. 294, 464 N.E.2d 1381 (1984).

[Section 10:23]

[1] Ch. 668, Acts of 1989, effective June 30, 1990.

then alive." However, the statute adds a "wait-and-see" rule by which an interest is valid if in fact it vests or terminates within ninety years of its creation. Other salient points in the statute include the following: (a) the rule is expressly applied to powers of appointment; (b) the possibility that a child will be born to an individual after the individual's death is to be disregarded; (c) specifics are set forth for determining the time of creation of an interest in various circumstances; (d) provision is made for judicial reformation of certain otherwise invalid dispositions "in the manner that most closely approximates the transferor's manifested plan of distribution"; (e) the rule is not applicable to: (i) "nondonative" transfers except certain types specified in M.G.L.A. c. 184A, § 4, (ii) various fiduciary powers, (iii) interests held in succession by charities or governments, (iv) interests in the nature of pension plans and the like, and (v) interests which were not subject to the common law rule against perpetuities or were excluded by statute; (f) with respect to options, first refusals, leases to commence in the future, nonvested easements in gross, and fee simples determinable or subject to right of entry for condition broken, the statute sets a fixed thirty year period for exercise, commencement in possession or vesting;[2] and (g) the statute does not invalidate or modify any limitation which would have been valid prior to January 1, 1955 (except as to determinable and conditional fees, as to which see § **10:16**).

---

[2]Peterson v. Tremain, 35 Mass. App. Ct. 422, 621 N.E.2d 385 (1993).

Part III

DETERMINING THE STATUS OF USABILITY

Chapter 11

Zoning

TOPIC A: HISTORY AND SCOPE OF ZONING

TOPIC B: ADOPTION AND AMENDMENT

TOPIC C: NONCONFORMANCE

TOPIC D: ZONING FREEZES

TOPIC E: VARIANCE

TOPIC F: SPECIAL PERMIT

TOPIC G: JUDICIAL REVIEW

TOPIC H: ENFORCEMENT

TOPIC I: BOSTON ZONING

KeyCite®: Cases and other legal materials listed in KeyCite Scope can be researched through the KeyCite service on Westlaw®. Use KeyCite to check citations for form, parallel references, prior and later history, and comprehensive citator information, including citations to other decisions and secondary materials.

TOPIC A: HISTORY AND SCOPE OF ZONING

§ 11:1   History

Massachusetts first adopted a zoning enabling act in 1920 and similar laws were adopted throughout the United States in the following decades. From the outset the basic scheme involved the establishment within a community of districts or zones designated for different uses, provision for preservation of existing uses and structures which did not conform with the new requirements, and provision for the granting of variances and exceptions from the new requirements. The Massachusetts statute was judicially approved before enactment and upheld afterwards.[1] A zoning law of that type adopted in Euclid, Ohio, was upheld as nationally constitu-

---

[Section 11:1]

[1]In re Opinion of the Justices, 234 Mass. 597, 127 N.E. 525 (1920); Building Inspector of Lowell v. Stoklosa, 250 Mass. 52, 145 N.E. 262 (1924).

tional in 1926.[2] The common reference to "Euclidian Zoning" refers to that case and not to the ancient Greek mathematician, although some of his geometric concepts may at times be discerned in zoning laws.

The zoning enabling laws have, in light of experience, continuing urbanization and new concepts of land use planning, been developed, amended, codified and recodified over the years. The original Massachusetts act was rewritten in 1933, again recodifed in 1954, and set forth in the present M.G.L.A. c. 40A in 1975, with many changes in each interim period and since 1975,[3] but with the essential scheme preserved. Zoning is in a sense the senior scheme of governmental land use and development control, followed in time, if not in importance or general impact, by subdivision control, wetland regulation and other environmental laws and regulations. Health and safety laws did to some extent precede zoning, but they have subsequently been broadened immensely in scope. All of these subjects are related, probably inextricably so, and modern zoning practice is often beset with problems of interrelation, and sometimes outright conflict, with other regulatory laws.

Consequently, despite the extensive legislative consideration and development of zoning laws and the extensive judicial consideration[4] of the many aspects of zoning, we cannot now regard zoning as a finished or settled art. One of the burdens of real estate development today, whether residential, commercial, industrial, institutional or governmental, is the need for multiple permits and approvals. In the area of zoning itself there is a significant and persistent trend, in the statute and in local zoning by-laws and ordinances adopted thereunder, toward the granting of special permits as the prerequisite to almost any real estate development—accompanied of course by a decline in the specification within the law itself of uses and structures which are permitted as a matter of right. Whether or not one has philosophical qualms about a shift from a government of laws to a government of men, it is inescapable that this trend makes real

---

[2]Village of Euclid, Ohio v. Ambler Realty Co., 272 U.S. 365, 47 S. Ct. 114, 71 L. Ed. 303, 4 Ohio L. Abs. 816, 54 A.L.R. 1016 (1926).

[3]Ch. 269, Acts of 1933; Ch. 368, Acts of 1954; Ch. 808, Acts of 1975. The many changes since 1975 are not listed here, but are referred to in the text or footnotes where they are deemed pertinent in light of prior case law.

[4]Complete listings of zoning decisions are annexed to the Massachusetts Zoning Manual, published by Massachusetts Continuing Legal Education, New England Law Institute, Inc., a most useful and comprehensive source of information about zoning law and practice.

estate development a much more "lawyer intensive" activity.

The practicing real estate lawyer must, therefore, become familiar with the subject of zoning in all its aspects, and that is a formidable task. The following sections of this chapter should not be taken as more than a beginning.

§ 11:2 Purposes

The present zoning statute, M.G.L.A. c. 40A, does not set forth the purposes of zoning. Chapter 808 of the Acts of 1975, by which it was adopted, specified its own purposes to be modernization and standardization of local zoning laws and implementation of the Home Rule Amendment to the Massachusetts Constitution,[1] and "suggests" that the objectives of zoning include protection of health and safety; lessening of congestion, overcrowding and concentration; facilitating provision of municipal services, schools and parks; encouraging housing for persons of all income levels; conserving property values and natural resources; and encouraging appropriate land use.

The types of local laws to be adopted to achieve such objectives are defined in Chapter 808 as including, but not limited to, laws restricting, prohibiting, permitting or regulating: uses of land, including wetlands, lands subjected to flooding, bodies of water and water courses; noxious uses; size, height, bulk, location and use of buildings and other structures; and signs, except those subject to M.G.L.A. c. 93, §§ 29 to 33 and to M.G.L.A. c. 93D; areas and dimensions of land and waters to be occupied or unoccupied by uses and structures; population density and intensity of use; accessory facilities and uses; and development of natural, scenic and aesthetic qualities.

The Home Rule Amendment vests police power, upon which zoning rests, directly in the cities and towns. Consequently, it is said that M.G.L.A. c. 40A is no longer actually an enabling act, but is a regulatory law which prescribes procedures by which communities may adopt and administer zoning laws. It follows that the scope of the local zoning power is not determined solely by historical or traditional concepts of zoning, but rather by the scope of the police power itself.

[Section 11:2]

[1]Article 89 of the Articles of Amendment, adopted in 1966.

§ 11:3 Examples

As every zoning practitioner knows, there is a great deal of diversity among local zoning laws, some of which exhibit considerable ingenuity. At the same time they are replete with standardized terms, such as "frontage," "height," "family" and "accessory use," variously defined. In view of the broad scope of the local police power under the Home Rule Amendment, the courts do not often revoke local zoning laws (except when they violate specific limitations, as referred to below), but they are often called upon to interpret the meaning and applicability of particular provisions.

A few interesting examples are as follows:
- When "frontage" was undefined, the court said it must have a "common and approved meaning" and rejected the combination of segments of continuity of land with a way, separated by land of intervening owners.[1] The importance of a frontage requirement is illustrated in the *Amberwood* case,[2] discussed below. The related requirements as to lot area were considered in *Petrillo*,[3] upholding a two-town lot on a finding of ambiguity in the bylaw, and in *Zanghi*,[4] involving exclusion of wetland area. And the very meaning of "lot" in the Cambridge zoning ordinance made a big difference to one developer.[5]
- As to the height of a building, the court rejected as irrational a measurement from the bed of an adjacent stream.[6] The court also rejected application of a height limitation to poles holding netting to catch errant golf balls.[7]
- Brookline's bylaw provided that "a group of five or more persons who are not within the second degree of kinship to each other . . . shall not be deemed to constitute a family," but the court held a household group comprising a mother, two sisters, their husbands and twelve children to

---

[Section 11:3]

[1]Valcourt v. Zoning Bd. of Appeals of Swansea, 48 Mass. App. Ct. 124, 718 N.E.2d 389 (1999).

[2]Amberwood Development Corp. v. Board of Appeals of Boxford, 65 Mass. App. Ct. 205, 837 N.E.2d 1161 (2005).

[3]Petrillo v. Zoning Bd. of Appeals of Cohasset, 65 Mass. App. Ct. 453, 841 N.E.2d 266 (2006), review denied, 446 Mass. 1106, 844 N.E.2d 1097 (2006).

[4]Zanghi v. Board of Appeals of Bedford, 61 Mass. App. Ct. 82, 807 N.E.2d 221 (2004).

[5]North Shore Realty Trust v. Com., 434 Mass. 109, 747 N.E.2d 107 (2001).

[6]McLendon v. Town of Stockbridge, 13 L.C.R. 241 (2005).

[7]Golftown, Inc. v. Bd. of Selectmen of Saugus, 5 L.C.R. 166 (1997).

be a permissible "single housekeeping unit."[8]

• The Appeals Court defined "accessory use" as a use which is "incidental," "subordinate," or "attendant or concomitant" to the principal use.[9] The Land Court rejected conversion of an apartment building into an assisted living facility because the required health-care part of the facility was not a permitted accessory use under the zoning ordinance,[10] but found a food service operation in a Costco store to be a lawful accessory use and not a fast-food establishment within the meaning of the zoning bylaw.[11] Upon challenge by a competitor the Land Court also upheld service bays as accessory in an auto parts store, observing that the purposes of zoning do not include "stifling competition."[12]

• In the absence of express permission in the zoning bylaw, the Land Court denied approval of a common driveway to serve several lots.[13] The Land Court also construed a zoning ordinance to allow a lawyer and his support staff, but not other associated lawyers, to use an office in the lawyer's residence, but the Appeals Court allowed employed associate lawyers also to use the office, holding that the ordinance language did not constitute an "express limitation."[14] The Appeals Court also held that a zoning provision that uses not specifically permitted are deemed prohibited did not bar permitting under a non-zoning earth removal bylaw.[15]

• Issues of conflict with other laws have been considered in a number of cases. The existence of a related town bylaw was held not to preclude application of a zoning bylaw.[16] A bylaw regulating trailers was upheld as a valid exercise of police power under the Home Rule Amendment even though the bylaw was not adopted in compliance with the

---

[8]Wolfson v. Town of Brookline, 9 L.C.R. 467 (2001).

[9]Gallagher v. Board of Appeals of Acton, 44 Mass. App. Ct. 906, 687 N.E.2d 1277 (1997).

[10]Apt Asset Management, Inc. v. Melrose Bd. of Appeals, 5 L.C.R. 178 (1997).

[11]Price Costco, Inc. v. Danvers Zoning Bd. of Appeals, 6 L.C.R. 107 (1998).

[12]Caruso v. City of Revere, 6 L.C.R. 212 (1998); see also Pep-Boys-Manny, Moe & Jack of Delaware,

Inc. v. Bd. of Aldermen of Everett, 6 L.C.R. 259 (1998).

[13]RHB Development, Inc. v. Duxbury Zoning Bd. of Appeals, 5 L.C.R. 166 (1997).

[14]Cunha v. City of New Bedford, 47 Mass. App. Ct. 407, 713 N.E.2d 385 (1999).

[15]Jaworski v. Earth Removal Bd. of Millville, 35 Mass. App. Ct. 795, 626 N.E.2d 19 (1994).

[16]Toda v. Board of Appeals of Manchester, 18 Mass. App. Ct. 317, 465 N.E.2d 277 (1984).

Zoning Act.[17] A board of health regulation attacked as a usurpation of zoning power was held valid, the court saying that ". . . different sources of land use control—zoning, planning, environmental controls, health regulations—overlap."[18]

§ 11:4   Special types

As noted by the Appeals Court, there are overlapping sources of land use control. The governmental regulations discussed in **Chapter 14**, are in that category, and in many respects they have a direct relationship to zoning. The Martha's Vineyard Commission and the Cape Cod Commission have powers of regulation which are equivalent to or have an effect similar to zoning laws. Land use is affected by the laws regulating manufactured housing, former railroad rights of way, solar energy systems, community preservation, governmental preemption rights, and of course "impact fees" or "linkage" payments. More specifically related to zoning are the provisions of M.G.L.A. c. 40B and of the federal Telecommunications Act, discussed in paragraph C of this section.

Also in the special category are "rate of development" bylaws adopted by several communities. In *Sturges v. Town of Chilmark,*[1] the SJC upheld the authority of a town to "impose reasonable time limitations on development, at least where those restrictions are temporary and adopted to provide controlled development while the municipality engages in comprehensive planning studies." In a wide-ranging decision (which should be considered required reading by every student of zoning law) Justice Wilkins upheld such a law as authorized by the statute and as constitutional. Such a bylaw in Blackstone was upheld.[2] The bylaw in Hadley was voided as failing to meet the test of *Sturges* because the Town had failed to implement an adopted plan for over ten years, leading the SJC to announce that "absent exceptional circumstances not present here," restrictions of unlimited duration on rate of development are "unconstitutional."[3] The application of a Templeton rate-of-development bylaw to a

---

[17]Cherkes v. Town of Westport, 393 Mass. 9, 468 N.E.2d 269 (1984).

[18]Hamel v. Board of Health of Edgartown, 40 Mass. App. Ct. 420, 664 N.E.2d 1199 (1996).

[Section 11:4]

[1]Sturges v. Town of Chilmark, 380 Mass. 246, 402 N.E.2d 1346 (1980).

[2]Advanced Development Concepts, Inc. v. Town of Blackstone, 33 Mass. App. Ct. 228, 597 N.E.2d 1372 (1992).

[3]Zuckerman v. Town of Hadley, 442 Mass. 511, 813 N.E.2d

61-lot subdivision was barred.[4]

A new category of "smart growth zoning district" was established by Ch. 141, Acts of 2005, under which a community may be eligible for "density bonus payments" under M.G.L.A. c. 40R.

§ 11:5   General limitations

As noted above, the scope of the municipal zoning power is governed essentially by the scope of the police power itself. Prior to the adoption of the Home Rule Amendment and the present M.G.L.A. c. 40A, the zoning power of the municipalities did derive from the predecessor zoning statute which prescribed specific purposes. Consequently, there is a body of judicial decisions which considered local zoning laws from the standpoint of compliance with the statute. These decisions are nevertheless still of interest because the courts generally upheld increasingly restrictive and diverse regulations, and justified them on general principles of reasonableness and on the scope of the police power, both of which remain applicable.

As Justice Wilkins said in *Sturges v. Town of Chilmark*: "The constitutional test . . . is whether the bylaw is clearly arbitrary and unreasonable, having no substantial relation to the public health, safety, morals, or general welfare," adding that "[The court's] role in review of zoning enactments is limited," and that "Every presumption is made in favor of the by-law, and, if its reasonableness is fairly debatable, it will be sustained," citing a number of decisions, many of which are cited in this section. Even when there is an allegation of violation of a constitutionally protected right, and especially when there is not, a heavy burden of proof of invalidity is on the person contesting the law or its application.

Abiding by those principles, the courts have sometimes, but not often, voided zoning laws or found them inapplicable in particular situations, considered under the following rubrics:

  • **Nexus.** In a few cases a reasonable nexus between the zoning regulation and a proper public purpose which it is intended to serve was found to be lacking because of: lack of public purpose,[1] improper conception of public pur-

---

843 (2004).

[4]Lorden v. Town of Templeton, 13 L.C.R. 319 (2005).

[Section 11:5]

[1]Nectow v. City of Cambridge, 277 U.S. 183, 48 S. Ct. 447, 72 L.

pose,[2] inappropriate district designation,[3] or inappropriate application to particular parcels.[4]

- **Equal Protection.** Racial discrimination in violation of the equal protection clause of the 14th Amendment has long been banned.[5]
- **Free Speech.** Protection of freedom of expression has been considered in relation to zoning regulating "adult" entertainment. While § 9A of M.G.L.A. c. 40A provides for the issuance of special permits for "adult" establishments, the cases generally turn upon First Amendment issues. The modern tests, set down by the U.S. Supreme Court, are known as the *Renton* rule,[6] and provide in brief that zoning laws (i) may not ban such establishments entirely, (ii) must be "content neutral," (iii) may impose "time, place and manner" regulations, (iv) must be designed to serve a substantial governmental interest, and (v) must not unreasonably limit alternative avenues of communication. In Massachusetts the courts have sometimes found compliance with the *Renton* rule,[7] and have sometimes found bylaws unenforceable for failure to meet the tests.[8]
- **Privacy.** A Framingham Bylaw prohibiting "abortion clinics" was held invalid as in conflict with the constitutionally protected right of privacy as enunciated in *Roe v. Wade*.[9]
- **Regulatory Taking.** The issue of when the effect of

Ed. 842 (1928); City of Pittsfield v. Oleksak, 313 Mass. 553, 47 N.E.2d 930 (1943) reversing Nectow v. City of Cambridge, 260 Mass. 441, 157 N.E.2d 618 (1927).

[2]122 Main St. Corp. v. City of Brockton, 323 Mass. 646, 84 N.E.2d 13, 8 A.L.R.2d 955 (1949).

[3]Barney & Casey Co. v. Town of Milton, 324 Mass. 440, 87 N.E.2d 9 (1949).

[4]Jenckes v. Building Com'r of Brookline, 341 Mass. 162, 167 N.E.2d 757 (1960); Aronson v. Town of Sharon, 346 Mass. 598, 195 N.E.2d 341 (1964).

[5]Buchanan v. Warley, 245 U.S. 60, 38 S. Ct. 16, 62 L. Ed. 149 (1917).

[6]City of Renton v. Playtime Theatres, Inc., 475 U.S. 41, 106 S. Ct. 925, 89 L. Ed. 2d 29 (1986), citing Young v. American Mini

Theatres, Inc., 427 U.S. 50, 96 S. Ct. 2440, 49 L. Ed. 2d 310 (1976).

[7]Town of West Springfield v. Olympic Lounge, Inc., 45 Mass. App. Ct. 923, 700 N.E.2d 1198 (1998); and see G.J.T., Inc. v. Boston Licensing Bd., 397 Mass. 285, 491 N.E.2d 594 (1986).

[8]T & D Video, Inc. v. City of Revere, 423 Mass. 577, 670 N.E.2d 162 (1996); and see 66 Mass.App.Ct. 461 (2006); A.F.M., Ltd. v. City of Medford, 428 Mass. 1020, 704 N.E.2d 184 (1999); Erenberg v. Town of Provincetown, 11 L.C.R. 125 (2003) and 13 L.C.R. 5 (2005); and see Highland Tap of Boston, Inc. v. Commissioner of Consumer Affairs and Licensing of Boston, 33 Mass. App. Ct. 559, 602 N.E.2d 1095 (1992).

[9]Framingham Clinic, Inc. v. Board of Selectmen of Southborough, 373 Mass. 279, 367 N.E.2d

regulation is such as to constitute a taking requiring compensation is as old as Euclid. Even before that Justice Holmes said in 1922:

> [W]hile property may be regulated to a certain extent, if regulation goes too far it will be recognized as a taking . . . [A] strong public desire to improve the public condition is not enough to warrant achieving the desire by a shorter cut than the constitutional way of paying for the change . . . [T]his is a question of degree—and therefore cannot be disposed of by general propositions.[10]

In 1972, the SJC upheld a zoning provision "even though there was a 'substantial diminution' in the value of the land," subject to a cautionary concurrence to the effect that the issue of unlawful taking had not been decided.[11]

The issue was brought to the fore by the federal cases, *First English Evangelical*,[12] posing the issue of recovery of damages on account of temporary or subsequently rescinded governmental action, and *Lucas v. South Carolina Coastal Council*,[13] involving a regulation that deprived a parcel of all economically beneficial uses and thus constituted a taking. In Massachusetts the case of *Lopes v. City of Peabody*[14] involved a zoning law establishing a wetland conservancy district prohibiting construction below elevation of the 88.5 foot contour. The Land Court upheld the regulation as valid and held that it did not constitute a taking. Responding to *Lucas*, the SJC reopened the taking issue and remanded to the Land Court which then "amended and established" the conservancy district to be at elevation 86.6 feet, which permitted an economically beneficial use of plaintiff's land. Accordingly, the Land Court found there was no "perma-

---

606 (1977).

[10]Pennsylvania Coal Co. v. Mahon, 260 U.S. 393, 43 S. Ct. 158, 67 L. Ed. 322, 28 A.L.R. 1321 (1922), quoted in Aronson v. Town of Sharon, 346 Mass. 598, 195 N.E.2d 341 (1964) and in MacNeil v. Town of Avon, 386 Mass. 339, 435 N.E.2d 1043 (1982).

[11]Turnpike Realty Co. v. Town of Dedham, 362 Mass. 221, 284 N.E.2d 891 (1972); MacGibbon v. Board of Appeals of Duxbury, 356 Mass. 635, 255 N.E.2d 347 (1970).

[12]First English Evangelical Lutheran Church of Glendale v. Los Angeles County, Cal., 482 U.S. 304, 107 S. Ct. 2378, 96 L. Ed. 2d 250 (1987).

[13]Lucas v. South Carolina Coastal Council, 505 U.S. 1003, 112 S. Ct. 2886, 120 L. Ed. 2d 798 (1992).

[14]Lopes v. City of Peabody, 417 Mass. 299, 629 N.E.2d 1312 (1994) (overruled on other grounds by, Gove v. Zoning Bd. of Appeals of Chatham, 444 Mass. 754, 831 N.E.2d 865 (2005)).

nent regulatory taking," but observed that "there does appear to have been a temporary taking as recognized in [First English Evangelical]." In later decisions plaintiff was denied costs, but held entitled to refund of real estate taxes paid during the period of the temporary taking.

• **Spot Zoning.** The singling out of a particular tract for special treatment of no significant public benefit, called "spot zoning" is proscribed both on equal protection grounds and on the basis of the provision in M.G.L.A. c. 40A, § 4, that zoning "shall be uniform within [each] district for each class or kind of structures or uses permitted."[15] However, charges of violation of the statutory requirement of uniformity or of spot zoning have often been rejected.[16]

A bylaw provision requiring a special permit for every business use even in a district zoned for business was held to violate the uniformity requirement and also the provision in M.G.L.A. c. 40A, § 9 authorizing special permits

[15]Leahy v. Inspector of Buildings of City of New Bedford, 308 Mass. 128, 31 N.E.2d 436 (1941); Town of Marblehead v. Rosenthal, 316 Mass. 124, 55 N.E.2d 13 (1944); Lamarre v. Commissioner of Public Works of Fall River, 324 Mass. 542, 87 N.E.2d 211 (1949); Whittemore v. Building Inspector of Falmouth, 313 Mass. 248, 46 N.E.2d 1016 (1943); Smith v. Board of Appeals of Salem, 313 Mass. 622, 48 N.E.2d 620 (1943); Caputo v. Board of Appeals of Somerville, 331 Mass. 547, 120 N.E.2d 753 (1954); McHugh v. Board of Zoning Adjustment of Boston, 336 Mass. 682, 147 N.E.2d 761 (1958); Beal v. Building Commissioner of Springfield, 353 Mass. 640, 234 N.E.2d 299 (1968); Canteen Corp. v. City of Pittsfield, 4 Mass. App. Ct. 289, 346 N.E.2d 732 (1976); Mastriani v. Building Inspector of Monson, 19 Mass. App. Ct. 989, 475 N.E.2d 408 (1985); National Amusements, Inc. v. City of Boston, 29 Mass. App. Ct. 305, 560 N.E.2d 138 (1990); Andrews v. Town of Amherst, 13 L.C.R. 528 (2005).

[16]Caires v. Building Com'r of Hingham, 323 Mass. 589, 83 N.E.2d 550 (1949); Halko v. Board of Appeals of Billerica, 349 Mass. 465, 209 N.E.2d 323 (1965); Muto v. City of Springfield, 349 Mass. 479, 209 N.E.2d 319 (1965); Mahoney v. Commissioner of Public Works of Lowell, 351 Mass. 697, 218 N.E.2d 93 (1966); Barrett v. Building Inspector of Peabody, 354 Mass. 38, 234 N.E.2d 884 (1968); Martin v. Town of Rockland, 1 Mass. App. Ct. 167, 294 N.E.2d 469 (1973); Woodland Estates, Inc. v. Building Inspector of Methuen, 4 Mass. App. Ct. 757, 358 N.E.2d 468 (1976); Sullivan v. Town of Acton, 38 Mass. App. Ct. 113, 645 N.E.2d 700 (1995), in which the court rejected the spot zoning contention "although the case is close"; W.R. Grace & Co.-Conn. v. Cambridge City Council, 56 Mass. App. Ct. 559, 779 N.E.2d 141 (2002); Van Renselaar v. City of Springfield, 58 Mass. App. Ct. 104, 787 N.E.2d 1148 (2003), and Land Court decisions in 5 L.C.R. 33 (1997), 6 L.C.R. 81 and 113 (1998), 8 L.C.R. 32 (2000), 9 L.C.R. 342 (2001).

only for "specific types of uses."[17] Based on the SCIT rule, or violation of uniformity, the Land Court has rejected rezoning in several cases,[18] and in the *Lordan* case ingeniously saved an otherwise valid bylaw by prescribing a specific permit standard.

   ● **Contract Zoning.** Often related to spot zoning the issue of "contract zoning" was faced in 1962 when the court upheld Newton's rezoning of a tract based upon inducements and negotiated restrictions proffered by the land owner, Sylvania.[19] Since then the inducements openly proffered by land owners seeking zoning favors have escalated, and the courts have generally upheld the rezonings.[20] In the leading *McLean Hospital* case the Appeals Court said that nothing in the law prohibited a municipality from "negotiating" for "receipt of benefits for desirable public purposes" assuming that "those benefits have some reasonable relationship to the site governed by the zoning." In *Durand* the money offered was for school construction, having nothing to do with the applicant's power plant, and the Land Court therefore declared the rezoning invalid, but the SJC reversed, holding that "the voluntary offer of public benefits beyond what might be necessary to mitigate the development of a parcel of land does not, standing alone, invalidate a legislative act of the town meeting." Three Justices dissented from this reasoning, finding in the record that the "parties struck a bargain" amounting to "a sale of the police power." However, they concurred in the judgment on the ground that the plaintiffs lacked standing.

§ 11:6   Statutory limitations

   M.G.L.A. c. 40A, § 3, specifies eleven specific limitations on the zoning power and three more partial limitations. Some of these provisions have had significant effect on zoning prac-

---

[17]SCIT, Inc. v. Planning Bd. of Braintree, 19 Mass. App. Ct. 101, 472 N.E.2d 269 (1984).

[18]Avalon Properties, Inc. v. City of Peabody, 6 L.C.R. 327; O'Brien v. City of Quincy, 9 L.C.R. 199 (2001); Lordan v. Town of Pepperell, 11 L.C.R. 252 (2003).

[19]Sylvania Elec. Products, Inc. v. City of Newton, 344 Mass. 428, 183 N.E.2d 118 (1962).

[20]Rando v. North Attleborough, 4 L.C.R. 63 (1996), aff'd 44 Mass.App.Ct. 603, 692 N.E.2d 544 (1998); McLean Hospital Corporation v. Town of Belmont, 8 L.C.R. 155 (2000), aff'd 56 Mass.App.Ct. 540, 778 N.E.2d 1016 (2002); Durand v. IDC Bellingham LLC, 10 L.C.R. 36 (2002), revs'd 440 Mass. 45, 793 N.E.2d 359 (2003); Hanna v. Town of Framingham, 10 L.C.R. 183 (2002), aff'd 60 Mass.App.Ct. 420, 802 N.E.2d 1061 (2004).

tices, and have received considerable judicial attention. It is important to note that the wording of the statute differs with respect to various prohibited items. The proscription may be of laws that "regulate or restrict," or that "unreasonably regulate or restrict or require a special permit for", and some are coupled with qualifying provisos.

The items as to which zoning regulation is banned, subject to specified exceptions, are as follows:

• **Building Materials.** The "use of materials or methods of construction of structures regulated by the state building code." M.G.L.A. c. 23B, § 16, sets forth the building code applicable throughout the Commonwealth. Zoning in violation of this ban has been voided.[1]

• **Agriculture.** The "use of land for the principal purpose of agriculture, horticulture, floriculture or viticulture," or "the use, expansion or reconstruction of existing structures thereon for the primary purpose of agriculture, horticulture, floriculture or viticulture, including those facilities for sale of produce, and wine and dairy products, provided that during the months of June, July, August, and September of every year or during the harvest season of the primary crop raised on land of the owner or lessee, the majority of such products for sale, based on either gross sales dollars or volume, have been produced by the owner or lessee of the land on which the facility is located, except that all such activities may be limited to parcels of more than five acres in areas not zoned for agriculture, horticulture, floriculture or viticulture," and provided further that for such purposes "land divided by a public or private way or a waterway shall be construed as one parcel" and that "the term horticulture shall include the growing and keeping of nursery stock and the sale thereof," which "nursery stock shall be considered to be produced by the owner or lessee of the land if it is nourished, maintained and managed while on the premises."

The basic proscription as to agriculture, horticulture, floriculture and viticulture is that zoning shall not "prohibit, unreasonably regulate or require a special permit for the use of land for the primary purpose" thereof. The courts have taken a broad view (an "expansive construction" in the words of the Appeals Court) of what constitutes "agriculture," including the keeping of pigs, raising

---

[Section 11:6]

[1]Enos v. City of Brockton, 354 Mass. 278, 236 N.E.2d 919 (1968); Peters v. Yarmouth, 5 L.C.R. 126 (1997); Meadowbrooks Development Corp. v. Medway, 6 L.C.R. 110 (1998).

horses, raising dogs, a slaughterhouse, and also of the other specified activites.[2] Although for other purposes, the broad definition of farming and agriculture in M.G.L.A. c. 111, § 1, may be germane. The statute provides protection for "existing" structures, but new structures deemed necessary or incidental to an agricultural operation have also been protected.[3] The provision as to sale of produce has also be generously construed, but lines have been drawn.[4]

• **Wetlands.** The exemption of "land or structures from flood plain or wetlands regulations established pursuant to general law."

• **Residence Interior.** The "interior area of a single family residential building." It may be noted that some towns do permit a single family residence to contain a separate "mother-in-law apartment" with cooking facilities. Also, special permits issued for condominium developments often regulate the number of bedrooms permitted in the Units.

• **Religion and Education.** The "use of land or structures for religious purposes or for educational purposes on land owned or leased by the Commonwealth or any of its agencies, subdivisions or bodies politic or by a religious sect or denomination or by a nonprofit educational corporation; provided, however, that such land or structures may be subject to reasonable regulations concerning

---

[2]Building Inspector of Mansfield v. Curvin, 22 Mass. App. Ct. 401, 494 N.E.2d 42 (1986); Steege v. Board of Appeals of Stow, 26 Mass. App. Ct. 970, 527 N.E.2d 1176 (1988); Town of Sturbridge v. McDowell, 35 Mass. App. Ct. 924, 624 N.E.2d 114 (1993); Modern Continental Const. Co., Inc. v. Building Inspector of Natick, 42 Mass. App. Ct. 901, 674 N.E.2d 247 (1997); Viera v. Zoning Bd. Of Appeals of Basrnstable, 4 L.C.R. 285 (1996); Darley v. Halifax, 5 L.C.R. 121 (1997); Cataument Garden Center, Inc. v. Bd. of Appeals of Bourne, 5 L.C.R. 131 (1997); Jarvin v. Planning Bd. of West Newbury, 6 L.C.R. 225 (1998); Prime v. Zoning Bd. of Appeals of Norwell, 42 Mass. App. Ct. 796, 680 N.E.2d 118 (1997).

[3]Modern Continental Const. Co., Inc. v. Building Inspector of Natick, 42 Mass. App. Ct. 901, 674 N.E.2d 247 (1997); Prime v. Zoning Bd. of Appeals of Norwell, 42 Mass. App. Ct. 796, 680 N.E.2d 118 (1997); Town of Tisbury v. Martha's Vineyard Com'n, 27 Mass. App. Ct. 1204, 544 N.E.2d 230 (1989); Volandre v. Bd. of Appeals of Norwell, 13 L.C.R. 465 (2005); but see Ring Road Realty Trust v. Plympton, 1 L.C.R. 172 (1993); Henry v. Board of Appeals of Dunstable, 418 Mass. 841, 641 N.E.2d 1334 (1994); Scott v. Town of Hawley, 8 L.C.R. 461 (2001); Tanner v. Board of Appeals of Boxford, 61 Mass. App. Ct. 647, 813 N.E.2d 578 (2004).

[4]Prime v. Zoning Bd. of Appeals of Norwell, 42 Mass. App. Ct. 796, 680 N.E.2d 118 (1997); but see Von Jess v. Bd. of Appeals of Littleton, 1 L.C.R. 170 (1993); Building Inspector of Peabody v. Northeast Nursery, Inc., 418 Mass. 401, 636 N.E.2d 269 (1994).

the bulk and height of structures and determining yard sizes, lot area, setbacks, open space, parking and building coverage requirements."

This provision, called the Dover Amendment,[5] is undoubtedly the most salient and hotly contested limitation in the statute. The courts have given a broad interpretation to "education."[6] In the cited *Campbell* case, upholding the educational status of a group residence for elderly mentally ill persons, the court said that "the proper test in deciding whether a nonprofit corporation is an educational one is whether its articles of organization permit it to engage in educational activities."

The Dover Amendment does not expressly bar the requirement of a special permit for an educational use, but the courts have so declared, and similarly as to site plan approval, and incidentally, also as to lodging house licenses.[7]

Before 1975 the Dover Amendment dealt only with use and made no mention of dimensional or physical regulations. Two leading cases addressed the issue and set forth a rule that a dimensional requirement could not be

---

[5]Arising from Attorney General v. Inhabitants of Town of Dover, 327 Mass. 601, 100 N.E.2d 1 (1951).

[6]Kurz v. Board of Appeals of North Reading, 341 Mass. 110, 167 N.E.2d 627 (1960); Radcliffe College v. City of Cambridge, 350 Mass. 613, 215 N.E.2d 892 (1966); Harbor Schools, Inc. v. Board of Appeals of Haverhill, 5 Mass. App. Ct. 600, 366 N.E.2d 764 (1977); Fitchburg Housing Authority v. Board of Zoning Appeals of Fitchburg, 380 Mass. 869, 406 N.E.2d 1006 (1980); Commissioner of Code Inspection of Worcester v. Worcester Dynamy, Inc., 11 Mass. App. Ct. 97, 413 N.E.2d 1151 (1980); Worcester County Christian Communications, Inc. v. Board of Appeals of Spencer, 22 Mass. App. Ct. 83, 491 N.E.2d 634 (1986); Gardner-Athol Area Mental Health Ass'n, Inc. v. Zoning Bd. of Appeals of Gardner, 401 Mass. 12, 513 N.E.2d 1272, 42 Ed. Law Rep. 381 (1987); Campbell v. City Council of Lynn, 32 Mass. App. Ct. 152, 586 N.E.2d 1009 (1992),

aff'd in part, rev'd in part, 415 Mass. 772, 616 N.E.2d 445, 84 Ed. Law Rep. 442 (1993); but see Whitinsville Retirement Soc., Inc. v. Town of Northbridge, 394 Mass. 757, 477 N.E.2d 407 (1985); Julia Ruth House, Inc. v. Board of Appeals of Westwood, 8 L.C.R. 451 (2001).

[7]Bible Speaks v. Board of Appeals of Lenox, 8 Mass. App. Ct. 19, 391 N.E.2d 279 (1979); Commissioner of Code Inspection of Worcester v. Worcester Dynamy, Inc., 11 Mass. App. Ct. 97, 413 N.E.2d 1151 (1980); Trustees of Tufts College v. City of Medford, 415 Mass. 753, 616 N.E.2d 433, 84 Ed. Law Rep. 430 (1993); Trustees of Boston College v. Schick, Land Court, No. 121573 (1987); Newbury Junior College v. Town of Brookline, 19 Mass. App. Ct. 197, 472 N.E.2d 1373, 22 Ed. Law Rep. 333 (1985). See also Trustees of Boston University v. Licensing Bd. of Boston, 24 Mass. App. Ct. 475, 510 N.E.2d 283, 40 Ed. Law Rep. 970 (1987).

enforced if it had the effect of "virtually nullifying" the educational use.[8] Those cases continue to be cited and to play an important role in the interpretation of the statutory language specifying "reasonable regulations" concerning certain specific dimensional factors. In the *Tufts College* case[9] the court said that physical requirements of the zoning ordinance that "do not facially discriminate against educational uses . . . are presumptively valid," but also said that "facially neutral requirements cannot be applied to educational uses without further inquiry into the outcome produced by such an application." The scope of and possibility of balance between the presumption of validity and further inquiry into outcome remain unresolved,[10] although balancing is indicated in a number of decisions.[11]

The scope of religious use has also been considered.[12] As to the application of dimensional requirements, the court upheld the right of the Mormon Church to build a steeple higher than the Belmont zoning law allowed.[13] The SJC rejected the trial court's inquiry into the association of steeple height with the proposed use as an inappropriate consideration of religious doctrine, but anomalously declared that "The record is replete with evidence that the steeple is integral to the specific character of the contem-

---

[8]Sisters of Holy Cross of Mass. v. Town of Brookline, 347 Mass. 486, 198 N.E.2d 624 (1964); Radcliffe College v. City of Cambridge, 350 Mass. 613, 215 N.E.2d 892 (1966).

[9]Trustees of Tufts College v. City of Medford, 415 Mass. 753, 616 N.E.2d 433, 84 Ed. Law Rep. 430 (1993).

[10]See E.C. Mendler, The Dover Amendment and the Judicial Role in Zoning—Where Do They Stand After Trustees of Tufts College v. Medford?, Massachusetts Law Review, Sept. 1994; Lasell College v. City of Newton, 36 Mass. App. Ct. 1122, 635 N.E.2d 277 (1994).

[11]Watros v. Greater Lynn Mental Health and Retardation Ass'n, Inc., 421 Mass. 106, 653 N.E.2d 589 (1995); Caldeira v. Zoning Bd. of Appeals of Taunton, 3 L.C.R. 195 (1995); Assembly of God Church of Attleboro & Vicinity, Inc. v. Hutchings, 7 L.C.R. 208 (1999); Capus Developments v. R.

(No. 2), 1975 WL 155925 (Fed. T.D. 1975); Spectrum Health Systems, Inc. v. Framingham Zoning Bd. of Appeals, 9 L.C.R. 113 (2001); Dzog Chen Community of America v. Town of Buckland, 10 L.C.R. 198 (2002); Seven Hills Community Services, Inc. v. Town of Saugus, 11 L.C.R. 92 (2003); Austen Riggs Center, Inc. v. Zoning Bd. of Appeals of Lenox, 12 L.C.R. 243 (2004).

[12]Needham Pastoral Counseling Center, Inc. v. Board of Appeals of Needham, 29 Mass. App. Ct. 31, 557 N.E.2d 43 (1990). Similarly, see Congregation of the Sisters of St. Joseph of Boston v. Town of Framingham, 2 L.C.R. 125 (1994); and see Collins v. Melrose Zoning Board of Appeals, 4 L.C.R. 178 (1996).

[13]Martin v. Corporation of Presiding Bishop of Church of Jesus Christ of Latter-Day Saints, 434 Mass. 141, 747 N.E.2d 131 (2001).

plated use," indicating perhaps less rigor and scrutiny of the relation of dimensional requirements to the use in religious cases than in educational cases.

• **Child Care Facilities.** The "use of land or structures, or the expansion of existing structures, for the primary, accessory or incidental purpose of operating a child care facility; provided, however, that such land or structures may be subject to reasonable regulations concerning the bulk and height of structures and determining yard sizes, lot area, setbacks, open space, parking and building coverage requirements," and provided further that "the term 'child care facility' shall mean a day care center or a school age child care program, as those terms are defined in [M.G.L.A. c. 28A, § 9]."

Patterned on the Dover Amendment, this provision sets forth the same list of permitted "reasonable regulations." The requirement of a special permit for such use is expressly barred. Space for child care facilities is encouraged in M.G.L.A. c. 40A, § 9C, by a statutory bonus in a building providing a child care facility of 10% of the floor area that would otherwise be allowed under the local bylaw or ordinance.

The courts have rejected special permit and site plan approval requirements for child care facilities and have regularly found the application of various dimensional requirements to be unreasonable in the circumstances, often citing Dover Amendment cases.[14]

• **Floating Zones.** So-called floating zones, i.e., districts with boundary lines "which may be changed without adoption of an amendment to the zoning ordinance or by-law." It may be noted that many bylaws provide for "overlay districts," and in some of those relating to floodplains or wetlands the actual boundaries may be defined by flood contours or wetland flora. Some overlays provide for alternative uses.

Conceptually related to this principle is the concept that a "more restricted" zoning district may not be used, even

---

[14]Petrucci v. Bd. of Appeals of Westwood, 5 L.C.R. 52 (1997); Cartwright v. Town of Braintree, 5 L.C.R. 238 (1998); Campbell v. Town of Weymouth, 6 L.C.R. 276 (1998); Rogers v. Town of Norfolk, 432 Mass. 374, 734 N.E.2d 1143 (2000); Shapiro v. Zoning Bd. of Appeals of Sudbury, 8 L.C.R. 332 (2000); Walker Realty, LLC v. Planning Bd. of Hopkinton, 10 L.C.R. 63 (2002); Kindercare Learning Centers, Inc. v. Town of Westford, 62 Mass. App. Ct. 924, 818 N.E.2d 594 (2004); The Teddy Bear Club, Inc. v, City of Newton, 12 L.C.R. 397 (2004).

incidentally, to serve an adjacent "less restricted" district.[15]

• **Mobile Homes.** The prohibition of use of a manufactured home on the site of a residence destroyed by casualty for a period not to exceed 12 months while the residence is being rebuilt. The more common use of mobile trailers as offices on construction sites ordinarily requires a special permit. The regulation of manufactured home parks is referred to in § **14:12**.

• **Handicap Access Ramps.** Application of dimensional lot requirements to access ramps for handicapped persons. This limitation on zoning should be considered in relation to federal and state laws relating to architectural barriers, discussed in § **14:11**, and otherwise assisting and banning discrimination against handicapped persons.

• **Solar Energy.** The "installation of solar energy systems or the building or structures that facilitate the collection of solar energy." The statute bans zoning provisions that "prohibit or unreasonably regulate" the foregoing "except where necessary to protect the public health, safety or welfare." Besides defining solar energy facilities and prohibiting zoning interference therewith, M.G.L.A. c. 40A, § 9B, provides for special permits to "create an easement to sunlight over neighboring property."

• **Amateur Antennas.** The "construction or use of an antenna structure by a federally licensed radio operator." But zoning "may reasonably regulate the location and height of such antenna structures for the purposes of health, safety, or aesthetics," but must "reasonably allow for sufficient height of such antenna structures so as to effectively accommodate amateur radio communications
. . ."

In addition to the foregoing the partial or conditional limitations or exemptions are as follows:

• **Public Service Corporations.** Land or structures used by a public service corporation may be exempted from zoning if the Department of Telecommunications and Energy (DTE) makes requisite findings. The general exemption from zoning regulation of land and structures of the Commonwealth and its instrumentalities devoted to

---

[15]Co-Ray Realty Co. v. Board of Zoning Adjustment of Boston, 328 Mass. 103, 101 N.E.2d 888 (1951); Harrison v. Building Inspector of Braintree, 350 Mass. 559, 215 N.E.2d 773 (1966); Harrison v. Town of Braintree, 355 Mass. 651, 247 N.E.2d 356 (1969); Sharon v. Keefe, 14 L.C.R. 230 (2006); but see Tofias v. Butler, 26 Mass. App. Ct. 89, 523 N.E.2d 796 (1988); King v. Zoning Bd. of Appeals of Chatham, 30 Mass. App. Ct. 938, 569 N.E.2d 855 (1991); Brewton v. Spiegel, 14 L.C.R. 468 (2006).

essential governmental functions was affirmed in Town of Freetown v. Zoning Bd. of Appeals of Dartmouth, 33 Mass. App. Ct. 415, 600 N.E.2d 1001 (1992), citing pertinent prior cases. A town water district was held not to be a state agency entitled to exemption, but a municipal one, subject to zoning.[16] M.G.L.A. c. 40A, § 9, ¶ 15, bars any municipal ordinance or bylaw from prohibiting the installation of solid waste transfer facilities in a district zoned for industrial use. The validity of that provision has been upheld, and a zoning provision barring such use was held invalid.[17]

• **Disabled Persons.** The statute provides broadly that "local land use and health and safety laws, regulations, practices, ordinances, by-laws and decisions of a city or town shall not discriminate against a disabled person," and particularly protects "congregate living arrangements among non-related persons with disabilities," and expressly includes Boston in its application.

• **Day Care Homes.** "Family day care home and large family day care home [as defined in M.G.L.A. c. 28A, § 9] shall be an allowable use unless [the local zoning law] prohibits or specifically regulate such use."

§ 11:7   Protection of lower cost housing

There is no sharp distinction between some of the "limitations" described in the preceding section, pursuant to which actions contrary to local zoning may be given sanction, and the "overrides" described in this and the following section. It seems appropriate, however, to refer to the following two areas of regulation as constituting overrides.

The "Low and Moderate Income Housing Act," adopted in 1969, sometimes known by the pejorative popular title of "anti-snob zoning act," enacted M.G.L.A. c. 40B, §§ 20 to 23. Acknowledging a shortage of housing available at costs attainable by persons having low or moderate income, and recognizing that both single family and multi-family housing could be built at lower costs, and sold or rented for less, if there were reduced or less stringent requirements for such things as minimum lot size, frontage, setbacks and side and

[16]Pierce v. Town of Wellesley, 336 Mass. 517, 146 N.E.2d 666 (1957); Shirley Water District v. Shirley Board of Appeals, 4 L.C.R. 129 (1996); and see Save the Bay, Inc. v. Department of Public Utilities, 366 Mass. 667, 322 N.E.2d 742 (1975).

[17]Town of Warren v. Hazardous Waste Facility Site Safety Council, 392 Mass. 107, 466 N.E.2d 102 (1984); Ricmer Properties, Inc. v. Ferruzzi, 7 L.C.R. 363 (1999).

rear yard, maximum height or floor area ratio, off-street parking, etc., the Act provided in effect a means of overriding such regulations.

Under 40B, as it is commonly called, a qualified applicant[1] seeking to build low or moderate income housing may apply to the local zoning board of appeals for a single permit for the project, comprehensive of all permits that would be required by all city or town boards. A historic district committee was held to be a local board for this purpose, but the Martha's Vineyard Commission was held not to be.[2] The statute requires boards of appeal to adopt rules and regulations for this purpose. The comprehension of multiple permits into a single approval is in itself a great time and expense saver to a developer, particularly perhaps in legal costs. Such a permit is meant to comply with the statutory prescription of regulations that are "consistent with local needs," notwithstanding the details of the actual local regulations.

If the board denies the permit or imposes conditions which make the project "uneconomic," the applicant may then appeal to the housing appeals committee in the Massachusetts Department of Housing and Community Development, which may overrule the local board if it finds the denial or conditions not to be "reasonable and consistent with local needs."[3]

The phrase "consistent with local needs" is defined in the statute in terms of the "regional needs" for low and moderate income housing and conventional health, safety and land use considerations. It is then expressly provided that local "requirements or regulations shall be consistent with local needs . . ." when (1) low and moderate income housing is in excess of 10 percent of housing units or on sites comprising 1 1/2 percent or more of the land area zoned for residential, commercial or industrial use in the community (excluding governmentally owned lands), or (2) the implementation of the pending application would result in commencement of construction of such housing on sites comprising more than 3/10ths percent of such land area or 10 acres, whichever is larger, in one calendar year.[4]

Even when a community has met the 10 percent test, its

[Section 11:7]

[1]M.G.L.A. c. 40B, § 21.

[2]Dennis Housing Corp. v. Zoning Bd. of Appeals of Dennis, 439 Mass. 71, 785 N.E.2d 682 (2003); Mavro v. CKA, LLC, 11 L.C.R. 46 (2003).

[3]M.G.L.A. c. 40B, § 23.

[4]In 2002 DHCD adopted amendments to its regulations under c. 40B (760 CMR 30.00), under which the definition of "low or moderate income housing" now includes certain additional housing provided

board of appeals may still issue a comprehensive permit under the Act.[5] When a project is permitted under 40B, it continues indefinitely to be subject to affordable housing requirements, notwithstanding a "cliff date" provided in a financing agreement with a state agency.[6]

The Act has been upheld, interpreted and applied in a number of cases, which have generally sustained its strict application.[7] Other cases have upheld 40B projects but did not pose issues under the statute.[8]

As part of the 2006 Act aimed at "streamlining and expediting permitting," Chapter 40B was amended by adding a new section 30 which among other things created a "technical assistance center," to promote "balanced development" of communities and otherwise to facilitate and

---

by a community under M.G.L.A. c. 44B, or otherwise.

[5]Boothroyd v. Zoning Board of Appeals of Amherst, 11 L.C.R. 187 (2003); Board of Appeals of Hanover v. Housing Appeals Committee in Dept. of Community Affairs, 363 Mass. 339, 294 N.E.2d 393 (1973).

[6]Zoning Bd. of Appeals of Wellesley v. Ardemore Apartments Ltd. Partnership, 436 Mass. 811, 767 N.E.2d 584 (2002).

[7]Board of Appeals of Hanover v. Housing Appeals Committee in Dept. of Community Affairs, 363 Mass. 339, 294 N.E.2d 393 (1973); Mahoney v. Board of Appeals of Winchester, 366 Mass. 228, 316 N.E.2d 606 (1974); Board of Appeals of Maynard v. Housing Appeals Committee in Dept. of Community Affairs, 370 Mass. 64, 345 N.E.2d 382 (1976); Board of Appeals of North Andover v. Housing Appeals Committee, 4 Mass. App. Ct. 676, 357 N.E.2d 936 (1976); Bailey v. Board of Appeals of Holden, 370 Mass. 95, 345 N.E.2d 367 (1976); Zoning Bd. of Appeals of Wellesley v. Housing Appeals Committee, 385 Mass. 651, 433 N.E.2d 873 (1982); Milton Commons Associates v. Board of Appeals of Milton, 14 Mass. App. Ct. 111, 436 N.E.2d 1236 (1982); Zoning Bd. of Appeals of Greenfield v. Housing Appeals Committee, 15 Mass. App. Ct. 553, 446 N.E.2d 748 (1983); Quinn v. Zoning Bd. of Appeals of Dalton, 18 Mass. App. Ct. 191, 464 N.E.2d 395 (1984); Pheasant Ridge Associates Ltd. Partnership v. Town of Burlington, 399 Mass. 771, 506 N.E.2d 1152 (1987); Bagley v. Illyrian Gardens, Inc., 401 Mass. 822, 519 N.E.2d 1308 (1988); Landers v. Board of Appeals of Falmouth, 31 Mass. App. Ct. 939, 579 N.E.2d 1375 (1991).

[8]Town of Bedford v. Cerasuolo, 62 Mass. App. Ct. 73, 818 N.E.2d 561 (2004); McKinley Investments, Inc. v. Middleborough Land, LLC., 62 Mass. App. Ct. 616, 818 N.E.2d 627 (2004); Lane v. Zoning Bd. of Appeals of Falmouth, 65 Mass. App. Ct. 434, 841 N.E.2d 260 (2006), review denied, 448 Mass. 1106, 862 N.E.2d 380 (2007); Town of Middleborough v. Housing Appeals Committee, 66 Mass. App. Ct. 39, 845 N.E.2d 1143 (2006), review granted in part, 447 Mass. 1105, 851 N.E.2d 1078 (2006) and judgment aff'd, 449 Mass. 514, 870 N.E.2d 67 (2007); and Land Court cases in 12 L.C.R. 127 (2004), 13 L.C.R. 271 and 279 (2005).

expedite the zoning permitting process.[9]

Procedural aspects of zoning under Chapter 40A have been held applicable to Chapter 40B as well, including issues of standing to contest a permit issued thereunder.[10] However, the SJC held that the standards for an appeal under Chapter 40B were not the same as for Chapter 40A, and that an abutter's standing was not sustained by evidence of diminished property value.[11] The jurisdictional interplay between a developer's administrative appeal and an abutter's appeal has been considered.[12]

§ 11:8 Federal protection of telecommunications

The federal Telecommunications Act of 1996[1] was aimed at fostering competition in the telecommunications industry. There seems to be plenty of that and many Massachusetts communities have faced applications for installation of new wireless communications facilities, including towers and antennas. The Act purports to protect local control "over decisions regarding the placement, construction and modification of personal wireless service facilities,"[2] but imposes several significant limitations and exceptions. Notably, no state or local government regulation may "prohibit or have the effect of prohibiting" the provision of personal wireless services, or "discriminate among providers," or deny applications unless "supported by substantial evidence," or be made "on the basis of the environmental effects of radio frequency emissions to the extent such facilities comply with the [FCC's] regulations concerning such emissions."

The Massachusetts Department of Telecommunications and Energy (formerly Department of Public Utilities) has in

---

[9]Chapter 205, Section 10, Acts of 2006.

[10]Stanley Realty Holdings, LLC v. Watertown Zoning Bd. of Appeals, 12 L.C.R. 301 (2004); Bell v. Zoning Bd. of Appeals of Gloucester, 429 Mass. 551, 709 N.E.2d 815 (1999); Planning Bd. of Hingham v. Hingham Campus, LLC, 438 Mass. 364, 780 N.E.2d 902 (2003); Cardwell v. Board of Appeals of Woburn, 61 Mass. App. Ct. 118, 807 N.E.2d 207 (2004); Town of Cohasset Water Commission v. Avalon Cohasset, Inc., 13 L.C.R. 130 (2005).

[11]Standerwick v. Zoning Bd. of Appeals of Andover, 447 Mass. 20,

849 N.E.2d 197 (2006); and see Lavin v. Norton, 14 L.C.R. 439 (2006); but see Russell v. Barrett, 14 L.C.R. 460 (2006).

[12]Taylor v. Board of Appeals of Lexington, 68 Mass. App. Ct. 503, 863 N.E.2d 79 (2007), review granted, 449 Mass. 1101, 865 N.E.2d 1140 (2007).

[Section 11:8]

[1]U.S.C.A. § 332(c)(7)(A), enacted as P.L. 104-104.

[2]Section 704(a)(7)(9A) of the Act.

several instances ruled wireless communication facilities to be entitled to the public service corporation exemption referred to in the preceding paragraph B.[3] Utility companies are required by Massachusetts law to afford "wireless providers" with "nondiscriminatory" access to their poles and rights of way, and to expand their facilities at the request and expense of a wireless provider.[4]

The federal limitations as well as the conditional exemption defined by DTE are of significant interest to communities seeking to frame new zoning provisions to deal with wireless communications facilities.

In some respects Massachusetts law has prevailed. In a careful and detailed analysis by Justice Marshall, the SJC held that neither the substantial evidence clause nor the provision for expedited review in the federal act precluded the established Massachusetts procedure, and sustained the judicial de novo review of a special permit issued for construction of a new 100 ft. tower.[5] The Appeals Court upheld a local order to remove a Nextel telecom tower from residential land in violation of zoning use and height restrictions, holding that Nextel was not a public utility entitled to Massachusetts statutory protection, and that no violation of the Telecommunications Act was involved.[6]

However, in most cases the federal law has effectively overridden local regulation. Federal and state courts have found local regulations and action to involve "effective prohibition," lack of "substantial evidence," "a naked attempt" to circumvent or an impermissible "collateral attack on" federal law.[7]

Permission to erect towers has also been upheld as a matter of application of local law.[8] In *Hill v. Upton Zoning Bd. of*

---

[3]But see Greater Boston Real Estate Bd. v. Department of Telecommunications and Energy, 438 Mass. 197, 779 N.E.2d 127 (2002).

[4]Chapter 143, Acts of 2006.

[5]Roberts v. Southwestern Bell Mobile Systems, Inc., 429 Mass. 478, 709 N.E.2d 798 (1999).

[6]Building Com'r of Franklin v. Dispatch Communications of New England, Inc., 48 Mass. App. Ct. 709, 725 N.E.2d 1059 (2000).

[7]Omnipoint Communications MB Operations, LLC v. Town of Lincoln, 107 F. Supp. 2d 108 (D. Mass. 2000); Nextel Communications of the Mid-Atlantic, Inc. v. Manchester-by-the-Sea, 115 F. Supp. 2d 65 (D. Mass. 2000); National Tower, LLC v. Plainville Zoning Bd. of Appeals, 297 F.3d 14 (1st Cir. 2002); Russell's Garden Center, Inc. v. Nextel Communications, 13 L.C.R. 179 (2005).

[8]New York Cellular Geographic Service Area, Inc. v. Planning Board of Hanover, 7 L.C.R. 42 (1999); Sangiolo v. Board of Aldermen of Newton, 57 Mass. App. Ct. 911, 783 N.E.2d 830 (2003);

Appeals,[9] the Land Court gave careful consideration to several of the practical issues. In a case involving action of the Cape Cod Commission (see **Chapter 14**) the Land Court found no violation of the anti-discrimination provision in the federal act.[10]

TOPIC B: ADOPTION AND AMENDMENT

§ 11:9 Law and procedure

The mechanics of adoption and amendment of zoning ordinances or by-laws are not complicated, but the procedural requirements are mandatory. It is undisputed among lawyers who have obtained, or sought to obtain, zoning amendments on behalf of a client or on behalf of a community board that the process is fraught with politics and public relations. Those are subjects not to be dealt with here, but any lawyer venturing into this field is certainly well advised to start by studying and getting to know the community, its history, people and officials. Knowledge of these will likely have a considerable effect on the manner in which the proposal is cast and presented.

The provisions for adoption and change of zoning ordinances (in cities) and by-laws (in towns) are set forth in M.G.L.A. c. 40A, § 5. A proposal for such adoption or change is initiated by submission thereof to the city council or board of selectmen. The proposal may originate with the city council or board of selectmen, or with the owner of land to be affected, a specified numbers of registered voters, a planning board or regional planning agency, or "by other methods provided by municipal charter."

Within 14 days of receipt, the selectmen or city council are to submit the proposal to the planning board for review. The planning board then gives notice of a hearing by publication and posting, and holds a public hearing within 65 days. Notice of the hearing is also to be given by mail to the Massachusetts Department of Housing and Community Development, the regional planning agency, if any, and the planning boards of all abutting cities and towns. Provision is also

---

Walters v. Voicestream Wireless, 11 L.C.R. 147 (2003).

[9]Hill v. Upton Zoning Bd. of Appeals, 12 L.C.R. 46 (2004).

[10]Industrial Communications & Electronics, Inc. v. Cape Cod Commission, 12 L.C.R. 464 (2004).

made in M.G.L.A. c. 40A, § 5, for notice by mail to non-resident property owners if such notice is provided for in the local zoning ordinance or by-laws. The statute further provides that "No defect in the form of any notice under this chapter shall invalidate any zoning by-laws or ordinances unless such defect is found to be misleading." If there is no planning board, such hearing is held by the city council or board of selectmen. The statutory wording suggests that in a city there should be hearings both by the planning board and the city council or a committee designated by it for the purpose.[1]

Action may not be taken on a proposed zoning ordinance or by-law until the planning board has submitted "a report with recommendations"[2] to the city council or town meeting, or until 21 days have elapsed after the planning board's hearing without the submission of such a report. The statute does not require the report to be in writing, but planning boards usually do render them both in writing and orally. The recommendations of the planning board are advisory and are not binding on the city council or town meeting.[3] If a city council fails to act on the matter within 90 days, or a town meeting within 6 months, after such hearing, they may then not act on the matter until the planning board has again held a hearing, with notice, and made a report as above.[4] When the city council or town meeting does act, it may "adopt, reject or amend any such proposed ordinance or by-law." The extent to which it may "amend" is subject to judicial review.[5]

A peculiar further provision in M.G.L.A. c. 40A, § 5, is that: "Prior to the adoption of any zoning ordinance or by-law or amendment thereto which seeks to further regulate matters established by [M.G.L.A. c. 131, § 40] or regulations

[Section 11:9]

[1]See Woods v. City of Newton, 351 Mass. 98, 217 N.E.2d 728 (1966).

[2]Whittemore v. Town Clerk of Falmouth, 299 Mass. 64, 12 N.E.2d 187(1937); but see Woods v. City of Newton, 351 Mass. 98, 217 N.E.2d 728 (1966).

[3]Vagts v. Superintendent and Inspector of Bldgs. of Cambridge, 355 Mass. 711, 247 N.E.2d 366 (1969); Wallace v. Building Inspector of Woburn, 5 Mass. App. Ct. 786, 360 N.E.2d 664 (1977).

[4]Carstensen v. Cambridge Zoning Bd. of Appeals, 11 Mass. App. Ct. 348, 416 N.E.2d 522 (1981).

[5]See Town of Burlington v. Dunn, 318 Mass. 216, 61 N.E.2d 243, 168 A.L.R. 1181 (1945); Doliner v. Town Clerk of Millis, 343 Mass. 10, 175 N.E.2d 925 (1961); Johnson v. Town of Framingham, 354 Mass. 750, 242 N.E.2d 420 (1968); Crall v. City of Leominster, 362 Mass. 95, 284 N.E.2d 610 (1972); Daly Dry Wall, Inc. v. Board of Appeals of Easton, 3 Mass. App. Ct. 706, 322 N.E.2d 780 (1975).

authorized thereunder relative to agricultural and aquacultural practices, the city or town clerk shall, no later than seven days prior to the city council's or town meeting's public hearing relative to the adoption of said new or amended zoning ordinances or by-laws, give notice of the said proposed zoning ordinances or by-laws to the farmland advisory board established pursuant to [M.G.L.A. c. 131, § 40]."

Adoption of a zoning ordinance in a city requires a 2/3rds vote of all the members of the city council, and adoption of a zoning by-law in a town requires a 2/3rds vote of a town meeting (at which a quorum is present). There are other provisions in M.G.L.A. c. 40A, § 5, with respect to communities having a commission form of government or a council of fewer than 25 members.[6]

When a zoning proposal is unfavorably acted upon, it cannot be considered again within two years unless the planning board recommends its adoption.

When a zoning by-law is adopted by a town, it must then be submitted to the attorney general for his approval pursuant to M.G.L.A. c. 40, § 32, together with an explanatory statement and maps or plans as appropriate, as provided by M.G.L.A. c. 40A, § 5. This submission is made by the town clerk, who certifies the by-law as adopted. The attorney general must state any reasons for disapproval, and his review is limited to legal considerations and not matters of legislative policy. The by-law is deemed approved if the attorney general fails to act on it within 90 days, extendable by agreement with town counsel for up to an additional 90 days.

If the attorney general notes a defect in procedure or notice, instead of rejecting the by-law he may notify the town clerk who then is to give public notice of the specified defect, and any resident or other party in interest may assert a claim that the defect was misleading or prejudicial. If no such claim is made, the attorney general may waive the defect, but if a claim is made, the 90-day period restarts.

Once approved by the attorney general the by-law is effective as of the date of adoption at town meeting. If disapproved, the prior by-law remains in effect. In a city, a zoning ordinance does not require approval of the attorney general and is effective when adopted by the city council. Once a zoning ordinance or by-law becomes effective a copy must be sent by the city or town clerk to the Massachusetts Department of Housing and Community Development.

Under M.G.L.A. c. 40, § 32, a town zoning by-law must

---

[6]See O'Brien v. City of Quincy,   6 L.C.R. 284 (1998).

then also be either (1) published in a "town bulletin or pamphlet" or posted in a specified number of public places, (2) published twice in a newspaper of general circulation (the usual method), or (3) delivered to every occupied dwelling in the town. Notice of adoption of a city zoning ordinance must be given by similar publication. It is provided in M.G.L.A. c. 40, § 32, that such publication "shall include a statement that claims of invalidity by reason of any defect in the procedure of adoption or amendment may only be made within ninety days of such posting or of the second publication." Challenges to zoning amendments on procedural grounds are not often sustained.[7]

TOPIC C: NONCONFORMANCE

§ 11:10   The statutory scheme

Section 6 of M.G.L.A. c. 40A covers the entire subject of pre-existing nonconforming uses, structures and lots, and freezes affected by perimeter plan endorsement and subdivision plan approval. Before the adoption of the current Chapter 40A these subjects were dealt with separately in §§ 5, 5A, 7A and 11 of the prior Chapter 40A, and consequently some of the applicable case law refers to the old section numbers.

The first three paragraphs of § 6 of M.G.L.A. c. 40A provide that:

> Except as hereinafter provided, a zoning ordinance or by-law shall not apply to structures or uses lawfully in existence or lawfully begun, or to a building or special permit issued before the first publication of notice of the public hearing on such ordinance or by-law required by section five, but shall apply to any change or substantial extension of such use, to a building or special permit issued after the first notice of said public hearing, to any reconstruction, extension or structural change of such structure and to any alteration of a structure begun after the first notice of said public hearing to provide for its use for a substantially different purpose or for the same purpose in a substantially different manner or to a substantially greater extent except where alteration, reconstruction, extension or structural change to a single or two-family residential structure does not increase the nonconforming nature of said structure. Pre-existing nonconforming structures or uses may be extended or altered, provided, that no such exten-

---

[7]Wolf v. Town of Mansfield, 67 Mass. App. Ct. 56, 851 N.E.2d 1115 (2006), review denied, 447 Mass. 1113, 856 N.E.2d 182 (2006); Bruni v. Brooks, 14 L.C.R. 411 (2006).

sion or alteration shall be permitted unless there is a finding by the permit granting authority or by the special permit granting authority designated by ordinance or by-law that such change, extension or alteration shall not be substantially more detrimental than the existing nonconforming [*] use to the neighborhood. This section shall not apply to establishments which display live nudity for their patrons, as defined in section nine A, adult bookstores, adult motion picture theaters, adult paraphernalia shops, or adult video stores subject to the provisions of section nine A.

A zoning ordinance or by-law shall provide that construction or operations under a building or special permit shall conform to any subsequent amendment of the ordinance or by-law unless the use or construction is commenced within a period of not more than six months after the issuance of the permit and in cases involving construction, unless such construction is continued through to completion as continuously and expeditiously as is reasonable.

A zoning ordinance or by-law may define and regulate nonconforming uses and structures abandoned or not used for a period of two years or more.

In reviewing those provisions, several basic points appear, as follows:

At the point indicated by [*] in the above quotation the courts have effectively inserted the words "structure or," making that provision, discussed in paragraph B of this section, applicable to structures as well as uses.[1] In *Willard* the court noted that the absence of those words created "an obscurity of the type which has come to be recognized as one of the hallmarks of the chapter."

The protection afforded by a building permit or special permit, as opposed to a structure or use actually in existence, is discussed in § **11:15**. It may be observed, however, that in both cases (permit and existence) the determining time is the date of first publication of notice of public hearing on the adoption or amendment of a proposed zoning ordinance or by-law, rather than the date of adoption of the ordinance or by-law.

With respect to pre-existing structures and uses the exemption is afforded only if they were "lawfully in existence or lawfully begun," and not when the structure or use was

---

[Section 11:10]

[1]Watros v. Greater Lynn Mental Health and Retardation Ass'n, Inc., 421 Mass. 106, 653 N.E.2d 589 (1995), citing Willard v. Board of Appeals of Orleans, 25 Mass. App. Ct. 15, 514 N.E.2d 369 (1987).

previously unlawful, even if allowed by a prior variance.[2] The statute of limitations provisions in § 7 of M.G.L.A. c. 40A, discussed below, are pertinent to this point. The creation of a new nonconformity may taint an otherwise protected nonconformity by "infectious invalidity."[3]

The statute does not permit local limitation or exclusion of the protection of pre-existing structures and uses, but local law may expand the protection.[4]

The last sentence quoted above permits local definition and regulation of non-conforming uses and structures which are either "abandoned" or "not used" for two years or more. Prior law referred only to abandonment, which rested on intent and voluntary conduct,[5] but that is no longer required and mere non-use may effect termination of protection of a non-conforming use or structure.[6]

So-called "adult" establishments are not entitled to any pre-existing nonconformance protections.

§ 11:11 Changes in use or structure

The statute clearly excludes from protection "any change or substantial extension" of a nonconforming use and "any reconstruction, extension or structural change" of a nonconforming structure. The exclusions from protection are, however, not absolute. Repeating the quotation of the second

---

[2]See Durkin v. Board of Appeals of Falmouth, 21 Mass. App. Ct. 450, 488 N.E.2d 6 (1986); Mendes v. Board of Appeals of Barnstable, 28 Mass. App. Ct. 527, 552 N.E.2d 604 (1990); Whitten v. Board of Appeals of Woburn, 38 Mass. App. Ct. 949, 648 N.E.2d 1310 (1995); Campos v. Chelsea Zoning Bd. of Appeals, 5 L.C.R. 128 (1997); Deignan v. Harwich Bd. of Appeals, 13 L.C.R. 244 (2005).

[3]Russo v. Bd. of Appeals of Watertown, 2 L.C.R. 171 (1994); Bouffard v. Peabody Zoning Bd., 3 L.C.R. 230 (1995); Pateuk v. Coppola, 6 L.C.R. 312 (1998).

[4]Murphy v. Kotlik, 34 Mass. App. Ct. 410, 611 N.E.2d 741 (1993); Frank v. Baker, 9 L.C.R. 330 (2001); Correia v. Brockton Zoning Bd. of Appeals, 12 L.C.R. 32 (2004).

[5]Pioneer Insulation & Modernizing Corp. v. City of Lynn, 331 Mass. 560, 120 N.E.2d 913 (1954).

[6]Fitzsimonds v. Board of Appeals of Chatham, 21 Mass. App. Ct. 53, 484 N.E.2d 113 (1985); Burlington Sand & Gravel, Inc. v. Town of Harvard, 26 Mass. App. Ct. 436, 528 N.E.2d 889 (1988); Ka-Hur Enterprises, Inc. v. Zoning Bd. of Appeals of Provincetown, 40 Mass. App. Ct. 71, 661 N.E.2d 120 (1996), judgment aff'd, 424 Mass. 404, 676 N.E.2d 838 (1997); Dawson v. Board of Appeals of Bourne, 18 Mass. App. Ct. 962, 469 N.E.2d 509 (1984); Haddigan v. Zoning Bd. of Appeals of Foxborough, 1 L.C.R. 15 (1993); Bartlett v. Board of Appeals of Lakeville, 23 Mass. App. Ct. 664, 505 N.E.2d 193 (1987); Bjorklund v. Bd. of Appeals of Scituate, 3 L.C.R. 141 (1995); Town of Orange v. Shay, 68 Mass. App. Ct. 358, 862 N.E.2d 393 (2007).

sentence the statute: "Pre-existing nonconforming structures or uses may be extended or altered, provided, that . . ." a specified "permit granting authority" makes a "finding" "that such change, extension or alteration shall not be substantially more detrimental than the existing nonconforming [structure or] use to the neighborhood."

As noted above, "structure or" was inserted into the statute by the courts. The word "finding" has been construed as involving a special permit, after notice and hearing, subject to "conditions, safeguards and limitations of time and use," and subject of course to judicial review.[1]

Before reaching that provision, however, we must consider the "except" clause at the end of the first sentence of the statute, which provides for single and two-family dwellings a test less stringent than absence of detriment, requiring only determination that the alteration does not increase the nonconformity. Considering that distinction the court determined that in order to apply the exception for one and two-family dwellings, the local board of appeals must identify the particular structural nonconformance and then determine whether the alteration intensified it.[2] When the alteration involved an increased footprint of the structure, that was held to constitute an increased nonconformity.[3] Based on that concept the Land Court allowed a vertical extension within the zoning height limit and without enlargement of the building footprint, but the Appeals Court reversed and remanded, holding that confinement to the prior footprint did not alone afford the exception, and required a specific finding that the alteration did not "intensify the nonconformity."[4]

In cases of one- and two-family residences which did not

[Section 11:11]

[1]See Murray v. Board of Appeals of Barnstable, 22 Mass. App. Ct. 473, 494 N.E.2d 1364 (1986); Texstar Const. Corp. v. Board of Appeals of Dedham, 26 Mass. App. Ct. 977, 528 N.E.2d 1186 (1988); Rockwood v. Snow Inn Corp., 409 Mass. 361, 566 N.E.2d 608 (1991); Shrewsbury Edgemere Associates Ltd. Partnership v. Board of Appeals of Shrewsbury, 409 Mass. 317, 565 N.E.2d 1214 (1991); Petit v. Bd. of Appeals of Millbury, 1 L.C.R. 156 (1993); Block v. Zoning Bd. of Appeals of Otis, 3 L.C.R. 1 (1994).

[2]Fitzsimonds v. Board of Appeals of Chatham, 21 Mass. App. Ct. 53, 484 N.E.2d 113 (1985); Willard v. Board of Appeals of Orleans, 25 Mass. App. Ct. 15, 514 N.E.2d 369 (1987); Norwell-Arch, LLC v. Norwell Zoning Bd. of Appeals, 12 L.C.R. 208 (2004).

[3]Willard v. Board of Appeals of Orleans, 25 Mass. App. Ct. 15, 514 N.E.2d 369 (1987).

[4]Goldhirsh v. McNear, 32 Mass. App. Ct. 455, 590 N.E.2d 709 (1992); Norwell-Arch, LLC v. Norwell Zoning Bd. of Appeals, 12 L.C.R. 208 (2004); Mandalos v. Mashpee ZBA, 13 L.C.R. 572 (2005);

meet the non-increase test, and in all other cases, the absence of detriment test is applicable. Those provisions have produced a hefty body of case law. Some decisions simply construe and apply the prohibition clauses, but special permits for relief are often sought and many cases also consider the issue of detriment to the neighborhood. The case law may be briefly analyzed under the following rubrics:

● **Uses Approved.** Use of Improved equipment or methods of operation, some degree of increased volume, modifications of a similar nature and purpose, somewhat extended periods of operation, and conversion to condominium, have been upheld as protected,[5] but all within limits indicated in the "rejection" cases cited below.

● **Uses Rejected.** When the courts see the change in use as involving a change in the character or quality of use or as an excessive increase in use, the change is rejected.[6]

● **Structures Approved.** The approval of enlarged, additional or replacement structures often turns on findings of permission found in the local zoning law.[7]

● **Structures Rejected.** But when the local law does

Mann v. Edgartown ZBA, 13 L.C.R. 576 (2005).

[5]Sullivan v. Board of Appeals of Harwich, 15 Mass. App. Ct. 286, 445 N.E.2d 174 (1983); Derby Refining Co. v. City of Chelsea, 407 Mass. 703, 555 N.E.2d 534 (1990); Murphy v. Kotlik, 34 Mass. App. Ct. 410, 611 N.E.2d 741 (1993); Simmons v. Zoning Bd. of Appeals of Newburyport, 60 Mass. App. Ct. 5, 798 N.E.2d 1025 (2003); Titcomb v. Board of Appeals of Sandwich, 64 Mass. App. Ct. 725, 835 N.E.2d 295 (2005); and Land Court cases in 3 L.C.R. 153 (1995) and 13 L.C.R. 542 (2005).

[6]Town of Bridgewater v. Chuckran, 351 Mass. 20, 217 N.E.2d 726 (1966); Vokes v. Avery W. Lovell, Inc., 18 Mass. App. Ct. 471, 468 N.E.2d 271 (1984); Tamerlane Realty Trust v. Board of Appeals of Provincetown, 23 Mass. App. Ct. 450, 503 N.E.2d 464 (1987); Hall v. Zoning Bd. of Appeals of Edgartown, 28 Mass. App. Ct. 249, 549 N.E.2d 433 (1990); Rockwood v. Snow Inn Corp., 409 Mass. 361, 566

N.E.2d 608 (1991); KA-Hur Enterprises, Inc. v. Zoning Bd. of Appeals of Provincetown, 2 L.C.R. 103 (1994), aff'd 40 Mass.App.Ct. 71, 661 N.E.2d 120 (1996), aff'd 424 Mass. 404, 676 N.E.2d 838 (1997); Cox v. Board of Appeals of Carver, 42 Mass. App. Ct. 422, 677 N.E.2d 699 (1997); Cumberland Farms, Inc. v. Zoning Bd. of Appeals of Walpole, 61 Mass. App. Ct. 124, 807 N.E.2d 245 (2004); and Land Court cases in 1 L.C.R. 211 and 216 (1993), 3 L.C.R. 158 (1995), 6 L.C.R. 309 (1998), 7 L.C.R. 1 and 87 (1999), 8 L.C.R. 239 (2000), 11 L.C.R. 165 (2003), 12 L.C.R. 60 and 273 (2004).

[7]Lomelis v. Board of Appeals of Marblehead, 17 Mass. App. Ct. 962, 458 N.E.2d 740 (1983); Nichols v. Board of Zoning Appeal of Cambridge, 26 Mass. App. Ct. 631, 530 N.E.2d 1257 (1988); Boulter Bros. Const. Co., Inc. v. Zoning Bd. of Appeals of Norfolk, 45 Mass. App. Ct. 283, 697 N.E.2d 997 (1998); Maselbas v. Zoning Bd. of Appeals of North Attleborough, 45 Mass. App. Ct. 54, 694 N.E.2d 1314

not show the way to approval, or the local board finds detriment, the courts reject structural additions.[8]

The cases cited in these categories reflect of course a great diversity of factual situations, often include both use and structure issues, and involve interpretation of complex and sometimes unclear local by-laws as well as the statute itself which is, as noted by the Appeals Court, beset with "obscurity." When faced with an issue in this area, a practitioner may well need to read through the lot of the cited cases to get a feel for how his case might come out. A few salient points stand out:

- In *Maselbas*, attaching an addition to a nonconforming structure would clearly have required a board of appeal finding, but when the addition was moved ten feet away from the existing structure, it qualified as a permitted accessory use.

- In *Britton* the Appeals Court showed deference to the board of appeals in its denial of a permit for enlargement of a nonconforming residence on grounds of aesthetics and bad precedent, even though the trial court perceived no significant "detriment."

- Deference to the local board was again displayed by a bare majority in *Bransford*, with dissent by three justices contending that denial solely on the basis of increased living space afforded too little weight to the language of the statute and legislative policy. No deference was given when the board had not rationally considered the effects on the neighborhood.[9]

- In *Rockwood* the court applied the "lawfully in existence" clause of the first sentence of the statute to the second sentence, holding in effect that a board of appeals could not permit extension of a nonconformance even if it found no "detriment" unless the extension complied with current zoning or was granted a variance. That rendered the second sentence substantially ineffective, or only an additional (or redundant) criterion for granting of a variance for the extension. Nevertheless, in *Hooper* both the local board and the land court judge seemed to regard a

---

(1998); and Land Court cases in 1 L.C.R. 91 and 122 (1993), 13 L.C.R. 608 (2005), 14 L.C.R. 28, 65, 199, 393, 506 and 556 (2006).

[8]Dougherty v. Board of Appeal of Billerica, 41 Mass. App. Ct. 1, 668 N.E.2d 363 (1996); Britton v. Zoning Bd. of Appeals of Gloucester, 59 Mass. App. Ct. 68, 794 N.E.2d

1198 (2003); Bransford v. Zoning Bd. of Appeals of Edgartown, 444 Mass. 852, 832 N.E.2d 639 (2005); and Land Court cases in 2 L.C.R. 151 (1994), 4 L.C.R. 297 (1996), 7 L.C.R. 39 (1999), 13 L.C.R. 244 (2005).

[9]Wojnowski v. Marquis, 14 L.C.R. 600 (2006).

"finding" under § 6 as an alternative to a variance.
- A nonconformance may be lost by abandonment.[10]
- The imposition of "conditions, safeguards and limitations" has been considered in several cases.[11]

§ 11:12 Pre-existing residential lots—The statute

The fourth paragraph of § 6 of M.G.L.A. c. 40A provides that:

> Any increase in area, frontage, width, yard, or depth requirements of a zoning ordinance or by-law shall not apply to a lot for single and two-family residential use which at the time of recording or endorsement, whichever occurs sooner was not held in common ownership with any adjoining land, conformed to then existing requirements and had less than the proposed requirement but at least five thousand square feet of area and fifty feet of frontage. Any increase in area, frontage, width, yard or depth requirement of a zoning ordinance or by-law shall not apply for a period of five years from its effective date or for five years after January first, nineteen hundred and seventy-six, whichever is later, to a lot for single and two family residential use, provided the plan for such lot was recorded or endorsed and such lot was held in common ownership with any adjoining land and conformed to the existing zoning requirements as of January first, nineteen hundred and seventy-six, and had less area, frontage, width, yard or depth requirements than the newly effective zoning requirements but contained at least seven thousand five hundred square feet of area and seventy-five feet of frontage, and provided that said five year period does not commence prior to January first, nineteen hundred and seventy-six, and provided further that the provisions of this sentence shall not apply to more than three of such adjoining lots held in common ownership. The provisions of this paragraph shall not be construed to prohibit a lot being built upon, if at the time of the building, building upon such lot is not prohibited by the zoning ordinances or by-laws in effect in a city or town.

§ 11:13 Pre-existing residential lots—Applications

That paragraph is surely a prime example of the obscurity which besets § 6. Although intended to clarify earlier versions of such provisions, it has left the courts to struggle with interpretation of its meaning. The special protections apply to lots "for single and two-family residential use." The first sentence affords permanent protection to lots having at

[10]Coleman v. Gionfriddo, 14 L.C.R. 284 (2006); Shuffain v. Mulvehill, 14 L.C.R. 311 (2006).

[11]Miscoe Springs, Inc. v. Mendon Zoning Bd. of Appeals, 12 L.C.R. 219 (2004); DiGiovanni v. Zoning Bd. of Appeals of Lincoln, 13 L.C.R. 384 (2005).

least 5000 sq. ft. area and 50 foot frontage which "conformed" to "existing requirements" [of zoning] at the time of the lots' "recording or endorsement" and were not then "held in common ownership with any adjoining land." The second sentence affords protection for five years to up to three lots having 7500 sq. ft. of area and 75 foot frontage which "conformed" to zoning requirements as of January 1, 1976 and were "held in common ownership with adjoining land." The third sentence seems to say that a local zoning law may permit any lot of any size or province to be built upon for any use.

Those brief paraphrases incorporate some of the interpretations that have been made, but leave many others open. The evolution of judicial analysis may be summarized as follows:

• The first paragraph of § 6 applies to residential structures; the fourth paragraph to vacant residential lots.[1]

• "Adjoining" lots do not include two lots meeting at a point,[2] nor lots separated by marshland,[3] but do include lots which have been "checkerboarded," or transferred to related parties, which practice will not bring lots into the protection of the first sentence.[4]

• "Recording" in the first sentence relates to the most recent instrument of record prior to the zoning change, and includes a deed or a plan.[5]

• The January 1, 1976, date in the second sentence applies only as the time for "conformance" with the then existing zoning requirements, and not as a starting date for the five year period, which may begin with the later re-

---

[Section 11:13]

[1]Willard v. Board of Appeals of Orleans, 25 Mass. App. Ct. 15, 514 N.E.2d 369 (1987); Dial Away Co., Inc. v. Zoning Bd. of Appeals of Auburn, 41 Mass. App. Ct. 165, 669 N.E.2d 446 (1996).

[2]Sturges v. Town of Chilmark, 380 Mass. 246, 402 N.E.2d 1346 (1980).

[3]Heavey v. Board of Appeals of Chatham, 58 Mass. App. Ct. 401, 792 N.E.2d 651 (2003).

[4]Sorenti v. Board of Appeals of Wellesley, 345 Mass. 348, 187 N.E.2d 499, 96 A.L.R.2d 1361 (1963); Wright v. Board of Appeals of Falmouth, 24 Mass. App. Ct. 409, 509 N.E.2d 923 (1987); Planning Bd. of Norwell v. Serena, 27 Mass. App. Ct. 689, 542 N.E.2d 314 (1989), aff'd, 406 Mass. 1008, 550 N.E.2d 1390 (1990); DiStefano v. Town of Stoughton, 1 L.C.R. 42 (1993), affirmed, 36 Mass.App.Ct. 642, 634 N.E.2d 584 (1994).

[5]Sieber v. Zoning Bd. of Appeals of Wellfleet, 16 Mass. App. Ct. 985, 454 N.E.2d 108 (1983); Adamowicz v. Town of Ipswich, 395 Mass. 757, 481 N.E.2d 1368 (1985); Rourke v. Rothman, 448 Mass. 190, 859 N.E.2d 821 (2007).

cording or endorsement of a plan of the lot.[6]

• To qualify for protection under the first sentence, the lot must be defined by some "recording."[7]

• The requisite "frontage" may be on an unbuilt way, and should not be determined by criteria of M.G.L.A. c. 41, § 81L, which has different purposes than Chapter 40A, § 6.[8]

• The combination of two pre-existing lots of less than 5000 sq. ft. area into one lot having more was rejected as producing a lot qualified for protection,[9] but two lots each entitled separately to protection lost it when "merged" in common ownership,[10] a concept opposed by the Massachusetts Conveyancers' Association and the Abstract Club.

• The provision in the second sentence as to not-more-than-three adjoining lots affords protection when there are more than three such adjoining lots to the first three for which permission to build is sought, and then to no more.[11]

Application of these provisions has been made in a number of additional cases.[12]

TOPIC D: ZONING FREEZES

§ 11:14 Introduction

As noted in § 11:10, the subject of zoning freezes as well as nonconformance is covered in M.G.L.A. c. 40A, § 6. The freeze provisions as well as the nonconformance provisions were assembled (and revised) from prior separate statutory

---

[6]Baldiga v. Board of Appeals of Uxbridge, 395 Mass. 829, 482 N.E.2d 809 (1985).

[7]Dowling v. Board of Health of Chilmark, 28 Mass. App. Ct. 547, 552 N.E.2d 866 (1990).

[8]LeBlanc v. Board of Appeals of Danvers, 32 Mass. App. Ct. 760, 594 N.E.2d 906 (1992); Marinelli v. Board of Appeals of Stoughton, 440 Mass. 255, 797 N.E.2d 893 (2003); Berg v. Town of Lexington, 68 Mass. App. Ct. 569, 863 N.E.2d 968 (2007).

[9]Burke v. Zoning Bd. of Appeals of Harwich, 38 Mass. App. Ct. 957, 650 N.E.2d 355 (1995).

[10]Preston v. Board of Appeals of Hull, 51 Mass. App. Ct. 236, 744 N.E.2d 1126 (2001).

[11]Marinelli v. Board of Appeals of Stoughton, 440 Mass. 255, 797 N.E.2d 893 (2003); Marinelli v. Board of Appeals of Stoughton, 65 Mass. App. Ct. 902 (2005).

[12]Ferzoco v. Board of Appeals of Falmouth, 29 Mass. App. Ct. 986, 562 N.E.2d 105 (1990) (overruled by, Rourke v. Rothman, 448 Mass. 190, 859 N.E.2d 821 (2007)); Priore v. Sawyer, 30 Mass. App. Ct. 943, 570 N.E.2d 167 (1991); Rourke v. Rothman, 64 Mass. App. Ct. 599, 834 N.E.2d 769 (2005), judgment rev'd, 448 Mass. 190, 859 N.E.2d 821 (2007).

sources to which the case law sometimes has reference. With respect to freezes, the "obscurity" of the statute referred to in § 11:10 is happily not present, the provisions in § 6 with respect to plan freezes being quite detailed and in most respects clear. It may be noted that "freeze" is a lawyers' epithet, now adopted by the courts, for a requirement of continued application of zoning provisions existing on the occurrence of a specified action for some specified period thereafter.

§ 11:15   Permit freeze

The first sentence of M.G.L.A. c. 40A, § 6, quoted above, equally protects both "structures or uses lawfully in existence" and "a building or special permit issued" before a specified date.

As to a building permit, a structure for which it has been issued before the specified date may be built even if a zoning provision adopted before it is built makes it nonconforming. A building permit properly issued does specify the use to which the structure is intended to be put, and it is reasonable to assume that such use is also protected. However, if the use is vaguely specified, as, say, "commercial," subsequent changes in the particular commercial activities that are allowed may become applicable.

As to a special permit, the specifics of the permit are important. If it specifies a use, that is protected. Sometimes special permits also deal with particular dimensional or physical issues as well, such as building size, or off-street parking, and those would also be protected.

The crucial date before which the building or special permit must be issued in order to be afforded such protection, or to effect a "freeze," as it is said, is the date of the first notice of hearing by the planning board on the proposed zoning change.[1] Further timing requirements of great importance are provided in the second paragraph of M.G.L.A. c. 40A, § 6, which mandates provision in every zoning ordinance and by-law that "the use or construction" under a building or special permit shall be "commenced" within six months after the issuance of the permit and that any construction shall be "continued through to completion as continuously and expeditiously as is reasonable," or the protection against subsequent zoning change will be lost.

The courts have considered questions of what constitutes

[Section 11:15]

[1]Collura v. Town of Arlington, 367 Mass. 881, 329 N.E.2d 733 (1975).

commencement of construction,[2] the effect of subsequent modification of a permit,[3] and excusable delays in commencement of construction.[4]

When there is a freeze effected by a plan, as discussed in the following Section C, a permit may then be issued during that freeze period after notice of hearing and adoption of zoning changes.[5]

Site plan approval may involve a special permit, but sometimes it is not and will not effect a freeze.[6]

§ 11:16 Plan freeze—The statute

The fifth through ninth paragraphs of M.G.L.A. c. 40A, § 6, provide as follows:

> If a definitive plan, or a preliminary plan followed within seven months by a definitive plan, is submitted to a planning board for approval under the subdivision control law, and written notice of such submission has been given to the city or town clerk before the effective date of ordinance or by-law, the land shown on such plan shall be governed by the applicable provisions of the zoning ordinance or by-law, if any, in effect at the time of the first such submission while such plan or plans are being processed under the subdivision control law, and, if such definitive plan or an amendment thereof is finally approved, for eight years from the date of the endorsement of such approval, except in the case where such plan was submitted or submitted and approved before January first, nineteen hundred and seventy-six, for seven years from the date of the endorsement of such approval. Whether such period is eight years or seven years, it shall be extended by a period equal to the time which a city or town imposes or has imposed upon it by a state, a federal agency or a court, a moratorium on construction, the issuance of permits or utility connections.

---

[2]Alexander v. Building Inspector of Provincetown, 350 Mass. 370, 214 N.E.2d 876 (1966); Smith v. Board of Appeals of Brookline, 366 Mass. 197, 316 N.E.2d 501 (1974); and see Murphy v. Board of Selectmen of Manchester, 1 Mass. App. Ct. 407, 298 N.E.2d 885 (1973); Rinaudo v. Zoning Bd. of Appeals of Plymouth, 383 Mass. 885, 421 N.E.2d 439 (1981).

[3]Smith v. Building Com'r of Brookline, 367 Mass. 765, 328 N.E.2d 866 (1975); Carstensen v. Cambridge Zoning Bd. of Appeals, 11 Mass. App. Ct. 348, 416 N.E.2d 522 (1981).

[4]Woods v. City of Newton, 351 Mass. 98, 217 N.E.2d 728 (1966); Papalia v. Inspector of Bldgs. of Watertown, 351 Mass. 176, 217 N.E.2d 911 (1966); Belfer v. Building Com'r of Boston, 363 Mass. 439, 294 N.E.2d 857 (1973); Murphy v. Board of Selectmen of Manchester, 1 Mass. App. Ct. 407, 298 N.E.2d 885 (1973).

[5]Nyquist v. Board of Appeals of Acton, 359 Mass. 462, 269 N.E.2d 654 (1971).

[6]See Towermarc Canton Limited Partnership v. Town of Canton (Land Court Case No. 131947, Oct. 26, 1989).

When a plan referred to in section eighty-one P of chapter forty-one has been submitted to a planning board and written notice of such submission has been given to the city or town clerk, the use of the land shown on such plan shall be governed by applicable provisions of the zoning ordinance or by-law in effect at the time of the submission of such plan while such plan is being processed under the subdivision control law including the time required to pursue or await the determination of an appeal referred to in said section, and for a period of three years from the date of endorsement by the planning board that approval under the subdivision control law is not required, or words of similar import.

Disapproval of a plan shall not serve to terminate any rights which shall have accrued under the provisions of this section, provided an appeal from the decision disapproving said plan is made under applicable provisions of law. Such appeal shall stay, pending either (1) the conclusion of voluntary mediation proceedings and the filing of a written agreement for judgment or stipulation of dismissal, or (2) the entry of an order or decree of a court of final jurisdiction, the applicability to land shown on said plan of the provisions of any zoning ordinance or by-law which became effective after the date of submission of the plan first submitted, together with time required to comply with any such agreement or with the terms of any order or decree of the court.

In the event that any lot shown on a plan endorsed by the planning board is the subject matter of any appeal or any litigation, the exemptive provisions of this section shall be extended for a period equal to that from the date of filing of said appeal or the commencement of litigation, whichever is earlier, to the date of final disposition thereof, provided final adjudication is in favor of the owner of said lot.

The record owner of the land shall have the right, at any time, by an instrument duly recorded in the registry of deeds for the district in which the land lies, to waive the provisions of this section, in which case the ordinance or by-law then or thereafter in effect shall apply. The submission of an amended plan or of a further subdivision of all or part of the land shall not constitute such a waiver, nor shall it have the effect of further extending the applicability of the ordinance or by-law that was extended by the original submission, but, if accompanied by the waiver described above, shall have the effect of extending, but only to extent aforesaid, the ordinance or by-law made then applicable by such waiver

§ 11:17 Plan freeze—Applications

Refreshingly detailed and clear, these provisions relate to plans which have been dealt with by a Planning Board under the Subdivision Control Law, discussed in **Chapter 12**.

● **ANR Plan.** The sixth paragraph of Chapter 40A, § 6, affords to land shown on a plan submitted to a planning board under § 81-P of M.G.L.A. c. 41, with written notice to the city or town clerk, for endorsement "approval not required," a "freeze" of the zoning provisions relating to use of the land in effect at the time of such submission, during the processing thereof and any appeal with respect thereto, and for a period of three years after the planning board so endorses the plan. The uses protected are those provided by the zoning law in effect at the time of submission of the plan,[1] and include those which require a special permit as well as those permitted as a matter of right.[2] Distinctions have been noted as to what uses are protected and as to the relation of some physical provisions of zoning to a permitted use.[3]

The freeze takes effect even if the plan was filed solely for freeze purposes, was not recorded or used for conveyance and was ignored when a permit was sought,[4] or when the plan was deemed endorsed by default of the Planning Board to act.[5]

● **Subdivision Plan.** The fifth and seventh paragraphs of Chapter 40A, § 6, afford to land shown on a plan submitted to a planning board as a definitive plan of subdivision, or a preliminary plan followed within seven months by a definitive plan, with due notice to the city or town clerk, a "freeze" of all zoning provisions applicable to the land shown on the plan in effect at the time of such submission, during the processing thereof, until any appeal from a denial of approval is resolved, and, if a definitive plan is finally approved, for a period of eight years thereafter. The eight years is further extended by a period equal to any lawfully imposed

---

[Section 11:17]

[1]See Bellows Farms, Inc. v. Building Inspector of Acton, 364 Mass. 253, 303 N.E.2d 728 (1973); Cape Ann Land Development Corp. v. City of Gloucester, 371 Mass. 19, 353 N.E.2d 645 (1976); McCaffrey v. Board of Appeals of Ipswich, 4 Mass. App. Ct. 109, 343 N.E.2d 154 (1976); Perry v. Building Inspector of Nantucket, 4 Mass. App. Ct. 467, 350 N.E.2d 733 (1976); Falcone v. Zoning Bd. of Appeals of Brockton, 7 Mass. App. Ct. 710, 389 N.E.2d 1032 (1979).

[2]Miller v. Board of Appeals of Canton, 8 Mass. App. Ct. 923, 396 N.E.2d 180 (1979); Samson v. San-Land Development Corp., 17 Mass. App. Ct. 977, 458 N.E.2d

1201 (1984).

[3]Stampfl v. Zoning Bd. of Appeals of Norwood, 33 Mass. App. Ct. 354, 599 N.E.2d 646 (1992); Katzen v. Town of Wellesley, 5 L.C.R. 134 (1997); Cicatelli v. Board of Appeals of Wakefield, 57 Mass. App. Ct. 799, 786 N.E.2d 1216 (2003); Cape Ann Land Development Corp. v. City of Gloucester, 371 Mass. 19, 353 N.E.2d 645 (1976).

[4]Long v. Board of Appeals of Falmouth, 32 Mass. App. Ct. 232, 588 N.E.2d 692 (1992).

[5]Katzen v. Town of Wellesley, 5 L.C.R. 134 (1997); Cumberland Farms, Inc. v. Planning Bd. of West Bridgewater, 64 Mass. App. Ct. 902, 833 N.E.2d 153 (2005).

moratorium on construction, the issuance of permits or utility connections, but was held not to have been tolled by a
rate-of-development bylaw.[6]

Because of the substantial freeze period and because it
bars the application of all zoning changes, this protection is
both coveted and contested.[7] The freeze is only of zoning
laws, and a landowner so protected may be subject to other
regulations.[8] It may be noted, however, that M.G.L.A. c. 111,
§ 127P, imposes a three year freeze on enforcement of certain
environmental and health laws.[9] A freeze was denied when,
after denial of approval of the original definitive, a revised
plan meeting objections was filed more than seven months
after the original filing.[10] Freeze was also denied to a pre-
existing lot adjacent to a subdivision and shown on the approved subdivision plan.[11] The period of freeze cannot be
extended or renewed by filing the same plan again.[12] Freezes
have withstood attacks in several cases,[13] including *Massachusetts Broken Stone* in which the local board and the
Appeals Court gutted the provision, but were fortunately reversed by the SJC. Several issues arising at the end of a
freeze period have been considered,[14] and the Land Court

[6]Sebastiao v. Zoning Bd. of
Appeals of Blackstone, 8 L.C.R. 189
(2000); and see M. DeMatteo Const.
Co. v. Board of Appeals of Hingham,
3 Mass. App. Ct. 446, 334 N.E.2d
51 (1975).

[7]R.C. Management Corp. v.
Planning Bd. of Southbridge, 31
Mass. App. Ct. 510, 580 N.E.2d
1045 (1991).

[8]Rayco Inv. Corp. v. Board of
Selectmen of Raynham, 368 Mass.
385, 331 N.E.2d 910 (1975); Island
Properties, Inc. v. Martha's
Vineyard Commission, 372 Mass.
216, 361 N.E.2d 385 (1977).

[9]See Independence Park, Inc.
v. Board of Health of Barnstable,
403 Mass. 477, 530 N.E.2d 1235
(1988).

[10]Arenstam v. Planning Bd. of
Tyngsborough, 29 Mass. App. Ct.
314, 560 N.E.2d 142 (1990).

[11]Astle v. Fall River Zoning Bd.
of Appeals, 5 L.C.R. 83 (1997).

[12]Charles Square Unit 908

Realty Trust v. Planning Bd. of
Weston, 1 L.C.R. 133 (1993).

[13]McCarthy v. Board of Appeals
of Ashland, 354 Mass. 660, 241
N.E.2d 840 (1968); Green v. Board
of Appeal of Norwood, 358 Mass.
253, 263 N.E.2d 423 (1970); Heritage
Park Dev. Corp. v. Town of Southbridge, 3 L.C.R. 93 (1995), aff'd, 424
Mass. 71, 674 N.E.2d 233 (1997);
Antonelli v. Planning Bd. of North
Andover, 4 L.C.R. 67 (1996); Kindercare Learning Centers, Inc. v. Town
of Westford, 62 Mass. App. Ct. 924,
818   N.E.2d   594   (2004);
Massachusetts Broken Stone Co. v.
Town of Weston, 430 Mass. 637,
723 N.E.2d 7 (2000).

[14]Falcone v. Zoning Bd. of
Appeals of Brockton, 7 Mass. App.
Ct. 710, 389 N.E.2d 1032 (1979);
but see Cape Ann Land Development Corp. v. City of Gloucester,
371 Mass. 19, 353 N.E.2d 645
(1976); Mullen Lumber Co., Inc. v.
Board of Appeals of Marshfield, 7
Mass. App. Ct. 917, 389 N.E.2d 736
(1979).

has considered a number of points.[15]

Under the last paragraph in Chapter 40A, § 6, a land-owner having the benefit of a freeze may "waive" the protections of § 6, allowing subsequently adopted zoning laws to become effective. The submission of an amended plan or further subdivision of all or part of the protected land does not by itself constitute a waiver,[16] but if accompanied by such a waiver it "shall have the effect of extending, but only to the extent aforesaid, the ordinance or by-law made then applicable by such waiver," the meaning of which is not clear.

TOPIC E: VARIANCE

§ 11:18   Criteria

As noted in § 11:1, zoning laws have from the outset included some provision for "variance" or exception from the application of particular zoning regulations. In Massachusetts the power to grant variances has always been narrowly stated and strictly construed,[1] as further indicated by the courts' rejection of "local prerogative," or a local bylaw "waiver"[2] and upholding denial of a variance even if the use sought was "inoffensive" and plaintiff's objection "mean spirited."[3] Furthermore, it is provided in M.G.L.A. c. 40A, § 10, that no "use variances" may be granted unless the local bylaw expressly permits them.

The criteria for the granting of a variance are that: (a) "owing to circumstances relating to the soil conditions, shape, or topography of such land or structures and especially affecting such land or structures but not affecting generally the zoning district in which it is located", (b) "a literal

[15]See 2 L.C.R. 1, 10, 97, 153; 3 L.C.R. 215; 4 L.C.R. 18, 203, 242; 5 L.C.R. 118, 150; 7 L.C.R. 81, 185; 8 L.C.R. 38; 9 L.C.R. 246, 429.

[16]Patelle v. Planning Bd. of Woburn, 20 Mass. App. Ct. 279, 480 N.E.2d 35 (1985).

[Section 11:18]

[1]Hammond v. Board of Appeal of Bldg. Dept. of Springfield, 257 Mass. 446, 154 N.E. 82 (1926); Coleman v. Board of Appeal of Building Department of Boston, 281 Mass. 112, 183 N.E. 166 (1932); Real Properties v. Board of Appeal of Boston, 319 Mass. 180, 65 N.E.2d 199, 168 A.L.R. 8 (1946); DiGiovanni v. Board of Appeals of Rockport, 19 Mass. App. Ct. 339, 474 N.E.2d 198 (1985).

[2]Tsagronis v. Board of Appeals of Wareham, 33 Mass. App. Ct. 55, 596 N.E.2d 369 (1992), judgment rev'd, 415 Mass. 329, 613 N.E.2d 893 (1993); Aloha Foundation v. Zoning Bd. of Appeals of Norwell, 4 L.C.R. 199 (1996).

[3]Brogle v. Martin, 20 Mass. App. Ct. 901, 477 N.E.2d 605 (1985).

enforcement of the provisions of the ordinance or by-law would involve substantial hardship, financial or otherwise, to the petitioner . . .," and (c) that "desirable relief may be granted without substantial detriment to the public good and without nullifying or substantially derogating from the intent or purpose of such ordinance or by-law."

All three criteria must be met for a variance to be lawful,[4] but even if the criteria are met the owner does not have a legal right to a variance.[5]

Each of the criteria has received substantial judicial review.

● **Land or Structure Conditions.** Conditions held to warrant variance have included: the presence of "pudding stone," location under high tension lines of a triangular lot with peaty soil and beset by clandestine dumping, location of a lot at a low point on which area drainage collected, unusual topography and presence of ledge, peculiar "pork chop" lot shape, and disuse of an old church, converted into an office building.[6] However, rejection is more frequent and it has been held that variance is not warranted by poor soil conditions present throughout the area, the end of a rail line, affecting other abutters as well, proximity to a gravel pit, mere lack of adequate frontage,[7] or generally any conditions which are not shown as "especially affecting" the particular site. Denial of a variance because of the unsafety of a long driveway was upheld.[8] When a variance had been granted for a garage in a set-back area, it was held that use of the structure for non-garage purposes would require a new

---

[4]Warren v. Board of Appeals of Amherst, 383 Mass. 1, 416 N.E.2d 1382 (1981); Kirkwood v. Board of Appeals of Rockport, 17 Mass. App. Ct. 423, 458 N.E.2d 1213 (1984).

[5]Bruzzese v. Board of Appeals of Hingham, 343 Mass. 421, 179 N.E.2d 269 (1962).

[6]Rodenstein v. Board of Appeal of Boston, 337 Mass. 333, 149 N.E.2d 382 (1958); Dion v. Board of Appeals of Waltham, 344 Mass. 547, 183 N.E.2d 479 (1962); Sherman v. Board of Appeals of Worcester, 354 Mass. 133, 235 N.E.2d 800 (1968); Broderick v. Board of Appeal of Boston, 361 Mass. 472, 280 N.E.2d 670 (1972); Johnson v. Board of Appeals of Wareham, 360 Mass. 872, 277 N.E.2d 695 (1972); Pauld-

ing v. Bruins, 18 Mass. App. Ct. 707, 470 N.E.2d 398 (1984).

[7]Bicknell Realty Co. v. Board of Appeal of Boston, 330 Mass. 676, 116 N.E.2d 570 (1953); Planning Bd. of Watertown v. Board of Appeals of Watertown, 5 Mass. App. Ct. 833, 363 N.E.2d 293 (1977); Costa v. Zoning Bd. of Appeals of Framingham, 6 Mass. App. Ct. 872, 374 N.E.2d 1239 (1978); Guiragossian v. Board of Appeals of Watertown, 21 Mass. App. Ct. 111, 485 N.E.2d 686 (1985).

[8]Chiancola v. Board of Appeals of Rockport, 65 Mass. App. Ct. 636, 843 N.E.2d 108 (2006), review denied, 446 Mass. 1107, 846 N.E.2d 780 (2006).

variance.[9]

• **Hardship.** As the wording of the statute makes clear, a "hardship" sufficient to warrant a variance must derive from physical circumstances especially affecting the land or structure itself. In the few cases in which variance was upheld the "hardship" was usually found in the substantial unsuitability of the property for residential use, thus warranting a commercial use. But again, rejection is much more common, and the requisite hardship does not arise from an owner's "financial squeeze," or from "deprivation of potential advantage, or costs personal to the owner, nor from impact on the lot owner's business prospects."[10] Furthermore, when insufficient frontage resulted from the owner's prior conveyance of adjoining land, such "self-imposed hardship" will not be accepted to warrant a variance.[11] However, when the short frontage resulted from a taking from an "innocent" owner, the variance was upheld.[12]

• **Detriment or Derogation.** Affirmative finding that a variance would not result in substantial detriment or derogation was made for: a government office in a residential neighborhood, a power plant in an urban renewal project, a medical building, a general store in a residential district, and a gas station replacing a dilapidated building.[13] Absent such an affirmative finding by the trial court, the test is not

---

[9]Lussier v. Zoning Bd. of Appeals of Peabody, 447 Mass. 531, 854 N.E.2d 1236 (2006).

[10]Real Properties v. Board of Appeal of Boston, 319 Mass. 180, 65 N.E.2d 199, 168 A.L.R. 8 (1946); Bruzzese v. Board of Appeals of Hingham, 343 Mass. 421, 179 N.E.2d 269 (1962); McLaughlin v. Rockland Zoning Bd. of Appeals, 351 Mass. 678, 223 N.E.2d 521 (1967); Abbott v. Appleton Nursing Home, Inc., 355 Mass. 217, 243 N.E.2d 912 (1969); Garfield v. Board of Appeals of Rockport, 356 Mass. 37, 247 N.E.2d 720 (1969); Planning Bd. of Barnstable v. Board of Appeals of Barnstable, 358 Mass. 824, 267 N.E.2d 923 (1971); Sullivan v. Board of Appeals of Belmont, 346 Mass. 81, 190 N.E.2d 83 (1963); Wolfson v. Sun Oil Co., 357 Mass. 87, 256 N.E.2d 308 (1970).

[11]Gordon v. Zoning Bd. of Appeals of Lee, 22 Mass. App. Ct.

343, 494 N.E.2d 14 (1986); DiCicco v. Berwick, 27 Mass. App. Ct. 312, 537 N.E.2d 1267 (1989); Karet v. Zoning Bd. of Appeals of Worcester, 27 Mass. App. Ct. 439, 539 N.E.2d 81 (1989); Chelmsford Planning Bd. v. Zoning Bd. of Appeals of Chelmsford, 7 L.C.R. 261 (1999); Minassian v. Eonas, 7 L.C.R. 287 (1999).

[12]Adams v. Brolly, 46 Mass. App. Ct. 1, 702 N.E.2d 400 (1998).

[13]O'Brian v. Board of Appeals of Brockton, 3 Mass. App. Ct. 740, 326 N.E.2d 728 (1975); Boston Edison Co. v. Boston Redevelopment Authority, 374 Mass. 37, 371 N.E.2d 728 (1977); Boyajian v Bd. of Appeal, 6 Mass.App.Ct. 283, 374 N.E.2d 1237 (1978); Cavanaugh v. DiFlumera, 9 Mass. App. Ct. 396, 401 N.E.2d 867 (1980); Kairis v. Board of Appeal of Cambridge, 337 Mass. 528, 150 N.E.2d 278 (1958); but see Di Rico v. Board of Appeals of Quincy, 341 Mass. 607, 171

met, but the judge's taking a view may suffice.[14] Rejected on grounds of detriment or derogation were: a boat business in a residential area, a restaurant in a residential area, and a parking area on a residential lot serving an adjacent supermarket.[15]

As to each of the criteria the analysis and outcome depend critically on the particular facts of the case. Consequently there is a great body of diverse findings of which the cases here cited are only a sampling. The SJC has said that "a decision of the board of appeals granting a variance cannot stand unless the board specifically finds that each statutory requirement has been met," and that on appeal the judge is to determine the facts for himself and may uphold the variance only if he finds that the prerequisites of the statute have been met.[16] In the cited case the variance was for an apartment house loading bay of 10 ft. height rather than 14 ft. as required by the bylaw. While conceding that the board of appeals findings were "meager," the court carefully analyzed the facts and found site-specific warrant of hardship. Similar accommodation for minor dimensional variances is indicated in other decisions.[17]

As to the imposition of conditions upon the grant of a variance, the issue of a time limit was left unresolved; an anti-subdivision condition was barred.[18]

§ 11:19   Application and procedure

A variance may be granted only by a Board of Appeals or a "zoning administrator," if one has been appointed by the board pursuant to M.G.L.A. c. 40A, § 13. The board of appeals is required to adopt rules for the conduct of its busi-

---

N.E.2d 144 (1961).

[14]Planning Bd. of Springfield v. Board of Appeals of Springfield, 355 Mass. 460, 245 N.E.2d 454 (1969); Broderick v. Board of Appeal of Boston, 361 Mass. 472, 280 N.E.2d 670 (1972); Kairis v. Board of Appeal of Cambridge, 337 Mass. 528, 150 N.E.2d 278 (1958).

[15]Atherton v. Board of Appeals of Town of Bourne, 334 Mass. 451, 136 N.E.2d 201 (1956); Benjamin v. Board of Appeals of Swansea, 338 Mass. 257, 154 N.E.2d 913 (1959); Cary v. Board of Appeals of Worcester, 340 Mass. 748, 166 N.E.2d 690 (1960).

[16]Josephs v. Board of Appeals of Brookline, 362 Mass. 290, 285 N.E.2d 436 (1972).

[17]Wolfman v. Board of Appeals of Brookline, 15 Mass. App. Ct. 112, 444 N.E.2d 943 (1983); Reeves v. Board of Zoning Appeal of Cambridge, 16 Mass. App. Ct. 1011, 455 N.E.2d 447 (1983); Great Woods, Inc. v. Bd. of Appeals of Mansfield, 6 L.C.R. 300 (1998).

[18]Maurice Callahan & Sons, Inc. v. Board of Appeals of Lenox, 30 Mass. App. Ct. 36, 565 N.E.2d 813 (1991); Webster v. Town of Bolton, 9 L.C.R. 380 (2001).

ness and file them with the city or town clerk, but that requirement has not been strictly enforced.[1] Unless the local bylaw or ordinance so provides, the board has no power to grant any use variance. Local laws may not otherwise enlarge the board's variance powers or restrict the statutory criteria.

An application for a variance should be filed with the board of appeals and the city or town clerk. The date of filing begins important time frames. The application should set forth the name of the petitioner, a description of the premises and the location thereof, the subject matter of the petition and a clear and sufficient description of the relief sought, specifying the particular zoning provisions sought to be varied. It may sometimes be useful to include assertions as to the basis of compliance with the statutory criteria, but of course the applicant should reserve the right to present other or further evidence at the public hearing. If the applicant intends to "save his rights," it is well to say so.[2]

The board must then give notice of a public hearing on the application. It is not remiss for an applicant's counsel to seek review of the form of notice before it is given in order to assure that it meets legal requirements. Some laxity in meeting notice requirements is allowed but there are limits.[3] Defects may be corrected by waiver, affidavit or supplemental notice, as provided in § 11 of Chapter 40A, or be determined to be non-prejudicial.[4]

M.G.L.A. c. 40A, § 11 provides that the notice must be given by the board by publication, posting and mail to "parties in interest," including "the petitioner, abutters, owners of the land directly opposite on any public or private street

---

[Section 11:19]

[1]Roman Catholic Archbishop of Boston v. Board of Appeal of Bldg. Dept. of City of Boston, 268 Mass. 416, 167 N.E. 672 (1929); Co-Ray Realty Co. v. Board of Zoning Adjustment of Boston, 328 Mass. 103, 101 N.E.2d 888 (1951); Lynch v. Board of Appeal of Boston, 1 Mass. App. Ct. 353, 297 N.E.2d 63 (1973); Burwick v. Zoning Bd. of Appeals of Worcester, 1 Mass. App. Ct. 739, 306 N.E.2d 455 (1974); Tenneco Oil Co. v. City Council of Springfield, 406 Mass. 658, 549 N.E.2d 1135 (1990).

[2]Cities Service Oil Co. v. Board of Appeals of Bedford, 338 Mass.

719, 157 N.E.2d 225 (1959).

[3]Kane v. Board of Appeals of City of Medford, 273 Mass. 97, 173 N.E. 1 (1930); Kasper v. Board of Appeals of Watertown, 3 Mass. App. Ct. 251, 326 N.E.2d 915 (1975); Chiuccariello v. Building Com'r of Boston, 29 Mass. App. Ct. 482, 562 N.E.2d 96 (1990); Franchi v. Zoning Bd. of Appeals of Norwood, 13 L.C.R. 491 (2005).

[4]Kasper v. Board of Appeals of Watertown, 3 Mass. App. Ct. 251, 326 N.E.2d 915 (1975); Ranney v. Board of Appeals of Nantucket, 11 Mass. App. Ct. 112, 414 N.E.2d 373 (1981).

or way, and abutters to the abutters within three hundred feet of the property line of the premises involved in the petition, as they appear on the most recent applicable tax list, notwithstanding that the land of any such owner is located in another city or town, the planning board of the city or town, and the planning board of every abutting city or town."

The publication must be once in each week for two successive weeks, the first at least 14 days before the public hearing, in a newspaper of general circulation in the community where the subject land lies. The determination of abutters to abutters within three hundred feet is sometimes tricky, and again applicant's counsel may properly concern himself with sufficiency of the notice even though it is the responsibility of the board. If, for instance, any land of a condominium lies within 300 feet of the subject land, it would appear that notice would need to be given to every unit owner of the condominium, although it is arguable (but unresolved) that notice to the condominium organization would suffice. It is provided in § 11 of Chapter 40A that a certification by the municipal assessors of names and addresses "shall be conclusive for all purposes."[5]

The board of appeals is to hold a public hearing within 65 days after receipt of an application for variance and make its decision within 100 days after such receipt, but each of those time limits may be extended by written agreement between the applicant and the board, filed with the city or town clerk. In the absence of prejudice some stretching of these periods has been allowed.[6] The grant of a variance requires that the decision of the board be unanimous by a three member board or by four of a five member board. Under § 11 of Chapter 40A the decision must identify the land and owner, specify compliance with the statutory criteria, and be filed with the city or town clerk and the planning board. A separate provision in § 15 requires the board to make a "detailed record" of its proceedings, indicating the vote of each member and "setting forth clearly the reason for its decision," to be filed within 14 days with the city or town clerk as a public record. The board is also to mail a "notice of the decision" to all parties in interest, specifying appeal rights. These provisions, though amended, may still merit the Appeal Court's epithet as the "notoriously confused text of M.G.L.A. c. 40A, § 15,

---

[5]Napier v. Bd. of Appeals of Tisbury, 1 L.C.R. 144 (1993).

[6]Casasanta v. Zoning Bd. of Appeals of Milford, 377 Mass. 67,

384 N.E.2d 1218 (1979); cf. Noe v. Board of Appeals of Hingham, 13 Mass. App. Ct. 103, 430 N.E.2d 853 (1982).

fifth par."[7] The 14-day period has been held to run from the end of the 100-day period even if the board has made its decision before 100 days ran out.[8]

A twenty-day appeal period follows such § 11 filing, and the decision does not take effect until the clerk certifies that the appeal period has expired with no appeal taken or that any appeal has been dismissed or denied, and then the decision together with such certification is duly recorded in the registry of deeds.

Failure of the board to act within 100 days, or any extended period,[9] "shall be deemed to be the grant of the appeal, application or petition," and the applicant may, within 14 days after such failure, then (i) give written notice to parties in interest of their rights of appeal, and (ii) twenty days later obtain certification from the city or town clerk that approval of the application has become final by failure of the board to act, and that the appeal period has expired without appeal or with appeal dismissed or denied. That certification becomes effective upon due recording.

It is provided in § 10 of Chapter 40A that "the rights authorized by a variance" "shall lapse" if they are not exercised within one year of the grant, provided that if application for extension is made within the year, the board may extend the time for up to six months. Issues of lapse have been litigated.[10] The one-year period runs from the date of grant of the variance, not the recording.[11]

In § 16 of Chapter 40A it is provided that if an application "has been unfavorably and finally acted upon" by the board, it may not be acted favorably upon within two years after the unfavorable action unless the board of appeals makes a finding by specified vote of "material changes," and "all but one of the members of the planning board consents." If

---

[7]O'Kane v. Board of Appeals of Hingham, 20 Mass. App. Ct. 162, 478 N.E.2d 962 (1985).

[8]Burnham v. Town of Hadley, 58 Mass. App. Ct. 479, 790 N.E.2d 1098 (2003); and see O'Kane v. Board of Appeals of Hingham, 20 Mass. App. Ct. 162, 478 N.E.2d 962 (1985), and Zuckerman v. Zoning Bd. of Appeals of Greenfield, 394 Mass. 663, 477 N.E.2d 132 (1985).

[9]See Petersen v. Cargill, 14 L.C.R. 403 (2006).

[10]Hogan v. Hayes, 19 Mass. App. Ct. 399, 474 N.E.2d 1158

(1985); Lopes v. Board of Appeals of Fairhaven, 27 Mass. App. Ct. 754, 543 N.E.2d 421 (1989); Laberis v. Building Inspector of Peabody, 2 L.C.R. 99 (1994); Buttaro v. Bd. of Appeals of Woburn, 4 L.C.R. 111 (1996); Alroy v. Zoning Bd. of Appeals of Newton, 5 L.C.R. 245 (1998); Asack v. Board of Appeals of Westwood, 47 Mass. App. Ct. 733, 716 N.E.2d 135 (1999); Tremblay v. Tewksbury Bd. of Appeals, 11 L.C.R. 206 (2003).

[11]Tremblay v. Tewksbury Bd. of Appeals, 11 L.C.R. 206 (2003).

unfavorable action appears to be imminent, an applicant might wish to withdraw, but once notice of a public hearing has been published, withdrawal without prejudice requires the approval of the board of appeals.

TOPIC F: SPECIAL PERMIT

§ 11:20 Types

Provision for special permit is made in § 9 of Chapter 40A, supplemented by § 9A, added in 1982, relating to "adult" establishments, and § 9B, added in 1985, relating to solar energy facilities. Section 9 itself, as well as § 9A, have subsequently been amended. The first paragraph of § 9 provides that "Zoning ordinances or by-laws shall provide for specific types of uses which shall only be permitted in specified districts upon issuance of a special permit," which "may be issued only for uses which are in harmony with the general purpose and intent of the ordinance or by-law, and shall be subject to general or specific provisions set forth therein; and such permits may also impose conditions, safeguards and limitations on time or use."

The following provisions were inserted in § 9 as part of the 2006 Act Relative to Streamlining and Expediting the Permitting Process:[1]

> In any city or town that accepts this paragraph, zoning ordinances or bylaws may provide that research and development uses, whether or not the uses are currently permitted as a matter of right, may be permitted as a permitted use in any non-residential zoning district which is not a residential, agricultural or open space district upon the issuance of a special permit provided the special permit granting authority finds that the uses do not substantially derogate from the public good. "Research and development uses" shall include any 1 or more of investigation, development, laboratory and similar research uses and any related office and, subject to the following limitations, limited manufacturing uses and uses accessory to any of the foregoing. "Limited manufacturing" shall, subject to the issuance of the special permit, be an allowed use, if the following requirements are satisfied: (1) the manufacturing activity is related to research uses; (2) no manufacturing activity customarily occurs within 50 feet of a residential district; and (3) substantially all manufacturing activity customarily occurs inside of buildings with any

---

[Section 11:20]

[1]Chapter 205, Acts of 2006.

manufacturing activities customarily occurring outside of buildings subject to conditions imposed in the special permit.

Also, as referred to in § **11:7**, that Act added a new § 30 to M.G.L.A. c. 40B, but the wording thereof would seem to apply to all zoning processes in a municipality that accepts the statute, as follows:

> Section 30. (a) There shall be within each regional planning district created under this chapter or by special act, a technical assistance center for the delivery of coordinated, comprehensive, and continuing technical services to and among local governments for the purpose of expediting permitting. The board of executive directors of the Massachusetts association of regional planning agencies shall develop a state-wide permitting model that municipalities may adopt. The model processes shall expedite local permitting and zoning consistent with chapter 43D. The board shall direct each regional planning agency to conduct an evaluation of its member cities' and towns' permitting processes and to report its findings to the board. It shall be the responsibility of each regional planning agency to work under the guidance of the board to assist in the development of a state-wide model.

The "specific types of uses" for which a special permit may be issued require express provisions in a zoning ordinance or bylaw, and some standards for the issuance must be set forth. A bylaw in the town of Egremont, authorized special permits for multi-family dwellings and for "retail business or consumer service establishments," which were upheld as adequately describing "specific types of uses," but an authorization of special permits for "[a]ny other use determined by the Planning Board and not offensive or detrimental to the neighborhood" was rejected as not adequately specific.[2]

Land uses and activities that are commonly subjected to special permit requirements include wetland controls, earth removal, recreational and social clubs or facilities in residential districts, variant housing accommodations, home occupations, dimensional variations, and site planning in relation to developments. Salient among these are the following:

● **Wetland Regulations** were specifically provided for in the 1975 zoning recodification, and provisions of that type have been upheld; some overlapping regulations under general laws, notwithstanding the limitation

---

[2]Gage v. Town of Egremont, 409 Mass. 345, 566 N.E.2d 597 (1991); Weld v. Board of Appeals of Gloucester, 345 Mass. 376, 187 N.E.2d 854 (1963); Board of Appeals of Hanover v. Housing Appeals Committee in Dept. of Community Affairs, 363 Mass. 339, 294 N.E.2d 393 (1973); Land Court decisions in 3 L.C.R. 1 (1994), 3 L.C.R. 74 (1995), 6 L.C.R. 268 (1998).

referred to in § **11:6**.[3]

• **Site Plan Approval.** In the *Y.D. Dugout* case[4] it was held that a bylaw in Canton providing for commercial uses of right could not also provide that they were subject to discretionary site plan approval. The popularity among zoning and planning officials of site plan review as a regulatory device has led to a series of cases in which the courts have further defined the distinction between a site plan review limited to determination of compliance with established and specified criteria, and site plan approval constituting in effect the discretionary grant of a special permit. A review of the pertinent cases has been provided by the appeals court.[5] A non-discretionary site plan review is not an appealable action.[6] An alternative approach tried in Braintree, making all uses in a business district subject to a discretionary special permit, was rejected in the *SCIT, Inc.* case[7] as violative of the uniformity requirement.

• **Dimensional Variations.** The "uses" for which a zoning bylaw may allow a special permit include dimensional modifications.[8]

• **Historic District Approval.** Although governed by M.G.L.A. c. 40C and not a zoning procedure, the issuance by a historic district commission of a "certificate of appropriateness" may involve issues analogous to those posed in special permit cases. See § **14:6** and § **14:7**.

The types of special permits which may be provided for in local zoning laws are not mandatory, and many of them do

---

[3]Turnpike Realty Co. v. Town of Dedham, 362 Mass. 221, 284 N.E.2d 891 (1972); S. Volpe & Co., Inc. v. Board of Appeals of Wareham, 4 Mass. App. Ct. 357, 348 N.E.2d 807 (1976); MacGibbon v. Board of Appeals of Duxbury, 369 Mass. 512, 340 N.E.2d 487 (1976); Golden v. Board of Selectmen of Falmouth, 358 Mass. 519, 265 N.E.2d 573 (1970); Lovequist v. Conservation Commission of Town of Dennis, 379 Mass. 7, 393 N.E.2d 858 (1979); S. Kemble Fischer Realty Trust v. Board of Appeals of Concord, 9 Mass. App. Ct. 477, 402 N.E.2d 100 (1980); Turner v. Town of Walpole, 10 Mass. App. Ct. 515, 409 N.E.2d 807 (1980); Farrugia v. Board of Appeals of Marshfield, 14 Mass. App. Ct. 720, 442 N.E.2d 1161 (1982).

[4]Y. D. Dugout, Inc. v. Board of Appeals of Canton, 357 Mass. 25, 255 N.E.2d 732 (1970).

[5]Osberg v. Planning Bd. of Sturbridge, 44 Mass. App. Ct. 56, 687 N.E.2d 1274 (1997).

[6]Dufault v. Millennium Power Partners, L.P., 49 Mass. App. Ct. 137, 727 N.E.2d 87 (2000).

[7]SCIT, Inc. v. Planning Bd. of Braintree, 19 Mass. App. Ct. 101, 472 N.E.2d 269 (1984).

[8]Emond v. Board of Appeals of Uxbridge, 27 Mass. App. Ct. 630, 541 N.E.2d 380 (1989); Berkshire Power Development, Inc. v. Zoning Bd. of Appeals of Agawam, 43 Mass. App. Ct. 828, 686 N.E.2d 1088 (1997); and Land Court cases in 3 L.C.R. 51 and 205 (1995), 13 L.C.R. 297 (2005).

not appear at all in local ordinances and bylaws. Beyond the generic requirement and customary types, other permissible special permits are defined, by prolix and often confusing provisions, in §§ 9, 9A and 9B of Chapter 40A as including the following:

- **Density and Intensity.** Increase in "density of population" or "intensity of a particular use" may be permitted in return for applicant's provision of such things as open space, low cost housing, traffic improvements, solar energy systems, or "other amenities." If a bylaw provides for this type of permit, it must specify the acceptable amenities and the maximum permissible increases in density or use.

- **Multi-Family Residences.** Multi-family residences may be permitted in nonresidential zones, subject to required findings.

- **Transfer of Development Rights.** Transfer of "development rights of land" within or between districts may be permitted in order to promote specified "community interests," and may include "incentives" such as increased density, floor space or lot coverage.

- **Cluster Development and Planned Unit Development.** Cluster development and planned unit development may be permitted, as defined in the statute and subject to specified requirements. Cluster plan approvals have been reviewed.[9]

- **Shared Elderly Housing.** The sharing of housing by elderly persons may be permitted for up to six occupants and subject to "any age requirements and any other conditions deemed necessary."

- **Scientific Activities.** Special permit may be granted for uses accessory to activities necessary in connection with scientific research or development or related production, subject to finding that such use "does not substantially derogate from the public good."

- **Hazardous Waste Facility.** A special permit may impose "reasonable conditions on the construction or operation" of a hazardous waste facility, which may, as the statute provides, be constructed as of right on any site "zoned for industrial use," subject to water supply and environmental protections.

- **Adult Establishments.** Various so-called "adult" establishments, including bookstore, motion picture theatre, paraphernalia store, video store, and "establishments

---

[9]Brewton v. Spiegel, 14 L.C.R. 468 (2006); J.A. Taylor Construc- tion Company, Inc. v. Ampagoom- ian, 14 L.C.R. 603 (2006).

which display live nudity," all as defined in § 9A with reference to M.G.L.A. c. 272, § 31. A zoning bylaw may provide certain locational controls, and pre-existing establishments of this type are required to apply for a permit within 90 days after a municipality adopts such zoning. As noted in § 11:5, the application of these provisions are generally governed by the so-called *Renton* rule.

• **Solar Energy Facilities.** Under § 9B a special permit may be issued "to protect access to direct sunlight for solar energy systems," which would "create an easement to sunlight over neighboring property." While such regulatory creation of an easement might strike lawyers as both drastic and dubious, it is clear that the salubrious legislative purpose was to "encourage the use of solar energy systems and protect solar access by regulation of orientation of streets, lots and buildings, maximum building height limits, minimum building set back requirements, limitations on the type, height and placement of vegetation and other provisions." Some of the "other provisions" are described in § 9B, and there are procedural provisions with respect to "notification of affected neighboring property owners, opportunity for a hearing, appeal process and recordation of such permits on burdened and benefited property deeds."

As these brief summaries indicate, these sections are in many respects unclear and subject to interpretation and challenge. Also, besides providing for special permits, they include several affirmative regulatory zoning provisions.

Section 9C of Chapter 40A, relating to Child Care Facilities, is in fact only a regulatory provision, and contains no reference at all to issuance of a special permit. It defines such a facility as a "day care center or a school age child care program," in reference to M.G.L.A. c. 28A, § 9. In effect it exempts the area of a building devoted to a child care facility from the zoning floor area requirements applicable to the building, up to 10 percent of the otherwise allowable floor area. Once such a bonus has been allowed, the child care facility cannot be discontinued except by a procedure like that for a variance, with a finding that "public interest and convenience" do not require the facility. There are also provisions limiting the amount the building owner may charge the operator of the facility, and provisions aimed at affording access to children from families with lower than average income.

§ 11:21 Application and procedure

A zoning ordinance or bylaw may provide for different

types or "classes" of special permit to be issued by different "special permit granting authorities" (SPGA). Most commonly designated are the zoning board of appeals and the planning board, but the board of selectmen, city council or other municipal body are sometimes specified. Each such board is required to adopt rules relative to the issuance of such permits and file them with the city or town clerk. The ordinance or bylaw may also require that a petition for a special permit be submitted to and reviewed by one or more of the board of health, planning board, city or town engineer, conservation commission "or any other town agency or board." Such boards are to "make such recommendations as they deem appropriate," and if not submitted within 35 days of receipt of the petition shall be deemed "lack of opposition thereto."

As implicit in the general grant of special permit power and specific with respect to several of the particular types, the zoning ordinance or bylaw and the rules adopted by the SPGA need to set forth standards for issuance of special permits. In upholding the standards for issuance of permit for cluster development the appeals court discussed this principle, citing several of the pre-1975 cases in which it was developed.[1] The standards or criteria must of course relate to legitimate zoning purposes; they are usually upheld unless found to be too broad or vague.[2]

The applicant for a special permit may sometimes be a person other than the owner of the affected land.[3] A petition or application for a special permit should be filed with the city or town clerk and with the appropriate special permit granting authority (SPGA), and all other boards specified, determined by review of the local zoning law. The SPGA must then give notice in accordance with § 11 of Chapter 40A in the same manner as described with respect to variance in § 11:19. As provided in § 9, and redundantly rephrased in § 9A, the SPGA is to hold a public hearing

[Section 11:21]

[1]Owens v. Board of Appeals of Belmont, 11 Mass. App. Ct. 994, 418 N.E.2d 635 (1981).

[2]Smith v. Board of Appeals of Fall River, 319 Mass. 341, 65 N.E.2d 547 (1946); Harrison v. Town of Braintree, 355 Mass. 651, 247 N.E.2d 356 (1969); Shuman v. Board of Aldermen of Newton, 361 Mass. 758, 282 N.E.2d 653 (1972); Tebo v. Board of Appeals of Shrewsbury, 22 Mass. App. Ct. 618, 495 N.E.2d 892 (1986).

[3]Marinelli v. Board of Appeal of Bldg. Dept. of City of Boston, 275 Mass. 169, 175 N.E. 479 (1931); Carson v. Board of Appeals of Lexington, 321 Mass. 649, 75 N.E.2d 116 (1947); and see Brady v. City Council of Gloucester, 59 Mass. App. Ct. 691, 797 N.E.2d 479 (2003).

within 65 days after filing of the application and to make its decision within 90 days after the public hearing. Those dates may be extended by written agreement between the applicant and the SPGA, filed with the clerk. As in variance cases, the courts have allowed some laxity in notice requirements and time periods when that is found not to be prejudicial.

The grant of a special permit requires a vote of two-thirds of a board of more than five members, four of a five member board, and all of a three member board. The provisions of § 11 and § 15 of Chapter 40A as to contents of a decision, "detailed record," filing, notice to all parties in interest, appeal period, certification by the city or town clerk, and recording in the registry of deeds, all as described in **§ 11:19**, apply to special permits as well as variances. The provisions of § 15 as to failure of the board to act and certification of permit by default by the city or town clerk, and as to the "detailed record," are redundantly repeated in § 9 of Chapter 40A. Grant by default has been considered in a number of cases, several of which illustrate the confusion between "final action" and the "detailed report" of § 15.[4]

It is provided in § 9 that the zoning ordinance or bylaw shall provide that any special permit shall lapse within a specified period, not more than two years, "if a substantial use thereof has not sooner commenced except for good cause or, in the case of permit for construction, if construction has not begun by such date except for good cause." The period is tolled by an appeal. Issues of lapse with respect to special

---

[4]Building Inspector of Attleboro v. Attleboro Landfill, Inc., 384 Mass. 109, 423 N.E.2d 1009 (1981); Shea v. Board of Aldermen of Chicopee, 13 Mass. App. Ct. 1046, 434 N.E.2d 214 (1982) (abrogated by, Board of Aldermen of Newton v. Maniace, 429 Mass. 726, 711 N.E.2d 565 (1999)); Girard v. Board of Appeals of Easton, 14 Mass. App. Ct. 334, 439 N.E.2d 308 (1982); Noe v. Board of Appeals of Hingham, 13 Mass. App. Ct. 103, 430 N.E.2d 853 (1982); Capone v. Zoning Bd. of Appeals of Fitchburg, 389 Mass. 617, 451 N.E.2d 1141 (1983); Elder Care Services, Inc. v. Zoning Bd. of Appeals of Hingham, 17 Mass. App. Ct. 480, 459 N.E.2d 832 (1984); Zuckerman v. Zoning Bd. of Appeals of Greenfield, 394 Mass. 663, 477 N.E.2d 132 (1985); O'Kane v. Board of Appeals of Hingham, 20 Mass. App. Ct. 162, 478 N.E.2d 962 (1985); Cameron v. Board of Appeals of Yarmouth, 23 Mass. App. Ct. 144, 499 N.E.2d 847 (1986); Angelus v. Board of Appeals of Canton, 25 Mass. App. Ct. 994, 521 N.E.2d 1373 (1988); Board of Appeals of Westwood v. Lambergs, 42 Mass. App. Ct. 411, 677 N.E.2d 270 (1997); Board of Aldermen of Newton v. Maniace, 429 Mass. 726, 711 N.E.2d 565 (1999); Town of Scituate v. Scituate Planning Bd., 13 L.C.R. 395 (2005).

permits have been considered by the courts.[5]

The provisions of § 16 of Chapter 40A, referred to in the last paragraph of § **11:19**, are applicable to special permits as well as variances. Issues as to the moratorium on reconsideration have been considered by the courts.[6]

As quoted in the first paragraph in § **11:20**, a special permit may "impose conditions, safeguards and limitations on time and use." Upon challenge some conditions have been upheld,[7] but many have been voided.[8] A challenge to such conditions must be made in a timely appeal from the granting of the permit, and may not be made by later separate action.[9]

The courts generally afford deference to the judgment of local SPGAs. When special permits are granted, they are usually upheld,[10] but some have been voided.[11] When the

---

[5]Neilson v. Planning Bd. of Walpole, 9 L.C.R. 57 (2001); Cohasset Heights Ltd. v. Zoning Bd. of Appeals of Cohasset, 7 L.C.R. 53 (1999); McDermott v. Board Of Appeals Of Melrose, 59 Mass. App. Ct. 457, 796 N.E.2d 455 (2003).

[6]Powers v. Leno, 24 Mass. App. Ct. 381, 509 N.E.2d 46 (1987); Hall v. Zoning Bd. of Appeals of Edgartown, 40 Mass. App. Ct. 918, 663 N.E.2d 264 (1996).

[7]Hopengarten v. Board of Appeals of Lincoln, 17 Mass. App. Ct. 1006, 459 N.E.2d 1271 (1984); and Land Court cases in 2 L.C.R. 68 (1994), 8 L.C.R. 29 (2000), 13 L.C.R. 512 (2005).

[8]Middlesex & Boston St. Ry. Co. v. Board of Aldermen of Newton, 371 Mass. 849, 359 N.E.2d 1279 (1977); Weld v. Board of Appeals of Gloucester, 345 Mass. 376, 187 N.E.2d 854 (1963); V.S.H. Realty, Inc. v. Zoning Bd. of Appeals of Plymouth, 30 Mass. App. Ct. 530, 570 N.E.2d 1044 (1991); Chambers v. Building Inspector of Peabody, 40 Mass. App. Ct. 762, 667 N.E.2d 895 (1996); Solar v. Zoning Bd. of Appeals of Lincoln, 33 Mass. App. Ct. 398, 600 N.E.2d 187 (1992); Castle Hill Apartments Ltd. Partnership v. Planning Bd. of

Holyoke, 65 Mass. App. Ct. 840, 844 N.E.2d 1098 (2006), review denied, 447 Mass. 1101, 848 N.E.2d 1211 (2006); and Land Court cases in 5 L.C.R. 3, 20 and 41 (1997), 9 L.C.R. 37 (2001), 12 L.C.R. 110 (2004), 13 L.C.R. 16 and 548 (2005), 14 L.C.R. 396 (2006).

[9]Iodice v. City of Newton, 397 Mass. 329, 491 N.E.2d 618 (1986); Klein v. Planning Bd. of Wrentham, 31 Mass. App. Ct. 777, 583 N.E.2d 892 (1992).

[10]Carson v. Board of Appeals of Lexington, 321 Mass. 649, 75 N.E.2d 116 (1947); Shoppers' World, Inc. v. Beacon Terrace Realty, Inc., 353 Mass. 63, 228 N.E.2d 446 (1967); Malcomb v. Board of Appeals of Southborough, 361 Mass. 887, 282 N.E.2d 681 (1972); Garvey v. Board of Appeals of Amherst, 9 Mass. App. Ct. 856, 400 N.E.2d 880 (1980); Knott v. Zoning Bd. of Appeals of Natick, 12 Mass. App. Ct. 1002, 429 N.E.2d 353 (1981); Planning Bd. of Sandwich v. Board of Appeals of Sandwich, 15 Mass. App. Ct. 971, 446 N.E.2d 1077 (1983); Walker v. Board of Appeals of Harwich, 388 Mass. 42, 445 N.E.2d 141 (1983); and Land Court cases in 5 L.C.R. 93 (1997), 12 L.C.R. 50, 63 and 444 (2004).

SPGA denies a special permit, that is generally upheld.[12] If the SPGA cites any valid reason for its action, that will suffice, notwithstanding the expression of other untenable reasons.[13] When the courts overrule a denial of special permit, there are often remands for further consideration,

---

[11]Franchi v. Zoning Bd. of Appeals of Worcester, 3 L.C.R. 133 (1995); Planning Bd. of Oxford v. Bd. of Appeals of Oxford, 4 L.C.R. 107 (1996); Vitale v. Hanson Zoning Bd. of Appeals, 9 L.C.R. 189 (2001).

[12]Raimondo v. Board of Appeals of Bedford, 331 Mass. 228, 118 N.E.2d 67 (1954); Pendergast v. Board of Appeals of Barnstable, 331 Mass. 555, 120 N.E.2d 916 (1954); Simeone Stone Corp. v. Oliva, 350 Mass. 31, 213 N.E.2d 230 (1965); Gulf Oil Corp. v. Board of Appeals of Framingham, 355 Mass. 275, 244 N.E.2d 311 (1969); Zaltman v. Board of Appeals of Stoneham, 357 Mass. 482, 258 N.E.2d 565 (1970); Strazzulla v. Building Inspector of Wellesley, 357 Mass. 694, 260 N.E.2d 163 (1970); Golden v. Board of Selectmen of Falmouth, 358 Mass. 519, 265 N.E.2d 573 (1970); Humble Oil & Refining Co. v. Board of Appeals of Amherst, 360 Mass. 604, 276 N.E.2d 718 (1971); Glacier Sand & Stone Co. v. Board of Appeals of Westwood, 362 Mass. 239, 285 N.E.2d 411 (1972); Vazza Properties, Inc. v. City Council of Woburn, 1 Mass. App. Ct. 308, 296 N.E.2d 220 (1973); Pioneer Home Sponsors, Inc. v. Board of Appeals of Northampton, 1 Mass. App. Ct. 830, 297 N.E.2d 73 (1973); Copley v. Board of Appeals of Canton, 1 Mass. App. Ct. 821, 296 N.E.2d 716 (1973); S. Volpe & Co., Inc. v. Board of Appeals of Wareham, 4 Mass. App. Ct. 357, 348 N.E.2d 807 (1976); Board of Appeals of Southampton v. Boyle, 4 Mass. App. Ct. 824, 349 N.E.2d 373 (1976); Subaru of New England, Inc. v. Board of Appeals of Canton, 8 Mass. App. Ct. 483, 395 N.E.2d 880 (1979); S. Kemble Fischer Realty Trust v. Board of Appeals of Concord, 9 Mass. App. Ct. 477, 402 N.E.2d 100 (1980); Kinchla v. Board of Appeals of Falmouth, 11 Mass. App. Ct. 927, 415 N.E.2d 882 (1981); Stivaletta v. Zoning Bd. of Appeals of Medfield, 12 Mass. App. Ct. 994, 429 N.E.2d 66 (1981); Goddard v. Board of Appeals of Concord, 13 Mass. App. Ct. 1001, 433 N.E.2d 98 (1982); Shea v. Town of Danvers, 21 Mass. App. Ct. 996, 490 N.E.2d 806 (1986); Nugent v. Board of Appeals of Granby, 22 Mass. App. Ct. 909, 491 N.E.2d 644 (1986); Texstar Const. Corp. v. Board of Appeals of Dedham, 26 Mass. App. Ct. 977, 528 N.E.2d 1186 (1988); Schiffone v. Zoning Bd. of Appeals of Walpole, 28 Mass. App. Ct. 981, 553 N.E.2d 1308 (1990); Old Colony Council-Boy Scouts of America v. Zoning Bd. of Appeals of Plymouth, 31 Mass. App. Ct. 46, 574 N.E.2d 1014 (1991); ACW Realty Management, Inc. v. Planning Bd. of Westfield, 40 Mass. App. Ct. 242, 662 N.E.2d 1051 (1996); Croteau v. Planning Bd. of Hopkinton, 40 Mass. App. Ct. 922, 663 N.E.2d 583 (1996); APT Asset Management, Inc. v. Board of Appeals of Melrose, 50 Mass. App. Ct. 133, 735 N.E.2d 872 (2000); Garabedian v. Westland, 59 Mass. App. Ct. 427, 796 N.E.2d 439 (2003); and Land Court cases in 2 L.C.R. 4, 29, 80, 117 and 158 (1994), 3 L.C.R. 3, 166 and 236 (1995), 4 L.C.R. 1, 81, 250, 258 and 291 (1997), 5 L.C.R. 16, 98, 103 and188 (1997), 12 L.C.R. 365 (2004).

[13]Vazza Properties, Inc. v. City Council of Woburn, 1 Mass. App. Ct. 308, 296 N.E.2d 220 (1973); Board of Appeals of Southampton v. Boyle, 4 Mass. App. Ct. 824, 349 N.E.2d 373 (1976).

and outright rejections or orders for issuance turn on findings that the action was arbitrary or capricious or not founded on any tenable legal basis.[14]

TOPIC G: JUDICIAL REVIEW

§ 11:22 Jurisdiction; procedure

The terms of § 17 of Chapter 40A, providing for judicial review of zoning actions, pose a number of tricky issues, several of which have been rather extensively litigated. In the first place, the right to seek review is conferred upon "any person aggrieved" and the meaning of that phrase has become so salient in zoning practice that an analysis thereof is the subject of the following Subsection B. Other significant points under § 17 include the following:

- Jurisdiction is conferred basically upon the land court and the superior court. The housing court may also have jurisdiction in Hampden County or "in a county region or area served by a division of the housing court." Also, except in Hampden County, an appeal may be filed in the district court, provided that any party may by appropriate action in effect require transfer of the case to the superior court.

- Appeal may be taken from "a decision of the board of appeals or any special permit granting authority" or "the failure" of such board or authority "to take final action . . . within the required time."

- Appeal may be taken by "any person aggrieved . . . whether or not previously a party to the proceeding, or any municipal officer or board."

- As to parties defendant, § 17 provides that: "If the

---

[14]MacGibbon v. Board of Appeals of Duxbury, 347 Mass. 690, 200 N.E.2d 254 (1964); Mahoney v. Board of Appeals of Winchester, 344 Mass. 598, 183 N.E.2d 850 (1962); Tambone v. Board of Appeal of Stoneham, 348 Mass. 359, 203 N.E.2d 802 (1965); Lombard v. Board of Appeal of Wellesley, 348 Mass. 788, 204 N.E.2d 471 (1965); Slater v. Board of Appeals of Brookline, 350 Mass. 70, 213 N.E.2d 394 (1966); Y. D. Dugout, Inc. v. Board of Appeals of Canton, 357 Mass. 25, 255 N.E.2d 732 (1970); Cumberland Farms of Conn., Inc. v. Zoning Bd. of Appeal of North Attleborough, 359 Mass. 68, 267 N.E.2d 906 (1971); SCIT, Inc. v. Planning Bd. of Braintree, 19 Mass. App. Ct. 101, 472 N.E.2d 269 (1984); Colangelo v. Board of Appeals of Lexington, 407 Mass. 242, 552 N.E.2d 541 (1990); Federman v. Board of Appeals of Marblehead, 35 Mass. App. Ct. 727, 626 N.E.2d 8 (1994); and Land Court cases in 1 L.C.R. 109 and 135 (1993), 2 L.C.R. 23 and 91 (1994), 3 L.C.R. 139 and 168 (1995), 4 L.C.R. 5 (1996), 9 L.C.R. 358 (2001), 12 L.C.R. 153 (2004); 13 L.C.R. 589 (2005).

complaint is filed by someone other than the original applicant, appellant or petitioner, such original applicant, appellant, or petitioner and all members of the board of appeals or special permit granting authority shall be named as parties defendant with their addresses." The statute does not specify the parties defendant when plaintiff *is* the original applicant, appellant or petitioner, but implies that they should include all members of the acting board or SPGA by the provision that: "To avoid delay in the proceedings, instead of the usual service of process, the plaintiff shall within fourteen days after the filing of the complaint, send written notice thereof, with a copy of the complaint, by delivery or certified mail to all defendants, including the members of the board of appeals or special permit granting authority."[1] It is also provided that: "Other persons may be permitted to intervene, upon motion."[2]

• The written notice referred to in the preceding paragraph must be followed by an affidavit that such notice has been given, filed with the clerk of the court within 21 days after entry of the complaint, and absent such filing, "the complaint shall be dismissed." It is also provided that any such action may be brought "within twenty days after the decision has been filed in the office of the city or town clerk," and that "Notice of the action with a copy of the complaint shall be given to such city or town clerk so as to be received within such twenty days." Compliance with this requirement is jurisdictional and strictly enforced,[3] although the courts have allowed a little "wiggle room," while still not condoning any lawyers' "procedural missteps."[4]

• The statute requires that: "The complaint shall allege

[Section 11:22]

[1]Twomey v. Board of Appeals of Medford, 7 Mass. App. Ct. 770, 390 N.E.2d 272 (1979).

[2]Butts v. Zoning Bd. of Appeals of Falmouth, 18 Mass. App. Ct. 249, 464 N.E.2d 108 (1984); Prudential Ins. Co. of America v. Board of Appeals of Westwood, 18 Mass. App. Ct. 632, 469 N.E.2d 501 (1984).

[3]O'Blenes v. Zoning Bd. of Appeals of Lynn, 397 Mass. 555, 492 N.E.2d 354 (1986); Cappuccio v. Zoning Bd. of Appeals of Spencer, 398 Mass. 304, 496 N.E.2d 646 (1986); Bingham v. City Council of Fitchburg, 52 Mass. App. Ct. 566, 754 N.E.2d 1078 (2001); Norfolk County v. Zoning Bd. of Appeals of Walpole, 16 Mass. App. Ct. 930, 450 N.E.2d 628 (1983); DeLuca v. Bd. of Appeals of Bedford, 5 L.C.R. 51 (1997); Cottone v. Bd. of Appeals of Truro, 7 L.C.R. 132 (1999); Schiller v. Charles River Country Club, Inc., 14 L.C.R. 234 (2006); Volandre v. Opdyke, 14 L.C.R. 384 (2006).

[4]Bjornlund v. Zoning Bd. of Appeals of Marshfield, 353 Mass. 757, 231 N.E.2d 365 (1967); Garfield

that the decision exceeds the authority of the board or authority, and any facts pertinent to the issue, and shall contain a prayer that the decision be annulled," and that a copy of the decision, certified by the city or town clerk, be attached.[5] The court is charged with hearing all evidence pertinent to the authority of the board or SPGA to act, determining the facts, and annulling the decision, if appropriate, or making "such other decree as justice and equity may require." While the trial court's findings are *de novo,* considerable deference is afforded to the local board's judgment,[6] but board actions are overruled when based on legally untenable grounds.[7] The power of the court to make "other decree" is illustrated in several cases.[8]

There are other procedural provisions, including exclusivity of the remedy and limitations on assessing costs. A declaration that such actions "shall have precedence over all other civil actions and proceedings" has not led to much relief from burdens of "the law's delay."

§ 11:23   Standing

A person may be a "party in interest" entitled to notice under §§ 11 and 15 of Chapter 40A, and yet not be a "person aggrieved" under § 17. As parties in interest, abutters and abutters to abutters are entitled to a presumption of standing under § 17, but if their standing is adequately contested, the burden shifts and they must then show that they are in fact "aggrieved." Those points were reviewed and confirmed

---

v. Board of Appeals of Rockport, 356 Mass. 37, 247 N.E.2d 720 (1969); Carr v. Board of Appeals of Saugus, 361 Mass. 361, 280 N.E.2d 199 (1972); Konover Management Corp. v. Planning Bd. of Auburn, 32 Mass. App. Ct. 319, 588 N.E.2d 1365 (1992); Moncare Chatfield-Taylor v. Nantucket Planning Bd., 13 L.C.R. 595 (2005).

[5]But see Carr v. Board of Appeals of Saugus, 361 Mass. 361, 280 N.E.2d 199 (1972).

[6]Lomelis v. Board of Appeals of Marblehead, 17 Mass. App. Ct. 962, 458 N.E.2d 740 (1983); Building Inspector of Chatham v. Kendrick, 17 Mass. App. Ct. 928, 456 N.E.2d 1151 (1983); Nugent v. Board of Appeals of Granby, 22 Mass. App. Ct. 909, 491 N.E.2d 644

(1986); Crittenton Hastings House of the Florence Crittenton League v. Board of Appeal of Boston, 25 Mass. App. Ct. 704, 521 N.E.2d 1374 (1988).

[7]Kirkwood v. Board of Appeals of Rockport, 17 Mass. App. Ct. 423, 458 N.E.2d 1213 (1984); Federman v. Board of Appeals of Marblehead, 35 Mass. App. Ct. 727, 626 N.E.2d 8 (1994); Quincy v. Planning Bd. of Tewksbury, 39 Mass. App. Ct. 17, 652 N.E.2d 901 (1995); Schey v. Bd. of Appeals of Marblehead, 8 L.C.R 142 (2000).

[8]Lopes v. City of Peabody, 3 L.C.R. 78 (1995); Nixon v. Ipswich Zoning Bd. of Appeals, 3 L.C.R. 121 (1995); Quincy v. Planning Bd. of Tewksbury, 39 Mass. App. Ct. 17, 652 N.E.2d 901 (1995).

in the *Barvenik* case,[1] which cited the earlier decisions establishing these principles. Subsequent cases confirmed these points, and in particular that the presumption of standing disappears when adequately contested, but remains in effect unless adequate evidence is proffered to contest it.[2]

In *Barvenik* the court said that in order "[t]o qualify for that limited class [of persons aggrieved], a plaintiff must establish—by direct facts and not by speculative personal opinion—that his injury is special and different from the concerns of the rest of the community," and "must show that his legal rights have been, or likely will be, infringed or his property interests adversely affected." The court added that a plaintiff "must provide specific evidence demonstrating a reasonable likelihood that the granting of a special permit will result, if not in a diminution in the value of his property, at least in his property or legal rights being more adversely affected by the activity authorized by the permit than (a) they are by present uses and activities or (b) they would be as a result of the uses and activities permitted as of right on the defendant's locus."

In the *Marashlian* case[3] the SJC said that *Barvenik*: "seem[s] to require that a plaintiff, in order to obtain standing, show a substantial likelihood of harm greater than that which could result from a use of the property permissible as of right." Noting that "[t]his line of cases appears to be a departure from those previously decided at the time of the judge's decision," the court said: "We decline to adopt such a rule, except to the extent that it requires specific facts to establish perceptible harm. Although the magnitude of the threat of harm to a potential plaintiff in relation to the threat of harm from a use permissible as of right is a factor that may be considered, it is not dispositive of the standing issue."

[Section 11:23]

[1]Barvenik v. Board of Aldermen of Newton, 33 Mass. App. Ct. 129, 597 N.E.2d 48 (1992).

[2]Cohen v. Zoning Bd. of Appeals of Plymouth, 35 Mass. App. Ct. 619, 624 N.E.2d 119 (1993); Jaffe v. Zoning Bd. of Appeals of Newton, 34 Mass. App. Ct. 929, 612 N.E.2d 693 (1993); Riley v. Janco Cent., Inc., 38 Mass. App. Ct. 984, 652 N.E.2d 631 (1995); Watros v. Greater Lynn Mental Health and Retardation Ass'n, Inc., 37 Mass. App. Ct. 657, 642 N.E.2d 599 (1994), aff'd, 421 Mass. 106, 653 N.E.2d 589 (1995); Marashlian v. Zoning Bd. of Appeals of Newburyport, 421 Mass. 719, 660 N.E.2d 369 (1996); Monks v. Zoning Bd. of Appeals of Plymouth, 37 Mass. App. Ct. 685, 642 N.E.2d 314 (1994); Valcourt v. Zoning Bd. of Appeals of Swansea, 48 Mass. App. Ct. 124, 718 N.E.2d 389 (1999).

[3]Marashlian v. Zoning Bd. of Appeals of Newburyport, 421 Mass. 719, 660 N.E.2d 369 (1996).

Supporting this, the court cited *Tsagronis*[4] in which the standing of a non-conforming abutter based on impairment of his view of Buzzards Bay was upheld, albeit with three dissents.

Following *Marashlian*, standing has been upheld in a number of cases[5] and rejected in others.[6] Provisions in a local bylaw may afford standing when it would not otherwise be available.[7] The right of "any municipal officer or board" to appeal has been limited to those that have duties to perform in relation to the subject matter of the decision, and "cross-town" suits have been rejected.[8]

The financial risks of proceeding with an appeal without having actual aggrievement have been demonstrated by award of costs and counsel fees.[9]

TOPIC H: ENFORCEMENT

§ 11:24   Jurisdiction; procedure

Under § 7 of Chapter 40A enforcement of the zoning ordinance or bylaw is the charge of the local building inspector or commissioner, or if none, the board of selectmen or

---

[4]Tsagronis v. Board of Appeals of Wareham, 415 Mass. 329, 613 N.E.2d 893 (1993).

[5]Chambers v. Building Inspector of Peabody, 40 Mass. App. Ct. 762, 667 N.E.2d 895 (1996); McGee v. Board of Appeal of Boston, 62 Mass. App. Ct. 930, 819 N.E.2d 975 (2004); Choate v. Zoning Bd. of Appeals of Mashpee, 67 Mass. App. Ct. 376, 853 N.E.2d 1089 (2006), review denied, 447 Mass. 1113, 857 N.E.2d 1094 (2006); Cottone v. Cedar Lake, LLC, 67 Mass. App. Ct. 464, 854 N.E.2d 456 (2006), review denied, 447 Mass. 1114, 857 N.E.2d 1095 (2006); and Land Court cases in 4 L.C.R. 57 (1996), 11 L.C.R. 96 and 248 (2003), 12 L.C.R. 63, 349 and 359 (2004), 13 L.C.R. 350, 486 and 494 (2005), 14 L.C.R. 52, 148 and 311 (2006).

[6]Denneny v. Zoning Bd. of Appeals of Seekonk, 59 Mass. App. Ct. 208, 794 N.E.2d 1269 (2003), judgment entered, 2003 WL 25333636 (Mass. Super. Ct. 2003); Butler v. City of Waltham, 63 Mass. App. Ct. 435, 827 N.E.2d 216 (2005); and Land Court cases in 8 L.C.R. 119 (2000), 10 L.C.R. 103 (2002), 11 L.C.R. 217 (2003), 13 L.C.R. 188, 202 and 211 (2005), 14 L.C.R. 3, 359, 533, 574 and 585 (2006).

[7]Monks v. Zoning Bd. of Appeals of Plymouth, 37 Mass. App. Ct. 685, 642 N.E.2d 314 (1994); Sheehan v. Zoning Bd. of Appeals of Plymouth, 65 Mass. App. Ct. 52, 836 N.E.2d 1103 (2005).

[8]Planning Bd. of Marshfield v. Zoning Bd. of Appeals of Pembroke, 427 Mass. 699, 695 N.E.2d 650 (1998); Town Council of Franklin v. Zoning Bd. of Appeals of Bellingham, 6 L.C.R. 334 (1998).

[9]Farnum v. Mesiti Development, 68 Mass. App. Ct. 419, 862 N.E.2d 425 (2007), review denied, 449 Mass. 1105, 868 N.E.2d 133 (2007).

other board designated by local ordinance or bylaw. The first means of enforcement provided is the withholding of a building permit, or related permit, for any building or structure which "would be in violation" of the local zoning law. Similarly, no permit or license shall be granted for "a new use" of any building, structure or land which would be in such violation.

The second means of enforcement is by response of the enforcement agent to the written request of any party for enforcement of zoning laws "against any person allegedly in violation of the same." If the enforcement agent does not take action in compliance with such a request, he is obliged to give written notice within 14 days to the requesting party, specifying the reasons for his "refusal to act."

Section 8 of Chapter 40A provides that "any person aggrieved" by the refusal of the zoning enforcement agent either to issue a permit or to take action against an alleged violation may "appeal to the permit granting authority as the zoning ordinance or by law may provide." Such an appeal may also be taken "by the regional planning agency in whose area the city or town is situated, or by any person including an officer or board of the city or town, or of an abutting city or town aggrieved by an order or decision of the inspector of buildings, or other administrative official, in violation of any provision of this chapter or any ordinance or by-law adopted hereunder."

The procedure for such an administrative appeal is governed by § 15 of Chapter 40A, as referred to in § **11:21**. It must be taken within 30 days from the date of the action appealed, and notice thereof filed with the city or town clerk, the officer or board whose action is being appealed and the permit granting authority, specifying the grounds for appeal. Substantially the same provisions apply when there is a "zoning administrator" appointed under § 13 of chapter 40A. The appeal is then referred to the board of appeals, and its procedures as to notice, hearing, timing, quantum of vote, failure to act,[1] and filing of a "public record" are as described in § **11:19**. When such an administrative appeal has been completed, judicial review under § 17, as described in § **11:22**, becomes possible. Judicial review is rejected when the

---

[Section 11:24]

[1]Cameron v. Board of Appeals of Yarmouth, 23 Mass. App. Ct. 144, 499 N.E.2d 847 (1986); Zuckerman v. Zoning Bd. of Appeals of Greenfield, 394 Mass. 663, 477 N.E.2d 132 (1985); O'Kane v. Board of Appeals of Hingham, 20 Mass. App. Ct. 162, 478 N.E.2d 962 (1985); and Land Court cases in 4 L.C.R. 111 (1996), 6 L.C.R. 210 (1998), 8 L.C.R. 300 (2000).

administrative remedy has not been pursued,[2] but that does not preclude all remedies or criminal enforcement.[3]

It is further provided in § 7 that (1) no local zoning law shall provide a penalty of more than $300 per violation, but each day of violation may be considered a separate offense;[4] (2) no enforcement action may be taken except in accordance with §§ 7, 8 and 17 of Chapter 40A; and (3) the superior court and land court have jurisdiction to enforce the statute and local zoning laws,[5] and may restrain violations by injunction. The framing of practical remedies for some zoning violations is difficult, and the courts have been quite reluctant to order the removal of existing structures.[6] However, after quite a bit of confused, hesitant and somewhat contradictory actions by town officials, and to some extent by trial judges, involving untenable assertion of "grandfather" status, a trial judge finally ordered, and the Appeals court affirmed, the removal of an unlawfully erected house.[7]

§ 11:25 Statutes of limitation

Section 7 of Chapter 40A contains two successive limitation provisions. The first is that: "if real property has been improved and used in accordance with the terms of the original building permit issued by a person duly authorized to issue such permits," no action upon a zoning violation may alter "the use allowed by said permit" or compel alteration of "any structure erected in reliance upon said permit" unless

[2]Neuhaus v. Building Inspector of Marlborough, 11 Mass. App. Ct. 230, 415 N.E.2d 235 (1981); McDonald's Corp. v. Town of Seekonk, 12 Mass. App. Ct. 351, 424 N.E.2d 1136 (1981); City of Woburn v. McNutt Bros. Equipment Corp., 16 Mass. App. Ct. 236, 451 N.E.2d 437 (1983).

[3]Hogan v. Hayes, 19 Mass. App. Ct. 399, 474 N.E.2d 1158 (1985); Com. v. A. Graziano, Inc., 35 Mass. App. Ct. 69, 616 N.E.2d 825 (1993); Cape Resort Hotels, Inc. v. Alcoholic Licensing Bd. of Falmouth, 385 Mass. 205, 431 N.E.2d 213 (1982); see M.G.L.A. c. 111, § 127-O; and see § 10:8, as to M.G.L.A. c. 240, § 14A.

[4]Burlington Sand & Gravel, Inc. v. Town of Harvard, 31 Mass.

App. Ct. 261, 576 N.E.2d 707 (1991).

[5]Town of Uxbridge v. Griff, 68 Mass. App. Ct. 174, 860 N.E.2d 972 (2007).

[6]Town of Marblehead v. Deery, 356 Mass. 532, 254 N.E.2d 234 (1969); Kelloway v. Board of Appeal of Melrose, 361 Mass. 249, 280 N.E.2d 160 (1972); Town of Sterling v. Poulin, 2 Mass. App. Ct. 562, 316 N.E.2d 737 (1974); Building Inspector of Falmouth v. Haddad, 369 Mass. 452, 339 N.E.2d 892 (1976); Berman v. Coutinho, 20 Mass. App. Ct. 969, 481 N.E.2d 222 (1985); but see Pelletier v. Bertrand, 14 L.C.R. 503 (2006).

[7]Wells v. Zoning Bd. of Appeals of Billerica, 68 Mass. App. Ct. 726, 864 N.E.2d 586 (2007).

the action is commenced and notice recorded in the registry of deeds within six years after the commencement of the alleged violation. The second provision makes no reference to a building permit and simply provides that no action to compel the removal, alteration, or relocation of any structure shall be maintained unless commenced and notice recorded within ten years after the commencement of the alleged violation. As noted by the appeals court, the 6-year provision protects uses and structures which are "in accordance with the terms" of a building permit, and the 10-year provision does not protect uses at all.[1] Plaintiffs seeking protection under these provisions have not enjoyed much success.[2]

TOPIC I: BOSTON ZONING

§ 11:26   History

As early as 1905, the legislature adopted laws regulating heights of buildings in Boston and establishing districts of use classification. In 1924, a general zoning law for Boston was enacted, and the current Boston enabling act was adopted in 1956,[1] under which the Zoning Commission of the City adopted the Boston Zoning Code, effective on December 31, 1964. That code was then more advanced and sophisticated than most other local zoning ordinances and bylaws, containing such items as control of bulk by floor-area ratios, provision for conditional uses, planned development, requirement of off-street parking, overlay districts, etc. All of these devices and techniques have now become widespread and common in most zoning ordinances and bylaws.

To say that the Boston Code itself has been further refined would be a gross understatement. In fact it has become a monumental exemplar of the art of urban land use planning. The Boston Redevelopment Authority (BRA) was established in 1957 and replaced the City Planning Board in 1960. It exercises all of the powers of urban redevelopment under M.G.L.A. c. 121A and 121B, and the powers of the planning

---

[Section 11:25]

[1]Lord v. Zoning Bd. of Appeals of Somerset, 30 Mass. App. Ct. 226, 567 N.E.2d 954 (1991).

[2]Moreis v. Oak Bluffs Bd. of Appeals, 62 Mass. App. Ct. 53, 814 N.E.2d 1132 (2004); Bruno v. Board of Appeals of Wrentham, 62 Mass. App. Ct. 527, 818 N.E.2d 199

(2004); and Land Court cases in 2 L.C.R. 93 (1993), 2 L.C.R. 141 (1994), 6 L.C.R. 215 (1998), 9 L.C.R. 326 (2001), 14 L.C.R. 573 (2006).

[Section 11:26]

[1]Chapter 665, Acts of 1956, amended by Chapter 371, Acts of 1987, Chapter 461, Acts.

board under Chapter 652, § 12, of the Acts of 1960. Under the BRA's initiative and guidance, particularly since 1989, the Boston Zoning Code has burgeoned in length and complexity. The entire Code may now be downloaded from the BRA website. A starting point is Article 80, providing for "development review" of four separate types for large projects, small projects, planned development areas, and institutional master plans.

In Boston changes in the zoning code, both as to text and zoning maps defining district boundaries, are not effected by the City Council, but rather by a statutory Zoning Commission, appointed by the Mayor. The BRA is of course the usual source of proposals for changes, which are sometimes challenged.[2]

§ 11:27   Similarities and differences

From the outset, the enabling acts for Boston and the codes adopted thereunder have been very similar in most respects to the enabling laws for other cities and towns and local zoning laws adopted pursuant thereto. Recognizing this, the courts have generally given these laws parallel interpretation, often so specifying.[1] In the *McGee* decision the court said that the Boston Code is analogous to Chapter 40A, so we "import teachings" therefrom. This principle is further illustrated by the many other Boston cases cited for general propositions in the preceding sections of this **Chapter 11**. Also, the legislature has made certain provisions applicable to Boston, including protection of disabled persons against discrimination,[2] the protection of child care facilities under Chapter 40A, § 3 (see § **11:6**),[3] and prohibition of any variance or special permit for a structure exceeding height limits which would cast a shadow on the Boston Commons.[4]

There are, however, several important differences in

---

[2]Manning v. Boston Redevelopment Authority, 400 Mass. 444, 509 N.E.2d 1173 (1987); National Amusements, Inc. v. City of Boston, 29 Mass. App. Ct. 305, 560 N.E.2d 138 (1990); KCI Management, Inc. v. Board of Appeal of Boston, 54 Mass. App. Ct. 254, 764 N.E.2d 377 (2002).

[Section 11:27]

[1]Rinaldi v. Board of Appeal of Boston, 50 Mass. App. Ct. 657, 741 N.E.2d 77 (2001); Lapidus v. Board of Appeal of Boston, 51 Mass. App. Ct. 723, 748 N.E.2d 495 (2001); McGee v. Board of Appeal of Boston, 62 Mass. App. Ct. 930, 819 N.E.2d 975 (2004).

[2]Chapter 106 and Chapter 341, § 117, Acts of 1989.

[3]Chapter 521, Acts of 1990.

[4]Chapter 362, Acts of 1990.

Boston. Mandamus continues to play a role;[5] the land court has no jurisdiction on appeal from the Boston Board of Appeal (*sic,* singular);[6] a bond is required upon appeal;[7] and there is no express time period for decision, prompting invocation of a Chapter 40A analogy.[8] After the adoption of Chapter 808, Acts of 1975, it was asserted that Chapter 40A became applicable to Boston, particularly as to the Dover Amendment (see § **11:6**), but the court rejected that,[9] and in fact Boston requires development review for educational and religious projects.

Also, Boston has "linkage." A system of special exactions, commonly known as linkage, was adopted in the Boston Zoning Code in 1983 and further provisions added in 1986. A challenge of the law, partly on the ground of absence of legislative authority, was rejected by the SJC because of lack of plaintiff's standing,[10] but in 1987 the legislature did authorize linkage, and provided for appeal by persons aggrieved in the superior court or land court.[11] Under the linkage system large scale commercial real estate developments involving new, enlarged or substantially rehabilitated floor area of 100,000 square feet or more are subject to special exactions, dedicated to the production of low and moderate income housing. The original provisions under Articles 26 and 26A of the Code have now been replaced by § 80B-7 of Article 80. Under authorization by Chapter 170, Acts of 2001, the maximum amount of exaction was increased to $7.18 for each square foot of the development over 100,000 square feet. The exaction is payable over a period of years, generally 7 years for developments in downtown locations and 12 years elsewhere in the City. In addition, there are requirements for contribution of $1 for each square foot over 100,000 square feet for purposes of job training and employment plans for persons of low and moderate income. The equiva-

---

[5]Dooley v. Munsell, 23 Mass. App. Ct. 1102, 498 N.E.2d 1078 (1986).

[6]Rinaldi v. Board of Appeal of Boston, 50 Mass. App. Ct. 657, 741 N.E.2d 77 (2001).

[7]Jack v. Board of Appeal of Boston, 15 Mass. App. Ct. 311, 445 N.E.2d 184 (1983); Feldman v. Board of Appeal of Boston, 29 Mass. App. Ct. 296, 559 N.E.2d 1263 (1990)

[8]National Amusements, Inc. v. Commissioner of Inspectional Services Dept. of Boston, 26 Mass. App. Ct. 80, 523 N.E.2d 789 (1988); Lapidus v. Board of Appeal of Boston, 51 Mass. App. Ct. 723, 748 N.E.2d 495 (2001).

[9]Emerson College v. City of Boston, 393 Mass. 303, 471 N.E.2d 336, 21 Ed. Law Rep. 672 (1984); see also Emerson College v. City of Boston, 391 Mass. 415, 462 N.E.2d 1098 (1984).

[10]Bonan v. City of Boston, 398 Mass. 315, 496 N.E.2d 640 (1986).

[11]Chapter 371, Acts of 1987.

lent of "linkage" in communities other than Boston is discussed in § **14:16**.

The Boston Code provides for and confers powers, at least advisory, upon various neighborhood groups or commissions, whose authority has sometimes been challenged.[12] The BRA's role under urban redevelopment laws may in some instances insulate its planning decisions,[13] but its powers are not unlimited.[14]

---

[12]Marr   v.   Back   Bay Architectural Com'n, 23 Mass. App. Ct. 679, 505 N.E.2d 534 (1987); Marr v. Back Bay Architectural Com'n, 32 Mass. App. Ct. 962, 592 N.E.2d 756 (1992).

[13]St. Botolph Citizens Commit-

tee, Inc. v. Boston Redevelopment Authority, 429 Mass. 1, 705 N.E.2d 617 (1999).

[14]South Boston Betterment Trust Corp. v. Boston Redevelopment Authority, 438 Mass. 57, 777 N.E.2d 812 (2002).

Chapter 12

Subdivision Control

TOPIC A: THE STATUTORY CONCEPT

§ 12:1 Statutory applicability

The Subdivision Control Law, comprising §§ 81K to 81GG of M.G.L.A. c. 41, was enacted in 1953,[1] replacing prior planning law. Except for Boston it is in effect in every city and town which has accepted it. Such acceptance is affected by the local planning board's filing with the register of deeds and recorder of the land court certified copies of the vote by which the city or town accepted the law and the rules and regulations adopted by the planning board to implement the statute. Some communities may possibly still retain planning control systems under prior statutes of special acts, and such cases call for ad hoc inquiry and study.[2]

The Act does not apply to Boston, which does not have a separate law for subdivision control. As noted in § **11:26**, the Boston Redevelopment Authority is the planning board of Boston, and it effectively controls subdivision under Article 80 of the zoning code. Also, the so-called Tregor Act[3] imposed a Boston city tax of $500 on each lot in excess of two in a subdivision, and Suffolk registry of deeds requires a certificate of payment or exception from the City Treasurer before recording of any subdivision plan.

Leading in to the Subdivision Control Law are provisions of §§ 81A through 81J of Chapter 41, providing for establishment and powers of planning boards and promulgation of a municipal master plan and official map, which may have determinative effects on a number of subdivision control issues.

§ 12:2 Definition of subdivision

The statute prohibits subdivision of land without approval

[Section 12:1]

[1]Chapter 674, Acts of 1953.

[2]See M.G.L.A. c. 41, § 81GG.

[3]Chapter 190, § 9, Acts of 1982.

of a plan thereof by the local planning board, and provides several means of enforcement, discussed in § 12:14. At the outset, the very definition of "subdivision" poses several questions. In brief it provides that subdivision means division of land into two or more lots, but there are several categories of exception, each posing its own questions, as follows:

• It is not a subdivision if every lot has frontage on a public way or way which the city or town clerk certifies "is maintained and used as a public way." But doubt often prevails as to whether a way is "a public way" or not. Towns may, and often do, maintain and repair private ways.[1] The status of ancient ways is often unclear.[2] A city or town clerk's certification is ordinarily conclusive, but may be rebuttable.[3]

• It is not a subdivision if every lot has frontage on a way shown on a subdivision plan previously approved under the subdivision control law. This may apply even before the way has been constructed, but violation of conditions of the approval or absence of assurance of construction may invalidate that qualification.[4]

• It is not a subdivision if every lot has frontage on "a way in existence when the subdivision control law became effective in the city or town in which the land lies, having, in the opinion of the planning board, sufficient width, suitable grades and adequate construction to provide for the needs of vehicular traffic in relation to the proposed use of the land abutting thereon or served thereby, and for the installation of municipal services to serve such land and the buildings erected or to be erected thereon." The "opinion" of the planning board may be contested, and of course involves a substantive judgment.[5] To qualify under this clause, the way must have been in existence when the

[Section 12:2]

[1]Casagrande v. Town Clerk of Harvard, 377 Mass. 703, 387 N.E.2d 571 (1979); Murphy v. Planning Board of Pembroke, 3 L.C.R. 200 (1995).

[2]Schulze v. Town of Huntington, 24 Mass. App. Ct. 416, 509 N.E.2d 927 (1987); Nasca v. Board of Appeals of Medway, 27 Mass. App. Ct. 47, 534 N.E.2d 792 (1989); Moncy v. Planning Bd. of Scituate, 50 Mass. App. Ct. 715, 741 N.E.2d 82 (2001); Recore v. Town of Conway, 8 L.C.R. 329 (2000); Zaskey v. Town of Whatley,

9 L.C.R. 126 (2001); White v. Donahue, 9 L.C.R. 111 (2001).

[3]Casagrande v. Town Clerk of Harvard, 377 Mass. 703, 387 N.E.2d 571 (1979); Matulewicz v. Planning Bd. of Norfolk, 438 Mass. 37, 777 N.E.2d 153 (2002).

[4]Richard v. Planning Bd. of Acushnet, 10 Mass. App. Ct. 216, 406 N.E.2d 728 (1980).

[5]Rettig v. Planning Bd. of Rowley, 332 Mass. 476, 126 N.E.2d 104 (1955); Linhares v. Medeiros, 14 Mass. App. Ct. 927, 436 N.E.2d 1233 (1982); and Land Court cases in 1 L.C.R. 150 (1993), 2 L.C.R. 74

city or town adopted the Subdivision Control Law,[6] but the condition of the way at that time is not pertinent, and subsequent improvements may qualify it.[7]

• Also not constituting a subdivision are "conveyances or other instruments adding to, taking away from or changing the size and shape of lots in such a manner as not to leave any lot so affected without the frontage [specified in the statute.]" This allows for creation of a "non-buildable" lot, to be consolidated with an abutter's property, or otherwise held as non-buildable.[8]

• And finally, not constituting a subdivision is "the division of a tract of land on which two or more buildings were standing when the subdivision control law went into effect in the city or town in which the land lies into separate lots on each of which one of such buildings remains standing." Such division has been considered and upheld.[9] In a case in which division into two lots made one lot meet zoning requirements and left the other lot too small to comply, the land court upheld ANR endorsement, but held that the small lot was tarnished by "infectious invalidity," and the barn thereon could not be replaced with a house.[10] The buildings must have been in existence when the town adopted the subdivision control law.[11]

The statute provides that "frontage" for the purposes of these exceptions "shall be of at least such distance as is then required by zoning or other ordinance or by-law, if any, of said city or town for erection of a building on such lot, and if no distance is so required, such frontage shall be of at least twenty feet." The minimum 20 ft. frontage requirement is anomalous, being akin to zoning regulation. The appeals court has spoken on the relation of this clause and planning

and 100 (1994), 3 L.C.R. 185 (1995), 4 L.C.R. 29, 94, 188 and 293 (1996), 13 L.C.R. 516 (2005).

[6]Coolidge Construction Co., Inc. v. Planning Bd. of Andover, 7 L.C.R. 75 (1999); Gould v. Bean, 7 L.C.R. 78 (1999); Centore v. Planning Bd. of Georgetown, 11 L.C.R. 1 (2003).

[7]Barton Properties, Inc. v. Planning Bd. of Concord, 4 L.C.R. 293 (1996).

[8]Bloom v. Planning Bd. of Brookline, 346 Mass. 278, 191 N.E.2d 684 (1963); Cricones v. Planning Bd. of Dracut, 39 Mass. App. Ct. 264, 654 N.E.2d 1204

(1995); and Land Court cases in 5 L.C.R. 27 (1997), 10 L.C.R. 231 (2002), 13 L.C.R. 375 (2005).

[9]Citgo Petroleum Corp. v. Planning Bd. of Braintree, 24 Mass. App. Ct. 425, 509 N.E.2d 284 (1987); Smalley v. Planning Bd. of Harwich, 10 Mass. App. Ct. 599, 410 N.E.2d 1219 (1980); and Land Court cases in 2 L.C.R. 96 (1994), 5 L.C.R, 30 (1997), 12 L.C.R. 173 (2004).

[10]Norton v. Duxbury Planning Bd., 12 L.C.R. 173 (2004).

[11]Libby v. Gaughan, 14 L.C.R. 214 (2006).

board regulations to zoning requirements of frontage.[12] The meaning of the phrase as to frontage "then required by zoning . . ." has itself received varied interpretations by the courts.[13]

A determination that a division of land does not constitute a "subdivision," by ANR endorsement of a plan, as discussed in the following § 12:3, does not establish that the lots shown on the plan comply with applicable zoning provisions or entitle any lot to a building permit.[14] That is an important context of the decisions referred to above, often referred to therein.

Beyond all this there is a line of cases casting further doubt on entitlement to ANR endorsement based on considerations of actual access to the lots asserted not to constitute a subdivision. In the *Gifford* case in 1978,[15] the SJC held that a plan showing "pork chop lots," each having requisite frontage on a public way "by a long, narrow neck turning at an acute angle" rendering "vehicular access to the main parts of these lots inadequate," was not entitled to ANR endorsement. The reason given was the *purpose* of the Subdivision Control Law, expressed in § 81-M of Chapter 41, described in § 12:10. Section 81-M refers specifically to "subdivisions," and this application thereof to divisions of land expressly excluded from the definition of "subdivision" came as a surprise to many conveyancers. In the *Gifford* decision the court said that: "We stress that we are concerned here with a quite exceptional case" and that its holding "is not to interfere with the sound application of the [ANR] technique."

Nevertheless, the concept stuck and has been developed further, in a somewhat checkered manner which seems not yet to have defined a bright line.

• Cases in which denial of ANR has been upheld include: *Hrenchuk*,[16] in which the frontage was on Interstate 95, a limited access highway, and actual access was provided by a

---

[12]Arrigo v. Planning Bd. of Franklin, 12 Mass. App. Ct. 802, 429 N.E.2d 355 (1981).

[13]Seguin v. Planning Bd. of Upton, 33 Mass. App. Ct. 374, 600 N.E.2d 185 (1992); Grandstaff v. Bd. of Appeals of Haverhill, 9 L.C.R. 173 (2001).

[14]Gattozzi v. Director of Inspection Services of Melrose, 6 Mass. App. Ct. 889, 376 N.E.2d 1266

(1978); Corrigan v. Board of Appeals of Brewster, 35 Mass. App. Ct. 514, 622 N.E.2d 1379 (1993); Shea v. Board of Appeals of Lexington, 35 Mass. App. Ct. 519, 622 N.E.2d 1382 (1993).

[15]Gifford v. Planning Bd. of Nantucket, 376 Mass. 801, 383 N.E.2d 1123 (1978).

[16]Hrenchuk v. Planning Bd. of Walpole, 8 Mass. App. Ct. 949, 397

private way. *Perry*,[17] in which frontage was on an unconstructed public way. *Poulos*,[18] in which impairment of access was attributed to a DPW guard rail and a slope, although the Land Court had noted that DPW's policy was to remove guard rails and there was no constraint on altering the slope. *Gates*,[19] in which access from the frontage way was "illusory" because of extensive wetlands, the crossing of which would have been an "environmental disaster" and an "economic calamity." *Ball*,[20] again finding an unconstructed way to be inadequate, and citing "tension" between *Perry* and *Sturdy*.

• Cases in which rejection of ANR was overruled or found improper include: *Gallitano*,[21] in which ANR had been denied only because of absence of "easy access to utility and municipal services." *Hutchinson*,[22] holding that ANR may not be withheld when it is determined that "the quality of access" is of the kind that public ways "normally provide." *Corcoran*,[23] in which there were wetlands between the frontage and building areas of some lots, but it was held that the need for regulatory approval for filling wetlands did not did not detract from actual access to the lots. The court here repeated a statement from *Gallitano* that the decision in *Gifford* "was not intended to broaden the powers of planning boards." *Sturdy*,[24] in which frontage was on an ancient way so physically deficient that it did "not satisfy the requirement of safe access." Rejecting inadequacy of access as a ground for withholding ANR endorsement the court declared the "more accurate formulation" to be that such endorsement may be denied only where the access is "illusory in fact." This decision was entered a few months before *Poulos*,

---

N.E.2d 1292 (1979).

[17]Perry v. Planning Bd. of Nantucket, 15 Mass. App. Ct. 144, 444 N.E.2d 389 (1983).

[18]Poulos v. Planning Bd. of Braintree, 413 Mass. 359, 597 N.E.2d 417 (1992).

[19]Gates v. Planning Bd. of Dighton, 48 Mass. App. Ct. 394, 722 N.E.2d 477 (2000).

[20]Ball v. Planning Bd. of Leverett, 58 Mass. App. Ct. 513, 790 N.E.2d 1138 (2003).

[21]Gallitano v. Board of Survey and Planning of Waltham, 10 Mass. App. Ct. 269, 407 N.E.2d 359 (1980).

[22]Hutchinson v. Planning Bd. of Hingham, 23 Mass. App. Ct. 416, 502 N.E.2d 572 (1987).

[23]Corcoran v. Planning Bd. of Sudbury, 406 Mass. 248, 547 N.E.2d 911 (1989); see also Long Pond Estates, Ltd. v. Planning Bd. of Sturbridge, 406 Mass. 253, 547 N.E.2d 914 (1989).

[24]Sturdy v. Planning Bd. of Hingham, 32 Mass. App. Ct. 72, 586 N.E.2d 11 (1992); see also Hastings v. Planning Bd. of Pelham, 2 L.C.R. 149 (1993); Jaxtimer v. Planning Bd., 4 L.C.R. 71 (1996), on remand from 38 Mass.App.Ct. 23, 643 N.E.2d 1064 (1995), rev. den. 419 Mass.1108, 646 N.E.2d 1071 (1995).

but not cited therein. In *Hobbs Brook Farm*,[25] the planning board had doubted access to Route 2 and declared it "extraordinarily unsafe and dangerous," but the court said that a "qualitative question is not a proper subject for planning board concern in the context of the ANR process," and that state curb cuts were sure to be granted.

• Faced with the issue, the Land Court analyzes the data presented and sometimes finds access to be illusory,[26] and sometimes not.[27]

In face of continuing uncertainties, developers may seek to effect street and lot improvements before filing plans for ANR endorsement. As to wetlands, see **Chapter 13**. As to street improvements, see **Chapter 15**.

TOPIC B: APPROVAL NOT REQUIRED

§ 12:3 Three modes

In order for a plan showing two or more lots to be accepted for recording by a registry of deeds, it must bear or be accompanied by specified certifications, showing either that it has been approved as a subdivision, as discussed in **Topic C of this Chapter**, or that it is not a subdivision. For the latter, there are three alternative forms of certification:

• One mode, of limited availability, is a statutorily prescribed certification by a registered surveyor on the face of the plan. The certification by a registered surveyor which entitles a plan to be recorded without any planning board endorsement is to the effect that: "The property lines shown are the lines dividing existing ownerships, and the lines of streets and ways shown are those of public or private streets or ways already established, and that no new lines for division of existing ownership or for new ways are shown." The property lines of existing ownership may have been shown on prior recorded plans or on unrecorded plans, or established by deed description without any plans. Similarly, the lines of some old ways may not previously have been shown on any plans. A

---

[25]Hobbs Brook Farm Property Co. Ltd. Partnership v. Planning Bd. of Lincoln, 48 Mass. App. Ct. 403, 721 N.E.2d 398 (2000).

[26]Walker Development Corp. v. Gore, 14 L.C.R. 280 (2006).

[27]Albemarle Realty Corp., 14 L.C.R. 45 (2006).

registered surveyor is of course required to make sufficient inquiry or record search to determine the accuracy of such a recital.

• The most common mode is an endorsement by a planning board that "Approval is not Required" or words to that effect. Any plan which does show new lots, not previously established by plan or deed, and which are asserted to meet one or more of the tests for exemption from the definition of a subdivision described in § 12:2, must be submitted to the planning board for such endorsement. The submission is made pursuant to § 81-P of Chapter 41; the form of application used by most planning boards is called Form A; and the endorsement sought is approval under the subdivision control law not required, or words of similar import. Such plans are, consequently, often referred to as "P plans," or "Form A plans," or, more often, simply as "ANR plans."

The filing is made with the planning board, with written notice to the city or town clerk, who should receipt for it. The notice must describe the land sufficiently for identification and state the date of filing and the name and address of the owner. Formal or procedural flaws may be grounds for denial of ANR endorsement.[1] Upon such filing, without any public hearing or further notice, the planning board shall, if it finds that the plan does not require approval, i.e. is not a subdivision, "forthwith" endorse it with the Approval Not Required language. The planning board's judgment is confined to determining whether the plan shows a subdivision,[2] and it must make that determination forthwith without waiting for a subsequent zoning change.[3] The endorsement should be signed by a majority of the planning board unless the board has authorized one or more of its members or other person to endorse for it, and has so notified the register of deeds in writing. In any event the Board's action requires a majority of the members, not just a quorum.[4]

If the planning board determines that in its opinion the plan does require approval under the subdivision control

---

[Section 12:3]

[1]See Land Court cases in 5 L.C.R. 163 (1997), 8 L.C.R. 346 (2000), 9 L.C.R. 62 (2001).

[2]Smalley v. Planning Bd. of Harwich, 10 Mass. App. Ct. 599, 410 N.E.2d 1219 (1980); Malaguti v. Planning Bd. of Wellesley, 3 Mass. App. Ct. 797, 339 N.E.2d 246 (1975).

[3]Bisson v. Planning Bd. of Dover, 43 Mass. App. Ct. 504, 684 N.E.2d 7 (1997).

[4]Duddy v. Mankewich, 66 Mass. App. Ct. 789, 851 N.E.2d 445 (2006).

law, it must so notify the applicant and the city or town clerk in writing within 21 days after submission of the plan. Notice to the applicant need not be in writing,[5] applicant may then submit the plan for approval, or he may appeal the board's determination to the superior court or land court, as further discussed in § **12:15**.

• If the planning board fails to act and notify the city or town clerk within 21 days of submission of the plan, it shall be deemed to have determined that the plan does not require approval, and it is then obligated to endorse the plan approval not required. If it does not do so, then the third mode comes into play: The city or town clerk may issue a certificate to the same effect; i.e., that 21 days have passed without planning board action and the plan is in effect deemed endorsed approval not required. This is usually a separate document, not written on the face of the plan. A planning board or municipal clerk may be compelled so to act by suit in the nature of mandamus.[6] In upholding a constructive grant of ANR the court rejected arguments as to the "purposes" of the statute.[7]

§ 12:4   Effect

It is provided in § 81-P that approval-not-required endorsements "shall be conclusive on all persons." It is, however, subject to judicial review,[1] and is not clear in what respect such endorsements are conclusive. Although the subdivision control law defines "lot" as "an area of land in one ownership, with definite boundaries, used, or available for use, as the site of one or more buildings," an approval-not-required endorsement does not constitute a determination that the lots shown meet the applicable zoning or septic disposal requirements,[2] nor in some instances the sufficiency of the way to meet ANR requirements.[3] It has been said that the endorsement is conclusive on the board itself, does not con-

---

[5]See Goodrich v. Duxbury Planning Bd., 8 L.C.R. 448 (2001).

[6]J & R Inv., Inc. v. City Clerk of New Bedford, 28 Mass. App. Ct. 1, 545 N.E.2d 1173 (1989).

[7]Kupperstein v. Planning Bd. of Cohasset, 66 Mass. App. Ct. 905, 845 N.E.2d 1141 (2006).

[Section 12:4]

[1]Lee v. Board of Appeals of Harwich, 11 Mass. App. Ct. 148, 414 N.E.2d 619 (1981).

[2]Gattozzi v. Director of Inspection Services of Melrose, 6 Mass. App. Ct. 889, 376 N.E.2d 1266 (1978); Smalley v. Planning Bd. of Harwich, 10 Mass. App. Ct. 599, 410 N.E.2d 1219 (1980); Corrigan v. Board of Appeals of Brewster, 35 Mass. App. Ct. 514, 622 N.E.2d 1379 (1993); Reagan v. Planning Bd. of Braintree, 37 Mass. App. Ct. 956, 642 N.E.2d 1054 (1994).

[3]Linhares v. Medeiros, 14 Mass. App. Ct. 927, 436 N.E.2d

stitute an approval under § 81U, and therefore cannot be revoked under § 81W.[4]

In *Marinelli v. Board of Appeals of Stoughton*,[5] a zoning "grandfather" case, the S.J.C. held, anomalously, that an ANR endorsement of a plan indicated the planning board's determination that the way shown thereon met the requirements applicable to ways for purposes of a subdivision plan and was "a way shown on a plan approved and endorsed in accordance with the Subdivision Rules, Regulations and Requirements in Stoughton." The confusion between ANR and subdivision approval arose from looking for definition of "frontage" for purposes of grandfather protection under M.G.L.A. c. 40A, § 6 (discussed in § **11:12**) in the definitions in M.G.L.A. c. 41, § 81L and local zoning provisions derived therefrom. In *Marinelli*, the court did cite *LeBlanc v. Board of Appeals of Danvers*,[6] which had made clear that "To define frontage in c. 40A, Section 6, by importing the criteria of c. 41, Section 81L, would not serve the purpose of" Chapter 40A, § 6, and that "the subdivision control law is inapplicable" in this situation, the two statutes being different as to frontage because their purposes are different.

TOPIC C: APPROVAL OF SUBDIVISION

§ 12:5   Preliminary plan

A preliminary plan is required for a nonresidential subdivision, and although optional as a precursor of a definitive plan for a residential subdivision, it is usually advisable to file one. The requirements of planning boards for preliminary plans as to form, engineering details and supporting documentation are usually somewhat less strict than for definitive plans, and economies of cost and time may be achieved by the informal review afforded by a preliminary plan. The minimum requirements for what a preliminary plan must show are set forth in the definition thereof in § 81-L of Chapter 41, as follows:

'Preliminary plan' shall mean a plan of a proposed subdivi-

1233 (1982); Woodridge Road Realty Trust v. Wayland Zoning Bd. of Appeals, 8 L.C.R. 351 (2000).

[4]Cassani v. Planning Bd. of Hull, 1 Mass. App. Ct. 451, 300 N.E.2d 746 (1973).

[5]Marinelli v. Board of Appeals of Stoughton, 440 Mass. 255, 797 N.E.2d 893 (2003).

[6]LeBlanc v. Board of Appeals of Danvers, 32 Mass. App. Ct. 760, 594 N.E.2d 906 (1992).

sion or resubdivision of land drawn on tracing paper, or a print thereof, showing (a) the subdivision name, boundaries, north point, date, scale, legend and title 'Preliminary Plan'; (b) the names of the record owner and the applicant and the name of the designer, engineer or surveyor; (c) the names of all abutters, as determined from the most recent local tax list; (d) the existing and proposed lines of streets, ways, easements and any public areas within the subdivision in a general manner; (e) the proposed system of drainage, including adjacent existing natural waterways, in a general manner; (f) the approximate boundary line of proposed lots, with approximate areas and dimensions; (g) the names, approximate location and widths of adjacent streets; (h) and the topography of the land in a general manner.

A preliminary plan is filed with the planning board and the local board of health, and written notice given to the city or town clerk, who should be asked to provide a receipt. Without public hearing, the planning board and the board of health then consider the plan and within 45 days notify the applicant and the city or town clerk of approval, approval with modifications, or disapproval for stated reasons. As a practical matter, this process usually involves informal meetings and discussions of the applicant and his surveyors and attorneys with the boards, and results in modifications making the plan acceptable to the planning board. It also affords a means to identify the particular waivers of requirements of the planning board's rules and regulations which will be sought and are likely to be granted upon approval of a definitive plan. Often there is also review of the preliminary plan by the conservation commission, police and fire chiefs and perhaps other officials, and give and take between them and the applicant is the norm.

Action on a preliminary plan is not subject to appeal.[1]

§ 12:6 Definitive plan

The submission of a definitive plan to the local planning board for approval is a prerequisite to subdivision. Section 81-O of Chapter 41 requires that the plan show the lots into which the land is to be divided, and the ways furnishing access thereto. As a practical matter the plan will also include all of the data referred to in the definition of a preliminary plan, set forth above, and other data and details required by the planning board rules and regulations, discussed in the following § 12:11. In addition to survey and engineering data,

[Section 12:5]

[1]Paul Livoli, Inc. v. Planning Bd. of Marlborough, 347 Mass. 330, 197 N.E.2d 785 (1964).

and requirements concerning the form and contents of the plan, Planning Boards often also require submission of traffic studies, wetland studies, demographic studies, and title information. At this stage survey and engineering data must be detailed and complete, and plans prepared in linen or Mylar transparency originals suitable for recording.

Submission of a definitive plan is effected by its being delivered at a meeting of the planning board or mailed to the board by registered mail, effective upon receipt. The statute also requires that written notice of submission of the plan be given to the city or town clerk. The notice must (as in the case of a § 81-P plan) describe the land sufficiently for identification, state the date of submission and the name and address of the owner, and it is here also important for the applicant to obtain a receipt from the clerk.

Under § 81-Q, a planning board is prohibited from requiring by its rules and regulations the "referral of a subdivision plan to any other board [other than the board of health] or person prior to its submission to the planning board." However, planning board rules and regulations usually require submission of a sufficient number of prints of a subdivision plan so that they may forthwith be distributed to the conservation commission, police chief, fire chief and sometimes other officials.

Section 81-U of Chapter 41 requires that a copy of the definitive plan also be filed with the local board of health. Within 45 days the board of health must report in writing to the planning board, with a copy to the applicant, its approval or disapproval, and in the latter case, specifying "areas shown on such plan [which] cannot be used for building sites without injury to the public health," including "specific findings and the reasons therefor," and "where possible, . . . recommendations for the adjustments thereof." Failure so to report shall be deemed to be approval by the board of health of the subdivision plan as filed.

If on-site septic disposal is proposed, then percolation and water table tests will generally have been made before submission of the plan, and the results thereof submitted to the planning board and the board of health with the plan. The board of health will then ordinarily specify any lots which cannot be used for building sites, stating as its reasons the inability of such lots to meet requirements of Title 5 (discussed in **§ 13:20**). The grounds for disapproval by a board of health are not limited to issues of septic disposal.[1]

§ 12:7 Planning board action

The planning board is required by § 81-T of Chapter 41 to hold a public hearing on the definitive plan, giving notice, at the applicant's expense, by publication in a local newspaper once a week for two successive weeks, the first publication at least 14 days before the hearing (or by posting if there is no local paper), and by mailing to the applicant and all abutters. After the public hearing and the report of the board of health (or lapse of 45 days where applicable), the planning board must enter its decision, certify its action to the city or town clerk and give notice of such action by registered mail to the applicant. Pendency of a town master plan was held not to justify delay in approval.[1] Although a definition in 81-L of Chapter 41 refers to action by "a majority" of the members of the planning board, there is in fact no specification in the statute. The SJC held that a majority of the whole board was required, distinguishing an earlier "quorum" concept.[2]

The time within which the planning board must take final action and certify such action to the city or town clerk is 90 days after submission of the definitive plan if there was a preliminary plan procedure or 135 days after submission of the definitive plan if there had been no preliminary plan procedure. The period was held to have been tolled by reference of the subdivision plan to the Martha's Vineyard Commission (see § 14:13).[3] In either case the time may be extended "at the written request of the applicant." Often it is the planning board which wants more time, and applicants usually deem it to be expedient to provide the board with a written request for extension. The planning board must notify the city or town clerk of such extension. If the board

[Section 12:6]

[1]See Independence Park, Inc. v. Board of Health of Barnstable, 403 Mass. 477, 530 N.E.2d 1235 (1988); K. Hovnanian at Taunton, Inc. v. Planning Bd. of Taunton, 32 Mass. App. Ct. 480, 590 N.E.2d 1172 (1992); Schroeder v. Planning Bd. of Groton, 9 L.C.R. 257 (2001); and see Abbott v. Board of Water and Sewer Com'rs of Hopkinton, 40 Mass. App. Ct. 495, 664 N.E.2d 1204 (1996).

[Section 12:7]

[1]Pieper v. Planning Bd. of

Southborough, 340 Mass. 157, 163 N.E.2d 14 (1959); and see Vitale v. Planning Bd. of Newburyport, 10 Mass. App. Ct. 483, 409 N.E.2d 237 (1980); Falk v. Peeso, 12 L.C.R. 123 (2004).

[2]McElderry v. Planning Bd. of Nantucket, 431 Mass. 722, 729 N.E.2d 1090 (2000).

[3]Crocker v. Martha's Vineyard Com'n, 407 Mass. 77, 551 N.E.2d 527 (1990).

does not take the necessary actions within the prescribed time, it is deemed to have approved the plan. Constructive approval has been upheld in some cases, rejected in others.[4]

Under § 81-U the decision of the planning board may be to approve the plan, modify and approve the plan, or disapprove the plan. Approval is a favored result. It is provided in § 81-M of Chapter 41 that:

> It is the intent of the subdivision control law that any subdivision plan filed with the planning board shall receive the approval of such board if said plan conforms to the recommendation of the board of health and to the reasonable rules and regulations of the planning board pertaining to subdivisions of land, . . .

That is to say, if the plan is approved by the board of health and complies with the provisions of the subdivision control law and the rules and regulations of the planning board in effect at the time of original submission of the plan or the preliminary plan preceding it, then the planning board is obliged to approve the plan.[5] On the other hand, if the board of health disapproves the plan, the planning board may not then approve it.[6]

When a planning board chooses to "modify and approve" that usually appears in the form of "conditions" of approval. Such conditions are often tested in light of planning board rules and regulations, discussed in **Topic D of this Chapter**. The scope of the power to modify and approve is not defined, but it certainly is aimed at achieving approval. The statute does state expressly that if the board of health

---

[4]Constructive approval upheld: Craig v. Planning Bd. Of Haverhill, 64 Mass. App. Ct. 677, 835 N.E.2d 270 (2005); New Bedford Management Systems, Inc. v. Planning Bd. of New Bedford, 10 L.C.R. 75 (2002); Eliades v. Callahan, 13 L.C.R. 225 (2005); Bernstein v. Planning Bd. of Stockbridge, 14 L.C.R. 266 (2006). Constructive approval rejected: Coolidge Construction Co., Inc. v. Planning Bd. of Andover, 8 L.C.R. 268 (2000); Ford v. Clark, 9 L.C.R. 454 (2001).

[5]Baker v. Planning Bd. of Framingham, 353 Mass. 141, 228 N.E.2d 831 (1967); Selectmen of Ayer v. Planning Bd. of Ayer, 3 Mass. App. Ct. 545, 336 N.E.2d 388 (1975); Chira v. Planning Bd. of Tisbury, 3 Mass. App. Ct. 433, 333 N.E.2d 204 (1975); Canter v. Planning Bd. of Westborough, 4 Mass. App. Ct. 306, 347 N.E.2d 691 (1976); Mac-Rich Realty Const., Inc. v. Planning Bd. of Southborough, 4 Mass. App. Ct. 79, 341 N.E.2d 916 (1976); Patelle v. Planning Bd. of Woburn, 6 Mass. App. Ct. 951, 383 N.E.2d 94 (1978); Vitale v. Planning Bd. of Newburyport, 10 Mass. App. Ct. 483, 409 N.E.2d 237 (1980).

[6]Fairbairn v. Planning Bd. of Barnstable, 5 Mass. App. Ct. 171, 360 N.E.2d 668 (1977); Loring Hills Developers Trust v. Planning Bd. of Salem, 5 Mass. App. Ct. 813, 361 N.E.2d 417 (1977), judgment aff'd, 374 Mass. 343, 372 N.E.2d 775 (1978).

shall so require, the approval of the planning board shall be on condition that no building or structure shall be built or placed upon areas designated without consent by the board of health. In practice that usually means that certain lots or portions of lots shown on the plan, are not qualified for on-site septic disposal without further consideration and approval by the board of health.

If a planning board disapproves a subdivision plan, it is obliged to "state in detail wherein the plan does not conform to the rules and regulations of the planning board or the recommendations of the health board or officer"[7] and is further obliged to "revoke its disapproval and approve a plan which, as amended conforms to such rules and regulations or recommendations." That is to say, an applicant whose plan is disapproved may modify it to dispose of the particular objections specified by the planning board, and then be forthwith entitled to have it approved. That provision may lead to remand to the planning board, but not always.[8] The statute does not by its terms require any resubmission of the plan or any further public hearing, but the court has held that to be necessary.[9] In any event, once the appeal period on an approval or disapproval has expired, it would seem that any remedy of modification would lie in the provisions of M.G.L.A. c. 41, § 81-W, discussed in § **12:9**.

In any case the planning board is obliged to file "a certificate of its action" with the city or town clerk.

§ 12:8 Securing performance

It is provided in § 81-U of Chapter 41 that:

Before endorsement of its approval of a plan, a planning board shall require that the construction of ways and the installation of municipal services be secured by one, or in part one and in part by another, of the methods described in the following clauses (1), (2), (3) and (4) which method or combination of methods may be selected and from time to time varied by the applicant.

• The first and second methods consist of providing the

---

[7]See O.I.B. Corpration v. Planning Bd. of Braintree, 6 L.C.R. 57 (1998).

[8]Ferguson v. Planning Bd. of Millis, 3 L.C.R. 45 (1995); Weinstein v. Planning Bd. of Haverhill, 4 L.C.R. 213 (1996); Fieldstone Meadows Development Corp. v. Planning Bd. of Andover, 12 L.C.R.

213 (2004).

[9]Patelle v. Planning Bd. of Woburn, 6 Mass. App. Ct. 951, 383 N.E.2d 94 (1978); and see Vitale v. Planning Bd. of Newburyport, 10 Mass. App. Ct. 483, 409 N.E.2d 237 (1980); Windsor v. Planning Bd. of Wayland, 26 Mass. App. Ct. 650, 531 N.E.2d 272 (1988).

planning board with a performance bond of an insurance company (method 1) or a deposit of money or negotiable securities (method 2), in either case sufficient in the opinion of the planning board to secure performance, and bearing "a direct and reasonable relationship to the expected cost including the effects of inflation, necessary to complete the work." The statute goes on to provide that:

> Such amount or amounts shall from time to time be reduced so that the amount bonded, deposited or retained continues to reflect the actual expected cost of work remaining to be completed.

If either of these methods is chosen, the planning board may require that the time be specified within which the construction and installation shall be completed, a period of two years being the norm. Such a time limit may be strictly enforced.[1] The city or town may avail itself of the bond or deposit to cover "the reasonable cost" of completing the work, but is not obligated to do so.[2]

• The third method is by a covenant executed and recorded by the owner of the subdivided land, running with the land, whereby the ways and services must be constructed and installed to serve any lot on the plan before such lot may be built upon or conveyed. Exceptions are that (a) lots may be mortgaged and such mortgage may be foreclosed, provided that the subsequent owners remain subject to the prohibition on building until the ways and services are provided to serve the lot, and (b) the entire tract or all lots not previously released from the covenant may be conveyed by a single deed, subject to the covenant. Any other deed is voidable by the grantee prior to release of the covenant with respect to the land conveyed and within three years after the date of the deed.

There is no express time limit provision with respect to performance secured by covenant, but planning boards often set time limits for performance in their rules and regulations, and these may apply regardless of the method of security. The planning board has been held not liable to enforce the terms of such a covenant.[3]

Since subdividers will ordinarily partially complete the construction of the ways and installation of municipal services before seeking to sell lots, the usual practice is to select

[Section 12:8]

[1]Antonelli v. Planning Bd. of North Andover, 4 L.C.R. 67 (1996).

[2]Marlborough Sav. Bank v. City of Marlborough, 45 Mass. App. Ct. 250, 697 N.E.2d 143 (1998).

[3]McGowan v. Town of Dennis, 3 L.C.R. 24 (1995).

the covenant method at the time of approval, avoiding the expense of a bond or the anteing up of marketable securities. Once the ways are sufficiently built to market the lots, then a bond, covering only the remaining cost of completion, is provided and the covenant is released. Since lot purchasers will then probably bring in construction equipment over the roads, it is advisable not to finish the road surface (the "skim coat") until later, and the bond will remain outstanding until that is done. Furthermore, the amount of the bond may be reduced from time to time.

In § 81-U it is provided that:

> Any covenant given under the preceding paragraph and any condition required by the health board or officer shall be either inscribed on the plan or contained in a separate document, referred to on the plan.

This clause has been cited by the courts as applicable in cases considering the validity of conditions of approval other than those required by a health board or the validity of waivers, discussed in § **12:13**.

There is a standard form of subdivision approval covenant used by most planning boards, but special provisions are sometimes included at the instance of either the applicant or the planning board, as indicated in **Appendix L**. For instance, the applicant may wish to clarify or to make special provisions for release of certain lots, or to exclude lots which are shown on the subdivision plan but have frontage on an existing public way, which lots would not otherwise be excluded from the covenant.[4] The planning board may wish to insert additional covenants which will continue to run with the land even after release of the lots from the prohibition on building and sale. In the latter case the covenant would never be released completely, and it will then be important for the applicant to obtain a certificate of completion stating specifically that all construction requirements have been met. It is also important to both the board and the applicant to make a record of any conditions of the approval and any waivers of regulations that have been granted, and this covenant may be an appropriate place to do so, at least when the planning board's "certificate of its action" does not do so. Even if the planning board's certificate filed with the city or town clerk does specify waivers granted and any other special conditions, it may be important to establish them of record by including them in the approval with covenant contract to be recorded in the registry

---

[4]Landgraf Associates, Inc. v. Building Commissioner of Springfield, 4 Mass. App. Ct. 840, 354 N.E.2d 887 (1976).

of deeds.

● The fourth method is an agreement by the subdivider and his construction mortgage lender whereby the latter agrees to hold and advance funds for completion of construction of the ways. This has little appeal to lenders and is rarely used.

Upon completion of all the work the subdivider is required so to state in writing, sent to the planning board and city or town clerk by registered mail. The planning board is then to release whatever security it still holds; or if the planning board disagrees with the statement, it must within 45 days give registered mail notice to the subdivider and the clerk specifying the deficiencies. Failure to do so within the 45-day period voids the security and the city or town clerk shall then so certify.

§ 12:9 Modifications

It is provided in § 81-O of Chapter 41 that:

> After the approval of a plan the location and width of ways shown thereon shall not be changed unless the plan is amended accordingly as provided in [§ 81-W]; but the number, shape and size of the lots shown on a plan so approved may, from time to time, be changed without action by the board, provided every lot so changed still has frontage on a public way or way shown on a plan approved in accordance with the subdivision control law of at least such distance, if any, as is then required by ordinance or by-law of said city or town for erection of a building on such lot, and if no distance is so required, has such frontage of at least twenty feet.

That is to say, so long as the approved street layout is not changed, the lots shown may be changed so long as they continue to comply with applicable zoning provisions. Such a change would require at least an ANR endorsement of a plan showing the altered lots, because otherwise it would not be recordable.

Once a subdivision plan has been approved, whether by planning board action or default thereof, the possibility of any change affecting the location or width of ways, or any other element that is fundamental to the approval, is governed by § 81-W of Chapter 41, which provides in the first paragraph thereof that:

> A planning board, on its own motion or on the petition of any person interested, shall have power to modify, amend or rescind its approval of a plan of a subdivision, or to require a change in a plan as a condition of its retaining the status of an approved plan. All of the provisions of the subdivision control

law relating to the submission and approval of a plan of a subdivision shall, so far as apt, be applicable to the approval of the modification, amendment or rescission of such approval and to a plan which has been changed under this section.

An ANR procedure may not be substituted for notice and hearing under § 81-W.[1] The § 81-W procedure has been used to correct errors, and impose overlooked conditions,[2] but is not always suitable for that purpose.[3]

It is further provided in § 81-W that no action thereunder "shall affect the lots in such subdivision which have been sold or mortgaged in good faith and for a valuable consideration subsequent to the approval of the plan," without the consent of the owner and mortgagee of the lots.[4] It is also provided in § 81-DD of Chapter 41 that any person who has "changed his position or made expenditures in reliance upon" a subdivision approval and is then "injured in his property by reason of the modification, amendment or rescission of the approval" under § 81-W without his consent, "may recover the damages so caused under chapter seventy-nine." M.G.L.A. c. 79 is the eminent domain statute, and the meaning of this obscure clause is far from clear.

In order for an action under § 81-W to take effect, specified recordings and endorsements must be made, and in the case of registered land, court action may be necessary.

TOPIC D: PLANNING BOARD RULES AND REGULATIONS

§ 12:10 Adoption; effect

The purposes of subdivision control, as set forth in § 81-M of Chapter 41, may succinctly be summarized as provision of ways which are safe and sufficient for access, provision of necessary services such as water, sewerage, drainage and utilities, coordination with other subdivisions and other municipal ways and services, assurance of compliance with zoning laws, and "due regard for . . . the use of solar energy."

These purposes are spelled out in the statute, but still

[Section 12:9]

[1]Hamilton v. Planning Bd. of Beverly, 35 Mass. App. Ct. 386, 620 N.E.2d 44 (1993).

[2]Mierzwa v. Planning Bd. of Haverhill, 7 L.C.R. 240 (1999).

[3]Norwell Planning Bd. v. Scituate Planning Bd., 6 L.C.R. 6 (1998).

[4]See Eliades v. Callahan, 13 L.C.R. 225 (2005); Terrill v. Planning Bd. of Upton, 14 L.C.R. 490 (2006).

broadly stated, and the meat on the bones must be provided by rules and regulations adopted by the local planning board. Under § 81-Q the adoption of such rules and regulations is mandatory, and once adopted they constitute substantive provisions with which a subdivision must comply unless they are duly waived by the planning board, as discussed in § **12:13**. In order to adopt or amend subdivision rules and regulations, a planning board must hold a public hearing, giving notice thereof by publication and posting.[1]

Once adopted, a true copy of the rules and regulations, with all amendments, must be kept on file and available for inspection at the offices of the planning board and the city or town clerk. A copy certified by the clerk must be sent to the register of deeds and recorder of the land court.[2] The rules and regulations in effect when a definitive plan is submitted shall govern that plan through its approval process. If a preliminary plan has been previously filed, the rules and regulations in effect at the time of the submission thereof shall govern the definitive plan derived therefrom provided that the definitive plan is duly submitted within seven months after the preliminary plan.[3] The Land Court has pointed out the distinction between a "freeze" of applicable subdivision rules and regulations and a zoning freeze under M.G.L.A. c. 40A, § 6.[4]

§ 12:11   General requirements

As the SJC said in the leading *Castle Estates* case,[1] such rules and regulations should be comprehensive, reasonably definite and carefully drafted so that owners may know in advance what is or may be required of them and what standards and procedures will be applied. That often cited principle was the basis of rejection of regulations requiring "attractiveness" and "livability,"[2] but "adequate access" was accepted as not too vague, being rather a statutory phrase

---

[Section 12:10]

[1]See Doliner v. Planning Bd. of Millis, 343 Mass. 1, 175 N.E.2d 919 (1961).

[2]See Stamell v. Dietz, 10 L.C.R. 57 (2002).

[3]See Doliner v. Planning Bd. of Millis, 343 Mass. 1, 175 N.E.2d 919 (1961).

[4]Falk v. Peeso, 12 L.C.R. 124 (2004).

[Section 12:11]

[1]Castle Estates, Inc. v. Park and Planning Bd. of Medfield, 344 Mass. 329, 182 N.E.2d 540 (1962); see also North Landers Corp. v. Planning Bd. of Falmouth, 382 Mass. 432, 416 N.E.2d 934 (1981).

[2]Chira v. Planning Bd. of Tisbury, 3 Mass. App. Ct. 433, 333 N.E.2d 204 (1975); see also Canter v. Planning Bd. of Westborough, 7 Mass. App. Ct. 805, 390 N.E.2d

expressing a basic goal of subdivision control,[3] and diverse regulations have been upheld.[4]

The fairly extensive provisions of § 81-Q set forth a number of particular matters which may and may not be governed by subdivision rules and regulations. The statute is rather discursive, and the provisions are herein regrouped in a bit more orderly manner, and are accompanied by analysis and case citations, as follows:

- As noted in § 12:6, the rules may not require referral of the plan to any other board or person (except the board of health) prior to submission to the planning board. A regulation requiring an applicant to have made arrangements with utility companies and town departments for furnishing utility services prior to submission of the subdivision plan was held valid.[5]

- The rules must be reasonable and not inconsistent with the subdivision control law or other provisions of a statute or of any valid ordinance or by-law of the city or town.

- Except insofar as it may require compliance with the requirements of zoning ordinances or by-laws, no rule or regulation shall relate to the size, shape, width, frontage or use of lots within a subdivision or buildings which may be constructed thereon, or shall be inconsistent with requirements of any other municipal board acting within its jurisdiction.

- The rules may, however, specify that not more than one building for dwelling purposes shall be erected on any lot in a subdivision, "or elsewhere in the city or town," without the consent of the planning board.

Such a one-building-for-dwelling-per-lot rule was held to bar a separate cat shelter building in addition to a dwell-

1128 (1979); Nahigian v. Town of Lexington, 32 Mass. App. Ct. 517, 591 N.E.2d 1095 (1992); DeSanctis v. Planning Board of Saugus, 2 L.C.R. 12 (1994); Sealund Sisters, Inc. v. Planning Bd. of Weymouth, 50 Mass. App. Ct. 346, 737 N.E.2d 503 (2000).

[3]North Landers Corp. v. Planning Bd. of Falmouth, 382 Mass. 432, 416 N.E.2d 934 (1981).

[4]See, e.g., Canter v. Planning Bd. of Westborough, 7 Mass. App.

Ct. 805, 390 N.E.2d 1128 (1979); Nahigian v. Town of Lexington, 32 Mass. App. Ct. 517, 591 N.E.2d 1095 (1992); O'Connell v. Planning Bd. of Hingham, 2 L.C.R. 157 (1994); Mac-Rich Realty Const., Inc. v. Planning Bd. of Southborough, 4 Mass. App. Ct. 79, 341 N.E.2d 916 (1976).

[5]Rounds v. Board of Water and Sewer Com'rs of Wilmington, 347 Mass. 40, 196 N.E.2d 209 (1964).

ing,[6] but not to preclude the use of a single building for multiple dwellings, as allowed by the local zoning.[7] This provision, particularly the "or elsewhere" clause, might be regarded as anomalous since it confers upon a planning board a power of regulation which could otherwise be effected only by a zoning law, but in the *Ellen M. Gifford* case the court did not find the planning board to have "engaged in any attempt to exercise an undelegated zoning power."

• The rules and regulations may prescribe the size, form, content, style and number of copies of plans and the procedure for submission and approval thereof, and shall be such as to make such plans recordable.

• The rules shall set forth the requirements of the board with respect to location, construction, width and grades of ways and installation of municipal services therein, all so as "to carry out the purposes" as set forth in § 81-M, and "giving due regard . . . to the prospective character of different subdivisions, whether open residence, dense residence, business or industrial, and the prospective amount of travel" upon the ways.

Since the provision of "adequate access" is so fundamental to subdivision control, issues under rules and regulations relating thereto are often litigated, and for that reason discussion thereof has been separated into Subsection 2 of this section.

• Notwithstanding the broad scope of such rules, it is provided, however, that rules regarding "the laying out, construction, alteration, or maintenance of ways" may not "exceed the standards and criteria commonly applied" by the city or town to "its publicly financed ways located in similarly zoned districts."

This did not bar application of rules as to underground utilites,[8] or off-site ways.[9]

• A turnaround may be required at the end of "a way which does not connect with another way," i.e., a dead-end way.

The statute contains express provisions partially disposing of easements in such a turnaround when the way is further extended.

---

[6]Ellen M. Gifford Sheltering Home Corp. v. Board of Appeals of Wayland, 349 Mass. 292, 208 N.E.2d 207 (1965).

[7]Selectmen of Ayer v. Planning Bd. of Ayer, 3 Mass. App. Ct. 545,

336 N.E.2d 388 (1975).

[8]Miles v. Planning Bd. of Millbury, 404 Mass. 489, 536 N.E.2d 328 (1989).

[9]Stamell v. Dietz, 10 L.C.R. 57 (2002).

• The rules may require underground installation of utility services, and may require that aboveground poles be provided for street lighting or police and fire alarm boxes.

• The rules may "encourage the use of solar energy systems and protect . . . access [thereof] to direct sunlight," and may include "restrictive covenants protecting solar access."

• The rules may not require that any land within a subdivision be dedicated to public use or conveyed to the commonwealth, the county, city or town, for use as a public way, public park or playground, or any other public purpose without just compensation to the owner.

A rule requiring provision of areas for community use was struck down,[10] but a rule requiring alignment and continuity of ways, which would have caused the developer to give up several lots, was upheld, the court finding therein no evidence of a requirement of dedication or conveyance to the public.[11]

Notwithstanding the foregoing prohibition, it is, provided in § 81-U of Chapter 41 that a planning board shall "in proper cases require the plan to show a park or parks suitably located for playground or recreation purposes or for providing light and air" and may require that no building be erected on such park for up to three years.

• And although not mentioned in 81-Q, it is clear under M.G.L.A. c. 44, § 53G, that a planning board may adopt rules "for the imposition of reasonable fees for the employment of outside consultants."

§ 12:12 Rules concerning ways

Planning board rules and regulations as to ways come in considerable variety, as do related rules with respect to installation therein of public utility, water service and drainage facilities. There are of course basic provisions with respect to width of pavement, radius of curvature, grades, sidewalks, and street construction specifications, but even those have some variants.

The matters which have been most often litigated may be reviewed under the rubrics set forth below, which do not, however, define sharp distinctions or categories, but involve overlapping principles and considerations.

---

[10]Aronson v. Town of Sharon, 346 Mass. 598, 195 N.E.2d 341 (1964).

[11]McDavitt v. Planning Bd. of Winchester, 2 Mass. App. Ct. 806, 308 N.E.2d 786 (1974).

- **Basic Access.** When the subdivider does not have or clearly prove basic access rights, the subdivision approval is denied or overturned.[1] In the *Beale* case the SJC said that § 81U had to be read "in conjunction with . . . § 81M." The ways do not necessarily have to be in usable condition.[2]

- **Offsite Ways.** The insufficiency of ways outside the subdivision but necessary to access thereto have often resulted in denial of approval, based again on § 81M considerations.[3] However, a condition of a subdivision approval requiring the developer to improve state highways was voided as arbitrary.[4]

- **Dead End Ways.** Upon the first consideration of this issue, the SJC upheld denial of subdivision approval because of violation of a planning board regulation limiting dead-end streets to 500 feet, which the court held to be reasonable under § 81-Q as serving the purposes set forth in § 81-M,[5] while acknowledging the lack of a definition of dead-end street. The appeals court later offered such definition from Webster's dictionary and Black's Law Dictionary, and said that such regulations reflected "concern that blockage of a dead-end street, as by a fallen tree or an automobile accident, will prevent access to the homes beyond the block-

---

[Section 12:12]

[1]Silva v. Planning Bd. of Somerset, 34 Mass. App. Ct. 339, 611 N.E.2d 257 (1993); Beale v. Planning Bd. of Rockland, 423 Mass. 690, 671 N.E.2d 1233 (1996); and Land Court cases in 9 L.C.R. 84, 149 and 179 (2001), 13 L.C.R. 42 (2005).

[2]Toothaker v. Planning Bd. of Billerica, 346 Mass. 436, 193 N.E.2d 582 (1963); LeBlanc v. Board of Appeals of Danvers, 32 Mass. App. Ct. 760, 594 N.E.2d 906 (1992); Berg v. Town of Lexington, 68 Mass. App. Ct. 569, 863 N.E.2d 968 (2007).

[3]Canter v. Planning Bd. of Westborough, 7 Mass. App. Ct. 805, 390 N.E.2d 1128 (1979); Federline v. Planning Bd. of Beverly, 33 Mass. App. Ct. 65, 596 N.E.2d 1028 (1992); Carbone v. Planning Bd. of Beverly, 33 Mass. App. Ct. 909, 596 N.E.2d 1031 (1992); Rattner v. Planning Bd. of West Tisbury, 45 Mass. App. Ct. 8, 695 N.E.2d 669

(1998); Stamell v. Dietz, 10 L.C.R. 57 (2002); Taylor v. Lexington Planning Bd., 13 L.C.R. 42 (2005); but see Adams v. Planning Bd. of Westwood, 64 Mass. App. Ct. 383, 833 N.E.2d 637 (2005); Rattner v. Planning Bd. of West Tisbury, 45 Mass. App. Ct. 8, 695 N.E.2d 669 (1998).

[4]Sullivan v. Planning Bd. of Acton, 38 Mass. App. Ct. 918, 645 N.E.2d 703 (1995); see also Nahigian v. Lexington, 1 L.C.R. 1 (1993); Design Housing, Inc. v. Town of Stoughton, 6 L.C.R. 51 (1998).

[5]Francesconi v. Planning Bd. of Wakefield, 345 Mass. 390, 187 N.E.2d 807 (1963); similarly Mac-Rich Realty Const., Inc. v. Planning Bd. of Southborough, 4 Mass. App. Ct. 79, 341 N.E.2d 916 (1976); Lakeside Builders, Inc. v. Planning Bd. of Franklin, 56 Mass. App. Ct. 842, 780 N.E.2d 944 (2002); and Land Court cases in 2 L.C.R. 133 (1994), 4 L.C.R. 209 (1996), 7 L.C.R. 155 (1999).

age, particularly by fire engines, ambulances, and other emergency equipment."[6] The nature and location of the "through street" from which the *cul de saq* (a French term for dead-end) is measured has also been considered and the application of such a regulation to a commercial subdivision called into question.[7]

When a planning board had approved a plan with two *cul de sacs* off another street without reference to its 600-feet-to-dead-end rule, an abutter's appeal was denied,[8] and when a planning board required a dead end instead of a through connection to an abutting street, its then denial of waiver of a 500 feet rule, found by the court not to be required for safety purposes, was held to be an abuse of discretion for ulterior purposes.[9]

● **Continuity.** A planning board regulation that "streets shall be continuous and in alignment with existing streets" was upheld,[10] and when a planning board ignored its own rule to that effect and approved a plan which did not comply, the court remanded for further action.[11] The concept plays a role in several of the cases cited under the preceding rubrics.

● **Utilities.** Rules and regulations with respect to utilities and applications thereof have generally been upheld—with respect to water supply,[12] sewer connection,[13] and requirement of underground installation.[14]

§ 12:13 Waiver

Section 81-R of Chapter 41 provides that:

[6]Wheatley v. Planning Bd. of Hingham, 7 Mass. App. Ct. 435, 388 N.E.2d 315 (1979); Federline v. Planning Bd. of Beverly, 33 Mass. App. Ct. 65, 596 N.E.2d 1028 (1992).

[7]Federline v. Planning Bd. of Beverly, 33 Mass. App. Ct. 65, 596 N.E.2d 1028 (1992); Nahigian v. Town of Lexington, 32 Mass. App. Ct. 517, 591 N.E.2d 1095 (1992).

[8]Sparks v. Planning Bd. of Westborough, 2 Mass. App. Ct. 745, 321 N.E.2d 666 (1974).

[9]Musto v. Planning Bd. of Medfield, 54 Mass. App. Ct. 831, 768 N.E.2d 588 (2002).

[10]McDavitt v. Planning Bd. of Winchester, 2 Mass. App. Ct. 806, 308 N.E.2d 786 (1974).

[11]Curtin v. Board of Survey & Planning of Waltham, 15 Mass. App. Ct. 978, 447 N.E.2d 15 (1983).

[12]Rounds v. Board of Water and Sewer Com'rs of Wilmington, 347 Mass. 40, 196 N.E.2d 209 (1964); Garabedian v. Water and Sewerage Bd. of Medfield, 359 Mass. 404, 269 N.E.2d 275 (1971).

[13]K. Hovnanian at Taunton, Inc. v. Planning Bd. of Taunton, 32 Mass. App. Ct. 480, 590 N.E.2d 1172 (1992); Abbott v. Board of Water and Sewer Com'rs of Hopkinton, 40 Mass. App. Ct. 495, 664 N.E.2d 1204 (1996).

[14]Sansoucy v. Planning Bd. of Worcester, 355 Mass. 647, 246 N.E.2d 811(1969); Miles v. Planning Bd. of Millbury, 404 Mass. 489, 536 N.E.2d 328 (1989).

A planning board may in any particular case, where such action is in the public interest and not inconsistent with the intent and purpose of the subdivision control law, waive strict compliance with its rules and regulations, and with the frontage or access requirements specified in said law, and may, where the ways are not otherwise deemed adequate, approve a plan on conditions limiting the lots upon which buildings may be erected and the number of buildings that may be erected on particular lots and the length of time for which particular buildings may be maintained without further consent by the planning board to the access provided.

In almost every subdivision several waivers are sought and often some are granted. In fact, planning boards may deliberately adopt very detailed and strict regulations governing every conceivable point, and then grant waivers *ad hoc* of those which are not generally essential in all subdivisions. Such a procedure certainly affords a desirable flexibility to planning boards, but from a subdivider's standpoint it falls short of meeting the *Castle Estates* test of letting them know in advance what is or may be required of them and what standards and procedures will be applied.

Any waivers which are granted should be expressly set forth in the decision of the planning board approving the plan, and the applicant should be sure to obtain and retain a certified copy of that decision, since the granting of waivers may not appear in the endorsement of approval on the face of the plan or anywhere else in a public record. It has been held that written specification of the rules and regulations being waived, while desirable, is not essential to validity of the waiver.[1] As suggested in § **12:8**, the covenant with the planning board for performance security may be the best place to set forth conditions and waivers. The courts have said that conditions and waivers cannot be relied on unless they are inscribed on the plan or set forth in a separate instrument referred to on the plan, an obvious reference to the statutory clause relating to covenants, although not syntactically apt.[2]

Annulment of subdivision approval was ordered when waivers granted were "inconsistent with the intent and

---

[Section 12:13]

[1]Meyer v. Planning Bd. of Westport, 29 Mass. App. Ct. 167, 558 N.E.2d 994 (1990); Howard v. Planning and Zoning Bd. of Easton, 3 L.C.R. 77 (1995).

[2]Green v. Board of Appeal of Norwood, 358 Mass. 253, 263 N.E.2d 423 (1970); M. DeMatteo Const. Co. v. Board of Appeals of Hingham, 3 Mass. App. Ct. 446, 334 N.E.2d 51 (1975).

purpose of the subdivision control law,"[3] and when the approved plan did not comply with rules and regulations which were ignored but not waived.[4] In appropriate cases the courts have upheld the denial of a waiver,[5] and have ordered the issuance of a waiver.[6]

TOPIC E: ENFORCEMENT; JUDICIAL REVIEW

§ 12:14   Enforcement

To begin with, § 81-X of Chapter 41 provides that: "No register of deeds shall record any plan showing a division of a tract of land into two or more lots, and ways, whether existing or proposed, . . ." unless the plan bears an endorsement of approval by a planning board or one of the endorsements or certifications indicating that approval is not required. In the case of an approved plan, it may not be recorded after elapse of six months from the endorsement of approval unless accompanied by a certificate of the city or town clerk, within thirty days before the recording, that the plan has not been changed.It is, incidentally, provided in M.G.L.A. c. 60, § 23, that a subdivision plan may not be recorded unless it is accompanied by a municipal lien certificate indicating that all taxes, assessments and charges on the land shown have been paid in full.

Next, it is provided in § 81-Y that (1) no "public way" shall be constructed and "no municipal service or improvement shall be constructed in a way within a subdivision," unless shown on an approved plan, except by proper vote of the city council or town meeting to lay out a public way, and (2) that no building permit shall be issued until the building inspector, or other building permit granting official, is satisfied that the lot for which a building permit is sought is shown on a plan entitled to be recorded, as aforesaid, and that planning board conditions have been met or waived.

It should be noted, however, that the board of appeals is given power to grant a building permit in cases of "practical

---

[3]Wheatley v. Planning Bd. of Hingham, 7 Mass. App. Ct. 435, 388 N.E.2d 315 (1979).

[4]Curtin v. Board of Survey & Planning of Waltham, 15 Mass. App. Ct. 978, 447 N.E.2d 15 (1983).

[5]Lakeside Builders, Inc. v. Planning Bd. of Franklin, 56 Mass. App. Ct. 842, 780 N.E.2d 944 (2002).

[6]Musto v. Planning Bd. of Medfield, 54 Mass. App. Ct. 831, 768 N.E.2d 588 (2002).

difficulty or unnecessary hardship, and if circumstances of the case do not require that the building be related to a way shown on such plan," even though the subdivision control law has not been complied with.

Section 81-Y also provides that if a subdivision is made without a duly recorded plan (which might possibly be accomplished by deed descriptions based on monuments), anyone executing and delivering a deed, mortgage or other instrument by which such subdivision was made shall be liable for all damages sustained by any subsequent owner "without notice or knowledge," which might be hard to prove in such circumstances. There is also provision for an innocent lot purchaser to obtain approval of a plan of his lot.

Finally, § 81-Y provides for enforcement action in the superior court or land court upon complaint of a planning board or ten taxpayers brought within one year after the act or failure to act complained of.

Section 81-Z of Chapter 41 provides for a board of appeals, which may be, and usually is, "the existing board of appeals" under the local zoning law. Its powers with respect to the subdivision control law, specified in § 81-AA, seem to be limited to the granting of a permit under § 81-Y, as referred to above.

§ 12:15   Judicial review

Section 81-BB of Chapter 41 provides that:

> Any person, whether or not previously a party to the proceedings, or any municipal officer or board, aggrieved by a decision of a board of appeals under section eighty-one Y, or by any decision of a planning board concerning a plan of a subdivision of land, or by the failure of such a board to take final action concerning such a plan within the required time, may appeal to the superior court for the county in which said land is situated or to the land court; provided, that such appeal is entered within twenty days after such decision has been recorded in the office of the city or town clerk or within twenty days after the expiration of the required time as aforesaid, as the case may be, and notice of such appeal is given to such city or town clerk so as to be received within such twenty days. The court shall hear all pertinent evidence and determine the facts, and upon the facts so determined, shall annul such decision if found to exceed the authority of such board, or make such other decree as justice and equity may require. The foregoing remedy shall be exclusive, but the parties shall have all rights of appeal and exceptions as in other equity cases.

These provisions are similar in most respects to those for zoning appeals. That is, the appellant must be "aggrieved," the appeal lies in the superior court or land court, must be filed within 20 days after the action or inaction complained of, and notice of the appeal must be given to the city or town clerk within the 20 day period. This remedy is exclusive, the appeal sounds in equity, and the court hears the matter de novo as to all facts. Such appeals are nominally entitled to be advanced for speedy trial over other civil actions.

Appellants have been rejected as not aggrieved when their claims were generalized or speculative,[1] or otherwise not well founded.[2] Appeals have sometimes been held to have been filed too late,[3] but not always, there being a distinction between § 81-BB of Chapter 41 and § 17 of Chapter 40A.[4] The failure of the town clerk to record the notice of appeal was held not to void the appeal.[5]

When a plan that has been modified pursuant to § 81-W, an appeal therefrom involves only matters that were modified, and will not reopen issues that could have been addressed upon an appeal from the original plan approval.[6]

It is also provided in § 81-BB that a city or town may provide a municipal officer or board with legal counsel in relation to appeals, and that costs shall not be allowed against a planning board unless it acted with gross negligence or in bad faith, and finally that the court shall require nonmunicipal appellants to post bond of two to fifteen thousand dollars to cover appellee's costs if the court finds the appellant acted "in bad faith of with malice." The court has upheld the award

---

[Section 12:15]

[1]Bringhurst v. Planning Bd. of Walpole, 1 L.C.R. 12 (1993); Manter v. Bourne Planning Bd., 3 L.C.R. 41 (1995); see also Howard v. Planning and Zoning Bd. of Easton, 3 L.C.R. 77 (1995); Putnam v. Town of Grafton, 9 L.C.R. 164 (2001); Kazanjian v. Planning Bd. of Haverhill, 12 L.C.R. 13 (2004).

[2]Reagan v. Planning Bd. of Braintree, 37 Mass. App. Ct. 956, 642 N.E.2d 1054 (1994); Newman v. Planning Bd. of Plymouth, 4 L.C.R. 253 (1996); and see Waldron v. Planning Bd. of Dartmouth, 2 L.C.R. 3 (1994).

[3]Cullen v. Planning Bd. of Hadley, 4 Mass. App. Ct. 842, 355 N.E.2d 490 (1976); Nantucket Land Council, Inc. v. Planning Bd. of Nantucket, 5 Mass. App. Ct. 206, 361 N.E.2d 937 (1977); Land Court cases in 3 L.C.R. 107 (1995), 5 L.C.R. 220 (1997); Calnan v. Planning Bd. of Lynn, 63 Mass. App. Ct. 384, 826 N.E.2d 258 (2005).

[4]Twomey v. Board of Appeals of Medford, 7 Mass. App. Ct. 770, 390 N.E.2d 272 (1979); Berg v. Town of Lexington, 8 L.C.R. 458 (2001); Falk v. Peeso, 12 L.C.R. 124 (2004).

[5]Hahn v. Planning Bd. of Stoughton, 24 Mass. App. Ct. 553, 511 N.E.2d 20 (1987).

[6]Sergi v. Planning Bd. of Kingston, 60 Mass. App. Ct. 918, 805 N.E.2d 1005 (2004).

of counsel fees to the victim of a frivolous appeal.[7]

It may be noted that § 81-BB refers to actions "concerning a plan of a subdivision of land" and makes no express provision for judicial appeal from an ANR endorsement. Section 81-P provides for appeal under § 81-BB from a planning board determination that a submitted plan is a subdivision, but also lacks any reference to appeal from an ANR endorsement. Nevertheless, appeals relating to ANR plans were accepted by the courts in many cases, referred to in the *Stefanick* decision and others.[8] In the *Stefanick* case,[9] affirming dismissal as too late of a declaratory judgment action attacking the validity of an ANR endorsement, Justice Kass took the opportunity to consider the issue from a jurisprudential standpoint, and concluded that appeals of that type would lie in certiorari within 60 days after the ANR endorsement is made, in accordance with M.G.L.A. c. 249, § 4.

§ 12:16 Legal effect

As discussed in § 12:4, the endorsement of "approval not required" is "conclusive on all persons," but of limited legal significance. On the other hand, the statute lacks such a provision with respect to a subdivision approval, but such approval has far greater significance. In the process of approval the planning board will have determined the compliance of each lot with requirements of the local zoning laws as to frontage, area and lot configuration, and the board of health will have determined the suitability thereof for on-site septic disposal or otherwise from the public health standpoint. Furthermore, the process will have involved public hearing, formal notifications and the opportunity for judicial review, affording a remedy specified to be exclusive. Consequently, one may conclude that subdivision approval with the appeal period expired and no appeal pending is indeed conclusive.

With respect to plans recorded before the subdivision control law took effect in the city or town where the land shown on the plan lies, the legal impact of the law is set

---

[7]Cohen v. Hurley, 20 Mass. App. Ct. 439, 480 N.E.2d 658 (1985).

[8]Carey v. Planning Bd. of Revere, 335 Mass. 740, 139 N.E.2d 920 (1957); Reagan v. Planning Bd. of Braintree, 37 Mass. App. Ct. 956, 642 N.E.2d 1054 (1994); Poirier v. Zoning Bd. of Appeals of Waltham, 1 L.C.R. 30 (1993); Pino v. Planning Bd. of Norton, 4 L.C.R. 188 (1996);

Dunham's Corner Residents Association, Inc. v. Edgartown Planning Bd., 12 L.C.R. 163 (2004); but see Johnson v. Planning Bd. of Edgartown, 4 L.C.R. 29 (1996); Hatem v. Burke, 5 L.C.R. 231 (1998).

[9]Stefanick v. Planning Bd. of Uxbridge, 39 Mass. App. Ct. 418, 657 N.E.2d 475 (1995).

forth in § 81-FF of Chapter 41. This sets forth a clear distinction between prior subdivisions of registered and unregistered land.

With respect to unregistered land § 81-FF provides that the recording of a subdivision plan before the subdivision control law became effective in the city or town in which the land is located does not exempt the land from the operation of the subdivision control law "except with respect to lots which have been sold and were held in ownership separate from that of the remainder of the subdivision when said law went into effect in such city or town, and to rights of way and other easements appurtenant to such lots." The exception poses some questions: When lots in an old subdivision are owned by numerous owners, some of whom owned one lot and some of whom owned several or many lots, which ones are in "separate ownership" and which, if any, constitute the "remainder"? What does it mean to say that the lots in separate ownership are "exempt"? For a lot which is not exempt, does this provision make it unbuildable even though it is protected as a building lot by a specific grandfather clause in the local zoning law? As a practical matter, the solution will usually lie in submission of a subdivision plan, based on the old plan, to the planning board for approval.[1] Of course, if the ways shown on the old plan exist and the planning board determines that they are sufficient, then the new plan may be endorsed "approval not required."

With respect to registered land, any subdivision plan registered before February 1, 1952, "shall have the same validity in all respects" as if the plan had been approved under the subdivision control law. Plans filed for registration after that date must comply with the subdivision control law if it is in effect in the city or town involved, and the land court has jurisdiction to determine "whether the subdivision control law has been complied with." Once the land court has so verified, and accepted the plan for registration, the plan shall "be deemed to be, and shall be invested with all the rights and privileges of, a plan approved pursuant to said law." The court has noted that these provisions are "not altogether clear," and declined to afford registered land lots on an ANR plan lawful status under the zoning laws.[2] If waivers or conditions were set forth by the planning board in connection with approval of a plan filed with the land

---

[Section 12:16]

[1]See Berg v. Town of Lexington, 68 Mass. App. Ct. 569, 863 N.E.2d 968 (2007).

[2]Shea v. Board of Appeals of Lexington, 35 Mass. App. Ct. 519, 622 N.E.2d 1382 (1993).

court for registration, the land court is required to cite them on its issued Land Court Plan or in a decree of confirmation or registration.

Finally, a very important legal effect of a subdivision plan, or an ANR plan, is of course the "plan freeze" provided for in the zoning act, M.G.L.A. c. 40A, § 6, discussed in § **11:16** and § **11:17**.

Chapter 13

Environmental Controls

KeyCite®: Cases and other legal materials listed in KeyCite Scope can be researched through the KeyCite service on Westlaw®. Use KeyCite to check citations for form, parallel references, prior and later history, and comprehensive citator information, including citations to other decisions and secondary materials.

TOPIC A: INTRODUCTION

§ 13:1   A complex subject

In recent decades environmental problems and concerns have generated whole new fields of law, and of policy and politics. The subject is of great complexity and the field of environmental law itself extends well beyond the concerns of Massachusetts real estate lawyers. Within that growing body of law there are surely, however, many facets which do have an impact, often direct and immediate, on the transactions and the issues with which real estate lawyers regularly contend.

The laws which have such an impact may be federal, state or local, and there is often a mélange or overlapping of several jurisdictional levels. The first task of the practicing real estate lawyer is thus to discern what environmental issues are posed by the matter he is working on, then to identify the laws that are applicable. Next he must decide what action is necessary in the circumstances, and finally, he may be required to express a formal opinion on the matter. An environmental review and opinion has become a standard requirement of mortgage lenders and in many other transactions.

To prepare for those tasks the lawyer may need to view the property, to obtain engineering analyses and reports thereon, to review local records and those of the Massachusetts Department of Environmental Protection (DEP), as well as United States Geological Survey maps, HUD flood insurance maps and local maps.

In light of all those considerations, the following sections of this Chapter should be considered to be only an introduction to the subject.

TOPIC B: ENVIRONMENTAL IMPACT REVIEW

§ 13:2 Federal regulation—NEPA

The National Environmental Policy Act[1] comes into play whenever a project involves action of a federal agency or the issuance of a federal permit or license, or a federal loan, loan guarantee, subsidy or the like. General regulations under the Act may be found in the Code of Federal Regulations (CFR),[2] and individual federal agencies may also have their own regulations with respect to implementation of NEPA.

§ 13:3 Massachusetts regulation—MEPA

The Massachusetts Environmental Policy Act (MEPA), set forth in M.G.L.A. c. 30, §§ 61 to 62H, is a counterpart of NEPA, applicable whenever a project involves action of a state agency, such as the granting of a permit or approval, or financial assistance. The statute defines "agency" broadly, including "any authority of any political subdivision" of the commonwealth, which comprises cities and town. However, the MEPA regulations, set forth in 301 CMR 11.00, exclude municipal boards and commissions from the definition of "agency" unless they are authorities specifically created and acting pursuant to a statute, such as a redevelopment authority.[1] The term "permit" is broadly defined in both the statute and the regulations, so as to include almost any action of an "agency" required for a project to proceed.

Typical of permits required for a real estate development project are: permits for curb cut onto a state highway (governed by M.G.L.A. c. 81, § 21), permits for connection to or extension of a sewer under state jurisdiction, Title 5 variance with respect to on-site sewage disposal, sewage treatment facilities requiring approval of DEP, permits for discharge of surface waters, and supervening orders of DEP

[Section 13:2]

[1]42 U.S.C.A. §§ 4321 et seq.

[2]40 C.F.R. 1500 to 1508.

[Section 13:3]

[1]Boston Preservation Alliance, Inc. v. Secretary of Environmental Affairs, 396 Mass. 489, 487 N.E.2d 197 (1986).

from local conservation commission orders.

Set forth in 301 CMR 11.03 is a fairly elaborate listing of Review Thresholds, commonly referred to as the triggers of MEPA applicability. If any one of them is applicable to a project of real estate development or expansion thereof, then an Environmental Notification Form (ENF) must be filed with the MEPA office in the Executive Office of Environmental Affairs (EOEA). The Review Thresholds list types of projects for which an Environmental Impact Report (EIR) will be mandatory, and types for which a less formal review by the MEPA office may suffice, subject to a subsequent determination that an EIR will be required.

The categories requiring mandatory EIR include those in which there is any one of: state financial assistance, project size affecting 50 acres or more or with impervious surface of 10 acres or more, project effect on an acre or more of salt marsh or vegetated wetlands, implication of the Wetlands Protection Act, withdrawal of certain levels of groundwater, wastewater treatment, generation of a high volume of traffic, and other touchstones. The Review Thresholds also list types of projects for which an ENF, though not an EIR, is mandatory, such as: a project affecting 25 acres or more or with 5 acres or more of impervious surface, any conversion of conservation, park or recreational land to other uses, conversion of agricultural land to nonagricultural uses, urban renewal, affecting significant wildlife habitat or endangered species, and other touchstones. It is also provided in 301 CMR 11.04 that even if a project does not invoke any review threshold, an ENF may be required by the Secretary of EOEA or on petition of any state agency involved or of ten persons.

The form of an ENF is prescribed in the regulations. When filed, it is published in the *Environmental Monitor*, followed by a period for public comment, and then decision by the Secretary as to requirement of an EIR in non-mandatory cases. Whenever an EIR is required, the project applicant and counsel may be summoned to a "scoping" session, and then a scope decision is issued, defining the issues the EIR must address. In any case an EIR must eventually receive the approval of the Secretary of EOEA. In many instances an EIR is filed as a draft, and later revised into a Final form, or FEIR, and sometimes there is a Supplemental Final form, or SFEIR.

In the event of any material change in a project, or significant lapse of time (3 or 5 years, depending on the review process) after an ENF was filed and published, a Notice of Project Change is required, initiating a new review.

Challenges to MEPA actions are provided for in M.G.L.A. c. 30, § 62H, and in 301 CMR 11.14, which provides that in most instances the matter challenged must have been raised during the MEPA review process.

A town's suit against the Secretary was rejected on both jurisdictional and substantive grounds.[2] A suit against the Secretary, who had approved an FEIR, and the developer, whose project was alleged to cause environmental damage, was allowed to proceed under M.G.L.A. c. 214, § 7A, against the developer, but not the Secretary who was held not to be a proper party under that statute, which provides in substance a remedy to citizens who may be harmed by environmental damage that is in violation of any statute or regulation intended to protect the environment.[3] However, citizens' suits, one challenging a determination by the Secretary that no EIR would be required,[4] and one challenging an approved FEIR,[5] were both rejected. In the latter, the *Enos* case, the SJC found no standing for the plaintiffs in the wording and purpose of the MEPA statute, overruling a carefully reasoned analysis by Gillerman, J., in the appeals court, and leading Abrams, J., to object that the decisions in both *Cummings* and *Enos* "exempt[ed] the Secretary's actions from judicial review by affected citizens" and that "The only person left to bring suit is the developer . . ." In a later action under M.G.L.A. c. 214, § 7A, the SJC distinguished *Enos* and affirmed plaintiffs' standing to contest an FSEIR after the approved permit had been issued.[6] The court discussed the appropriate standard of review, and upheld the FSEIR as sufficient.

In fact a developer had succeeded in asserting its standing to challenge a scoping decision, and to establish that in a private project, subject to MEPA solely because of a permit, the scope of an EIR is limited to the effect of the permit.[7]

It is fair to say that the MEPA office usually has a goal of making the scope of an EIR as broad as possible, and that in

---

[2]Town of Walpole v. Secretary of the Executive Office of Environmental Affairs, 405 Mass. 67, 537 N.E.2d 1244 (1989).

[3]Boston Investments Ltd. v. Secretary of Environmental Affairs, 35 Mass. App. Ct. 391, 619 N.E.2d 991 (1993).

[4]Cummings v. Secretary of Executive Office of Environmental Affairs, 402 Mass. 611, 524 N.E.2d 836 (1988).

[5]Enos v. Secretary of Environmental Affairs, 432 Mass. 132, 731 N.E.2d 525 (2000).

[6]Villages Development Co., Inc. v. Secretary of Executive Office of Environmental Affairs, 410 Mass. 100, 571 N.E.2d 361 (1991).

[7]Sierra Club v. Commissioner of Dept. of Environmental Management, 439 Mass. 738, 791 N.E.2d 325 (2003).

cases of mandatory EIR, all potential environmental impacts of the project must be covered in the report, and measures must be proposed for mitigation of perceived environmental damage.

If no EIR is required, a state agency may proceed with its action related to the project. But if there is an EIR, the state agency may not act until it (or the FEIR or SFEIR) has been approved and the challenge period expired. Provision is made in 301 CMR 11.11 for issuance of waivers of MEPA by the Secretary of EOEA if its application would impose undue hardship on an applicant and would not avoid or minimize damage to the environment.

TOPIC C: WATERS, WATERWAYS AND WETLANDS

§ 13:4   Background

Laws relating to waters, waterways and wetlands are not new, particularly to Massachusetts. The Colonial Ordinance of 1641–1647 set the limits of littoral ownership on tidelands and great ponds and established the public's rights of fishing, fowling and navigation in the marginal sea. Common law rules as to riparian ownership, use and flowage of water in streams, and discharge and diversion of surface waters have long prevailed, and in many cases been incorporated into Massachusetts statutes. The pertinent statutes include: M.G.L.A. c. 253, dealing with many aspects of non-navigable waterways, including mills, dams, cranberry bogs and reservoirs; M.G.L.A. c. 91, and its predecessors, dealing with tidewaters and great ponds; M.G.L.A. c. 131 dealing with fisheries; M.G.L.A. c. 111, dealing with public health; and M.G.L.A. c. 252, providing for "reclamation."

A former provision in M.G.L.A. c. 111, § 132, defining a wetland as a "nuisance" was repealed some decades ago. The concept of "reclaiming" wetlands by filling them is of course in disfavor, and M.G.L.A. c. 252 survives because it governs mosquito control procedures. Beginning in the 1960's there arose a new wave of policy and law aimed at protecting the environment. The jurisdiction over the "general oversight and care of inland waters and streams" was transferred under M.G.L.A. c. 111, § 159, from the Department of Public Health to the Department of Environmental Protection, and the administration of M.G.L.A. c. 91 was transferred from the Department of Public Works to the Department of Environmental Protection (formerly known as the Department of Environmental Quality Engineering, or DEQE).

There are now many and varied laws, both federal and state, relating to the specific environmental aspects of waters, waterways and wetlands, and those are the subject of the following paragraphs of this **Topic C**.

§ 13:5 Federal water pollution control

Since 1899 the Rivers and Harbors Act[1] has governed the construction of dams, dikes, piers or other structures in navigable waters, and the filling thereof or discharge of refuse therein. The modern environmental supplement thereto is the Federal Water Pollution Control Act,[2] which deals with wide-ranging causes of water pollution. Among the programs most frequently affecting real estate developments is the National Pollutant Discharge Elimination System (NPDES), under which a permit is required for any discharge of pollutants into waters of the United States. Although all runoff water from roofs and parking lots is technically a pollutant under the regulations, and substantially all runoff discharge systems lead the water eventually to "waters of the United States," the factual situations in which an NPDES permit will be required are quite convoluted,[3] requiring careful analysis by a developer's attorney. If the "point source" of the discharge is large, industrial or likely to impact a water supply, then an NPDES permit will in all probability be required.

The Act, as amended, is now usually known as the Clean Water Act, and promotes federal-state cooperation in various forms. Under § 404 of the Act a permit from the Army Corps of Engineers is required "to make deposits in any tidal harbor or river . . ." Under regulations and judicial construction that includes wetlands that are "adjacent" to such waters, and consequently a real estate project that involves filling or regrading of wetlands may require a § 404 permit. Some actions may be covered by a "Programmatic General Permit" issued by the Army Engineers. The application of the § 404 permit requirement to wetlands that are "adjacent" to regulated waters, as well as the determination of what constitutes adjacency, have long been controversial and contested.[4]

[Section 13:5]

[1]33 U.S.C.A. § 407.

[2]33 U.S.C.A. §§ 1251 et seq., including an amendment called the

Water Quality Act.

[3]See 40 C.F.R. 9, 122 to 124.

[4]U.S. v. Riverside Bayview Homes, Inc., 474 U.S. 121, 106 S.

§ 13:6 Federal drinking water quality control

The Safe Drinking Water Act[1] establishes standards for water supply systems and provides (as do a number of federal environmental acts) for cooperative federal-state enforcement systems. The administration of this Act is conducted by the Massachusetts DEP, which has adopted appropriate regulations.[2] The regulations may be pertinent to any project in the vicinity of a water supply system or an aquifer designated by DEP as a drinking water source.

§ 13:7 Flood insurance

The federal program is discussed in § 14:10, and should be taken into account in any project in which any flood-prone land is included.

§ 13:8 Massachusetts clean water control

Massachusetts has its own Clean Waters Act,[1] pursuant to which the Massachusetts Department of Environmental Protection, through its Division of Water Pollution Control, regulates discharges to surface waters, ground waters or into sewerage systems. DWPC permits for discharge are ordinarily issued in conjunction with a federal NPDES permit. M.G.L.A. c. 21, § 1 includes ground water in the definition of "waters of the Commonwealth," and consequently any discharge thereto requires such a permit. This applies not only to discharge of runoff surface waters into "dry wells," but also to on-site subsurface sewage discharge under Title 5 of the Environmental Code, referred to again in § 13:20. The grant of a groundwater discharge permit for a municipal wastewater treatment plant was upheld.[2]

With respect to connection to or extension of sewer systems, DWPC has broad regulatory authority.[3] Other controls are imposed by municipalities and other agencies,

---

Ct. 455, 88 L. Ed. 2d 419 (1985); U.S. v. Wilson, 133 F.3d 251, 48 Fed. R. Evid. Serv. 384 (4th Cir. 1997); U.S. v. Banks, 115 F.3d 916, 37 Fed. R. Serv. 3d 1108 (11th Cir. 1997); American Min. Congress v. U.S. Army Corps of Engineers, 951 F. Supp. 267 (D.D.C. 1997), judgment aff'd, 145 F.3d 1399 (D.C. Cir. 1998).

[Section 13:6]

[1]42 U.S.C.A. §§ 300f et seq.

[2]310 CMR 22.00 et seq.

[Section 13:8]

[1]M.G.L.A. c. 21, §§ 26 to 53A.

[2]Friends and Fishers of Edgartown Great Pond, Inc. v. Department of Environmental Protection, 446 Mass. 830, 848 N.E.2d 393 (2006).

[3]M.G.L.A. c. 21, § 43(2); 314 CMR 7.00.

such as the Metropolitan District Commission, that own and operate sewage systems, including restrictions on access thereto based on limitations of capacity.

Besides controls on discharge of waters there are controls on the withdrawal of water from private water supplies, as set forth in M.G.L.A. c. 21G and regulations in 310 CMR 36. 00. Also, a developer or user of land in or near an aquifer must take into account the Watershed Management Act, M.G.L.A. c. 92A 1/2, replacing an earlier Act. An owner who had obtained an Order of Conditions under the Wetland Protection Act, discussed in the following paragraph, nevertheless ran afoul of the Watershed Management Act provisions.[4]

§ 13:9   Massachusetts wetland protections

The Wetlands Protection Act in M.G.L.A. c. 130, § 40, provides in brief that no one may alter an area "bordering on inland waters" without first giving Notice of Intent to do so to the local Conservation Commission and, after public hearing, obtaining an Order of Conditions from the Commission permitting the action. Since "inland waters" exist almost everywhere in Massachusetts, it is a rare real estate project that does not implicate this statute. The statute itself is complex and the DEP regulations thereunder are very detailed and extensive.[1] These regulations have evolved over the years, involving more than a little controversy and conflict, but have generally survived judicial scrutiny.[2]

Terms describing regulated bordering areas, such as bogs, swamps, meadows and marshes, are defined broadly, partly by reference to typical wetland flora. The regulations provide for a Buffer Zone, 100 feet wide adjacent to regulated areas, with respect to activity in which a Notice of Intent is required unless the Conservation Commission has ruled otherwise in response to application for a Determination of Applicability.[3] The regulations speak of "simplified review criteria" for areas within the buffer, but more than 50 feet away from a regulated area, and provide expressly that there

---

[4]Com. v. Blair, 60 Mass. App. Ct. 741, 805 N.E.2d 1011 (2004).

[Section 13:9]

[1]310 CMR 10.00.

[2]Citizens for Responsible Environmental Management v. Attleboro Mall, Inc., 400 Mass. 658, 511 N.E.2d 562 (1987); Baker v. Department of Environmental Protection, 39 Mass. App. Ct. 444, 657 N.E.2d 480 (1995); Warcewicz v. Department of Environmental Protection, 410 Mass. 548, 574 N.E.2d 364 (1991).

[3]See Yellin v. Conservation Com'n of Dover, 55 Mass. App. Ct. 918, 774 N.E.2d 1155 (2002).

is no regulation under the statute beyond the Buffer Zone.

Rivers were included in wetland coverage by the Rivers Protection Act, an amendment of M.G.L.A. c. 130, § 40.[4] As defined, a "river" includes almost every perennial stream, with exceptions for "intermittent streams." A "riverfront area" extends generally 200 feet from mean high water, but only 25 feet in specified cities and 100 feet with respect to proposed agricultural activities. The regulations contemplate a minimum of a "100 foot wide area of undisturbed vegetation." Further, there is a presumption of applicability of regulatory protection in the riverfront area, rebuttable upon a showing of absence of a practicable and substantially equivalent economic alternative to the proposed activities, defined by elaborate regulations in 310 CMR 10.58.

When a Notice of Intent is filed with a Conservation Commission (or if none, the Selectmen or Mayor), the applicant must also notify "all abutters within one hundred feet of the property line of the land where the activity is proposed." The Commission must then hold a public hearing within 21 days, giving notice by publication at least 5 days before. The Commission's charge is to determine whether the area on which the proposed work is to be done is significant to protection of water supply, groundwater supply, flood control, storm damage prevention, prevention of pollution, protection of shellfish, wildlife habitat, fisheries or riverfront.

Within 21 days after the hearing the Commission must issue its Order of Conditions, specifying procedures for and limitations on the proposed work. Within 10 days thereafter the applicant, or any person aggrieved, abutter or 10 residents may appeal to DEP which may within 70 days issue a Supervening Order of Conditions. An original or supervening order of conditions does not take effect, and no work may be done, until it is recorded in the registry of deeds.

There are provisions for posting a sign on the site with the DEP file number, for default approval, for Certificate of Compliance when work pursuant to an Order of Conditions is completed, for certain exemptions such as for mosquito control, agricultural maintenance and emergency actions. There are also provisions for enforcement orders and for civil and criminal penalties for violations, and for adjudicatory hearing by DEP and appeal to the superior or land court.

Pertinent judicial decisions include the following (some of which refer to the Department of Environmental Quality

---

[4]Chapter 258, Acts of 1996.

Engineering, abbreviated to DEQE, the former name of DEP):

- An appeal from an Order of Conditions was dismissed because plaintiff showed no injury differing from that of the general public.[5]
- A town's illegal filling of wetlands for high school fields was allowed to stand.[6]
- Exemptions were strictly construed.[7]
- The classification as an "agricultural use" is a matter for determination by the local conservation commission.[8]
- While a conservation commission may enter private land for which a notice of intent has been filed, it may not enter in search of violations.[9]
- A condition in an order of conditions purporting to regulate future projects was rejected.[10]
- An order of conditions denying a right to build a house because of incursion on a wetland was held not to constitute a regulatory taking.[11]
- Criminal indictments for violation of the wetland protection act were upheld.[12]
- The Land Court observed that clearing in exercise of a view easement over wetlands would likely require Conservation Commission approval.[13]

§ 13:10 Local controls

It must be noted that a number of towns have adopted bylaws which are essentially copies of the Wetland Protection Act, in some instances incorporating additional elements of protection. These usually combine local procedure with that under the state act, and require a local permit along with an order of conditions, the two being almost identical,

---

[5]Friedman v. Conservation Com'n of Edgartown, 62 Mass. App. Ct. 539, 818 N.E.2d 208 (2004).

[6]DiCicco v. Department of Environmental Protection, 64 Mass. App. Ct. 423, 833 N.E.2d 654 (2005).

[7]Department of Environmental Quality Engineering v. Town of Hingham, 15 Mass. App. Ct. 409, 446 N.E.2d 406 (1983).

[8]Department of Environmental Quality Engineering v. Cumberland Farms of Connecticut, Inc., 18 Mass. App. Ct. 672, 469 N.E.2d 1286 (1984).

[9]Com. v. John G. Grant & Sons Co., Inc., 403 Mass. 151, 526 N.E.2d 768 (1988).

[10]North Andover Land Corporation v. Town of North Andover, 6 L.C.R. 185 (1998).

[11]Giovanella v. Conservation Com'n of Ashland, 447 Mass. 720, 857 N.E.2d 451 (2006), cert. denied, 127 S. Ct. 1826, 167 L. Ed. 2d 321 (U.S. 2007).

[12]Com. v. Clemmey, 447 Mass. 121, 849 N.E.2d 844 (2006).

[13]Patterson v. Paul, 14 L.C.R. 128 (2006).

but separately enforceable. These local laws have been upheld and applied.[1] The question of whether the local permit
is subject to a supervening order of DEP depends on whether
the local law provided greater protection than the statute or
was not more stringent.[2] Some of these cases consider an
interplay with Chapter 91 licensing, discussed in paragraph
5 below.

In many cities and towns the zoning laws include provisions as to flood plain and watershed protection.

§ 13:11 Massachusetts wetland restrictions

Under M.G.L.A. c. 131, § 40A, with respect to "inland
wetlands," and M.G.L.A. c. 130, § 105, with respect to
"coastal wetlands," the commissioner of environmental
protection is authorized to adopt orders regulating, restricting or prohibiting alteration of such wetlands. In each case
there must first be a public hearing in the municipality
where the affected lands are situated and notice to the owners of such lands. Once adopted, such an order along with
plans of the land affected must be recorded in the registry of
deeds and copies sent to every land owner affected. Such
orders may be enforced by actions in the superior court and
there are criminal penalties for violation.

Any owner, lessee for 25 years or more, or mortgagee[1] of
affected land may within 90 days petition the superior court
for determination whether the "order constitutes the equivalent of taking without compensation." If the court so finds,
the court's finding shall be recorded in the registry of deeds
and the regulatory order shall then not apply to the land of
the petitioner, but that does not affect any other land. In the

---

[Section 13:10]

[1]Lovequist v. Conservation
Commission of Town of Dennis, 379
Mass. 7, 393 N.E.2d 858 (1979);
Fogelman v. Town of Chatham, 15
Mass. App. Ct. 585, 446 N.E.2d
1112 (1983); Fafard v. Conservation
Com'n of Reading, 41 Mass. App.
Ct. 565, 672 N.E.2d 21 (1996);
Fafard v. Conservation Com'n of
Barnstable, 432 Mass. 194, 733
N.E.2d 66 (2000); Com. v. Muise,
59 Mass. App. Ct. 562, 796 N.E.2d
1289 (2003); Dubuque v. Conserva-
tion Com'n of Barnstable, 58 Mass.
App. Ct. 824, 793 N.E.2d 1244
(2003).

[2]DeGrace v. Conservation
Com'n of Harwich, 31 Mass. App.
Ct. 132, 575 N.E.2d 373 (1991); FIC
Homes of Blackstone, Inc. v. Conser-
vation Com'n of Blackstone, 41
Mass. App. Ct. 681, 673 N.E.2d 61
(1996); Hobbs Brook Farm Property
Co. Ltd. Partnership v. Conserva-
tion Com'n Of Lincoln, 65 Mass.
App. Ct. 142, 838 N.E.2d 578 (2005),
review denied, 446 Mass. 1104, 843
N.E.2d 639 (2006).

[Section 13:11]

[1]The statutes say "mortgagor," an obvious solecism or spoo-
nerism.

event of such a finding the commissioner is authorized to take the excluded land by eminent domain under M.G.L.A. c. 79. This remedy is exclusive. Assertions of regulatory taking thereunder have not succeeded.[2]

There are certain exclusions from the application of these statutes, including, as to inland wetlands, land used for agriculture.

§ 13:12 Massachusetts licensing of structures and fill

M.G.L.A. c. 91 provides for the licensing of any structures or fill within tidewaters, great ponds (10 acres or more as defined in the statute) or the Connecticut River or Merrimack River, or any other river or stream on which public funds have been expended.

The statute (having origins in the 19th century) and regulations thereunder were amended after considerable discussion and controversy in the 1980s and 1990s, during which time there were periods of "amnesty" for the late filing of applications for licensing of unauthorized fill and structures built before 1984. The main thrust of the revised statute, and regulations in 310 CMR 9.00, is to limit development in the regulated areas so far as possible to "water-dependent uses," which understandably conflicts with the desires of developers who regard waterfront sites as very attractive for such things as hotels, restaurants and condominiums, which the regulations specifically decree to be not water-dependent. The DEP is invested with a power, akin to zoning discretionary permit power, to determine whether a proposed use is appropriate and to govern design and dimensions of a development.

In view of the fact that large parts of Boston are filled land, formerly flowed by the sea, issues of the validity of title thereto and freedom from Chapter 91 regulation have naturally come to the fore. In the leading case on the subject[1] the SJC overruled a Land Court registration of title of Boston Waterfront Development Corporation to its property

---

[2]Moskow v. Commissioner of Dept. of Environmental Management, 384 Mass. 530, 427 N.E.2d 750 (1981); Englander v. Department of Environmental Management, 16 Mass. App. Ct. 943, 450 N.E.2d 1120 (1983); similarly, see Roberts v. Department of Environmental Quality Engineering, 404 Mass. 795, 537 N.E.2d 154 (1989); Leonard v. Town of Brimfield, 423 Mass. 152, 666 N.E.2d 1300 (1996); FIC Homes of Blackstone, Inc. v. Conservation Com'n of Blackstone, 41 Mass. App. Ct. 681, 673 N.E.2d 61 (1996).

[Section 13:12]

[1]Boston Waterfront Development Corp. v. Com., 378 Mass. 629, 393 N.E.2d 356 (1979).

comprising Lewis Wharf, a filled structure, most of which lies between historic high and low water lines and part of which lies beyond historic low water. Strongly asserting the "public trust doctrine" to the effect that any grant by the sovereign of rights or title to flowed land remains subject to a condition of continued use for the public benefit, the court rationalized the terms of the statutes authorizing the fill in the 19th century and the line of cases construing them as grants of title. The history and the analysis in the decision are both fascinating and an important background for anyone dealing with such issues.

The regulations in 310 CMR 9.00 make specific reference to the *BWDC* decision and the public trust doctrine. They set forth presumptions that a privately owned area seaward of mean low tide (or 100 rods below mean high, as specified in the Colonial Ordinance of 1641–1647) is a "Commonwealth Tideland" and that such an area landward of such line is not. The locations of "historic" mean high and low water marks are determined by DEP, rebuttable only by a "clear showing" of "natural accretion."

The regulations' limited concession to title concerns in Boston and elsewhere was a definition of "Landlocked Tidelands" as filled tidelands separated from any flowed tidelands by a public way and more than 250 feet from the high water line. However, in 2007 the SJC voided that regulation as beyond the powers of DEP.[2] The court pointed out that a proposal in 1990 to enact such an exemption of so-called landlocked tidelands did not pass, and that the 1983 amendment of Chapter 91 authorized DEP to permit non-water-dependent uses on filled tidelands only upon a specific finding after public hearing that the proposed use constituted a "proper public purpose." The proposed project, on 48 acres of abandoned rail yards in East Boston whose "very nature would preclude any [water-dependent] use," was to include residential, office, retail and park uses. Seeking to allay concerns of excessive regulation, the court said that the filled tidelands of Back Bay and South Boston had been wholly released from public rights by legislative acts in the 19th century.

Application for a Chapter 91 license requires a form, specifying the specific purposes and uses proposed, and a detailed plan meeting prescribed specifications. The filing fee may be hefty and may depend on the volume of tidewater

---

[2]Moot v. Department of Environmental Protection, 448 Mass. 340, 861 N.E.2d 410 (2007).

displaced, if not elsewhere replicated.[3] The procedure involves notice to the local planning board, which may hold a public hearing and is charged with making a recommendation to DEP, further notice to selectmen or mayor and to the conservation commission of the municipality, further procedures upon proposals for nonwater dependent uses, and certification by the city or town clerk that the proposed work is not in violation of zoning. When issued, the license and its accompanying plan must be recorded in the registry of deeds within 60 days and notice thereof given to DEP or the license becomes void. All licenses are voidable by DEP, subject to notice requirements. Provision is made for adjudicatory review, but standing must be shown.[4]

§ 13:13 Other Massachusetts controls

In addition to the foregoing, one might consider the following, which are not intended to be or to complete an exhaustive list of laws applicable to environmental controls of waters, waterways and wetlands:

● **Coastal Zone Management.** There are federal and state laws on the subject[1] and a coastal zone management office under the Massachusetts Department of Environmental Protection. The coastal zone is defined as extending from the three-mile offshore state jurisdictional limit to 100 feet inland from specified shore area roads and rail lines.

● **Ocean Sanctuaries.** Under a Massachusetts statute[2] most of the coastal areas of the Commonwealth within the three-mile limit are designated as sanctuaries in which environmentally damaging activities are prohibited.

● **Scenic Rivers.** Under a Massachusetts statue and regulations thereunder,[3] a river or stream may be subjected to a scenic river order, restricting activities on the water or banks thereof. Such orders are recorded in the registry of deeds. The North River, exiting to the sea in Scituate,

[3]Trio Algarvio, Inc. v. Commissioner of Dept. of Environmental Protection, 440 Mass. 94, 795 N.E.2d 1148 (2003).

[4]Higgins v. Department of Environmental Protection, 64 Mass. App. Ct. 754, 835 N.E.2d 610 (2005).

[Section 13:13]

[1]16 U.S.C.A. §§ 1451 et seq.; see also Chapter 589, Acts of 1983;

301 CMR 20.00 et seq. and 21.00 et seq.

[2]M.G.L.A. c. 132A, §§ 13, 14, 15, 16, and 18; 302 CMR 5.00.

[3]M.G.L.A. c. 21, § 17B; 302 CMR 3.00.

has been so designated, and is the site of a Massachusetts Audubon Wildlife Sanctuary.

• **Interstate Compacts.** Massachusetts has entered into compacts with adjoining states relating to water pollution control, water resources, and several rivers, including the Merrimack, the Thames and the Connecticut.[4]

TOPIC D: HAZARDOUS SUBSTANCES; SEWAGE

§ 13:14   Federal RCRA

Federal regulation of hazardous wastes begins with the Resource Conservation and Recovery Act[1] (RCRA, or "recra"). Under this Act the federal Environmental Protection Agency identifies hazardous wastes and sources of generation thereof, and regulates the storage, transportation and disposal thereof through a permit system. Disposal, and land sites for disposal, are particularly strictly regulated.

One of the programs under RCRA regulates underground storage tanks (USTs), including those for service stations holding gasoline, diesel fuel or waste oil, and tanks holding heating oil, both commercial and residential. This is administered through state agencies which are required to establish systems complying with EPA standards set forth in 40 C.F.R. 280. The designated agency in Massachusetts is the Department of Public Safety, and the state action is further discussed in the following subsection B.

Owners and operators of USTs are required to notify the DPW of a tank's existence and location. Detection and prevention of tank leaks are primary goals, and owners are held responsible for consequences of leaks. Under EPA rules a mortgagee which forecloses or assumes management of property containing USTs may avoid liability as an owner or operator by emptying the tanks and divesting itself of the property in a reasonably expeditious manner.

§ 13:15   Federal CERCLA

The second major federal statute with respect to hazardous waste is the Comprehensive Environmental Response,

---

[4]Chapter 421, Acts of 1947; Chapter 621, Acts of 1959; Chapter 608, Acts of 1956; Chapter 616, Acts of 1957; Chapter 716, Acts of 1981.

[Section 13:14]

[1]42 U.S.C.A. §§ 6901 et seq.

Compensation, and Liability Act[1] (CERCLA), providing for cleaning up of existing hazardous waste disposal sites. It is known as the "Superfund Statute" because it affords federal funding along with procedures for recovering costs of cleanup from owners and operators of disposal sites and from persons or organizations which, directly or indirectly, arranged for or allowed delivery of hazardous wastes to such a site. Allocation of costs among "potentially responsible parties" is often a touchy issue.[2] CERCLA provides for the recording by EPA of a notice of lien to secure the payment of EPA's response costs. The "innocent owner" and "lender liability" provisions are of particular interest to real estate lawyers. Following considerable contest of the lien and liability provisions,[3] Congress limited liability of lenders and fiduciaries under both RECRA and CERCLA, and reinstated regulation (40 C.F.R. 307) under which actions short of "participation in management" may be taken without subjecting the lender or fiduciary to liability as an "owner or operator."

§ 13:16 Federal brownfields tax

Federal tax law provides an incentive for environmental cleanup by allowing for deduction, rather than capitalization, of privately incurred cleanup costs.

§ 13:17 Massachusetts hazardous waste management law

While the federal acts led the way and promulgated the framework for dealing with hazardous wastes, the arena has been dominated by state laws and actions.

The Hazardous Waste Management Act[1] is the Massachusetts equivalent of RCRA, administered by the Division of Hazardous Waste in the Department of Environmental Protection. Pursuant to the Act and regulations in 310

[Section 13:15]

[1]26 U.S.C.A. §§ 4611 et seq.; 42 U.S.C.A. §§ 9601 et seq.

[2]Harmon Industries, Inc. v. Browner, 191 F.3d 894 (8th Cir. 1999); Acushnet Co. v. Mohasco Corp., 191 F.3d 69, 162 A.L.R. Fed. 717 (1st Cir. 1999); Bardon Trimount, Inc. v. Guyott, 49 Mass. App. Ct. 764, 732 N.E.2d 916 (2000).

[3]Reardon v. U.S., 947 F.2d 1509, 116 A.L.R. Fed. 667 (1st Cir.

1991); John S. Boyd Co., Inc. v. Boston Gas Co., 992 F.2d 401 (1st Cir. 1993); U.S. v. Fleet Factors Corp., 901 F.2d 1550 (11th Cir. 1990); In re Bergsoe Metal Corp., 910 F.2d 668 (9th Cir.1990); Waterville Industries, Inc. v. Finance Authority of Maine, 984 F.2d 549 (1st Cir. 1993); Kelley v. E.P.A., 15 F.3d 1100 (D.C. Cir. 1994).

[Section 13:17]

[1]M.G.L.A. c. 21C.

CMR 30.000 et seq. a license from DEP is required for the collection, transportation, treatment and disposal of hazardous waste. With respect to designation of sites for disposal of hazardous waste, provision is made in M.G.L.A. c. 21D, and M.G.L.A. c. 111, §§ 150A and 150B, must also be taken into account. The provisions thereunder govern the siting and operation of facilities for disposition of waste materials (other than sewerage), whether hazardous or not.[2]

§ 13:18   Massachusetts hazardous materials release law

The Oil and Hazardous Material Release Prevention and Response Act[1] is the Massachusetts equivalent of CERCLA and is called the State Superfund Act. Like CERCLA it provides for recovery from responsible parties, up to treble the amount of cleanup costs, for joint and several liability of contributors to the hazardous waste being cleaned up,[2] and for liens on the property of hazardous waste site owners and generators of the wastes.

The lien provisions are complex as to priority, depending on notice and the status of the property and its owner, and include some protections for innocent parties and mortgagees who have not been involved in management of the property. Secured lenders who acquire contaminated property are allowed 36 months to divest and must notify DEP and purchasers of known contamination. Tenants of a contaminated site may be exempted, subject to proof they are not contributors; and down gradient owners of polluted land are exempt, but may also bear a burden of proof.

The procedures for cleanup of contaminated sites and for assessment and recovery of cleanup costs are governed by the Massachusetts Contingency Plan, set forth in 310 CMR 40.0000 et seq., which regulations are very lengthy and complex. In a nutshell, they provide for identification and classification of hazardous materials, require notice to DEP

---

[2]General Chemical Corp. v. Department of Environmental Quality Engineering, 19 Mass. App. Ct. 287, 474 N.E.2d 183 (1985); Clean Harbors of Braintree, Inc. v. Board of Health of Braintree, 409 Mass. 834, 570 N.E.2d 987 (1991); TBI, Inc. v. Bd. of Health of North Andover, 431 Mass. 9, 725 N.E.2d 188 (2000); Goldberg v. Board of Health of Granby, 444 Mass. 627, 830 N.E.2d 207 (2005).

[Section 13:18]

[1]M.G.L.A. c. 21E.

[2]Martignetti v. Haigh-Farr Inc., 425 Mass. 294, 680 N.E.2d 1131 (1997); Hill v. Metropolitan Dist. Com'n, 439 Mass. 266, 787 N.E.2d 526 (2003); Com. v. Boston Edison Co., 444 Mass. 324, 828 N.E.2d 16 (2005).

of any release or threat of release thereof, specify the types and scope of response action that is appropriate, set forth "tier classifications" for response actions and time frames, provide for Licensed Site Professionals (LSP) qualified to conduct cleanup and response activities, and provide for the recovery of costs incurred by the Commonwealth.

Among the means of subsequent control of contaminated land are an Environmental Restriction or an Activity and Use Limitation, provided for in M.G.L.A. c. 21E, § 6 and 310 CMR 40.1099. In either case the instrument would specify prohibited and permitted activities and uses, aimed at implementing cleanup, avoidance of further contamination and exclusion of risks to public health and safety. A notice of AUL may be required by DEP, to be signed by the landowner, and an LSP.

Chapter 21E, as well as the Massachusetts Contingency Plan, also contain so-called Brownfield provisions, aimed at promoting "cleanup and redevelopment of contaminated sites in economically distressed areas." An "eligible person," who owns or operates contaminated property, but did not own it at the time of the contaminating release, did not cause or contribute to the release, and meets other requirements, may be exempted from liability to the Commonwealth or to third parties. (But this does not affect federal CERCLA liability.) Qualification for such exemption rests on determination that redevelopment of the site is of economic benefit to the community, and cooperation with DEP, including payment of costs of response action incurred by the Commonwealth, which may be reduced by negotiation in light of future economic benefit and ability to pay. A non-eligible person who settles with the Commonwealth may also be granted a limited exemption from liability. The Attorney General may in appropriate cases bind the Commonwealth by a covenant not to sue.

Leaving aside Brownfields exemptions, the courts have taken a broad view of the Commonwealth's right to recover.[3] Parties who have incurred costs of environmental cleanup have sought to recover under general liability insurance policies. Such policies usually contain a "pollution exclusion," subject to an exception for "sudden and accidental" occurrences, and the courts have considered those issues.[4] Claims against title insurers based on the incurring of a

---

[3]Com. of Mass. v. Pace, 616 F. Supp. 815 (D. Mass. 1985); Acme Laundry Co., Inc. v. Secretary of Environmental Affairs, 410 Mass.

760, 575 N.E.2d 1086 (1991).
[4]Hazen Paper Co. v. U.S. Fidelity and Guar. Co., 407 Mass. 689, 555 N.E.2d 576 (1990); Lumber-

Chapter 21E lien have not succeeded.[5]

Not only the Commonwealth, but also private parties who purchased contaminated property, or are owners of "down-gradient property," may recover under Chapter 21E for damage caused by release and diffusion of hazardous materials.[6] The purchaser of contaminated property who did not become an "operator" thereof was held not liable to a harmed abutter.[7]

In addition to requirements of notice to DEP, the disclosure, or failure thereof, of the existence or release of hazardous substances may have important commercial consequences. Failure so to disclose may be grounds for rescission of a purchase and sale agreement or for assertion of an unfair trade practice under M.G.L.A. c. 93A.[8]

§ 13:19   Underground storage tanks

As noted in § 13:14, the RCRA requirements with respect to underground storage tanks (USTs) are administered by the Massachusetts Department of Public Safety, through the fire prevention board. Under M.G.L.A. c. 148, § 13, the use of premises for storage of explosive or flammable substances, including petroleum, must be licensed. Such a license may be revoked for failure to meet applicable requirements, but

---

mens Mut. Cas. Co. v. Belleville Industries, Inc., 407 Mass. 675, 555 N.E.2d 568 (1990); Jussim v. Massachusetts Bay Ins. Co., 415 Mass. 24, 610 N.E.2d 954 (1993); Hakim v. Massachusetts Insurers' Insolvency Fund, 424 Mass. 275, 675 N.E.2d 1161 (1997); Liberty Mut. Ins. Co. v. SCA Services, Inc., 412 Mass. 330, 588 N.E.2d 1346 (1992); Highlands Ins. Co. v. Aerovox Inc., 424 Mass. 226, 676 N.E.2d 801 (1997).

[5]Chicago Title Ins. Co. v. Kumar, 24 Mass. App. Ct. 53, 506 N.E.2d 154 (1987); South Shore Bank v. Stewart Title Guar. Co., 688 F. Supp. 803 (D. Mass. 1988), judgment aff'd, 867 F.2d 607 (1st Cir. 1988).

[6]Bisson v. Eck, 40 Mass. App. Ct. 942, 667 N.E.2d 276 (1996); Graves v. R.M. Packer Co., Inc., 45

Mass. App. Ct. 760, 702 N.E.2d 21 (1998); Taygeta Corp. v. Varian Associates, Inc., 436 Mass. 217, 763 N.E.2d 1053 (2002); Black v. Coastal Oil New England, Inc., 45 Mass. App. Ct. 461, 699 N.E.2d 353 (1998); Hill v. Metropolitan Dist. Com'n, 439 Mass. 266, 787 N.E.2d 526 (2003).

[7]Scott v. NG U.S. 1, Inc., 67 Mass. App. Ct. 474, 854 N.E.2d 981 (2006), review granted, 448 Mass. 1101, 859 N.E.2d 432 (2006).

[8]V.S.H. Realty, Inc. v. Texaco, Inc., 757 F.2d 411 (1st Cir.1985); Sheehy v. Lipton Industries, Inc., 24 Mass. App. Ct. 188, 507 N.E.2d 781 (1987); Waste Management of Massachusetts, Inc. v. Carver, 37 Mass. App. Ct. 694, 642 N.E.2d 1058 (1994); Graves v. R.M. Packer Co., Inc., 45 Mass. App. Ct. 760, 702 N.E.2d 21 (1998).

not on grounds ulterior to the purposes of the statute.[1]

Under regulations in 527 CMR 9.00 et seq., the installation of a UST, and underground pipes serving it, must meet design and performance specifications, including in most cases devices for leak detection, and requires prior notice to and approval of the local fire department. Installation may only be done by a licensed professional, and the regulations make provision for abandonment or removal of tanks.

A program for funding of costs of replacement and cleanup of leaking or defective existing tanks at "dispensing facilities," such as gasoline service stations, is provided for in M.G.L.A. c. 21J, and regulations thereunder in 503 CMR 2.00, which establish rules for eligibility, claims and reimbursements. The regulations do set forth procedural rules, but a service station owner who sued for "interest" because of delay in responding to its claim, was not successful.[2]

§ 13:20   On-site sewage disposal

There are many communities in Massachusetts, even in metropolitan areas, where there are no sewers connected to a public treatment and disposal system. In such locations the disposition of sewage is accomplished by in-ground facilities, governed by provisions in the State Environmental Code, in 310 CMR 15.000 et seq., known as Title 5. Thereunder systems for disposing of less than 10,000 gallons per day, primarily for residences, are under the jurisdiction of local authority, usually the local Board of Health. Primary jurisdiction remains in the Massachusetts Department of Environmental Protection with respect to larger systems, variances granted by local boards, shared systems,[1] alternative systems, effluent treatment systems, and other elements. Improvements in the technology of small treatment systems and reduction in their costs have made them more prevalent, and consequently the requirements and procedures of DEP with respect to treatment systems has become of more interest.

[Section 13:19]

[1]Derby Refining Co. v. Board of Aldermen of Chelsea, 407 Mass. 718, 555 N.E.2d 584 (1990).

[2]Snaxin, Inc. v. Underground Storage Tank Petroleum Cleanup Fund Administrative Review Bd., 62 Mass. App. Ct. 224, 815 N.E.2d 1087 (2004); and see Williams Auto Elec. Services, Inc. v. Hebert, 63 Mass. App. Ct. 182, 824 N.E.2d 878 (2005).

[Section 13:20]

[1]GPT-Acton, LLC v. Department Of Environmental Protection, 64 Mass. App. Ct. 103, 831 N.E.2d 396 (2005).

A standard system consists of a septic tank in which solids settle and from which liquid effluent is discharged into a soil absorption system, commonly known as a leaching field. The regulations contain detailed specifications for the design and construction of septic tanks and leaching fields, the sizes of which depend on the use of the property and, for residences, number of bedrooms, or for commercial properties, the floor area. There are also requirements of setback from building foundation, property line, water supply, wetlands, etc., which may impose severe limitations on the development of smaller lots—a factor sometimes taken into account in zoning law minimum lot sizes. Municipalities may impose more stringent requirements if certain statutory standards are met.[2]

To install a system, it is first necessary to determine that there is an adequate area and that the soil conditions are suitable for leaching disposal. This is done by percolation and "deep hole" tests performed by a licensed engineer. Next, one must obtain permits from the Board of Health for the installer and the construction, and the system may not be used until the board issues a certificate of compliance. It is also usually necessary to obtain a groundwater discharge permit under 314 CMR 6.00. Discharge into "waters of the commonwealth," broadly defined, as specified in **§ 13:5** will not be allowed.

The Title 5 regulations also contain provision with respect to failed systems, which in some cases may be subject to mandatory replacement. Older systems are particularly suspect, and upon any sale of a residence it is ordinarily necessary to obtain a recertification of the system from the local board of health.[3]

TOPIC E: OTHER LAWS

§ 13:21   Air pollution controls

The federal Clean Air Act[1] mandates regulation of air quality and of polluting emissions from both stationary and mobile sources. The Act is administered by the federal Environmental Protection Agency, and calls also for state

---

[2]Hamel v. Board of Health of Edgartown, 40 Mass. App. Ct. 420, 664 N.E.2d 1199 (1996); Padden v. West Boylston, 64 Mass. App. Ct. 120, 831 N.E.2d 927 (2005).

[3]Breuing v. Callahan, 50 Mass. App. Ct. 359, 737 N.E.2d 507 (2000).

[Section 13:21]

[1]42 U.S.C.A. §§ 7401 et seq; and see 40 C.F.R. 60; 40 C.F.R. 86.

implementation plans (SIPs).

With respect to stationary sources, such as power generation and other industrial facilities burning fossil fuels, an
EPA permit is required if the emissions therefrom are of
certain types or exceed specified tonnage levels. Of the many
air pollutants listed in the Act and regulations, sulfur dioxide
is one of the most significant, along with various volatile
organic compounds.

Under M.G.L.A. c. 111, § 142A, the Massachusetts Department of Environmental Protection has adopted air pollution
control regulations in 310 CMR Chapters 6, 7 and 8, in effect
constituting the Massachusetts SIP. The regulations require
periodic registration of sources of air pollutants, prior approval of plans for construction or alteration of facilities, and
DEP review of proposed operating permits, to be submitted
by DEP to EPA.

With respect to moving sources, mainly highway vehicles,
the federal controls include the so-called "CAFE" standards
for average fuel mileage of each automobile manufacturer's
fleet. Federal and Massachusetts SIP requirements include
regulation of gasoline pump hoses and nozzles, and other
measures for suppression of vapor and organic solvent emissions, and also carpool programs and preferred highway
lanes for carpools and buses. Limitations on idling of vehicles
is aided by "right-on-red" rules, and limitations or "freeze"
on new parking spaces has sometimes been deemed important, such as that applying to the vicinity of Logan Airport
under 310 CMR 7.33.

M.G.L.A. c. 111, § 31C, authorizes local boards of health to
regulate atmospheric pollution, and most of them have
adopted regulations to do so. The Boston Air Pollution
Control Commission limits the use of fuels of high sulfur
content or high particulate emission characteristics, bans
most outdoor open burning, and regulates "abrasive
blasting." The demolition of buildings is a source of airborne
pollutants and is regulated under the Massachusetts SIP
and local regulations. A 20-day advance notice to DEP is
required for demolition of any commercial, industrial or
institutional building or residential building containing 20
or more dwelling units. The suppression of dissemination of
asbestos is a particular target, regulated under M.G.L.A. c.
149, §§ 6A to 6F and 453 CMR 6.00.

Smoke from fires and carbon monoxide are public health
hazards, and requirements of detectors are discussed in
§ 14:11. Mold is also a potential air pollutant. Tobacco smoke
and "secondary smoke" therefrom are well-known pollutants

and health hazards, which a number of municipalities have now undertaken to restrict.

There are federal and state programs for the abatement of radon within schools and residences. The disposition of radioactive wastes, both low level and high level, is a federal priority and also subject to state regulation. Finally, there are controls over the ambient levels and frequencies of electromagnetic radiation, and as noted in § **11:8**, the federal Telecommunications Act in some respects preempted that field.

§ 13:22 Other controls

Other regulatory controls of matters which have some manner of environmental impact include the following:

- Limitations on disposition of park and conservation lands, discussed in § **2:10**.
- The Endangered Species Act, M.G.L.A. c. 131A, and 321 CMR 10.00, under which a permit is required for alteration of a designated habitat.
- The Public Shade Tree Act, M.G.L.A. c. 87, protecting trees within public ways.
- The Scenic Road Act, M.G.L.A. c. 40, § 15C, providing for protection by local designation. A challenge to a local scenic road by law was rejected.[1]
- The Scenic Mountains Act, M.G.L.A. c. 131, § 39A, allowing municipalities in Berkshire County to regulate development in mountain areas.
- Historical protection by the Massachusetts Historical Commission under M.G.L.A. c. 9, §§ 26 to 28 and 950 CMR 71.00, and by a local Historic District Commission under M.G.L.A. c. 40C, discussed in § **14:6** and § **14:7**.
- Preemptive rights of municipalities with respect to lands classified under M.G.L.A. c. 61, 61A or 61B, as forest land, agricultural land or recreational land, and under M.G.L.A. c. 40, § 54A, with respect to former railroad lands, as discussed in § **14:5**.
- Conservation, agricultural preservation and historic preservation restrictions voluntarily imposed, as discussed in **Topic D of Chapter 15**.
- Environmental Restrictions or Activity and Use Limitations, granted to or imposed by DEP, as referred to in § **13:18**, and in **Topic D of Chapter 15**.

[Section 13:22]

[1]Scott v. NG U.S. 1, Inc., 67 Mass. App. Ct. 474, 854 N.E.2d 981 (2006), review granted, 448 Mass. 1101, 859 N.E.2d 432 (2006).

• Earth removal, regulated under M.G.L.A. c. 40, § 21, and local bylaws.

• Signs and billboards, regulated under M.G.L.A. c. 93, §§ 29 to 33, and local bylaws.

• The Energy Facilities Siting Board, an agency of DTE, is charged with providing energy facilities "with a minimum impact on the environment at the lowest possible cost." The SJC upheld the board's approval of electric transmission lines to serve the proposed "Cape Wind" project, subject to federal approval of the wind tower sitings in federal waters.[2]

---

[2]Alliance to Protect Nantucket Sound, Inc. v. Energy Facilities Siting Bd., 448 Mass. 45, 858 N.E.2d 294 (2006).

Chapter 14

Governmental Regulations Affecting Use and Sale

TOPIC A: INTRODUCTION

§ 14:1 The basics

The primary and most salient governmental regulations affecting the use and sale of real estate are, of course, zoning laws, subdivision control laws, and environmental controls, discussed in the preceding **Chapter 11, Chapter 12,** and **Chapter 13.** The financing of real estate transactions is affected by the truth-in-lending law and laws regulating interest rates, prepayment, balloon payment, etc., discussed in **Chapter 21.** The provisions of M.G.L.A. c. 93A with respect to unfair trade practices, discussed in § **5:4,** also have a significant regulatory effect on the sale of real estate. Other laws and regulations of general applicability and obvious impact on the use of real estate are the state building code[1] and related provisions, the state fire prevention code[2] and regulation of blasting.[3] There are also governmental assistance programs, federal and state, which come in considerable number and variety, some of which may be found in M.G.L.A. Chapters 21J, 23A, 23B, 23D, 23F, 23G, 40E, 40G, 40H, 40J, 40L, 40O, 40Q, 40R, and 121B and 121C; and as to housing, 12 U.S.C.A. §§ 1701 et seq. and 42 U.S.C.A. §§ 5301 et seq.

In addition to all of those (and urban renewal), there are a number of other governmental regulations with which a real estate lawyer needs to be familiar. Those most often encountered are the subject of the following sections of this chapter.

§ 14:2 Urban renewal

This is a subject of considerable breadth, here touched upon only briefly. The basis and establishment of urban re-

---

[Section 14:1]

[1]M.G.L.A. c. 143, §§ 93 to 95.

[2]M.G.L.A. c. 148.

[3]Worcester Sand & Gravel Co., Inc. v. Board of Fire Prevention Regulations, 400 Mass. 464, 510 N.E.2d 267 (1987).

334

newal plans are governed by M.G.L.A. c. 121B, and varied aspects of provisions thereof have been considered by the courts.[1] The sale of real estate by a redevelopment authority to a redeveloper is referred to in § 2:6. Urban redevelopment corporations are provided for in M.G.L.A. c. 121A, which affords tax exemptions that have also been litigated.[2]

TOPIC B: REGULATION OF SALE OR USE

§ 14:3 Interstate land sales

The Interstate Land Sales Full Disclosure Act[1] makes it unlawful to use the mails or any other means of communication in interstate commerce to sell or lease any lot of land unless statutory requirements are met. This effectively applies to any sale or lease to a person who is not resident of and present in Massachusetts. The Act applies to the sale or lease of unimproved land, not existing buildings. It contains a categorical exemption of the sale or lease of "any improved land on which there is a residential, commercial, condomin-

---

[Section 14:2]

[1]Electronics Corp. of America v. City Council of Cambridge, 348 Mass. 563, 204 N.E.2d 707 (1965); Moskow v. Boston Redevelopment Authority, 349 Mass. 553, 210 N.E.2d 699 (1965); Charbonnier v. Amico, 367 Mass. 146, 324 N.E.2d 895 (1975); Reid v. Acting Com'r of Dept. of Community Affairs, 362 Mass. 136, 284 N.E.2d 245 (1972); Commissioner of Dept. of Community Affairs v. Boston Redevelopment Authority, 362 Mass. 602, 289 N.E.2d 867 (1972); Trager v. Peabody Redevelopment Authority, 367 F. Supp. 1000 (D. Mass. 1973); Bronstein v. Prudential Ins. Co. of America, 390 Mass. 701, 459 N.E.2d 772 (1984); Charles River Park, Inc. v. Boston Redevelopment Authority, 28 Mass. App. Ct. 795, 557 N.E.2d 20 (1990); St. Botolph Citizens Committee, Inc. v. Boston Redevelopment Authority, 429 Mass. 1, 705 N.E.2d 617 (1999); Russell v. Zoning Bd. of Appeals of Brookline, 349 Mass. 532, 209 N.E.2d 337 (1965); LeBeau v. Board of Selectmen of East Brookfield, 13 Mass. App. Ct. 942, 431 N.E.2d 257 (1982); Gardner v. Governor Apartments Associates, 396 Mass. 661, 488 N.E.2d 3 (1986); Christensen v. Boston Redevelopment Authority, 60 Mass. App. Ct. 615, 804 N.E.2d 947 (2004).

[2]In re Opinion of the Justices, 324 Mass. 724, 85 N.E.2d 222 (1949); Opinion of the Justices, 334 Mass. 760, 135 N.E.2d 665 (1956); Opinion of the Justices to the Senate and the House of Representatives, 341 Mass. 760, 168 N.E.2d 858 (1960); Dodge v. Prudential Ins. Co. of America, 343 Mass. 375, 179 N.E.2d 234 (1961); Prudential Ins. Co. of America v. City of Boston, 369 Mass. 542, 340 N.E.2d 858 (1976); Anderson Street Associates v. City Of Boston, 442 Mass. 812, 817 N.E.2d 759 (2004).

[Section 14:3]

[1]15 U.S.C.A. §§ 1701 to 1720.

ium, or industrial building, or . . . land under a contract obligating the seller or lessor to erect such a building thereon within a period of two years." The two-year clause accounts for the provision, which one often encounters in purchase and sale agreements for condominiums being built or to be built, by which the seller commits delivery of possession to the unit within 2 years of the buyer's first reservation deposit, notwithstanding any other provisions as to time for performance or extension (which usually expire anyway before the 2 year backstop limit).

The Act also contains a categorical exemption of subdivisions containing less than 25 lots. Besides that, there are other specific exemptions which it is useful for one dealing with this subject to review. Some are full exemptions and some only exemptions from registration and disclosure requirements. One important exemption is of land which is zoned for industrial or commercial development, or restricted of record to such use, and meets other statutory tests. None of the exemptions apply, however, if a method of sale is "adopted for the purpose of evasion" of the law.

Exemption from registration and disclosure requirements is provided for (1) subdivisions of fewer than 100 lots, (2) sale of fewer than 12 lots per year, (3) certain small noncontiguous subdivisions, (4) lots of 20 acres or more, (5) subdivisions meeting specified requirements of local controls, availability of utilities, form of deed, title insurance, on-site inspection by purchasers, and absence of specified marketing techniques, (6) certain mobile home sites, (7) intrastate marketing, subject to on-site inspection and other requirements, and (8) sales of lots in a subdivision of fewer than 300 lots to purchasers within the same standard metropolitan statistical area.

The Secretary of Housing and Urban Development has promulgated regulations[2] with respect to these exemptions, defining eligibility for various exemptions, and setting forth formats of required exemption statements.

When no exemption of any kind is available, the required registration includes a good deal of detailed data, specified in the statute and the HUD regulations, about the developer and his financial record and prospects, the project and its location, the community and surroundings, and a variety of factors which may enable the buyer to make some estimate of the future of the development. All of this is to be set forth in a Property Report, a copy of which must be given to each

---

[2]24 C.F.R. 1710.

buyer before he signs a contract. Although HUD must approve the Property Report, it must contain disclaimers as to federal approval of the project and other warnings to buyers to the effect that the Property Report is not a binding commitment of the developer.

The federal Act provides for "certification" of a State upon determination by HUD that the State has and enforces laws and regulations applicable to the sale or lease of lots which require disclosures equivalent to those required by the Act. Massachusetts has not been so certified.

Whether or not "certified" under the federal Act, a number of states do have registration and marketing disclosure laws with respect to the sale of condominium units, and some may assert a long reach of protection of their residents. When a Massachusetts developer wishes to offer his vacant lots or unbuilt units for sale on the market in another state, he will have to meet the registration requirements of that state. However, even when an effort is made to confine all marketing activity to Massachusetts, it remains a fact that Massachusetts newspapers, and radio and television broadcasts, do find their way into other states. That alone should not afford a basis for applicability of the federal Act, or the law or jurisdiction of any other state, nor should they apply when a resident of another state enters Massachusetts to purchase a condominium unit and the transaction is conducted entirely in this state, but those points have not been judicially confirmed.

§ 14:4   Preemptive rights: forest, agricultural and recreational lands

M.G.L.A. Chapters 61, 61A and 61B provide for special reduced assessment, evaluation and taxation of land on the basis of particular classifications of use. Chapter 61 applies to forest land use, Chapter 61A to agricultural or horticultural use, and Chapter 61B to recreational use. The statutes provide for procedures for so classifying such lands and for the termination of such classification upon removal of land so classified from such use. The statutes provide that upon such removal there shall be a "withdrawal penalty tax" under Chapter 61, or "conveyance tax" or "roll-back tax" under Chapter 61A or 61B.

Furthermore, prior to sale of such land or conversion thereof to other use, each of the statutes provides that notice must be given by the seller to the city or town in which the land is located, and the city or town has, for 120 days, a first refusal option to meet a bona fide offer to purchase the land, or an option to purchase at full and fair market value. This does not apply to foreclosure of a mortgage, but the holder of a mortgage on land so classified is required to give the city or town 90 days prior notice of the time and place of any foreclosure sale.

These provisions were extensively amended in 2006,[1] including new definitions, procedures of assessment, and detailed regulation of "conveyance tax" and timing and scaling thereof, and "roll-back tax." Also provided were detailed requirements for notice of conversion or intent to sell, and municipal response thereto. Evidently responding to issues posed in earlier cases, cited below, the statute as amended in 2006 now (i) excludes from "bona fide offer" an offer that is dependent on zoning change or other contingencies, or with a variable price, (ii) permits withdrawal of a notice to convert, and (iii) generally tightens up procedures.

Municipal actions under the pre-2006 versions of these statutes and judicial reaction thereto was somewhat checkered. Pertinent decisions dealt as follows with several of the specified aspects:

• As to the nature, sufficiency and effect of notice to the city or town:[2] The *Billerica* case held that notice once given and acted upon cannot be withdrawn; now reversed by statute. In *Town of Sudbury v. Scott* (reluctantly followed in the *Petersham* case) actions of a prospective buyer indicating an "intent" to discontinue agricultural use were held to have the effect of notice by the seller; now effectively overruled.

• As to the timing and effect of response to notice:[3] A subsequent resale at a higher price was held not to inure to the town's benefit (*Town of Sudbury v. Mahoney*). The 120-day period was held not to have been "tolled" by delay in determination of fair market value (*Wareham*), nor by the town's attempt to negotiate a price (*Franklin v. Wyllie*).

• As to the nature of the sale contract of which notice is

[Section 14:4]

[1]Chapter 394, Acts of 2006.

[2]Town of Billerica v. Card, 11 L.C.R. 195 (2002); Town of Sudbury v. Scott, 439 Mass. 288, 787 N.E.2d 536 (2003); Town of Petersham v. Peck Realty, LLP, 11 L.C.R. 177 (2003).

[3]Meachen v. Selectmen of Sudbury, 6 L.C.R. 235 (1998); Town of Sudbury v. Mahoney, 9 L.C.R. 297 (2001); Town of Boylston v. Dovetail Homes, Inc., 11 L.C.R. 132 (2003); Wareham Land Trust v. A.D. Makepeace Company, 12 L.C.R. 204 (2004); Town of Franklin v. Wyllie, 443 Mass. 187, 819 N.E.2d 943 (2005).

given:[4] The *Farmer* case held that an option does not trigger the statute. In *Franklin v. Wyllie*, when notice was given to the town of a contract with price dependent on subdivision approval, it was held that the town did not have the right to negotiate another deal, but in *Newburyport v. Woodman*, also involving a contract with a price dependent on later approvals, the Land Court distinguished *Wyllie* and enjoined the sale until after trial. The statute now excludes such contracts from the definition of "bona fide offer."

The first refusal options under Chapter 61 on forest land and under Chapter 61B on recreational land may be assigned, with proper notice given, to qualified non-profit conservation organizations, which will upon acquisition be obliged to continue the specified use. Exercise of a so-assigned right of first refusal has been upheld.[5]

The Division of Forests and Parks has promulgated guidelines for classification and taxation of forest lands under Chapter 61, set forth in 304 CMR 8.00. Furthering the purposes of M.G.L.A. c. 61A, there are provisions in M.G.L.A. c. 40L, which authorize cities and towns to establish so-called agricultural incentive areas. In such areas land may not, subject to limited exceptions, be sold for or converted to other than agricultural uses without notice to the city or town and the Department of Food and Agriculture. For a period of 60 days after such notice, the city or town and the Commonwealth have a right of first refusal to meet a bona fide offer or an option to purchase at full and fair market value to be determined by impartial appraisal. A mortgagee is required to give 30 days prior notice of foreclosure.

The statute requires that maps of land so classified "shall be made available in one or more public places," but there is no requirement of recording of a designation of an agricultural incentive area in the registry of deeds in a manner in which a title examiner would ordinarily be sure to find it.

§ 14:5   Former railroad lands

Pursuant to M.G.L.A. c. 40, § 54A, no permit to build any structure on land formerly used as a railroad right-of-way,

---

[4]The Trust for Public Land v. Farmer, 4 L.C.R. 90 (1996); Town of Franklin v. Wyllie, 443 Mass. 187, 819 N.E.2d 943 (2005); City of Newburyport v. Woodman, 13 L.C.R. 325 (2005).

[5]Wareham Land Trust v. A.D. Makepeace Company, 12 L.C.R. 204 (2004); Raffi v. Johnson, 5 L.C.R. 139 (1997); Carlisle Land Trust v. Pannell, 8 L.C.R. 101 (2000).

or property appurtenant thereto, may be issued without the consent, after public hearing, of the secretary of the executive office of transportation and construction. If the secretary denies consent with respect to land purchased from a railroad company before 1976, the owner may recover eminent domain damages.

Failure to comply with the statute proved to be costly to several parties.[1] Plaintiff bank had advanced large sums to a developer whose construction of condominiums was well along when the city, at the request of the attorney general, issued a cease and desist order based on § 54A. The law firm acting for the bank and as agent for defendant title insurer had issued a policy to the bank. The court noted that prior railroad use was readily determinable by title examination, that § 54A was not "recondite" but well-known to conveyancers, that the law firm was "quite likely . . . at fault," and was being sued by the bank. The defendant was held not contractually liable under the policy, but possibly liable in negligence depending upon its undertakings.

TOPIC C: HISTORIC PRESERVATION

§ 14:6   State action

M.G.L.A. c. 9, §§ 26 to 26D provide for the Massachusetts Historical Commission and define its duties and powers. This includes the establishment of the State Register of Historic Places, and the means of nomination of sites for inclusion therein, using as a guide the criteria for listing in the National Register of Historic Places.[1]

Procedures and controls are set forth in §§ 27 to 27D of Chapter 9, the salient elements of which include the following:

• The Commission itself may and often does initiate a proposal for certification of a site as an historic landmark and inclusion thereof in the Register. Such certification requires "the written consent of the person or persons claiming ownership, and such others having recorded interests as the commission shall deem necessary." Once

[Section 14:5]

[1]Somerset Sav. Bank v. Chicago Title Ins. Co., 420 Mass. 422, 649 N.E.2d 1123 (1995).

[Section 14:6]

[1]16 U.S.C.A. § 470a.

so certified, effective upon recording of a notice in the registry of deeds, the site may not "be altered in such a manner as would seriously impair its historical values" without the permission of the Commission, following public hearing, and subject to enforcement by action in the Superior Court. The statute provides that such permission shall not be required by "persons having recorded interests who have not given written consent to the certification and those claiming under them," which seems anomalous in light of the provision that certification could not have been made in the first place without such persons' consent.

• With respect to any project which is undertaken by a state body or is a private project in any way subject to "funding or licensing" by a state body (which includes of course almost all real estate projects), the state body so acting must notify the Historical Commission "[a]s early as possible in the planning process." The Commission may then make a determination within 30 days "whether such project will have any adverse effect, direct or indirect, on any property listed in the state register of historic places." When such a determination is made, both the state agency and the project proponent are obliged to "consult to discuss ways to eliminate, minimize or mitigate the adverse effects," and to "adopt all prudent and feasible means to eliminate, minimize, or mitigate the adverse effects."

The Commission's review "shall not be limited to the subject matter of the license, but shall extend to the entire project whether licensed or funded in whole or in part." There is no statutory time limit for such consultation and review, and consequently developers are subject to considerable pressure to accede to the Commission's desires, notwithstanding the provisions about "consent" of private owners.

§ 14:7   Local action

Under M.G.L.A. c. 40C, §§ 1 to 17, a municipality may, by ordinance or bylaw adopted by two-thirds vote of a city council or a town meeting, establish historic districts, based upon review and report on historic elements, and after public hearing, with 14 days prior written notice to owners of all properties proposed to be included in such district. Maps showing the boundaries of the districts are to be filed with the city or town clerk and recorded in the registry of deeds.

Once established, no building or structure within a historic district may be "constructed or altered in any way that affects exterior architectural features unless the commission shall first have issued a certificate of appropriateness, a certificate of non-applicability or a certificate of hardship with respect to such construction or alteration." An ordinance or bylaw establishing a historic district may, however, exclude from the control of the local historic commission various aspects of building or site alteration.

When a certificate of appropriateness, non-applicability or hardship is applied for, the commission must respond within 14 days, and if it determines that protected values would be impaired, then it is to hold a public hearing, with notice to applicants, abutters and others deemed to be "materially affected." Hearing may be waived by consent of all persons entitled to notice. If the Commission does not act within 60 days, a certificate of hardship is deemed issued. Persons aggrieved by an action of the commission may appeal to the Superior Court.[1]

TOPIC D: CONSUMER WARRANTIES

§ 14:8   Federal regulation

The Magnuson-Moss Warranty—Federal Trade Commission Improvement Act[1] applies to any warranty made with respect to any "consumer product." The statute does not precisely define the term "consumer product," and although a residence is not in itself included, any house or condominium unit certainly contains consumer products. Particularly with respect to newly constructed condominiums, developers usually offer some form of warranty, and it is of course advisable to cast them in compliance with the federal act.

Under the Act and regulations promulgated pursuant thereto,[2] the particular requirements include (1) clear identification of the names and addresses of the warrantors, (2) identification of parties to whom the warranty is extended, (3) products or parts covered, (4) a statement of what the warrantor will do, at whose expense, and for what period

---

[Section 14:7]

[1]Anderson v. Old King's Highway Regional Historic Dist. Com'n, 397 Mass. 609, 493 N.E.2d 188 (1986); McIntyre v. Board of Selectmen of Ashby, 31 Mass. App. Ct. 735, 584 N.E.2d 1137 (1992); Harris v. Old King's Highway Regional Historic Dist. Com'n, 421 Mass. 612, 658 N.E.2d 972 (1996); Tortorella v. Board of Health of Bourne, 39 Mass. App. Ct. 277, 655 N.E.2d 633 (1995); Rudders v. Building Com'r of Barnstable, 51 Mass. App. Ct. 108, 744 N.E.2d 83 (2001).

[Section 14:8]

[1]15 U.S.C.A. §§ 2301 to 2312.
[2]16 C.F.R. 701.

of time, (5) a statement of what the consumer must do and expenses he must bear, (6) exceptions and exclusions from the warranty, (7) step-by-step procedure for consumer enforcement of the warranty, (8) information as to the availability of informal procedures for settlement of disputes, (9) a brief, general description of the legal remedies, and (10) further similar specifications.

The Act sets forth specific federal minimum standards for a "full" warranty, and any warranty which does not meet them in all respects must be "conspicuously designated a 'limited warranty'." A full warranty may not exclude or limit consequential damages "unless such exclusion or limitation conspicuously appears on the face of the warranty." If any full or limited warranty does exclude or limit consequential damages, that provision must be accompanied by the statement that "Some states do not allow the exclusion or limitation of incidental or consequential damages, so the above limitation or exclusion may not apply to you."

In a limited warranty any implied warranties may be limited in duration to the period of a warranty "of reasonable duration" only if such limitation is "conscionable" and is set forth "in clear and unmistakable language and prominently displayed on the face of the warranty." Common practice is to use all capital letters for such a clause and to place it on the first page of a multi-page warranty form. The regulations also specifically require that such a limitation be accompanied by the statement that "Some states do not allow limitations on how long an implied warranty lasts, so the above limitation may not apply to you."

§ 14:9   Massachusetts warranty of habitability

This subject is discussed in § 5:5, as a judicially imposed remedy for breach of contract with respect to new houses and condominiums. It is also in effect a governmental regulation, and its terms might well be incorporated into the forms of warranty proffered by developers of new dwelling units of any type.

TOPIC E: REGULATION OF PHYSICAL CONDITIONS

§ 14:10   Flood prone lands

In response to major damage from hurricanes in 2005, the federal government provided large amounts of funding for restoration in the Gulf Coast and elsewhere, and also sought to bolster and improve operations of the Federal Emergency Management Agency (FEMA) in many respects. Long antedating that, however, and little changed since, the Flood Disaster Protection Act of 1973,[1] established a program, administered by FEMA pursuant to regulations in 44 C.F.R. 59 et seq., making flood insurance available, which was otherwise not available from commercial insurers.

The statute prohibits federally insured or regulated lending institutions, which includes practically all mortgage lenders, including state chartered banks participating in FDIC, from making mortgage loans on properties in defined flood hazard areas unless flood insurance is available. That strongly induces participation in the program by all communities containing any flood hazard areas. The definition and locations of flood hazard areas are determined by FEMA, and shown on maps as described below.

In order to qualify for the program, a city or town must adopt land use regulations (usually zoning laws) limiting or controlling use and development in areas subject to flood hazard, in accordance with federally established standards. The existing flood plain, wetland and watershed zoning provisions are in many cases sufficient, and some municipalities have adopted zoning laws specifically for this purpose, closely following the federal regulatory text.

Flood Hazard Boundary Maps define generally the flood hazard areas identified by FEMA. Flood Insurance Rate Maps are more detailed and specify Zone B, above the 100 year flood level, Zone A, below the 100 year flood level, Zone V, a so-called "velocity zone" in which there may be wave action, and other zone classifications. Zone lines are often based on elevation contours, and maps are usually available locally, or may be obtained from the Flood Plan Management office of FEMA in Boston.

When acting for a mortgage lender, the conveyancer should examine the pertinent Maps for the area in which the property is located, and if the property is in an affected area, notify the borrower that flood insurance will be required. The borrower's attorney, or his seller's attorney will often already have the pertinent information available. The lender may not rely solely on the borrower's certification, and lenders usually require an opinion of counsel as to compliance, which often rests upon a surveyor's certification.

[Section 14:10]

[1]42 U.S.C.A. §§ 4001 to 4128.

§ 14:11   Building elements

There are many different physical elements of buildings and substances commonly found or used in buildings which are subject to regulation, including at least the following:

• **Architectural Barriers.** M.G.L.A. c. 22, § 13A, creates an Architectural Access Board empowered to make and enforce rules and regulations to make "public buildings," construed broadly, accessible to physically handicapped persons. The statute specifically requires that in rental housing containing 20 or more units at least 5 percent of the units be so accessible. A shopping mall was held to be a public building within the meaning of the statute.[1] The Board may grant variances in cases of hardship, but the burden of proof is on the applicant and in several cases has not been carried.[2]

The subject of architectural barriers is also dealt with by Title III of the Americans with Disabilities Act of 1990 (ADA).[3] The Act affects new construction and substantial remodeling of nearly all publicly accessible and commercial facilities, and requires design to afford ready access and usability to persons with disabilities. Pertinent regulations are in 36 C.F.R. 1192.

Under M.G.L.A. c. 22, § 13A, and M.G.L.A. c. 151B, §§ 1 and 4, Massachusetts provides similar protection for disabled tenants. Owners of housing accommodations of 10 or more units may be required to make physical modifications of the premises to meet the needs of persons with disabilities, including impaired sight and hearing. A property owner may be exempted on account of undue hardship, taking into account the nature and cost of the modification, the impact on marketability of the property and the size and business character of the project, but such instances will be rare, as indicated above. The Act also mandates reasonable adaptation of managerial policies and rules to avoid discrimination against handicapped persons. Evictions of handicapped persons have been barred where the court found the policy of protecting them to outweigh their relatively minor violations of rules or

---

[Section 14:11]

[1]Pyramid Co. of Hadley v. Architectural Barriers Bd., 403 Mass. 126, 525 N.E.2d 1328, 82 A.L.R.4th 113 (1988).

[2]Winn v. Architectural Access Bd., 25 Mass. App. Ct. 41, 514 N.E.2d 860 (1987); Home-Like Apartments, Inc. v. Architectural Access Bd., 27 Mass. App. Ct. 851, 545 N.E.2d 58 (1989); Hotel Dynamics, Inc. v. Architectural Access Bd., 30 Mass. App. Ct. 277, 568 N.E.2d 616 (1991).

[3]42 U.S.C.A. §§ 12101 et seq.

conditions of the tenancy.[4]

• **Lead Paint.** M.G.L.A. c. 111, § 197, provides that whenever a child under age 6 resides in any premises in which paint, plaster or other accessible material contains proscribed levels of lead, the owner is required to abate or contain it. If a buyer of a residence brings a child under 6 into the premises, it is the buyer's responsibility to do so within 90 days. There are provisions for containment and control of lead-bearing materials on an "interim basis" if approved by a licensed inspector.

The process of abating or containing lead-bearing material may be removal, but the alternative of encapsulating or containing the leaded material so as to make it inaccessible to a child under age 6 is also possible, although repainting alone will not suffice. Areas accessible to young children include, but are not limited to, areas below the 4 foot level above the floor.

Following § 197 there are a number of succeeding sections of M.G.L.A. c. 111, from 197A to 199A, which contain further provisions pertinent to the subject, including: requirements of notice, specification of violations and penalties therefore, liabilities of the owner, licensing of lead paint inspectors, provision affording lenders who take possession up to 90 days to comply with the statute or divest the property, and provisions relating to discrimination under M.G.L.A. c. 151B. The anti-discrimination provisions make it unlawful to refuse to sell or lease residential premises to persons who have children under 6 on the ground of presence of lead-bearing materials. However, a landlord may "reasonably delay," for not more than 30 days, the commencement of the tenancy, and may provide an existing tenant with alternate quarters in order to make the premises available for being brought into compliance with lead materials abatement requirements. M.G.L.A. c. 167, § 48, similarly prohibits discrimination in lending.

A mortgagee who engaged an agent to collect rents under a collateral assignment of rents was held not thereby to have become an "owner" under the statute.[5] A landlord, unaware of the presence of lead paint at the time of a lease, was held not to be liable when the tenants later

---

[4]Whittier Terrace Associates v. Hampshire, 26 Mass. App. Ct. 1020, 532 N.E.2d 712 (1989); City Wide Associates v. Penfield, 409 Mass. 140, 564 N.E.2d 1003 (1991).

[5]Com. v. Advantage Bank, 406 Mass. 885, 550 N.E.2d 1388 (1990).

had a child who suffered from the effects of lead.[6] Regulations defining a technical method of determining the presence of lead were upheld.[7] In egregious circumstances a statute affording tort claim immunity was held not to release the Boston Housing Authority from lead paint liability,[8] and in another case "justice and equity" allowed a claim to stand despite running out of a one-year statute of limitations.[9]

The federal program under 42 U.S.C.A. §§ 4851 et seq., implemented by regulations in 24 C.F.R. 35.80 et seq. and 40 C.F.R. 745.61 et seq., is aimed primarily at structures built before 1978 when use of lead paint was prevalent, including housing, schools and other facilities where children under 6 are present. The regulations contain extensive provisions with respect to disclosure, any renovation or modification of the target structures, and licensing of professionals in the field.

• **Pesticides.** M.G.L.A. c. 132B controls the sale and use of pesticides and requires notices of such use to be given. This Act also pursues state conformity with federal law under 21 U.S.C.A. § 346a, referred to in 40 C.F.R. 1.43, and other statutes. The Massachusetts Act was held to have preempted the field and a local bylaw regulating use of pesticides was therefore voided.[10]

• **Insulation; UFFI; Asbestos.** Regulations of the Federal Trade Commission in 16 C.F.R. 460, arising under 15 U.S.C.A. §§ 41 et seq., require that the type, thickness and R-value of insulation installed in any new residences, including condominium units, be stated by insulation vendors in the sales contract or in a document incorporated by reference therein. If a sales contract is entered before the type of insulation to be installed is determined, the seller may advise the buyer of this data as soon as it is known. R-value is a measure of resistance to heat flow, and the statute specifies the methods by which it must be tested.

The use of urea formaldehyde foam insulation, known as UFFI, was formerly prevalent. The sale and use thereof

---

[6]Underwood v. Risman, 414 Mass. 96, 605 N.E.2d 832, 19 A.L.R. 5th 964 (1993).

[7]Massachusetts Rental Housing Ass'n, Inc. v. Lead Poisoning Control Director, 49 Mass. App. Ct. 359, 729 N.E.2d 673 (2000).

[8]Campbell v. Boston Housing Authority, 443 Mass. 574, 823 N.E.2d 363 (2005).

[9]In re Estate of Grabowski, 444 Mass. 715, 831 N.E.2d 291 (2005).

[10]Town of Wendell v. Attorney General, 394 Mass. 518, 476 N.E.2d 585 (1985).

has now been banned under both federal and Massachusetts laws concerning hazardous substances, and regulations adopted pursuant thereto.[11] An interim Massachusetts statute, now repealed, required sellers of dwellings to inspect for and disclose the presence of UFFI.[12] However, provisions prohibiting discrimination on account of the presence of UFFI by mortgage lenders still appear in the statute book.[13]

Strict application of the regulations banning UFFI was upheld, and subsequent attempts to avoid the consequences were not successful.[14] A homeowner who engaged a contractor to install UFFI failed to recover for later discovered consequences.[15]

Another hazardous substance formerly used for insulation is asbestos, which has been the subject of major federal and state removal programs. A Massachusetts law, extending the time for the recovery by state and local governments of the costs of asbestos removal was upheld.[16]

● **Sprinklers; Smoke and Heat Detectors; CO Detectors.** The requirements with respect to sprinkler systems, automatic fire warning systems, smoke and heat detectors, and carbon monoxide detectors are set forth in M.G.L.A. c. 148, §§ 26 to 26I. There has been a progression over the years of additional and more broad-reaching sections of this statute, the requirements of which may presently be summarized as follows:

(1) Automatic sprinklers are required in all buildings over 70 feet in height, including buildings constructed before 1975, for which there was a phase-in period for retrofitting, ending in March 1998, absent an ad hoc extension. Automatic sprinklers are also required in bars, nightclubs and the like, and in lodging and boarding houses. In cities and towns which accept applicable provisions of the statute, automatic sprinklers are also required in (a) all buildings and additions over 7500

---

[11]15 U.S.C.A. §§ 1261 et seq.; M.G.L.A. c. 94B; 105 CMR 650.017.

[12]M.G.L.A. c. 255, 121, repealed by Chapter 248, Acts of 2002.

[13]M.G.L.A. c. 167, § 47.

[14]Borden, Inc. v. Commissioner of Public Health, 388 Mass. 707, 448 N.E.2d 367, 38 A.L.R.4th 1036 (1983); Anderson Insulation Co., Inc. v. Department of Public Health, 48 Mass. App. Ct. 80, 717 N.E.2d 662 (1999); Anderson Insulation Co., Inc. v. Department Of Public Health, 61 Mass. App. Ct. 913, 814 N.E.2d 1100 (2004).

[15]Rice v. James Hanrahan & Sons, 20 Mass. App. Ct. 701, 482 N.E.2d 833, 41 U.C.C. Rep. Serv. 1641 (1985).

[16]City of Boston v. Keene Corp., 406 Mass. 301, 547 N.E.2d 328 (1989).

square feet in floor area, with specified exceptions, and (b) all new construction of multiple dwellings containing four or more units.

(2) An automatic fire warning system or heat and smoke detectors of the kinds specified in the statute are required in all buildings under 70 feet in height, all places in which there is lodging in six or more units, and all one to five family dwellings; that is, all dwelling structures.

(3) Carbon monoxide alarms of specified types are required in all buildings containing dwellings that have any form of fossil fuel burning equipment, including but not limited to a furnace, or enclosed parking.

(4) Upon the sale or transfer of any dwelling, inspection for compliance by the local fire department is required.

Exceptions under § 26A 1/2 of the statute, which are no longer applicable, at least as to condominiums, were considered by the courts.[17]

• **Oil Tanks.** Regulations relating to oil storage tanks, including those used for home heating fuel, are discussed in § **13:14**.

• **Solar Energy Systems.** As referred to in § **11:6**, zoning laws may not bar solar energy systems or structures for "collection of solar energy." Further, as discussed in § **11:20**, provision is made in § 9B of M.G.L.A. c. 40A purporting to allow the creation by means of a special permit of "an easement to sunlight over neighboring property." Beyond that, the act[18] introducing those provisions also inserted in M.G.L.A. c. 41, § 81Q, a right of planning boards to adopt rules and regulations (discussed in § **12:10**) encouraging use of solar energy systems and requiring "restrictive covenants protecting solar access." Furthermore, a new § 23C was added to M.G.L.A. c. 184 voiding provisions in instruments "which purport to forbid or unreasonably restrict the installation or use of a solar energy system." And finally, M.G.L.A. c. 187 was amended by inserting a new § 1A which provides that: "An easement of direct sunlight may be acquired over the land of another by express grant or covenant, or by a solar access permit as set forth in [Chapter 40A, § 9B]," and also defines the contents of a solar energy easement.

---

[17]Brook House Condominium Trust v. Automatic Sprinkler Appeals Bd., 414 Mass. 303, 607 N.E.2d 744 (1993); AT&T v. Automatic Sprinkler Appeals Bd., 52 Mass. App. Ct. 11, 750 N.E.2d 505 (2001).

[18]Chapter 637, Acts of 1985.

- **Psychological Impacts.** It is provided in M.G.L.A. c. 93, § 108, that the "fact or suspicion that real property may be or is psychologically impacted" does not require disclosure by a seller, lessor or real estate broker, provided that misrepresentation or false statement is not thereby excused. Real property may bear a psychological impact because of the occurrence thereon of: HIV or other disease not transmittable through mere occupancy, felony, suicide or homicide, or "parapsychological or supernatural phenomenon."
- **Home Inspections.** Under M.G.L.A. c. 112, §§ 201 to 206, persons conducting "home inspections" must be licensed, and are subject to penalties for performing such services without being licensed.

§ 14:12   Manufactured housing

M.G.L.A. c. 140, §§ 32F to 32S regulate manufactured housing communities, formerly called mobile home parks. Section 32F provides that no land may be used for such purposes unless the owner or occupant is licensed under § 32B. Under § 32G manufactured homes may be subject to license fees and exempt from property tax. Sections 32L to 32Q set forth requirements as to rental and sale of manufactured houses. Section 32R regulates sale or lease of land on which a manufactured housing community is located, and grants a first refusal to any group or association of residents representing at least 51% of the manufactured home owners.

The statute has been held constitutional and not a regulatory taking,[1] and applied, including a Chapter 93A claim against a non-complying developer.[2]

TOPIC F: REGIONAL CONTROLS

§ 14:13   Martha's Vineyard

The Martha's Vineyard Commission (MVC) was created in 1977[1] as a regional planning and land use agency for the six towns in Dukes County, but excluding Indian Common

[Section 14:12]

[1]Greenfield Country Estates Tenants Ass'n., Inc. v. Deep, 423 Mass. 81, 666 N.E.2d 988 (1996).

[2]Quinn v. Rent Control Bd. of Peabody, 45 Mass. App. Ct. 357, 698 N.E.2d 911 (1998); Danusis v. Longo, 48 Mass. App. Ct. 254, 720 N.E.2d 470 (1999).

[Section 14:13]

[1]Chapter 831, Acts of 1977.

Lands and the Elizabeth Islands. The Commission is authorized, after notice and public hearing, to designate "districts of critical planning concern" (DCPC), the development of which must then be governed by municipal regulations approved by MVC, or in the absence of local action, adopted by the Commission. MVC also is charged with defining standards and criteria for identification of projects which affect more than one community, called developments of regional impact (DRI), but a broad-brush assertion of that authority was rejected.[2]

Whenever a local board receives an application for any permit, license, etc. for a project which constitutes a DRI, it must refer the same to MVC, which first reviews the application to determine if it is deemed complete, and within 30 days holds a public hearing, and renders a decision within 60 days after the close of the hearing, which period may be extended by agreement of MVC and the applicant. MVC has established a land use planning committee (LUPC) which conducts review of the application and the project. Pending decision by MVC local boards may not approve an application, and all applicable time periods (e.g., under M.G.L.A. c. 40A, § 9 or § 15, or M.G.L.A. c. 41, § 81U) are tolled.[3] The statute provides that MVC shall permit the referring agency to grant a development permit only if MVC finds among other things that the development will have probable benefit exceeding probable detriment, will not interfere with local or Dukes County planning goals, and meets any applicable DCPC regulations. Denial by MVC on such grounds of a permit for a service station in Tisbury was upheld.[4] However, a DCPC regulation was held ineffective in Tisbury because of the town's failure to adopt appropriate rules.[5]

While the local board may not grant a permit without MVC approval, nor waive conditions imposed by MVC, it may deny an MVC approved application or impose additional conditions. The Act provides for appeal to the superior court (but not the land court[6]) from a decision of MVC within 20 days after filing thereof with the town clerk and notice to the applicant.

---

[2]Morey v. Martha's Vineyard Com'n, 409 Mass. 813, 569 N.E.2d 826 (1991).

[3]See Crocker v. Martha's Vineyard Com'n, 407 Mass. 77, 551 N.E.2d 527 (1990).

[4]Tisbury Fuel Service, Inc. v. Martha's Vineyard Com'n, 68 Mass. App. Ct. 773, 864 N.E.2d 1229 (2007).

[5]Crane v. Town of Tisbury, 14 L.C.R. 250 (2006).

[6]Nab's Corner Realty Trust v. Martha's Vineyard Com'n, 9 L.C.R. 444 (2001).

Acknowledging judicial "concern for the unique status of the Vineyard," the land court held that MVC is not a "local board" within the meaning of M.G.L.A. c. 40B, and thus not subject to override thereunder, as discussed in § 11:7.[7]

§ 14:14　Cape Cod

The Cape Cod Commission was created in 1989,[1] replacing a prior commission. The Commission is charged with formulating a regional policy plan for Barnstable County. Municipalities in the county may adopt local comprehensive plans, subject to certification of consistency by the Commission. Similarly to Martha's Vineyard, the Act provides for designation of DCPCs, but in this case as proposed by the Commission or other county or municipal agency, and effective only upon adoption of an ordinance by the County Assembly of Delegates. Once adopted, the towns affected must adopt consistent implementing regulations, or in the absence of local action, the Commission may propose such regulations for approval by the Assembly. The designation of the entire town of Barnstable as a DCPC was upheld.[2]

There is also provision for designation of developments of regional impact (DRIs), which include any project for which an ENF or EIR must be filed under MEPA, as discussed in § 13:2, subject to the right of an applicant to apply to the Commission for an exemption. The Commission's public hearing on a DRI application is to be opened within 60 days and closed within 90 days, and its decision is to be rendered within 60 days after close of the hearing. Failure of the Commission to act within this time results in the DRIs being deemed approved. The Act provides that a municipal agency's review shall be suspended until the Commission has reviewed the proposed development. Once approved by the Commission a DRI may be permitted by the municipality at any time with 7 years thereafter.

The criteria for approval by the Cape Cod Commission are similar to those for MVC, including the benefit-over-detriment test. The Act provides for appeal from a decision of the Commission to the Barnstable superior court or the land court within 30 days after filing thereof with the town clerk and notice to the applicant. The denial of approval of a DRI survived attacks on grounds of regulatory taking, equal

---

[7]Mavro v. DKA, LLC, 11 L.C.R. 46 (2003).

[Section 14:14]

[1]Chapter 716, Acts of 1989.

[2]Home Builders Ass'n Of Cape Cod, Inc. v. Cape Cod Com'n, 441 Mass. 724, 808 N.E.2d 315 (2004).

protection and due process, through extended litigation,[3] and an unsuccessful attempt by a successor owner to reopen the matter.[4] Denial of exemption from DRI status was held to be appealable.[5]

The Act also provides expressly for development agreements between applicants and the Commission and/or a municipality. It is further provided that the Commission may adopt regulations governing the procedures by which it or municipalities may calculate, assess and impose "impact fees." The Act does not apply to projects with a building permit or other permits or subdivision approval issued before its effective date.[6]

TOPIC G: FINANCIAL EXACTIONS

§ 14:15   Boston linkage

Special exaction of payments for zoning review of proposed real estate development projects, commonly known as "linkage," was initiated in the Boston Zoning Code in the 1980s, and is now regarded (with whatever misgivings) as a regular element of the procedure. The specifics of Boston's linkage program are discussed in § **11:27**.

§ 14:16   Other municipalities

In communities other than Boston basis for special exactions may be found in the provision in M.G.L.A. c. 40A, § 9, that:

> Zoning ordinances or by-laws may also provide for special permits authorizing increases in the permissible density of population or intensity of a particular use in a proposed development; provided that the petitioner or applicant shall, as a condition for the grant of said permit, provide certain open space, housing for persons of low or moderate income, traffic or pedestrian improvements, installation of solar energy systems, protection for solar access, or other amenities. Such

---

[3]Daddario v. Cape Cod Com'n, 4 L.C.R. 143 (1996), appeal, 425 Mass. 411, 681 N.E.2d 833 (1997), cert. den. 522 U.S. 1036, 118 S.Ct. 644, 139 L.Ed.2d 621 (1997), remand, 7 L.C.R. 324 (1999); 8 L.C.R. 336 (2000); 56 Mass.App.Ct. 764, 780 N.E.2d 124 (2002).

[4]Giuffrida v. Zoning Bd. Of Appeals Of Falmouth, 68 Mass. App. Ct. 396, 862 N.E.2d 417 (2007).

[5]Striar v. Cape Cod Com'n, 4 L.C.R. 221 (1996).

[6]Taylor v. Cape Cod Com'n, 6 L.C.R. 49 (1998).

zoning ordinances or by-laws shall state the specific improvements or amenities or locations of proposed uses for which the
special permits shall be granted, and the maximum increases
in density of population or intensity of use which may be authorized by such special permits.

Apart from invoking that provision, and linkage contributions from developers on an ostensibly voluntary basis, a
legal basis for financial exactions is found in M.G.L.A. c. 44,
§ 53G, which provides for imposition of fees for employment
of consultants pursuant to rules promulgated under M.G.L.A.
c. 40, § 8C (by a conservation commission), M.G.L.A. c. 40A,
§ 9 or § 12, or M.G.L.A. c. 40B, § 21 (by a zoning board),
M.G.L.A. c. 4, § 81Q (by a planning board), or M.G. L. c. 111,
§ 31 (by a board of health). The statute defines procedures
for engaging consultants and determining their
qualifications. It also provides that such fees shall be placed
in an account separate from other municipal funds, and that
upon completion of a project any excess attributable to the
project shall be available, with interest, to the applicant.

As noted in § **14:14**, the Cape Cod Commission has specific
statutory authority for assessment of "impact fees" on
proposed developments in accordance with defined criteria.

A town bylaw providing for a "school impact fee" assessed
on developers of housing, and based on a formula relating to
the expected number of additional children in the public
schools, was voided as "an invalid and unauthorized tax."[1]

IRS Revenue Ruling 2002-9 allows impact fees to be
capitalized and depreciated.

§ 14:17 Community Preservation Act

The Community Preservation Act, set forth in M.G.L.A. c.
44B, has the purposes of promoting or assisting "the acquisition, creation and preservation of open space; the acquisition, preservation, rehabilitation and restoration of historic
resources; the acquisition, creation and preservation of land
for recreational use; for the acquisition, creation, preservation and support of community housing; and the rehabilitation or restoration of open space, land for recreational use
and community housing that is acquired or created as
provided in" the statute. In municipalities that vote to accept the Act, the funding for these purposes is provided from
two sources: One is a surcharge of not over 3 percent on real

---

[Section 14:16]

[1]Greater Franklin Developers
Ass'n, Inc. v. Town of Franklin, 49
Mass. App. Ct. 500, 730 N.E.2d 900
(2000).

estate tax levies, subject to certain exemptions, and the other is surcharges on recording or registration fees for most real estate instruments, added to the basic recording and registration fees as governed by M.G.L.A. c. 262, §§ 38 and 39. That surcharge is $20 for a deed, mortgage or almost any other instrument, and $10 for a certificate of municipal liens. Exempt from recording surcharge are: declaration of homestead, child support and medical assistance liens, federal tax liens, and charges for extra pages, oversize plans, marginal references and the like.

The funds are paid into a Community Preservation Trust Fund, and there is a community board that makes recommendations for expenditures in accordance with the stated purposes.

TOPIC H: EXPEDITED PERMITTING

§ 14:18 A renewed effort

While most of the matters discussed in this Chapter are considered by the real estate community to be impediments (however rational) to development, the subject of this section is, on the contrary, the "Streamlining and Expediting [of] The Permitting Process In The Commonwealth," as proposed in the Act of that name.[1] Some of the elements of that Act have been discussed in § **11:7**, with respect to Chapter 40B, and in § **11:20**, with respect to special permits, and in § **8:2**, with respect to Land Court jurisdiction.

Beyond that, this Act enacted a new M.G.L.A. c. 43D, replacing an earlier version. The provisions of Chapter 43D are applicable in any city or town that accepts it, the process of acceptance not being specified therein. The actions to which it applies include a wide variety of permits, approvals, orders of condition and the like with respect to zoning, subdivision control, wetlands, septic disposal, filling of bordering wetlands and garaging of motor vehicles with fuel. Extensive provisions are made for procedures aimed at expediting the processes of permitting, consolidating permitting actions, and achieving "final action" within 180 days, with appeal rights also expedited.

In one essential respect, however, the applicability of

[Section 14:18]

[1]Chapter 205, Acts of 2006.

Chapter 43D is unclear. It contains a definition of a "priority development site," as one that is commercially or industrially zoned and eligible under applicable zoning provisions for a building of at least 50,000 square feet of floor area, and has been designated as a priority development site. At a couple of places the Chapter refers to "priority development permit," but it does not expressly limit its applicability to permits for a so-defined priority development site, and the ambiguity calls for attention by the legislature or the courts. If it is applicable only to 50,000 square foot commercial or industrial projects, then it falls short of the promise of the caption of the 2006 Act.

Chapter 15

Servitudes: Easements and Restrictions

TOPIC A: INTRODUCTION

§ 15:1 Servitudes

The law of servitudes is of ancient origin, arising from Roman law, developed in English common law, diversified among American states, and putatively reconsolidated and brought up to date by the Restatement (Third) of Property: Servitudes, published in 2002. Massachusetts law has followed the pattern of diversification among American states, and has in some respects moved forward toward adoption of the broader and more liberal positions expounded in the new Restatement.

The very term "servitudes" is now seen as somewhat archaic, and is not commonly used by real estate lawyers. As defined in the Restatement, it comprises "profits, easements, and covenants." For present purposes, in keeping with a focus on contemporary practice in Massachusetts, the classification is reduced to easements, which include "profits" as a form thereof, and restrictions, being the type of covenant of most interest to real estate practitioners.

Among the principles espoused for servitudes in the 2002 Restatement are (as paraphrased) that: (1) any form is valid unless illegal, unconstitutional or against public policy; (2) the intent and expectations of the parties should govern; (3) they run with title to both the benefited and burdened land; and (4) they may be in gross and assignable, and enforceable by a holder who does not own benefited land. The following sections of this chapter will indicate the manner and extent in which Massachusetts law has come to abide with or approach these concepts.

§ 15:2 Private easements

An easement is defined as a right of a person to use the real property of another person for some specified purpose that is not inconsistent with or wholly exclusive of the affected owner's use of the property. It is distinguished from a lease in that a lessee acquires possession of the leased premises to the exclusion of the owner. In contrast, it has been stated that the owner of an estate subject to an easement may use the affected area "for all purposes except those that are inconsistent with the holder of an easement right."[1] It is distinguished from a license in that an easement is a recognized interest in the land itself, and a license is only a permission for use, ordinarily revocable.[2] It differs from a *profit à prendre* in that the latter includes the right to remove materials from the affected real estate, such as crops, timber, soil or minerals.[3] A restriction, on the other hand, is not a right of use, but an impediment or limitation on the use of property by the owner thereof. The word "restriction," did not, however, bar the finding that an affirmative easement arose from a provision barring obstruction of view for 999 years.[4]

An easement may be held by a person who does not own land adjoining the land upon which he has an easement, or does not own any land at all. In that case it is called a "personal servitude," or more commonly, an easement in gross. Unless the instrument creating it provides otherwise, it may be assigned by the holder.

More frequent are easements held by a land owner over land of other neighboring or nearby landowners. That is what used to be called a "predial servitude," and is now referred to as an appurtenant easement. The land of the owner or the holder of the easement is the "dominant estate," and the land affected or "burdened" by the easement is the "servient estate." Such an easement runs with the land; i.e., it continues to remain in effect as a benefit to the dominant estate and a burden on the servient estate, regardless of any change of ownership of either. That is true of course only if the instrument creating the easement was properly recorded as referred to in **Chapter 6**, and if it does not provide

---

[Section 15:2]

[1]Nab Asset Venture III, L.P. v. Gillespie, 7 L.C.R. 375 (1999); Hyde Park Liquors II, Inc. v. Nahabedian, 8 L.C.R. 23 (2000).

[2]Sturnick v. Watson, 336 Mass. 139, 142 N.E.2d 896 (1957).

[3]Fielding v. Old Tuck Cranberry Corp., 10 L.C.R. 205 (2002); 14 L.C.R. 202 (2006); Jenkins v. Johnson, 14 L.C.R. 521 (2006).

[4]Cotton v. Moscow, 8 L.C.R. 65 (2000); and see Patterson v. Paul, 14 L.C.R. 125 (2006); Clarke v. Town of Hingham, 14 L.C.R. 465 (2006).

otherwise.

TOPIC B: EASEMENTS

§ 15:3   Origin and status

• **Grant.** An easement usually has its origin in a grant or reservation set forth in a recorded instrument. A grant of an easement may be made by a separate recorded instrument, but is often made in a deed of land in which is included a clause to the effect that "said premises are hereby conveyed together with the right and easement . . . " Or in some cases the deed may convey the premises "subject to the right and easement hereby reserved to the grantor . . ." Such a reservation is equivalent to, and should be regarded as the same as, a granted easement.[1]

In some circumstances an easement may be created by an order of court, including a decree of partition, as to which see **§ 6:41**. An easement so created in 1844 was referred to by the Land Court as "a conveyancer's nightmare" because it was not again referred to of record within a normal title examination period, but remained in effect.[2]

In any instrument it is always desirable to spell out the particulars of appurtenance of the easement. That is, the grant or reservation should specify that the easement is "appurtenant to the premises hereby conveyed," or in the case of a reservation, that it is "appurtenant to the remaining (or adjoining, or other specified) premises of the grantor." In the latter case, it should be noted that in a deed of A to B, A cannot grant an easement to C unless the instrument names C as a grantee; nor can A "reserve" an easement to C, a third-party beneficiary. If A has the intention of giving C an easement, he should grant it to C before he deeds his property to B.

There are some instances, perhaps not frequent, in which it is desirable or useful to grant an easement that is "personal" or "in gross," i.e., not appurtenant to any land, but exercisable by the grantee named and his assignees. If it is desired to limit such an easement to the named grantee, or a particular group, then the instrument should expressly state that the rights granted are not assignable, or are as-

---

[Section 15:3]

[1]See Barlow v. Chongris & Sons, Inc., 38 Mass. App. Ct. 297, 647 N.E.2d 437 (1995).

[2]Boudreault v. Silva, 8 L.C.R. 1 (2000).

signable only to specified persons. In any case, if an easement in gross is intended, that must be made very clear in
the instrument for the simple reason that in Massachusetts
there is a strong presumption of appurtenance of easements.
The court has said that "an easement is not presumed to be
personal unless it cannot be construed fairly as appurtenant
to some estate."[3] This subject is considered again in reference to Overburden; Surcharge, below.

In any grant of easement it is important to specify carefully the particular rights granted, the location or geographical scope of the easement, the temporal limitations, if any,
the land to which it is appurtenant, the scope or limits or
rights to make physical changes or changes in use of the
easement, and in some cases, provisions for termination or
relocation. Failure to do so leads to endless litigation, some
of which is referred to in the following subsections.

● **Implication.** When the owner of a tract subdivides it
into separate lots or parcels having frontage on new ways
shown on the subdivision plan, every such lot or parcel
acquires by implication of law a right of way over the ways
shown on the plan to the extent necessary for access to a
public way.[4] The cited *Murphy* decision referred to "the familiar rule that when a grantor conveys land bounded on a
street or way, he and those claiming under him are estopped
to deny the existence of such street or way, and the right
. . . acquired by the grantee . . . [is at least] an easement of
way . . . [along] the entire length of the way, as it is then
laid out or clearly indicated." It was also stated that: "This
rule is applicable even if the way is not yet in existence, so
long as it is contemplated and sufficiently designated," and
that it "seems to have become a rule of law rather than a
mere canon of construction."

The mere showing of a street on a recorded plan does not,
however, create any easements,[5] but an easement was held
to exist in a way despite lack of approval by a planning
board, and in an area marked "reserved for future roadway"

[3]Southwick v. Planning Bd. of
Plymouth, 65 Mass. App. Ct. 315,
839 N.E.2d 351 (2005), review
denied, 446 Mass. 1106, 844 N.E.2d
1097 (2006), citing Jones v. Stevens,
276 Mass. 318, 177 N.E. 91, 76
A.L.R. 591 (1931).

[4]Wellwood v. Havrah Mishna
Anshi Sphard Cemetery Corp., 254
Mass. 350, 150 N.E. 203 (1926);
Casella v. Sneirson, 325 Mass. 85,

89 N.E.2d 8 (1949); Murphy v. Mart
Realty of Brockton, Inc., 348 Mass.
675, 205 N.E.2d 222 (1965); Jackson
v. Knott, 418 Mass. 704, 640 N.E.2d
109 (1994); Estes v. DeMello, 61
Mass. App. Ct. 638, 814 N.E.2d 1
(2004).

[5]Patel v. Planning Bd. of North
Andover, 27 Mass. App. Ct. 477,
539 N.E.2d 544 (1989).

on a plan.[6] The prevalent practice of subdividers is to spell out in their deeds, or by a prior, recorded "declaration of easements," the rights granted to lot owners and those reserved to the grantor.

An implication of rights beyond access to a public way, or in other respects, may arise from the intent of the parties, discerned from their conduct or circumstances, of various kinds, relating to the creation of an easement by grant. When rights of way leading to a beach were granted, an implication of rights to use the beach have been so found in several cases.[7] Easements in "parks" shown on an 1873 plan were held to have arisen by implication from the intention of the subdivider, indicated by marketing history.[8] On the other hand, express easements may negate further implication.[9]

• **Necessity.** A way by necessity arises when a division of land leaves a part of it without any access to a public way. When such a way arises, the owner of the isolated parcel may use "a way of convenient width for all ordinary uses of free passage to and from [the landlocked] land."[10] In the cited *Town of Bedford v. Cerasuolo* case, the landlocked parcel had long been used for agriculture, served by a 7 foot wide cart path, but the court allowed the construction of a 24 foot wide road and installation of utilities to serve a Chapter 40B housing project, finding that the transition from agriculture to residential use was reasonable and foreseeable.

When a formerly landlocked parcel entitled to an easement by necessity becomes accessible to a later layout of an abutting public way, the easement by necessity terminates.[11]

• **Estoppel.** As noted above, a way by implication from a plan arises out of the "estoppel" of the person who recorded the plan showing the way and gave deeds of lots fronting on the way from denying the way's existence or his grantees' rights to use it. Consequently, courts often speak of an easement by "estoppel,"[12] but it was stated in one case that no

---

[6]E. Whitehead, Inc. v. Gallo, 357 Mass. 215, 258 N.E.2d 25 (1970).

[7]Labounty v. Vickers, 352 Mass. 337, 225 N.E.2d 333 (1967); Murphy v. Olsen, 63 Mass. App. Ct. 417, 826 N.E.2d 249 (2005).

[8]Reagan v. Brissey, 446 Mass. 452, 844 N.E.2d 672 (2006).

[9]Zotos v. Armstrong, 63 Mass. App. Ct. 654, 828 N.E.2d 551 (2005).

[10]Town of Bedford v. Cerasuolo, 62 Mass. App. Ct. 73, 818 N.E.2d 561 (2004).

[11]Barrett v. Lyons, 4 L.C.R. 235 (1996), citing Hart v. Deering, 222 Mass. 407, 111 N.E. 37 (1916); Grant v. Spring, 9 L.C.R. 84 (2001).

[12]Czerwonka v. W.D. Cowls,

easement "by estoppel" or "*in pais*" exists in Massachusetts.[13] The assertion that a private easement of travel arose in abutters upon the discontinuance of a public way was firmly rejected by the SJC[14] but an easement in a former public way may persist from a prior implication or from prescription.[15]

• **Prescription.** Easements arising by prescription are discussed in § **7:18**.

§ 15:4 M.G.L.A. c. 183, § 58

As noted at the end of § **15:3**, a well-drafted grant of easement will include all necessary specifications. When they are lacking, or when an easement arises solely by implication or necessity, courts may need to, and often do, provide the missing specifications, exercising broad powers in equity.

There are two statutory provisions which assist their determinations. The first is M.G.L.A. c. 183, § 58, which provides that:

> Every instrument passing title to real estate abutting a way, whether public or private, watercourse, wall, fence or other similar linear monument, shall be construed to include any fee interest of the grantor in such way, watercourse or monument, unless (a) the grantor retains other real estate abutting such way, watercourse or monument, in which case, (i) if the retained real estate is on the same side, the division line between the land granted and the land retained shall be continued into such way, watercourse or monument as far as the grantor owns, or (ii) if the retained real estate is on the other side of such way, watercourse or monument between the division lines extended, the title conveyed shall be to the center line of such way, watercourse or monument as far as the grantor owns, or (b) the instrument evidences a different intent by an express exception or reservation and not alone by bounding by a side line.

This enacts a long-standing principle of law[1] that, as expressed in brief, fee title to land abutting a way extends to

---

Inc., 3 L.C.R. 29 (1995); Gray v. Flynn, 6 L.C.R. 345 (1998); Pratt v. Commonwealth, 13 L.C.R. 75 (2005); Adams v. Planning Bd. of Westwood, 64 Mass. App. Ct. 383, 833 N.E.2d 637 (2005); Lane v. Zoning Bd. of Appeals of Falmouth, 65 Mass. App. Ct. 434, 841 N.E.2d 260 (2006), review denied, 448 Mass. 1106, 862 N.E.2d 380 (2007).

[13]Cappa v. Murray, 13 L.C.R. 67 (2005).

[14]Nylander v. Potter, 423 Mass. 158, 667 N.E.2d 244 (1996).

[15]Czerwonka v. W.D. Cowls, Inc., 3 L.C.R. 29 (1995); DiCarlo v. Bird, 5 L.C.R. 232 (1998).

[Section 15:4]

[1]City of Boston v. Richardson, 95 Mass. 146, 13 Allen 146, 1866 WL 4969 (1866).

the center line. It should be noted that the statute passes the entire fee interest of the grantor in the abutting way, which may in some circumstances include the full width of the way. Before enactment of the statute in 1971 and amendment in 1990, bounding the lot "by the sideline" of the way was sufficient to exclude conveyance of the fee in the way, and in rare circumstances, involving land registered or confirmed before 1972, or where reliance has been made on a contrary court decision, the old rule may still be pertinent.

The statute, referred to as the "derelict fee statute," applies not only to private ways but also to public ways unless the layout thereof was by fee taking. This is important because, as stated in § 6:29, a taking for street purposes establishes only an easement of public travel unless the fee is expressly taken. The statute applies even if the way is an unconstructed "paper street,"[2] and it also applies to a "watercourse, wall, fence or other similar linear monument." A number of points have been subject to judicial consideration.[3] The cited *Tattan* case affords an analysis of the statute and prior decisions. The cited case of *Cross v. Young* held that an oil pipeline location was not a linear monument or a way under the statute. However, in the cited *Rowley* case the SJC held in 2003 that the statute did apply to a railroad easement acquired by the old "filed location" procedure, thus resolving an issue posed by this author in 1967.[4]

§ 15:5   M.G.L.A. c. 187, § 5

The second statute guiding judicial determinations is M.G.L.A. c. 187, § 5, which provides that:

> The owner or owners of real estate abutting on a private way who have by deed existing rights of ingress and egress upon such way or other private ways shall have the right by implication to place, install or construct in, on, along, under and upon said private way or other private ways pipes, conduits, manholes and other appurtenances necessary for the transmission of gas, electricity, telephone, water and sewer service,

---

[2]Brennan v. DeCosta, 24 Mass. App. Ct. 968, 511 N.E.2d 1110 (1987); Tattan v. Kurlan, 32 Mass. App. Ct. 239, 588 N.E.2d 699 (1992); Estes v. DeMello, 61 Mass. App. Ct. 638, 814 N.E.2d 1 (2004); Dellert v. Geryk, 13 L.C.R. 37 (2005).

[3]Tattan v. Kurlan, 32 Mass. App. Ct. 239, 588 N.E.2d 699 (1992); Rowley v. Massachusetts Elec. Co., 438 Mass. 798, 784 N.E.2d 1085 (2003); Zora Enterprises, Inc. v. Burnett, 61 Mass. App. Ct. 341, 810 N.E.2d 835 (2004); and Land Court cases in: 2 L.C.R. 65, 8 L.C.R. 111, 9 L.C.R. 67, 446 and 463.

[4]See *Who Owns the Railroad Bed?*, E.C. Mendler, Massachusetts Law Quarterly, June 1967.

provided such facilities do not unreasonably obstruct said private way or other private ways, and provided that such use of the private way or other private ways does not interfere with or be inconsistent with the existing use by others of such way or other private ways; and, provided further, that [all such work is done in accordance with applicable requirements of utility companies and municipal regulations.]

This statute has been broadly applied.[1] It is retroactive, and it applies to a private driveway, as stated in the *Barlow* decision. It applies to an easement by implication or necessity, deemed to have arisen "by deed," as held in the cited *Adams* and *Lane* decisions, although it does not apply to a prescriptive easement.[2] As pointed out in the *Adams* decision, the right to install utilities arises solely from the statute and not from common law, as upheld in a prior case,[3] although the "vitality" of the old rule was "subject to question."

The application of this statute, providing for installation of utilities, has a functional relationship to other improvements of a way, discussed below, and sometimes to issues of surcharge or overburdening of an easement, also discussed below.

Beyond the foregoing statutory applications, the courts have considered other aspects of easements and filled in gaps in their terms.

§ 15:6 Location; relocation

When the location or width of a right of way is inadequately specified, the courts provide the data.[1] A right to go "across" a street was held not to include a right to go along it.[2] An easement located by reference to a natural water line was held not to have been altered by unauthorized fill, but the court acknowledged that natural erosion or accretion

---

[Section 15:5]

[1]Barlow v. Chongris & Sons, Inc., 38 Mass. App. Ct. 297, 647 N.E.2d 437 (1995); Adams v. Planning Bd. of Westwood, 64 Mass. App. Ct. 383, 833 N.E.2d 637 (2005); Lane v. Zoning Bd. of Appeals of Falmouth, 65 Mass. App. Ct. 434, 841 N.E.2d 260 (2006), review denied, 448 Mass. 1106, 862 N.E.2d 380 (2007).

[2]Cumbie v. Goldsmith, 387 Mass. 409, 439 N.E.2d 815 (1982).

[3]Nantucket Conservation Foundation, Inc. v. Russell Management, Inc., 2 Mass. App. Ct. 868, 316 N.E.2d 625 (1974).

[Section 15:6]

[1]Rajewski v. McBean, 273 Mass. 1, 172 N.E. 882 (1930); Ramey v. Dover General, Inc., 2 L.C.R. 27 (1994); Belkin v. Bateman, 3 L.C.R. 225 (1995); Haugh v. Simms, 11 L.C.R. 156 and 232 (2003); Femc v. Cohen, 12 L.C.R. 106 (2004).

[2]Crook v. Jacobson, 11 L.C.R. 21 (2003).

would have that effect.[3]

When a grant of easement specifies the location thereof, the common law rule is that the location cannot be changed without the consent of the owner of the dominant estate. The land court applied that rule with expressed regret and criticism, and upon appeal,[4] the SJC in 2004 disposed of the rule and adopted "as the law of the Commonwealth" the modern rule set forth in the Restatement (Third) of Property: Servitudes, which provides in § 4.8.(3) that: "Unless expressly denied by the terms of an easement, as defined in § 1.2, the owner of the servient estate is entitled to make reasonable changes in the location or dimensions of an easement, at the servient owner's expense, to permit normal use or development of the servient estate, but only if the changes do not (a) significantly lessen the utility of the easement, (b) increase the burdens on the owner of the easement in its use and enjoyment, or (c) frustrate the purpose for which the easement was created."

In a case decided before *M.P.M. Builders*, the appeals court referred to the old rule, but found an acquiescence to the proposed change of location.[5] It has been suggested that the principle of *M.P.M. Builders* may apply also to the servient owner of land flowed by water pursuant to a prescriptive easement.[6]

§ 15:7 Uses; encroachment

The extent and nature of activities allowed by the terms of an easement, or deemed to be collateral or incidental thereto, have been considered with respect to: mowing grass over a septic disposal area,[1] mooring boats in an easement area for recreational boating,[2] barring construction of a house as interference with rights to pass over and "enjoy the benefits" of a parcel.[3] In many cases parking of a vehicle within a right of way was held not to be included in the easement,[4]

---

[3]Bergh v. Hines, 44 Mass. App. Ct. 590, 692 N.E.2d 980 (1998).

[4]M.P.M. Builders, LLC v. Dwyer, 442 Mass. 87, 809 N.E.2d 1053 (2004).

[5]Proulx v. D'Urso, 60 Mass. App. Ct. 701, 805 N.E.2d 994 (2004).

[6]Trenz v. Town of Norwell, 68 Mass. App. Ct. 271, 861 N.E.2d 777 (2007).

[Section 15:7]
[1]Sawdy v. Zuber, 8 L.C.R. 60 (2000).

[2]Seascape Association, Inc. v. Cavaretta, 7 L.C.R. 35 (1999).

[3]Burritt v. Lilly, 40 Mass. App. Ct. 29, 661 N.E.2d 102 (1996).

[4]Harrington v. Lamarque, 42 Mass. App. Ct. 371, 677 N.E.2d 258 (1997); Kostorizos v. Samia, 9 L.C.R. 117 (2001), citing In re Opinion of

but was sometimes found to be allowed.[5] In *Broude v. Massachusetts Bay Lines, Inc.*[6] the land court looked to the intent of an urban renewal plan and held that an easement for a marina at Harbor Towers on the Boston waterfront was for pleasure boats only and could not be used commercially by the defendant.

Structural encroachments that interfere with the use or enjoyment of an easement are regularly ordered to be removed,[7] but may be allowed to remain if *de minimis*.[8]

§ 15:8 Improvement

In *Guillet v. Livernois*,[1] the SJC cited prior cases for the propositions that "when an easement or other property right is created, every right necessary for its enjoyment is included by implication," that the right to make reasonable repairs and improvements in a way was well established, and that the reasonableness of improvements was "largely a question of fact." In that case the court upheld substantial regrading of the way, including construction of retaining walls, even though that harmed other abutters as to grade and drainage. In later cases the right to improve ways established by prescription was upheld, including paving of the way.[2]

It was held that a Chapter 91 license (see § **13:12**) for a ramp and float over private flats could be issued to the holder of an easement notwithstanding objection of the fee owner,[3] but an easement running to "mean high water" was held insufficient to permit construction of a walkway over flats to low water.[4] As noted above, the improvement of a way often interplays with other issues, as indicated in a number of

---

the Justices, 297 Mass. 559, 8 N.E.2d 179 (1937); Lanzillo v. Mabardy, 11 L.C.R. 23 (2003).

[5]Brassard v. Flynn, 352 Mass. 185, 224 N.E.2d 221 (1967); BDS Realty, LLC v. Broutsas, 11 L.C.R. 94 (2003).

[6]Broude v. Massachusetts Bay Lines, Inc., 13 L.C.R. 332 (2005).

[7]Harrington v. Lamarque, 42 Mass. App. Ct. 371, 677 N.E.2d 258 (1997); Brodeur v. Lamb, 22 Mass. App. Ct. 502, 495 N.E.2d 324 (1986); Gustenhoven v. Smith, 3 L.C.R. 85 (1995); Goulding v. Cook, 422 Mass. 276, 661 N.E.2d 1322 (1996); Rondeau v. Caputi, 5 L.C.R. 144 (1997).

[8]Capodilupo v. Vozzella, 46 Mass. App. Ct. 224, 704 N.E.2d 534 (1999).

[Section 15:8]

[1]Guillet v. Livernois, 297 Mass. 337, 8 N.E.2d 921, 112 A.L.R. 1300 (1937).

[2]Glenn v. Poole, 12 Mass. App. Ct. 292, 423 N.E.2d 1030 (1981); Stagman v. Kyhos, 19 Mass. App. Ct. 590, 476 N.E.2d 257 (1985).

[3]Tindley v. Department of Environmental Quality Engineering, 10 Mass. App. Ct. 623, 411 N.E.2d 187 (1980).

[4]Sheftel v. Lebel, 44 Mass. App. Ct. 175, 689 N.E.2d 500

cases, some of which are cited above.[5]

§ 15:9   Overburden; surcharge

The term "overburden" is usually applied to the use of an easement for purposes for which it was not established or to an extent beyond that for which it was established. The term "surcharge" is usually applied to the use of an easement to serve land to which it is not appurtenant. However, the usage of the terms is often mixed by lawyers and courts. In both cases they obviously involve questions of the scope of the easement, various aspects of which are discussed in the preceding paragraphs.

Use by motor vehicles of old farm ways created before there were such, is not held to be an overburden, even when the use of the way is substantially increased and the vehicles are hauling gravel and not agricultural produce.[1] The basic principle is that use of a way is not limited to or by the use of the dominant estate at the time of creation of the easement,[2] and it has been applied in a variety of circumstances.[3] But if a limited use is specified, such as "with teams only" that may control.[4]

On the other hand, the use of a way to serve land other than or beyond the estate that was the dominant estate when the easement was established, is generally rejected.[5] When the instrument is vague, the court may define both the scope

---

(1998).

[5]Barlow v. Chongris & Sons, Inc., 38 Mass. App. Ct. 297, 647 N.E.2d 437 (1995); Adams v. Planning Bd. of Westwood, 64 Mass. App. Ct. 383, 833 N.E.2d 637 (2005); Lane v. Zoning Bd. of Appeals of Falmouth, 65 Mass. App. Ct. 434, 841 N.E.2d 260 (2006), review denied, 448 Mass. 1106, 862 N.E.2d 380 (2007); Town of Bedford v. Cerasuolo, 62 Mass. App. Ct. 73, 818 N.E.2d 561 (2004); Selwyn v. Schwartz, 4 L.C.R. 137 (1996); Digital Equipment Corporation v. Leto, 4 L.C.R. 194 (1996); Boudreault v. Silva, 8 L.C.R. 1 (2000).

[Section 15:9]

[1]Swensen v. Marino, 306 Mass. 582, 29 N.E.2d 15, 130 A.L.R. 763 (1940); Hodgkins v. Bianchini, 323 Mass. 169, 80 N.E.2d 464 (1948).

[2]Mahon v. Tully, 245 Mass. 571, 139 N.E. 797 (1923).

[3]Cornell-Andrews Smelting Co. v. Boston & P.R. Corp., 215 Mass. 381, 102 N.E. 625 (1913); Pion v. Dwight, 11 Mass. App. Ct. 406, 417 N.E.2d 20 (1981).

[4]Clarkin v. Duggan, 292 Mass. 263, 198 N.E. 170 (1935).

[5]Randall v. Grant, 210 Mass. 302, 96 N.E. 672 (1911); Murphy v. Mart Realty of Brockton, Inc., 348 Mass. 675, 205 N.E.2d 222 (1965); Brassard v. Flynn, 352 Mass. 185, 224 N.E.2d 221 (1967); McLaughlin v. Board of Selectmen of Amherst, 38 Mass. App. Ct. 162, 646 N.E.2d 418 (1995), aff'd, 422 Mass. 359, 664 N.E.2d 786 (1996); DiTullio v. Streeter, 9 L.C.R. 179 (2001); Southwick v. Planning Bd. of Plymouth, 65 Mass. App. Ct. 315, 839 N.E.2d 351 (2005), review denied, 446 Mass.

of the easement and the dominant estate.[6] And in some circumstances use of a way to serve additional, or "after acquired" property may be warranted, including the "unique nature of a condominium."[7]

As noted in § 15:1, the principles espoused by the Restatement call for broad interpretation and application of servitudes in accordance with "the intent and expectations of the parties." In the *Southwick* case[8] the grants of easements from the developer to the town were broadly phrased, making the intent and expectations of the parties rather clear. Yet the appeals court strictly applied narrow rules of appurtenance and surcharge. The SJC had previously indicated an openness to reconsideration of "common law rules concerning the creation, validity and enforcement of servitudes [that] may no longer be sound,"[9] and had otherwise taken note of the Restatement,[10] as the appeals court itself did later, noting that the benefit or burden of a servitude may be both appurtenant and personal.[11]

§ 15:10   Termination

As noted in § 15:2, an easement is an interest in land. It is so recognized in common law and it follows that an easement, whether established by grant or by implication, is not terminated by lack of exercise, or "non-user," thereof, even for a long time.[1] An easement "from the garage to [the]

1106, 844 N.E.2d 1097 (2006).

[6]Rajewski v. McBean, 273 Mass. 1, 172 N.E. 882 (1930).

[7]Barrett v. Lyons, 4 L.C.R. 235 (1996); Bateman v. Board of Appeals of Georgetown, 56 Mass. App. Ct. 236, 775 N.E.2d 1276 (2002).

[8]Southwick v. Planning Bd. of Plymouth, 65 Mass. App. Ct. 315, 839 N.E.2d 351 (2005), review denied, 446 Mass. 1106, 844 N.E.2d 1097 (2006).

[9]Bennett v. Commissioner of Food and Agriculture, 411 Mass. 1, 576 N.E.2d 1365 (1991).

[10]Garland v. Rosenshein, 420 Mass. 319, 649 N.E.2d 756 (1995).

[11]Well-Built Homes, Inc. v.

Shuster, 64 Mass. App. Ct. 619, 834 N.E.2d 1213 (2005).

[Section 15:10]

[1]Dubinsky v. Cama, 261 Mass. 47, 158 N.E. 321 (1927); Delconte v. Salloum, 336 Mass. 184, 143 N.E.2d 210 (1957); Sorel v. Boisjolie, 330 Mass. 513, 115 N.E.2d 492 (1953); First Nat. Bank of Boston v. Konner, 373 Mass. 463, 367 N.E.2d 1174 (1977); Yagjian v. O'Brien, 19 Mass. App. Ct. 733, 477 N.E.2d 202 (1985); Brodeur v. Lamb, 22 Mass. App. Ct. 502, 495 N.E.2d 324 (1986); Lasell College v. Leonard, 32 Mass. App. Ct. 383, 589 N.E.2d 342 (1992); and Land Court cases in: 1 L.C.R. 78 and 192 (1993), 2 L.C.R. 127 (1994), 4 L.C.R. 205 (1996), 7 L.C.R. 33 (1999), 8 L.C.R. 1 (2000).

street" was held not extinguished by removal of the garage.[2] An easement may of course be terminated by a voluntary recorded instrument of release or termination executed by the holder of the easement. Termination of an easement by "abandonment" by the holder is rarely found,[3] even when there has been adverse use or blockage of the easement, or subdivision of the dominant estate.[4] Compelling evidence of abandonment or physical blockage for a long time may result in termination of an easement.[5] Further, an easement may be terminated by "frustration" of its purpose, such as by taking of the servient estate and easements thereover,[6] or by "merger" when the dominant and servient estates come into common ownership.[7] And finally, there are powers of governmental authorities over private ways, including power to discontinue, as referred to in the following section.

§ 15:11 Public easements

An easement in favor of the public at large is usually established by a taking under the power of eminent domain. There may be easements, though not always designated as such, for sewers (M.G.L.A. c. 83), common landing places (M.G.L.A. c. 88), water mains, and a variety of other public facilities. The most common public easements are of course those for highways—federal, state and local. It may be noted that a landowner may "dedicate" a way to public use, but as specifically provided in M.G.L.A. c. 84, § 25, that does not make it a public way unless it is laid out and established in accordance with the law. The Appeals Court noted that prior to 1846 dedication to public use was effective to establish the status of public way, and that such status could be effected

[2]Hamouda v. Harris, 66 Mass. App. Ct. 22, 845 N.E.2d 374 (2006).

[3]Chopelas v. Plymouth Zoning Bd. of Appeals, 1 L.C.R. 78 (1993); Sea Rock Estate v. Sturt, 1 L.C.R. 102 (1993); Smith v. Leonard, 2 L.C.R. 127 (1994).

[4]King v. Nickerson, 3 L.C.R. 26 (1995); Kurtz v. Salter, 8 L.C.R. 113 (2000); Brooks v. Geraghty, 13 L.C.R. 154 (2005); Murray v. Sullivan, 13 L.C.R. 193 (2005); Sullivan v. Leonard, 13 L.C.R. 482 (2005).

[5]Yagjian v. O'Brien, 19 Mass. App. Ct. 733, 477 N.E.2d 202 (1985); Lasell College v. Leonard, 32 Mass. App. Ct. 383, 589 N.E.2d 342 (1992); Dyer v. Key, 4 L.C.R. 205 (1996); Merry v. White, 13 L.C.R. 339 (2005).

[6]New England Continental Media, Inc. v. Town of Milton, 32 Mass. App. Ct. 374, 588 N.E.2d 1382 (1992); New England Mutual Life Ins. Co. v. Agorianitis, 7 L.C.R. 33 (1999); Brooker v. Motiva Enterprises, LLC, 11 L.C.R. 102 (2003).

[7]Daly v. O'Pray, 3 L.C.R. 183 (1995).

by prescription.[1]

The laws on the subject are complex, diverse and in many respects, confusing. The problem is compounded because various authorities are given power not only to layout, accept, manage, repair, and discontinue public ways, but also power to layout, alter, repair and even discontinue, private ways. The complexity of the subject is well beyond the scope of this treatise, and it must suffice here to pass over the law of the federal highway system and to make note only of the principal Massachusetts sources of law.

The Massachusetts Turnpike is governed by M.G.L.A. c. 81A. All other state highways are governed by M.G.L.A. c. 81, administered by the Department of Highways, established by M.G.L.A. c. 16. Among the salient points in Chapter 81 are those relating to: access by abutters (§ 21); limited access highways (§ 7C); barring of adverse possession or prescription within highways (§ 22); removal of abutting vegetation (§ 14); The distinction between "discontinuance," reverting the state highway to a town way, and "abandonment," reverting title in the owner at the time of the taking (§ 12); and leasing for 99 years of "air rights" over state highways (§ 7L). The Department of Highways' authority with respect to private ways is covered by §§ 24 to 27A of Chapter 81.

Under M.G.L.A. c. 82, County Commissioners (insofar as they still exist) are authorized to layout ways between communities and within communities. With respect to abolished counties, all their interests in county roads have been transferred to their "successor councils of governments" or to the municipalities in which the roads are situated, with a number of specified exceptions.[2]

Under § 17 of Chapter 82 cities and towns are given concurrent jurisdiction within their own limits. A provision in § 1 of Chapter 82 limits the power of cities and towns to exclude motor vehicle traffic from their ways within 500 yards of an adjoining community without state approval. Power to layout, relocate and discontinue private ways is conferred on cities, towns and county commissioners by §§ 21, 29 and 30 of Chapter 82. Discontinuance is governed by § 32A. Powers with respect to footways and bicycle paths are covered in §§ 33 to 38. Provision is also made in M.G.L.A. c. 40, § 6N, for repair of private ways by cities and towns.

[Section 15:11]

[1]Martin v. Building Inspector of Freetown, 38 Mass. App. Ct. 509,

649 N.E.2d 779 (1995).

[2]Chapter 336, Acts of 2006.

A very important principle with respect to takings in general is that they are limited to the interest needed for the purpose of the taking to be fulfilled.[3] With respect to highway takings that means that only an easement for highway purposes is established by the taking unless the order of taking expressly takes the fee title. When the federal or state government lays out major highways, intended and expected to remain in service for long terms, and often specified as having limited access, the taking of the fee title does make sense. For takings of local or county highways, however, the practice of taking fee titles (by some communities in some eras) is of dubious value, and leads to serious complications when there is need for relocation or discontinuance.

TOPIC C: PRIVATE RESTRICTIONS

§ 15:12   Introduction

As stated in § 15:2, a restriction is an impediment or limitation on the use of property by the owner thereof, enforceable by some other person. Although enforceable only in equity, a restriction has been held to be an "equitable servitude" and a "property right," equivalent in that respect to an easement.[1] The applicable principles of equity were developed in the common law, and the use of restrictions as a planning tool has a long history in Massachusetts. In the 1850s the Back Bay area in Boston was created by filling in tidal mudflats adjacent to what is now the Charles River Basin. The Commonwealth sold lots in that area subject to a set of restrictions which are still reflected in the predominant architectural style, and which continued to have legal significance for many decades.[2]

As noted in § 15:1, the Restatement (Third) of Property: Servitudes, refers to "conditions," and that term is frequently related or even equated to restrictions. It should, however,

---

[3]Inhabitants of Town of Lexington v. Suburban Land Co., 235 Mass. 108, 126 N.E. 360 (1920); Leroy v. Worcester St. Ry. Co., 287 Mass. 1, 191 N.E. 39 (1934).

N.E. 244 (1917).

[2]Blakeley v. Gorin, 365 Mass. 590, 313 N.E.2d 903 (1974).

[Section 15:12]

[1]Riverbank Improvement Co. v. Chadwick, 228 Mass. 242, 117

be sharply distinguished from a common law "condition" on title for the breach of which a right of entry may be asserted.[3] As set forth in § 10:16, assertion of a right of entry or a possibility of reverter has been limited by statute, and while that time limitation has a similarity to time limits on restrictions, they are not related.

As described in the following sections of this chapter, a statutory time limitation on the enforceability of restrictions was first imposed in 1887. In 1961 further statutory provisions were adopted, incorporating equitable principles and setting additional limits of time and enforcement.

§ 15:13 Thirty-year limitation

M.G.L.A. c. 184, § 23, first adopted in 1887, provides that:

> Conditions or restrictions, unlimited as to time, by which the title or use of real property is affected, shall be limited to the term of thirty years after the date of the deed or other instrument or the date of the probate of the will creating them, except in cases of gifts or devises for public, charitable or religious purposes. This section shall not apply to conditions or restrictions existing on July sixteenth, eighteen hundred and eighty-seven, to those contained in a deed, grant or gift of the commonwealth, or to those having the benefit of section thirty-two.

It will be noted that restrictions existing prior to July 16, 1887, could have continued in effect forever, until the adoption of the 1961 statute discussed below.[1] The Back Bay restrictions were not only prestatute, they were imposed by deed of the Commonwealth. As for restrictions created thereafter, the statute has been applied in many cases.[2] The term "unlimited as to time" has been held to apply not only to the absence of a time limit but to a period or term which is indefinite.[3] It has been said that: "The word 'unlimited'

---

[3]Gray v. Blanchard, 25 Mass. 284, 8 Pick. 284, 1829 WL 1862 (1829); Carlson v. Czerpak, 3 L.C.R. 58 (1995).

[Section 15:13]

[1]Jones v. Murphy, 60 Mass. App. Ct. 1, 799 N.E.2d 595 (2003).

[2]Flynn v. Caplan, 234 Mass. 516, 126 N.E. 776 (1920); Riverbank Imp. Co. v. Bancroft, 209 Mass. 217, 95 N.E. 216 (1911); Burke

v. Metropolitan Dist. Commission, 262 Mass. 70, 159 N.E. 739 (1928); Snow v. Van Dam, 291 Mass. 477, 197 N.E. 224 (1935); Baker v. Seneca, 329 Mass. 736, 110 N.E.2d 325 (1953); Jones v. Murphy, 60 Mass. App. Ct. 1, 799 N.E.2d 595 (2003).

[3]Flynn v. Caplan, 234 Mass. 516, 126 N.E. 776 (1920); Burke v. Metropolitan Dist. Commission, 262 Mass. 70, 159 N.E. 739 (1928).

means without confines, unrestricted, boundless."[4] The specification of a statutory time period does not preclude denial of enforcement of restrictions at an earlier date on general equitable grounds.[5] Nor, of course, can a restriction be enforced when the statute of limitations on a violation thereof has long expired.[6]

Besides excepting restrictions created by deed of the Commonwealth, the 30-year limitation does not apply "in cases of gifts or devises for public charitable or religious purposes." Also note that the last clause in the statute was added in 1969, exempting conservation and other restrictions having the benefit of M.G.L.A. c. 184, § 32.

A covenant not to build or obstruct view seems to have a resemblance to an easement in that the beneficiary of the covenant has a right, at least of view, over the subject land. This was called a "negative easement," and has been held to be equivalent to a restriction, and therefore subject to the 30-year limitation.[7]

§ 15:14 The modern scheme

In 1961 §§ 26, 27, 28, 29 and 30 were inserted in M.G.L.A. c. 184,[1] and some modifications were subsequently adopted. These new sections in effect codified and elaborated equitable principles which had evolved over the years, and added procedural means of making the effect of restrictions clear, certain and definite in time.[2] Each of the sections has a particular role and function, as referred to below:

● **Section 26** sets the stage, so to speak, by specifying that §§ 26 to 30 shall apply to all restrictions, broadly defined, with specified exceptions. Section 26 also sets forth simple definitions of "subject land," "benefited land, and

[4]City of Boston v. Roxbury Action Program, Inc., 68 Mass. App. Ct. 468, 862 N.E.2d 763 (2007), review denied, 449 Mass. 1101, 865 N.E.2d 1140 (2007).

[5]Loud v. Pendergast, 206 Mass. 122, 92 N.E. 40 (1910).

[6]City of Boston v. Roxbury Action Program, Inc., 68 Mass. App. Ct. 468, 862 N.E.2d 763 (2007), review denied, 449 Mass. 1101, 865 N.E.2d 1140 (2007), a case in which the City sought to recover from its own bad management by pursuing contrived theories through the Land Court and the Appeals Court.

[7]Labounty v. Vickers, 352 Mass. 337, 225 N.E.2d 333 (1967); Myers v. Salin, 13 Mass. App. Ct. 127, 431 N.E.2d 233 (1982); but see Cotton v. Moscow, 8 L.C.R. 65 (2000).

[Section 15:14]

[1]Chapter 448, Acts of 1961, which also inserted new §§ 10A, 10B and 10C in M.G.L.A. c. 240, referred to in § **10:6**, and added provisions to 184A, § 3, and M.G.L.A. c. 260, § 31A, referred to in § **10:16**.

[2]Labounty v. Vickers, 352 Mass. 337, 225 N.E.2d 333 (1967).

"public records," as well as specification of adequacy of land description, and provisions as to "common scheme" restrictions. The precise terms of § 26 are important, and it is useful to consider them piecemeal. The first sentence provides that:

> All restrictions on the use of land or construction thereon which run with the land subject thereto and are imposed by covenant, agreement, or otherwise, whether or not stated in the form of a condition, in any deed, will or other instrument executed by or on behalf of the owner of the land or in any order of taking shall be subject to this section and sections twenty-seven to thirty, inclusive, except . . .

As indicated below, questions as to whether a restriction affected "use of the land" and the issue of "run with the land" have been considered by the courts. The "except" clauses are a bit more complicated, as follows:

> (a) restrictions in leases, mortgages and other security instruments, (b) restrictions in orders of taking by the commonwealth or a political subdivision or public instrumentality thereof made before January first, nineteen hundred and seventy and (c) conservation, preservation, agricultural preservation, and affordable housing restrictions, as defined in section thirty-one which have the benefit of section thirty-two, and other restrictions held by any governmental body, if the instrument imposing such conservation, preservation, agricultural preservation, affordable housing or other restriction is duly recorded and indexed in the grantor index in the registry of deeds or registered in the registry district of the land court for the county or district wherein the land lies so as to affect its title, and describes the land by metes and bounds or by reference to a recorded or registered plan showing its boundaries.

The clause as to "other restrictions held by a governmental body" leads to a definition of "governmental body," as follows:

> 'Governmental body', as referred to in this section and sections thirty-two and thirty-three, means the United States or the commonwealth, acting through any of its departments, divisions, commissions, boards or agencies, or any political subdivision or public instrumentality thereof or any public authority or any quasi-public entity or any instrumentality created pursuant to chapter forty F, whether acting for its own account, or as agent or designee for or assignees of any private individual or private entity which has been required to place such restriction in its chain of title as a condition to receiving financial or other assistance from the United States or the commonwealth, acting through any of its depart-

ments, divisions, commissions, boards or agencies, or any political subdivision or public instrumentality thereof or any public authority or any quasi-public entity or any instrumentality created pursuant to said chapter forty F.[3]

As to "gifts or devises for public, charitable or religious purposes" under § 23 and "other restrictions held by any governmental body" under § 26, it was held that a provision in a deed in 1947 from a City to the Boy Scouts that "the grantee shall never deed or grant the premises to any other than the grantor" was enforceable as a restriction exempt from the 50-year limitation in § 28 and from the 30-year limitation in § 23 because it was a gift for public or charitable purposes.[4]

As to common scheme restrictions, § 26 provides as follows:

Restrictions may be deemed imposed as part of a common scheme if imposed of record on various parcels in such manner that each owner is entitled to enforce the restrictions against the other parcels, although there may be variations in the restrictions among the various parcels. Unless the instrument imposing the restriction provides otherwise, it is to be presumed that a restriction imposed as part of a common scheme is enforceable for the benefit of any land only when such land either (a) is bounded by a street by which the subject parcel is bounded or (b) lies in a block surrounded by the same streets as the subject parcel, or (c) is contiguous to said block except for streets or ways.

This provision, and others in the succeeding sections of M.G.L.A. c. 184, indicate a degree of preferential protection for common scheme restrictions which had been developed in earlier case law. When there is evidence of a general scheme for restricting the use of lots carved out from a large tract, it has been held that the existence of such a scheme permits all lot owners in the area covered by the scheme to enforce the restrictions against all other lot owners who took their titles with notice of the scheme.[5] Notice of the scheme must be a matter of record in a purchaser's

---

[3]The "quasi-public entity" under M.G.L.A. c. 40F is a Community Development Finance Corporation, and evidently there may be such until July 1, 2010, pursuant to a repeal of that statute by Ch. 324, § 6, Acts of 1987; Ch. 528, § 6, Acts of 1990.

[4]Town of Chelmsford v. Greater Lowell Council, Inc.-Boy Scouts of America, 9 L.C.R. 225 (2001).

[5]Snow v. Van Dam, 291 Mass. 477, 197 N.E. 224 (1935); Guillette v. Daly Dry Wall, Inc., 367 Mass. 355, 325 N.E.2d 572 (1975).

actual chain of title, or the purchaser must have some other actual notice of it.[6] There are, however, circumstances in which a common scheme does not arise. If the restrictions do not appear to be intended for the benefit of land retained by the grantor, then the restrictions are merely a contract between the two parties to the deed, and grantees of other lots cannot enforce them.[7]

• **Section 27** applies to restrictions created after 1961, and limits the enforcement thereof as follows:

(a) The person seeking enforcement must be either a party to the instrument and stated therein to be benefited, or successor to such party, or the owner of an interest in benefited land which either adjoins the subject parcel or is described and stated to be benefited in the instrument creating the restriction. When these tests are not met, enforcement of a restriction is generally denied,[8] but the land court has indicated some latitude.[9]

(b) If it is not a common scheme restriction "applicable to four or more parcels contiguous except for any intervening streets or ways," in order to be enforced after 30 years from its creation, a "notice of restriction" must be recorded before the expiration of the 30 years and before the expiration of each succeeding 20-year period.

It is important to note that § 23 still applies: a restriction unlimited as to time expires in 30 years, as does a restriction for a stated term of 30 years, and neither can be "extended" by a notice of restriction under § 27. Although sometimes questioned, that proposition has been clearly confirmed.[10] Such an extension of enforceability is possible only if the instrument originally imposing the

[6]Roak v. Davis, 194 Mass. 481, 80 N.E. 690 (1907); Houghton v. Rizzo, 361 Mass. 635, 281 N.E.2d 577 (1972).

[7]Hill v. Levine, 252 Mass. 513, 147 N.E. 837 (1925); Lowell Inst. v. City of Lowell, 153 Mass. 530, 27 N.E. 518 (1891); Patrone v. Falcone, 345 Mass. 659, 189 N.E.2d 228 (1963).

[8]Rudnick v. Oppenheim, 3 L.C.R. 164 (1995); Fetterer v. Rock Ridge Lake Shores Property Owners Association, 6 L.C.R. 69 (1998); Old Harvard Estates Homeowners Association, Inc. v. Habitech, Inc., 6 L.C.R. 101 (1998); Chalet Suisse International, Inc. v. Town of Saugus, 6 L.C.R. 164 (1998); Brear v. Fagan, 447 Mass. 68, 849 N.E.2d 211 (2006).

[9]Samuel v. Scorton Shores Ass'n, Inc., 10 L.C.R. 11 (2002).

[10]Brear v. Fagan, 447 Mass. 68, 849 N.E.2d 211 (2006); Stop & Shop Supermarket Co. v. Urstadt Biddle Properties, Inc., 433 Mass. 285, 740 N.E.2d 1286 (2001); Jones v. Murphy, 60 Mass. App. Ct. 1, 799 N.E.2d 595 (2003).

restriction provides for a period of enforceability in excess of 30 years and the specified period is not "unlimited."

A "notice of restriction" must be signed by "a person then entitled of record to the benefit of the restriction", and must describe such person's benefited land, describe the subject land, name one or more persons then appearing of record as owners of the subject parcel, and state a recording reference to the instrument imposing the restriction.

(c) If the restriction is "imposed as part of a common scheme applicable to four or more parcels contiguous except for any intervening streets or ways," then it may be extended only if "provision is made in the instrument or instruments imposing it for extension for further periods of not more than twenty years at a time by owners of record, at the time of recording of the extension, of fifty percent or more of the restricted area in which the subject parcel is located," and if "an extension in accordance with such provision is recorded before the expiration of the thirty years or earlier date of termination specified in the instrument and names or is signed by one or more of the persons appearing of record to own the subject parcel at the time of such recording," and as for further extension, only if "a further like extension" is recorded within "twenty years, or the specified extension term if less than twenty years."

This provision is similar to that for non-common-scheme restrictions in that extension is possible only if the creating instrument provides for it, and extensions require recorded notice within 30 years of the creation of the restriction and each 20 years thereafter. It is more limiting, however, in that it requires participation of owners of 50% of the commonly "restricted area." The reference to the "subject parcel" does not detract from that, but suggests that 50% of the owners of the commonly restricted land may, if the creating instrument so allows, extend the restrictions piecemeal or selectively upon parcels within the restricted area.

• **Section 28** applies to restrictions created before 1962. In practical effect it sets a limit on the enforcement of restrictions of fifty years from the creation thereof. It does not supersede the thirty year limitation under § 23 and it does not allow "extension" to fifty years of a restriction for a specified period of less than fifty years.[11]

This statute contains no exception for restrictions imposed by deed of the Commonwealth, or for gifts or devises for public charitable or religious purposes. It is applicable thereto, but it has been held that it does not affect public charitable trusts.[12]

Restrictions imposed before 1962 for specified terms of more than fifty years are rare indeed. To the extent that they exist, the statute provides that they may continue to be enforced only if a notice of restriction is recorded before the expiration of fifty years, and each twenty years thereafter. The required notice of restriction is as provided in § 27.

In an unusual case, the land court considered a 1926 provision affecting registered land which imposed a "restriction" for 999 years prohibiting structures or plantings "as would obstruct the view of the water" from benefited parcels. No notice of restriction had been recorded. The land court held that the provision established an affirmative easement, not governed by the restriction statutes.[13] Actual extension of restrictions by agreement among the parties are of course valid.[14]

In the case of common scheme restrictions the requirements for extension of enforceability are similar but not identical to those specified in § 27. Under § 28 the notice of restriction to preserve enforceability of a common scheme restriction must (1) be signed by a person then entitled of record to the benefit of the restriction, and describe his benefited land, (2) describe the subject parcels, (3) specify the way or ways, public or open to public use, upon which each such parcel abuts, or nearest to which it is located and its street number if any, and (4) specify the instrument imposing the restriction and its recording reference.

The statute further provides that the record holder of a mortgage may sign in place of an owner if the notice, in addition to the foregoing, specifies the mortgage and its recording reference, and names one or more of the persons then appearing to own the land.

• **Section 29** deals solely with due recording or registration of a notice or extension of restriction under §§ 27 and

---

[11]Jones v. Murphy, 60 Mass. App. Ct. 1, 799 N.E.2d 595 (2003).

[12]Manning v. New England Mut. Life Ins. Co., 399 Mass. 730, 506 N.E.2d 870 (1987); Dunphy v. Com., 368 Mass. 376, 331 N.E.2d 883 (1975).

[13]Cotton v. Moscow, 8 L.C.R. 65 (2000).

[14]Moore v. Holt, 8 L.C.R. 304 (2000).

28, and the effectiveness thereof. It provides as follows:

> No notice or extension of restriction under sections twenty-seven or twenty-eight shall be effective against a subject parcel (a) if its title is registered, unless the notice or extension is noted on the certificate or certificates of title thereof or (b) if its title is not registered, unless (1) the notice or extension is indexed in the grantor index under the names of the persons named therein as owners of the subject parcel, (2) if the instrument imposing the restriction is recorded at a registry of deeds, the notice or extension is noted on the margin of the record of the instrument, and (3) if the instrument imposing the restriction is a will, a duplicate or certified copy of the notice or extension is filed with the records of the probate of the will. No notice under clause (b) of section twenty-eight shall be effective unless indexed in a special index which each register shall maintain arranged alphabetically by city or town and within each city or town, by the ways named, in which are listed the books and pages of record of the notices of restriction and of the instruments therein specified as creating them. Where an instrument imposes more than one restriction a notice or extension may, if it so specifies, apply only to a particular restriction or restrictions. A notice under section twenty-seven or twenty-eight may be given with respect to any number of parcels subject to the restriction and may be joined in by the owners of any number of parcels having the benefit thereof and may be signed in behalf of any person by an attorney or agent and on behalf of any person under disability by a guardian, conservator or parent. No notice given under section twenty-seven or twenty-eight shall entitle any person to enforce a restriction other than the person giving the notice and his successors in title, nor entitle anyone to enforce a restriction if at the time of recording of the notice the restriction is for any reason no longer enforceable.

The salient point is that the requirements are detailed and specific, such that strict application is to be expected, and careful drafting is therefore important.[15] The last clause is also important in view of the statutory articulation of equitable principles relating to enforcement of restrictions.

• **Section 30** turns from procedural matters to substantive considerations with respect to enforcement of restrictions. There are two basic touchstones. The first point is that enforcement of the restriction must be "of actual and substantial benefit" to the person seeking enforcement. The statute states a presumption against the existence of such benefit, and spells out exceptions and

---

[15]Lariviere v. Peat Meadows   Association, Inc., 9 L.C.R. 95 (2001).

criteria for rebutting that presumption. The second point is that, even when there is such benefit, enforcement of the restriction may be limited to award of money damages unless specified equitable criteria are met. The details of the criteria are important in both cases.

As to the presumption against actual benefit, the first exception therefrom is that it does not apply "in cases of gifts or devises for public, charitable or religious purposes." A planning board was held to be a governmental body entitled to enforce restrictions without holding benefited land.[16] The second exception is that it applies only if the subject land (or part thereof) lies in a city or town with a population of over 100,000. In smaller communities a plaintiff does not have to overcome a contrary presumption, but must still show actual and substantial benefit. Since some Massachusetts communities may hover around the 100,000 population mark, the enforcement of restrictions therein may pose special problems for plaintiffs and courts.

When the presumption against actual benefit does apply, the person seeking enforcement may overcome it by meeting one or more of the following tests: (1) When imposed, the restriction was not more burdensome as to "lot size, density, building height, setback, or other yard dimensions" than those applicable by restrictions on the benefited land; (2) The restriction is part of a common scheme applicable to four or more parcels contiguous except for any intervening streets or ways to land "purported to be benefited thereby"; or (3) a simple showing that the "restriction is in favor of contiguous land of the grantor," the word "grantor" presumably being intended to mean the person who first imposed the restriction.

With respect to limitation to award of money damages, the statute provides as follows:

> No restriction determined to be of such benefit shall be enforced or declared to be enforceable, except in appropriate cases by award of money damages, if (1) changes in the character of the properties affected or their neighborhood, in available construction materials or techniques, in access, services or facilities, in applicable public controls of land use or construction, or in any other conditions or circumstances, reduce materially the need for the restriction or the likelihood of the restriction accomplishing its original purposes or render it obsolete or inequitable to enforce except by award of money damages, or (2) conduct

---

[16]Murphy v. Planning Bd. of   Hopkinton, 14 L.C.R. 143 (2006).

of persons from time to time entitled to enforce the restriction has rendered it inequitable to enforce except by award of money damages, or (3) in case of a common scheme the land of the person claiming rights of enforcement is for any reason no longer subject to the restriction or the parcel against which rights of enforcement are claimed is not in a group of parcels still subject to the restriction and appropriate for accomplishment of its purposes, or (4) continuation of the restriction on the parcel against which enforcement is claimed or on parcels remaining in a common scheme with it or subject to like restrictions would impede reasonable use of land for purposes for which it is most suitable, and would tend to impair the growth of the neighborhood or municipality in a manner inconsistent with the public interest or to contribute to deterioration of properties or to result in decadent or substandard areas or blighted open areas, or (5) enforcement, except by award of money damages, is for any other reason inequitable or not in the public interest.

These provisions are of course at the heart of the equitable considerations that courts must take into account when asked to enforce a restriction. Pertinent cases are discussed in § 15:15.

Section 30 of M.G.L.A. c. 184 ends with the provision that: "Nothing herein shall prevent a court from issuing a temporary injunction or restraining order pending determination of enforceability of a restriction."

§ 15:15   Interpretation and enforcement

In several cases decided after M.G.L.A. c. 184, § 30, was adopted, restrictions considered in light thereof were upheld and specifically enforced, based upon findings of actual benefit, common scheme, and intent.[1] However, when the SJC denied enforcement to the old Commonwealth Restrictions affecting Back Bay, the decision prompted a sharp dissent by two Justices.[2] The majority conceded that it was settled law in Massachusetts that restrictions of that type established

---

[Section 15:15]

[1]Walker v. Sanderson, 348 Mass. 409, 204 N.E.2d 108 (1965); Harrod v. Rigelhaupt, 1 Mass. App. Ct. 376, 298 N.E.2d 872 (1973); Gulf Oil Corp. v. Fall River Housing Authority, 364 Mass. 492, 306 N.E.2d 257 (1974) (abrogated by, Bennett v. Commissioner of Food and Agriculture, 411 Mass. 1, 576 N.E.2d 1365 (1991)).

[2]Blakeley v. Gorin, 365 Mass. 590, 313 N.E.2d 903 (1974).

"property interests in land,"[3] but held that § 30 was not unconstitutional, and its enforcement did not constitute a taking. The court found enforcement of those restrictions not to be equitable or in the public interest, and remanded only for assessment of money damages for loss of light and air which would result from construction contrary to the restrictive provisions. The dissent deemed the denial of specific enforcement of the restrictions to be a taking of a valuable property right.

In later cases the courts have sometimes found restrictions to be of substantial benefit to those seeking enforcement,[4] sometimes not,[5] and in the cited cases the land court has construed and applied particular restrictive provisions. A restriction on a lot in effect prohibiting its joint development with adjoining property was rejected by the SJC[6] as not being of benefit to the land, but only of personal benefit to the owner, aimed at achieving a "hold up price."

The case of *Atwood v. Walter*[7] involved a developer's "Declaration of Covenants, Restrictions and Reservations" which included a restriction requiring residences in the subdivision to have wood shingle roofs. The Appeals Court carefully considered all of the provisions in M.G.L.A. c. 184, § 30, and held the restriction to be of substantial benefit to plaintiff and enforceable in kind against the defendant who had replaced his roof with asphalt shingles. However, the plaintiff-developer had also replaced the roof of his own house with asphalt shingles, and the court gave him ten days to opt between an order that both houses be reshingled with wood roofs, or dismissal of the case with prejudice.

An example of "instruments [that] might have been drafted with greater precision" is found in *Well-Built Homes, Inc. v. Shuster*.[8] In a divorce settlement allocating lots in a subdivision the husband and wife had created it was provided that

---

[3]Riverbank Improvement Co. v. Chadwick, 228 Mass. 242, 117 N.E. 244 (1917).

[4]Cogliano v. Lyman, 370 Mass. 508, 348 N.E.2d 765 (1976); Exit 1 Properties Ltd. Partnership v. Mobil Oil Corp., 44 Mass. App. Ct. 571, 692 N.E.2d 115 (1998); Connaughton v. Payne, 56 Mass. App. Ct. 652, 779 N.E.2d 683 (2002); Talbot v. DuPrat, 4 L.C.R. 134 (1996); Cape Cod Conservatory of Music and Arts, Inc., 8 L.C.R. 472 (2001); Tage Associates Limited Partnership v.

Katz, 10 L.C.R. 245 (2002); Weston Design and Development Corp. v. Rojik, 13 L.C.R. 28 (2005).

[5]Hess v. Gilson, 4 L.C.R. 98 (1996); Bresnick v. Lautenberg, 8 L.C.R. 127 (2000); McGarr v. Dugas, 11 L.C.R. 135 (2003).

[6]Garland v. Rosenshein, 420 Mass. 319, 649 N.E.2d 756 (1995).

[7]Atwood v. Walter, 47 Mass. App. Ct. 508, 714 N.E.2d 365 (1999).

[8]Well-Built Homes, Inc. v.

"there will be restrictions and obligations imposed upon all the buildable lots . . . which have yet to be prepared," in accordance with further, also indefinite, specifications and limitations. This was followed by deeds, resubdivision, sale of some of the lots by the wife to a developer, and its recording of a declaration of restrictions. Upon elaborate analysis the Appeals Court held that the divorce agreement did run with the land, reversing the Land Court, and that the developer could impose restrictions affecting the husband's lots, remanding to the Land Court for determination of the substance of acceptable restrictions.

§ 15:16 Touch and concern

Related to other equitable principles is the old concept that in order for a restriction to be enforceable, it must "touch and concern" the land. The common law principle that a restriction which did not "touch and concern" the land itself did not run with the land and could not be enforced against subsequent owners was well established in Massachusetts.[1] However, that concept became outmoded and in disfavor, particularly with respect to business non-competition restrictions which were deemed to be of increasing value and importance in a competitive economy. Following a forewarning in 1967,[2] the SJC in 1979 held that henceforth reasonable covenants against competition may be considered to run with the land when they "serve a purpose of facilitating orderly and harmonious development for commercial use."[3] Non-competition restrictions have subsequently been upheld and enforced.[4] A peculiar provision rendering void a geographical non-competition provision in any agreement with a psychologist was enacted by Chapter 209, Acts of 2004.

As referred to in the above § 15:9, the courts have sometimes indicated a willingness to reconsider other com-

Shuster, 64 Mass. App. Ct. 619, 834 N.E.2d 1213 (2005).

[Section 15:16]

[1]Norcross v. James, 140 Mass. 188, 2 N.E. 946 (1885) (overruled by, Whitinsville Plaza, Inc. v. Kotseas, 378 Mass. 85, 390 N.E.2d 243 (1979)); Shade v. M. O'Keeffe, Inc., 260 Mass. 180, 156 N.E. 867 (1927) (overruled by, Whitinsville Plaza, Inc. v. Kotseas, 378 Mass. 85, 390 N.E.2d 243 (1979)).

[2]Shell Oil Co. v. Henry Ouellette & Sons Co., 352 Mass. 725, 227 N.E.2d 509, 25 A.L.R.3d 888 (1967) (overruled by, Whitinsville Plaza, Inc. v. Kotseas, 378 Mass. 85, 390 N.E.2d 243 (1979)).

[3]Whitinsville Plaza, Inc. v. Kotseas, 378 Mass. 85, 390 N.E.2d 243 (1979).

[4]Exit 1 Properties Ltd. Partnership v. Mobil Oil Corp., 44 Mass. App. Ct. 571, 692 N.E.2d 115 (1998).

mon law rules concerning the creation, validity and enforce-ment of servitudes.

§ 15:17   Time limits

In addition to the time limitations on enforcement of restrictions discussed in preceding sections of this Chapter, there is a specific statute of limitations on certain types of enforcement, set forth in M.G.L.A. c. 184, § 23A, as follows:

> No action, suit, or proceeding shall be maintained either at law or in equity in any court to recover damages or to compel the removal, alteration, or relocation of any structure by rea-son of any violation of any private restriction or condition in the nature of a restriction by which the use of real property is affected in regard to: (a) building set-back requirements from front, side, or rear property lines, (b) the size, type, number of dwelling units, or number of stories of any structure, (c) the addition of any porch, garage, sign, bay window or similar ad-dition, or the location or construction of any driveway, fence or wall, or (d) the materials used or the expenditures made for construction, unless such action, suit, or proceeding is com-menced within six years next after the completion of such building, addition or other construction.

> For the purposes of this section, the record of assessment of any house or other structure for taxation shall be prima facie evidence of the completion of such house or structure by the first day of January of the year of assessment.

> This section shall not be construed as extinguishing, limit-ing or abridging any defense against any such action, suit or proceeding which would otherwise be available nor as affect-ing sections nineteen to twenty-three, inclusive, or sections twenty-four to thirty, inclusive.

The six-year limitation on suit applies to recovery of money damages as well as to specific structural enforcement. The statute leaves some questions open which courts may have to resolve. It does not relate to all structures, but only speci-fied elements, which include the "number of stories," but not height, and specific or "similar" additions, but not every addition. The provisions that this section does not affect "de-fenses" or specified sections of Chapter 184 further il-lustrates the limited scope of this statute.

§ 15:18   Protected subjects

Chapter 184 contains §§ 23C and 23D providing as follows:

> Section 23C. "Any provision in an instrument relative to the ownership or use of real property which purports to forbid or unreasonably restrict the installation or use of a solar energy system as defined in section one A of chapter forty A or the building of structures that facilitate the collection of solar

energy shall be void."

Section 23D. "Any restriction, reservation, condition, exception, or covenant in any subdivision plan, deed or other instrument of or pertaining to the transfer, sale, lease or use of property which would permit residential use of property but would prohibit a community residence for disabled persons shall, to the extent of such prohibition, be void."

§ 15:19   Discrimination

Section 23B of Chapter 184 provides that:

> A provision in an instrument relating to real property which purports to forbid or restrict the conveyance, encumbrance, occupancy, or lease thereof to individuals of a specified race, color, religion, national origin or sex shall be void. Any condition, restriction or prohibition, including a right of entry or a possibility of reverter, which directly or indirectly limits the use for occupancy of real property on the basis of race, color, religion, national origin or sex shall be void, excepting a limitation on the basis of religion on the use of real property held by a religious or denominational institution or organization or by an organization operated for charitable or educational purposes which is operated, supervised or controlled by or in connection with a religious organization.

As pointed out in § **10:16**, this provision also applies to possibilities of reverter and rights of entry. Restrictions discriminating on racial or ethnic grounds, once rather common in Massachusetts as well as elsewhere in the United States, have long been held unenforceable on constitutional grounds of equal protection. Laws with respect to discrimination on grounds of age, sex and sexual orientation are of more recent provenance, and obviously controversial in some respects, although perhaps less so in relation to real estate dispositions.

General laws of broad scope against discrimination are set forth in M.G.L.A. c. 151B. Provisions with respect to housing accommodations are found in §§ 4, 6 and 7. Protected persons include those with disabilities or impairments. Enforcement powers are vested in the Massachusetts Commission Against Discrimination and in Boston, the Boston Fair Housing Commission.

A prohibition of discrimination on grounds of marital status was held to impinge upon the constitutional rights of free speech of defendants who had refused to rent quarters to an unwed cohabiting couple.[1] A public housing authority was allowed to evict a tenant, elderly and disabled, who had persisted in disruptive, noisy actions after repeated attempts at mediation.[2]

Both federal law and provisions in Chapter 151B allow for housing specifically limited to persons of age 55 or over, or 62 or over, there being two categories of exemption from laws against age discrimination. A zoning by-law authorizing developments limited to persons aged 55 or older and the eviction therefrom of younger persons was upheld.[3] The size of parcels eligible for such elderly housing was changed for some communities by special Acts.[4] A minimum of 5 acres for such use was eliminated in 2006 and replaced with a requirement of biennial registration with the Department of Housing and Community Development.[5] Provisions intended to accommodate such age related exemption in a condominium are set forth in Section 17 of **Appendix N**.

An act of 1675 which prohibited Indians from being in Boston was repealed in 2005.[6]

TOPIC D: PUBLIC RESTRICTIONS

§ 15:20 Introduction

Restrictions for the purposes of conservation, agricultural preservation, historic preservation, watershed preservation and affordable housing are provided for in §§ 31, 32 and 33 of M.G.L.A. c. 184, first enacted in 1969 and supplemented since then. The original aim of the statutes was to insulate conservation restrictions from the infirmities of private restrictions under the common law and the statutes discussed above. The other types of restrictions deemed worthy of such protection were added later.

These are herein referred to as "public restrictions," differing from private restrictions in several respects. The differences are recognized in the statutes governing "private restrictions," including § 23 and §§ 26 to 30 of Chapter 184.

[Section 15:19]

[1]Attorney General v. Desilets, 418 Mass. 316, 636 N.E.2d 233 (1994).

[2]Andover Housing Authority v. Shkolnik, 443 Mass. 300, 820 N.E.2d 815 (2005).

[3]Town of Northborough v. Collins, 38 Mass. App. Ct. 978, 653 N.E.2d 598 (1995).

[4]Chapter 415, Acts of 2004; Chapter 429, Acts of 2004.

[5]Chapter 291, Acts of 2006.

[6]Chapter 25, Acts of 2005.

All of the public restrictions have the benefit of § 32 of Chapter 184 and are specifically excepted in § 23 from the 30-year limitation therein and in § 26 from all of the provisions in §§ 26 to 30.

In short, such public restrictions may be imposed for and continue to be effective for unlimited and unspecified time periods; they run with the land regardless of other tests thereof, they are generally free from attack on equitable grounds, and specifically, as provided in § 32, they need not meet any tests of privity of estate or contract.

Section 31 defines the various types, § 32 sets forth the legal requirements for their validity and protection, and § 33 provides for the special recording thereof in the registries of deeds.

Section 15:24 describes an entirely different kind of "public restriction."

§ 15:21 Definitions

The definitions of these restrictions set forth in § 31 are as follows:

• **Conservation Restriction:** "a right . . . appropriate to retaining land or water areas predominantly in their natural, scenic or open condition or in agricultural, farming or forest use, to permit public recreational use, or to forbid or limit any or all (a) construction or placing of buildings, roads, signs, billboards or other advertising, utilities or other structures on or above the ground, (b) dumping or placing of soil or other substance or material as landfill, or dumping or placing of trash, waste or unsightly or offensive materials, (c) removal or destruction of trees, shrubs or other vegetation, (d) excavation, dredging or removal of loam, peat, gravel, soil, rock or other mineral substance in such manner as to affect the surface, (e) surface use except for agricultural, farming, forest or outdoor recreational purposes or purposes permitting the land or water area to remain predominantly in its natural condition, (f) activities detrimental to drainage, flood control, water conservation, erosion control or soil conservation, or (g) other acts or uses detrimental to such retention of land or water areas."

• **Preservation Restriction** (referring to historic preservation): "a right . . . appropriate to preservation of a structure or site historically significant for its architecture, archeology or associations, to forbid or limit any or all (a) alterations in exterior or interior features of the structure, (b) changes in appearance or condition of the site, (c) uses not historically appropriate, (d) field investigation, as defined in section twenty-six A of chapter nine, without a permit as provided by section twenty-seven C of said chapter, or (e) other acts or uses detrimental to appropriate preservation of the structure or site."

• **Agricultural Preservation Restriction:** "a right . . . appropriate to retaining land or water areas predominately in their agricultural farming or forest use, to forbid or limit any or all (a) construction or placing of buildings except for those used for agricultural purposes or for dwellings used for family living by the land owner, his immediate family or employees; (b) excavation, dredging or removal of loam, peat, gravel, soil, rock or other mineral substance in such a manner as to adversely affect the land's overall future agricultural potential; and (c) other acts or uses detrimental to such retention of the land for agricultural use."

• **Watershed Preservation Restriction:** "a right . . . appropriate to retaining land predominantly in such condition to protect the water supply or potential water supply of the commonwealth, to forbid or limit any or all (a) construction or placing of buildings; (b) excavation, dredging or removal of loam, peat, gravel, soil, rock or other mineral substance except as needed to maintain the land and (c) other acts or uses detrimental to such watershed."

• **Affordable Housing Restriction:** "a right . . . appropriate to (a) limiting the use of all or part of the land to occupancy by persons, or families of low or moderate income in either rental housing or other housing or (b) restricting the resale price of all or part of the property in order to assure its affordability by future low and moderate income purchasers or (c) in any way limiting or restricting the use or enjoyment of all or any portion of the land for the purpose of encouraging or assuring creation or retention of rental and other housing for occupancy by low and moderate income persons and families."

In each case it is provided that such a right may arise "whether or not stated in the form of a restriction, easement, covenant or condition in any deed, mortgage, will, agreement, or other instrument executed by or on behalf of the owner of the land." With respect to conservation restrictions and historic preservation restrictions, the statute also recognizes that they may be established by an "order of taking."

With respect to conservation restrictions and affordable housing restrictions it is provided that they may be "either in perpetuity or for a specified number of years." With respect to an agricultural preservation restriction, it is provided that it "shall be in perpetuity except as released under the provisions of section thirty-two," and also provided that: "All other customary rights and privileges of ownership shall be retained by the owner including the right to privacy and to carry out all regular farming practices." Similarly, with respect to a watershed preservation restriction it is provided that it "shall be in perpetuity except as released under the provisions of section thirty-two," and that: "All other customary rights and privileges of ownership shall be retained by the owner including the right to privacy."

Further, with respect to affordable housing restrictions it is also provided that: "Without in any way limiting the scope of the foregoing definition, any restriction, easement, covenant or condition placed in any deed, mortgage, will, agreement or other instrument pursuant to the requirements of [various specified programs for low and moderate income housing] or pursuant to the requirements of any regulations or guidelines promulgated pursuant to any of the foregoing, shall be deemed to be an affordable housing restriction within the meaning of this paragraph."

It may be observed that the definition of a conservation restriction encompasses or includes much of the definition of an agricultural preservation restriction. The choice between one or the other may depend on the particular goals or on application for state or federal funding for the purpose of protection of agricultural lands.

It may also be noted that, while the statute permits restrictions for a term of years, in order to be qualified for a federal income tax deduction, a conservation restriction must be perpetual.

§ 15:22 Legal status; enforcement; termination

Section 32 of Chapter 184 provides that, if specified requirements are met, no restriction of any of these types "shall be unenforceable on account of lack of privity of estate or contract or lack of benefit to particular land or on account of the benefit being assignable or being assigned to any other governmental body or to any charitable corporation or trust with like purposes, or on account of the governmental body the charitable corporation or trust having received the right to enforce the restriction by assignment."

The requirements begin with the type of entity by which the restriction is held. The entity may be "any governmental body" or "a charitable corporation or trust" whose purposes include appropriate activities. The appropriate purposes are: with respect to a conservation, agricultural or watershed restriction, "conservation of land or water areas or of a particular such area"; with respect to a historical preservation restriction, "preservation of buildings or sites of historical significance or of a particular such building or site"; with respect to an affordable housing restriction, "creating or retaining or assisting in the creation or retention of affordable rental or other housing for occupancy by persons or families of low or moderate income."

The other requirements relate to governmental approval of the restriction. If the restriction is held by a city or town or an instrumentality thereof, then the required approval is by the Secretary of Environmental Affairs for a conservation restriction; the Commissioner of the MDC for a watershed restriction; the Commissioner of Food and Agriculture for an agricultural restriction; the Massachusetts Historical Commission for a historical preservation restriction; or the Director of Housing and Community Development for an affordable housing restriction.

If the restriction is held by a charitable corporation or trust, then it must be approved by the mayor or city manager and city council, or the selectmen or town meeting of a town, and also by the pertinent one of the state officials above specified.

The specified state officials generally have subordinate officers who perform the approval function for them. DEP has a standard form for its approval. If one encounters delays in obtaining such approvals and the donor of the restriction is facing a tax deadline, it may be worthwhile to record the restriction without the approvals and re-record it later when the approvals are obtained.

Section 32 also sets forth enforcement provisions, the right of the holder of the restriction to reasonable entry on the land, the power of the Department of Telecommunications and Energy to make takings for utility lines over so restricted lands, and for release of such restrictions.

Release of such a public restriction requires a public hearing and approvals by the mayor or city manager and city council, or selectmen of a town, and by the state-level official whose approval was required to establish the restriction. Additional requirements apply in certain cases: If the restriction was established with the application of state funds, then release is limited to repurchase by the land owner "at its then current fair market value." An agricultural preservation restriction may be released "only if the land is no longer deemed suitable for agricultural or historical purposes." The statute does not say who is authorized so to "deem." A

watershed preservation restriction may be released only if
the Commissioner of the MDC and the Secretary of Environmental Affairs deem it "to no longer be of any importance to
the water supply or potential water supply of the
commonwealth." In either of the latter cases a release may,
alternatively, be approved by "two-thirds of both branches of
the general court, by a vote taken by yeas and nays," for the
public good.

The language as to two-thirds vote by yeas and nays tracks
that of Article XLIX (as amended by Article XCVII) of the
Amendments to the Massachusetts Constitution, but the
actual provisions of § 32 of Chapter 184 make it clear that
the constitutional requirement is not applicable. Although
legislative action for release of a conservation restriction is
not required, adoption of a special act for that purpose has
often been sought and obtained.

Enforcement of public restrictions has been considered in
a number of cases. A conservation restriction was held to be
too vague, lacking description of the affected land, but the
SJC later reversed itself and upheld the restriction.[45] The
compliance of particular structures to the terms of a conservation restriction were considered as to a fence,[46] a swimming pool,[47] and a walkway over marshland.[48] The scope of
authority of the Commissioner of Food and Agriculture under
the terms of an agricultural preservation restriction was upheld in one case,[49] rejected in another.[50] The courts rejected
allegations of laches and waiver, and ordered removal of a
barn erected in violation of a conservation restriction.[51]

§ 15:23 Recording

Section 33 of Chapter 184 provides for the establishment
and use of a "public restriction tract index" in the registries
of deeds in which public restrictions may be indexed with
reference to appropriate maps. Such maps may also be used
for indexing of orders or licenses issued by a governmental
body, the boundaries of historic or architectural control
districts under M.G.L.A. c. 40C, landmarks certified under
M.G.L.A. c. 9, § 27, and other data concerning titles or
interests in land of governmental bodies. The implementation of this statute is not mandatory and has not been widely
accomplished.

Since public restrictions establish an interest in land by
the holder, it is important that they be duly recorded in the
registry of deeds and indexed so as to appear in the chain of
title of the land owner, since they constitute encumbrances
on title.

§ 15:24 Environmental restrictions

As mentioned in § 13:18, M.G.L.A. c. 21E, § 6 authorizes the use of restrictions as a device for control of property which has been subjected to environmental contamination. Under the Massachusetts Contingency Plan (MCP) this is implemented by means of so-called Activity and Use Limitations (AUL). These may be imposed by order of the Department of Environmental Protection, by a grant of an Environmental Restriction or by a Notice of Activity and Use Limitation. Forms of such documents are provided in 310 CMR 40.1099. Each of these forms calls for specification of prohibited and permitted activities and uses, aimed at implementing cleanup, avoidance of further contamination and exclusion of risks to public health and safety. The Environmental Restriction is a more formal document, requiring approval of DEP and including a grant of easements to DEP. The Notice form may be executed by the property owner and a Licensed Site Professional. Both forms call for description of the property and title reference. The restrictions may be in perpetuity or for a specified number of years. Similarly to conservation and preservation restrictions, the statute provides that such an AUL shall not "be unenforceable on account of lack of privity of estate or contract or lack of benefit to particular land," adding "or on account of the benefit being assignable or being assigned to any other governmental body, provided that such restrictions or assignments are approved by the commissioner of the department."

Part IV

FORMS OF OWNERSHIP

Chapter 16

Individual and Business Forms

TOPIC A: INDIVIDUAL FORMS

TOPIC B: BUSINESS FORMS

TOPIC C: TRUSTS AND NOMINEES

> **KeyCite®:** Cases and other legal materials listed in KeyCite Scope can be researched through the KeyCite service on Westlaw®. Use KeyCite to check citations for form, parallel references, prior and later history, and comprehensive citator information, including citations to other decisions and secondary materials.

TOPIC A: INDIVIDUAL FORMS

§ 16:1   Sole ownership

The ownership of real estate by a single individual poses

no legal issues of form. At common law and under early statutes a married woman could own property, but could not convey real estate without her husband's consent. One may occasionally encounter an old deed in which the grantors are "John Doe and Mary Doe, his wife, in her own right," which indicates that it is the wife's separate property being conveyed. Separate ownership by a married woman has been statutorily protected since 1855. Dower and curtesy were eliminated as of January 1, 1966, by M.G.L.A. c. 189, § 1, and either a husband or a wife may convey his or her own property without any joinder or release by the other. As referred to in § **16:5**, equality in a tenancy by the entirety was enacted in 1979.

An individual who does business in his own name, owning the real and personal assets of the business in his own name, is taxed on the income and losses of the business on Schedule C of his own Form 1040. Operating losses of a sole proprietorship may be carried back two years and forward twenty years.[1] IRAs and other retirement plans are available to sole proprietorships.

§ 16:2　Homestead

M.G.L.A. c. 188, § 1, provides that a "homestead estate" may be acquired by the "owner or owners of a home" (or lessees) "who occupy or intend to occupy said home as a principal residence," but "that only one owner may acquire an estate of homestead in any such home for the benefit of his family." The statute goes on to provide that "For the purposes of this chapter, an owner of a home shall include a sole owner, joint tenant, tenant by the entirety or tenant in common," and that "the word 'family' shall include either a parent and child or children, a husband and wife and their children, if any, or a sole owner."

In response to a federal court which found the statute to be "internally inconsistent," the SJC held a declaration of homestead by a husband and wife to be valid as to the husband, the first to sign, and the wife's signature to be a legal nullity.[1] Homestead exemptions have been upheld notwithstanding faulty filing.[2]

A homestead estate is exempt from attachment and debts

[Section 16:1]

[1]26 U.S.C.A. § 172(b)(1).

[Section 16:2]

[1]Dwyer v. Cempellin, 424　Mass. 26, 673 N.E.2d 863 (1996).

[2]In re Cempellin, 175 B.R. 1 (Bankr. D. Mass. 1994); Shamban v. Masidlover, 429 Mass. 50, 705 N.E.2d 1136 (1999).

with certain exceptions. Since the exceptions include "a debt contracted prior to the acquisition of said estate of homestead," the date of the homestead declaration and the amount of the homestead estate thereby established are important. The amount of the homestead estate was increased from $50,000 to $60,000 in 1983, to $100,000 in 1985, to $300,000 as of November 2, 2000, and to $500,000 as of October 28, 2004.[3] The figures apply to the owner's equity in the property, not the total value including prior existing mortgage debt.[4] Issues of the status of a debt as prior to the homestead have been considered.[5]

A homestead estate may be established by designation in the deed by which the property is acquired or by a separate recorded declaration. The statute makes special provisions for protection of persons over age 62 "regardless of marital status" and for disabled persons. It also includes a "manufactured home" (see § 14:12) in the eligible property, with respect to which the filing is with the city or town clerk.

It has been held that a trust is not eligible even if the principal beneficiary occupies the property as his residence.[6] It was also held that a declaration of homestead by one co-tenant cannot bar partition by the other co-tenants.[7]

§ 16:3 Tenancy in common

The basic characteristic of a tenancy in common is that the tenants have separate fractional interests in the whole, with no survivorship among them. Each tenant in common may convey or devise his separate interest.[1] Tenants in common do have some duty to each other, and it is a principle of common law that each of several tenants in common is entitled to the possession and use of the property.[2] In the usual context that would mean that one of several tenants in common who gives a lease would be obligated to account to his co-tenants. As a corollary of the principle it is said that

---

[3]Chapter 218, Acts of 2004.

[4]M.G.L.A. c. 188, § 6; In re Giarrizzo, 128 B.R. 321 (Bankr. D. Mass. 1991).

[5]Gruet v. F.D.I.C., 879 F. Supp. 153 (D. Mass. 1995); Winsper v. Winsper, 4 L.C.R. 13 (1996); In re Weinstein, 164 F.3d 677 (1st Cir. 1999).

[6]Assistant Recorder of North Registry Dist. of Bristol County v. Spinelli, 38 Mass. App. Ct. 655, 651

N.E.2d 411 (1995).

[7]Ladd v. Swanson, 24 Mass. App. Ct. 644, 511 N.E.2d 1112 (1987).

[Section 16:3]

[1]Altobelli v. Montesi, 300 Mass. 396, 15 N.E.2d 463 (1938).

[2]Altobelli v. Montesi, 300 Mass. 396, 15 N.E.2d 463 (1938); Goldsmith v. Barron, 288 Mass. 176, 192 N.E. 509 (1934).

co-tenants may not have adverse possession against each other, but that is not categorically true. If possession by one tenant in common is sustained long enough and is adverse enough to constitute an ouster, that tenant may thereby acquire title against his co-tenants.[3] Upon a claim adequately sustained by the evidence, co-tenants were held to hold title upon a resulting trust for one of them.[4]

§ 16:4   Joint tenancy

The essence of joint tenancy is the right of survivorship. On the death of one joint tenant the surviving joint tenants take the entire estate in the property by virtue of the joint estate created by the original conveyance, and not by virtue of a transfer taking effect upon the death of the first tenant.[1] There is no limitation on the number of persons who may be joint tenants, and the title passes by survivorship successively to the last survivor, who takes the whole. Obviously only natural persons may be joint tenants, since corporations and other entities cannot "survive."

At common law there was a preference for joint tenancy, but that was overturned by statute as early as 1785. Since then the opposite has been true and the law has expressed "the public policy of the commonwealth that joint tenancies are looked upon with disfavor."[2] M.G.L.A. c. 184, § 7, provides expressly that: "A conveyance or devise of land to two or more persons or to husband and wife, except a mortgage or a devise or conveyance in trust, shall create an estate in common and not in joint tenancy, unless it is expressed in such conveyance or devise that the grantees or devisees shall take jointly, or as joint tenants, or in joint tenancy, or to them and the survivor of them, or unless it manifestly appears from the tenor of the instrument that it was intended to create an estate in joint tenancy." Because of that it is customary, if not compulsory, to create a joint tenancy by convey-

---

[3]Nickerson v. Nickerson, 235 Mass. 348, 126 N.E. 834 (1920); Allen v. Batchelder, 17 Mass. App. Ct. 453, 459 N.E.2d 129 (1984); Duncan v. DiFranco, 2 L.C.R. 85 (1994).

[4]Simmons v. Smith, 20 Mass. App. Ct. 775, 482 N.E.2d 887 (1985).

[Section 16:4]

[1]Chippendale v. North Adams Savings Bank, 222 Mass. 499, 111

N.E. 371 (1916); Attorney General v. Clark, 222 Mass. 291, 110 N.E. 299 (1915); Foster v. Smith, 211 Mass. 497, 98 N.E. 693 (1912).

[2]Pineo v. White, 320 Mass. 487, 70 N.E.2d 294 (1946); Fulton v. Katsowney, 342 Mass. 503, 174 N.E.2d 366 (1961).

ance to A and B "as joint tenants and not as tenants in common" or "as joint tenants with the right of survivorship." In any event, express words are necessary to create a joint tenancy. The words "share and share alike, or to the survivor" and a conveyance to two persons as "tenants for life, remainder to their heirs forever" were held to created interests in common and not in joint tenancy.[3]

The same statute contains other provisions expressly relating to tenancy by the entirety, considered below, and also provides that: "In a conveyance or devise to three or more persons, words creating a joint tenancy shall be construed as applying to all of the grantees, or devisees, regardless of marital status, unless a contrary intent appears from the tenor of the instrument." This provision of the statute became effective on July 22, 1973, and earlier conveyances or devises similarly phrased may have created a tenancy by the entirety between married couples among the grantees or devisees.

In 1979 another amendment of M.G.L.A. c. 184, § 7, was made, providing: "A conveyance or devise of land to two persons as tenants by the entirety, who are not married to each other, shall create an estate in joint tenancy and not a tenancy in common." This provision is applicable only to conveyances and devises after August 30, 1979, it having been held previously that such a conveyance created a tenancy in common.[4]

As to mortgages, the statutory exception serves as a rule of construction under which several mortgagees may be determined to hold jointly or in common, depending on the circumstances. The exception as to devise or conveyance in trust applies to the trustees, not the beneficiaries, but the wording of the trust may make the beneficiaries joint tenants as well.[5]

At common law a joint tenancy could not arise unless all of the joint tenants acquired their interests together, meeting the "four unities" of time, title, interest and possession.[6] To achieve that, deeds to a straw and back are still used to

---

[3]Cross v. Cross, 324 Mass. 186, 85 N.E.2d 325 (1949); Hurley v. A'Hearn, 338 Mass. 695, 157 N.E.2d 223 (1959); Knight v. Travell, 13 Mass. App. Ct. 1008, 433 N.E.2d 464 (1982).

[4]Bernatavicius v. Bernatavicius, 259 Mass. 486, 156 N.E. 685, 52 A.L.R. 886 (1927); Fuss v. Fuss, 373 Mass. 445, 368 N.E.2d 276 (1977).

[5]Bowditch v. Attorney General, 241 Mass. 168, 134 N.E. 796, 28 A.L.R. 713 (1922); Collier v. Napierski, 357 Mass. 516, 258 N.E.2d 789 (1970).

[6]Dane v. Delaney, 125 F. Supp. 594 (D. Mass. 1954).

create joint tenancies among persons who, or some of whom, already have interests in the property. While that common law rule has been considerably softened, it should not be regarded as wholly repealed by M.G.L.A. c. 184, § 8 which provides: "Real estate, including any interest therein, may be transferred by a person to himself jointly with another person in the same manner in which it might be transferred by him to another person, and a conveyance of real estate by a person to himself and his spouse as tenants by the entirety shall create a tenancy by the entirety."

A joint tenancy is terminated by conveyance by any one of the joint tenants of his interest in the joint tenancy, which constitutes the grantee a tenant in common, although the remaining owners are still joint tenants with right of survivorship among themselves.[7] The same is true if the interest of a joint tenant is taken or sold by his creditor; that is, the creditor or its purchasers become a tenant in common with the remaining tenant or tenants, who remain joint tenants among themselves. A joint tenancy may also be terminated by an action of partition, in which a presumption of equality of interests may be overcome by contrary evidence.[8]

§ 16:5   Tenancy by the entirety

This form of joint tenancy may exist only between husband and wife.[1] It derived from the common law concept of the unity of a husband and wife as one person, and constituted a single indivisible estate in the couple and the survivor.[2] It differs from the ordinary form of joint tenancy only in that it may not be severed or terminated by the voluntary conveyance of either spouse to a third person. Beyond that, not much remains of the common law concepts, most of which have been disposed of by statutes, particularly the concept of masculine control of the "unity."

Under M.G.L.A. c. 184, § 8, quoted above, a tenancy by the entirety may be created by a deed from one spouse to both. A tenancy by the entirety may be terminated by conveyance of

---

[7]Attorney General v. Clark, 222 Mass. 291, 110 N.E. 299 (1915); Foster v. Smith, 211 Mass. 497, 98 N.E. 693 (1912); Dwyer v. Cempellin, 424 Mass. 26, 673 N.E.2d 863 (1996).

[8]Moat v. Ducharme, 28 Mass. App. Ct. 749, 555 N.E.2d 897 (1990).

[Section 16:5]

[1]Morris v. McCarty, 158 Mass. 11, 32 N.E. 938 (1893).

[2]Licker v. Gluskin, 265 Mass. 403, 164 N.E. 613 (1929).

one spouse to the other.[3] It is also terminated by divorce, and thereupon becomes a tenancy in common,[4] although other provision for disposition of martial property may be made by the court having jurisdiction over the divorce.[5]

A common law feature of tenancy by the entirety was the entitlement of the husband to the possession of the premises and to the rents and profits thereof during the joint lives of husband and wife.[6] That feature was abolished by a 1979 amendment of M.G.L.A. c. 209, § 1, which now reads as follows: "The real and personal property of any person shall, upon marriage, remain the separate property of such person, and a married person may receive, receipt for, hold, manage and dispose of property, real and personal, in the same manner as if such person were sole. A husband and wife shall be equally entitled to the rents, products, income or profits and to the control, management and possession of property held by them as tenants by the entirety. The interest of a debtor spouse in property held as tenants by the entirety shall not be subject to seizure or execution by a creditor of such debtor spouse so long as such property is the principal residence of the nondebtor spouse; provided, however, both spouses shall be liable jointly or severally for debts incurred on account of necessaries furnished to either spouse or to a member of their family."

Under § 1A, added to Chapter 209 in 1989, pre-1979 tenancies by the entirety were permitted to become subject to § 1 by an election by a recorded instrument. As time goes on, pre-1979 ownerships become more rare, but the somewhat confusing cases still need to be considered, as discussed in § **16:6**.

As noted above, the statutory disfavor of joint tenancies applies to a deed to a husband and wife, which creates a tenancy in common unless a contrary intention is expressed. Before 1973 a conveyance to a husband and wife as joint tenants was construed to create a tenancy by the entirety, but M.G.L.A. c. 184, § 7, now provides that: "A conveyance or devise of land to a person and his spouse which expressly states that the grantees or devisees shall take jointly or as joint tenants, or in joint tenancy, or to them and the survivor of them shall create an estate in joint tenancy and not a tenancy by the entirety." The statute does, however, provide

---

[3]Hale v. Hale, 332 Mass. 329, 125 N.E.2d 142 (1955).

[4]Bernatavicius v. Bernatavicius, 259 Mass. 486, 156 N.E. 685, 52 A.L.R. 886 (1927).

[5]Finn v. Finn, 348 Mass. 443, 204 N.E.2d 293 (1965).

[6]Collins v. Croteau, 322 Mass. 291, 77 N.E.2d 305 (1948).

that: "A devise of land to a person and his spouse shall, if the instrument creating the devise expressly so states, vest in the devisees a tenancy by the entirety."

§ 16:6 Survivorship

One may have heard a suggestion (not often from a lawyer) that it is advantageous to hold property in joint ownership in order to "avoid probate." It is clear, however, to practitioners in the real estate and probate fields that joint ownership more often creates problems than solves them, and it is never a substitute for estate planning.

When one of several joint owners dies, the presumption is made, with important exceptions, for estate tax purposes, both federal and state, that the entire value of the jointly owned property is includable in the decedent's estate.[1] The presumption may be rebutted, but only by clear and convincing proof, which is frequently lacking, of contribution to the cost of the property by the surviving owners out of funds which were not provided by the decedent.

The exceptions to the foregoing relate to property owned by husband and wife as tenants by the entirety or as joint tenants. If there are no estate planning reasons to the contrary, it may well be advisable for a husband and wife to own their residence as joint tenants or tenants by the entirety. Under 26 U.S.C.A. § 2040(b) only one-half of the value of property so owned is includable in the estate of the first to die of the spouses. The exemption provided in M.G.L.A. c. 65, § 1, is of an "interest arising or accruing by survivorship of a husband or wife in a tenancy by the entirety or joint tenancy" either (a) "in single family residential property occupied by such husband and wife as a domicile," to the extent of the value of the property, or (b) "in multiple family residential property so occupied," to the extent of $25,000 of its value.[2]

§ 16:7 Creditors' claims in probate

As noted in § 16:4, a creditor of a joint tenant who takes his interest in the property thereby severs the joint tenancy and becomes a tenant in common. His interest then is not affected by any right of survivorship.

With respect to a tenancy by the entirety, however, the

[Section 16:6]

[1]I.R.C. § 2040(a); M.G.L.A. c. 65, § 1.

[2]See Evans v. Commissioner of Corporations and Taxation, 339 Mass. 754, 162 N.E.2d 310 (1959).

creditor is subject to some limitations. In the first place, both § 1 and § 1A of M.G.L.A. c. 209 were held not to have retroactive effect.[1] However, a filing under § 1A made after an attachment was held valid.[2] A federal tax lien may possibly reach the interest of the non-taxed spouse.[3] It was held that the statute bars "seizure or execution," but not attachment.[4] On the other hand the wife's interest in a common law tenancy by the entirety could not be attached, and the statutes did not change that.[5] A mortgage by a husband alone was held to be valid, but subject to defeasance if title passed to his wife as survivor.[6] The statute does not protect against debts for necessaries furnished to either spouse or a member of their family, which may call for some judicial interpretation.[7]

TOPIC B: BUSINESS FORMS

§ 16:8 General partnership

The law of partnership has its origins in the common law, arising out of the actions and intentions of the parties doing business together, and leading to the principles of mutual agency and mutual liability. Partnership is now largely defined and governed by statute, the Massachusetts version of the Uniform Partnership Act being set forth in M.G.L.A. c. 108A.

There are explicit statutory rules for determining the existence of a partnership. It must be a voluntary association of two or more persons to carry on a business for profit. Carrying on a business involves the risk of loss as well as the possibility of profit, and both must be shared for a partnership to exist. The sharing of profits alone is prima facie evidence of the existence of a partnership, subject to explicit statutory exceptions to such inference, but joint tenancy, tenancy in common, tenancy by the entirety or other shared ownership

---

[Section 16:7]

[1]Turner v. Greenaway, 391 Mass. 1002, 459 N.E.2d 821 (1984); Maynard Realty Corporation v. Testa, 12 L.C.R. 1 (2004).

[2]Patriot Portfolio, LLC v. Joseph, 7 L.C.R. 130 (1999).

[3]U.S. v. Rodgers, 459 U.S. 1031, 103 S. Ct. 438, 74 L. Ed. 2d 597 (1982).

[4]Peebles v. Minnis, 402 Mass. 282, 521 N.E.2d 1372 (1988).

[5]Levy v. Crawford, 33 Mass. App. Ct. 932, 600 N.E.2d 597 (1992).

[6]Coraccio v. Lowell Five Cents Sav. Bank, 415 Mass. 145, 612 N.E.2d 650 (1993).

[7]See Veterans' Agent of Randolph v. Rinaldi, 21 Mass. App. Ct. 901, 483 N.E.2d 829 (1985).

does not of itself establish a partnership, even if profits are shared. Sometimes joint tenants or tenants in common do share both the expenses and income of the property, and it may not be clear whether they intend to carry on a business or to constitute themselves as partners.[1] In such a case there may be no mutual agency, and one dealing with them should require all to sign.

The principle of mutual agency is also statutorily defined, and there are express exceptions as to acts "not apparently for the carrying on of the business of the partnership in the usual way" and as to other specified acts of kinds which are not ordinarily regarded as being in the usual course of business. The statutory provisions as to agency and apparent authority have been held to be substantially an expression of the common law.[2]

Partners hold title to property as tenants in partnership, also a common law form now defined by statute. The incidents of such tenancy include (a) equal rights among the partners to possession of partnership property for partnership purposes, but no right of possession for other purposes, (b) nonseverability of any partner's interest in partnership property, (c) exemption of a partner's interest from attachment or execution except on a claim against the partnership, and non-eligibility for homestead exemption, (d) survivorship among partners, and (e) exemption of a partner's interest from dower, curtesy or any allowance to widows, heirs or next of kin.

As to survivorship, the partnership property vests in the surviving partners, and the estate of the decedent partner is entitled to an accounting.[3] The death of a partner causes dissolution, but it is quite common, of course, for partnership agreements to provide for continuance of the business by the surviving partners. The conveyancer may well encounter situations in which he will need to make a careful study and application of particular provisions of the statute relating to dissolution and winding up of the partnership, or to continuation of the business by the surviving partners.

The term "joint venture" usually designates a partnership formed for a particular purpose or project. The participants often wish to avoid any appearance of mutual agency or

---

[Section 16:8]

[1]Bova v. Clemente, 278 Mass. 585, 180 N.E. 611 (1932).

[2]Warner v. Modano, 340 Mass. 439, 164 N.E.2d 904 (1960); Century

Indem. Co. v. Bloom, 329 Mass. 508, 109 N.E.2d 166 (1952).

[3]Cavazza v. Cavazza, 317 Mass. 200, 57 N.E.2d 558 (1944); Wellman v. North, 256 Mass. 496, 152 N.E. 886 (1926).

ostensible authority between themselves except in relation to the specific property or project which they are jointly undertaking.[4] For that purpose a nominee trust may sometimes be used, or an ad hoc instruments of limitation of authority may be recorded as a control device.

A partnership is not a taxable entity, but is a conduit through which income, gains, losses, deductions and credits are passed through to the several partners. When a person contributes money or property to a partnership in exchange for an interest in the partnership, he does not thereby realize any gain or loss for tax purposes. Losses of a partnership may be passed through to the partners to the extent of the particular partner's investment in the partnership, including not only money and property contributed, but also the partner's share of partnership liabilities, subject to "at risk" and "passive loss" rules. Partnerships file federal information returns on Form 1065, and furnish their partners with Schedule K-1, which individual partners use to complete Schedule E to their own Form 1040s.

§ 16:9   Limited partnership

A limited partnership is not a common law entity, but is a statutory creation.[1] Nevertheless, it has its roots in the common law of partnership, and the statute provides expressly that: "Except as provided in this chapter, a general partner of a limited partnership is subject to the liabilities of a partner in a partnership without limited partners and, except as provided in this chapter or in the partnership agreement, has the rights and powers and is subject to the restrictions of a partner in a partnership without limited partners." The words "except as provided" or "unless otherwise provided" are characteristic of this statute, and the obvious result is that one dealing with a limited partnership must always carefully consider the provisions of the partnership agreement and the certificate of limited partnership for their own substantive terms and for compliance with the statute. The essence of a limited partnership is that the limited partners are *not* liable for the debts or actions of

---

[4]Eastern Elec. Co. v. Taylor Woodrow Blitman Const. Corp., 11 Mass. App. Ct. 192, 414 N.E.2d 1023 (1981).

[Section 16:9]

[1]M.G.L.A. c. 109, the Massachusetts version of the Uniform

Limited Partnership Act.

the partnership and do not have mutual agency. There must be at least one general partner who is so liable, and if there are more than one general partners, they have mutual liability and agency. Approval of all limited partners is required for admission of a new general partner.

A limited partnership is formed by the filing of a certificate of limited partnership with the office of the secretary of state. Among the provisions of the act which are of particular interest to a conveyancer are: (1) a requirement that the name of any limited partnership include those words in full, without abbreviation; (2) a requirement that the limited partnership maintain an office in Massachusetts and keep there a current list of names and addresses of partners, a copy of the certificate of limited partnership and all amendments thereto, and other records, and (3) specified events which causes a general partner to cease to be such, "unless otherwise provided in the certificate of limited partnership."

The office of the secretary of state will provide a certificate, somewhat akin to a corporate certificate of legal existence, and Land Court rules require the filing thereof for dealing with registered land by a limited partnership. Under M.G.L.A. c. 110, § 6, no filing of a business name certificate is required for a limited partnership with those words in its name.

In the case of *Wagley v. Danforth*,[2] the court reviewed the origin and purposes of clauses in a limited partnership agreement, weighed them against statutory provisions and concluded that unanimous agreement of the general partners was required for a sale of the partnership's real estate, and held the sale void, there not having been unanimous agreement. Limited partners may have rights, like those of shareholders in a corporation, to maintain derivative action against the general partners.[3]

The taxation of a limited partnership and its partners is the same in most respects as for a general partnership. Under the "at risk" rules only debt that is completely nonrecourse to the partnership may be included in the partners' bases for their partnership interests.

§ 16:10 LLP

Amendments of M.G.L.A. c. 108A and c. 109, effective in

---

[2]Wagley v. Danforth, 46 Mass. App. Ct. 15, 702 N.E.2d 822 (1998).

[3]See Smyth v. Marshall Field, Fifth, 40 Mass. App. Ct. 625, 666 N.E.2d 1008 (1996).

1996, provided for limited liability partnerships. In an LLP, a partner is not liable "directly or indirectly, including, without limitation, by way of indemnification, contribution, assessment or otherwise, for debts, obligations and liabilities of or chargeable to such partnership, whether in tort, contract or otherwise arising while the partnership is a registered limited liability partnership," except for liability arising from the partner's "own negligence, wrongful acts, errors or omissions." It is further provided that the liability of a partner in a LLP engaged in rendering professional services shall not be less than that of a shareholder in a M.G.L.A. c. 156A professional corporation engaged in rendering such services. The SJC has set forth Rule 3.06 on the use of limited liability entities by professional organizations.[1]

Registration is accomplished by a filing with the Secretary of State, stating the name of the partnership, including LLP or the like, the address of its principal office, its federal employer identification number and a brief statement of its business or profession, and certain additional information for a professional services LLP. The registration may also name the partners authorized to execute instruments affecting real estate. There are a filing fee and an annual report fee. Foreign registered LLPs may register in and do business in Massachusetts.

There is provision for issuance by the State Secretary of a certificate of good standing, certifying as to legal existence, payment of all required fees, and the identity of partners named in the registration as authorized to act with respect to real property instruments. Any recordable instrument executed in the name of an LLP by a partner identified in the registration as so authorized is binding in favor of all persons relying thereon in good faith, "notwithstanding any inconsistent provisions of the partnership agreement, side agreements among the partners, by-laws or rules, resolutions or votes of the registered limited liability partnership."

§ 16:11   Corporation

The characteristics of a corporation which have made it the most widely used form of business entity are limited liability and the simple fact that it constitutes a legal person. The basic source of corporate authority and power is statutory. Business corporations are governed by M.G.L.A. c. 156D, adopted in 2003 as the Massachusetts version of the

---

[Section 16:10]

[1]421 Mass. 1306 (1995).

uniform business corporations act.[1] Section 17.01 thereof makes Chapter 156D applicable to all corporations whether formed before or after 1994, with certain exceptions as to specialized types of corporations. Its predecessors, Chapters 155, 156 and 156B, have not been repealed, and may still have applicability in certain respects. Chapter 156D contains provisions with respect to foreign corporations, and former Chapter 181 was repealed.

Many other chapters of the General Laws apply to specialized types of corporations: Chapter 156A, professional corporations; Chapters 157 and 157A, cooperative corporations; Chapter 158, "certain miscellaneous corporations"; Chapters 159, 159A and 159B, various common carriers; Chapter 160, railroads; Chapter 161, street railways; Chapter 161A, Massachusetts Bay Transportation Authority; Chapters 161B, 161C and 161D, other transportation facilities; Chapter 162, electric railroads; Chapter 163, trackless trolley companies; Chapter 164, corporations for manufacture and sale of gas and electricity; Chapter 164A, New England power pool; Chapter 165, water and aqueduct companies; Chapter 166, telephone and telegraph companies; Chapter 166A, CATV systems; Chapter 167A to 167H, Chapters 168, 169, 170, 171, 172 and 172A, various banks and credit unions; Chapters 175 and 175G, insurance companies; Chapter 176, fraternal benefit societies; Chapter 176A to 176P, various medical, insurance and legal service corporations; Chapter 67, religious corporations; Chapter 114, cemetery corporations; Chapter 121A, urban redevelopment corporations, Chapter 121B, housing authorities, and Chapter 121C, economic development corporations.

Chapters 180 and 180A govern non-profit membership corporations. In addition some corporations were organized by special acts of the legislature and derived their powers therefrom.

The powers of a business corporation to hold, purchase, convey, mortgage or lease real estate for business purposes are broadly granted in M.G.L.A. c. 156D, § 3.02, unless otherwise provided in the articles of organization. Such a limitation in the articles of organization of a corporation formed under the earlier statute was considered.[2] Under § 2.06 of Chapter 156D the by-laws may contain any provi-

---

[Section 16:11]

[1]Chapter 127, § 17, Acts of 2003; Chapter 178, Acts of 2004, amended a number of other statutes to coordinate them with Chapter 156D.

[2]Moseley v. Briggs Realty Co., 320 Mass. 278, 280, 69 N.E.2d 7 (1946).

sion not inconsistent with law or the articles of organization. As to the adoption of by-laws for some specialized corporations M.G.L.A. c. 155, § 7 may still have pertinence.

For federal tax purposes most business corporations are classified as C corporations, the income of which is taxed to it, not its stockholders. C corporations report their taxable income on Form 1120, and report dividends paid to stockholders on Form 1096, (to the IRS), and on Form 1099 (to stockholders). Stockholders report dividends received as income on Form 1040, Schedule B.

A great variety of pension plans, profit sharing plans and stock bonus plans are available to C corporations, as well as other benefits which a corporation may offer employees without taxability to them, such as medical cost coverage, group term life insurance and death benefits, all subject to statutory limitations. Accumulation of income and distribution upon liquidation both call for careful attention by knowledgeable tax counsel.

Some corporations are classified as S corporations, a status achieved by election of the stockholders, which makes it a pass-through to the stockholders of income, gains, losses deductions and credits, instead of a taxable entity at the corporate level. It is in this respect similar to a partnership. There are limitations with respect to pass-through of capital gains and losses. S corporation status is available only if (a) the corporation has no more than 100 stockholders, (b) all stockholders are individuals, or certain acceptable estates or trusts, (c) no stockholder is a non-resident alien, (d) there is only one class of stock (although the class may have differing voting rights), and (e) all of the stockholders consent.

For Massachusetts income tax purposes, there is no such thing as a pass-through corporation. An S corporation and its stockholders are taxed the same as if it were a C corporation.[3]

§ 16:12 LLC

M.G.L.A. c. 156C[1] provides for the creation of limited liability companies in Massachusetts and the registration of foreign limited liability companies doing business in

---

[3]M.G.L.A. c. 63, §§ 29 and 32D.

[Section 16:12]

[1]Enacted by Ch. 281, Acts of 1995, effective January 1, 1996.

Massachusetts. This form of organization affords limited liability to the owners, referred to as members, along with pass-through taxation like a partnership, although taxation as a corporation may in some circumstances result from corporate-like features or may possibly be elected.

The entity, formed by at least two members, is created upon filing of a simple certificate of organization with the secretary of state, specifying the name of the company, including LLC or the like, and minimal other data. The members need not be named in the certificate, but any manager(s) must be. It is not mandatory that persons authorized to execute documents affecting real estate be named, but it is advisable to do so for conveyancing purposes.

The structure, operation and financial details may be set forth in an operating agreement which is not filed with the commonwealth. There are filing fees and an annual report fee. An LLC is a legal entity which may hold title to real estate in its own name. The interests of the members are personalty, and they have no interest in properties owned by the LLC. The statute provides for issuance of a certificate of good standing, which covers legal existence, payment of requisite fees, and identification of managers and persons authorized to execute real estate documents.

Any recordable instrument executed in the name of an LLC by a person identified in such a certificate as authorized to execute real estate documents is binding in favor of all persons relying thereon in good faith, notwithstanding any inconsistent provisions of the operating agreement, side agreements, by-laws or rules, regulations or votes of the LLC. An LLC may consolidate or merge with other business entities, such action to be specified in a certificate filed with the secretary of state, but such filing may be subsequent to the effectiveness of the consolidation or merger. Furthermore, an LLC may be dissolved by actions or occurrences which would not appear on records of the secretary. Consequently, conveyancers will need to look to certifications by the managers and their counsel.

§ 16:13 Massachusetts business trust

The principal characteristics of a so-called Massachusetts business trust are that it has divisible transferable shares of beneficial interest and that the shareholders constitute a voluntary association for the conduct of a business enterprise under the management of the trustees. Such associations are governed by provisions of M.G.L.A. c. 182. It is possible to create a trust with transferable shares but without any

association of the beneficiaries, whose interests are only equitable and who have no legal power or control over the
management of the trust or choice of the trustees.[1] In that
case it would not be subject to M.G.L.A. c. 182 and would
not have the characteristics of a corporation which a true
business trust has.

The formation of the business trust requires the filing of a
copy of the trust instrument with the secretary of state and
the city or town clerk of each municipality in which the association has a place of business. The usual business of such
trusts is in real estate and the instrument creating the trust
is also ordinarily recorded in the registry of deeds.[2] Evidence
of issuance of shares need not be recorded in order to make a
trust effective. Such a trust may not be named so as to
conflict with any corporate names; it may be sued and its
property is subject to attachment and execution "in like manner as if it were a corporation, and service of process upon
one of the trustees shall be sufficient," and it may have a
seal. Nevertheless, such a trust is not a legal entity, and it is
the trustees, not the trust, who have power to act and
contract.[3] The trustees' powers are defined by the trust
instrument, which may be deemed analogous to a corporate
charter and broadly construed.[4] The rule of unanimity for actions of trustees still applies except as the trust instrument
expressly provides otherwise. And a trustee is personally liable for his contracts unless the other party thereto expressly
agrees to look only to the trust property.[5] Mere reference to
himself as "trustee" will not absolve him of liability,[6] and in
addition to signing "as trustee as aforesaid and not individually," it is usually advisable to set forth an express non-
recourse clause.

The "association" of shareholders of such a trust usually
consists of their common interest in the business of the trust
and their power to elect the trustees. In order that the

[Section 16:13]

[1]Bouchard v. First People's Trust, 253 Mass. 351, 148 N.E. 895 (1925); Pope & Cottle Co. v. Fairbanks Realty Trust, 124 F.2d 132 (C.C.A. 1st Cir. 1941).

[2]Swartz v. Sher, 344 Mass. 636, 184 N.E.2d 51 (1962).

[3]Peterson v. Hopson, 306 Mass. 597, 29 N.E.2d 140, 132 A.L.R. 1 (1940); Griswold v. U.S., 36 F. Supp. 714 (D. Mass. 1941), judgment aff'd, 124 F.2d 599 (C.C.A. 1st Cir. 1941); Commissioner of Corporations and Taxation v. City of Springfield, 321 Mass. 31, 71 N.E.2d 593 (1947).

[4]Bomeisler v. M. Jacobson & Sons Trust, 118 F.2d 261 (C.C.A. 1st Cir. 1941).

[5]Tebaldi Supply Co. v. Macmillan, 292 Mass. 384, 198 N.E. 651 (1935).

[6]Larson v. Sylvester, 282 Mass. 352, 185 N.E. 44 (1933).

shareholders not become liable as partners, they should not, however, participate in the management of the business.[7]

Such trusts are required to file annual reports with the secretary of state specifying the name of the trust, the addresses of its places of business in Massachusetts and elsewhere, the number of its outstanding shares and the names and addresses of the trustees.

For federal income tax purposes a trust with transferable shares is treated the same as a C corporation in substantially all respects. For Massachusetts purposes, however, it is given hybrid treatment: its income is taxed to it as if it were an individual, but in relation to reorganization or liquidation it is in some respects treated as if it were a corporation.[8]

TOPIC C: TRUSTS AND NOMINEES

§ 16:14   Trusts

Besides business trusts, discussed in the previous section, and nominee trusts, discussed below, other forms of trust are often found of record in Massachusetts. Many of these are intended for purposes of real estate management or estate planning, some carefully drawn by lawyers skilled in the fields, and some concocted ad hoc with little attention to appropriate refinements. Those with deficiencies or lack of clarity lead to litigation.[1]

Some of the basic elements of trusts with respect to purchase and sale transactions have been discussed in § **1:14**, and land court requirements are discussed in § **8:9**. The statutes dealing with "unrecorded" trusts or amendments thereof, as referred to in § **10:22**, indicate a desire of conveyancers not to be burdened with the intricacies of trust law. Nevertheless, as stated therein, failure to record trust instruments is generally an indication of a conveyancing

---

[7]Williams v. Inhabitants of Milton, 215 Mass. 1, 102 N.E. 355 (1913).

[8]M.G.L.A. c. 62, §§ 1(j), 8, 10(c). See Marco Realty Trust v. Commissioner of Revenue, 385 Mass. 798, 434 N.E.2d 200 (1982).

[Section 16:14]

[1]National Shawmut Bank of Boston v. Joy, 315 Mass. 457, 53 N.E.2d 113 (1944); Harrison v. Marcus, 396 Mass. 424, 486 N.E.2d 710 (1985); Kirby v. Board of Assessors of Medford, 350 Mass. 386, 215 N.E.2d 99 (1966); Roberts v. Roberts, 419 Mass. 685, 646 N.E.2d 1061 (1995).

lapse. While it is not necessary for a conveyancer to become an authority on the extensive law of trusts, it is important to understand the basics, and to be able, when a trust is encountered of record, to determine who the trustees are, that they are properly in office, and that they have the power and authority to take the actions they purport to take.

§ 16:15 Nominees

There is a difference between a "straw" and a "nominee." A straw was defined as one who holds a naked title for the benefit of another.[1] He is not a trustee or an agent, and has no powers, duties or obligations except to revest the title in the true owner. The traditional qualifications of a straw were absolute reliability, such limited financial status as to be essentially judgment-proof, and exemplary conduct so as to be an unlikely defendant either in contract or tort. For one reason or another it became harder to find available individuals, and the corporate straw was introduced. But then the strictures of tax laws made it cumbersome and risky to leave title of income producing and depreciable real estate in a corporation which was not the owner.

Individual and corporate straws are sometimes used as a "pass-through" to hold title momentarily or for a short term for the purpose of changing the form of ownership among several persons, or of executing a note and mortgage where the loan transaction is a non-recourse one. In the latter case, however, it is generally simpler, more straightforward and preferable in all respects to have the principal who is the borrower sign all of the documents and to set forth therein specific and precise nonrecourse provisions.

When, however, there is need to hold title for more than a moment in a name other than that of the principal or beneficial owner, that role may be fulfilled by a so-called nominee trust.[2] Nominee trusts are used typically when the beneficiaries are: (a) a group of widely scattered heirs or other tenants in common who have selected one of their number or their attorney to deal with the property, (b) a partnership with a complex structure of general partners, including possibly foreign corporations, or (c) an individual or corporation having diverse business or investment interests with need for the nominee to serve as one of several "hats." Since it is

---

[Section 16:15]

[1]Collins v. Curtin, 325 Mass. 123, 89 N.E.2d 211 (1949); Sandler v. Scullen, 290 Mass. 106, 194 N.E. 827 (1935); Cohen v. Simon, 304 Mass. 375, 23 N.E.2d 863 (1939).

[2]A form of nominee trust is set forth in **Appendix R**.

not necessary to record a designation of beneficiaries, a nominee trust may serve the sometimes dubious purpose of concealing the identity of the true owners. The usual purpose, however, is simply convenience and ease of dealing with record title and property management when there are multiple owners.

A nominee trust differs from a traditional straw in several respects. The trustees do have an active trusteeship function; they are, at least to some extent, agents of the principals, and in many instances the trustee or trustees are one or more of the actual principals.

The primary characteristic of a nominee trust is that the trustees are therein prohibited from exercising any of their specified powers except as and in the manner that they are specifically authorized and directed to do so by the beneficiaries in writing. Variants have been devised by lawyers, providing that some powers may be exercised without beneficiary authorization and some only when there is such authorization, or providing that all powers may be exercised unless the beneficiaries specify otherwise. Such variants are not always well-drafted or clear in their intent or effect.

In view of the prohibition on action without beneficiary authorization, nominee trusts usually contain a so-called bootstrap clause whereby the trustees' own certification that they have been so authorized and directed is conclusive and may be relied upon by third persons dealing with them. Variants of the bootstrap clause have also been devised, also with mixed results. Cautious lawyers usually require not only a trustees' certification of authorization by the beneficiaries, which is recorded with the documents on the transaction, but also a certification signed by the beneficiaries themselves that they have so authorized the trustees, which is usually not recorded.

While a nominee trust is ordinarily seen as an agency of the beneficiaries,[3] it may also contain provisions which take effect as in an ordinary or "true" trust.[4] In some instances a nominee trust was found to have little or no effect on the beneficiaries rights: Income tax deductions were allowed to beneficiaries for losses incurred on property held in nominee trusts.[5] The tort liability limit on charities protected the ben-

---

[3]Apahouser Lock and Sec. Corp. v. Carvelli, 26 Mass. App. Ct. 385, 528 N.E.2d 133 (1988).

[4]Roberts v. Roberts, 419 Mass. 685, 646 N.E.2d 1061 (1995).

[5]Druker v. State Tax Commission, 374 Mass. 198, 372 N.E.2d 208 (1978), with a dissent by Braucher,

eficiary of a nominee trust.[6] A federal tax lien on the beneficiary of a nominee trust (who was also the trustee) was held not to reach the trust property.[7] On the other hand, an individual who was entitled to a real estate tax exemption lost it by putting his property in his name as trustee of a nominee trust.[8]

A purchase and sale agreement may not bind the trust when signed by the trustee of a nominee trust without authority,[9] or when signed by the trustee without disclosure that he was acting as trustee of a nominee trust.[10]

A mortgage signed on behalf of a nominee trust by a person not appointed trustee in accordance with its terms was held unenforceable.[11] A lender was not permitted to reach the property of a nominee trust of which the beneficiaries were liable on the debt,[12] but that may turn on the parties' intent.[13] The guarantor of a debt did not protect his property from the lender's claim by putting it into a nominee trust because he failed to make any designation of beneficiaries, nullifying the trust.[14]

A nominee trust is not a federally taxable entity. Any income, gains or losses of such a trust pass through to the beneficiaries and are reportable by them. The trust itself should report as a grantor trust on a separate statement attached to Form 1041. The Massachusetts Department of Revenue issued a directive that sales and transfers of beneficial interest in nominee trusts are subject to the deed excise tax.

J.

[6]Morrison v. Lennett, 415 Mass. 857, 616 N.E.2d 92 (1993).

[7]Zuroff v. First Wisconsin Trust Co., 41 Mass. App. Ct. 491, 671 N.E.2d 982 (1996).

[8]Moscatiello v. Board of Assessors of Boston, 36 Mass. App. Ct. 622, 634 N.E.2d 147 (1994), citing Kirby v. Board of Assessors of Medford, 350 Mass. 386, 215 N.E.2d 99 (1966).

[9]Penta v. Concord Auto Auction, Inc., 24 Mass. App. Ct. 635, 511 N.E.2d 642 (1987).

[10]Rogaris v. Albert, 431 Mass. 833, 730 N.E.2d 869 (2000).

[11]Plunkett v. First Federal Sav. and Loan Ass'n of Boston, 18 Mass. App. Ct. 294, 464 N.E.2d 1381 (1984); Levin v. Schnell, 3 L.C.R. 217 (1995).

[12]Shamrock, Inc. v. F.D.I.C., 36 Mass. App. Ct. 162, 629 N.E.2d 344 (1994).

[13]F.D.I.C. v. Porter, 46 Mass. App. Ct. 241, 704 N.E.2d 1203 (1999).

[14]Arlington Trust Co. v. Caimi, 414 Mass. 839, 610 N.E.2d 948, 20 U.C.C. Rep. Serv. 2d 1167 (1993).

Chapter 17

Condominiums

> **KeyCite®:** Cases and other legal materials listed in KeyCite Scope can be researched through the KeyCite service on Westlaw®. Use KeyCite to check citations for form, parallel references, prior and later history, and comprehensive citator information, including citations to other decisions and secondary materials.

TOPIC A: INTRODUCTION

§ 17:1   Background

Massachusetts first adopted a condominium law, M.G.L.A. c. 183A, in 1963. The condominium form of home ownership has mushroomed ever since. As use of this form of owner-ship grew and issues arose in condominium practice, some amendments of the statute were made to deal with them, but the basic scheme has not been changed, and the Mas-sachusetts statute may still fairly be characterized as a "first generation" act. Many states have now adopted a version of the "Uniform Condominium Act" which contains many provi-sions lacking in our statute and affords considerably greater flexibility. Several of the respects in which that is true will be referred to below.

Fortunately, there is a basis in Chapter 183A for broad in-terpretation of the statute, and the courts have recognized the need for flexibility. Section 2 of the statute states that "The provisions of this chapter shall not be deemed to preclude or regulate the creation or maintenance of other interests in real property not expressly declared by the owner or owners to be subject hereto." The definitions in § 1 of the statute are all subject to the proviso "unless the context otherwise requires," and the definition of "common areas and facilities" is stated to be "except as otherwise provided or stipulated in the master deed." Also, § 12 permits the adop-tion of by-laws containing "Such other provisions as may be deemed necessary for the management and regulation of the organization of unit owners or the condominium not incon-sistent with this chapter and the master deed."

Taking into account the legislative history and the nature of condominiums, in 1981 the SJC took the beneficial view that "Statutes like c. 183A which imprint the condominium with legislative authorization are essentially enabling statutes," and that "This statute provides planning flexibility to developers and unit owners,"[1] and in 2002 strongly confirmed that "Such flexibility is particularly important with respect to phased condominium developments where long-term financial and market conditions may be uncertain."[2]

Based on that concept lawyers have, in order to meet the needs of condominium developers, imaginatively conceived a great variety of condominium forms and provisions for which no express authority is found in the statute. As will appear below, the courts have generally accepted and accommodated these innovations, but there have been hitches along the way, and the interpretation of some statutory provisions remains uncertain.

§ 17:2 The condominium concept

The essence of the condominium concept is (a) the separate ownership by several owners of "units," ordinarily an apartment or other enclosed space in a building, (b) the common ownership by all of the several "unit" owners, each having a specified fractional interest as a tenant in common, of those portions of the land, the structure of buildings, appurtenances and related facilities, as are, by their nature or by intent or desire, common to the needs, protection or benefit of all of the owners, (c) the recognition for legal purposes as separate pieces of real estate of each "unit" together with its share of undivided interest in the commonly owned property, and (d) an organizational structure by which the unit owners may manage and control such common areas and facilities and the relationships among themselves.

§ 17:3 Statutory particulars

The elements mentioned above are all provided for in the statute.

• **Unit.** The statute defines "unit" as: "a part of the condominium including one or more rooms with appurtenant areas such as balconies, terraces and storage lockers if any are

---

[Section 17:1]

[1]Barclay v. DeVeau, 384 Mass. 676, 429 N.E.2d 323 (1981).

[2]Queler v. Skowron, 438 Mass. 304, 780 N.E.2d 71 (2002).

stipulated in the master deed as being owned by the unit owner, occupying one or more floors or a part or parts thereof, including the enclosed space therein, intended for any type of use, and with a direct exit to a street or way or to a common area leading to a street or way."

The references to "rooms," "floors," and "enclosed space" are certainly apt in most condominiums, but do they preclude use of the condominium form for, say, open air boat slips in a marina? Since all the definitions are prefaced by "unless the context otherwise requires," it is at least arguable that the marina condominium could be established in Massachusetts, as it has elsewhere. Perhaps a locker on the dock could be a "room," and the boat slip itself an "appurtenant area." The reference to "balconies" and "terraces" poses the issue of whether they are, although not rooms and not enclosed, part of the unit itself or are "limited common areas and facilities" appurtenant to the unit. Since balconies and terraces affect the external visual aesthetics of a project, it is customary to put them in the latter category so that they may be restricted and regulated as common areas.

The Uniform Condominium Act defines "unit" in effect as any physical portion of a condominium designated for separate ownership or occupancy with defined boundaries.

• **Common Areas and Facilities.** The basic definition of "common areas and facilities" includes a listing of items in some detail, including in short, the land, the structure of buildings, utilities and apparatus serving common use, and community and recreational facilities. All are included "except as otherwise provided or stipulated in the master deed." That exception makes it possible to create a condominium with very little "in common," such as a group of detached single-family dwellings with their own exclusive yards, and perhaps the roadway serving them as the only true common area and facility.

In 1994 an amendment of the statute first added a definition of "limited common area and facilities" as: "a portion of the common areas and facilities allocated by the master deed or any amendment thereto for the exclusive use of one or more but fewer than all of the units," thereby legitimizing a practice that was then already common in condominium practice, particularly with respect to balconies and terraces. The practice had already been upheld with respect to elevators and other facilities designated as limited or special common areas and facilities appurtenant to some but not all units.[1]

• **Real Estate.** Section 3 of Chapter 183A specifically makes a "unit together with its undivided interest in the common areas and facilities" an item or entity of "real estate."[2] In 1985 that was made applicable "whether or not such unit is built on owned or leased land." The details of leasehold condominiums will be discussed below, but that clause poses interesting questions as to the legal status of leasehold condominium units. In any event, with respect to a condominium we no longer have "land" and "buildings," but rather only "units" which comprise all of the land and buildings included in the condominium.

• **Organization.** Finally, an organization of unit owners is an essential element of a condominium. It is defined as: "the corporation, trust or association owned by the unit owners and used by them to manage and regulate the condominium." There are a number of provisions in the statute as to the structure and functions of that organization, again with both specific requirements and areas of flexibility, as is discussed below.

TOPIC B: CREATION OF A CONDOMINIUM

§ 17:4 Master deed basics

A Master Deed is not a deed of conveyance, but is a declaration by which a condominium is established. In the language of the statute it is the instrument by which the condominium property "is submitted to the provisions" of Chapter 183A, a phrase usually included in the opening paragraph of a master deed. In many states that instrument is called a "Declaration," and in Massachusetts the person or entity executing a master deed is usually called the Declarant. The term "Sponsor" is sometimes seen, as is "Grantor," which is inapt.

Section 2 of Chapter 183A provides that it "shall apply" only when the owner of the land, or a lessee thereof under a lease meeting specified requirements, "submits" the land by executing and recording a master deed "containing a state-

---

[Section 17:3]

[1]Tosney v. Chelmsford Village Condominium Ass'n, 397 Mass. 683, 493 N.E.2d 488 (1986).

[2]Associated Industries of Massachusetts, Inc. v. C. I. R., 378 Mass. 657, 393 N.E.2d 812 (1979).

ment to the effect that the owner or lessee proposes to create a condominium to be governed by the provisions of this chapter." Although not specifically stated, that clause suggests that the word "Condominium" should be included in the name of every such entity, or otherwise specified as identifying the entity. It is provided in § 9 of the statute that the name of a leasehold condominium must contain the word "Lease" or "Leasehold."

Such a leasehold condominium could be created only after April 6, 1993, the term of the lease must be at least 60 years, and the lessor must "assent." Further requirements as to leasehold condominiums are set forth in § 8A of Chapter 183A. Before that statutory date a leasehold condominium might have been created with a lease term meeting the requirements of M.G.L.A. c. 186, § 1, and full joinder of the lessor in submitting the land to the statute.

Section 8 of Chapter 183A sets forth detailed requirements for the contents of the master deed, including:

- The submission statement referred to above;
- Descriptions of the land, the buildings, stating the number of stories, the number of units, and the principal materials of which they are constructed;
- A letter or number designation of each unit, and a statement of its location, approximate area, number of rooms, and immediate common area to which it has access;
- Description of the common areas and facilities and the proportionate interest of each unit therein;
- Floor plans "showing the layout, location, unit numbers and dimensions of the units, stating the name of the building or that it has not a name, and bearing the verified statement of a registered architect, registered professional engineer, or registered land surveyor, certifying that the plans fully and accurately depict the layout, location, unit number and dimensions of the units as built";
- A statement of the purposes for which the building and each of the units are intended and the restrictions, if any, as to their use;
- The method by which the master deed may be amended;
- The name of the corporation, trust or association which has been formed and through which the unit owners will manage and regulate the condominium, together with a statement that such corporation, trust or association has enacted by-laws pursuant to this chapter, and if a trust or association, other data and substantive requirements, as set forth in clause (i) of § 8. Although the bylaws

of the organization are not required to be recorded, its address and the names of the trustees or managers must be set forth in the master deed.

The detailed descriptive data called for by these provisions are usually set forth in tabular form, attached as exhibits to the master deed, as indicated at the end of **Appendix N**.

§ 17:5   Descriptions and plans

A full metes and bounds perimeter description of the land included in the condominium should be set forth in the Master Deed or attached as an exhibit thereto. This may be based on a previously recorded survey plan or on a "site plan" prepared for purposes of the condominium.

• **Site Plan.** While § 8 calls for "floor plans," the data required includes the "location" of the buildings, and that in effect calls for a "site plan" which locates the buildings on the land and the units within the buildings. Section 8 refers to the plans as "contained" in the master deed, but of course they are recorded therewith, and they must meet requirements of the registers of deeds as to form and size. As to condominiums on registered land, the requirements of the Land Court are referred to in § 8:10. The site plan will show the perimeter of the land and the footprints of the buildings thereon. The location of the buildings should be established by offsets therefrom to land boundaries or monuments, sufficient to eliminate any floating or reorientation. Separate buildings or portions of buildings which constitute common areas and facilities should be shown on the site plan, but dimensioning and layout of the interior thereof is not required, nor is any certification with respect thereto.

In a condominium which is to be constructed in phases (**Topic D of this Chapter**) the usual approach is to have a site plan recorded with the master deed which shows the perimeter of the entire tract of land, but only the then built buildings which are to constitute the first phase. If a site plan is recorded which shows footprints of any proposed future buildings, it should be clearly specified that these have not been built and are not included in the condominium.

• **Floor Plans.** The key requirements are "layout" and "dimensions." The depiction of the "layout" would seem to include interior walls dividing the unit into rooms, but there is no compelling reason for a strict construction of the term, and a condominium unit may presumably be sold in "shell" form with the interior partitioning to be provided by the purchaser. When this is done, it is desirable, even if not required by the statute, to record a supplemental plan showing the room layout of the unit when it is completed.

The dimensions of the units may be shown by any effective means, and are sometimes shown as running between wall center lines, but are more often shown as running between finished surfaces of interior walls. In either case, it is well to specify the mode because the unit boundaries usually run to the face of structural walls, not finished surfaces. It is not necessary to show dimensions of every room, but only sufficient dimensions to indicate the size and shape of the unit.

Anticipating the requirements for certification of the plan to accompany the first deed of units (§ **17:18**), the floor plans should also show the approximate area of each unit and indicate its main entrance by an arrow or other means. Developers usually provide well-prepared floor plans for marketing purposes.

The layout of units, specifying the rooms and facilities included, is ordinarily described verbally in the master deed, often with a bit of marketing flair. Also, since the term "units" is rather sterile, some developers prefer to call them "homes," relating that term and others to their statutory equivalents by a definitional clause in the master deed.

• **As Built.** The certification of plans recorded with the master deed must show the units "as built." That is, a unit cannot be included in a condominium in Massachusetts until it has been built. It need not be completed, or even "substantially completed" in the customary architect's term, because the statutory specifics for the as-built certification can be met when the frame of the building and the walls between the units and common areas therein are established. When the structure of a building has reached that stage, it may be included in a condominium. Since the floor plans then may hardly be distinguishable from floor plans of the same units when completed, any developer who records a master deed at that stage should be most diligent in making full disclosure of the incomplete state of the building.

In any event the plans recorded must meet the statutory specifics and bear a "verified statement . . . certifying that the plans fully and accurately depict the layout, location, unit number and dimension of the units as built." The certification usually uses those very words and is verified simply by the signature and registration seal of the requisite architect, professional engineer or land surveyor. In many cases it is appropriate for the site plan to be so certified by a surveyor and the floor plans by an architect.

• **Unit Boundaries.** Since structural elements of buildings—floors, ceilings and walls—are ordinarily included in common areas and facilities (or common elements, as they are often called), and Units comprise space enclosed therein, it is important to specify the boundaries between them. When there is a wall within a Unit that does not contribute to the support of the building, a provision allowing the Unit Owner to remove it is perfectly in order. But bearing walls require more attention. A Unit owner may in some cases be permitted to make alterations in a bearing wall, but such a wall is a common element, and the condominium organization should carefully control such activity.

At the every-day level, there are issues as to exterior doors, window glass, screens, balconies, and even picture hooks in walls. While, as noted above, dimensions of Units are often taken from finished interior surfaces, it is common to extend the boundaries of Units to the actual structure, e.g., the wall studs, making the interior lath and plaster or other wall-finish material a part of the Unit. Doors to the exterior, outside screens and the glass in all windows are often included as part of the unit. An example of a detailed specification of unit boundaries may be found in paragraph 6 of **Appendix N**.

• **Encroachment.** A so-called encroachment clause is commonly included, dealing with the possibility that a unit might move due to settling or shifting of a building in which it is contained, or because of locational variation upon rebuilding after casualty. The clause permits such encroachments and protects them by easement. The condominium statutes of some states obviate an encroachment clause by providing in effect that the unit is still defined by its surrounding structure even if it has moved. That concept suggests the possibility of a condominium of boats, floating on the tide, but so far no one has had the audacity to create the "sampan condo" in Massachusetts.

• **Common Areas and Facilities.** A full and detailed description of common areas and facilities should be set forth in the master deed, carefully tailored to the particular elements of the project, including any recreational or social facilities, and more particularly with respect to limited common areas and facilities allocated to specific Units. An example may be found in paragraph 7 of **Appendix N**. Some of such facilities are often depicted on the site plan of the condominium.

§ 17:6   Unit percentages

Section 5(a) of Chapter 183A provides that: "Each unit owner shall be entitled to an undivided interest in the common areas and facilities in the percentage set forth in the master deed. Such percentage shall be in the approximate relation that the fair value of the unit on the date of the master deed bears to the then aggregate fair value of all the units."

In keeping with the statutory term, unit owners' shares of undivided interest are usually specified as percentages, adding up to 100. When there are many and diverse units, percentages are sometimes expressed to the second or third decimal point, adding to, say, 100.000. Sometimes one sees percentages expressed as decimal fractions, 1% being .01, adding up to 1. or to 1.000.

The unit percentages so established will serve several purposes: under § 6(a) of the statute they govern shares of common expenses and common profits; under § 10(a) they govern interest and voting powers in the organization of unit owners; under § 13 they govern liability for claims involving the common areas and facilities; under § 14 they govern liabilities for betterment assessments, water and sewer charges; under § 18 they govern voting on improvements, and under § 19 they govern the interest of the unit owners in the proceeds in the event of dissolution of the condominium. That is to say, the same percentage figures govern the sharing of both expenses and capital value, which poses a problem since the actual load of units on common expenses often has only a limited relation to their capital value.

The principal indicia of expense load include such things as floor area, number and size of appurtenant balconies, patios, etc., appurtenant garage or outdoor parking space, and in elevator buildings, the floor level. To some extent, capital value relates to the same factors: larger units with more appurtenances are generally more valuable, and in high-rise buildings the higher units are usually more valuable. But capital value and initial sale prices are often heavily influenced by other factors such as location and view, and a smaller unit may be sold for a substantially higher price than a larger unit. Yet the common expense load of the larger unit is certainly greater than that of the smaller unit. In a high-rise building a unit on, say, the 15th floor may have a sale price much greater than that for an identical unit on the 5th floor, yet their common expense load will be substantially equal, with only some differential attributable to elevator operation and maintenance costs.

To most unit purchasers the monthly common charge is the important matter, and a share in proceeds if the condominium should be dissolved, a very remote consideration.

Consequently, the term "fair value" in § 5(a) has been taken by many creators of condominiums to apply to the principal purpose thereof of allocating common expenses. In short, value for that purpose may not be determined strictly by the initial sale prices of units, but rather by considerations of the more fundamental or inherent proportional value of the units. Such a distinction is perhaps supported by the fact that §§ 17 and 18, dealing with capital matters, use the term "fair market value," instead of "fair value" as in § 5(a). Determinations of percentages taking various factors into account have been upheld.[1]

Under the Uniform Condominium Act the percentages of interest in the common elements may be allocated according to any formula set forth in the declaration of condominium, and common expenses are to be assessed in accordance therewith, except that the declaration may provide for special assessments to particular units having the benefit of limited common elements, allocation of insurance costs according to risks, and allocation of utility costs according to usage. With respect to distribution of proceeds upon termination of a condominium, the Uniform Condominium Act does not look to the percentages of interest in the common elements at all, but provides for appraisal at the time of termination of the condominium of the fair market values of the units and their appurtenances. Such a two-tiered or multi-tiered approach to unit shares is certainly more sound analytically than the one-percentage-for-all-purposes approach of M.G.L.A. c. 183A.

The adoption of the 1994 amendment providing for limited common areas and facilities allowed assessment of costs relating thereto to the Unit Owners served thereby, thus affording (or regularizing) some relief at the operational level.

§ 17:7 Purposes and restrictions

The purposes for which units may be used is an important specification, somewhat akin to use provisions in a zoning law. It is advisable to specify purpose of some common elements as well. An example is paragraphs 10 and 11 in **Appendix N**.

Restrictions on the use of units should also be carefully considered. In order to be effective, they must be set forth in the master deed, as provided in clause (g) of § 8, or in the

---

[Section 17:6]

[1]Podell v. Lahn, 38 Mass. App. Ct. 688, 651 N.E.2d 859 (1995);

Tosney v. Chelmsford Village Condominium Ass'n, 397 Mass. 683, 493 N.E.2d 488 (1986).

bylaws of the condominium organization, as provided in clause (e) of § 11 of Chapter 183A. Restrictions so set forth are usually upheld.[1]

Restrictions affecting the use of units may not be created by, and are not subject to, the rules-and-regulation power of the trustees or managing board. The power to make "administrative rules and regulations" under clause (d) of § 11 applies only to the common areas and facilities.[2] Even a regulation of common areas and facilities may be voided if it has the effect of prohibiting or inhibiting a permitted use of a unit.[3] In unusual circumstances, however, in a "mixed" condominium, mostly residential but with some commercial units, actions by the condominium trustees regulating use of a commercial restaurant unit were upheld.[4] The court held that such actions, even though beyond the trustees' powers, were not necessarily improper, and anyway that plaintiff had by its conduct waived the trustees' breaches.

The sample master deed in **Appendix N** contains restrictions affecting units in paragraph 11 thereof. Administrative rules and regulations affecting common elements are referred to in Article V, section 6, of the related condominium trust in **Appendix O**. An initial set of such rules and regulations is sometimes annexed to the condominium bylaws at the outset.

Restrictions affecting units set forth in a master deed or condominium trust are expected to remain in effect as long as the condominium exists; that is, for an unspecified time. In paragraph 11 of the sample master deed in **Appendix N**, provision is made for extension of restrictions "as permitted or required by law for the continued enforceability thereof." It is not certain that the restriction statutes (§ **15:13**, § **15:14**) are applicable to a condominium, but caution is advisable.

§ 17:8 Other master deed matters

The remaining statutory requirements for inclusion in a master deed are: designation of the organization of unit owners, discussed in § **17:3**, the "method by which the master deed may be amended," and in the case of a leasehold condo-

---

[Section 17:7]

[1]Franklin v. Spadafora, 388 Mass. 764, 447 N.E.2d 1244, 39 A.L.R.4th 77 (1983); Noble v. Murphy, 34 Mass. App. Ct. 452, 612 N.E.2d 266 (1993).

[2]Johnson v. Keith, 368 Mass.

316, 331 N.E.2d 879 (1975).

[3]Granby Heights Ass'n, Inc. v. Dean, 38 Mass. App. Ct. 266, 647 N.E.2d 75 (1995).

[4]KACT, Inc. v. Rubin, 62 Mass. App. Ct. 689, 819 N.E.2d 610 (2004).

minium, the name of the lessor and the recording data of the lease.

A sample of a provision with respect to amendment of the master deed is in paragraph 14 of **Appendix N**. As indicated therein, there may be different majorities of vote required for different types of amendment.

In addition to covering the mandatory matters and customary related provisions as discussed above, master deeds often also contain provisions intended to qualify mortgages of units for sale on the secondary market to entities such as Federal Home Loan Mortgage Corporation or Federal National Mortgage Association. The regulations and requirements of those agencies need to be studied in order to tailor the particular clauses.

Provisions granting a right of first refusal to the condominium organization with respect to sales of units are sometimes included, or provision is made for adoption of such right by subsequent vote of the unit owners.[1]

If the condominium is to be constructed or established in phases, there will, of course, also be provisions dealing with that. The subject of phasing is discussed in **Topic D of this Chapter**.

In order for a master deed to take effect, it must of course be recorded or registered. As to the latter, see § **8:10**.

TOPIC C: ORGANIZATION OF UNIT OWNERS

§ 17:9 Types

As noted above, a condominium organization of unit owners may be a corporation, a trust or an association. It is not clear what the statutory draftsmen had in mind when referring to a corporation. A business corporation organized under M.G.L.A. c. 156D (or its predecessors) could lawfully be used, with shares of stock issued to unit owners in numbers proportionate to their interests in the common areas and facilities. However, such a corporation is prima facie a business entity formed to conduct a business for profit, and that is not the usual purpose of a condominium organization, certainly not a residential condominium. A non-profit

---

[Section 17:8]

[1]See Morris v. Tewksbury

Junction Condominium Association, 14 L.C.R. 537 (2006).

membership corporation would seem to be an ideal entity, but there are two problems. The first is that the purposes for which such a corporation may be formed under M.G.L.A. c. 180 are limited by the statute and do not include condominium organizations. The second is that the voting power in a condominium is proportionate to the interests of the unit owners in the common areas and facilities, usually varying percentages, and it is not clear that M.G.L.A. c. 180 permits any mode other than one member-one vote.

Unincorporated associations are sometimes used for condominium organizations. Such an association is formed by a group of original members who hold a meeting to adopt some form of articles of association and by-laws, and to elect a board of managers. The minutes of the organizational meeting are not recorded, but should be preserved and kept with the condominium documents in the possession of the board of managers. When a condominium is registered, the land court may wish to have a copy of those minutes for its files. The bylaws of an unincorporated association serving as a condominium organization should preferably be recorded, attached as an exhibit to the master deed. Such an association so formed and serving as a condominium organization is not and should not be deemed to be "a voluntary association" under or subject to M.G.L.A. c. 182 because the beneficial interests in a condominium are not "transferable certificates of participation or shares" within the meaning of that statute. Although unincorporated associations ordinarily lack the capacity to sue or be sued, § 10(b)(4) of Chapter 183A creates an exception for condominium associations.[1]

The trust form of organization of unit owners is widely used and is the most prevalent form. Trusts are familiar entities in Massachusetts; once recorded there are no annual filing requirements or fees; and the record in the registry of deeds of the trust, all amendments thereof and all instruments effecting changes of trustees, affords a convenient safeguard to the continuing integrity of the organization. The essential and common provisions of such a trust are contained in the sample included in **Appendix O**.

It should be noted that Chapter 183A calls for the organization of unit owners to have been formed prior to the execution of the Master Deed. In practice these are usually simultaneous events, and both documents are recorded together.

[Section 17:9]

[1]Belson v. Thayer & Associates, Inc., 32 Mass. App. Ct. 256, 588 N.E.2d 695 (1992).

§ 17:10 Developer control

It is common for the developer of a condominium project to retain control of the board of trustees or managers until he has sold a substantial percentage of the units. The propriety of doing so is the issue which was litigated in *Barclay v. DeVeau*, the leading case cited above. In essence the decision therein indicates that a developer may retain effective control during the "marketing phase," which may be limited to a reasonable time during the continuation of bona fide efforts to sell units, and that provisions of the Uniform Condominium Act (UCA), even though not enacted in Massachusetts, may be looked to as guidelines. Those provisions call for relinquishment of control by the developer upon the earliest of (i) 60 days after sale of 75% of the units (including future phase units which may be created), (ii) 2 years after the declarant ceases to offer units for sale in the ordinary course of business, and (iii) 2 years after any development right to add new units was last exercised. There is also provision for representation of unit owners other than the declarant on the board to the extent of 25% of the board 60 days after 25% of the units have been sold, and 33% of the board 60 days after 50% of the units have been sold.

In a phased condominium, i.e., one to be built in separate stages or parts, the relationship of the three periods might be particularly pertinent to the possibility of retention of control by the developer.

In any event, provisions for retention of developer control, although rarely following the literal terms of UCA cited above, seem to have withstood the tests of the marketplace. A clause in ¶ (m) of § 10 of the statute at least recognizes that the phenomenon exists.

§ 17:11 Bylaw provisions

As in any organization it is advisable for the bylaws to cover all aspects of the management, operations and contingencies that may be entailed. The bylaws should of course dovetail with the provisions of the master deed and with the statutory requirements. Sections 10, 11 and 12 of Chapter 183A are focused primarily on bylaws, but there are other provisions that need to be reflected in the bylaws, including those in §§ 17, 18 and 19, some in § 4, and extensive provisions in §§ 5 and 6, mostly added to the statute by amendments in the 1990s.

Section 10 provides first that the unit owners' interests in the organization shall be the same as their interests in the common areas and facilities and shall not be separated from ownership of the units. It also sets forth:

- Basic powers and governance provisions of the organization, including powers to own, deal with and dispose of real estate, to insure property, to litigate, to impose charges for late payment of common expense assessments and fees for violation of condominium document requirements, and to engage a manager to administer the condominium.

- Extensive and detailed provisions with respect to the keeping of records and financial reports and access of the unit owners and mortgagees thereto, and the duties of a manager with respect thereto, and requirements of maintenance of fidelity insurance and of a reserve fund.

- Power of the organization to install "energy saving devices" of a variety of types, including some plumbing devices and windows, in all units, and to assess the costs as common charges, notwithstanding any contrary provisions in the master deed. Similar provisions appear in § 6, discussed below.

- Action by a majority of the trustees or managing board when the organization is a trust or unincorporated association, and for reliance by third parties on the identity and actions of the trustees or managing board as appears of record.

The statute does not require the organizational instruments or the by-laws to be recorded, but that is most desirable and almost universally done, either by means of a declaration of trust such as the one in **Appendix O**, or, when the organization is an unincorporated association, by appending the instrument to the master deed as an exhibit.

Section 11 of the statute requires that the bylaws provide for methods and procedures for: maintenance, repair and replacement of common areas and facilities and payment therefore and approval of payment vouchers; collection of common expenses; hiring of personnel and a manager; adoption and amendment of administrative rules and regulations governing the details of the operation and use of the common areas and facilities and such restrictions on and requirements respecting the use and maintenance of the units and the use of the common areas and facilities, not set forth in the master deed, as are designed to prevent unreasonable interference with the use of their respective units and of the common areas and facilities by the several unit owners.

As mentioned in § **17:7**, there is a clear distinction between rules and regulations concerning use of common areas and facilities, which may be adopted by the board of trustees or managers, and restrictions or requirements affecting the use of units, which must appear in the master deed or the by-laws, and may not be imposed by regulation of the board.

Section 12 of the statute permits other by-law provisions, including: methods for arbitration of the fair market value of units for purposes of application of §§ 17 and 18; procedures for arbitration of certain disputes; and a right of first refusal in favor of the organization on sale of units. First refusal provisions are fairly common, often set forth in the master deed, and must be cast so as to meet the statutory specifics of a 30-day time limit on exercise and prohibition of discriminatory exercise.

§ 17:12   Assessments and collection

The assessment and collection of funds from unit owners needed for the operation, maintenance and management of the common areas and facilities are of course fundamental duties of the condominium organization. Common expenses, as they are called, are dealt with in § 6 of Chapter 183A, which begins with the provision that, with important exceptions, they must be assessed in accordance with the units' percentages of interest, and assessed at least annually (monthly being the usual practice), based on an annual budget. Provisions to that effect should be included in the bylaws.

The exceptions are that: (i) expenses incurred because of failure of a unit owner to abide by requirements of the condominium documents, or misconduct of a unit owner, his family, tenant or invitee, may be charged against the unit owner; (ii) expenses related to a limited common area or facility may be charged to the owner of the unit to which it is appurtenant, allocated or designated; (iii) the direct costs of energy conservation devices required to be installed in a unit may be charged to that unit, subject to waiver by the board of trustees or managers; and (iv) water and utility costs may be assessed according to meters attached to units, if a majority of unit owners so approves at a duly noticed meeting. Section 6 provides for an appeal to the condominium board which seems to apply to all of such assessments. It also states that the statutory provision prevails over contrary provisions in the condominium documents, but any newly drafted condominium should take them into account, and existing condominiums might benefit from accepting amendment.

All of such assessments are the personal liability of the unit owner assessed, and also a lien on the unit. The provisions with respect to delinquency and collection are set forth at length in § 6. They interrelate with provisions in § 4 with respect to notice to mortgagees and provisions in § 5 with respect to changes in percentages, all of which are discussed in § 17:21.

TOPIC D: PHASING

§ 17:13 Background

There are no provisions in M.G.L.A. c. 183A expressly permitting phasing of a condominium; that is, the construction of buildings on contiguous parcels in stages and the inclusion thereof in the condominium by amendment subsequent to the recording of the original master deed. However, the economics and practicalities of real estate development, construction and financing require such staged creation of all but the smallest condominiums, and draftsmen have produced provisions for such phasing within the bounds of and consistently with provisions of the condominium statute. In 1995, the appeals court observed in a footnote that: " 'Phasing' is not a statutory term, but is a usage that has grown out of the general enabling provisions of G.L. c.183A."[1]

As noted above, the statute has always contained provisions contemplating amendment of a master deed, and has been construed to afford flexibility. Amendments in the late 1990s of Chapter 183A contain clauses which clearly recognize the practice of phasing, and to some extent assist in its accomplishment. Section 5(b)(1) of Chapter 183A provides that: "The percentage of the undivided interest of each unit owner in the common areas and facilities as expressed in the master deed shall not be altered without the consent of all unit owners whose percentage of the undivided interest is materially affected, expressed in an amendment to the master deed duly recorded; provided, however, that the acceptance and recording of the unit deed shall constitute consent by the grantee to the addition of subsequent units or land or both to the condominium and consent to the reduction of the undivided interest of the unit owner if the master deed at the time of the recording of the unit deed provided for the addition of units or land and made possible an accurate determination of the alteration of each unit's undi-

---

[Section 17:13]

[1]Podell v. Lahn, 38 Mass. App.
Ct. 688, 651 N.E.2d 859 (1995).

vided interest that would result therefrom."

And it is provided in § 5(b)(2) that: "The organization of unit owners, acting by and through its governing body, shall have the power and authority, as attorney in fact on behalf of all unit owners from time to time owning units in the condominium, except as provided in this subsection, to: * * *(iii) Extend, revive or grant rights to develop the condominium, including the right to add additional units or land to the condominium; provided, however, that the rights to add additional units are set forth in or specifically authorized by the master deed,* * *"

These provisions were enacted in response to, and in effect to overrule, certain judicial decisions that seemed to reflect a lack of understanding of the condominium statute, and certainly had the effect of frustrating practices that were both established and necessary in condominium development and management. The course of analysis has been somewhat checkered, and a brief review is needed for an understanding of the current situation and the issues that are yet unresolved.

In 1991, in *Kaplan v. Boudreaux*,[2] the court equated percentage interest in common areas with the use of common areas and, based on the then § 5(b) of the statute, voided an amendment of by-laws adopted by over three-quarters of the unit owners allocating use of a small walkway to the one unit it served, with no actual change in any unit percentage. The concept that any modification of common areas constituted an alteration of percentages of undivided interest was repeated in 1994 in *Strauss v. Oyster River Condominium Trust*,[3] in which the court erroneously refers to "the common area owned by the condominium" and says that plaintiff unit owners "are not the owners of the common area." In that case a master deed provision expressly authorizing expansion of units with the consent of the condominium trustees (which had been given) was held unlawful and contrary to the statute. The long-existing unit additions were, however, allowed to remain, based upon equitable considerations, and the order of the land court to amend the master deed with recast unit descriptions and percentages was upheld.

Next came *Suprenant v. First Trade Union Savings Bank, FSB*,[4] in which the court voided an amendment adopted by a

---

[2]Kaplan v. Boudreaux, 410 Mass. 435, 573 N.E.2d 495 (1991).

[3]Strauss v. Oyster River Condominium Trust, 417 Mass. 442, 631 N.E.2d 979 (1994).

[4]Suprenant v. First Trade

70% vote, and then *Viola v. Millbank II Associates,*[5] overruling the trial court and holding that a columnar menu in the master deed of unit percentages for successive phases of development did not constitute an alteration of percentage interests in violation of § 5(b), but there was a lengthy dissent.

The cases just cited were not governed by the statutory amendments quoted above, nor was *Newman v. Warshaw,*[6] in which the land court nevertheless upheld the addition of a phase and rejected the contention that 100% approval was required, saying that: "If accepted, Plaintiffs' arguments would amount to a general prohibition on phasing unless the developer obtains unanimous approval of all unit owners in the prior phases. M.G.L.A. c. 183A, § 5(b) does not compel such a result. Indeed, if I were to accept Plaintiffs' arguments, the Court would effectively be rendering phased condominiums impractical, given the uncertainty that the developer could ever obtain unanimous approval."

The current provision in § 5(b)(1), quoted above, certainly does make phased addition of units lawful if it is provided for in the master deed, the consent of unit owners thereto being implicit in "the acceptance and recording of the unit deed." The reduction of the percentages of undivided interests of existing unit owners in the common areas and facilities resulting from the addition of new units acquiring percentages of interest is also made lawful and deemed consented to, provided that the master deed "made possible an accurate determination of the alteration of each unit's undivided interest." That is a bit more tricky, and is discussed below, as are other issues of phasing.

§ 17:14 Simple

In the simplest situation the land which is ultimately to be included in the condominium may be divided into separate parcels, each of which is a lawful lot for zoning and subdivision control purposes. Then the condominium can be established when the building or buildings on the first lot are constructed, and the master deed may simply provide that when buildings are completed on the other lots, they may be included in the condominium by amendment executed by the declarant. When the declarant reserves such a

---

Union Sav. Bank, FSB, 40 Mass. App. Ct. 637, 666 N.E.2d 1026 (1996).

    [5]Viola v. Millbank II Associates, 44 Mass. App. Ct. 82, 688 N.E.2d 996 (1997).

    [6]Newman v. Warshaw, 4 L.C.R. 22 (1996); see also Lane v. Provost, 9 L.C.R. 324 (2001).

power to himself, he should, of course, specify in the master deed with reasonable precision the number and types of the future units and any new common facilities. If these are known precisely at the time of the master deed, then the exact percentages of interest of the original units and future units can be determined at the outset and set forth in tabular form in the master deed.

This approach is possible even if there are several future phase lots and the developer is not certain at the outset of the order in which they will be included. If the "unit types" are specified at the outset, and the number of each in each future phase is determined, then a columnar or "menu" approach to specification of each future phase remains possible, as well as specification of the unit percentages at every point in the phasing program.

§ 17:15 Complex

Complexity may arise from (i) land configuration, (ii) diversity of unit types, and (iii) means of establishing unit percentages.

• **Land Configuration.** The first complexity arises when the tract of land intended to be included in the condominium in several phase is not subdividable. That is to say, it cannot be divided into separate parcels each of which will meet subdivision and zoning requirements for separate development. Section 15 of Chapter 183A provides that: "The subdivision control law shall not apply to the division of a building into units." The statute does not in any way exempt land included in a condominium from the subdivision control law.

There may be, for instance, a tract of, say, 100 acres, all zoned for multiple housing, but with existing frontage of no more than the minimum required by the zoning law. The roads to be built within the tract to serve condominium units do not need to be built to standard planning board specifications, and often town boards do not want them to become public ways, so they will not afford legal frontage when they are built. Then the first phase of the condominium development may occupy all of the existing frontage and the future phases are on "back" areas having no frontage.

In such a case it is necessary to include the entire tract in the condominium at the outset, and the declarant must reserve to himself the right to build future phase buildings on land which has thus become part of the common areas, and thus will belong to the owners of the first phase units when they are sold. Such a reservation must be carefully and clearly stated. The reserved parcels should be indicated on the site plan, at least by dotted lines. The master deed may state that only the land included in the first phase is part of the common areas and facilities, and that the developer reserves the "future phase" parcels to himself. However, the developer cannot reserve separate title to those back parcels without entailing a violation, technical at least, of the subdivision control law. This distinction is not always recognized by developers or their lawyers, and in fact issues of disposition of such parcels remain in some respects unresolved.

A device (initiated by this author) to afford protection in such circumstances is the "condominium phasing lease" recorded prior to the master deed, an example of which is set forth in **Appendix P**. The lease, held by an affiliate or nominee of the developer, confers upon the lessee the right to construct buildings and improvements, and to own them, all until they are included in the condominium by amendment of the master deed. When the developer obtains construction financing for such future phase units, the mortgagee, too, gains a significant security by taking a mortgage on or assignment of the leasehold estate.

The basic principle was established in *DiBiase Corp. v. Jacobowitz*[1] that land included in a condominium as part of the common areas and facilities held for future phase development, but not so used within an applicable time period, remained part of the common areas and facilities. But the waters became murkier in *Levy v. Reardon*,[2] in which the developer "removed" a parcel from a condominium and established a new condominium thereon, to which he granted easements to use the swimming pool in the first condominium. The appeals court voided both the removal clause in the master deed and the easement, and left it to the land court to sort out the consequences, which it did.[3] Next came the saga of the *Stonehedge Farm* cases[4] in which title to "Phase III" land was held to have passed by foreclo-

---

[Section 17:15]

[1]DiBiase Corp. v. Jacobowitz, 43 Mass. App. Ct. 361, 682 N.E.2d 1382 (1997), aff'd, 427 Mass. 1004, 691 N.E.2d 548 (1998).

[2]Levy v. Reardon, 43 Mass. App. Ct. 431, 683 N.E.2d 713 (1997) (overruled by, Queler v. Skowron, 438 Mass. 304, 780 N.E.2d 71 (2002)).

[3]Anderson v. Monaghan, 7 L.C.R. 224 (1999), 9 L.C.R. 351 (2001).

[4]Stonehedge Farm Condominium Associates v. American Stonehenge, Inc., 6 L.C.R. 286 (1998); Palm v. Stonehedge Farm Condominium Trust, 13 L.C.R. 171 (2005); Stonehedge Farm Condominium Trust v. American Stonehenge, Inc.,

sure of a mortgage thereon recorded before the master deed, notwithstanding the provision in the master deed that the Phase III land "shall be considered a Common Element, a part of the Condominium," which decision led of course to further litigation.

Then came *Queler v. Skowron*,[5] in which the SJC overruled *Levy v. Reardon*, and upheld provision in a master deed that land not "included" in a future phase by a "termination date" would be "deemed to be removed" from the condominium and the interests of the unit owners would "terminate" and "revest" in the developer. The message for lawyers acting for unit purchasers is that the phasing provisions should be analyzed in detail with care, because such "remove" and "revest" clauses may be less than salient in a lengthy and complex document.

● **Unit Types.** A second difficulty arises when there are a variety of unit types, and future phases may include a different "mix" than the first phase, or even include types not appearing in the first phase. A declarant may at the outset offer unit types A, B, C and D, each type having a different size, layout and features. Naturally, the declarant wants to meet the market demand, and it is surely desirable from the consumers' standpoint that he do so. In the first phase the declarant builds some of each type, but only after marketing can he know which types are the more popular, and in future phases he will naturally build more of those and fewer of the less popular types.

The various types may come in mirror-image forms, which should be specified but makes no substantive difference. There may also be variants, designated for instance as types A1, A2, etc. And finally there may be new types, perhaps E, F and G. In all such cases it is most important for the developer to be as definite and specific as possible in describing the units that may be included in the condominium

● **Unit Percentages.** Whenever there are multiple unit types and the "mix" is not established for future phases, predetermined percentage numbers for each unit in each future phase are impossible, and a formula is necessary. Such a formula needs to be prepared with the greatest care, so that—regardless of the final unit mix, and even if the developer ultimately completes the condominium with fewer units than the maximum number originally proposed—the percentages of interest of the units in the condominium will

---

13 L.C.R. 176 (2005).   304, 780 N.E.2d 71 (2002).

[5]Queler v. Skowron, 438 Mass.

always remain, as each phase is added, in the same proportions to each other and in the same proportions to fair value.

Section 5(a) of Chapter 183A provides that: "Each unit owner shall be entitled to an undivided interest in the common areas and facilities in the percentage set forth in the master deed. Such percentage shall be in the approximate relation that the fair value of the unit on the date of the master deed bears to the then aggregate fair value of all the units."

In relation to phasing it is reasonable to construe that to require that the percentages for first phase units be set forth in the master deed in numerical form, adding to 100. The master deed may provide a formula for the determination of percentages for future phases, and when each future phase is added, the percentages for units therein, computed pursuant to the formula, are set forth numerically in the amendment of the master deed including that phase. The percentages of units in the first phase are thereby reduced proportionately, and the total for all the old and new units still adds up to 100. That is clearly contemplated by the provision in § 5(b)(1) quoted in § **17:13**.

It must be noted that § 5(a) refers to proportionate fair value on the date of the master deed. In volatile real estate markets subject to changes or even fads in popularity of unit types, the proportionate values of unit types may well be different upon the adoption of a phasing amendment than they were at the time of the master deed. Also to be noted is that in a building of say, five units, a given type may be more valuable if it is located on the end of the building rather than in the middle, and that the value of units of the same type may vary because of view, proximity to a desirable element of the common areas and facilities or other locational aspect. The court upheld a formula based on the floor areas of units, duly "weighted," and taking into account special common areas and facilities appurtenant to units.[6]

The key is a formula which is so constructed and defined as to meet statutory tests of fairness, proportionality and "accurate determination," as specified in § 5(b)(1). The formula in Section 13 of the master deed set forth in **Appendix N** is held out as meeting those tests. A variety of formulas have been used in phased condominiums, and as to some of them, even if approved by the land court, it is hard to see how they meet the tests.

When a phase is actually added, a phasing amendment,

----

[6]Podell v. Lahn, 38 Mass. App. Ct. 688, 651 N.E.2d 859 (1995).

such as set forth in **Appendix Q**, should recite all pertinent data to indicate compliance with the phasing provisions of the master deed.

§ 17:16 Timing; tax

The right reserved to a developer to add phases to a condominium is appropriately limited in time, usually seven years or less, conforming with regulations of FHLMC and FNMA in order to make unit mortgages eligible for the secondary market.

Before the adoption of the statutory amendments cited above, the courts regularly rejected extension of time for phasing without approval of 100% of the unit owners.[1] Under the present § 5(b)(2) of the statute the managing board of a condominium organization may on its own authority "extend, revive or grant" rights to "add additional units or land to the condominium" if such rights are authorized by the master deed.

Among the factors considered in relation to delay in phasing are compliance with a zoning permit,[2] and foreclosure of the developer's mortgage,[3] in which case the purchaser was allowed to exercise such rights. But construction of a phase after the developer's rights to do so had expired is of course unlawful.[4]

It is provided in § 14 of Chapter 183A that the common areas and facilities of a condominium "shall not be deemed to be a taxable parcel." Based on that it was held that land included as common areas and facilities and held for future phase development were not subject to real estate tax,[5] but the court expressed some doubts about "reasonable fiscal

[Section 17:16]

[1]Suprenant v. First Trade Union Sav. Bank, FSB, 40 Mass. App. Ct. 637, 666 N.E.2d 1026 (1996); DiBiase Corp. v. Jacobowitz, 43 Mass. App. Ct. 361, 682 N.E.2d 1382 (1997), aff'd, 427 Mass. 1004, 691 N.E.2d 548 (1998); Lebowitz v. Heritage Heights, Inc., 4 L.C.R. 48 (1996).

[2]Bernstein v. Chief Building Inspector, 52 Mass. App. Ct. 422, 754 N.E.2d 133 (2001).

[3]Dudley Corporation v. Pizzi Farms, Inc., 4 L.C.R. 75 (1996).

[4]Crasper v. Bondsville Partners, Inc., 14 L.C.R. 432 (2006).

[5]Spinnaker Island and Yacht Club Holding Trust v. Board of Assessors of Hull, 49 Mass. App. Ct. 20, 725 N.E.2d 1072 (2000); First Main Street Corp. v. Board of Assessors of Acton, 49 Mass. App. Ct. 25, 725 N.E.2d 1076 (2000).

policy."

TOPIC E: SALE AND PURCHASE

§ 17:17   Marketing; sale agreement

The marketing of condominium units often begins before construction is completed. Usually a few model units will have been completed, and in addition to the opportunity to inspect the models the prospective purchaser will be given a condominium "presentation." This presentation usually includes a narrative description of the project (and often of the developer's prior projects), a site plan, sample floor plans, copies of the condominium documents themselves, the forms of purchase and sale agreement, unit deed, limited warranty and management agreement, and a pro forma estimated first year budget.

This is a sizable package and a prospective unit purchaser will wish to study it and have his attorney examine the documents before he signs a purchase and sale agreement. Sometimes this package is offered only upon receipt from the prospective purchaser of a "reservation deposit" which he may cancel and have his deposit refunded if he does not enter into a binding purchase and sale agreement within a specified reservation period.[1]

A purchase and sale agreement for a condominium unit needs to contain all of the standard terms, the "boiler plate," appropriate to any purchase and sale of real estate, plus several additional provisions relating to the particulars of the condominium form and to marketing disclosure mandates.

The additional provisions may include the following: (1) recital that the buyer has read the presentation documents, (2) reservation to the developer of the right to make limited changes in the condominium or the documents, but not in the unit being sold or its percentage, (3) requirement that the purchaser pay 1 or 2 month's common expenses as a contribution to a condominium working capital fund, (4) reference to insurance carried by the condominium organization, (5) provision for selection by the purchaser of interior colors, fixtures, etc., (6) agreement of the seller to provide a 6(d) Certificate (referred to below) at closing, (7) the right of the seller to specify the closing date, within a time limit, by no-

---

[Section 17:17]

[1]See Langton v. LaBrecque,   25 Mass. App. Ct. 463, 519 N.E.2d 1361 (1988).

tice to the buyer, and (8) agreement of the developer to give a limited warranty, usually for one year.

Developers often present their forms as more-or-less non-negotiable, for the understandable reason that it is inconsistent with sound marketing practice to give special accommodation to one purchaser and not to all, and needlessly expensive in staff and legal costs to negotiate every agreement separately.

As to warranty, the implied warranty of habitability, described in § **5:5**, applies to newly built condominium units, and the claim against the builder-vendor may be brought by individual unit purchasers or by the organization of unit owners.[2]

Occasionally there are elements intended to be appurtenant to units which are sold and allocated as "extras," such as parking spaces, gardening plots, or even preferred access to an amenity of the condominium, such as a recreational facility. In any such case, the master deed should specify those items as limited common areas and facilities and specify the procedures by which the declarant (or the condominium managers) may allocate them. If a developer intends to sell any such features within a condominium to persons other than unit owners, the right to do so should be clearly established by an instrument, such as a lease or grant of easement, recorded before the master deed and referred to therein as an encumbrance to which the condominium is subject. Absent such a clear reservation, the developer cannot withhold a portion of the common areas.[3] When a parking space had been made appurtenant to a unit, it was held that it could not then be leased to a third party.[4]

In the first impression of such a case where there was a record reservation[5] the court majority said the parking space had been "conveyed" by the master deed to the condominium trust and suggested that the reserved lease of the space might constitute a violation of § 5(c) of the statute. However, when the case arose again on the merits,[6] the reserved lease was upheld, following the decision in another case in which

---

[2]Berish v. Bornstein, 437 Mass. 252, 770 N.E.2d 961 (2002).

[3]Locke v. Spaulding, 24 Mass. App. Ct. 977, 512 N.E.2d 1145 (1987).

[4]Schwartzman v. Schoening, 41 Mass. App. Ct. 220, 669 N.E.2d 228 (1996); Brady v. Zimmerman, 7 L.C.R. 101 (1999).

[5]Beaconsfield Towne House Condominium Trust v. Zussman, 401 Mass. 480, 517 N.E.2d 816 (1988).

[6]Beaconsfield Towne House Condominium Trust v. Zussman, 416 Mass. 505, 623 N.E.2d 1115 (1993).

the developer's right to control and charge for on-site parking, established of record before the master deed, was upheld and found not to be in violation of § 5(c).[7] Related parking issues are discussed in § **17:20**.

§ 17:18   Unit deed; 6(d) certificate

Section 9 of Chapter 183A sets forth required contents of deeds of units, including the following:
   • Reference to the condominium as subject to Chapter 183A.
   • A description of the land as set forth in the master deed or the post office address of the property, and in either case the book, page and date of recording of the master deed. It is much simpler to recite a post office address than to set forth the whole land description. Sometimes it takes a bit of negotiation with the local post office to obtain addresses for newly built condominium units. It should be noted that the *date* of recording is required.
   • The unit designation set forth in the master deed, and "any other data necessary for its proper identification." Usually a Unit number and a building name or number will suffice.
   • A statement of the use for which the unit is intended and the restrictions, if any, on its use. It may be necessary to quote such provisions in full from the master deed, although unit deed forms provided by the Land Court and by REBA seem to suggest that these may be incorporated by reference.
   • The undivided interest appertaining to the unit in the common areas and facilities. In a phased condominium where that number may later be reduced, it is well to say so in the deed.
   • The *first* deed of each unit, that is the initial conveyance thereof by the declarant of the condominium, must also have "attached thereto, as part thereof, a copy of the portion or portions of the plans theretofore filed with the master deed to which copy shall be affixed the verified statement of a registered architect, registered professional engineer or registered land surveyor certifying that they show the unit designation of the unit being conveyed and of immediately adjoining units, and that they fully and accurately depict the layout of the unit, its location, dimen-

---

[7]Commercial Wharf East Condominium Ass'n v. Waterfront Parking Corp., 407 Mass. 123, 552 N.E.2d 66 (1990).

sions, approximate area, main entrance and immediate common area to which it has access, as built."

The registries of deeds, including land court registry districts, may not always require that plan copies attached to unit deeds be in recordable form. They may be paper prints, usually in reduced size and actually attached to the deed. The statutory reference to "a copy of the portion or portions of the plans theretofore filed with the master deed" need not be taken literally, but allows some flexibility of reproduction. Of course paper plan copies will ordinarily not be copied into the record books along with the deeds.

It is to be noted that the certification under § 9 differs from that under § 8(f) by adding requirements of certification of approximate area, main entrance and immediate common area to which the unit has access, and also the unit designations of "immediately adjoining units," which may be taken to mean laterally adjoining units, not those on floors above and below In multi-storied buildings.

There have been instances in which a declarant followed the recording of the master deed with a deed of all of the units to a straw, accompanied by a full set of the plans recorded with the master deed, and then a deed of the straw back to the declarant. Then on individual sales of units to purchasers, no plans were attached because these were not "the first deed" of the unit. That practice defeats the purpose of the statute and is unethical.

The term **6(d) Certificate** (initiated by this author some 40 years ago) refers to a certificate under § 6(d) of Chapter 183A, signed and acknowledged by a trustee or member of the board of managers of the condominium organization, stating that there are no unpaid common expenses assessed to the unit. When recorded, such a certificate has a binding effect and discharges the unit of any lien for unpaid charges. The statute requires that such a certificate be delivered within ten days after written request, and that a reasonable fee may be charged for it, except to a foreclosing mortgagee who has given notice. A condominium manager was absolved of negligent misrepresentation for stating that no special assessments had been made or were planned in an affidavit made a few months before the condominium announced a substantial special assessment of correct construction defects.[1]

[Section 17:18]

[1]Eisenberg v. Phoenix Ass'n Management, Inc., 56 Mass. App. Ct. 910, 777 N.E.2d 1265 (2002).

§ 17:19   Resales; foreclosure

When a condominium unit is resold, the buyer's interests are much the same as those of the initial purchaser: he will wish to examine the condominium documents, the budget and master insurance policies, to obtain and record a certificate under § 6(d) and to obtain whatever information he can about the status of maintenance and repair of the premises and buildings. The buyer will, of course, examine the unit itself and its fixtures and appliances, but he has a substantial interest also in determining the soundness of the entire building in which the unit is located, as well as other buildings and all of the common areas and facilities, because the costs of any needed repairs thereof will be covered in future assessments in which he must share.

The seller may be induced to take the responsibility for providing all of the information, but the buyer and his attorney should not hesitate to make inquiry directly of the manager or board of the condominium. It is often useful to review the operating statements of receipts and expenses over the preceding several years, and also the minutes or reports of meetings of the unit owners. The nature and extent of grants of rights in limited common areas and facilities, and all provisions with respect to future phasing should be reviewed. It is also important to check for the existence of reserves for maintenance and repair and the budgeting of adequate annual additions thereto. Also, as noted above, initial purchasers of condominium units are usually required to pay in 1 or 2 months common expenses to a working capital fund. All such funds are an asset of the unit owner, to the extent of his percentage of interest therein, which will pass with title to the unit, and should be specifically provided for as an adjustment.

The Greater Boston Real Estate Board publishes a copyrighted Standard Form Condominium Purchase and Sale Agreement which is similar to the agreement set forth in **Appendix A**, with changes suitable to the resale of a condominium unit. REBA Form 21a is a condominium supplement to its form of purchase and sale agreement. Since most condominiums are covered by title insurance, it is advisable for a buyer's attorney to examine an existing policy before the purchase and sale agreement is signed and to become generally familiar with the title exceptions. The seller's attorney will ordinarily wish to provide in the agreement that the premises are to be sold subject to provisions of the master deed and of all easements, restrictions, agreements, etc., therein set forth or referred to, but that broad a clause poses

446

as much risk for a condominium unit buyer as for the buyer of any other real estate. If the existing policy shows a satisfactory state of title and exceptions, the buyer may supplement the title clause in the agreement with a requirement that he be able to obtain a new unit owner's policy in the specified form at standard rates.

Most condominium unit purchasers finance their purchase with a mortgage loan, and the mortgagee will of course wish to have the benefit of clause (5) of § 4 of Chapter 183A, providing for listing with the condominium organization and notice of its actions.

A resale of a condominium unit may occur while the developer still has future phases under construction and subject to a development construction loan. In any such case Section 22 of Chapter 183A is pertinent. It provides that: "In the event of a foreclosure upon a condominium development the lender taking over the project shall succeed to any obligations the developer has with the unit owners and to the tenants, except that the developers shall remain liable for any misrepresentations already made and for warranties on work done prior to the transfer." This section is certainly unclear in several respects, but raises cautions to lenders and leaves doubts to purchasers. When a bank took a deed in lieu of foreclosure and completed and sold unfinished units in a condominium, the court held § 22 to be applicable, saying that reading "foreclosure" as not including "deed in lieu" would leave § 22 "devoid of practical effect."[1]

TOPIC F: OPERATION AND MANAGEMENT

§ 17:20 Basic management

Clause (c) in § 10 of Chapter 183A provides for professional management of a condominium and spells out the duties of the manager in some detail. Some requirements are applicable only to condominiums with more than 50 units, but professional management is desirable for all condominiums except possibly those with only a few residential units. A condominium management agreement usually confers broad powers and duties of management on the professional, reserving to the board of trustees or managers

---

[Section 17:19]

[1]Moloney v. Boston Five Cents Sav. Bank FSB, 422 Mass. 431, 663 N.E.2d 811 (1996).

themselves only a policy making role, a power of approval of budgets, exercise of first refusal rights, and other fundamental decisions which are not appropriate to delegate.

Condominium developers are often also experienced property managers and they make the initial condominium management agreement with themselves or their affiliated management companies. This not only affords the developer protection during the initial marketing phase but also works distinctly to the benefit of the unit owners, whose interests in many cases lie in keeping the original developer in a management role even after he has sold the units. The statute provides that a management contract must be terminable without cause on no more than 90 days notice and for cause on 10 days notice with an opportunity to cure. Similar requirements and limitation of the management contract term may be required by FNMA and FHLMC.

The fundamental duties of condominium managers are discussed in the following paragraphs B, C and D of this section. Several managerial issues which do not readily fall within those categories are worth mention.

A recurring issue is that of control and allocation of parking spaces. As noted in § **17:17**, a developer's reservation of parking control was upheld, but when a successor developer modified the parking arrangements unilaterally without consent of the condominium association, those actions were voided.[1] An attempt to modify a parking clause without amendment of the master deed was also rejected.[2] A long-term lease to a third party of a parking space appurtenant to a unit was voided.[3] However, an amendment of the master deed of a condominium comprising residential and commercial units granting to the successor developer control over parking areas was upheld upon the conclusion that the developer had valid business reasons for retaining parking control and that the deal had been extensively negotiated with unit owners represented by counsel.[4] When a master deed recognized a possible prescriptive right of plaintiff's unit to a parking space and driveway, plaintiff was allowed to sue to assert the claim without meeting derivative suit

---

[Section 17:20]

[1]Commercial Wharf East Condominium Ass'n v. Waterfront Parking Corp., 412 Mass. 309, 588 N.E.2d 675 (1992).

[2]Howell v. Glassman, 33 Mass. App. Ct. 349, 600 N.E.2d 173 (1992).

[3]McElligott v. Lukes, 42 Mass. App. Ct. 61, 674 N.E.2d 1108 (1997).

[4]CBK Brook House I Ltd. Partnership v. Berlin, 64 Mass. App. Ct. 913, 834 N.E.2d 1251 (2005).

requirements.[5]

Actions of unit owners in violation of provisions of the condominium documents or without requisite permission of the association have been invalidated and wrongful structures ordered removed.[6] A balcony built by a unit owner was ordered removed, but the condominium trustees who had mistakenly authorized it were exonerated from liability.[7]

As to other matters: An owner of a residential unit was held to have standing to seek a zoning variance to change to commercial use when the condominium documents did not prohibit that action.[8] A condominium organization was required to file bond to appeal an abutter's zoning permit in Boston.[9] A condominium was held not to be a "public building" subject to strict liability for injury under M.G.L.A. c. 143, § 51, applicable to places of assembly, theatres, and other buildings.[10] A prospective purchaser of a commercial unit and associated parking spaces, frustrated in the acquisition by opposition and actions of the condominium board and unit owners, sued them for allegedly tortious wrongs, but the suit was dismissed under the anti-SLAPP statute.[11] When some unit owners claimed that their condominium association had acquired adjoining land as part of its common areas and facilities by adverse possession, a complex series of proceedings led eventually to a conclusion that the condominium association was the appropriate plaintiff, but the court allowed unit owners to pursue the case on a derivative basis.[12]

§ 17:21 Assessment and collection of common expense funds

One of the most important functions of a condominium organization is, as mentioned in § 17:12, to plan, budget for, assess and collect the common expense charges, and to disburse the funds in accordance with the budget. Usually it

---

[5]Beckman v. Bard, 9 L.C.R. 261 (2001).

[6]Xifaras v. Andrade, 59 Mass. App. Ct. 789, 798 N.E.2d 291 (2003); Pashman v. Eliachar, 7 L.C.R. 48 (1999); Leone v. Silverman, 12 L.C.R. 460 (2004).

[7]Lilley v. Rich, 27 Mass. App. Ct. 1212, 545 N.E.2d 622 (1989).

[8]39 Joy Street Condominium Ass'n v. Board of Appeal of Boston, 426 Mass. 485, 688 N.E.2d 1363 (1998).

[9]Jack v. Board of Appeal of Boston, 15 Mass. App. Ct. 311, 445 N.E.2d 184 (1983).

[10]Osorno v. Simone, 56 Mass. App. Ct. 612, 779 N.E.2d 645 (2002).

[11]Office One, Inc. v. Lopez, 437 Mass. 113, 769 N.E.2d 749 (2002).

[12]Sea Pines Condominium III Ass'n v. Steffens, 61 Mass. App. Ct. 838, 814 N.E.2d 752 (2004).

is the professional manager who prepares the annual budget within guidelines laid down by the board, and then presents it to the board of trustees or managers for their approval. In most condominiums the budget-setting power is vested in the board, which prepares or approves it and presents it to the unit owners, who do not have any veto. The remedy of the unit owners, if they are dissatisfied with the budget, is to elect a new board of trustees at the next opportunity. Once duly assessed, common expenses constitute a lien upon the units pursuant to § 6(a)(i) and are a personal liability of the unit owner pursuant to § 6(b) of Chapter 183A.

Section 6(c), extensively amended in the 1990s, sets forth the provisions for collection. The condominium organization must first give notice by certified mail, specifying the delinquent amount, when any assessment has been delinquent for 60 days, and also within 30 days of filing an enforcement action, to the unit owner and to a first mortgagee of the unit which has informed the organization of its name and address. Provisions calling for written notices to and from mortgagees are set forth in § 4(5) of the statute.

The enforcement of such a lien is "in the manner provided in" the mechanics lien statute, M.G.L.A. c. 254, §§ 5 and 5A, the latter section having been adopted for the specific purpose of condominium liens, and having withstood legal attack.[1] It is provided in § 6(c) that the lien has priority over all liens and encumbrances on the unit except for those established prior to the master deed, real estate taxes and assessments, and a first mortgage on the unit recorded before the date of the delinquency, subject to provisos. The statutory provisos sound like, and probably were, a negotiated deal between lawyers representing condominium organizations and lawyers representing mortgage lenders to unit owners. In brief, it is provided that the condominium lien has priority even over such a mortgage to the extent of six months of duly assessed, ordinary common expense charges, plus costs and attorneys fees, but a mortgagee faced with such a prospect can prevent action to foreclose the lien by paying up the six months charges and expenses and agreeing to pay future ordinary common expense assessments. The agreement to pay future assessments passes to a purchaser upon foreclosure of the mortgage and the mortgagee is no longer liable.

Beyond that, if a unit is rented to a tenant, the condomin-

[Section 17:21]
[1]Bankers Trust Company of California, N.A. v. Halliday, 6 L.C.R. 122 (1998).

ium organization is given the right to collect the rent when the unit owner landlord is 25 days delinquent in paying common charges. That is subject to notice requirements and a non-judicial exchange of certifications, under which a unit owner may be subject to treble damages for misrepresentations. Section 4(6) of Chapter 183A requires unit owners to provide to the condominium organization the names of tenants and occupants of the unit "other than visitors for less than thirty days." The statute prohibits "retaliatory action" by a unit owner against a tenant who pays rent to the condominium organization, and permits the condominium organization to pursue other remedies against the defaulting unit owner. If a first mortgagee asserts an assignment of rents, it may collect thereunder, but then becomes liable for all assessments and costs, past and future.

It has been held that no set-offs may be asserted against an action to collect unpaid common charges.[2] When a town took a tax title on condominium units, it was held to have become liable for payment of common assessments, including those for the period between the taking and the tax title foreclosure.[3]

§ 17:22 Maintenance and repair

The basic obligation of the organization of unit owners or its hired managers is of course to maintain and repair the common areas and facilities in good order and condition. The trustees or managers who fail to do so may be held liable for their own actions[1] or for the negligence of a contractor they hired,[2] but negligence must be adequately demonstrated.[3] The condominium organization may sue the developer[4] or the architect[5] for faulty work, but must do so in a timely manner.[6] A unit owner's suit against the condominium developer because of a leaky roof was upheld even though

---

[2]Trustees of Prince Condominium Trust v. Prosser, 412 Mass. 723, 592 N.E.2d 1301 (1992); Baker v. Monga, 32 Mass. App. Ct. 450, 590 N.E.2d 1162 (1992); Blood v. Edgar's, Inc., 36 Mass. App. Ct. 402, 632 N.E.2d 419 (1994).

[3]Town of Milford v. Boyd, 434 Mass. 754, 752 N.E.2d 732 (2001).

[Section 17:22]

[1]McEneaney v. Chestnut Hill Realty Corp., 38 Mass. App. Ct. 573, 650 N.E.2d 93 (1995).

[2]O'Brien v. Christensen, 422 Mass. 281, 662 N.E.2d 205 (1996).

[3]Hawkins v. Jamaicaway Place Condominium Trust, 409 Mass. 1005, 568 N.E.2d 1126 (1991).

[4]Libman v. Zuckerman, 33 Mass. App. Ct. 341, 599 N.E.2d 642 (1992).

[5]Aldrich v. ADD Inc., 437 Mass. 213, 770 N.E.2d 447 (2002).

[6]Beaconsfield Townhouse Condominium Trust v. Zussman, 49

the condominium association had executed a release affecting the common areas and facilities, it being held that the trustees of the association had no authority to settle claims of individual unit owners.[7] That principle was further recognized, but a unit owner's suit against the developer resting on negligent construction of common areas and facilities was rejected.[8] A unit owner may require the condominium organization to take such action only through proper assertion of a derivative claim.[9] When four unit owners (out of five in all) were effectively in control of the condominium organization, they were held to have standing to sue for allegedly improperly done repairs to the condominium property.[10]

§ 17:23 Casualty; insurance

Section 17 of Chapter 183A provides for rebuilding after fire or other casualty as part of "the necessary work of maintenance, repair and replacement, using common funds, including the proceeds of any insurance, for that purpose," subject to the important proviso that the "loss does not exceed ten per cent of the value of the condominium prior to the casualty."

If the loss exceeds that amount, then there is a choice to be made by the unit owners within 120 days after the casualty occurs. If 75% of the unit owners do not agree within the 120-day period to proceed with repairs or restoration, then the condominium may be terminated by a partition proceeding. If they do agree to proceed with repairs or restoration, then the costs in excess of common funds, including insurance proceeds, is a common expense, and if such excess is greater than 10% of the value of the condominium prior to the casualty, then any unit owner who did not join in the agreement may, by a proceeding in the superior court, require the condominium organization to purchase his unit at fair market value.

That right of a non-agreeing unit owner to a "bail out" could serve as a lever or an inducement to refrain from agreeing to restoration, which in most cases is undesirable. Consequently, that feature has been wholly eliminated from

---

Mass. App. Ct. 757, 733 N.E.2d 141 (2000).

[7]Golub v. Milpo, Inc., 402 Mass. 397, 522 N.E.2d 954 (1988).

[8]Cigal v. Leader Development Corp., 408 Mass. 212, 557 N.E.2d 1119 (1990).

[9]Cote v. Levine, 52 Mass. App. Ct. 435, 754 N.E.2d 127 (2001); Turner v. Wright, 12 L.C.R. 134 (2004).

[10]Bedfordor Limited Partnership v. Forgione, 14 L.C.R. 20 (2006).

the Uniform Condominium Act.

Mortgagees of condominium units often require that the power of agreement to restoration in the event of casualty be exercised by, or only with the consent of, the mortgagee, even when there has been no default in the loan.

Like all property owners, condominium managers need to weigh and balance costs against risks, and to make judgments as to insurance amounts, types and deductibles. Casualty insurance as well as public liability insurance held by a condominium organization is usually made payable to members of the board of trustees or managers, or some of them, as "insurance trustees for the benefit of the unit owners and their mortgagees." The individual unit owners and their unit mortgagees may be issued certificates by the insurer certifying as to the total amount of coverage and the unit percentages of the particular units.

It is generally advisable to require in the condominium documents that the board carry 100% replacement cost insurance and that a periodic (usually annual) insurance appraisal be made to determine the appropriate amount. Mortgagees of units should not expect the kind of loss payment rights they customarily require on non-condominium loans. The proceeds of insurance on a condominium must always be available in the first instance to the condominium board for restoration, but the vote of the unit owner on the question of restoration after substantial casualty may be taken over by the mortgagee.

The established insurance industry definition of a building, and the criteria of elements included in the building, are such that they go beyond the usual condominium definition of common areas and facilities and include portions of the condominium units. In particular, the standard master policy will include interior lath and plaster, non-bearing partitions, and to some extent wall finishing materials and built-in features. If there is a casualty loss, the proceeds of insurance should be applied to restoration of these elements of units as well as the common areas and facilities. However, if a unit owner has added such things as wall paneling, additional non-bearing partitions, built-ins, etc., he should not look to the master policy but should insure these special features himself. The insurer who issues the master policy will ordinarily make available to unit owners individual policies covering their unit improvements and contents, and individual public liability of the unit owner.

Drawing the line between coverage by the master policy and individual unit elements which are not covered is sometimes difficult. This is particularly so when unit owners have made substantial interior improvements or modifications, and in many condominiums there are provisions requiring unit owners to furnish the board with notice and specification of all interior changes. In any event, it is advisable to vest some power of reasonable allocation of insurance proceeds in the board, first to restoration of common areas and facilities, and then, as to any remaining proceeds, among unit owners in proportion to the damage to their respective units. This principle also applies to differential assessments for repairs.[1] Ordinarily the condominium board will contract for all of the restoration, and not dole out funds to unit owners.

§ 17:24 Improvements

The distinction between "maintenance and repair" for which common assessment may be made, and "improvement," subject to provisions of § 18 of Chapter 183A is not always clear. When normal aging and wear and tear brings an element of the common areas and facilities to a condition in which it needs to be replaced, it is natural and sensible to do so with the most durable and up-to-date materials and products. It is also natural for the managers of such a project to assert that they have made an "improvement." That term, however, should be reserved entirely for facilities that did not previously exist in the condominium, and should not be applied to replaced facilities, even if they are in some way or to some extent "better" than the old one.

The reason for such caution is that § 18 provides that (a) if 50% or more but less than 75% of the unit owners agree "to make an improvement to the common areas and facilities," the cost is to be borne by those so agreeing, and (b) if 75% or more so agree, then the cost is assessed as a common charge to all unit owners, but again, similarly to the case of restoration of casualty loss as referred to in the preceding paragraph D, if the cost of the improvement is in excess of 10% of the value of the condominium, a non-agreeing owner may by a superior court proceeding require purchase of his unit by the condominium organization at fair market value. The obvious flaw in this approach is that it invites dissension and ill-feeling between a majority who want the improvement and may have to pay for it themselves and the "holdouts" in the additional 25% they must persuade to join them in order to

---

[Section 17:23]

[1]Belson v. Thayer & Associ-   ates, Inc., 32 Mass. App. Ct. 256, 588 N.E.2d 695 (1992).

have it charged as a common expense. The holdouts may be regarded as looking for a free ride since they will benefit from the improvement unless the over-10% provision applies and they in fact opt out of the condominium.

Happily, in 2005 the Land Court lead the way on this subject in the right direction. Plaintiff unit owners brought a derivative action contesting the authority of the condominium trustees of the 50–60 Longwood Avenue Condominium to impose a large special assessment for alleged improvements not authorized by the unit owners.[1] As a matter of first impression Judge Piper found most of the proposed work to be "repairs" and not "improvements." Referring to "real world distinctions" he noted that adding elements of new technology which were previously lacking "does not, by itself, bring the project within the realm of an improvement." While giving weight to the discretion of the trustees and the potential urgency of some repairs, he noted that a proposed glass enclosure of the loggia did seem to be an improvement. Although the condominium is on registered land, Judge Piper also observed that many of the issues posed "concern matters generally not part of the Land Court's customary diet of cases" and possibly should be referred to the Superior Court.

Sometimes unit owners desire to make additions to their own units at their own expense which in effect involve modification of the common areas and facilities; the addition of a fireplace and chimney being an example. The statute does not preclude permitting this by appropriate master deed and bylaw provisions, without requiring unit owners' votes under § 18, and such provisions are sometimes included in condominium documents.

TOPIC G: SPECIAL TYPES

§ 17:25 Conversion

When an existing building containing previously rental apartments is to be converted to the condominium form of ownership, some special considerations are involved. In defining the units in the master deed, one should take into account the definitions of the same apartments which were previously set forth in leases. A tenant who is purchasing a unit which he has long occupied as an apartment should not

---

[Section 17:24]

[1]Bonderman v. Naglich, 13 L.C.R. 406 (2005).

be faced with any surprises as to the boundaries of his unit, its included facilities, or appurtenances such as parking spaces.

It has been a common practice for the converting owner to offer the units in the first instance for sale to the tenants, often at a discount from the market prices. From the tenants' standpoint it may be desirable for them to form a committee and seek common or coordinated legal representation. The interests of the tenants collectively lie in establishing the good order, repair and condition of the buildings, and in having the condominium documents in a form which is generally satisfactory to them. Their interests may include participation in the managing board as the developer's control is relinquished, the means of determining the common expense budget, the provisions therein for reserve funds, the disposition of parking spaces and other appurtenances, and also the protection through the remaining terms of their leases of tenants who are not purchasing their units.

From the late 1970s until the mid-1990s many Massachusetts communities struggled to preserve the availability of rental housing by means of rent control and strict regulation of conversion of rental housing accommodations to condominiums for sale. Statewide regulation of conversion of rental housing to condominium or cooperative form was enacted by Chapter 527, Acts of 1983, which also validated local controls. Complex regulatory controls and judicial interpretation thereof ensued. The cases are not cited or discussed herein because M.G.L.A. c. 40P, effective in 1995, wholly abolished rent control and all state and local regulation of conversions. However, some of the decisions may have zoning implications outside the realm of rent control and anti-conversion, relating to definition of "multi-family residential use,"[1] or change of non-conforming use.[2] In 1996 Boston adopted an ordinance regulating eviction of tenants in buildings converted to condominium or cooperative, but that was invalidated as contrary to M.G.L.A. c. 40P.[3]

§ 17:26 Interval ownership

M.G.L.A. c. 183B, enacted in 1987, provides for interval

[Section 17:25]

[1]Boston Redevelopment Authority v. Charles River Park C Co., 21 Mass. App. Ct. 777, 490 N.E.2d 810 (1986).

[2]Gamsey v. Building Inspector of Chatham, 28 Mass. App. Ct. 614, 553 N.E.2d 1311 (1990).

[3]Greater Boston Real Estate Bd. v. City of Boston, 428 Mass. 797, 705 N.E.2d 256 (1999).

ownership, or "time-share" of units of real estate. Condominium units are of the appropriate type, and may be included in a time-share scheme, but Chapter 183B stands alone and is not a sub-part of Chapter 183A, nor dependent on it. Consequently, the time-share form of "ownership" is considered separately in **Topic C of Chapter 18**.

In a case arising before enactment of Chapter 183B, involving real estate taxation of condominium units subject to a time-share scheme, the trial court held that time-sharing was not a legally permissible interest in real estate.[1]

Section 11 of Chapter 183B provides that: "If all of the documents constituting the project instrument are recorded, time-shares shall not be created in any unit in a project unless expressly permitted by the project instrument. No amendment to a project instrument which is recorded shall permit the creation of time-shares unless the owners of at least eighty per cent of the units, or any larger vote required by the project instrument or by law, consent to such amendment." Nevertheless, if it desired to exclude time-sharing from a condominium, as is often the case, it should be so provided in the master deed.

§ 17:27 Commercial and mixed; municipal participation; other

Section 21 of Chapter 183A provides that: "If a condominium does not contain any unit which is designed for occupancy by only one family or household, or if the floor area of all those units which are designed for occupancy by only one family or household does not in the aggregate exceed ten percent of the floor area of all units in the condominium, then the following provisions shall be applicable notwithstanding any other provisions of this chapter, and such condominium shall be considered a commercial condominium."

The "following provisions" are exceptions from the requirements set forth in other sections of Chapter 183A. It is important to note that if 10% or more of the total floor area of a condominium is devoted to residential units, then the commercial units therein, even if occupying 90% of the floor area, are not entitled to any exceptions, and the entire condominium must abide by the "regular" provisions of the statute. Because of that, § 21 is not applicable or pertinent to most "mixed" condominiums, containing both residential and commercial units. Thus, commercial condominiums are

---

[Section 17:26]

[1]McCabe v. Board of Asses-

sors of Provincetown, 402 Mass. 728, 525 N.E.2d 640 (1988).

usually exclusively so. Such an arrangement may be suitable for, say, an office building for a group of medical doctors or other professionals. Each unit owner therein may then take deductions for his own real estate taxes as well as the common expense charges and depreciation of the unit cost.

The exceptions which are allowed in a commercial condominium include permission for the by-laws to provide (1) for allocations of common profits, common expenses and voting rights in proportions other than those of the percentages of interest of the units in the common areas and facilities, (2) for exemption of unit owners from personal liability for common expenses (but the lien remains), (3) for limitation of the priority of first mortgage liens over common expense liens, (4) for use of "other impartial determination" as well as arbitration for dispute resolution, (5) for vesting control of the management board in any one or more unit owners, regardless of percentages of interest, and (6) for exemption from or provisions differing from subsection (c) of § 6, subsections (c) through (k) and (m) of § 10, and §§ 17, 18 and 19. It is also provided that the master deed need not state the number of rooms in a commercial unit, and may require trustees or managers to act by more than a majority of their number.

These broad exceptions permit the application of economic and managerial criteria to such condominiums. For instance: common expenses may be determined and allocated according to various measures, such as floor area, insurance risks, utility usage and even volume and type of traffic and usage of facilities generated by particular business activities; charges for capital repairs and improvements may be allocated according to floor areas, cubic footage of space or appraised values; managerial powers may be distributed among the several unit owners or may be retained largely or wholly by one dominant unit owner; there may be rights of preemption as well as first refusal; there may be restrictions limiting use to particular businesses or professions, and protecting unit owners against competitive activities within the condominium.

Section 20 of Chapter 183A provides for participation by cities and towns in the form and use of condominiums. A municipality may become a unit owner, be liable for common expenses, and participate in the condominium organization. Or a municipality may contract for the construction of a condominium building for municipal purposes, or itself be the declarant of a condominium wholly or partly for municipal purposes, and may sell units therein not needed for municipal purposes.

Finally, it should be noted that Chapter 183A does not wholly pre-empt the field of horizontal or complex disposition of spaces into separate ownerships. There are several other statutory provisions dealing with so-called air rights. M.G.L.A. c. 40, § 22E, permits cities and towns to lease air rights in municipal properties other than park and conservation land, M.G.L.A. c. 81, § 7L permits the state department of highways to lease space over public highways, and M.G.L.A. c. 81A, § 15, does the same for the Massachusetts Turnpike Authority, in each case for a term not to exceed 99 years, and any buildings erected pursuant thereto to be taxable to the lessee.

Furthermore, the common law did not preclude separate ownership of spaces not directly associated with underlying land. Such dispositions were sometimes made before the condominium statute was enacted, and common law divisions of the condominium type may still be useful and particularly suitable in some circumstances. Examples may be the combination in a given building or complex of buildings of, say, (i) public and private housing, a parking garage or a transportation terminal and retail stores, (ii) a hotel and residences, or (iii) a hospital or clinic and offices. In such cases the basic divisions between the disparate uses may be accomplished by agreements and instruments devised by creative lawyers based upon common law principles, and the uses which involve multiple spaces may then be dealt with in the form of a statutory condominium.

Chapter 18

Cooperatives; Homeowners' Associations; Time Shares

KeyCite®: Cases and other legal materials listed in KeyCite Scope can be researched through the KeyCite service on Westlaw®. Use KeyCite to check citations for form, parallel references, prior and later history, and comprehensive citator information, including citations to other decisions and secondary materials.

TOPIC A: COOPERATIVES

§ 18:1   The concept; federal tax considerations

A cooperative, like a condominium, is a form of ownership in which there is a combination of individual possession of separate spaces and management in common of the several spaces. The manner in which this is accomplished differs markedly between the two forms.

In the cooperative form the ownership of the real estate and the management thereof is vested in a corporation, and the individuals obtain possession of their separate spaces by means of a so-called proprietary lease to which they become entitled by owning stock in the corporation. Pursuant to state laws condominium units are deemed to be separate parcels of real estate, and are separately subject to real estate tax and separately mortgageable, entitling the unit owner to federal tax deduction of amounts paid for real estate taxes and mortgage interest. In a cooperative the taxes are assessed to and paid by the corporation, and the entire property is mortgaged by the corporation. Therefore, in order for the owner of a space in a cooperative to deduct his share of the taxes and the mortgage interest requires an accommodation under the federal tax laws. Those laws do so provide, and in that sense a cooperative is a creature of the federal income tax law.

In order to qualify as a "cooperative housing corporation" under the Internal Revenue Code[1] a corporation must meet the following tests:

(1) It must have only one class of stock;

(2) Each of its stockholders must be entitled, solely by reason of his ownership of stock of the corporation, to occupy for dwelling purposes a house, or an apartment in a building, owned or leased by the corporation;

(3) No stockholder may be entitled to receive any distribution not out of earnings and profits of the corporation except on a complete or partial liquidation of the corporation; and

(4) 80% or more of its gross income for an applicable taxable year must be derived from tenant-stockholders.

The tenant-stockholders are also subject to Internal Revenue Code tests. In order to be entitled to the deductions, the tenant-stockholder must be an individual, and he must have paid for his shares of stock in full "in an amount not less than an amount shown to the satisfaction of the Secretary [of the Treasury] as bearing a reasonable relationship to the portion of the value of the corporation's equity in the houses or apartment building and the land on which situated which is attributable to the house or apartment which such individual is entitled to occupy."

If those tests are met, then the tenant-stockholders may individually take federal income tax deductions for their proportionate shares of real estate taxes paid by the cooperative housing corporation on the cooperative real estate, and

---

[Section 18:1]

[1]I.R.C. § 216.

of the interest on indebtedness of the corporation incurred in the acquisition, construction, alteration, rehabilitation or maintenance of the premises.

There are certain exceptions to the requirement that the cooperative housing corporation derive 80% of its gross income from the tenant-stockholders, as follows:

(1) Stock owned and apartments leased by the federal or state government or agencies thereof for the purpose of providing housing facilities are not taken into account;

(2) Stock and apartment leaseholds acquired by a lending institution by foreclosure or instrument in lieu of foreclosure are treated as owned by a tenant-stockholder for up to three years from the date of acquisition; and

(3) Payments by a person who sold property to a cooperative and owned stock therein, i.e., the developer, is considered income derived from a tenant-stockholder for three years from such seller's acquisition of the stock even though the seller is not an individual.

In addition to deductibility of real estate taxes and mortgage interest, there are other tax benefits available to the tenant-stockholders. If a tenant-stockholder uses his cooperative apartment premises in a trade or business for the production of income, his stock may be depreciable. When a tenant-stockholder buys or sells stock and a proprietary lease in a cooperative housing corporation and uses the premises as his principal residence, the transaction is qualified for "rollover," or nonrecognition of gain, just as with any other sale and purchase of a principal residence.

§ 18:2   The Massachusetts statute

M.G.L.A. c. 157B, enacted in 1983, provides for cooperative housing corporations. The salient points include the following:

• Corporations organized as cooperatives under former, now repealed, § 3A of M.G.L.A. c. 157, may comply with the new act by acceptance.

• The name of a cooperative corporation must include that word, and other use of the word is subject to penalty.

• The power to make, amend or repeal bylaws must be reserved to the stockholders.

• The articles or by-laws of the corporation may provide for voting per member or per unit rather than by shares, mail ballots, redemption or recall of stock, termination of membership rights or privileges of a stockholder and standards of eligibility to become a stockholder.

• The board must make annual apportionment in

prescribed alternative manners, of the net savings of the corporation.

• Termination of all proprietary leases is permitted with the consent of lessees holding 80 percent of the stock, or more if so provided in the by-laws.

• Stockholders of such a corporation are referred to as "members." A "proprietary lease" is simply defined as "an agreement between a cooperative corporation and its stockholder for occupancy of a dwelling unit owned by the cooperative corporation."

• Finally, and importantly, the statute provides that: "Any financial institution organized under the laws of the commonwealth and supervised either by the commissioner of banks or the commissioner of insurance shall be authorized to make loans secured by a pledge of a proprietary lease and the appurtenant stock of a cooperative corporation upon the same terms and with the same limitations as loans secured by mortgages of real property." This provision makes it possible for a purchaser of a cooperative apartment, i.e. of stock and a proprietary lease, to finance the purchase with a mortgage loan in the same manner as a purchaser of a condominium unit might do so.

§ 18:3   Share interests; proprietary lease

In order that each member or proprietor have an interest in the cooperative corporation proportionate to his investment, he is ordinarily issued or sold a number of shares of stock which bears the same relationship, as may be reasonably determined, to the total number of shares issued as the value of his apartment bears to the total value of the cooperative premises. Then, if each share has one vote, the voting power of the proprietors would be proportionate to the values of their apartments. However, as noted above, the statute permits variations in voting power.

The respective powers, functions and duties of the stockholders as such, the board of directors, and the officers of the cooperative corporation are ordinarily similar to those in a business corporation. The precise terms thereof, however, as set forth in the by-laws of the corporation, are of interest to the tenant-stockholders, and they may wish to have reserved to themselves as stockholders some prerogatives or judgments which in a true business corporation would more often be left to the directors or officers.

A key feature of a cooperative, as well as of a condominium, is the non-severability of the possessory rights to an apartment from the basic ownership rights. In a cooperative that is accomplished by provisions, which ordinarily appear in the proprietary lease and may also appear in the corporate documents, that a tenant-stockholder may transfer his shares of stock and proprietary lease only as a unit, and may not transfer either of them separately. It is also common to provide a first refusal on any sale by a tenant-stockholder in favor of the cooperative corporation.

The proprietary leases themselves are of primary importance to the cooperative owners. They are ordinarily written for a long term, something under 100 years. The rent, or monthly charges as they may be called, cover the tenant-stockholder's proportionate share of real estate taxes, mortgage carrying charges and all expenses of operation, maintenance and management of the entire premises, and a reserve fund for long-term maintenance and repair. These leases give each tenant-stockholder the right to exclusive occupancy and possession of his own apartment and the right to use common facilities in common with all other tenants-stockholders. As stated above, the tenant-stockholder cannot assign his lease or possessory rights separately from a sale of his entire interest, including his stock, and there is usually a requirement of consent of the board of the cooperative corporation to any such sale or any subletting. The eminent domain provisions in a proprietary lease are generally similar to those in any apartment lease, but, of course, there may be special considerations in some cases.

Default under a cooperative proprietary lease poses special problems, but, subject to statutory provisions, the cooperative cooperation may be given a right to evict the defaulting tenant-stockholder and to require surrender of his stock, which may be canceled if he does not do so.

The sale of shares of stock representing a cooperative apartment was treated as real estate and afforded specific performance.[1]

In representing a purchaser of a cooperative apartment, a conveyancer should consider all of the foregoing, and should not, of course, forget the basic conveyancer's interest in good title in the cooperative corporation.

§ 18:4 Management

In cooperatives the proprietors' interest in management issues is much the same as those of condominium unit own-

---

[Section 18:3]

[1]Blum v. Kenyon, 29 Mass. App. Ct. 417, 560 N.E.2d 742 (1990).

ers. In the case of cooperatives the proprietors' degree of control and remedies will depend much more on the bylaws of the corporation and the terms of the proprietary leases, since there is no regulatory scheme as extensive as that applicable to condominiums.

A cooperative was held to be sufficiently similar to a condominium to be entitled to a specific statutory exemption of condominiums from a sprinkler retrofit requirement.[1] Cooperative shareholder-proprietors were held not to be entitled to residential real estate tax exemptions under M.G.L.A. c. 59, § 5C.[2] The conversion of a cooperative into a condominium upon vote of 80% of the shares was upheld once the court was satisfied that tests of fair dealing and good faith had been met.[3]

TOPIC B: HOMEOWNERS' ASSOCIATIONS

§ 18:5   The concept

The term homeowners' association is sometimes used generically to include condominiums and cooperatives, but the form considered here is one in which the dwellings and the lots on which they are situated are separately owned, and the development includes other land and facilities serving all of the homeowners which is owned by a separate entity, usually a trust or a nonprofit membership corporation, controlled by the homeowners. This may be a simple subdivision development, but might otherwise be a "cluster development," a "planned development," a "townhouse development," or even a "gated community" containing a golf course, in the Florida style.

The land and facilities held for the common benefit of the homeowners may of course take many forms. There are ordinarily recreational facilities, such as swimming pool, tennis courts, club house, and even a golf course, or water sports where the development includes or adjoins a waterway. There may also be parcels set aside for garden-

---

[Section 18:4]

[1]1010 Memorial Drive Tenants Corp. v. Fire Chief of Cambridge, 424 Mass. 661, 677 N.E.2d 219 (1997).

[2]Born v. Board of Assessors of Cambridge, 427 Mass. 790, 696 N.E.2d 142 (1998).

[3]Dennis Seashores, Inc., 7 L.C.R. 369 (1999), 12 L.C.R. 177 (2004).

ing, farming, or simply conservation.

In cluster developments and planned unit developments, provided for in the zoning act, the common land is ordinarily owned by a separate entity, which may be a conservation organization or one which is controlled by the lot owners. Under M.G.L.A. c. 59, § 11, such common land may be assessed as an additional assessment to each individual lot owner.

Such a development is initiated by a declaration, recorded in advance of lot or house sales, requiring each homeowner to be a member of the governing entity and to pay assessments and to abide by all of the rules and restrictions set forth in the declaration and the bylaws of the organization. The restrictions ordinarily prescribe permitted housing types, architectural style, building and grounds maintenance, use of vehicles, and the like.

§ 18:6   The association

As in the case of a condominium, the association owning the common lands and facilities may be a trust, and there are some hurdles to the use of a nonprofit membership corporation. M.G.L.A. c. 180 permits the formation of a nonprofit membership corporation only for specified purposes, and a homeowners' association as such is not among them. Sometimes, however, a homeowners' association may be formed to serve one or more of the permitted purposes, such as civic, educational, athletic, raising of choice breeds of domestic animals, agricultural or horticultural, or improving the physical aspects of a city or town and furthering the recreation and enjoyment of inhabitants thereof.

In any case such an association needs to have bylaws covering all of the elements that are covered in the bylaws of a condominium association. That includes election of trustees, managers and officers, meetings of the homeowner members, voting rights, etc., as to which considerable flexibility is possible since there are no statutory constraints. It also includes procedures for assessment of charges and collection thereof. In a condominium the organization has by statute both personal liability of the owner and a lien for such charges, but in a homeowners' association any such liability or lien rests on contractual commitments. Since there may be issues as to whether such provisions run with the land, it is advisable to have each initial and subsequent homeowner agree thereto in writing.

§ 18:7   Legal status

A homeowners' association might in some circumstances

qualify as a tax exempt organization as a "civic league" under
I.R.C. § 501(c)(4), or as a "social and recreational club" under
§ 501(c)(7). More likely, if its annual assessments account for
60% or more of its annual gross income, it would be classified as a homeowners' association under § 528 of the code.

Aside from tax considerations, the principal issues raised
with respect to homeowners' associations have arisen (mostly
in other states) from the observation that such associations,
or at least large ones comprising hundred of housing units,
act as if they were governmental entities. Their regulations
and restrictions are equivalent to and enforced like zoning
laws, and their assessments are like real estate taxes. Their
governance may not conform with democratic principles, and
sometimes they are even guilty of improper discrimination.
The office of the Attorney General of New York addresses
some of the issues on its website.

Massachusetts has no general regulation of homeowners'
associations, and problems with them have not come to the
fore. Lawyers representing developers wishing to use this
form of organization should of course take such issues into
account and be astute to abide by the prevailing Massachusetts rules of full disclosure and fair dealing in all
respects.

TOPIC C: TIME SHARES

§ 18:8   The concept

Chapter 183B, the Real Estate Time-Share Act, adopted in
1987, defines "time-share" as "a time-share estate or a time
share license." The term "time-share estate" is defined as "a
right to the occupancy of a unit or any of several units during five or more separated time periods over a period of at
least five years, including extension or renewal options,
coupled with a freehold estate or an estate for years in a
time-share property or a specified portion thereof," and the
term "Time-share license" is defined as "a right to the occupancy of a unit or any of several units during five or more
separated time periods not coupled with a freehold estate or
an estate for years." These rather cryptic definitions came
from a "model" act, intended to be as broad, permissive and
unrestrictive as possible.

In simple terms, a time-share is a right of occupancy for
part of a year, usually a week or two, of a residential unit or
apartment which will be occupied at other times by other
owners of a time-share in the same apartment. The statu-

tory clauses quoted above add a few refinements: First, it is not necessary to specify a particular unit; the right of occupancy may apply to any one of several units. Second, the time period for occupancy need not be the same each year for successive years, but may be any "separated time periods," of which there must be at least five during at least five years. Third, in order to be called an "estate," the right of occupancy must be "coupled with a freehold estate or an estate for years," the meaning of which is not clear at all. Those terms are not defined in the statute, but presumably depend on common law or other statutory definitions, and there is no indication of what "coupled with" means or how it is to be accomplished.

§ 18:9   Legal status

A bit (no more) of clarity is added by § 18 of the statute which provides:

A time-share estate, coupled with a freehold estate, shall be evidenced by a time-share deed, and a time-share estate, coupled with an estate for years shall be evidenced by a notice of time-share lease. A time-share license shall be evidenced by a notice of time-share license. Said deed, notice of time-share lease or notice of time-share license shall be recorded in the registry of deeds or land registration office for the district in which the time-share property is located; provided however, that the number of time-shares in a time-share property is more than twelve. The time-share deed shall include the information required by law to be set forth in a deed of real property and the notice of time-share lease or notice of time-share license shall include the information required by law to be set forth in a notice of lease. In addition such deed or notice shall include:

(1) a statement that the instrument relates to a time-share and is subject to the provisions of this chapter;

(2) a description of the time-share including designation of the unit or units, and the time-share property in which it is located;

(3) the book, page and date of recording of all time-share instruments denominating, creating or regulating the time-share;

(4) a statement of the use for which the time-share is intended and the restrictions, if any, on its use;

(5) the time-share expense liability and any voting rights assigned to the time-share; and

(6) any further provisions which the parties may deem desirable to set forth, consistent with the time-share instruments and the provisions of this chapter.

From this it appears that a time-share license is only a license and that a time-share estate coupled with an estate for years is only a leasehold.

Now for the assertion of a time-share estate being coupled with a "freehold estate," we turn to Section 3 of the statute, as follows:

> Section 3. (a) Except as otherwise provided in this chapter and notwithstanding any contrary rule of common law, a grant of an estate in a unit conferring the right of possession during a potentially infinite number of separated time periods creates an estate in fee simple having the character and incidents of such an estate at common law, and a grant of an estate in a unit conferring the right of possession during five or more separated time periods over a finite number of years equal to five or more, including extension or renewal options, creates an estate for years having the character and incidents of such an estate at common law.
>
> (b) Each time-share estate constitutes for all purposes a separate estate in real property; provided, however, that a time-share property shall be considered one parcel of real estate for the assessment and collection of real estate taxes, betterment assessments or portions thereof, annual sewer use charges, water rates and charges, and all other assessments or portions thereof, rates and charges of every nature, due to a city, town or district with respect to the time-share property. Notices of assessments and bills for taxes shall be furnished to and paid by the managing entity, if any, as agent the time-share owners.
>
> (c) A document transferring or encumbering a time-share estate may not be rejected for recording because of the nature or duration of such estate.

Clause (a) says that if the time-share right of occupancy is forever (potentially infinite), it is a fee simple, and clause (b) says it is a "separate estate in real property," except as to real estate taxes and such. However, notwithstanding those provisions, it is obvious that there are multiple owners of rights of occupancy in the same apartment or unit of real estate. Are they tenants-in-common? Can one finance a time-share purchase by mortgaging a two-week right of occupancy? Can one leave a time-share by will to anyone, regardless of transfer-control provisions in the time-share project documents? One may ask in fact whether those provisions as to "fee simple" and "separate estate" are legally sound or are just puff.

§ 18:10　The documents

A time-share project is created by a "time-share instrument," setting forth a "time-share plan," which may incorporate a "project instrument," setting forth "restrictions or covenants regulating the use, occupancy, or disposition of units in a project." A lawyer reviewing a proposed "sale contract" for a time-share should of course review all of those documents carefully, analyzing them and, as suggested above, the statute itself, with a grain of salt. The repute and track-record of the project developers and managers are always pertinent. The statute does contain provision that assessments for time-share expenses are liens on the time-share, enforceable in the manner provided in M.G.L.A. c. 254, § 5, and having priority over other liens similar to those for condominium common charges.

The interests of dues-paying members of a recreational camping club affording them use of a seasonal camping site for 25 years were held to be a "time-share license" under Chapter 183B. The club antedated Chapter 183B and the plaintiffs were allowed to avail themselves only of § 6 thereof upon their claims of violation of requirements of good faith.[1]

The statute does contain many provisions aimed at assuring disclosure and fairness, and referring to the potential securities-offering aspects of such projects. Beyond that, there are provisions with respect to "multi-location plans" and "exchange programs" pursuant to which time-share owners may take turns at various resorts all over the country and even beyond. The appeal of such vacation freedom seems to be growing, but it is not an easy job for a lawyer to tell his client what he is getting into.

[Section 18:10]

[1]Tiffany v. Sturbridge Camping Club, Inc., 32 Mass. App. Ct. 173, 587 N.E.2d 238 (1992).

Part V

DOCUMENTS AND CLOSING

Chapter 19

Deeds

TOPIC A: FORMS; COVENANTS

TOPIC B: ELEMENTS

TOPIC C: EXECUTION

TOPIC D: DELIVERY AND ACCEPTANCE; RECORDING

TOPIC A: FORMS; COVENANTS

§ 19:1 Forms

In 1913, the legislature provided for "statutory forms" of deeds and mortgages, and these, or versions of them, have become the norm. Forms printed by law-blank publishers follow these forms. There are so-called "short forms" of "warranty deed" and "quitclaim deed."[1] The latter is by far the most usual form of deed in Massachusetts.

A conveyance may be made by an instrument which is neither a quitclaim deed nor a warranty deed, but is simply a "grant," which by statute is sufficient to effect conveyance and imports no covenants. Such a deed is commonly referred to as a "release deed."

There is no prohibition on the use of old common law forms, and one may possibly encounter a deed in which the grantor "gives, grants, bargains sells and conveys" to the grantee "and his heirs and assigns," but none of those quoted words are necessary to effect a conveyance in fee simple.

The statute also provides that a "deed to uses" may be made, distinguished from a deed "in trust." That is, a deed running to "A to the use of B" will vest title in B. There may be a few situations in which that device is useful, although it is likely to confuse registry clerks and tax officials.

§ 19:2 Covenants

A deed which recites that it conveys "with warranty covenants" includes: "covenants on the part of the grantor, for himself, his heirs, executors, administrators and successors, with the grantee, his heirs, successors and assigns, that, at the time of the delivery of such deed, (1) he was lawfully seized in fee simple of the granted premises, (2) that the granted premises were free from all encumbrances, (3) that he had good right to sell and convey the same to the grantee

---

[Section 19:1]

[1]M.G.L.A. c. 183, §§ 1 to 7.

and his heirs and assigns, and (4) that he will, and his heirs, executors and administrators shall, warrant and defend the same to the grantee and his heirs and assigns against the lawful claims and demands of all persons." The "free from all encumbrances" provision may of course be limited by specifying in the deed the encumbrances to which the premises are subject.

A deed which recites that it conveys "with quitclaim covenants" includes: "covenants on the part of the grantor, for himself, his heirs, executors, administrators and successors, with the grantee, his heirs, successors and assigns, that at the time of the delivery of such deed the premises were free from all encumbrances made by him, and that he will, and his heirs, executors and administrators shall, warrant and defend the same to the grantee and his heirs and assigns forever against the lawful claims and demands of all persons claiming by, through or under the grantor, but against none other."

The salient differences are that the warranty deed applies to "all encumbrances" and to "all persons," while the quitclaim deed applies only to "encumbrances made by [the grantor]" and only to "persons claiming by, through or under the grantor."

It is important to note that the Massachusetts quitclaim deed warrants against encumbrances "made" by the grantor, but not against encumbrances "made or suffered" by the grantor,[1] as is the case under a limited warranty or special warranty deed, often called a quitclaim deed, in other states. Examples of encumbrances "suffered" but not "made" by a grantor might include rights of way established by prescription, governmental orders for layout or improvement of streets, sidewalks or the like, and betterment assessments.

In any event reliance is rarely placed upon deed covenants, and is more usually and sensibly placed upon the opinion of a qualified conveyancer based upon a properly prepared title abstract, and on title insurance issued pursuant to such opinion and abstract.

When the grantor is a fiduciary, a "fiduciary deed without covenants" may be appropriate. Since executors, administrators and conservators do not hold title and their deeds convey the title of the decedent or ward, covenants by such fiduciaries are not apt. However, trustees and guardians do hold

---

[Section 19:2]

[1]Silverblatt v. Livadas, 340 Mass. 474, 164 N.E.2d 875 (1960), overruling a prior decision and citing George P. Davis' first edition of this book.

title and may well make encumbrances thereon, and some trusts are business entities, so there is no evident reason for their deeds to be without covenants.

TOPIC B: ELEMENTS

§ 19:3   Parties; addresses

Grantors should be named so as to identify them as the same persons who hold record title to the property being conveyed. If names have changed by marriage or legal action, or if aliases are used, all the pertinent facts should be recited.

Grantees names come in the first instance from a purchase and sale agreement, but it is usually desirable to ask the purchasers or their attorney to specify exactly how they wish to take title. That will include the specification as to whether co-grantees are to be tenants in common, joint tenants, tenants by the entirety or other. If the purchase and sale agreement contains a clause permitting the designation of a nominee to take title, that must be taken into account.

M.G.L.A. c. 183, § 6, begins with the provision that: "Every deed presented for record shall contain or have endorsed upon it the full name, residence and post office address of the grantee and . . ." (the rest of it being quoted in the following section B.) A similar provision with respect to registered land appears in M.G.L.A. c. 185 § 61, requiring grantees' addresses also on mortgages and other instruments.

M.G.L.A. c. 183, § 6B, provides that: "All documents to be recorded in the land court or registry of deeds shall, where applicable, set forth in the margin the street address of the property which is affected by such document; provided, however, that failure to include such address shall not affect the validity of the document or the recording thereof."

Since failure to comply with these provisions "shall not affect the validity" of the deed, they serve largely as exhortations to draftsmen, though they are enforced to some extent by the registries of deeds.

§ 19:4   Consideration

M.G.L.A. c. 183, § 6, provides that: "Every deed presented for record shall contain . . . a recital of the amount of the full consideration thereof in dollars or the nature of the other consideration therefore, if not delivered for a specific monetary sum. The full consideration shall mean the total price for the conveyance without deduction for any liens or encumbrances assumed by the grantee or remaining thereon. All such endorsements and recitals shall be recorded as part of the deed. Failure to comply with this section shall not affect the validity of any deed. No register of deeds shall accept a deed for recording unless it is in compliance with the requirements of this section."

Usually the consideration is stated simply as a dollar amount. The full consideration includes the amount of any continuing lien or encumbrance to which the property remains subject, whether or not assumed by the grantee. Such continuing lien or encumbrance should be identified and the amount thereof specified. Failure to comply does not void the deed, but the registry will not accept it for recording without that data, and registry clerks are often reluctant to accept recitals as to "other consideration" that do not add up to a determinable dollar amount.

In the case of an exchange of property the stated "nature of the other consideration" might be "real estate having a value of $X." Deeds of gift should make it clear that it is a gift, and often refer to "nominal, non-monetary consideration", the "nature" of which might be described as "love and affection" or "the donative intent of the grantor." The consideration for some deeds, (such as in the resolution of a dispute) may be difficult to quantify in dollars, but doing so may be necessary to meet this statute and for purposes of deed excise tax stamps, discussed in § 6:14.

In any event a deed should recite that consideration was paid.[1] Such a recital may not be conclusive: a contingent additional consideration might be collected,[2] or an inadequate consideration might indicate a fraudulent conveyance upon which claims of grantor's creditors could arise.[3]

§ 19:5 Words of conveyance, covenants, habendum

The operative word of conveyance is usually "grant," but "convey" or possibly "release" will suffice. None of these words imports any covenants, and usually the deed will

---

[Section 19:4]

[1]Boynton v. Rees, 25 Mass. 329, 8 Pick. 329, 1829 WL 1869 (1829); Bartlett v. Bartlett, 86 Mass. 440, 4 Allen 440, 1862 WL 3771 (1862).

[2]Bressel v. Jolicoeur, 34 Mass.

App. Ct. 205, 609 N.E.2d 94 (1993).

[3]Fleet Nat. Bank of Massachusetts v. Merriam, 45 Mass. App. Ct. 592, 699 N.E.2d 1266 (1998); First Federal Sav. & Loan Ass'n of Galion, Ohio v. Napoleon, 428 Mass. 371, 701 N.E.2d 350 (1998).

grant "with quitclaim covenants," having the meaning quoted in § **19:2**. Some deeds may grant "with warranty covenants," the meaning of which is also there quoted.

In order to convey a fee simple estate at common law a deed would contain a habendum reciting "to have and to hold the said premises unto the grantee and his heirs and assigns forever." The statute makes that unnecessary and provides directly that: "A deed or reservation of real estate shall be considered to convey or reserve an estate in fee simple, unless a different intention clearly appears in the deed."[1]

When one wishes to convey an estate other than a fee simple, then the use of a habendum is still an appropriate device to accomplish the end. For instance, a deed to uses might begin with a grant from A to B, and then contain a habendum: "to have and to hold said premises unto said B and his heirs, but to the use of C and his heirs and assigns forever," which would vest fee simple title in C. A fee simple determinable might be created by a habendum: "to have and to hold said premises unto B and his heirs and assigns until the reverter date herein defined and no longer," with, of course, a defined reverter date, usually relating to the occurrence of a pertinent event. A condition subsequent might be created by a habendum: "to have and to hold said premises unto B and his heirs and assigns, subject, however, to the condition that . . .," followed by a defined condition and an express right of entry for condition broken. The distinction between a reverter and a right of entry for condition broken may not always be clear.[2] A life estate might be created by a granting clause from A to B for life and then to C, and preferably the words of grant are accompanied by a habendum to the same purport.[3]

§ 19:6 Description

The basic styles of describing a parcel of land are called a "bounding" description and a "running" description. Examples are set forth in the following paragraph 2.

Bounding descriptions are the norm in Massachusetts, and are uniformly required by the Land Court. To write a bounding description, stand on the parcel and look outward, perpendicularly to a property line. The direction in which

---

[Section 19:5]

[1]M.G.L.A. c. 183, § 13.

[2]Howson v. Crombie Street Congregational Church, 412 Mass. 526, 590 N.E.2d 687 (1992).

[3]Bernat v. Kivior, 22 Mass. App. Ct. 957, 494 N.E.2d 425 (1986).

you are looking is the direction by which that line "bounds" the parcel. It is customary to describe with reference to eight points of the compass rose, i.e., (as abbreviated here, but preferably not in deeds): N, NE, E, SE, S, SW, W, NW. Keep in mind that in Massachusetts magnetic North is 11 or 12 degrees west of true North, and that the difference between the two changes quite a bit over the course of a hundred years. Since bounding descriptions have long prevailed, it is usually advisable to stick with them, repeating the same description as in the last deed of the same parcel. However, slavish consistency is not called for; errors should be noted and corrected, and new information may be added.

A running description begins at a specified point, usually a monument in the ground, and proceeds, usually clockwise, along the boundary lines of the parcel, describing each by bearing and length, separating the line descriptions by "turning and running," and eventually returning to "the point of beginning." Some or all of the "bounding" information is often included. It is obvious that a thoroughly prepared running description contains much more detailed information than does a simple bounding description. Running descriptions are favored by surveyors, in part because they lend themselves to mathematical (computer) programs for determining "closure," i.e., that the stated bearings and distances will in fact get one back to the starting point.

Most parcels of land in urban and suburban areas, and many parcels in more rural areas, are now shown on recorded plans. It is possible to convey such a parcel by specifying it as "Lot No. . . ., as shown on a plan entitled ". . .", dated . . ., by . . ., registered land surveyor, recorded with . . . Registry of Deeds, Book . . ., Page . . .," without including any perimeter description at all. If the parcel has a street address, that should also be set forth. While deeds in such simplified form are not yet common, it seems likely that they will become more so in the future. The addition to such a plan reference of "and bounded and described as follows:" with a metes and bounds description set forth in the deed can serve the useful purpose of imparting information to buyers and sellers of the details of the transaction. However, that purpose is served only if the lawyers involved understand the descriptions and know how to explain them to their clients in reference to what they have seen on the site.

§ 19:7 Examples

The sample plan below is intended to show some of the elements involved in drafting descriptions and to illustrate the differences between bounding and running descriptions. It is of course not an engineered plan, and does not show bearings, distances, radii of curvature, road widths, lot areas and dimensions, and scale data, all of which would be shown on a properly engineered plan. The data of those kinds in the following sample descriptions are at least plausible in relation to the sample plan, but the numbers themselves were simply fabricated for the purpose of illustration. Based on the sample plan, examples of a bounding description and a running description of the land shown thereon (excepting Lot 7) are set forth below.

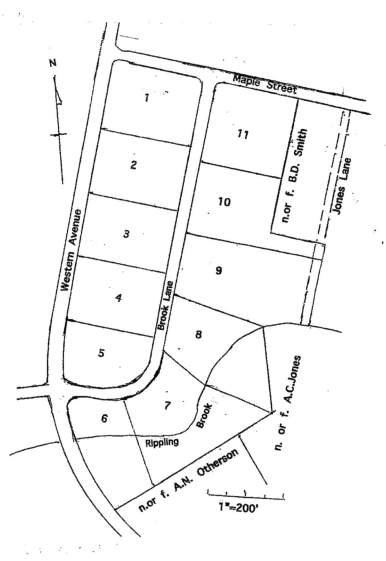

Bounding description:

SOUTHWESTERLY, WESTERLY and NORTHWEST-
ERLY by Western Avenue, 1,192.50 feet;

NORTHERLY by a curved line forming the intersection of
Western Avenue and Maple Street, 31.60 feet;

NORTHEASTERLY by Maple Street, 600.00 feet;

SOUTHEASTERLY by land shown on said plan as now or
formerly of B.D. Smith, 361.25 feet;

NORTHEASTERLY by the same, 148.00 feet;

SOUTHEASTERLY again by the same, 218.50 feet;

SOUTHERLY by Rippling Brook, by land shown on said
plan as now or formerly of A.C. Jones, 108 feet, more or less;

EASTERLY by said land now or formerly of A.C. Jones,
212.84 feet;

SOUTHWESTERLY by Lot 7 as shown on said plan by
two lines measuring, respectively, 195 feet, more or less, and
132 feet, more or less;

SOUTHEASTERLY by Brook Lane, 150.00 feet;

NORTHEASTERLY by said Lot 7, 250.00 feet; and

SOUTHEASTERLY by land shown on said plan as now or
formerly of A.N. Otherson, 125.00 feet;

Comprising Lots 1 through 6 and 8 through 11 as shown
on said plan, together with all right, title and interest of the
grantor in and to the fee and soil of Brook Lane, containing
in all 9.62 acres, more or less; subject to rights in and with
respect to Brook Lane appurtenant to said Lot 7, as set forth
in . . . Book . . . Page . . ., and to rights of others in Jones
Lane shown on said plan, set forth in . . . Book . . . Page
. . .

Running description:

Beginning at a point on the easterly side of Western Avenue at the southwesterly corner of the premises hereby
conveyed, and thence running NORTHWESTERLY.

NORTHERLY and NORTHEASTERLY by Western Ave-
nue by a line curving to the right, having a radius of 400.00
feet, a distance of 497.25 feet, including the intersection of
Brook Lane with Western Avenue; thence running

NORTH 15° 30′ EAST by Western Avenue, 685.25 feet;
thence turning and running

EASTERLY by the intersection of Western Avenue with
Maple Street, by a line curving to the right, having a radius
of 20.00 feet, a distance of 31.60 feet; thence running

SOUTH 74° 30′ EAST by Maple Street, 600.00 feet, including the intersection of Brook Lane with Maple Street; thence turning and running

SOUTH 15° 30′ WEST, bounded southeasterly by land shown on said plan as now or formerly of B.D. Smith, 361.25 feet; thence turning and running

SOUTH 74° 30′ EAST by the same, 148.00 feet; thence turning and running

SOUTH 15° 30′ WEST again by the same, by the southeasterly side of Jones Lane as shown on said plan, 218.50 feet; thence turning and running

WESTERLY by Rippling Brook, bounded southerly by land shown on said plan as now or formerly of A.C. Jones, 108 feet, more or less; thence turning and running

DUE SOUTH by the same, 212.84 feet; thence turning and running

NORTH 67° 10′ WEST, 195 feet, more or less, and NORTH 48o 30′ WEST, 132 feet, more or less, bounded southwesterly by Lot 7 shown on said plan; thence turning and running

SOUTHWESTERLY by Brook Lane by a line curving to the right, having a radius of 80.00 feet, a distance of 150.00 feet; thence turning and running

SOUTH 17° 50′ EAST, bounded northeasterly by said Lot 7, 250.00 feet; thence turning and running

SOUTH 62° 05′ WEST, bounded southeasterly by land shown on said plan as now or formerly of A.N. Otherson, 125.00 feet to the point and place of beginning;

Comprising [same as in bounding description]

§ 19:8 Title reference

M.G.L.A. c. 183, § 6A, provides that:

No instrument conveying unregistered land shall be accepted for recording unless (a) the instrument indicates that the land conveyed is the same as described in or conveyed by prior recorded instruments identified sufficiently to locate the place of recording within the registry, or states that the instrument does not create any new boundaries, or (b) the instrument identifies the land conveyed either by reference to a plan or plans previously recorded in the same registry of deeds and identified sufficiently to locate the place of recording therein, or by reference to a plan or plans recorded with the conveyance. Failure to comply with this section shall not affect the validity of any instrument.

This falls short of requiring a clear title reference. In the first place, most deeds do contain reference to a recorded plan, and in any event failure to comply has no consequences.

Nevertheless, inclusion of an appropriate title reference is important and should be considered as such by every draftsman of deeds. The reference should include specification of the deed, including the book and page of recording, by which the grantor acquired title. If there are multiple sources, all should be referred to. If the grantor acquired from an estate, the deed should identify the decedent, county and docket number, and the deed by which the decedent acquired title.

The common phrasing is "Being the same premises conveyed to the grantor by" the specified deed. Sometimes the recital is: "Meaning and intending to convey and hereby conveying the same premises . . ." If only part of the grantor's land is being conveyed, the title reference should so state and should specify with reasonable particularity which part.

§ 19:9   Other

Other items that are important to specify in a deed include encumbrances and appurtenances. As to encumbrances, the deed should recite that: "Said premises are hereby conveyed subject to the following:" with a listing of the instruments, along with their book and page numbers, by which such encumbrances were established. As to appurtenances, the recital may be that: "Said premises are hereby conveyed together with the rights and easements appurtenant thereto, to . . .," specifying the nature of such rights and the instruments by which they were established. Some recorded instruments, such as zoning permits, conservation orders of conditions and the like, often create both encumbrances and appurtenances, and in that case the recital may be that: "The premises are hereby conveyed subject to and with the benefit of the following:" again with a list of the instruments.

When new encumbrances are to be created by the deed, they should of course be spelled out and described with particularity.

With respect to real estate taxes, it is well to recite that the premises are conveyed "subject to taxes assessed as of January 1, [the year of or the year before the date of conveyance], which the grantee by acceptance hereof assumes and agrees to pay." Such acceptance and agreement is effective by "deed poll" without a signature of the grantee. The phrasing and dating of that clause is apt even when the grantor is going to pay part or most of the taxes assessed as of the specified date as an adjustment at the closing.

If there are other encumbrance obligations which the grantee is to assume and agree to, it is often advisable not to rely on deed poll, but to have the grantee sign the deed "in acceptance hereof and agreement to the provisions herein contained."

As noted in § **16:2**, a homestead estate may be established by recital in the deed by which the property is acquired.

TOPIC C: EXECUTION

§ 19:10   Signature

As stated in § **19:3**, the signature of a grantor should match his name as recited, which should match his name in the title-source instrument. If the title-source instrument incorrectly stated the grantor's name, or if names have changed by marriage or legal action, or if aliases are used, all the pertinent facts should be recited and errors corrected. A woman who was married after acquiring title and adopted her husband's name should use her current name and recite the name by which she was "formerly known as."

An illiterate person may sign with an X placed inside a box formed by his first and last names with a space in between and the words His Mark placed above and below the space. A blind person may sign his own name or may direct a person to sign for him in his presence. In any such case it is advisable for the pertinent facts to be stated before the notary and recited in the acknowledgment form.

A deed executed in blank with only oral authority to fill in the blanks is invalid.[1]

§ 19:11   Acknowledgement

A properly executed deed may be effective between the parties without acknowledgment, but in order to be recorded and to be effective with respect to third parties, it must be acknowledged. A deed between husband and wife is a special case and is not effective even between the parties unless it is acknowledged.[1] Within Massachusetts acknowledgment must be made before a notary public or justice of the peace. M.G.L.A. c. 222, § 8, provides that a person taking an acknowledge-

---

[Section 19:10]   N.E.2d 806 (1946).

[1]Macurda v. Fuller, 225 Mass. 341, 114 N.E. 366 (1916).

[Section 19:11]

[1]M.G.L.A. c. 209, § 3; McOuatt v. McOuatt, 320 Mass. 410, 69

ment shall print or type his name below his signature and state the date on which "my commission expires," but "failure to comply" does not invalidate the instrument or the record thereof.

Acknowledgment implicitly involves the personal appearance of the signatory before the notary, and it is improper for a notary to certify acknowledgement when the signatory did not either sign or identify his signature in the notary's presence. In one such case the court found no recoverable damages, but said of the notary that "his conscious lapse violates the most fundamental duty of a notary and our opinion should not be read as condoning the sloppy and grievous exercise of notary public commissions."[2]

The form of acknowledgement is not prescribed by statute. Traditionally it was stated as: "Then personally appeared the above-named [grantor] and acknowledged the foregoing instrument to be his free act and deed, before me, [notary public]." M.G.L.A. c. 183, § 42, provides that: "The forms set forth in the appendix to this chapter for taking acknowledgments to deeds and other instruments and for certifying the authority of officers taking proofs or acknowledgments may be used; but this shall not prevent the use of any other forms heretofore lawfully used."

In December 2003, the Governor of Massachusetts issued an Executive Order prescribing a form of acknowledgement as follows:

On this _____ day of _____, 20__, before me, the undersigned notary public, personally appeared _____, proved to me through satisfactory evidence of identification, which were _____, to be the person whose name is signed on the preceding or attached document, and acknowledged to me that *(he)(she)* signed it voluntarily for its stated purpose.

The Executive Order also prescribed related rules as to acknowledgments and jurats, including requirements that (1) evidence of identification must include either personal knowledge or at least one current governmentally issued document bearing photo and signature of the individual, and (2) all notarizations must bear an official seal including the notary's name, the words notary public and Commonwealth of Massachusetts, recital that my commission expires on (specified date), and a facsimile of the great seal of Massachusetts.

When an instrument is executed elsewhere in the United

---

[2]Bernal v. Weitz, 54 Mass.   (2002).
App. Ct. 394, 765 N.E.2d 798

States, or a "territory, district or dependency" thereof, an acknowledgment may be taken by a justice of the peace or notary public of another state, with an official seal or stamp affixed,[3] or by a "magistrate or commissioner appointed therefore by the governor of" Massachusetts, or by "any other officer therein authorized to take acknowledgments of deeds," provided that in the latter case there is attached a certificate of authority executed by the secretary of state or a clerk of court of the other state, meeting statutory requirements.[4]

Provision is made in M.G.L.A. c. 183, § 30(c), for acknowledgment of an instrument intended to be recorded in Massachusetts which is executed outside the United States. Pursuant to an international Convention this is now accomplished by a certificate known as an apostille, which is attached to the document as an allonge. The identity of foreign officials who are authorized to execute an apostille may be obtained from a United States consular office.

When an instrument executed in Massachusetts is to be recorded in or otherwise made effective in a foreign country, it may be acknowledged before a Massachusetts notary public, whose appointment is verified by a certificate of the Massachusetts Secretary of State, and then authenticated by an apostille executed by an official of the federal public records office or the clerk of the United States District Court or Court of Appeals.

Special provision is made in M.G.L.A. c. 222, § 11, for acknowledgment by persons in or with the military service, including dependents, as follows:

> Persons serving in or with the armed forces of the United States or their dependents, wherever located, may acknowledge any instrument, in the manner and form required by the laws of this commonwealth, before any commissioned officer in the active service of the armed forces of the United States with the rank of second lieutenant or higher in the army, air force or marine corps, or ensign or higher in the navy or United States coast guard. Any such instrument shall contain a statement that the person executing the instrument is serving in or with the armed forces of the United States or is a dependent of a person serving in or with the armed forces of the United States, and in either case the statement shall include the serial number of the person so serving. No such instrument shall be rendered invalid by the failure to state therein the place of execution or acknowledgment.

No authentication of the officer's certificate of acknowledg-

---

[3]Ashkenazy v. R.M. Bradley & Co., 328 Mass. 242, 103 N.E.2d 251 (1952).

[4]M.G.L.A. c. 183, §§ 30, 33.

ment shall be required.

Instruments so acknowledged outside of the commonwealth, if otherwise in accordance with law, shall be received and may be used in evidence, or for any other purpose, in the same manner as if taken before a commissioner of the commonwealth appointed to take depositions in other states.

Finally, it should be noted that an executed but unacknowledged instrument may be given effect pursuant to procedures under §§ 34 to 41 of Chapter 183, depending on proof by a subscribing witness.

§ 19:12 Corporate authority

The execution of a deed on behalf of a corporation properly and usually results from deliberate corporate action, ordinarily involving authorization by the board of directors, specifying the officers entitled to execute a purchase and sale agreement and a deed pursuant thereto, and otherwise to conduct a closing of the transaction. When the business of the corporation is buying and selling real estate, the authorizations may be broadly given. In any event, as discussed in § **1:8** and § **6:10**, execution of a deed by the president or vice president and the treasurer or assistant treasurer, who may be the same person, will bind the corporation with respect to any person who relied thereon in good faith. From the corporate standpoint, as well as that of sound conveyancing practice, it is desirable to have a paper record of proper authorization. From the conveyancer's standpoint it is at least prudent to ascertain that the persons signing did in fact hold the corporate offices specified.

§ 19:13 Power of attorney

As stated in § **6:11**, M.G.L.A. c. 201B, the Uniform Durable Power of Attorney Act, governs the subject. It is important that the signature of the grantor set forth in a deed executed under a power of attorney be the grantor's name, made "by . . ., his attorney-in-fact," who then signs his own name. The attorney-in-fact should also refer specifically to the power of attorney by date and place of recording, and should recite that it remains in full force and effect at the time of execution of the deed.

§ 19:14 Formalities

The few remaining formalities are relics of substantive requirements of the past. A seal or recital of seal is now wholly unnecessary, but deeds and other instruments still usually recite "witness our hands and seals." No recital of release of dower or curtesy is required in any deed, and a married person owning real estate may convey it without the joinder of a spouse, although one may occasionally find a deed in which a married woman is said to convey "in her own right." No witness to a deed is required, but as noted in § **19:11**, a subscribing witness is necessary to proof of an unacknowledged deed.

§ 19:15   Alterations

When a deed is carefully drawn and reviewed by counsel before execution, there should then be no occasion for alteration. Nevertheless, deeds are sometimes executed before review by the grantee and the grantee may then desire modification of the identity of the grantee or specification of the form in which multiple grantees take title. As referred to in § **6:12**, alterations made before execution of a deed are generally effective, but it is often impossible to determine after the fact when the alterations were made. A clean retyping is the best solution, but if alterations must be made, each one should be confirmed by initialing in the margin, or a recital specifying alterations should be set forth in the acknowledgment.

A buyer's attorney who requests authority to insert or modify the grantee designation, or otherwise to modify a deed, after execution, should obtain such authority in writing, because such post-execution alteration will be effective only in the absence of any fraud, and the burden of proving authority will be on the grantee. The alteration of a deed, back-dated by the grantee after delivery to him, was upheld in unusual circumstances.[1] Under M.G.L.A. c. 36, § 15, a register of deeds "shall note on the record, before attesting the

---

[Section 19:15]

[1]Graves v. Hutchinson, 39 Mass. App. Ct. 634, 659 N.E.2d 1212 (1996) (abrogated by, Cleary v. Cleary, 427 Mass. 286, 692 N.E.2d 955 (1998)).

same, all erasures and interlineations . . . ."

TOPIC D: DELIVERY AND ACCEPTANCE; RECORDING

§ 19:16 Delivery and acceptance

In order to be effective to pass title, a deed must be delivered by the grantor and accepted by the grantee.[1] Delivery and acceptance are ordinarily effected by the parties' attorneys on their behalf. Although not commonly done, it is an advisable precaution to have declarations of delivery and acceptance made at a closing and to memorialize the fact in a closing memorandum. Once delivered, a deed may not be cancelled by the grantor.[2]

M.G.L.A. c. 183, § 5, affords assurance about delivery by providing that: "The record of a deed, lease, power of attorney or other instrument, duly acknowledged or proved as provided in this chapter, and purporting to affect the title to land, shall be conclusive evidence of the delivery of such instrument, in favor of purchasers for value without notice claiming thereunder." However, recording alone is not proof of acceptance. Acceptance may be implied from subsequent conduct of the grantee, but only if at the time of such conduct the grantee had actual knowledge of the conveyance to him.[3]

§ 19:17 Recording

It should not be forgotten that deeds and other instruments must pass a test of acceptability for recording by Registry personnel, who may insist on printed names beneath signatures (M.G.L.A. c. 36, § 18A), legibility sufficient for photocopying (M.G.L.A. c. 36, § 12A), and other less warranted requirements. M.G.L.A. c. 36, § 24B, authorizes registries to require further information as to amounts involved in transactions and terms of financing, which information is then to be transmitted to the Department of Revenue and to the assessors of the community in which the affected land is located. M.G.L.A. c. 36, § 31A, requires registers of deeds to notify the Department of Revenue of the

---

[Section 19:16]

[1]Juchno v. Toton, 338 Mass. 309, 155 N.E.2d 162, 74 A.L.R.2d 988 (1959).

[2]Trial v. Rodrigues, 3 L.C.R.

232 (1995).

[3]Juchno v. Toton, 338 Mass. 309, 155 N.E.2d 162, 74 A.L.R.2d 988 (1959).

recording of every declaration of trust and deed to a trustee. Instruments with facsimile signatures may be rejected by Registries, but the impact of M.G.L.A. c. 110G, the Uniform Electronic Transactions Act, is not yet clear.

§ 19:18   Confirmatory deeds

A confirmatory deed is sometimes a useful device for correcting an error made in the deed being confirmed, or even for correcting a prior title defect. A grantor may be asked to give a confirmatory deed after the title has passed from his grantee to others, and in that case the deed should run to the original grantee "and to those persons claiming by, through or under him by instruments of record."

Since the confirmatory deed is usually given without new consideration paid, it is appropriate to make it a simple release or grant without covenants, even if the deed being corrected and confirmed contained covenants. A confirmatory deed should contain reference to the earlier deed, a statement that it is given to confirm the prior conveyance and an appropriate statement obviating deed excise tax stamps. It is also often useful to state briefly the error or defect which is intended to be cured.

With respect to registered land there is no such thing as a confirmatory deed, since the original deed either was or was not sufficient to be accepted for registration and the issuance of a certificate of title to the grantee. Deeds purporting to be confirmatory of a conveyance of registered land will not be accepted for conveyance. The procedure for correction of errors in registered documents is a petition to the Land Court, as discussed in § 8:13.

Chapter 20

Mortgages

KeyCite®: Cases and other legal materials listed in KeyCite Scope can be researched through the KeyCite service on Westlaw®. Use KeyCite to check citations for form, parallel references, prior and later history, and comprehensive citator information, including citations to other decisions and secondary materials.

TOPIC A: INTRODUCTION

§ 20:1   Basics

The financing of real estate transactions is a subject of great scope and complexity. This Chapter deals only with the common mortgage aspects of such financing. The principal sources of financing are banks, insurance companies and their mortgage lending subsidiaries, and also finance companies, credit unions, pension plans and federal and state agencies. When acting for a lender, a lawyer may begin by acquiring some familiarity with the rather extensive and diverse statutes applicable to the field. Chapters 167, 167A, 167B, 167C, 167D, 167E, 167F, 167G, 168, 168 Apx., 169, 170, 171, 172 and 172A of the General Laws are pertinent in one way or another. Particularly pertinent to mortgage loans is M.G.L.A. c. 167E, which applies to savings banks, cooperative banks and trust companies subject to state supervision. Loans by credit unions are governed by M.G.L.A. c. 171, § 24, and loans by Morris Plan banks by M.G.L.A. c. 172A, § 7.

The terms and status of loan commitments and loan restructuring agreements are a subject of considerable importance, as illustrated by a number of judicial decisions.[1]

In addition to institutional loans, private financing is often involved, including purchase money financing by sellers to buyers.

Massachusetts is a "title theory" state in which a mortgagee is considered to have legal title to the land, subject only to the mortgagor's right to redemption on satisfaction of the conditions of the mortgage.[2] The mortgagor holds "the equity of redemption" and unless the mortgage specifically provides otherwise the mortgagor may do anything he wishes with the property until or unless there occurs a breach any of the mortgage conditions.[3] The mortgagor may sell the property subject to the mortgage, it may be attached, or may be further mortgaged, or otherwise dealt with in all respects like any other real estate. Thus, the mortgagee holds the bare legal title and the effect is the same as in a "lien theory" state until a breach by the mortgagor occurs and foreclosure become necessary to protect the mortgagee's interest. The mortgagee can, however, maintain in its own right an action against any persons injuring or wasting the land, even though no breach of the mortgage has occurred.[4] On foreclosure the estate in fee in the mortgagee, which had been only conditional until that time, becomes absolute.[5]

§ 20:2 Mortgage covenants

Most mortgages in Massachusetts use or are based on the statutory short form,[1] although there are a great variety of printed forms, proprietary to banks and other lending

---

[Section 20:1]

[1]Rhode Island Hosp. Trust Nat. Bank v. Varadian, 419 Mass. 841, 647 N.E.2d 1174 (1995); Den Norske Bank v. First Nat. Bank of Boston, 1993 WL 773796 (D. Mass. 1995), vacated, 75 F.3d 49 (1st Cir. 1996); Federico v. Brockton Credit Union, 39 Mass. App. Ct. 57, 653 N.E.2d 607 (1995).

[2]Cooperstein v. Bogas, 317 Mass. 341, 58 N.E.2d 131 (1944); Krikorian v. Grafton Co-op. Bank, 312 Mass. 272, 44 N.E.2d 665 (1942).

[3]M.G.L.A. c. 183, § 26.

[4]M.G.L.A. c. 183, § 26; Menard v. Courchaine, 278 Mass. 7, 179 N.E. 167 (1931).

[5]Maglione v. BancBoston Mortg. Corp., 29 Mass. App. Ct. 88, 557 N.E.2d 756 (1990).

[Section 20:2]

[1]M.G.L.A. c. 183, §§ 19, 20, 21, 22, 23 and 24 with respect to coop-

institutions. The key recitals to take advantage of the statutory provisions are that the mortgage is granted with "mortgage covenants," is upon the "mortgage conditions" and includes the statutory "power of sale."

The recital that the grant is made "with mortgage covenants" includes covenants, similar to "warranty covenants," that: "The mortgagor, for himself, his heirs, executors, administrators and successors covenants with the mortgagee and his heirs, successors and assigns, that he is lawfully seized in fee simple of the granted premises; that they are free from all encumbrances; that the mortgagor has good right to sell and convey the same; and that he will, and his heirs, executors, administrators and successors shall, warrant and defend the same to the mortgagee and his heirs, successors and assigns forever against the lawful claims and demands of all persons; and that the mortgagor and his heirs, successors, or assigns, in case a sale shall be made under the power of sale, will, upon request, execute, acknowledge and deliver to the purchaser or purchasers a deed or deeds of release confirming such sale; and that the mortgagee and his heirs, executors, administrators, successors and assigns are appointed and constituted the attorney or attorneys irrevocable of the said mortgagor to execute and deliver to the said purchaser a full transfer of all policies of insurance on the buildings upon the land covered by the mortgage at the time of such sale."

§ 20:3   Mortgage conditions

The recital that the grant is made upon "mortgage conditions" includes provision that: "Provided, nevertheless, except as otherwise specifically stated in the mortgage, that if the mortgagor, or his heirs, executors, administrators, successors or assigns shall pay unto the mortgagee or his executors, administrators or assigns the principal and interest secured by the mortgage, and shall perform any obligations secured at the time provided in the note, mortgage or other instrument or any extension thereof, and shall perform the condition of any prior mortgage and until such payment and performance shall pay when due and payable all taxes, charges, and assessments to whomsoever and wherever laid or assessed, whether on the mortgaged premises or on any interest therein or on the debt or obligation received thereby; shall keep the building on said premises insured against fire in a sum not less than the amount secured by the mortgage

---

erative banks.

or as otherwise provided therein for insurance for the benefit of the mortgagee and his executors, administrators and assigns, in such form and at such insurance office as they shall approve, and at least two days before the expiration of any policy on said premises, shall deliver to him or them a new and sufficient policy to take the place of the one so expiring, and shall not commit or suffer any strip or waste of the mortgaged premises or any breach of any covenant contained in the mortgage or in any prior mortgage, then the mortgage deed, as also the mortgage note or notes, shall be void."

§ 20:4 Power of sale

And a recital that the conveyance is subject to the statutory power of sale includes provision that: "But upon any default in the performance or observance of the foregoing or other conditions, the mortgagee or his executors, administrators, successors or assigns, may sell the mortgaged premises or such portion thereof, either as a whole or in parcels, together with all improvements that may be thereon, by public auction on or near the premises then subject to the mortgage, or if more than one parcel is subject thereto, on or near one of said parcels, or at such place as may be designated for that purpose in the mortgage, first complying with the terms of the mortgage and with the statutes related to the foreclosure of mortgages by the exercise of a power of sale, and may convey the same by proper deed or deeds to the purchaser or purchasers absolutely and in fee simple, and such sale shall forever bar the mortgagor and all persons claiming under him from all rights and interest in the mortgaged premises, whether at law or in equity."

§ 20:5 Other forms

Most institutional lenders have their own standard forms of mortgage, which contain these statutory recitals and also set forth additional covenants and conditions. The statutory conditions cover payment and performance of the secured obligations, payment and performance of any prior mortgage obligations, payment of taxes, keeping the premises insured, and not committing or suffering strip or waste. Printed forms usually elaborate on these subjects, and add other provisions as to due-on-sale, due-on-encumbrance, assignment of leases and rents, etc.

Although very rare and certainly inadvisable, it is still possible to make an effective mortgage without referring to the statutory provisions. A conveyance will be construed to be a mortgage if it contains a defeasance clause, i.e. a provision that the conveyance becomes void upon performance of a specified obligation.[1] In old style mortgages this is usually a "provided, nevertheless" clause, in substance the same as the statutory condition. The defeasance clause may even be in a separate instrument, but it must be of record.

TOPIC B: SECURITY PROVISIONS

§ 20:6   Security clause

The style of the statutory short form of mortgage is: A grants to B with mortgage covenants "to secure the payment of . . . dollars in . . . years with . . . percent interest per annum, payable semi-annually, as provided in . . . note of even date . . ."[1] Many mortgages state only the principal amount of the debt "with interest as provided in a note of even date" and omit reference to the term of years, interest rate and other payment terms. It is actually not necessary to state the principal amount, and a mortgage "to secure payment of a certain amount as provided in a note of even date" is valid and good security for the amounts advanced under the note at the time of the mortgage.

On the other hand, it is often advisable to elaborate the clause further. It is usual to refer to "a note of even date given by the mortgagor to the mortgagee." If the note was dated earlier, or if there are parties to it other than the mortgagor and mortgagee, those facts should certainly be specified. Furthermore, the mortgage is often stated to secure not only the payment of the note but also "the performance and fulfillment of the terms, provisions, covenants and conditions set forth herein and in the other security instruments hereinafter defined," and then to define the security instruments as including the note, mortgage and any others given, such as collateral assignments of rents and leases, additional mortgages on other property, security agreements on personalty, etc.

When a debtor has several loans from a lender secured by mortgages on several different properties, the lender may wish to have "cross-collaterization," or application of all of the security to all of the debts. Such cross-collateralization

<hr/>

[Section 20:5]

[1]M.G.L.A. c. 183, § 53; see Murley v. Murley, 334 Mass. 627, 137 N.E.2d 909 (1956); Jacobson v. Jacobson, 334 Mass. 658, 138 N.E.2d

206 (1956).

[Section 20:6]

[1]M.G.L.A. c. 184, App. (5).

and so-called "dragnet clauses" have been considered in a number of cases.[2]

§ 20:7   Future advances

A mortgage which secures amounts to be advanced after the mortgage is recorded creates a valid lien for those amounts when they are advanced. If there is an intervening encumbrance, e.g., a second mortgage recorded after the first mortgage but before an advance of funds is made under the first mortgage, then the lien for the amount of that advance will be superior to the lien of the second mortgage only if the mortgagee of the first mortgage had a binding obligation to make the future advance.[1] The security clause in a mortgage on a construction loan should recite: "To secure the payment of all sums advanced and to be advanced under and pursuant to a promissory note of the mortgagor to the mortgagee of even date . . ."

The most common form of future advance mortgage is a construction loan, and construction lenders generally do not wish to be subject to a binding obligation to make advances. On the contrary, the prudent construction lender sets forth in the construction loan agreement numerous preconditions to its obligation to make advances. Consequently, before making each advance the lender requires that examination of title be continued in order to determine that there are no intervening encumbrances, and if any are found, that they be expressly subordinated to the advance to be made. However, as referred to in § 6:22, in some circumstances a construction lender may not be able to withhold advances because of an intervening mechanics lien.

Another statute to consider in relation to construction loan advances is M.G.L.A. c. 266, § 38A, which imposes a criminal penalty for application of construction proceeds "to any use other than payment for labor and/or materials" before such labor and materials have been paid for in full. A literal application of that provision would be quite difficult to achieve for any construction lender, and it was not strictly

[2]In re Ballarino, 180 B.R. 343 (D. Mass. 1995); Daly v. Westworth Ventures, Inc., 4 L.C.R. 27 (1996); Hull v. North Adams Hoosac Sav. Bank, 49 Mass. App. Ct. 514, 730 N.E.2d 910 (2000); NAB Asset Venture III, L.P. v. Brockton Credit Union, 62 Mass. App. Ct. 181, 815 N.E.2d 606 (2004).

[Section 20:7]
[1]Barry v. General Mortg. & Loan Corp., 254 Mass. 282, 150 N.E. 293 (1926).

applied.[2]

Another type of future advance is that made to cover costs of repairs, improvements or replacements to the mortgaged premises or payment of taxes or charges thereon. Even if made by a mortgagee without any obligation at all to do so, these are covered by the original mortgage lien by virtue of the provisions of M.G.L.A. c. 183, § 28A that: "Any sum or sums which shall be loaned by the mortgagee to the mortgagor at any time after the recording of any mortgage of real estate, to be expended for paying for repairs, improvements, lead paint removal or replacements to, fuel for, or for taxes or other municipal liens, charges or assessments or condominium common expense assessment, including legal fees on, the mortgaged premises, shall be equally secured with and have the same priority as the original indebtedness, to the extent that the aggregate amount outstanding at any one time when added to the balance due on the original indebtedness shall not exceed the amount originally secured by the mortgage. The provisions of this section shall apply to all forms of mortgages on real estate." While the meaning of the phrase "at any one time" was found to be less than clear, in ordinary circumstances, the lien for advances for improvements is upheld.[3]

Provision is made in M.G.L.A. c. 183, § 28B, and in M.G.L.A. c. 140D, for an "open-end credit plan" under which sums are lent by a mortgagee to a mortgagor "from time to time," up to a specified amount. The latter statute extends the mortgage lien to all sums so advanced with "the same priority as would any such sum disbursed as of the time of the recording of such mortgage."

§ 20:8   Non-recourse

As stated above, a mortgage is usually given to secure the payment of a promissory note. When the lender is willing to look only to the security of the mortgaged property for payment of the mortgage debt and to relieve the borrower of any obligation or risk other than losing the mortgaged premises, that is accomplished by a non-recourse clause. An example which might appear in a mortgage is as follows: "By acceptance hereof the mortgagee hereby agrees that in the event of any default hereunder, a foreclosure of this mortgage or

---

[2]Albre v. Sinclair Const. Co., 345 Mass. 712, 189 N.E.2d 563 (1963).

[3]Wellfleet Sav. Bank v. Swift, 340 Mass. 62, 162 N.E.2d 799 (1959); Zaltman v. Melrose Sav. Bank, 7 Mass. App. Ct. 930, 389 N.E.2d 1039 (1979).

any other legal proceeding to collect the note and other obligations secured hereby, the mortgagee's sole claim shall be against the mortgaged premises, and that the mortgagor shall not be personally or individually liable for or with respect to the note secured hereby or the debt evidenced thereby, nor for any deficiency not realized from the mortgaged premises; but except as herein specifically provided, nothing herein shall be deemed or construed to abrogate, impair, preclude the exercise of, or otherwise adversely affect, the rights, benefits and remedies afforded to the mortgagee under the note or this mortgage." A similar clause may also be set forth in the note itself.

§ 20:9 UCC filings

The Uniform Commercial Code, appearing in Massachusetts as M.G.L.A. c. 106, is a statute of considerable scope. Of primary concern to a conveyancer is Article 9, comprising §§ 9-101 to 9-507 of Chapter 106, covering secured transactions. Only a few salient points are discussed herein. Conveyancers regularly encounter the Code in relation to fixtures and personal property included in real estate mortgage security. Since construction lenders usually make advances for materials stored on site but not yet incorporated into the work, that is an area of particular interest.

The essential instruments include a "security agreement," which means an agreement which creates or provides for a security interest, and a "financing statement," which constitutes the notice of the transaction. A real estate mortgage, serving as a security agreement under the Code, should contain an express statement that it "creates a security interest," and it is customary and desirable to caption the instrument as a "mortgage and security agreement." If the loan security involves, in addition to real estate and personalty directly related thereto, any extensive other personalty, such as stock in trade or receivables, it will likely be advisable to cover those in a separate security agreement.

As to fixtures, § 9-313 of M.G.L.A. c. 106, provides in subsections (2) and (3) that: "(2) A security interest under this Article may be created in goods which are fixtures or may continue in goods which become fixtures, but no security interest exists under this Article in ordinary building materials incorporated into an improvement on land. (3) This Article does not prevent creation of an encumbrance upon fixtures pursuant to real estate law." Following these are subsections (4) and (5), specifying conditions (which warrant careful study) in which a security interest in fixtures has priority over the conflicting interest of an encumbrancer or owner of the real estate. Clause (6) then provides that, subject to those subsections (4) and (5), with one specified exception, "a security interest in fixtures is subordinate to a construction mortgage recorded before the goods become fixtures if the goods become fixtures before the completion of the construction. To the extent that it is given to refinance a construction mortgage, a mortgage has this priority to the same extent as the construction mortgage." And subsection (7) provides: "In cases not within the preceding subsections, a security interest in fixtures is subordinate to the conflicting interest of an encumbrancer or owner of the related real estate who is not the debtor."

In any event notice of a security interest is given by recording a financing statement. The contents are specified in § 9-402, and the form of UCC-1 is widely available. Subsection (6) of § 9-402 provides that:

> (6) A mortgage is effective as a financing statement filed as a fixture filing from the date of its recording if (a) the goods are described in the mortgage by item or type; and (b) the goods are or are to become fixtures related to the real estate described in the mortgage; and (c) the mortgage complies with the requirements for a financing statement in this section other than a recital that it is to be filed in the real estate records; and (d) the mortgage is duly recorded.

On real estate transactions financing statements need to be recorded only in the registry of deeds. A financing statement remains effective for 5 years from the date of filing unless extended within that period by a continuation statement. Termination of a financing statement is dealt with under § 9-404 and Assignment under § 9-405. The common printed form UCC-3 is generally used in relation to assignment, subordination, partial release or other disposition with respect to a security interest. When a real estate mortgage is discharged in the usual manner by acknowledgment of satisfaction of the debt, the security interest is thereby terminated. Nevertheless, care should be taken to sign and deliver UCC termination statements; § 9-404 provides for a penalty for failure to do so.

§ 20:10   Collateral assignments

Provisions for the assignment of rents and leases are often included in the text of real estate mortgages. In commercial loan transactions, particularly on multi-tenanted buildings, institutional lenders often supplement the mortgage with separate forms of collateral assignment of specified leases and catch-all collateral assignment of rents. These forms usually prohibit modification or termination of any lease, or acceptance of rent in advance, without the prior written consent of the lender, but permit continued collection of rent by the borrower until there is a default.

Such forms are often associated with agreements of subordination, attornment and non-disturbance between the tenants and the lender. In a case in which a lease is of record prior to a mortgage and the lender wishes to preserve that lease as a valuable source of funds to meet the debt service, it may still be desirable to have a subordination, attornment and non-disturbance agreement. That puts the parties in the same possessory positions as before, but has the advantage of creating a privity of contract between the tenant and the lender.

The bankruptcy court has held that a mortgagee is not entitled to collect rents unless it is in actual possession of the property, applying a fairly strict definition of actual possession.[1]

In relation to construction loans, collateral assignments to the lender of architectural and construction contracts are often made, and sometimes assignments of permits, licenses or franchise agreements. Commercial lenders may have their own standard forms, and there are forms promulgated by the American Institute of Architects.

§ 20:11   Other

Lenders often require the personal guaranty of principals of a business entity to which a loan is made, usually by a separate document.[1] A signature on a promissory note constitutes a personal endorsement unless it is clearly specified to be for another purpose.[2] Under the UCC the liability of a guarantor is the same as that of a co-maker of a note.[3]

A pledge of life insurance on the mortgagor is another

[Section 20:10]

[1]In re Prichard Plaza Associates Ltd. Partnership, 84 B.R. 289 (Bankr. D. Mass. 1988); In re Ledgemere Land Corp., 116 B.R. 338 (Bankr. D. Mass. 1990); and see In re Milford Common J.V. Trust, 117 B.R. 15 (Bankr. D. Mass. 1990).

[Section 20:11]

[1]Chestnut Manor, Inc. v. Abraham, 16 Mass. App. Ct. 960, 452 N.E.2d 258 (1983).

[2]First Safety Fund Nat. Bank v. Friel, 23 Mass. App. Ct. 583, 504 N.E.2d 664, 3 U.C.C. Rep. Serv. 2d 1021 (1987); and see Seronick v. Levy, 26 Mass. App. Ct. 367, 527 N.E.2d 746 (1988).

[3]D'Annolfo v. D'Annolfo Const. Co., Inc., 39 Mass. App. Ct. 189, 654 N.E.2d 82, 27 U.C.C. Rep. Serv. 2d 493 (1995).

means of security. And "mortgage insurance," per se, is sometimes required.

TOPIC C: PAYMENT PROVISIONS

§ 20:12 Direct reduction

On residential loans the basic format for payment is so-called "direct reduction." The payments thereunder are constant in monthly amount, applied first to interest on the unpaid balance and then to principal. The portion of the fixed payment going to interest gradually declines and the portion going to principal gradually increases. The monthly payment amount is set so that the loan will amortize completely in a specified term. The fixed monthly payment is an important feature to most residential borrowers, and is often retained under variant mortgage payment modes described below. Fixed terms of 20 to 30 years and fixed interest rates are less common than they once were.

§ 20:13 Variants

There are many possible variants of payment terms, including the following:

• **Variable Rate.** Salient among the variants is the reservation by the lender of the right to change the interest rate, which necessarily affects the monthly payment and the term of years of the loan. With respect to loans on one to four family, owner occupied, residences (herein called "personal residence loans") such a change is permitted, and regulated, under M.G.L.A. c. 183, §§ 60 and 63A.

• **Balloon.** When a note is written to mature at, say, ten years, but the monthly payments are such that it would take, say, thirty years to amortize the principal amount, then a "balloon" of principal becomes due upon maturity. With respect to personal residence loans that practice is regulated under M.G.L.A. c. 183, § 60.

• **Interest Only.** A personal residence loan may, under provisions of Chapter 167E, § 3A, provide for payment of interest only for up to ten years, and thereafter payments that will fully amortize the loan over its stated term. If that term were very little longer than the interest-only period, then the required principal payments would be quite large, of the type sometimes called "Bullets."

• **Reverse Mortgage Loans.** A so-called "reverse mortgage loan" is in essence one in which the lender makes payments, usually periodically, to the borrower, and the borrower has no obligation to repay until he dies or sells the mortgaged property. This device is supposed to be of benefit to older people who do not have sufficient income or means to make mortgage payments, but have an equity value in their residence. M.G.L.A. c. 183, § 67, prohibits reverse mortgage loans except in accordance with M.G.L.A. c. 167E, § 2B. ¶ 14A, which sets forth strict rules and a requirement of approval by the commissioner of banks for any such loan.

• **Commercial Loans.** With respect to commercial loans there is of course much greater flexibility as to modes of payment. Direct reduction is sometimes replaced by fixed periodic principal payments, with interest payable on the balance from time to time outstanding. The applicable interest rate may vary on a regular basis, even month to month, based upon some indexed figure, such as "prime rate," a federal bureau of labor statistics datum, or "LIBOR," a London-based banking measure.

§ 20:14 Prepayment; late payment; points

With respect to personal residence loans (i.e., on one to four family, owner-occupied, residences) the matters of prepayment, late payment and points are regulated by statutes.

Under M.G.L.A. c. 183, § 56, a prepayment charge may not exceed the balance of the first year's interest or three months interest, whichever is less, except that if prepayment is made within three years for the purpose of refinancing with another financial institution, an additional three months' interest may be required. There is a proviso with respect to FHA loans. If prepayment is occasioned by a taking for public purposes, under § 57 no prepayment charge may be made.[1]

Under M.G.L.A. c. 183, § 59, no late charge may be imposed with respect to a payment made within 15 days after the due date, or in an amount in excess of three percent of the late payment of interest and principal, excluding any tax escrow payment. This is applicable also to mortgages on condominium units.

Under M.G.L.A. c. 183, § 63, a lender is prohibited from charging "points" or a loan fee unless such charge has been "previously disclosed to the mortgagor in writing." When "points" are paid, the amount may be deductible as interest,

---

[Section 20:14]

[1]M.G.L.A. c. 183, § 57, applies to 3 or less, rather than 4 or less, dwellings; a legislative aberration.

subject to compliance with provisions of the Internal Revenue Code and applicable case law.

With respect to commercial loans, which are not subject to the statutes cited above, prepayment charges, late fees and points are common and usually enforceable as a matter of contract.[2] However, a prepayment charge may be struck down as an unenforceable penalty,[3] or barred by acceleration upon default.[4]

§ 20:15 Usury

The Massachusetts usury law, M.G.L.A. c. 271, § 49, is a criminal statute, making it a crime punishable by fine and imprisonment, to charge interest and expenses of more than twenty percent per annum on a loan. For that purpose, interest and expenses include not only interest as such but also "brokerage, recording fees, commissions, services, extensions of loan, forbearance to enforce payment, and all other sums charged against or paid or to be paid by the borrower for making or securing directly or indirectly the loan, and shall include all such sums when paid by or on behalf of or charged against the borrower for or on account of making or securing the loan, directly or indirectly, to or by any person other than the lender, if such payment or charge was known to the lender at the time of making the loan, or might have been ascertained by reasonable inquiry." It is a crime to possess, knowingly, papers specifying such a loan, subject also to fine and imprisonment.

A loan in violation may be declared void by a court on petition of a borrower.

Paragraph (d) of the statute then provides that those provisions "shall not apply to any person who notifies the attorney general of his intent to engage in a transaction or transactions which, but for the provision of this paragraph, would be proscribed . . . providing any such person maintains records of any such transaction."

That is to say, there is no prohibition on usurious lending in Massachusetts for any lender who notifies the Attorney General's office in advance of intent to make such a loan or loans. A notification so given is valid for two years and ap-

---

[2]Clean Harbors, Inc. v. John Hancock Life Ins. Co., 64 Mass. App. Ct. 347, 833 N.E.2d 611 (2005).

[3]In re A.J. Lane & Co., Inc.,

113 B.R. 821 (Bankr. D. Mass. 1990).

[4]Ferreira v. Yared, 32 Mass. App. Ct. 328, 588 N.E.2d 1370 (1992).

plies to all loans made during that period.[1] The lender must keep records of all such loan transactions, and they are available to the Attorney General.

The statute further provides that it shall not apply to any loan on which the rate of interest is regulated by law or to any lender subject to control, regulation or examination by any state or federal regulatory agency, thereby completely excluding banks and insurance companies from the provision. However, business corporation subsidiaries of such institutional lenders are subject to the statute, and it is important for them to comply strictly with the statute. When co-lenders advanced funds in the morning, but did not file statutory notices until the afternoon, the court remanded for forming of an equitable remedy for that breach.[2]

§ 20:16 Small loans

M.G.L.A. c. 140, § 90, applies to all loans of less than $1000, and §§ 90A to 90E apply to loans in excess of $1500, secured by a mortgage other than a first mortgage, of real estate having an assessed value of not over $40,000 and having thereon a dwelling with six or fewer household units "occupied in whole or in part at the time the loan is made as a home by any obligor on the mortgage debt or by any person granting or releasing any interest under said mortgage." The statute sets a maximum interest rate of 18% per annum, including all related fees and charges paid by the borrower to the lender, broadly construed, and grants a prepayment privilege. It also provides for separate statements of principal and interest, giving of receipts to the borrower for payments made, and remedies, forfeitures and penalties for violations of these requirements. Under § 95 some of these provisions may not apply to persons who have been licensed under § 96 to engage in the business of making loans of $6000 or less with interest and expenses exceeding 12% per annum.

TOPIC D: CONDITIONS

§ 20:17 Statutory

As set forth in § **20:3**, the statutory conditions call for a

---

[Section 20:15]

[1]Albano v. City Nat. Bank of Connecticut, 11 Mass. App. Ct. 973, 417 N.E.2d 998 (1981).

[2]Clean Harbors, Inc. v. John Hancock Life Ins. Co., 64 Mass. App. Ct. 347, 833 N.E.2d 611 (2005).

mortgagor to pay and perform obligations under the note and mortgage, to perform the condition of any prior mortgage, to pay taxes, to keep the property insured, and not to commit or suffer waste. Such provisions are often elaborated in the "boiler-plate" of institutional mortgage forms, and other requirements are added, as set forth in the following sections.

An example of the elaboration of mortgage covenants and the addition of requirements beyond the statutory conditions is provided in **Appendix S**. Significant items among these are set forth in the following sections.

§ 20:18   Due on sale or encumbrance

It is common practice in Massachusetts mortgages to include a clause that the holder may call the entire loan immediately due if the title to the mortgaged premises is sold or conveyed to a person other than the mortgagor. The enforceability of such a provision may be limited in other states, but it is enforced in Massachusetts.[1] The usual clause is broadly phrased, applying not only to sale, but to any conveyance or vesting of title in a person other than the mortgagor. More sophisticated clauses sometimes specify that a change in the controlling interest in a mortgagor corporation, partnership, limited partnership or other business entity shall be deemed to be a sale or conveyance of the premises and thus an occasion for acceleration of the debt by the holder.

M.G.L.A. c. 208, § 34A, provides that a transfer from one spouse to another under a divorce decree or a separation agreement shall not trigger a mortgage due on sale clause.

A provision in a mortgage authorizing the holder to accelerate the debt in the event of a junior mortgage lien poses equitable issues beyond those of due-on-sale. Massachusetts favors flexibility in and enforcement of contractual undertakings, and a due-on-encumbrance clause was allowed to stand.[2] Federal law may be more limiting with respect to mortgages held by federally chartered lenders.

§ 20:19   Real estate tax

The statutory condition requiring the mortgagor to pay

[Section 20:18]

[1]Dunham v. Ware Sav. Bank, 384 Mass. 63, 423 N.E.2d 998 (1981); and see Fidelity Federal Sav. and Loan Ass'n v. de la Cuesta, 458 U.S. 141, 102 S. Ct. 3014, 73 L. Ed. 2d 664 (1982).

[2]Egbert v. Freedom Federal Sav. and Loan Ass'n, 14 Mass. App. Ct. 383, 440 N.E.2d 22 (1982).

taxes, charges and assessments is often supplemented by an affirmative covenant of the mortgagor. Residential lenders sometimes require payment of a monthly tax reserve, but the prevalence of that practice declined upon adoption of M.G.L.A. c. 183, § 61, requiring lenders to pay interest on such funds, and § 62, requiring holders of such reserves to pay them over to cities and towns when taxes are due. In any event, if a mortgagor fails to pay taxes, the mortgagee may do so and under M.G.L.A. c. 183, § 28A, add the amount thereof to the mortgaged debt.

§ 20:20   Other

Among common other covenants are those dealing with insurance, leasing of the premises, keeping the premises in good order, repair and condition and conferring upon the mortgagee additional rights in the event of a breach and foreclosure. Insurance requirements on residence loans are limited by M.G.L.A. c. 183, § 66. A mortgagee was not allowed to retain, after casualty and foreclosure, insurance proceeds in excess of the mortgage debt.[1]

TOPIC E: GOVERNMENTAL REGULATIONS

§ 20:21   Truth in lending

M.G.L.A. c. 140D, the Consumer Credit Cost Disclosure Act, contains the Massachusetts truth-in-lending provisions. The Act is of broad application, and does not apply to credit transactions in which the total amount financed exceeds $25,000 unless the transaction involves a security interest in realty or personalty "used or expected to be used as the principal dwelling of the consumer."[1] Among the salient points from the standpoint of the conveyancer are the following:

● The commissioner of banks has power to prescribe rules and regulations, provided they do not provide "less stringent disclosure requirements than afforded . . . under the Federal Consumer Protection Act and Regulation Z . . ."

[Section 20:20]

[1]Rodriguez v. First Union Nat. Bank, 61 Mass. App. Ct. 438, 810 N.E.2d 1282 (2004).

[Section 20:21]

[1]Levites v. Chipman, 30 Mass. App. Ct. 356, 568 N.E.2d 639 (1991).

• The "finance charge" is defined to include: "(1) Interest, time price differential, and any amount payable under a point, discount, or other system of additional charges; (2) Service or carrying charge; (3) Loan fee, finder's fee, or similar charge; (4) Fee for an investigation or credit report; (5) Premium or other charge for any guarantee or insurance protecting the creditor against the obligor's default or other credit loss." Certain insurance charges may also be included, subject to specified exceptions.

• Disclosure by the lender to the person obligated (which would include a guarantor) of "the information required under this chapter" is called for by § 7, within tolerances for numerical disclosures as may be determined by the commissioner of banks.

• The borrower who mortgages his "principal dwelling" as security has a right to rescind the transaction "until midnight of the third business day following the consummation of the transaction or the delivery of the information and rescission forms required under this section together with a statement containing the material disclosures required by this chapter, whichever is later, by notifying the creditor, in accordance with regulations of the commissioner, of his intention to do so."[2] It is provided, however, that such right to rescind does not apply when the loan is for the purpose of financing the acquisition or initial construction of such dwelling.

In addition to M.G.L.A. c. 140D, other lender disclosure requirements were set forth in M.G.L.A. c. 184, §§ 17C and 17D, repealed in 2006.[3] Under § 17B, amended in the cited 2006 Act, a lender is required to advise borrowers as to engaging counsel.

§ 20:22 Prohibited discrimination

M.G.L.A. c. 183, § 64, provides that: "No mortgagee shall discriminate, on a basis that is arbitrary or unsupported by a reasonable analysis of the lending risks associated with a residential mortgage transaction, in the granting, withholding, extending, modifying or renewing, or in the fixing of the rates, terms, conditions or provisions of any residential mortgage loan or in any written application therefore on residential real property located in the commonwealth of four or fewer separate households occupied or to be occupied in

---

[2]Chapter 63, § 4B, Acts of 2006.

[3]See Mayo v. Key Financial Services, Inc., 424 Mass. 862, 678 N.E.2d 1311 (1997).

whole or in part by the applicant, that is within the reasonable service area of such mortgagee, on the basis such property is located in a specific neighborhood or geographical area . . . Nor shall any mortgagee use lending or underwriting standards, policies, systems or practices, that discriminate in practice or that discriminate in effect, on a basis that is arbitrary or unsupported by a reasonable analysis of the lending risks associated with a residential mortgage transaction."

The first sentence proscribes the practice known as redlining and the second sentence is of broad and general scope. The statute contains further provisions specifying what a mortgagee may and may not do, and requiring written notice to a loan applicant of "the specific reasons for any adverse action."

An aggrieved person is given the remedy of a civil action, subject to exhaustion of administrative remedies under M.G.L.A. c. 167, § 14A, in the district court, or housing court, where applicable, of the county in which the mortgagee is located. Upon a finding of violation, the court may award actual damages or punitive damages of $5000, whichever is greater, but in no event less than $2500, and may award costs and attorney's fees.

A claimant who is found by the court to have "intentionally misrepresented a material fact in the mortgage application," or to have filed a frivolous suit, is subject to an award in favor of the mortgagee of its actual damages or punitive damages of $500, whichever is greater, and also costs and attorney's fees.

§ 20:23 Predatory practices

M.G.L.A. c. 183C, enacted in 2004, is entitled the Predatory Home Loan Practices Act. It defines a "high cost home mortgage loan" as one with an interest rate 8 or 9 percentage points over the yield on U.S. Treasury securities having a comparable period of maturity, or requiring points or fees over 5% of the loan amount. Such loans are not wholly barred, but lenders are prohibited from making them unless they comply with a set of requirements, standards and limitations set forth in the statute, including a duly approved program for counseling borrowers. The statute affords a borrower of such a loan with a cause of action for violation of the statute, and the court with broad equitable remedies. The statute also provides standards and corrective procedures by which a lender may avoid being deemed in violation.

A related provision is § 28C of M.G.L.A. c. 183, which

prohibits a lender from making a home loan to payoff all or part of a home loan made within the preceding 60 months unless the new loan is in the "borrowers interest," as determined in accordance with standards set forth in the statute.

§ 20:24   Attorney certification requirements

M.G.L.A. c. 93, § 70, provides that:

In connection with the granting of any loan or credit to be secured by a purchase money first mortgage on real estate improved with a dwelling designed to be occupied by not more than four families and occupied or to be occupied in whole or in part by the mortgagor, an attorney acting for or on behalf of the mortgagee shall render a certification of title to the mortgaged premises to the mortgagor and to the mortgagee.

For the purposes of this section, said certification shall include a title examination which covers a period of at least fifty years with the earliest instrument being a warranty or quitclaim deed which on its face does not suggest a defect in said title; provided, however, that in the case of registered land, it shall be sufficient to start the said examination with the present owner's certificate of title issued by the land court, except that bankruptcy indices and federal and state liens shall be examined. The term record title, as used herein, shall mean the records of the registry of deeds or registry district in which the mortgaged premises lie and relevant records of registries of probate.

The certification shall include a statement that at the time of recording the said mortgage, the mortgagor holds good and sufficient record title to the mortgaged premises free from all encumbrances, and shall enumerate exceptions thereto. The certification shall further include a statement that the mortgagee holds a good and sufficient record first mortgage to the property, subject only to the matters excepted by said certification.

The liability of any attorney rendering such certification shall be limited to the amount of the consideration shown on the deed with respect to the mortgagor, and shall be limited to the original principal amount secured by the mortgage with respect to the mortgagee. Said certification shall be effective for the benefit of the mortgagor so long as said mortgagor has title to the mortgaged premises, and shall be effective for the benefit of the mortgagee so long as the original debt secured by the mortgage remains unpaid.

Willful failure by an attorney to render a certification to the mortgagor as required by the provisions of this section shall constitute an unfair or deceptive act or practice under the provisions of chapter ninety-three A.

§ 20:25   Government mortgage market requirements

The Veterans Administration and the Federal Housing

Administration have long had programs of guarantee or insurance of loans made by banks on single family residences. The FHA has also been a primary source of loan funds, at various times under several different federal programs, for construction and rehabilitation of public housing and housing for families of low and moderate income. Another source for similar purposes is the Massachusetts Housing Finance Agency. There are a number of federal and state agencies which provide, or help arrange for, loan funds for purposes other than housing, including the Farmers Home Administration, the Massachusetts Industrial Finance Agency, and the Massachusetts Health and Education Facilities Authority.

The principal agencies involved in providing a secondary market for mortgage loans are the Federal Home Loan Mortgage Corporation, known as FHLMC or Freddie Mac, the Federal National Mortgage Association, known as FNMA or Fannie Mae, and to some extent the Government National Mortgage Association, known as GNMA or Ginny Mae. The sale of condominium unit loans and single family residence loans by banks to these agencies is quite extensive.

Both the primary and the secondary lenders have requirements of their own. These may apply not only to the use of prescribed forms, but also to the loan terms, loan documentation, and in the case of condominiums, the organization and management thereof. The applicable provisions may be found in sellers' or servicers' guides or other publications issued by the lending or loan purchasing agencies.

TOPIC F: POST-CLOSING ACTIONS

§ 20:26   Partial release

There are often situations in which a mortgagor will need to obtain partial releases of the security and will have bargained for them in negotiating the loan. Common examples are the sale of Units in a condominium development or house lots in a subdivision. A mortgage clause might provide that: "By acceptance hereof the mortgagee hereby agrees to release from the lien of this mortgage [a unit in said condominium; or a lot shown on said subdivision plan] upon the payment to the mortgagee on account of the principal of said note secured hereby of the sum of $X for each [unit; lot] so released . . ." Alternatively, instead of a fixed amount for each unit or lot released, the release payment may be specified as a sum equal to, say, 85% of the gross price at which the mortgagor is then selling the unit or lot. The mortgagee will wish to insert protective conditions as to the mortgage being in good standing, the minimum prices at which units or lots may be sold, the bona fides of the sales, etc., and will always wish to set these terms so that the remaining security retains a value substantially in excess of the unpaid balance of the mortgage.

The mortgagor, on the other hand, will wish to be sure of obtaining the partial releases as and when he needs them for unit or lot sale closings. A partial release will not be required if the mortgage contains no provision for it,[1] or is in default.[2] It is also important to remembered that a partial release of a mortgage is not a grant, and consequently, does not generally carry appurtenances or implications. Thus each subdivision lot, for instance, should be released expressly "together with the rights and easements appurtenant thereto . . ." to use the necessary streets and ways, utility lines, etc., which serve it. The condominium statute makes units nonseverable from their appurtenant interest in the common areas and facilities, but a broad "together with" clause in a unit partial release is still advisable.

§ 20:27 Subordination

When a mortgagor intends to make substantial repairs, improvements or redevelopment of the property and needs new financing for that, the lender will ordinarily require that it receive a first mortgage lien. The holder of an existing first mortgage, which perhaps financed the original purchase of the property, may be unable or unwilling to finance the new development, and may be called upon to subordinate its mortgage to the new development mortgage.

That might have been bargained for with the original mortgagee, and a clause might have provided that: "By acceptance hereof the mortgagee agrees with the mortgagor to subordinate the lien of this mortgage to a first mortgage to a bank or other lending institution in an amount not in excess of $x, subject to the conditions hereinafter set forth, and upon the written request of the mortgagor to execute and deliver such instrument of subordination as the mortgagee

---

[Section 20:26]

[1]Rhode Island Hosp. Trust Nat. Bank v. Post, 27 Mass. App. Ct. 1207, 544 N.E.2d 592 (1989).

[2]Sheehan v. Aniello, 19 Mass. App. Ct. 621, 476 N.E.2d 263 (1985).

shall reasonably request."[1] The mortgagor will wish to have as much flexibility as possible in the terms of the new mortgage to which the original mortgagee will subordinate. The original mortgagee, on the other hand, wants to assure that the unpaid balance on its loan is fairly protected, and that it will not be cut off by, or forced to assume, an overly burdensome first mortgage. In short, the subordinating mortgagee has a very considerable interest in the terms of the mortgage to which it is subordinating, and should be particularly concerned to see that proceeds thereof go directly to the improvement of the mortgaged premises and enhancement of the value thereof.

Whenever there are serial mortgages, their respective priorities come into question, and the terms of subordinations may affect such priorities. A basic proposition is that a prior mortgagee may not modify the terms of its loan to the detriment of a junior mortgagee without the latter's consent.[2] Furthermore, encumbrances known to and contemplated by a mortgagee may be held subordinate to the mortgage even though recorded before it.[3] In *NAB Asset Venture III, L.P. v. Brockton Credit Union*,[4] a first mortgage was subordinated to a second mortgage held by defendant which contained a dragnet clause, but the subordination did not specifically refer to future advances by defendant and such advances later made by defendant under a third mortgage to it were held not to be covered by the subordination.

§ 20:28 Consent to condominium

A construction mortgage loan on a condominium project would naturally describe the mortgaged property as "the land with the buildings thereon or to be erected thereon." However, when the master deed is recorded, that ceases to be apt since the property has then become Units in the condominium, comprising their appurtenant interests in the common areas and facilities. An instrument by which a mortgagee recognizes that change was formerly (and sometimes still is) called a "subordination," but is now more properly called a Consent to Condominium and Amendment

---

[Section 20:27]

[1]See REBA Form 12.

[2]Shane v. Winter Hill Federal Sav. and Loan Ass'n, 397 Mass. 479, 492 N.E.2d 92 (1986).

[3]O'Brien v. Wainwright Bank & Trust Company, 6 L.C.R. 85 (1998).

[4]NAB Asset Venture III, L.P. v. Brockton Credit Union, 62 Mass. App. Ct. 181, 815 N.E.2d 606 (2004).

of Mortgage.[1] By such an instrument the mortgagee recognizes that the property consists of Units, and that a foreclosure will not terminate the condominium, but will effect sale only of the Units therein which have not previously been released from the mortgage. Sometimes such an instrument is used to spell out the terms upon which the mortgagee will give releases of Units. It is also advisable for the instrument to recognize the change in the status of casualty insurance, ordinarily then becoming payable to the condominium trustees or managers as insurance trustees, and applicable in accordance with provisions of the master deed and Chapter 183A.

§ 20:29 Assignment

Assignments of mortgages are very common, particularly since home loans are widely distributed in the secondary mortgage market. The word "assign" is sufficient under the customary form which provides simply that: "A, holder of a mortgage given by B to A, dated . . . recorded with . . . Registry of Deeds, Book . . ., Page . . ., assigns said mortgage and the note and claim secured thereby to C."[1] The holder of many mortgages may list and assign all of them in one such instrument, but the recording fee will be charged for each mortgage listed.[2] When a subsequent holder, C, re-assigns a mortgage to D, the same form may be used, referring to a mortgage from B to A, and it is not required that C identify itself as more than the "holder." It would ease title examination, and perhaps the mortgage discharge problems discussed below, if every assignment were required to specify all prior assignments.

TOPIC G: DISCHARGE

§ 20:30 The statutes

Ranking in inevitability with death and taxes, it is surprising how complex the process of mortgage discharge has become. Old timers will remember that when the last monthly payment was made, the bank treasurer signed and handed you a discharge. The form specified the mortgage by

---

[Section 20:28]

[1]See REBA Form 14.

[Section 20:29]

[1]M.G.L.A. c. 183, § 28.

[2]Bank for Savings v. Zamperelli, Middlesex Superior Court, C.A. No. 82-215.

parties, date and recording, referred to "the debt secured thereby," and provided that the bank "acknowledged satisfaction of the same." The paid note, and often the original mortgage, were also handed over.

Discharge of mortgage is now governed principally by M.G.L.A. c. 183, § 55, supplemented by §§ 54, 54A, 54B, 54C and 54D, and also by M.G.L.A. c. 240, § 15, most of which were rewritten in 2006.[1] The principal elements include the following:

• Section 55 requires that a "mortgagee, mortgage servicer or note holder who receives full payment and satisfaction of the conditions of a mortgage shall, within 45 days of receipt of payment," either cause a discharge to be recorded or send an executed discharge to the person who submitted the payoff. In the latter case, if the discharge is sent to anyone other than "a closing attorney or settlement agent," it must be accompanied by notice in large bold-face type warning of the importance of having the discharge recorded.

• Section 55 requires the discharge to be executed by a person authorized by the holder of the mortgage, and specifies at some length the means of identifying and verifying such authorization.

• Section 55 provides that when full payment in accordance with "a payoff statement" has been accepted, but the discharge has not been recorded or delivered within 45 days, the party so failing shall be liable for the greater of $2,500 or actual damages, and attorneys' fees; and a closing attorney, settlement agent or other person to whom a discharge is delivered may also be so liable to the current owner of the property, all subject to limitation of liability if corrective action is taken within 30 days.

• Section 55 provides also for the possibility of discharge of a mortgage by affidavit of an attorney-at-law in good standing and licensed to practice in Massachusetts, pursuant to requirements and procedures spelled out in the statute.

• Section 55 provides in addition that a discharge of a mortgage on a 1 to 4 family residential property may be effected by recording the note endorsed as paid, which may be attached to an affidavit under § 5B.

• Section 54 sets forth definitions:

Discharge" means: "a duly executed and acknowledged

[Section 20:30]

[1]Chapter 63, Acts of 2006.

deed of release of a mortgage or other written instrument that, by its terms, discharges or releases a mortgage or the lien thereof or acknowledges payment or satisfaction of a mortgage or the debt or obligation secured by a mortgage or the conditions therein contained, or, in the case of a partial release, a duly executed and acknowledged instrument that, by its terms, discharges or releases a mortgage or the lien thereof from less than all of the property encumbered by the mortgage.

"Payoff statement" means: "a statement in writing, including a written print-out by facsimile or other electronic transmission, issued at the request of the mortgagor or an authorized person on his behalf by a mortgagee, mortgage servicer or note holder indicating the amount of the unpaid balance of the mortgage loan, including principal, interest and other charges assessed pursuant to the mortgage loan, which may include the interest on a per diem basis with respect to the unpaid principal balance of the mortgage. A payoff statement shall include, where the context permits, a statement provided to the mortgagor or an authorized person on his behalf by a mortgagee, mortgage servicer or note holder, indicating the amount of the unpaid balance of the mortgage loan or other obligation that must be paid in order to issue a partial release of a mortgage."

There are also definitions of "Mortgagee," which includes assignees of record, "Mortgage servicer," which includes a party required to provide a "payoff statement," and "Note holder," which contemplates that such party may not be the holder of record of the mortgage.

• Section 54B provides that discharges and acknowledgments of payment or satisfaction, as well as partial releases, assignments, subordinations and other such instruments, when executed before a notary public, justice of the peace or other officer entitled to acknowledge instruments in Massachusetts or elsewhere, are effective if executed "by a person purporting to hold the position of president, vice president, treasurer, clerk, secretary, cashier, loan representative, principal, investment, mortgage or other officer, agent, asset manager, or other similar office or position, including assistant to any such office or position, of the entity holding record title thereto on behalf of such entity acting in its own capacity or as a general partner or co-venturer of the entity holding record title, shall be binding upon such entity and shall be entitled to be recorded or filed, and no vote of the entity affirming such authority shall be required to permit recording of filing."

• Section 54C provides for the validity of recorded discharges so executed by a "mortgagee, mortgage servicer or note holder," when accompanied by supporting documents under § 55, or, in the case of mortgages on 1 to 4 family residential property, when there has been a payoff statement issued in accordance with requirements and procedures set forth in § 54C.

• Section 54D provides that a "mortgagee, mortgage servicer or note holder who is receiving payments" is required to provide a "payoff statement" within 30 days after request, pursuant to requirements and procedures set forth in § 54D.

• Section 54A provides that when a mortgage was held by husband and wife and discharged by only one of them, no action toward foreclosure may be taken after 10 years from recording of the discharge unless within the 10-year period the non-signing spouse has recorded a notice of claim, to be marginally noted on the mortgage.[2]

• M.G.L.A. c. 240, § 15, providing a judicial procedure for discharge of old mortgages, discussed in § **10:5**, was rewritten in 2006 to accommodate the new provisions of M.G.L.A. c. 183, § 55.

§ 20:31 Mistakes

When the holder of a mortgage discharges it by mistake, the courts will sometimes order reinstatement of the mortgage,[1] but not always,[2] depending on the circumstances. When there have been intervening encumbrances, the solution sometimes lies in subrogation to a former security position, again depending critically on the circumstances of the error.[3] But an erring lender who failed to record an assign-

---

[2]Partly reversing Pineo v. White, 320 Mass. 487, 70 N.E.2d 294 (1946).

[Section 20:31]

[1]Fleet Bank of Massachusetts v. Cassin, 2 L.C.R. 9 (1994); Federal Deposit Insurance Corporation v. DeVito, 2 L.C.R. 161 (1994); South Boston Savings Bank v. IAG Federal Credit Union, 3 L.C.R. 223 (1995); Coffee v. Federal Savings Bank, 5 L.C.R. 172 (1997); RFC Special Assets I, Inc. v. Mulligan, 9 L.C.R. 52 (2001); Washington Mutual Home Loans, Inc. v. DeMello, 14 L.C.R. 374 (2006).

[2]NationsBanc Mortg. Corp. v. Eisenhauer, 49 Mass. App. Ct. 727, 733 N.E.2d 557 (2000); World Savings Bank, FSB v. Chen, 11 L.C.R. 90 (2003).

[3]Jeanne D'Arc Credit Union v. Northern States Tire Corporation, 2 L.C.R. 132 (1994); Fleet Bank of Massachusetts v. Cassin, 2 L.C.R. 9 (1994); Federal Deposit Insurance Corporation v. DeVito, 2 L.C.R. 161 (1994); South Boston Savings Bank v. IAG Federal Credit Union, 3

ment to it was not rescued by the court.[4]

Furthermore, under M.G.L.A. c. 260, § 33, referred to in § **10:12**, failure to extend a mortgage beyond its maturity date or after 35 years at most will result in its being "considered discharged."

TOPIC H: FORECLOSURE

§ 20:32 Introduction

Foreclosure of a mortgage in Massachusetts is customarily accomplished by possession and sale. Either alone may be effective to accomplish foreclosure, but in practice foreclosure sale is the principal means and entry for possession is a nearly universal back-up. No judicial procedure is involved, except for action under the Soldiers and Sailors Civil Relief Act. It is, nevertheless, possible to foreclose by judicial procedure, but that is rarely done in Massachusetts. Some of the pertinent points are discussed in the following sections, but mortgage foreclosure is a large and complex subject and many important points and cases are not covered herein.

Massachusetts has "strict" foreclosure; that is, under M.G.L.A. c. 244, § 18, no redemption is allowed after foreclosure, except in one limited case, mentioned in paragraph D.4 below.

Under M.G.L.A. c. 260, §§ 33 to 35, discussed in § **10:12**, no foreclosure may be initiated more than 5 years after the maturity date of a mortgage, or if none, more than 35 years after recording of the mortgage.

§ 20:33 Soldiers' and Sailors' Civil Relief Act

Beginning in 1918 and again in 1940, Congress enacted laws to protect persons in the military service with respect to various civil actions to which they might not be able to respond in time or effectively. The 1940 Act made invalid all foreclosures by sale made during the mortgagor's period of military service or within three months thereafter, unless the foreclosures were made upon order of a court of competent jurisdiction, and it was later amended to apply to fore-

---

L.C.R. 223 (1995); East Boston Savings Bank v. Ogan, 5 L.C.R. 186 (1997).

[4]FBS Mortgage Corporation v. BayBank Middlesex, N.A., 4 L.C.R. 3 (1996).

closure by entry.[1]

In 1943, Massachusetts established a judicial procedure, in the Land Court or Superior Court, to deal with the federal Act. The procedure involves a petition for an order authorizing foreclosure by entry and sale, and an order approving the entry and sale once completed. These orders are recorded with the foreclosure deed, and are conclusive as to compliance with the federal Act. Notice is given by publication and by mail to owners of interests in the equity of redemption, and an affidavit is filed as to equity owners not being in active military service. If an equity owner is on active duty and does not voluntarily appear, the Court may appoint a "military attorney," akin to a guardian ad litem, to represent the serviceman's interest, without necessarily delaying the foreclosure. Amendments of the statute and judicial decisions have narrowed the scope of the proceeding.[2] Protection of the statute does not extend to corporate or other non-individual record owners of the equity of redemption, and has been held not to apply to the beneficiary of a trust which acquired title before the beneficiary entered military service, to a person who was already in the military service when he executed the note and mortgage, nor in other cases.[3]

Mortgages are sometimes foreclosed in Massachusetts without any Soldiers and Sailors procedure, and any impairment of marketability resulting from such "fast-track" foreclosure may be cured by a release deed from the holder of the foreclosed equity of redemption, or by subsequent judicial action.[4] REBA Title Standard 7 provides that a title involving a foreclosure without compliance with the Soldiers' and Sailors' Civil Relief Act (or Servicemembers' CRA) is not to be deemed unmarketable after the passage of 20 years, provided that no adverse claim of ownership appears of record in that period.

[Section 20:33]

[1]50 U.S.C.A. §§ 501 et seq.; § 532 re mortgages.

[2]Chapter 57, Acts of 1943; Chapter 120, Acts of 1945; Chapter 105, Acts of 1959; Chapter 127, Acts of 1982; Chapter 496, Acts of 1990; Chapter 142, Acts of 1998.

[3]Guleserian v. Pilgrim Trust Co., 331 Mass. 431, 120 N.E.2d 193 (1954); Beaton v. Land Court, 367 Mass. 385, 326 N.E.2d 302 (1975); Farmers Savings Bank v. Close, (Land Court, Case No. 119336, 1987); Massey v. Cloutier, 26 Mass. App. Ct. 1003, 530 N.E.2d 359 (1988); Source One Mortgage Services Corp. v. Glenn, 1 L.C.R. 27 (1993); Homeside Lending, Inv. v. Hurley, 6 L.C.R. 104 (1998); Global Financial Services, Inc. v. Eresian, 7 L.C.R. 382 (1999).

[4]Guarnty-First Trust Co. v. Sullivan, 1993 WL 13154824 (Mass. Land Ct. 1993); George v. Thornton, 6 L.C.R. 127 (1998).

§ 20:34 Entry and possession

M.G.L.A. c. 244, § 1, provides that: "A mortgagee may, after breach of condition of a mortgage of land, recover possession of the land mortgaged by an open and peaceable entry thereon, if not opposed by the mortgagor or other person claiming it, or by action under this chapter; and possession so obtained, if continued peaceably for three years from the date of recording of the memorandum or certificate as provided in section two, shall forever foreclose the right of redemption."

Under § 2 of that statute, the "memorandum" of entry may be made by the mortgagor on the mortgage, but usually there is a certificate of entry, executed by two competent witnesses to the entry itself, which must be recorded in the registry of deeds in order to be effective to begin the three-year period necessary for foreclosure. Such entry is often made immediately prior to foreclosure sale, and the certificate recorded along with a foreclosure deed and affidavit. A recorded certificate of entry may be vitiated by subsequent action, such as discharge of the mortgage.[1]

In order to be effective, the entry must be "open and peaceable" and result in "possession." If possession cannot be obtained peaceably, it may be obtained by judicial procedure under other provisions of Chapter 244. It is also provided in §§ 9 and 10 of Chapter 244 that a mortgagee is not barred from taking possession before breach and from making such possession effective after breach for purposes of foreclosure.

Taking possession in advance of foreclosure sale has the usual purpose of collecting rents. In any event notice to residential tenants, and to the local tax officials, is required by § 15A of Chapter 244. The rights of a mortgagee to collect rents has been considered in bankruptcy situations and otherwise.[2] A lease recorded after the mortgage is not necessarily terminated by possession to foreclose, but may be accepted by the mortgagee's voluntary attornment.[3]

In some instances peaceable possession is not obtained even after foreclosure sale, and judicial action is required.[4]

[Section 20:34]

[1]Goff v. White, 37 Mass. App. Ct. 128, 636 N.E.2d 1369 (1994).

[2]In re Ledgemere Land Corp., 116 B.R. 338 (Bankr. D. Mass. 1990); O'Brien v. Wainwright Bank & Trust Company, 6 L.C.R. 90 (1998).

[3]HRPT Advisors, Inc. v. MacDonald, Levine, Jenkins & Co., P.C., 43 Mass. App. Ct. 613, 686 N.E.2d 203 (1997).

[4]Attorney General v. Dime Sav. Bank of New York, FSB, 413

§ 20:35 Foreclosure by sale

It is provided in M.G.L.A. c. 244, § 14, that under a mortgage containing a power of sale the holder "may, upon breach of condition and without action, do all the acts authorized or required by the power." Power of sale may be derived or inferred from language in a mortgage other than reference to the statutory power of sale.[1]

The just quoted clause in § 14 is followed, however, by a proviso that no such sale "shall be effectual to foreclose a mortgage, unless, previous to such sale," notice has been given in the manner prescribed in the statute. Strict compliance with the statute is necessary to the validity of a foreclosure,[2] but actual notice may bar a contest.[3]

Notice must be given as follows: (1) By publication; the timing, repetition and newspaper all being specified in the statute; (2) By registered mail to "the owner or owners of record of the equity of redemption as of thirty days prior to the date of sale," and again the statute is specific as to timing and addresses; and (3) By registered mail to "all persons of record as of thirty days prior to the date of sale holding an interest in the property junior to the mortgage being foreclosed," again with specific requirements as to timing and addresses. If the mortgage requires additional or other notice, that must be given also.

The statute allows for waiver of notice by persons holding junior interests, but not otherwise. Junior interests would include prior mortgages, leases or other encumbrances which have been subordinated to the mortgage being foreclosed, and possibly even a tax lien.[4] In the case of a condominium unit, that would also include the lien for common expenses held by the organization of unit owners, which is an interest of record.

The form of notice is set forth in § 14, which provides that it may be altered, which is often done, and that other forms

Mass. 284, 596 N.E.2d 1013 (1992); Boston Rent Equity Bd. v. Dime Sav. Bank of New York, FSB, 415 Mass. 48, 611 N.E.2d 245 (1993).

[Section 20:35]

[1]The Massachusetts Company v. Midura, 3 L.C.R. 138 (1995); Greater Worcester Habitat for Humanity, Inc. v. Tolson, 12 L.C.R. 73 (2004).

[2]Moore v. Dick, 187 Mass.

207, 72 N.E. 967 (1905); Clapp v. Gardner, 237 Mass. 187, 130 N.E. 47 (1921); Gladstone v. Treasurer and Receiver General, 337 Mass. 48, 147 N.E.2d 786 (1958).

[3]Hull v. Attleboro Sav. Bank, 33 Mass. App. Ct. 18, 596 N.E.2d 358 (1992).

[4]Zuroff v. First Wisconsin Trust Co., 41 Mass. App. Ct. 491, 671 N.E.2d 982 (1996).

may be used, which is seldom done. The form is in brief as follows:

MORTGAGEE'S SALE OF REAL ESTATE.

By virtue and in execution of the Power of Sale contained in a certain mortgage given by . . . to . . . dated . . . and recorded with . . . Deeds, Book . . ., page . . ., of which mortgage the undersigned is the present holder, . . . (If by assignment, or in any fiduciary capacity, give reference.) for breach of the conditions of said mortgage and for the purpose of foreclosing the same will be sold at Public Auction at . . . o'clock, ...M. on the . . . day of . . . A.D. (insert year), (place) all and singular the premises described in said mortgage, (In case of partial releases, state exceptions.)

To wit: "(Description as in the mortgage, including all references to title, restrictions, encumbrances, etc., as made in the mortgage.)"

Terms of sale: (State here the amount, if any, to be paid in cash by the purchaser at the time and place of the sale, and the time or times for payment of the balance or the whole as the case may be.)

Other terms to be announced at the sale.

(Signed)
Present holder of said mortgage

Several points are worth noting: Assignments of the mortgage and partial releases are to be specified. The description of the premises is to be quoted from the mortgage itself. If there have been partial releases, that should be specified, but the notice description itself should not be changed. And if encumbrances cited in the mortgage are no longer extant, that should be noted, as well as additional encumbrances to which the mortgage has become subject by subordination or otherwise. Terms of sale specified in such notice often include a certified check deposit by all bidders and execution of a purchase and sale agreement soon after the sale. A mortgagee's statement announced at the sale that if the highest bidder defaulted, the second bidder would become the purchaser, was upheld.[5]

§ 20:36 Auction sale

The sale itself is conducted by a licensed auctioneer,

---

[5]146 Dundas Corp. v. Chemical Bank, 400 Mass. 588, 511 N.E.2d 520 (1987).

engaged by the foreclosing mortgagee, who is ordinarily paid the equivalent of a broker's fee or commission, and may be authorized to bid for the mortgagee.[1] The auctioneer begins by reading the notice of sale and announcing any additional terms of sale. The opening bid is often made by the mortgagee (or its agent) in the amount of the unpaid principal balance of the secured debt. As other bids are made, the mortgagee is likely to follow them up to the aggregate amount of the principal plus unpaid interest, charges and costs, including the costs of foreclosure. The mortgagee is not required to bid even if there are no other bidders.[2] Adjournment of the sale to a later date (within reason) may be announced by the auctioneer at the time and place advertised for the sale, and no further notice need be given.[3] The amount bid and the value of the property have posed issues in relation to bankruptcy, as discussed below.

§ 20:37 Foreclosure deed and affidavit

A foreclosure deed itself is fairly simple. The grantor is the mortgagee, acting "by power conferred by said mortgage and every other power." The deed identifies the mortgage, states the consideration, which is the amount of the highest bid (or a lower bid if that became effective) at the auction sale, and names the grantee, who is usually the highest bidder, which may have been the mortgagee, or possibly a nominee under or assignee of an auction sale contract made by the auctioneer with the highest bidder. The description may simply be "the premises conveyed by said mortgage," which is legally sufficient. However, it may need to be supplemented (a) to exclude parcels which had previously been partially released from the mortgage, (b) to refer to easements or other rights subsequently granted and to which the mortgage had been subordinated, or (c) to refer to a new plan, description, title reference or other corrective or supplementary data.

It is provided in § 14 of Chapter 244 that if sale is made pursuant to notice duly given, as described in paragraph 1 above, then: "the deed thereunder shall convey the premises,

---

[Section 20:36]

[1]Flynn v. Curtis & Pope Lumber Co., 245 Mass. 291, 139 N.E. 533 (1923).

[2]Manning v. Liberty Trust Co., 234 Mass. 544, 125 N.E. 691, 8 A.L.R. 999 (1920); Boyajian v. Hart, 292 Mass. 447, 198 N.E. 764 (1935);

DesLauries v. Shea, 300 Mass. 30, 13 N.E.2d 932 (1938).

[3]Fitzgerald v. First Nat. Bank of Boston, 46 Mass. App. Ct. 98, 703 N.E.2d 1192 (1999), rejecting In re Ruebeck, 55 B.R. 163 (Bankr. D. Mass. 1985).

subject to and with the benefit of all restrictions, easements, improvements, outstanding tax titles, municipal or other public taxes, assessments, liens or claims in the nature of liens, and existing encumbrances of record created prior to the mortgage, whether or not reference to such restrictions, easements, improvements, liens or encumbrances is made in the deed; but no purchaser at the sale shall be bound to complete the purchase if there are encumbrances, other than those named in the mortgage and included in the notice of sale, which are not stated at the sale and included in the auctioneer's contract with the purchaser."

As to the "affidavit," § 15 of Chapter 244 provides that: "The person selling, . . . shall, after the sale, cause a copy of the notice and his affidavit, fully and particularly stating his acts, . . . to be recorded in the registry of deeds for the county or district where the land lies, with a note or reference thereto on the margin of the record of the mortgage deed, if it is recorded in the same registry. If the affidavit shows that the requirements of the power of sale and of the statute have in all respects been complied with, the affidavit or a certified copy of the record thereof, shall be admitted as evidence that the power of sale was duly executed."

Such an affidavit, executed by the mortgagee, an officer of a corporate mortgagee, or attorney acting under a recorded power of attorney, is usually appended to or recorded with the foreclosure deed, although a time limit for its recording has been repealed. The affidavit should recite that: (i) there was a breach or default of the mortgage, (ii) notice was given by mail and publication in accordance with the statute, including a full copy of the advertised notice (which may be a newspaper clipping), (iii) sale took place at the time and place specified in the notice or pursuant to specified adjournments, and (iv) sale was made by public auction by a licensed auctioneer to a named highest bidder in a specified amount.

§ 20:38 Bankruptcy issues

When the mortgagor or owner of the equity of redemption files in bankruptcy, that effects an automatic stay on foreclosure. Bankruptcy courts may be persuaded to lift the stay and allow foreclosure to proceed, but there has been concern generally about the propriety and fairness of non-judicial foreclosures. Following a series of cases developing the concerns, the courts arrived at the rules which seem to prevail, as set forth or epitomized by two decisions.[1] In *BFP v. Resolution Trust Corp.*, the U.S. Supreme Court (albeit by a 5 to 4 decision) rejected the earlier "Durrett rule" and held that under the Bankruptcy Code "reasonably equivalent value" is the price in fact paid at foreclosure sale, so long as the requirements of state foreclosure law have been complied with. Similarly, in Massachusetts it was held in *Pemstein v. Stimpson*, that neither low price nor mortgagee's being the sole bidder indicated bad faith or lack of diligence, and that the UCC Article 9 standard of commercial reasonableness was not applicable to foreclosure of a real estate mortgage. Massachusetts courts have regularly upheld foreclosures when the statutory procedures were followed.[2]

In response to the spate of "bad loans" and bank failures in the 1980s, Congress granted special rights to the Federal Deposit Insurance Corporation (FDIC) and the Resolution Trust Corporation (RTC) to redeem for 1 year after foreclosure by sale of a mortgage having priority over the interest of FDIC or RTC held other than as receiver or equivalent. When either agency does act as receiver, the property so held is not subject to foreclosure (or attachment or other legal process) without its consent. When FDIC or RTC acts as receiver for a financial institution and it is desired to obtain a discharge, partial release or other instrument relating to a mortgage held by the institution, there is a pattern of documentation to be followed. This ordinarily includes an order appointing FDIC or RTC as receiver of the insolvent institution, transfer to FDIC as receiver of a successor financial institution, power of attorney from FDIC to a managing agent, and certificate of authority and incumbency of persons signing for the managing agent. Research of pertinent statutes and cases might begin with those here cited.[3]

[Section 20:38]

[1]BFP v. Resolution Trust Corp., 511 U.S. 531, 114 S. Ct. 1757, 128 L. Ed. 2d 556 (1994); Pemstein v. Stimpson, 36 Mass. App. Ct. 283, 630 N.E.2d 608, 23 U.C.C. Rep. Serv. 2d 877 (1994).

[2]Coldwell Banker Residential Real Estate Services, Inc. v. Somerset Savings Bank, 2 L.C.R. 122 (1994); Kostigen v. Leone, 4 L.C.R. 89 (1996); Fitzgerald v. First National Bank of Boston, 4 L.C.R. 131 (1996); Largenton v. Fleet Finance, Inc., 4 L.C.R. 219 (1996); Burne v. IAG Federal Credit Union, 4 L.C.R. 247 (1996).

[3]28 U.S.C.A. § 2410(c); 12 U.S.C.A. § 1825(b); 12 U.S.C.A. § 1821(n)(3)(iv); McLaughlin v. F.D.I.C., 796 F. Supp. 47 (D. Mass. 1992); McAndrews v. New Bank of New England, N.A., 796 F. Supp. 613 (D. Mass. 1992), judgment aff'd, 989 F.2d 13 (1st Cir. 1993); Botschafter v. F.D.I.C., 33 Mass. App. Ct. 595, 603 N.E.2d 235 (1992),

§ 20:39　Other issues

When a foreclosing mortgagee receives funds, it must duly account for them in relation to the mortgage debt. Accounting for rents collected by a mortgagee in possession before foreclosure is provided for in M.G.L.A. c. 244, § 20. The courts have considered various aspects,[1] including (a) forgery on a mortgage of a co-owners signature, (b) a mortgage securing two notes separately held, (c) a mortgage subordinate by actual knowledge, (d) insurance proceeds, and (e) the effect of subordination.

Other issues were faced and remedies framed when the court found a foreclosure to have been induced by ulterior, improper motivations.[2]

§ 20:40　Foreclosure by action

Foreclosure by action under M.G.L.A. c. 244, §§ 3 to 8, and 11 to 13, is exceedingly rare in Massachusetts. The statute provides that a mortgagee may bring a writ of entry in the land court for a judicial determination of his right of entry. If the court finds that the mortgagee has such a right it will give him a conditional judgment. The conditional judgment gives the possession of the premises to the mortgagee unless the mortgage debt is paid within two months of judgment. The mortgagee's possession must still be continued for three years to cut off the mortgagor's right of redemption.

If a conditional judgment is entered upon a mortgage containing a power of sale, the court will at the request of the plaintiff order the property to be sold pursuant to such power, effecting foreclosure.

§ 20:41　Deficiency

Section 17B of Chapter 244 provides that: "No action for a deficiency shall be brought . . . by the holder of a mortgage note or other obligation secured by mortgage of real estate after a foreclosure sale by him . . . unless a notice in writing

---

aff'd in part, appeal dismissed in part, 416 Mass. 1004, 621 N.E.2d 1171 (1993); Resolution Trust Corp. v. Carr, 13 F.3d 425 (1st Cir. 1993).

[Section 20:39]

[1](a) Sheeran v. Page, 6 L.C.R. 201 (1998), (b) Citizens Savings Bank v. Bankers Trust of California, N.A., 10 L.C.R. 122 (2002), (c) Moore v. Gerrity Co., Inc., 62 Mass. App. Ct. 522, 818 N.E.2d 213 (2004), (d) Rodriguez v. First Union Nat. Bank, 61 Mass. App. Ct. 438, 810 N.E.2d 1282 (2004), (e) NAB Asset Venture III, L.P. v. Brockton Credit Union, 62 Mass. App. Ct. 181, 815 N.E.2d 606 (2004).

[2]Kattar v. Demoulas, 433 Mass. 1, 739 N.E.2d 246 (2000).

of the mortgagee's intention to foreclose the mortgage has been mailed, postage prepaid, by registered mail with return receipt requested, to the defendant sought to be charged with the deficiency at his last address then known to the mortgagee, together with a warning of liability for the deficiency, in substantially the form below, not less than twenty-one days before the date of the sale under the power in the mortgage, and an affidavit has been signed and sworn to, within thirty days after the foreclosure sale, of the mailing of such notice. A notice mailed as aforesaid shall be a sufficient notice, and such an affidavit made within the time specified shall be prima facie evidence in such action of the mailing of such notice. The notice and affidavit, respectively, shall be in substantially the following forms:

Notice of Intention to Foreclose and of Deficiency After Foreclosure of Mortgage

To A.B.   Street

You are hereby notified, in accordance with the statute, of my intention, on or after ___, to foreclose by sale under power of sale for breach of condition, the mortgage held by me on property on ___ Street in ___ in the County of ___ dated ___ and recorded with ___ deeds Book ___ page ___ to secure a note (or other obligation) signed by you, for the whole, or part, of which you may be liable to me in case of a deficiency in the proceeds of the foreclosure sale.

Yours very truly,
C.D. Holder of said mortgage.

Affidavit.

I hereby certify on oath that on the ___ day of ___ *(insert year)* I mailed by registered mail, postage prepaid and return receipt requested, the notice, a copy of which appears below, directed to the persons or person at the addresses therein named which were the last addresses of such persons known to me at the time of mailing.

(Here insert copy)

Signed and sworn to before me this ___ day of ___ *(insert year)*"

The giving of such a "Deficiency Notice" is in addition to the required notice of foreclosure described in section D.1 above. It is not compulsory, but is an essential prerequisite to a suit for payment on the note or other obligation secured by a mortgage and not fully satisfied by the proceeds of a foreclosure sale. Section 17A of Chapter 244 provides a statute of limitations on deficiency suits of two years after foreclosure,[1] and § 17C bars the waiver of §§ 17A and 17B.

When a § 17B notice is not given, recovery is barred.[2] When such notice is given, a deficiency may be recovered, even if in some circumstances the party charged did not receive it.[3] A § 17B notice given on a first mortgage may cover junior mortgages foreclosed simultaneously.[4] The requirements of § 17B do not apply when the debt or deficiency sued upon arises from foreclosure of an out-of-state mortgage.[5]

Section 35 of Chapter 244 provides that: "If, after the foreclosure of a mortgage not containing a power of sale, the person entitled to the debt recovers judgment for any part thereof on the ground that the value of the land mortgaged at the time of the foreclosure was less than the amount due, such recovery shall open the foreclosure, and the person entitled may redeem the land although the three years limited therefore have expired, if suit for redemption is brought within one year after the recovery of such judgment."

Although applicable only where the mortgage foreclosed did not contain a power of sale, a rare circumstance, and a deficiency is recovered, this provision is odd in that it allows a redemption after a foreclosure.

§ 20:42 Further assurances; deed in lieu

It is often advisable to include in a mortgage a provision requiring the mortgagor to give "further assurances" of title when requested by the mortgagee. This can be set forth as an independent covenant, applicable before or after breach

---

[Section 20:41]

[1]Pagliarini v. Iannaco, 57 Mass. App. Ct. 601, 785 N.E.2d 1233 (2003), aff'd, 440 Mass. 1032, 800 N.E.2d 696 (2003).

[2]IAG Federal Credit Union v. Laterman, 40 Mass. App. Ct. 116, 661 N.E.2d 945 (1996); Framingham Sav. Bank v. Turk, 40 Mass. App. Ct. 384, 664 N.E.2d 472 (1996); SKW Real Estate Ltd. Partnership v. Gold, 428 Mass. 520, 702 N.E.2d 1178 (1998); Bead Portfolio, LLC v. Follayttar, 47 Mass. App. Ct. 533, 714 N.E.2d 372 (1999).

[3]Fairhaven Sav. Bank v. Callahan, 391 Mass. 1011, 462 N.E.2d 112 (1984); First Nat. Bank of Boston v. Ibarra, 47 Mass. App. Ct. 660, 716 N.E.2d 647 (1999); Carmel Credit Union v. Bondeson, 55 Mass. App. Ct. 557, 772 N.E.2d 1089 (2002).

[4]BankBoston, N.A. v. Yodice, 54 Mass. App. Ct. 901, 763 N.E.2d 80 (2002).

[5]Senior Corp. v. Perine, 16 Mass. App. Ct. 967, 452 N.E.2d 1160 (1983); Wornat Development Corp. v. Vakalis, 403 Mass. 340, 529 N.E.2d 1329 (1988).

of conditions and even after foreclosure. Once a foreclosure has been completed, a deed from the mortgagor confirming the conveyance is most desirable, particularly if there has been no Soldiers and Sailors proceeding. The statutory mortgage covenants themselves contain a covenant that in case of foreclosure sale, the mortgagor will give "a deed or deeds of release confirming such sale."

If, however, a deed is taken with the mortgage and is subject to an agreement that it not be recorded unless there is a default, then surely it is another security instrument, and the title it would convey upon recording without foreclosure proceedings is subject to question. Furthermore, whether executed with the mortgage or after default, it can convey only mortgagor's title, and at the time of default on a mortgage there are usually numerous junior encumbrances. Foreclosure of the prior mortgage would cut them off, but a deed from the mortgagor would merge the prior mortgage and leave the junior encumbrances outstanding. Nevertheless, there are circumstances in which a "deed in lieu of foreclosure" is advisable and will be held valid.[1]

Furthermore, a foreclosing mortgagee is not precluded from making financing or other business arrangements with a prospective bidder or prospective lessee.[2]

[Section 20:42]

[1]J & W Wall Systems, Inc. v. Shawmut First Bank & Trust Co., 413 Mass. 42, 594 N.E.2d 859 (1992).

[2]Nicholas McPickolus Realty Corp. v. Jamaica Plain Co-op. Bank, 16 Mass. App. Ct. 964, 452 N.E.2d 285 (1983); International Paper Co. v. Priscilla Co., 281 Mass. 22, 183 N.E. 58 (1932).

Chapter 21

Conducting the Closing

TOPIC A: PREPARATIONS

TOPIC B: THE CLOSING ITSELF

KeyCite®: Cases and other legal materials listed in KeyCite Scope can be researched through the KeyCite service on Westlaw®. Use KeyCite to check citations for form, parallel references, prior and later history, and comprehensive citator information, including citations to other decisions and secondary materials.

TOPIC A: PREPARATIONS

§ 21:1   Agenda

A closing is a meeting of a number of parties and involves a procedure with a number of steps. This calls for an Agenda; that is, a document specifying the participants and the actions to be taken by each. The person in charge of organizing such a meeting and managing the conduct of the closing is often the attorney for the lender financing the purchase. It is that person who should draw up an Agenda and distribute it to all other participants, serving as a guide or checklist for documents and actions expected of them. The caption of such a Closing Agenda may specify the address of the premises, the names of buyer, seller, any nominees acting for either, the mortgage lender, tenants or other parties to be involved at closing, and the closing date. It is also important to identify by name, address and telephone number each attorney acting for each party, and all other expected participants, who usually include a title insurance agent, and sometimes include architects, surveyors and contractors.

The categories and items included in the Closing Agenda may then proceed as follows:

- Items basic or preliminary to the closing, such as the purchase and sale agreement, loan commitment, title examination documents, including abstracts, existing leases and tenant rosters, title insurance binders or commitments, plans, engineering studies, zoning studies, certificates of municipal liens and copies of current tax, water, and utility bills, adjustment data, and mortgage payment figures, as well as instruments, affidavits, tax lien releases or other documents necessary to clear the seller's title of defects and encumbrances, and with respect to business entities, appropriate certificates of their formation or good standing, and if any of the parties to the transaction are using new business entities or nominees, their organizational documents.

- Basic title transfer documents between seller and buyer, including the deed or deeds, any bills of sale, assignments of leases, licenses, franchises or contractual rights which are involved in the transaction, and such evidences or certificates of authority to act as may be appropriate for corporate officers, partners, joint venturers or trustees.

- The loan documents, including the note, mortgage, and any collateral loan documents such as a loan agreement, collateral assignments of leases and rents, personal guarantees, etc.

- Any new leases or amendment of existing leases, and notices of lease relating thereto, a subordination and attornments agreements, and any necessary authorizational documents for the execution thereof.

- A closing statement setting forth the figures of the transaction and supporting data, and also disclosure statements, casualty insurance policies, opinions of counsel, notices to tenants, receipts for broker's commission, etc.

- Any post-closing documents, including things to be provided after the closing, such as a schedule of recording data, the title insurance policy, and, if there are any escrows or agreements with respect to deferred delivery of possession or for some other purposes, the documents which will evidence performance of the conditions and final distribution of funds.

§ 21:2   Closing documents

Usually the deed is prepared by the seller's attorney, the loan documents by the lender's attorney, and any buyer organizational and authorization documents by the buyer's attorney. The attorneys for the buyer and the lender usually need to see and to have the opportunity to comment on all of the proposed documents prior to the closing, and there is often reason for the seller's attorney to be interested also in the whole transaction.

In acting for a seller, and preparing and distributing the proposed deed, a conveyancer should give careful consideration to the disclosure of encumbrances. M.G.L.A. c. 184, § 21 provides that: "If real property upon which any encumbrance exists is conveyed by deed or mortgage, the grantor, in whatever capacity he may act, shall before the consideration is paid, by exception in the deed or otherwise make known to the grantee the existence and nature of such prior encumbrance so far as he has knowledge thereof."

And M.G.L.A. c. 184, § 22 provides that: "Whoever conveys real property by a deed or mortgage which contains a covenant that it is free from all encumbrances shall, if it appears by a public record that an actual or apparent encumbrance, known or unknown to him, exists thereon, be liable in an action of contract to the grantee, his heirs, executors, administrators, successors or assigns, for all damages sustained in removing the same."

§ 21:3   Time and place

The time and place of closing will ordinarily have been specified in a purchase and sale agreement, but in practice the attorneys for the parties customarily make their own agreement on these subjects. The registries of deeds are hectic places, and closings are more often conducted in lawyers' offices, commonly following the rule of "going where the money is."

The time should, of course, not be postponed by more than a few hours without dealing with it as an extension, and when a place other than the registry is set for the closing, the attorneys should agree that funds will be held until the documents are in fact recorded.

TOPIC B: THE CLOSING ITSELF

§ 21:4   In general

Assuming that preparations have been made along the

lines suggested in the preceding section, and that every party and lawyer who needs to do so has read and understood the documents, there is no reason why a closing, even of a fairly complex transaction, should take more than two or three hours. The closing of simple transactions should take less than an hour. When all necessary parties are present and the documents are laid out in an orderly fashion, it does not take long to have them signed and notarized.

As the purchase and sale agreement will provide, time is of the essence, and all parties should be there on time, and ready to proceed with the signing. A closing is not the occasion for negotiating the deal or modifications thereof. It is not the occasion to review the documents or the import of clauses therein. It is not the occasion to question the figures; even the adjustments should usually have been computed in advance. A lawyer who causes, or allows his client to cause, delay in or postponement of a closing for any of those reasons does not do a service to his client or himself, and certainly not to the other parties and lawyers involved.

§ 21:5   Escrow closing

Escrow closings, common in other jurisdictions, are not unheard of in Massachusetts. The essence of the arrangement is for the parties, seller and buyer, to deposit documents and funds with a third party, usually a title insurance company, with instructions to close the transaction and go to record upon the fulfillment of specified requirements. The specifications should, of course, include deadline dates and means of undoing the deal if the requirements are not met. This technique may be useful when one or both parties are out of state or do not have local counsel when preliminary title clearing is called for, or when there is an exchange transaction involved.

The escrow should be with a responsible party and the escrow instructions need to be detailed and clear, as illustrated by several cases.[1] The escrow holder should have undivided loyalty and be free from conflict of interest.[2]

§ 21:6   RESPA

The federal Real Estate Settlement Procedures Act applies

[Section 21:5]

[1]Kaarela v. Birkhead, 33 Mass. App. Ct. 410, 600 N.E.2d 608 (1992); F.D.I.C. v. Holbrook & Johnston, 36 Mass. App. Ct. 424, 632 N.E.2d 424 (1994); Connecticut National Bank v. First Security Mortgage Corporation, 3 L.C.R. 82 (1995).

[2]Matter of Discipline of Two Attorneys, 421 Mass. 619, 660 N.E.2d 1093 (1996).

to all closings involving a "federally related mortgage loan" (which encompasses practically all loans) secured by a first lien on residential property, including condominiums and cooperatives, designed for occupancy of 1 to 4 families. Pursuant to the statute, the Secretary of the Department of Housing and Urban Development has prescribed a form of statement of settlement costs which must be used for subject closings, and must be completed and displayed to the borrower at or before the closing. The statute also contains provisions prohibiting "kickbacks" and tie-ins to title insurers, and limiting escrow deposits which may be required of a borrower. Regulations are set forth in 24 C.F.R. 3500.

§ 21:7 Funds

Purchase and sale agreements commonly call for payment by certified checks or checks of a bank issued by its cashier or treasurer, preferably drawn on a local bank, and payable to the buyer who endorses them at closing. A certified check is still subject to clearance, which may cause delay, although it may be "cashed" by the drawee bank or a depositee bank.

On larger transactions, particularly those involving interstate transfers of funds, the practice of wire transfer is common. While the purpose is to expedite transfer, delays are sometimes encountered. It may be useful to make inquiries of the banks involved about their procedures, and to keep in touch by telephone with bank personnel handling the transfer. Article 4A of the UCC, M.G.L.A. c. 106, governs funds transfers.

An attorney who receives funds for a client should, of course, not use them or mingle them with his own funds without specific instructions from the client,[1] and must comply with IOLTA requirements.[2]

As to the disbursement of mortgage loan proceeds, it is necessary to take into account the provisions of M.G.L.A. c. 183, § 63B, the so-called "good funds law," that: "No mortgagee who makes a loan to be secured by a mortgage or lien on real estate located in the commonwealth in conjunction with which, a mortgage deed evidencing the same is to be recorded in a registry of deeds or registry district in the commonwealth, shall deliver said deed or cause the same to be delivered into the possession of such registry of deeds or registry district for the purpose of the recording thereof un-

---

[Section 21:7]

[1]Matter of Discipline of an Attorney, 392 Mass. 827, 468 N.E.2d 256 (1984).

[2]Massachusetts Rules of Professional Conduct, Rule 1.15.

less prior to the time said deed is so delivered for recording, said mortgagee has caused the full amount of the proceeds of such loan due to the mortgagor pursuant to the settlement statement relevant thereto given to said mortgagor or in the instance of any such loan in which the full amount of the proceeds due to the mortgagor pursuant to the terms thereof are not to be advanced prior to said recording, so much thereof as is designated in the loan agreement, to be transferred to the mortgagor, the mortgagor's attorney or the mortgagee's attorney in the form of a certified check, bank treasurer's check, cashier's check or by a transfer of funds between accounts within the same state or federally chartered bank or credit union, or by the funds-transfer system owned and operated by the Federal Reserve Banks, or by a transfer of funds processed by an automated clearinghouse; provided, however, that neither the mortgagor's attorney or the mortgagee's attorney shall be required to make disbursements or deliver said proceeds to the mortgagor in such form; provided, however, that the provisions of this section shall not apply to the commonwealth, its agencies or political subdivisions."

There are REBA Practice Standards on the subject of funds and related matters.[3]

§ 21:8   IRC requirements

Compliance with the Foreign Investment in Real Property Tax Act,[1] known as FIRPTA, is required whenever funds are paid to a seller, unless the amount is less than $300,000 and the buyer is acquiring the property as his residence. Compliance is usually accomplished by an affidavit of the seller (or "transferor") setting forth the seller's name, address, social security or taxpayer identification number, and a certification that the transferor is not a foreign person within the meaning of the Act. Forms are specified in regulations.[2] The certification must be retained by the transferee for 5 years and made available to the IRS upon request.

If the transferor is in fact a foreign person, the transferee is required to withhold from the consideration paid an amount equal to 10 percent thereof, and within 20 days after the closing, pay it over to the IRS. The amount may be reduced or eliminated by certification by the IRS.

[3]See REBA Practice Standards 1, 2, 5, 7, 9, 15, 16, 18 and 22.

[2]See IRS Publication 515.

[Section 21:8]

[1]26 U.S.C.A. § 1445.

It is also necessary to comply with broader requirements of reporting of information with respect to real estate transfers under IRC provisions and regulations,[3] applicable to sale or exchange of all types of real estate, but excluding gifts, refinances, foreclosures and transfers in lieu of foreclosure. Also exempt are transactions by corporate and governmental transferors and certain "volume transferors" who conduct 25 or more transactions per year in the ordinary course of business. The person required to report is the settlement agent designated on the settlement statement of the transaction, or a person designated by agreement of the parties, or the person otherwise identified pursuant to the regulations. The information required must be set forth on Form 1099, and include the name, address and taxpayer identification number of the transferor, a general description of the real estate, date of closing, the gross proceeds, including non-cash consideration, name, address, and TIN of the party responsible for reporting, and other information. A separate return must be filed for each of multiple transferors, with an allocation of gross proceeds, but husband and wife are treated as a single transferor unless the reporting person receives an uncontested allocation of gross proceeds between them.

The Form 1099s must be filed with the IRS by February 28 of each year for the preceding year's transactions. A reporting person with 250 or more transactions to report must submit the returns on magnetic media, unless exception is made. The reporting person must also furnish the pertinent information to the transferor whose transaction is being reported.

§ 21:9 Opinions and certifications

A title opinion is called for in practically every real estate purchase and sale or loan transaction. An attorney is liable for loss or damages arising from a flawed opinion.[1] The claim runs from discovery or notice of the flaw, not from the date of the opinion, and liability may be extended by "continuing representation."[2] Upon annual registration with the Board of Bar Overseers, attorneys are required to disclose whether

---

[3]26 U.S.C.A. § 6045.

[Section 21:9]

[1]Republic Oil Corp. v. Danziger, 9 Mass. App. Ct. 858, 400 N.E.2d 1315 (1980); Fall River Sav. Bank v. Callahan, 18 Mass. App. Ct. 76, 463 N.E.2d 555 (1984).

[2]Hendrickson v. Sears, 365 Mass. 83, 310 N.E.2d 131 (1974); Salin v. Shalgian, 18 Mass. App. Ct. 467, 467 N.E.2d 475 (1984); Murphy v. Smith, 411 Mass. 133, 579 N.E.2d 165 (1991).

they are covered by professional liability insurance,[3] and that is an inquiry often made of counsel by lending institutions. Under M.G.L.A. c. 93, § 70, quoted in **§ 20:24**, the lender's counsel in certain loan transactions on residential properties is required to certify the title to the mortgagor as well as the mortgagee. That statute is not applicable to loans on vacant land.[4] Title certifications under that statute are often given on standard forms prepared for the purpose, which recite the exact statutory language of certification and of limitation of liability and time of effectiveness.

When a purchase and sale agreement provided that the buyer's obligations were contingent on approval of title by the buyer's attorney, the buyer was held to be entitled to refund of his deposit when his attorney declined to approve the title, even though the attorney's opinion, honestly made, as the putative encumbrance, may have been flawed.[5]

In most other cases title certification is given by a letter on the certifying attorney's letterhead, or if the certification is to a title insurance company, on a form provided by the title insurer. While purchase and sale agreements customarily call for a "good and clear record and marketable title," attorneys often wish to limit their certifications to "good and satisfactory" or "sufficient and satisfactory" record title. Sometime an attorney's certification of "marketability" is also required, and in that case the opinion will ordinarily specifically except any matters adversely affecting marketability which do not appear of record. In fact, even certifications which do not by their terms cover marketability usually contain an exception for "such state of facts as an accurate survey and an examination of the premises might disclose," intended to exclude from the certification any assertion of prescriptive or other off-record claims.

With respect to any such non-record matters which might be discerned by physical examination of the property, the appropriate certification is by a registered surveyor who has in fact made a survey and examined the premises. Such a "surveyor's certification" is of an importance commensurate with record title certification and is widely called for.

On residential mortgage loans banks generally accept a simple "plot plan" showing the house and other structures on the lot, usually located only by visual observation of ap-

[3]Massachusetts Rules of Professional Conduct, Rule 4.02.

[4]Page v. Frazier, 388 Mass. 55, 445 N.E.2d 148 (1983).

[5]Smith v. Allmon, 17 Mass. App. Ct. 712, 461 N.E.2d 1237 (1984).

parent boundaries and measurement by stadia. One of the purposes of such a plot plan is to determine compliance with zoning laws, and a mortgagee bank which did not disclose that information, it was held liable for misrepresentation.[6] In a commercial transaction, however, an instrument survey and a full surveyor's report, on a form prepared by the attorney or an ALTA or title insurance company form, is usually required. See **Appendix G**.

In addition, attorneys' opinions are often required on compliance of the premises with all aspects of the applicable zoning laws, and also a wide range of potentially applicable environmental regulatory laws. These usually pose issues, problems, and considerable discussion and give and take among the attorneys involved. They almost always involve dimensional and physical matters on which the attorney must rely on the reports of surveyors and engineers. While counsel to a lender will always want as broad and all-inclusive an opinion as possible, the attorney giving the opinion will want to express his reliance on survey and engineering reports so that the attorney will not be liable if they are not accurate, and also to avoid giving any catchall "there are none other" opinions, particularly with respect to environmental matters.

Another attorney's opinion which is regularly called for is one of the due organization and standing of a borrowing business entity and the authority and power to act of the officials thereof to execute the loan documents and the effectiveness of the loan documents for their stated purposes.

Guidelines on legal opinions in real estate transactions have been developed by and are available from committees of the American Bar Association (ABA) Section on Real Property and the American College of Real Estate Lawyers (ACREL).

§ 21:10   Post-closing tasks

The closing of a real estate transaction is not the end of the matter. When the conveyance documents are recorded, usually immediately following the closing, they will be given "instrument numbers," or "document numbers," keyed into registry computers. The determination by the registry of the record Book and Page numbers of the instruments may take from a few hours to a day or two, depending on the registry. It is desirable to obtain these numbers as quickly as possible

---

[6]Danca v. Taunton Sav. Bank,   (1982).
385 Mass. 1, 429 N.E.2d 1129

and to report them to the title insurer so that the policy will recite book and page numbers, and not just daily sheet instrument numbers, which alone are poor references for future title source and examination purposes.

Once the title insurance policies, owner's and mortgagee's, are issued, the attorneys for those parties should examine them carefully to be sure that they conform with the commitment for insurance if one was previously issued. If there was only a binder and not a formal commitment, the lawyer should then check the property description and consider the form of characterization of each exception. The original policies will, of course, be sent to the client, but the lawyer should retain a copy for inclusion in his "bible" of the transaction.

The original recorded instruments (except registered land documents) will be returned by the registry within a matter of days or weeks, depending on the registry and its current volume of business, which increases at the end of the year. Generally it is preferable to mark instruments for return to the attorneys rather than directly to the parties. In this way the attorneys can keep track of the disposition of instruments which they have recorded, and can confirm the book and page numbers written on the instruments. In substantial transactions the mortgagee's attorney may wish to have all of the instruments returned to him, and then he will distribute them to the seller and buyer, or their attorneys, and to the mortgagee, as appropriate.

In a transaction in which there are express agreements for post-closing actions, such as deferred delivery of possession, meter readings and payment of utility bills, collection and remittal of overdue rents or escalator payments, real estate tax readjustment, etc., the conveyancer's job includes seeing to the conclusion of these matters. Some of them, such as a real estate tax readjustment, may not occur until many months after the closing.

Finally, there is the preparation of a "bible" of the transaction. The schedule of documents used as an Agenda in preparation for the closing can often serve as the basis of an index of such a bible. Generally, it is desirable to make the bible a complete compendium of the pertinent documents. If there is an instrument which was called for or contemplated by the original purchase and sale agreement or by a loan commitment, but was then waived, superseded or for some reason made unnecessary, it should nevertheless be included in the bible with a brief notation thereon stating why it was not used. And, of course, if there are additional instruments not originally contemplated but found to be necessary or desirable, and actually used, they should be included. Full copies of the conveyance instruments, conformed as to signatures and dates, should be included, and the recording date and book and page numbers should be noted thereon or in the bible index. Also to be included are copies of the closing statements, checks delivered and endorsements thereon, the title insurance policies and documents relating to and showing fulfillment of post-closing actions as referred to above. It is also advisable to include copies of the letters by which documents were transmitted to other attorneys and clients. In short, the bible should be a complete record of the transaction. Often such bibles are made in multiple copies for distribution to the several attorneys and parties involved in the transaction.

APPENDICES

APPENDIX A

GBREB Standard Form of Purchase and Sale Agreement

STANDARD FORM PURCHASE & SALE AGREEMENT

From the Office of:_____

This_____ day of_____, 20_____

1. PARTIES AND MAILING ADDRESSES
(fill in)

hereinafter called the SELLER, agrees to SELL and

hereinafter called the BUYER or PURCHASER, agrees to BUY, upon the terms hereinafter set forth, the following described premises:

2. DESCRIPTION
(fill in and include title reference)

3. BUILDINGS, STRUCTURES, IMPROVEMENTS, FIXTURES
(fill in or delete)

Included in the sale as a part of said premises are the buildings, structures, and improvements now thereon, and the fixtures belonging to the SELLER and used in connection therewith including, if any, all wall-to-wall carpeting, drapery rods, automatic garage door openers, venetian blinds, window shades, screens, screen doors, storm windows and doors, awnings, shutters, furnaces, heaters, heating equipment, stoves, ranges, oil and gas burners and fixtures appurtenant thereto, hot water heaters, plumbing and bathroom fixtures, garbage disposers, electric and other lighting fixtures, mantels, outside television antennas, fences, gates, trees, shrubs, plants and, ONLY IF BUILT IN, refrigerators, air conditioning equipment, ventilators, dishwashers, washing machines and dryers; and

but excluding

4. TITLE DEED
(fill in)
include here by specific reference any restrictions, easements, rights and obligations in party walls not included in (b), leases, municipal and other liens, other encumbrances, and make provision to protect SELLER against BUYER's breach of SELLER's covenants in leases, where necessary.

Said premises are to be conveyed by a good and sufficient quitclaim deed running to the BUYER, or to the nominee designated by the BUYER by written notice to the SELLER at least seven _____ days before the deed is to be delivered as herein provided, and said deed shall convey a good and clear record and marketable title thereto, free from encumbrances, except

a. Provisions of existing building and zoning laws;
b. Existing rights and obligations in party walls which are not the subject of written agreement;
c. Such taxes for the then current year as are not due and payable on the date of the delivery of such deed;
d. Any liens for municipal betterments assessed after the date of this agreement;
e. Easements, restrictions and reservations of record, if any, so long as the same do not prohibit or materially interfere with the current use of said premises;
*f.

5. PLANS

If said deed refers to a plan necessary to be recorded therewith the SELLER shall deliver such plan with the deed in form adequate for recording or registration.

6. PURCHASE PRICE
(fill in) space is allowed to spell out the amounts if desired

The agreed purchase price for said premises is $

dollars, of which

$ have been paid as a deposit this day and
$
$ are to be paid at the time of delivery of the deed in cash, or by certified, cashier's,check(s).

$ _____
$ TOTAL

App. A-1

7. REGISTERED TITLE

In addition to the foregoing, if the title to said premises is registered, said deed shall be in form sufficient to entitle the BUYER to a Certificate of Title of said premises, and the SELLER shall deliver with said deed all instruments, if any, necessary to enable the BUYER to obtain such Certificate of Title.

8. TIME FOR PERFORMANCE; DELIVERY OF DEED
(fill in)

Such deed is to be delivered at_____o'clock (am/pm)_____on the_____day of_____20   , at the_____
_____
Registry of Deeds, unless otherwise agreed upon in writing. It is agreed that time is of the essence of this agreement.

9. POSSESSION and CONDITION of PREMISE
(attach a list of exceptions, if any)

Full possession of said premises free of all tenants and occupants, except as herein provided, is to be delivered at the time of the delivery of the deed, said premises to be then (a) in the same condition as they now are, reasonable use and wear thereof excepted, and (b) not in violation of said building and zoning laws, and (c) in compliance with the provisions of any instrument referred to in clause 4 hereof. The BUYER shall be entitled personally to enter said premises prior to the delivery of the deed in order to determine whether the condition thereof complies with the terms of this clause.

10. EXTENSION TO PERFECT TITLE OR MAKE PREMISES CONFORM
(Change period of time if desired).

If the SELLER shall be unable to give title or to make conveyance, or to deliver possession of the premises, all as herein stipulated, or if at the time of the delivery of the deed the premises do not conform with the provisions hereof, then any payments made under this agreement shall be forthwith refunded and all other obligations of the parties hereto shall cease, and this agreement shall be void without recourse to the parties hereto, unless the SELLER elects to use reasonable efforts to remove any defects in title, or to deliver possession as provided herein, or to make the said premises conform to the provisions hereof, as the case may be, in which event the SELLER shall give written notice thereof to the BUYER at or before the time for performance hereunder, and thereupon the time for performance hereof shall be extended for a period of thirty _____ days.

11. FAILURE TO PERFECT TITLE OR MAKE PERMISES CONFORM, etc.

If at the expiration of the extended time the SELLER shall have failed so to remove any defects in title, deliver possession, or make the premises conform, as the case may be, all as herein agreed, or if at any time during the period of this agreement or any extension thereof, the holder of a mortgage on said premises shall refuse to permit the insurance proceeds, if any, to be used for such purposes, then any payments made under this agreement shall be forthwith refunded and all other obligations of the parties hereto shall cease and this agreement shall be void without recourse to the parties hereto.

12. BUYER's ELECTION TO ACCEPT TITLE

The BUYER shall have the election, at either the original or any extended time for performance, to accept such title as the SELLER can deliver to the said premises in their then condition and to pay therefore the purchase price without deduction, in which case the SELLER shall convey such title, except that in the event of such conveyance in accord with the provisions of this clause, if the said premises shall have been damaged by fire or casualty insured against, then the SELLER shall, unless the SELLER has previously restored the premises to their former condition, either
   a. pay over or assign to the BUYER, on delivery of the deed, all amounts recovered or recoverable on account of such insurance, less any amounts reasonably expended by the SELLER for any partial restoration, or_____
   b. if a holder of a mortgage on said premises shall not permit the insurance proceeds or a part thereof to be used to restore the said premises to their former condition or to be so paid over or assigned, give to the BUYER a credit against the purchase price, on delivery of the deed, equal to said amounts so recovered or recoverable and retained by the holder of the said mortgage less any amounts reasonably expended by the SELLER for any partial restoration.

13. ACCEPTANCE OF DEED

The acceptance of a deed by the BUYER or his nominee, as the case may be, shall be deemed to be a full performance and discharge of every agreement and obligation herein contained or expressed, except such as are, by the terms hereof, to be performed after the delivery of said deed.

14. USE OF MONEY TO CLEAR TITLE

To enable the SELLER to make conveyance as herein provided, the SELLER may, at the time of delivery of the deed, use the purchase money or any portion thereof to clear the title of any or all encumbrances or interests, provided that all instruments so procured are recorded simultaneously with the delivery of said deed.

15. INSURANCE
*Insert amount (list additional types of insurance and amounts as agreed)

Until the delivery of the deed, the SELLER shall maintain insurance on said premises as follows:

Type of Insurance	Amount of Coverage
a. Fire & Extended Coverage	*$
b.	*$
c.	*$

16. ADJUSTMENTS
(list operating expenses, if any, or attach schedule)

Collected rents, mortgage interest, water and sewer use charges, operating expenses (if any) according to the schedule attached hereto or set forth below, and taxes for the then current fiscal year, shall be apportioned and fuel value shall be adjusted, as of the day of performance of this agreement and the net amount thereof shall be added to or deducted from, as the case may be, the purchase price payable by the BUYER at the time of delivery of the deed. Uncollected rents for the current rental period shall be apportioned if and when collected by either party.

17. ADJUSTMENT OF UNASSESSED AND ABATED TAXES

If the amount of said taxes is not known at the time of the delivery of the deed, they shall be apportioned on the basis of the taxes assessed for the preceding fiscal year, with a reapportionment as soon as the new tax rate and valuation can be ascertained; and, if the taxes which are to be apportioned shall thereafter be reduced by abatement, the amount of such abatement, less the reasonable cost of obtaining the same, shall be apportioned between the parties, provided that neither party shall be obligated to institute or prosecute proceedings for an abatement unless otherwise herein agreed.

18. BROKER's FEE
(fill in fee with dollar amount or percentage; also name of Brokerage firm(s))

A Broker's fee for professional services of_____

is due from the SELLER to_____

the Broker(s) herein, but if the SELLER pursuant to the terms of clause 21 hereof retains the deposits made hereunder by the BUYER, said Broker(s) shall be entitled to receive from the SELLER an amount equal to one-half the amount so retained or an amount equal to the Broker's fee for professional services according to this contract, whichever is the lesser.

19. BROKER(S) WARRANTY
(fill in name)

The Broker(s) named herein_____

warrant(s) that the Broker(s) is (are) duly licensed as such by the Commonwealth of Massachusetts.

20. DEPOSIT
(fill in name)

All deposits made hereunder shall be held in escrow by_____

as escrow agent subject to the terms of this agreement and shall be duly accounted for at the time for performance of this agreement. In the event of any disagreement between the parties, the escrow agent may retain all deposits made under this agreement pending instructions mutually given in writing by the SELLER and the BUYER.

21. BUYER's DEFAULT; DAMAGES

If the BUYER shall fail to fulfill the BUYER's agreements herein, all deposits made hereunder by the BUYER shall be retained by the SELLER as liquidated damages unless within thirty days after the time for performance of this agreement or any extension hereof, the SELLER otherwise notifies the BUYER in writing.

22. RELEASE BY HUSBAND OR WIFE

The SELLER's spouse hereby agrees to join in said deed and to release and convey all statutory and other rights and interests in said premises.

23. BROKER AS PARTY

The Broker(s) named herein join(s) in this agreement and become(s) a party hereto, insofar as any provisions of this agreement expressly apply to the Broker(s), and to any amendments or modifications of such provisions to which the Broker(s) agree(s) in writing.

24. LIABILITY OF TRUSTEE, SHAREHOLDER, BENEFICIARY, etc.

If the SELLER or BUYER executes this agreement in a representative or fiduciary capacity, only the principal or the estate represented shall be bound, and neither the SELLER or BUYER so executing, nor any shareholder or beneficiary of any trust, shall be personally liable for any obligation, express or implied, hereunder.

25. WARRANTIES AND REPRESENTATIONS
(fill in) if none, state "none"; if any listed, indicate by whom each warranty or representation was made

The BUYER acknowledges that the BUYER has not been influenced to enter into this transaction nor has he relied upon any warranties or representations not set forth or incorporated in this agreement or previously made in writing, except for the following additional warranties and representations, if any, made by either the SELLER or the Broker(s):

26. CONTINGENCY CLAUSE
    (omit if not provided for in Offer to Purchase)

In order to help finance the acquisition of said premises, the BUYER shall apply for a conventional bank or other institutional mortgage loan of $_____ at prevailing rates, terms and conditions. If despite the BUYER's diligent efforts a commitment for such loan cannot be obtained on or before_____, 20_____, the BUYER may terminate this agreement by written notice to the SELLER and/or the Broker(s), as agent(s) for the SELLER, prior to the expiration of such time, whereupon any payments made under this agreement shall be forthwith refunded and all other obligations of the parties hereto shall cease and this agreement shall be void without recourse to the parties hereto. In no event will the BUYER be deemed to have used diligent efforts to obtain such commitment unless the BUYER submits a complete mortgage loan application conforming to the foregoing provisions on or before_____, 20_____.

27. CONSTRUCTION OF AGREEMENT

This instrument, executed in multiple counterparts, is to be construed as a Massachusetts contract, is to take effect as a sealed instrument, sets forth the entire contract between the parties, is binding upon and enures to the benefit of the parties hereto and their respective heirs, devisees, executors, administrators, successors and assigns, and may be cancelled, modified or amended only by a written instrument executed by both the SELLER and the BUYER. If two or more persons are named herein as BUYER their obligations hereunder shall be joint and several. The captions and marginal notes are used only as a matter of convenience and are not to be considered a part of this agreement or to be used in determining the intent of the parties to it.

28. LEAD PAINT LAW

The parties acknowledge that, under Massachusetts law, whenever a child or children under six years of age resides in any residential premises in which any paint, plaster or other accessible material contains dangerous levels of lead, the owner of said premises must remove or cover said paint, plaster or other material so as to make it inaccessible to children under six years of age.

29. SMOKE DETECTORS

The SELLER shall, at the time of the delivery of the deed, deliver a certificate from the fire department of the city or town in which said premises are located stating that said premises have been equipped with approved smoke detectors in conformity with applicable law.

30. CARBON MONOXIDE DETECTORS

For properties sold or conveyed after March 30, 2006, the Seller shall provide a certificate from the fire department of the city or town in which the premises are located, either in addition to or incorporated into the certificate described above, stating that the premises have been equipped with carbon monoxide detectors in compliance with M.G.L. c. 148 § 26F1/2 or that the Premises are otherwise exempted the Statute.

31. ADDITIONAL PROVISIONS

The initialed riders, if any, attached hereto, are incorporated herein by reference.

FOR RESIDENTIAL PROPERTY CONSTRUCTED PRIOR TO 1978, BUYER MUST ALSO HAVE SIGNED LEAD PAINT "PROPERTY TRANSFER NOTIFICATION CERTIFICATION"

NOTICE: This is a legal document that creates binding obligations. If not understood, consult an attorney.

SELLER:_____   BUYER:_____
Print Name:_____   Print Name:_____
Taxpayer ID/Social Security No._____   Taxpayer ID/Social Security No._____
SELLER (or Spouse):_____   BUYER:_____
Print Name:_____   Print Name:_____
Taxpayer ID/Social Security No._____   Taxpayer ID/Social Security No._____

BROKER(S)

APPENDIX B

GBREB Sewage Disposal System Contingency Addendum

SEWAGE DISPOSAL SYSTEM CONTINGENCY ADDENDUM

ıe Buyer, if checked, hereby incorporates the following contingencies to this agreement.

SEWAGE DISPOSAL SYSTEM CONTINGENCY ADDENDUM

The property is serviced by an on-site subsurface sewage disposal system (the "System") regulated by Title 5 of the Massachusetts State Environmental Code ("Title 5"). As required by Title 5, the SELLER will make arrangements to have the System inspected at the SELLER's expense by a person authorized to perform such inspections (the "System Inspector"). The condition of the property shall not be deemed to violate the terms of this agreement because the SELLER is not reasonably able, before the time of the delivery of the deed, to restore any landscaped areas affected by such inspection. Unless, on or before _____, 20____.

1. The SELLER furnishes to the BUYER a certification from the System Inspector, in the form prescribed by the Massachusetts Department of Environmental Protection, stating that the System Inspector has not found any information which indicates that the System fails to adequately protect public health or the environment as defined in Title 5; and

2. In those instances where Title 5 instructs local officials to review the condition, design and operation of the System, such officials determine that the System is functioning properly;

the BUYER shall have the option of revoking this agreement by written notice to the SELLER and/or the Broker(s), on or before _____, 20____. If the BUYER so elects to revoke this agreement, all deposits made by the BUYER shall be forthwith refunded and this agreement shall become null and void without further recourse to either party.

tials:

_____   _____
Seller (or spouse)   Seller

_____   _____
Buyer   Buyer

_____
Broker(s)

APPENDIX C

GBREB Oil and Hazardous Material Inspection Contingency Addendum

INSPECTION CONTINGENCY ADDENDUM
Oil and Hazardous Material

The Buyer, if checked, hereby incorporates the following contingencies to this agreement.

☐ **INSPECTION CONTINGENCY ADDENDUM Oil and Hazardous Material**
  The BUYER may, at his own expense and on or before _____, 20___, have the property professionally inspected for the presence of oil or hazardous material (as such terms are defined in the Massachusetts Oil and Hazardous Material Release Prevention and Response Act, General Laws Chapter 21E). If it is the opinion of such inspector that any such substance is present on the property or that there is a substantial likelihood of a release of any such substance from or at the property, then the BUYER shall have the option of revoking the agreement by written notice to the SELLER and/or the Broker, prior to the expiration of such time, which notice shall be accompanied by a copy of the inspector's opinion and any related inspection report, whereupon all deposits made by the BUYER to the SELLER shall be forthwith refunded and this agreement shall become null and void and without further recourse to any party.

Initials:

_____
Seller (or spouse)

_____
Buyer

_____
Seller

_____
Buyer

_____
Broker(s)

APPENDIX D

GBREB Offer to Purchase Real Estate

OFFER TO PURCHASE REAL ESTATE

TO _____   Date:_____
(Seller and Spouse)   From the Office of : _____
_____
_____

The property herein referred to is identified as follows: _____

Special provisions (if any) re fixtures, appliances, etc. _____

hereby offer to buy said property, which has been offered to me by _____
_____ as the Broker(s) under the following terms and conditions:

CHECK ONE:
☐ Check, subject to collection
☐ Cash

1. I will pay therefore $_____, of which
   (a) $_____ is paid herewith as a deposit to bind this Offer
   (b) $_____ is to be paid as an additional deposit upon the execution of the Purchase and Sale Agreement provided for below.
   (c) $_____ is to be paid at the time of delivery of the Deed in cash, or by certified, cashier's, treasurer's or bank check(s).
   (d) $_____
   (e) $_____ Total Purchase Price

2. This Offer is good until _____ A.M. P.M. on _____, 20_____ at or before which time a copy hereof shall be signed by you, the Seller and your (husband) (wife), signifying acceptance of this Offer, and returned to me forthwith, otherwise this Offer shall be considered as rejected and the money deposited herewith shall be returned to me forthwith.

3. The parties hereto shall, on or before _____ A.M. P.M. _____, 20_____ execute the applicable Standard Form Purchase and Sale Agreement recommended by the Greater Boston Real Estate Board or any form substantially similar thereto, which, when executed, shall be the agreement between the parties hereto.

4. A good and sufficient Deed, conveying a good and clear record and marketable title shall be delivered at 12:00 Noon on _____, 20_____ at the appropriate Registry of Deeds, unless some other time and place are mutually agreed upon in writing.

5. If I do not fulfill my obligations under this Offer, the above mentioned deposit shall forthwith become your property without recourse to either party. Said deposit shall be held by _____ as escrow agent subject to the terms hereof provided however that in the event of any disagreement between the parties, the escrow agent may retain said deposit pending instructions mutually given in writing by the parties. A similar provision shall be included in the Purchase and Sale Agreement with respect to any deposit held under its terms.

6. Time is of the essence hereof.

7. Disclosures: For one to four family residences, the Buyer hereby acknowledges receipt of the Home Inspectors: Facts for Consumers brochure produced by the Office of Consumer Affairs. For residential property constructed prior to 1978, Buyer must also sign Lead Paint "Property Transfer Notification."

8. The initialed riders, if any, attached hereto are incorporated herein by reference. Additional terms and conditions, if any:
   _____
   _____

NOTICE: This is a legal document that creates binding obligations. If not understood, consult an attorney. WITNESS MY HAND AND SEAL.

_____   _____
Buyer   Buyer

_____   _____
Address/City/State/Zip   Phone Numbers (Work & Home)

Receipt of deposit check for transmittal by: (Agent/Facilitator)_____
Check shall not be deposited unless offer is accepted.

This Offer is hereby accepted upon the foregoing terms and conditions at _____ A.M. / P.M. on _____, 20_____
WITNESS my (our) hand(s) and seal(s)

_____   _____
Seller (or spouse)   Seller

RECEIPT FOR DEPOSIT

Date _____

Received from _____ Buyer the sum of $_____ as deposit under the terms

and conditions of above Offer, to be held by _____ as escrow agent.

Under regulations adopted pursuant to the Massachusetts license law:
All offers submitted to brokers or salespeople to purchase real property   _____
that they have a right to sell shall be conveyed forthwith to the owner   Agent for Seller
of such real property.

APPENDIX E

Option Agreement

Option Agreement

THIS AGREEMENT made this _____ day of _____, 2007, by and between Aaron V. Endor, of _____ Massachusetts (hereinafter referred to as "Seller") and William T. Perch, of _____ Massachusetts (hereinafter referred to as "Purchaser"), WITNESSETH THAT:

1. Seller owns the land with the buildings and improvements thereon situated at _____ in the Town of _____, _____ County, Massachusetts, described in Exhibit A attached hereto and hereby made a part hereof, including rights and easements appurtenant thereto, as specified in Exhibit A, all together herein referred to as "the Premises"; and Seller is willing to sell and convey the Premises to Purchaser upon the terms and conditions herein set forth.

2. Purchaser desires to and is willing to purchase the Premises, provided that certain conditions with respect to the use thereof and the financing of the development thereof can be met within a reasonable time.

3. For and in consideration of the sum _____ dollars ($_____), herein called the Option Payment, the receipt of which is hereby acknowledged, Seller hereby gives and grants to Purchaser an option, exercisable as hereinafter set forth, to purchase the Premises, all upon the terms, covenants, conditions and provisions hereinafter set forth.

4. Said option may be exercised by Purchaser by, on or before the Notice Date, hereinafter specified, (a) giving written notice to Seller that said option is exercised, (b) delivering to Seller the sum of _____ dollars, ($_____) in good current funds, as a deposit on the purchase price for the Premises, herein called the Deposit, and (c) specifying a date and hour for the closing of the purchase of the premises by the Purchaser, which date shall be not less than twenty (20) days nor more than ninety (90) days after the date on which such notice is given, herein called the Closing Date.

5. For purposes of this Agreement, the Notice Date shall

be _____, 2008, provided, however, that the Purchaser
may extend the Notice Date by thirty days, or less, by paying to the Seller the sum of _____ dollars ($_____),
herein called the First Extension Payment, and if such
extension is made, the Purchaser may thereafter further
extend the Notice Date for thirty days, or less, by paying
to the Seller the sum of _____ dollars ($_____),
herein called the Second Extension Payment.

6. If and when the option is exercised pursuant to provisions of paragraph 4 hereof, then the Premises shall be
conveyed to Purchaser by a good and sufficient quitclaim
deed conveying a good and clear record and marketable
title to the same, free and clear of all encumbrances, except
for real estate taxes for the then current fiscal year not
due and payable on the date of delivery of the deed, any
liens for municipal betterments assessed after the date
hereof, and such other exceptions as may be approved by
Purchaser in its sole and uncontrolled discretion. Seller
agrees to use its best efforts to remove, on or before the
Closing Date any and all restrictions, liens, encumbrances,
rights, title and interests in others affecting the Premises
which may now exist or which may arise before said time.
Seller further agrees that from and after the time of the
exercise of said option there shall not be created, and there
shall not be, any new restrictions, liens, encumbrances,
rights, title or interests in others, all without limitation as
aforesaid.

7. For such deed and conveyance Purchaser shall pay as
the purchase price the sum of _____ dollars ($_____).
The Deposit paid by the purchaser pursuant to provisions
of paragraph 4 hereof shall be credited against the
purchase price, but the Option payment pursuant to
paragraph 3 hereof and any First Extension Payment and
Second Extension Payment pursuant to provisions of
paragraph 5 hereof shall not be credited against the
purchase price, and shall be and remain the property of
the Seller in all events. The balance of the purchase price
shall be paid by certified or bank cashier's check or checks
drawn upon a bank situated in and lawfully doing business in Massachusetts, upon delivery of the deed.

8. Time shall be of the essence of this Agreement in all
respects.

9. Purchaser may, at Purchaser's own expense, have an
accurate as-built or lot line survey of the Premises made
by a Registered Surveyor. In the event that such survey
shows (i) the frontage of the Premises on _____ Street

to be less than that specified in Exhibit A, or (ii) the area of the Premises to be less than that specified in Exhibit A, or (iii) any encroachments upon the Premises, or (iv) any of the buildings or other improvements on the Premises to be encroaching upon adjoining lands, then and in any such event Purchaser may, at Purchaser's election, cancel this Agreement, in which event all sums paid by Purchaser hereunder shall immediately be refunded to Purchaser, and thereupon the rights and obligations of each of parties to this Agreement shall cease and terminate.

10. Seller hereby authorizes Purchaser and Purchaser's agents, employees and representatives to enter upon the Premises from time to time and to perform such soil boring and compacting tests, test well and water table, soil porosity and liquid absorption tests, and such other various engineering tests which Purchaser may in its discretion desire to perform and to inspect the Premises, including all buildings and improvements thereon, provided that all expenses of and for such tests and inspections shall be the sole responsibility of the Purchaser.

11. Seller acknowledges being advised by Purchaser that if said option is exercised, Purchaser intends to use the Premises for the specific purposes of _____. Therefore, Seller agrees to cooperate with Purchaser if Purchaser attempts to obtain appropriate zoning classifications, variances or special permits, building permits or necessary utility services for such purpose, and, where necessary, agrees to permit the use of Seller's name in connection therewith. Seller shall execute such instruments as Purchaser may reasonably request in reference to any application by Purchaser therefore, whether in the name of Purchaser or Seller or both, Seller hereby consenting to all such applications, including, without limitation such action as is necessary or appropriate to accomplish any or all of the foregoing; but all services performed in connection therewith and all costs incurred in the exercise of any of the rights of Purchaser pursuant to this Section shall be at Purchaser's expense. Purchaser shall not be obligated to commence or pursue any such activities.

12. Seller hereby represents that (a) there are no present violations of any applicable zoning by-laws and, if applicable, wetlands and other land use or subdivision control laws and regulations and that there is no proceeding presently instituted to correct any such alleged violation; (b) it is presently in possession of the Premises, as Owner, and that there are no contractual obligations which would in any manner prevent Seller from freely selling the

Premises or otherwise complying with the terms of this Agreement; (c) it has no knowledge of any Proceeding instituted by any Municipal, State or Federal Agency to condemn or acquire the Premises or any portion thereof, by eminent domain. Anything herein set forth to the contrary notwithstanding, if upon investigation by Purchaser it should be determined that any of the aforementioned representations are incorrect, then and in such event Purchaser may, at its election, either (a) cancel this Agreement by written notice to Seller, in which event all sums paid by Purchaser hereunder shall be forthwith returned to Purchaser and, thereupon, the rights and obligations of each of the parties to this Agreement and each other shall cease and terminate, or (b) accept delivery of the deed of the Premises, and in such latter event Purchaser will at its option either pay the full purchase price therefore, and shall have assigned to it the amount of any award or awards allocable to any portion of the Premises taken by eminent domain.

13. Seller will at closing of title deliver possession of the Premises vacant, unoccupied, free of any occupancy, tenancy and rights under license, the buildings and other improvements thereon, all of the same to be then in the same condition as they now are, reasonable wear and use thereof only excepted, and the Premises to be then in conformity with all applicable zoning and building laws and any other applicable environmental or land use control laws and regulations.

14. Real estate taxes, water and/or sewer charges, and fuel value, if any, shall be adjusted and prorated as of the closing.

15. All notices and other communications hereunder shall be in writing and shall be deemed given and delivered when mailed, by registered or certified mail, postage and registration or certification charges prepaid, addressed, in the case of Seller, to Seller at _____ and, in the case of Purchaser, to Purchaser at _____ except that either party may by written notice to the other designate another address which shall thereupon become the effective address of such party for the purposes of this.

16. The parties agree that Seller shall be solely responsible for any broker or finder fee, commission or other compensation payable in connection with this Agreement or the sale of the Premises hereunder, and Seller agrees to exonerate and indemnify Purchaser against all claims, suits, obligations, liabilities and damages, including at-

torneys' fees, arising out of any such broker or finder fee, commission or other compensation or any claim therefore.

WITNESS the execution hereof under seal the day and year first above written.

[signatures and acknowledgement]

APPENDIX F

Agreement of First Refusal

AGREEMENT OF FIRST REFUSAL

This Agreement, made this _____ day of _____, 2007, by and between John G. Iver, of _____, Massachusetts, hereinafter referred to Iver, and James R. Seaver, of _____, Massachusetts, hereinafter referred to as Seaver, Witnesseth That:

1. Iver is the owner of certain premises (hereinafter called the Subject Premises) situated at _____ in _____, Massachusetts, being the premises conveyed to Iver by deed of _____, dated _____, recorded with _____ Registry of Deeds in Book _____, Page _____.

2. For purposes of this Agreement, Iver and every other person who is an Entitled Person, as hereinafter defined, and who becomes an owner of the Subject Premises, shall be, and is hereinafter referred to as a Subject Owner, and included in the meaning of the term Subject Owner.

3. For consideration paid, receipt of which is hereby acknowledged, Iver, for himself and every other Subject Owner, hereby covenants and agrees with Seaver that for and during the period of twenty-one (21) years from the date hereof, neither Iver nor any other Subject Owner of the Subject Premises, or any part thereof, will sell or convey the same to any person other than an Entitled Person, unless (1) the Subject Owner has received a bona fide offer to purchase the same; (2) the Subject Owner has given Seaver written notice containing both (a) the name and address of the offeror, a description of the premises to which the offer applies, the amount and terms and conditions of said offer and the encumbrances, if any, to which the property is to be conveyed pursuant to said offer, and (b) an offer by the Subject Owner to sell the same to Seaver upon all and the same terms and conditions as set forth in said bona fide offer, and (3) Seaver has not, within ten (10) days after the giving of such notice, mailed or otherwise given the Subject Owner written reply notice stating that he accepts the offer and intends to purchase the offered premises in accordance with said offer.

4. In the event that Seaver has given a reply notice as aforesaid stating his intention to purchase, the deed shall be delivered and the consideration paid at said Registry of Deeds at 10 A.M. on the 15th day after the date of the giving of such reply notice, unless Seaver and the Subject Owner shall otherwise agree in writing.

5. If Seaver shall not have given any reply notice as aforesaid stating his intention to purchase, or in the event that Seaver, having given such reply notice, shall fail to complete such purchase in accordance with the offer so made to him and the provisions of paragraph 4 hereof, then the Subject Owner (without prejudice to any rights against Seaver on account of such failure) shall be free thereafter to sell and convey the premises covered by the offer to the offeror named in the Subject Owner's notice to Seaver at a price not lower than that specified therein, but the Subject Owner shall not sell or convey said premises to any other person or at any lower price without again offering the same to Seaver in the manner aforesaid.

6. If the Subject Owner shall make and record with said Registry of Deeds an affidavit stating (1) that a conveyance by said Subject Owner is made pursuant to a bona fide offer to purchase, (2) that the Subject Owner gave notice to Seaver as required pursuant to the provisions of this Agreement; (3) that he has not received written reply notice of Seaver's intention to purchase, or that Seaver has failed to complete the purchase in accordance with the provisions hereof; and (4) that the conveyance is made to the person named in such notice at a price not lower than that therein stated, then such affidavit shall be conclusive evidence of compliance with the requirements of this Agreement with respect to such conveyance in favor of the grantee therein and all persons claiming by, through or under such grantee.

7. For purposes of this Agreement, the term Entitled Person shall mean and include: (a) Iver, a lineal descendant of Iver, a spouse of Iver or of any such lineal descendant of Iver, (b) a charitable organization to which Iver or any Subject Owner has made a gift of the Subject Premises or an interest therein, and (c) the holder of a bona fide mortgage of the Subject Premises or any part thereof, or, provided that prior notice in writing has been given to Seaver of the sale or other proceeding for the foreclosure of any such bona fide mortgage, a person who acquires title pursuant to such foreclosure.

8. For purposes of this Agreement, a lease or tenancy or

occupancy agreement for a term of more than _____ (_____) years shall be deemed to be equivalent to a sale, and Seaver shall have the right hereunder of first refusal with respect to any such lease, tenancy or occupancy, exercisable in the manner aforesaid insofar as applicable.

9. Neither Iver nor any other Subject Owner shall be liable hereunder for breaches hereof except such as occur during his or such Subject Owner's ownership of the Subject Premises or portion thereof.

10. Any notice hereunder shall be deemed to have been duly given when mailed by registered or certified mail, all charges prepaid, return receipt requested, addressed (a) to Seaver at the address stated above, and (b) to Iver and to any Subject Owner at the Address of Iver stated above; provided that any of Seaver, Iver or any Subject Owner may from time to time specify another address for himself or herself by written notice to the other parties hereto, given as aforesaid.

Witness the execution hereof under seal as of the day and year first above written.

[signatures and acknowledgement]

APPENDIX G

ALTA Owner's Policy

American Land Title Association

Owner's Policy
Adopted 6/17/06

OWNER'S POLICY OF TITLE INSURANCE
Issued by
Blank Title Insurance Company

Any notice of claim and any other notice or statement in writing required to be given to the Company under this Policy must be given to the Company at the address shown in Section 18 of the Conditions.

COVERED RISKS

SUBJECT TO THE EXCLUSIONS FROM COVERAGE, THE EXCEPTIONS FROM COVERAGE CONTAINED IN SCHEDULE B, AND THE CONDITIONS, BLANK TITLE INSURANCE COMPANY, a Blank corporation (the "Company") insures, as of Date of Policy and, to the extent stated in Covered Risks 9 and 10, after Date of Policy, against loss or damage, not exceeding the Amount of Insurance, sustained or incurred by the Insured by reason of:

1. Title being vested other than as stated in Schedule A.

2. Any defect in or lien or encumbrance on the Title. This Covered Risk includes but is not limited to insurance against loss from

    (a) A defect in the Title caused by

        (i) forgery, fraud, undue influence, duress, incompetency, incapacity, or impersonation;

        (ii) failure of any person or Entity to have authorized a transfer or conveyance;

        (iii) a document affecting Title not properly created, executed, witnessed, sealed, acknowledged, notarized, or delivered;

        (iv) failure to perform those acts necessary to create a document by electronic means authorized by law;

        (v) a document executed under a falsified, expired, or otherwise invalid power of attorney;

        (vi) a document not properly filed, recorded, or indexed in the Public Records including failure to perform those acts by electronic means authorized by law; or

        (vii) a defective judicial or administrative proceeding.

    (b) The lien of real estate taxes or assessments imposed on the Title by a governmental authority due or payable, but unpaid.

    (c) Any encroachment, encumbrance, violation, variation, or adverse circumstance affecting the Title that would be disclosed by an accurate and complete land survey of the Land. The term "encroachment" includes encroachments of existing improvements located on the Land onto adjoining land, and encroachments onto the Land of existing improvements located on adjoining land.

3. Unmarketable Title.

4. No right of access to and from the Land.

5. The violation or enforcement of any law, ordinance, permit, or governmental regulation (including those relating to building and zoning) restricting, regulating, prohibiting, or relating to

    (a) the occupancy, use, or enjoyment of the Land;

    (b) the character, dimensions, or location of any improvement erected on the Land;

    (c) the subdivision of land; or

(d) environmental protection

if a notice, describing any part of the Land, is recorded in the Public Records setting forth the violation or intention to enforce, but only to the extent of the violation or enforcement referred to in that notice.

6. An enforcement action based on the exercise of a governmental police power not covered by Covered Risk 5 if a notice of the enforcement action, describing any part of the Land, is recorded in the Public Records, but only to the extent of the enforcement referred to in that notice.

7. The exercise of the rights of eminent domain if a notice of the exercise, describing any part of the Land, is recorded in the Public Records.

8. Any taking by a governmental body that has occurred and is binding on the rights of a purchaser for value without Knowledge.

9. Title being vested other than as stated in Schedule A or being defective

(a) as a result of the avoidance in whole or in part, or from a court order providing an alternative remedy, of a transfer of all or any part of the title to or any interest in the Land occurring prior to the transaction vesting Title as shown in Schedule A because that prior transfer constituted a fraudulent or preferential transfer under federal bankruptcy, state insolvency, or similar creditors' rights laws; or

(b) because the instrument of transfer vesting Title as shown in Schedule A constitutes a preferential transfer under federal bankruptcy, state insolvency, or similar creditors' rights laws by reason of the failure of its recording in the Public Records
   (i) to be timely, or
   (ii) to impart notice of its existence to a purchaser for value or to a judgment or lien creditor.

10. Any defect in or lien or encumbrance on the Title or other matter included in Covered Risks 1 through 9 that has been created or attached or has been filed or recorded in the Public Records subsequent to Date of Policy and prior to the recording of the deed or other instrument of transfer in the Public Records that vests Title as shown in Schedule A.

The Company will also pay the costs, attorneys' fees, and expenses incurred in defense of any matter insured against by this Policy, but only to the extent provided in the Conditions.

[Witness clause optional]

BLANK TITLE INSURANCE COMPANY

BY: **PRESIDENT**

BY: **SECRETARY**

SCHEDULE A

Name and Address of Title Insurance Company:

[File No.:   ]   Policy No.:
Address Reference:
Amount of Insurance: $ [Premium: $]
Date of Policy: [at a.m./p.m.]

1. Name of Insured:

2. The estate or interest in the Land that is insured by this policy is:

3. Title is vested in:

4. The Land referred to in this policy is described as follows:

SCHEDULE B

[File No.   ]   Policy No.

EXCEPTIONS FROM COVERAGE

This policy does not insure against loss or damage, and the Company will not pay costs, attorneys' fees, or expenses that arise by reason of:

1.   [Policy may include regional exceptions if so desired by the issuing
2.   Company.]
3.   [Variable exceptions such as taxes, easements, CC&R's, etc., shown here]
4.

EXCLUSIONS FROM COVERAGE

The following matters are expressly excluded from the coverage of this policy, and the Company will not pay loss or damage, costs, attorneys' fees, or expenses that arise by reason of:

1. (a) Any law, ordinance, permit, or governmental regulation (including those relating to building and zoning) restricting, regulating, prohibiting, or relating to

    (i) the occupancy, use, or enjoyment of the Land;

    (ii) the character, dimensions, or location of any improvement erected on the Land;

    (iii) the subdivision of land; or

    (iv) environmental protection;

    or the effect of any violation of these laws, ordinances, or governmental regulations. This Exclusion 1(a) does not modify or limit the coverage provided under Covered Risk 5.

    (b) Any governmental police power. This Exclusion 1(b) does not modify or limit the coverage provided under Covered Risk 6.

2. Rights of eminent domain. This Exclusion does not modify or limit the coverage provided under Covered Risk 7 or 8.

3. Defects, liens, encumbrances, adverse claims, or other matters

    (a) created, suffered, assumed, or agreed to by the Insured Claimant;

    (b) not Known to the Company, not recorded in the Public Records at Date of Policy, but Known to the Insured Claimant and not disclosed in writing to the Company by the Insured Claimant prior to the date the Insured Claimant became an Insured under this policy;

    (c) resulting in no loss or damage to the Insured Claimant;

    (d) attaching or created subsequent to Date of Policy (however, this does not modify or limit the coverage provided under Covered Risk 9 and 10); or

    (e) resulting in loss or damage that would not have been sustained if the Insured Claimant had paid value for the Title.

4. Any claim, by reason of the operation of federal bankruptcy, state insolvency, or similar creditors' rights laws, that the transaction vesting the Title as shown in Schedule A, is

    (a) a fraudulent conveyance or fraudulent transfer; or

    (b) a preferential transfer for any reason not stated in Covered Risk 9 of this policy.

5. Any lien on the Title for real estate taxes or assessments imposed by governmental authority and created or attaching between Date of Policy and the date of recording of the deed or other instrument of transfer in the Public Records that vests Title as shown in Schedule A.

SCHEDULE A

Name and Address of Title Insurance Company:

[File No.:   ]   Policy No.:
Address Reference:
Amount of Insurance: $ [Premium: $]
Date of Policy: [at a.m./p.m.]

1. Name of Insured:

2. The estate or interest in the Land that is insured by this policy is:

3. Title is vested in:

4. The Land referred to in this policy is described as follows:

SCHEDULE B

[File No.   ]   Policy No.

EXCEPTIONS FROM COVERAGE

This policy does not insure against loss or damage, and the Company will not pay costs, attorneys' fees, or expenses that arise by reason of:

1.   [Policy may include regional exceptions if so desired by the issuing
2.   Company.]
3.   [Variable exceptions such as taxes, easements, CC&R's, etc., shown here]
4.

CONDITIONS

1. DEFINITION OF TERMS

The following terms when used in this policy mean:

(a) "Amount of Insurance": The amount stated in Schedule A, as may be increased or decreased by endorsement to this policy, increased by Section 8(b), or decreased by Sections 10 and 11 of these Conditions.

(b) "Date of Policy": The date designated as "Date of Policy" in Schedule A.

(c) "Entity": A corporation, partnership, trust, limited liability company, or other similar legal entity.

(d) "Insured": The Insured named in Schedule A.

(i) the term "Insured" also includes

(A) successors to the Title of the Insured by operation of law as distinguished from purchase, including heirs, devisees, survivors, personal representatives, or next of kin;

(B) successors to an Insured by dissolution, merger, consolidation, distribution, or reorganization;

(C) successors to an Insured by its conversion to another kind of Entity;

(D) a grantee of an Insured under a deed delivered without payment of actual valuable consideration conveying the Title

(1) if the stock, shares, memberships, or other equity interests of the grantee are wholly-owned by the named Insured,

(2) if the grantee wholly owns the named Insured,

(3) if the grantee is wholly-owned by an affiliated Entity of the named Insured, provided the affiliated Entity and the named Insured are both wholly-owned by the same person or Entity, or

(4) if the grantee is a trustee or beneficiary of a trust created by a written instrument established by the Insured named in Schedule A for estate planning purposes.

(ii) with regard to (A), (B), (C), and (D) reserving, however, all rights and defenses as to any successor that the Company would have had against any predecessor Insured.

(e) "Insured Claimant": An Insured claiming loss or damage.

(f) "Knowledge" or "Known": Actual knowledge, not constructive knowledge or notice that may be imputed to an Insured by reason of the Public Records or any other records that impart constructive notice of matters affecting the Title.

(g) "Land": The land described in Schedule A, and affixed improvements that by law constitute real property. The term "Land" does not include any property beyond the lines of the area described in Schedule A, nor any right, title, interest, estate, or easement in abutting streets, roads, avenues, alleys, lanes, ways, or waterways, but this does not modify or limit the extent that a right of access to and from the Land is insured by this policy.

(h) "Mortgage": Mortgage, deed of trust, trust deed, or other security instrument, including one evidenced by electronic means authorized by law.

(i) "Public Records": Records established under state statutes at Date of Policy for the purpose of imparting constructive notice of matters relating to real property to purchasers for value and without Knowledge. With respect to Covered Risk 5(d), "Public Records" shall also include environmental protection liens filed in the records of the clerk of the United States District Court for the district where the Land is located.

(j) "Title": The estate or interest described in Schedule A.

(k) "Unmarketable Title": Title affected by an alleged or apparent matter that would permit a prospective purchaser or lessee of the Title or lender on the Title to be released from the obligation to purchase, lease, or lend if there is a contractual condition requiring the delivery of marketable title.

2. CONTINUATION OF INSURANCE

The coverage of this policy shall continue in force as of Date of Policy in favor of an Insured, but only so long as the Insured retains an estate or interest in the Land, or holds an obligation secured by a purchase money Mortgage given by a purchaser from the Insured, or only so long as the Insured shall have liability by reason of warranties in any transfer or conveyance of the Title. This policy shall not continue in force in favor of any purchaser from the Insured of either (i) an estate or interest in the Land, or (ii) an obligation secured by a purchase money Mortgage given to the Insured.

3. NOTICE OF CLAIM TO BE GIVEN BY INSURED CLAIMANT

The Insured shall notify the Company promptly in writing (i) in case of any litigation as set forth in Section 5(a) of these Conditions, (ii) in case Knowledge shall come to an Insured hereunder of any claim of title or interest that is adverse to the Title, as insured, and that might cause loss or damage for which the Company may be liable by virtue of this policy, or (iii) if the Title, as insured, is rejected as Unmarketable Title. If the Company is prejudiced by the failure of the Insured Claimant to provide prompt notice, the Company's liability to the Insured Claimant under the policy shall be reduced to the extent of the prejudice.

4. PROOF OF LOSS

In the event the Company is unable to determine the amount of loss or damage, the Company may, at its option, require as a condition of payment that the Insured Claimant furnish a signed proof of loss. The proof of loss must describe the defect, lien, encumbrance, or other matter insured against by this policy that constitutes the basis of loss or damage and shall state, to the extent possible, the basis of calculating the amount of the loss or damage.

5. DEFENSE AND PROSECUTION OF ACTIONS

(a) Upon written request by the Insured, and subject to the options contained in Section 7 of these Conditions, the Company, at its own cost and without unreasonable delay, shall provide for the defense of an Insured in litigation in which any third party asserts a claim covered by this policy adverse to the Insured. This obligation is limited to only those stated causes of action alleging matters insured against by this policy. The Company shall have the right to select counsel of its choice (subject to the right of the Insured to object for reasonable cause) to represent the Insured as to those stated causes of action. It shall not be liable for and will not pay the fees of any other counsel. The Company will not pay any fees, costs, or expenses incurred by the Insured in the defense of those causes of action that allege matters not insured against by this policy.

(b) The Company shall have the right, in addition to the options contained in Section 7 of these Conditions, at its own cost, to institute and prosecute any action or proceeding or to do any other act that in its opinion may be necessary or desirable to establish the Title, as insured, or to prevent or reduce loss or damage to the Insured. The Company may take any appropriate action under the terms of this policy, whether or not it shall be liable to the Insured. The exercise of these rights shall not be an admission of liability or waiver of any provision of this policy. If the Company exercises its rights under this subsection, it must do so diligently.

(c) Whenever the Company brings an action or asserts a defense as required or permitted by this policy, the Company may pursue the litigation to a final determination by a court of competent jurisdiction, and it expressly reserves the right, in its sole discretion, to appeal any adverse judgment or order.

6. **DUTY OF INSURED CLAIMANT TO COOPERATE**

(a) In all cases where this policy permits or requires the Company to prosecute or provide for the defense of any action or proceeding and any appeals, the Insured shall secure to the Company the right to so prosecute or provide defense in the action or proceeding, including the right to use, at its option, the name of the Insured for this purpose. Whenever requested by the Company, the Insured, at the Company's expense, shall give the Company all reasonable aid (i) in securing evidence, obtaining witnesses, prosecuting or defending the action or proceeding, or effecting settlement, and (ii) in any other lawful act that in the opinion of the Company may be necessary or desirable to establish the Title or any other matter as insured. If the Company is prejudiced by the failure of the Insured to furnish the required cooperation, the Company's obligations to the Insured under the policy shall terminate, including any liability or obligation to defend, prosecute, or continue any litigation, with regard to the matter or matters requiring such cooperation.

(b) The Company may reasonably require the Insured Claimant to submit to examination under oath by any authorized representative of the Company and to produce for examination, inspection, and copying, at such reasonable times and places as may be designated by the authorized representative of the Company, all records, in whatever medium maintained, including books, ledgers, checks, memoranda, correspondence, reports, e-mails, disks, tapes, and videos whether bearing a date before or after Date of Policy, that reasonably pertain to the loss or damage. Further, if requested by any authorized representative of the Company, the Insured Claimant shall grant its permission, in writing, for any authorized representative of the Company to examine, inspect, and copy all of these records in the custody or control of a third party that reasonably pertain to the loss or damage. All information designated as confidential by the Insured Claimant provided to the Company pursuant to this Section shall not be disclosed to others unless, in the reasonable judgment of the Company, it is necessary in the administration of the claim. Failure of the Insured Claimant to submit for examination under oath, produce any reasonably requested information, or grant permission to secure reasonably necessary information from third parties as required in this subsection, unless prohibited by law or governmental regulation, shall terminate any liability of the Company under this policy as to that claim.

7. **OPTIONS TO PAY OR OTHERWISE SETTLE CLAIMS; TERMINATION OF LIABILITY**

In case of a claim under this policy, the Company shall have the following additional options:

(a) To Pay or Tender Payment of the Amount of Insurance.

To pay or tender payment of the Amount of Insurance under this policy together with any costs, attorneys' fees, and expenses incurred by the Insured Claimant that were authorized by the Company up to the time of payment or tender of payment and that the Company is obligated to pay.

Upon the exercise by the Company of this option, all liability and obligations of the Company to the Insured under this policy, other than to make the payment required in this subsection, shall terminate, including any liability or obligation to defend, prosecute, or continue any litigation.

(b) To Pay or Otherwise Settle With Parties Other Than the Insured or With the Insured Claimant.

    (i) to pay or otherwise settle with other parties for or in the name of an Insured Claimant any claim insured against under this policy. In addition, the Company will pay any costs, attorneys' fees, and expenses incurred by the Insured Claimant that were authorized by the Company up to the time of payment and that the Company is obligated to pay; or

    (ii) to pay or otherwise settle with the Insured Claimant the loss or damage provided for under this policy, together with any costs, attorneys' fees, and expenses incurred by the Insured Claimant that were authorized by the Company up to the time of payment and that the Company is obligated to pay.

Upon the exercise by the Company of either of the options provided for in subsections (b)(i) or (ii), the Company's obligations to the Insured under this policy for the claimed loss or damage, other than the payments required to be made, shall terminate, including any liability or obligation to defend, prosecute, or continue any litigation.

8. DETERMINATION AND EXTENT OF LIABILITY

This policy is a contract of indemnity against actual monetary loss or damage sustained or incurred by the Insured Claimant who has suffered loss or damage by reason of matters insured against by this policy.

(a) The extent of liability of the Company for loss or damage under this policy shall not exceed the lesser of

    (i) the Amount of Insurance; or

    (ii) the difference between the value of the Title as insured and the value of the Title subject to the risk insured against by this policy.

(b) If the Company pursues its rights under Section 5 of these Conditions and is unsuccessful in establishing the Title, as insured,

    (i) the Amount of Insurance shall be increased by 10%, and

    (ii) the Insured Claimant shall have the right to have the loss or damage determined either as of the date the claim was made by the Insured Claimant or as of the date it is settled and paid.

(c) In addition to the extent of liability under (a) and (b), the Company will also pay those costs, attorneys' fees, and expenses incurred in accordance with Sections 5 and 7 of these Conditions.

9. LIMITATION OF LIABILITY

(a) If the Company establishes the Title, or removes the alleged defect, lien, or encumbrance, or cures the lack of a right of access to or from the Land, or cures the claim of Unmarketable Title, all as insured, in a reasonably diligent manner by any method, including litigation and the completion of any appeals, it shall have fully performed its obligations with respect to that matter and shall not be liable for any loss or damage caused to the Insured.

(b) In the event of any litigation, including litigation by the Company or with the Company's consent, the Company shall have no liability for loss or damage until there has been a final determination by a court of competent jurisdiction, and disposition of all appeals, adverse to the Title, as insured.

(c) The Company shall not be liable for loss or damage to the Insured for liability voluntarily assumed by the Insured in settling any claim or suit without the prior written consent of the Company.

10. REDUCTION OF INSURANCE; REDUCTION OR TERMINATION OF LIABILITY

All payments under this policy, except payments made for costs, attorneys' fees, and expenses, shall reduce the Amount of Insurance by the amount of the payment.

11. LIABILITY NONCUMULATIVE

The Amount of Insurance shall be reduced by any amount the Company pays under any policy insuring a Mortgage to which exception is taken in Schedule B or to which the Insured has agreed, assumed, or taken subject, or which is executed by an Insured after Date of Policy and which is a charge or lien on the Title, and the amount so paid shall be deemed a payment to the Insured under this policy.

12. PAYMENT OF LOSS

When liability and the extent of loss or damage have been definitely fixed in accordance with these Conditions, the payment shall be made within 30 days.

13. RIGHTS OF RECOVERY UPON PAYMENT OR SETTLEMENT

(a) Whenever the Company shall have settled and paid a claim under this policy, it shall be subrogated and entitled to the rights of the Insured Claimant in the Title and all other rights and remedies in respect to the claim that the Insured Claimant has against any person or property, to the extent of the amount of any loss, costs, attorneys' fees, and expenses paid by the Company. If requested by the Company, the Insured Claimant shall execute documents to evidence the transfer to the Company of these rights and remedies. The Insured Claimant shall permit the Company to sue, compromise, or settle in the name of the Insured Claimant and to use the name of the Insured Claimant in any transaction or litigation involving these rights and remedies.

If a payment on account of a claim does not fully cover the loss of the Insured Claimant, the Company shall defer the exercise of its right to recover until after the Insured Claimant shall have recovered its loss.

(b) The Company's right of subrogation includes the rights of the Insured to indemnities, guaranties, other policies of insurance, or bonds, notwithstanding any terms or conditions contained in those instruments that address subrogation rights.

14. ARBITRATION

Either the Company or the Insured may demand that the claim or controversy shall be submitted to arbitration pursuant to the Title Insurance Arbitration Rules of the American Land Title Association ("Rules"). Except as provided in the Rules, there shall be no joinder or consolidation with claims or controversies of other persons. Arbitrable matters may include, but are not limited to, any controversy or claim between the Company and the Insured arising out of or relating to this policy, any service in connection with its issuance or the breach of a policy provision, or to any other controversy or claim arising out of the transaction giving rise to this policy. All arbitrable matters when the Amount of Insurance is $2,000,000 or less shall be arbitrated at the option of either the Company or the Insured. All arbitrable matters when the Amount of Insurance is in excess of $2,000,000 shall be arbitrated only when agreed to by both the Company and the Insured. Arbitration pursuant to this policy and under the Rules shall be binding upon the parties. Judgment upon the award rendered by the Arbitrator(s) may be entered in any court of competent jurisdiction.

15. LIABILITY LIMITED TO THIS POLICY; POLICY ENTIRE CONTRACT

(a) This policy together with all endorsements, if any, attached to it by the Company is the entire policy and contract between the Insured and the Company. In interpreting any provision of this policy, this policy shall be construed as a whole.

(b) Any claim of loss or damage that arises out of the status of the Title or by any action asserting such claim shall be restricted to this policy.

(c) Any amendment of or endorsement to this policy must be in writing and authenticated by an authorized person, or expressly incorporated by Schedule A of this policy.

(d) Each endorsement to this policy issued at any time is made a part of this policy and is subject to all of its terms and provisions. Except as the endorsement expressly states, it does not (i) modify any of the terms and provisions of the policy, (ii) modify any prior endorsement, (iii) extend the Date of Policy, or (iv) increase the Amount of Insurance.

16. SEVERABILITY

In the event any provision of this policy, in whole or in part, is held invalid or unenforceable under applicable law, the policy shall be deemed not to include that provision or such part held to be invalid, but all other provisions shall remain in full force and effect.

17. CHOICE OF LAW; FORUM

(a) Choice of Law: The Insured acknowledges the Company has underwritten the risks covered by this policy and determined the premium charged therefor in reliance upon the law affecting interests in real property and applicable to the interpretation, rights, remedies, or enforcement of policies of title insurance of the jurisdiction where the Land is located.

Therefore, the court or an arbitrator shall apply the law of the jurisdiction where the Land is located to determine the validity of claims against the Title that are adverse to the Insured and to interpret and enforce the terms of this policy. In neither case shall the court or arbitrator apply its conflicts of law principles to determine the applicable law.

(b) Choice of Forum: Any litigation or other proceeding brought by the Insured against the Company must be filed only in a state or federal court within the United States of America or its territories having appropriate jurisdiction.

18. NOTICES, WHERE SENT

Any notice of claim and any other notice or statement in writing required to be given to the Company under this policy must be given to the Company at [fill in].

APPENDIX H

ALTA Loan Policy

American Land Title Association

Loan Policy
Adopted 6/17/06

LOAN POLICY OF TITLE INSURANCE
Issued by
Blank Title Insurance Company

Any notice of claim and any other notice or statement in writing required to be given to the Company under this Policy must be given to the Company at the address shown in Section 17 of the Conditions.

COVERED RISKS

SUBJECT TO THE EXCLUSIONS FROM COVERAGE, THE EXCEPTIONS FROM COVERAGE CONTAINED IN SCHEDULE B, AND THE CONDITIONS, BLANK TITLE INSURANCE COMPANY, a Blank corporation (the "Company") insures as of Date of Policy and, to the extent stated in Covered Risks 11, 13, and 14, after Date of Policy, against loss or damage, not exceeding the Amount of Insurance, sustained or incurred by the Insured by reason of:

1. Title being vested other than as stated in Schedule A.

2. Any defect in or lien or encumbrance on the Title. This Covered Risk includes but is not limited to insurance against loss from

    (a) A defect in the Title caused by

       (i) forgery, fraud, undue influence, duress, incompetency, incapacity, or impersonation;

       (ii) failure of any person or Entity to have authorized a transfer or conveyance;

       (iii) a document affecting Title not properly created, executed, witnessed, sealed, acknowledged, notarized, or delivered;

       (iv) failure to perform those acts necessary to create a document by electronic means authorized by law;

       (v) a document executed under a falsified, expired, or otherwise invalid power of attorney;

       (vi) a document not properly filed, recorded, or indexed in the Public Records including failure to perform those acts by electronic means authorized by law; or

       (vii) a defective judicial or administrative proceeding.

    (b) The lien of real estate taxes or assessments imposed on the Title by a governmental authority due or payable, but unpaid.

    (c) Any encroachment, encumbrance, violation, variation, or adverse circumstance affecting the Title that would be disclosed by an accurate and complete land survey of the Land. The term "encroachment" includes encroachments of existing improvements located on the Land onto adjoining land, and encroachments onto the Land of existing improvements located on adjoining land.

3. Unmarketable Title.

4. No right of access to and from the Land.

5. The violation or enforcement of any law, ordinance, permit, or governmental regulation (including those relating to building and zoning) restricting, regulating, prohibiting, or relating to

    (a) the occupancy, use, or enjoyment of the Land;

    (b) the character, dimensions, or location of any improvement erected on the Land;

    (c) the subdivision of land; or

App. H-1

(d) environmental protection

if a notice, describing any part of the Land, is recorded in the Public Records setting forth the violation or intention to enforce, but only to the extent of the violation or enforcement referred to in that notice.

6.   An enforcement action based on the exercise of a governmental police power not covered by Covered Risk 5 if a notice of the enforcement action, describing any part of the Land, is recorded in the Public Records, but only to the extent of the enforcement referred to in that notice.

7.   The exercise of the rights of eminent domain if a notice of the exercise, describing any part of the Land, is recorded in the Public Records.

8.   Any taking by a governmental body that has occurred and is binding on the rights of a purchaser for value without Knowledge.

9.   The invalidity or unenforceability of the lien of the Insured Mortgage upon the Title. This Covered Risk includes but is not limited to insurance against loss from any of the following impairing the lien of the Insured Mortgage

(a) forgery, fraud, undue influence, duress, incompetency, incapacity, or impersonation;

(b) failure of any person or Entity to have authorized a transfer or conveyance;

(c) the Insured Mortgage not being properly created, executed, witnessed, sealed, acknowledged, notarized, or delivered;

(d) failure to perform those acts necessary to create a document by electronic means authorized by law;

(e) a document executed under a falsified, expired, or otherwise invalid power of attorney;

(f) a document not properly filed, recorded, or indexed in the Public Records including failure to perform those acts by electronic means authorized by law; or

(g) a defective judicial or administrative proceeding.

10. The lack of priority of the lien of the Insured Mortgage upon the Title over any other lien or encumbrance.

11. The lack of priority of the lien of the Insured Mortgage upon the Title

(a) as security for each and every advance of proceeds of the loan secured by the Insured Mortgage over any statutory lien for services, labor, or material arising from construction of an improvement or work related to the Land when the improvement or work is either

(i) contracted for or commenced on or before Date of Policy; or

(ii) contracted for, commenced, or continued after Date of Policy if the construction is financed, in whole or in part, by proceeds of the loan secured by the Insured Mortgage that the Insured has advanced or is obligated on Date of Policy to advance; and

(b) over the lien of any assessments for street improvements under construction or completed at Date of Policy.

12. The invalidity or unenforceability of any assignment of the Insured Mortgage, provided the assignment is shown in Schedule A, or the failure of the assignment shown in Schedule A to vest title to the Insured Mortgage in the named Insured assignee free and clear of all liens.

13. The invalidity, unenforceability, lack of priority, or avoidance of the lien of the Insured Mortgage upon the Title

(a) resulting from the avoidance in whole or in part, or from a court order providing an alternative remedy, of any transfer of all or any part of the title to or any interest in the Land occurring prior to the transaction creating the lien of the Insured Mortgage because that prior transfer constituted a fraudulent or preferential transfer under federal bankruptcy, state insolvency, or similar creditors' rights laws; or

(b) because the Insured Mortgage constitutes a preferential transfer under federal bankruptcy, state insolvency, or similar creditors' rights laws by reason of the failure of its recording in the Public Records

    (i) to be timely, or

    (ii) to impart notice of its existence to a purchaser for value or to a judgment or lien creditor.

14. Any defect in or lien or encumbrance on the Title or other matter included in Covered Risks 1 through 13 that has been created or attached or has been filed or recorded in the Public Records subsequent to Date of Policy and prior to the recording of the Insured Mortgage in the Public Records.

The Company will also pay the costs, attorneys' fees, and expenses incurred in defense of any matter insured against by this Policy, but only to the extent provided in the Conditions.

[Witness clause optional]

BLANK TITLE INSURANCE COMPANY

BY: **PRESIDENT**

BY: **SECRETARY**

EXCLUSIONS FROM COVERAGE

The following matters are expressly excluded from the coverage of this policy, and the Company will not pay loss or damage, costs, attorneys' fees, or expenses that arise by reason of:

1. (a) Any law, ordinance, permit, or governmental regulation (including those relating to building and zoning) restricting, regulating, prohibiting, or relating to

    (i) the occupancy, use, or enjoyment of the Land;

    (ii) the character, dimensions, or location of any improvement erected on the Land;

    (iii) the subdivision of land; or

    (iv) environmental protection;

    or the effect of any violation of these laws, ordinances, or governmental regulations. This Exclusion 1(a) does not modify or limit the coverage provided under Covered Risk 5.

    (b) Any governmental police power. This Exclusion 1(b) does not modify or limit the coverage provided under Covered Risk 6.

2. Rights of eminent domain. This Exclusion does not modify or limit the coverage provided under Covered Risk 7 or 8.

3. Defects, liens, encumbrances, adverse claims, or other matters

    (a) created, suffered, assumed, or agreed to by the Insured Claimant;

    (b) not Known to the Company, not recorded in the Public Records at Date of Policy, but Known to the Insured Claimant and not disclosed in writing to the Company by the Insured Claimant prior to the date the Insured Claimant became an Insured under this policy;

    (c) resulting in no loss or damage to the Insured Claimant;

    (d) attaching or created subsequent to Date of Policy (however, this does not modify or limit the coverage provided under Covered Risk 11, 13, or 14); or

    (e) resulting in loss or damage that would not have been sustained if the Insured Claimant had paid value for the Insured Mortgage.

4. Unenforceability of the lien of the Insured Mortgage because of the inability or failure of an Insured to comply with applicable doing-business laws of the state where the Land is situated.

5. Invalidity or unenforceability in whole or in part of the lien of the Insured Mortgage that arises out of the transaction evidenced by the Insured Mortgage and is based upon usury or any consumer credit protection or truth-in-lending law.

6. Any claim, by reason of the operation of federal bankruptcy, state insolvency, or similar creditors' rights laws, that the transaction creating the lien of the Insured Mortgage, is

    (a) a fraudulent conveyance or fraudulent transfer, or

    (b) a preferential transfer for any reason not stated in Covered Risk 13(b) of this policy.

7. Any lien on the Title for real estate taxes or assessments imposed by governmental authority and created or attaching between Date of Policy and the date of recording of the Insured Mortgage in the Public Records. This Exclusion does not modify or limit the coverage provided under Covered Risk 11(b).

SCHEDULE A

Name and Address of Title Insurance Company:

[File No.:   ]   Policy No.:
Loan No.:
Address Reference:
Amount of Insurance: $ [Premium: $]
Date of Policy: [at a.m./p.m.]

1. Name of Insured:

2. The estate or interest in the Land that is encumbered by the Insured Mortgage is:

3. Title is vested in:

4. The Insured Mortgage and its assignments, if any, are described as follows:

5. The Land referred to in this policy is described as follows:

[6. This policy incorporates by reference those ALTA endorsements selected below:

4-06	(Condominium)
4.1-06	
5-06	(Planned Unit Development)
5.1-06	
6-06	(Variable Rate)
6.2-06	(Variable Rate--Negative Amortization)
8.1-06	(Environmental Protection Lien) Paragraph b refers to the following state statute(s):
9-06	(Restrictions, Encroachments, Minerals)
13.1-06	(Leasehold Loan)
14-06	(Future Advance-Priority)
14.1-06	(Future Advance-Knowledge)
14.3-06	(Future Advance-Reverse Mortgage)
22-06	(Location) The type of improvement is a _____, and the street address is as shown above.]

SCHEDULE B

[File No.   ]   Policy No.

EXCEPTIONS FROM COVERAGE

[Except as provided in Schedule B - Part II,] t[or T]his policy does not insure against loss or damage, and the Company will not pay costs, attorneys' fees, or expenses that arise by reason of:

[PART I

PART II

In addition to the matters set forth in Part I of this Schedule, the Title is subject to the following matters, and the Company insures against loss or damage sustained in the event that they are not subordinate to the lien of the Insured Mortgage:]

CONDITIONS

1. DEFINITION OF TERMS

The following terms when used in this policy mean:

(a) "Amount of Insurance": The amount stated in Schedule A, as may be increased or decreased by endorsement to this policy, increased by Section 8(b) or decreased by Section 10 of these Conditions.

(b) "Date of Policy": The date designated as "Date of Policy" in Schedule A.

(c) "Entity": A corporation, partnership, trust, limited liability company, or other similar legal entity.

(d) "Indebtedness": The obligation secured by the Insured Mortgage including one evidenced by electronic means authorized by law, and if that obligation is the payment of a debt, the Indebtedness is the sum of

  (i) the amount of the principal disbursed as of Date of Policy;

  (ii) the amount of the principal disbursed subsequent to Date of Policy;

  (iii) the construction loan advances made subsequent to Date of Policy for the purpose of financing in whole or in part the construction of an improvement to the Land or related to the Land that the Insured was and continued to be obligated to advance at Date of Policy and at the date of the advance;

  (iv) interest on the loan;

  (v) the prepayment premiums, exit fees, and other similar fees or penalties allowed by law;

  (vi) the expenses of foreclosure and any other costs of enforcement;

  (vii) the amounts advanced to assure compliance with laws or to protect the lien or the priority of the lien of the Insured Mortgage before the acquisition of the estate or interest in the Title;

  (viii) the amounts to pay taxes and insurance; and

  (ix) the reasonable amounts expended to prevent deterioration of improvements;

but the Indebtedness is reduced by the total of all payments and by any amount forgiven by an Insured.

(e) "Insured": The Insured named in Schedule A.

  (i) The term "Insured" also includes

    (A) the owner of the Indebtedness and each successor in ownership of the Indebtedness, whether the owner or successor owns the Indebtedness for its own account or as a trustee or other fiduciary, except a successor who is an obligor under the provisions of Section 12(c) of these Conditions;

    (B) the person or Entity who has "control" of the "transferable record," if the Indebtedness is evidenced by a "transferable record," as these terms are defined by applicable electronic transactions law;

    (C) successors to an Insured by dissolution, merger, consolidation, distribution, or reorganization;

    (D) successors to an Insured by its conversion to another kind of Entity;

    (E) a grantee of an Insured under a deed delivered without payment of actual valuable consideration conveying the Title

(1) if the stock, shares, memberships, or other equity interests of the grantee are wholly-owned by the named Insured,

(2) if the grantee wholly owns the named Insured, or

(3) if the grantee is wholly-owned by an affiliated Entity of the named Insured, provided the affiliated Entity and the named Insured are both wholly-owned by the same person or Entity;

(F) any government agency or instrumentality that is an insurer or guarantor under an insurance contract or guaranty insuring or guaranteeing the Indebtedness secured by the Insured Mortgage, or any part of it, whether named as an Insured or not;

(ii) With regard to (A), (B), (C), (D) , and (E) reserving, however, all rights and defenses as to any successor that the Company would have had against any predecessor Insured, unless the successor acquired the Indebtedness as a purchaser for value without Knowledge of the asserted defect, lien, encumbrance, or other matter insured against by this policy.

(f) "Insured Claimant": An Insured claiming loss or damage.

(g) "Insured Mortgage": The Mortgage described in paragraph 4 of Schedule A.

(h) "Knowledge" or "Known": Actual knowledge, not constructive knowledge or notice that may be imputed to an Insured by reason of the Public Records or any other records that impart constructive notice of matters affecting the Title.

(i) "Land": The land described in Schedule A, and affixed improvements that by law constitute real property. The term "Land" does not include any property beyond the lines of the area described in Schedule A, nor any right, title, interest, estate, or easement in abutting streets, roads, avenues, alleys, lanes, ways, or waterways, but this does not modify or limit the extent that a right of access to and from the Land is insured by this policy.

(j) "Mortgage": Mortgage, deed of trust, trust deed, or other security instrument, including one evidenced by electronic means authorized by law.

(k) "Public Records": Records established under state statutes at Date of Policy for the purpose of imparting constructive notice of matters relating to real property to purchasers for value and without Knowledge. With respect to Covered Risk 5(d), "Public Records" shall also include environmental protection liens filed in the records of the clerk of the United States District Court for the district where the Land is located.

(l) "Title": The estate or interest described in Schedule A.

(m) "Unmarketable Title": Title affected by an alleged or apparent matter that would permit a prospective purchaser or lessee of the Title or lender on the Title or a prospective purchaser of the Insured Mortgage to be released from the obligation to purchase, lease, or lend if there is a contractual condition requiring the delivery of marketable title.

2. CONTINUATION OF INSURANCE

The coverage of this policy shall continue in force as of Date of Policy in favor of an Insured after acquisition of the Title by an Insured or after conveyance by an Insured, but only so long as the Insured retains an estate or interest in the Land, or holds an obligation secured by a purchase money Mortgage given by a purchaser from the Insured, or only so long as the Insured shall have liability by reason of warranties in any transfer or conveyance of the Title. This policy shall not continue in force in favor of any purchaser from the Insured of either (i) an estate or interest in the Land, or (ii) an obligation secured by a purchase money Mortgage given to the Insured.

3. NOTICE OF CLAIM TO BE GIVEN BY INSURED CLAIMANT

The Insured shall notify the Company promptly in writing (i) in case of any litigation as set forth in Section 5(a) of these Conditions, (ii) in case Knowledge shall come to an Insured of any claim of title or interest that is adverse to the Title or the lien of the Insured Mortgage, as insured, and that might cause loss or damage for which the Company may be liable by virtue of this policy, or (iii) if the Title or the lien of the Insured Mortgage, as insured, is rejected as Unmarketable Title. If the Company is prejudiced by the failure of the Insured Claimant to provide prompt notice, the Company's liability to the Insured Claimant under the policy shall be reduced to the extent of the prejudice.

4. PROOF OF LOSS

In the event the Company is unable to determine the amount of loss or damage, the Company may, at its option, require as a condition of payment that the Insured Claimant furnish a signed proof of loss. The proof of loss must describe the defect, lien, encumbrance, or other matter insured against by this policy that constitutes the basis of loss or damage and shall state, to the extent possible, the basis of calculating the amount of the loss or damage.

5. DEFENSE AND PROSECUTION OF ACTIONS

(a) Upon written request by the Insured, and subject to the options contained in Section 7 of these Conditions, the Company, at its own cost and without unreasonable delay, shall provide for the defense of an Insured in litigation in which any third party asserts a claim covered by this policy adverse to the Insured. This obligation is limited to only those stated causes of action alleging matters insured against by this policy. The Company shall have the right to select counsel of its choice (subject to the right of the Insured to object for reasonable cause) to represent the Insured as to those stated causes of action. It shall not be liable for and will not pay the fees of any other counsel. The Company will not pay any fees, costs, or expenses incurred by the Insured in the defense of those causes of action that allege matters not insured against by this policy.

(b) The Company shall have the right, in addition to the options contained in Section 7 of these Conditions, at its own cost, to institute and prosecute any action or proceeding or to do any other act that in its opinion may be necessary or desirable to establish the Title or the lien of the Insured Mortgage, as insured, or to prevent or reduce loss or damage to the Insured. The Company may take any appropriate action under the terms of this policy, whether or not it shall be liable to the Insured. The exercise of these rights shall not be an admission of liability or waiver of any provision of this policy. If the Company exercises its rights under this subsection, it must do so diligently.

(c) Whenever the Company brings an action or asserts a defense as required or permitted by this policy, the Company may pursue the litigation to a final determination by a court of competent jurisdiction, and it expressly reserves the right, in its sole discretion, to appeal any adverse judgment or order.

6. DUTY OF INSURED CLAIMANT TO COOPERATE

(a) In all cases where this policy permits or requires the Company to prosecute or provide for the defense of any action or proceeding and any appeals, the Insured shall secure to the

Company the right to so prosecute or provide defense in the action or proceeding, including the right to use, at its option, the name of the Insured for this purpose.

Whenever requested by the Company, the Insured, at the Company's expense, shall give the Company all reasonable aid (i) in securing evidence, obtaining witnesses, prosecuting or defending the action or proceeding, or effecting settlement, and (ii) in any other lawful act that in the opinion of the Company may be necessary or desirable to establish the Title, the lien of the Insured Mortgage, or any other matter as insured. If the Company is prejudiced by the failure of the Insured to furnish the required cooperation, the Company's obligations to the Insured under the policy shall terminate, including any liability or obligation to defend, prosecute, or continue any litigation, with regard to the matter or matters requiring such cooperation.

(b) The Company may reasonably require the Insured Claimant to submit to examination under oath by any authorized representative of the Company and to produce for examination, inspection, and copying, at such reasonable times and places as may be designated by the authorized representative of the Company, all records, in whatever medium maintained, including books, ledgers, checks, memoranda, correspondence, reports, e-mails, disks, tapes, and videos whether bearing a date before or after Date of Policy, that reasonably pertain to the loss or damage. Further, if requested by any authorized representative of the Company, the Insured Claimant shall grant its permission, in writing, for any authorized representative of the Company to examine, inspect, and copy all of these records in the custody or control of a third party that reasonably pertain to the loss or damage. All information designated as confidential by the Insured Claimant provided to the Company pursuant to this Section shall not be disclosed to others unless, in the reasonable judgment of the Company, it is necessary in the administration of the claim. Failure of the Insured Claimant to submit for examination under oath, produce any reasonably requested information, or grant permission to secure reasonably necessary information from third parties as required in this subsection, unless prohibited by law or governmental regulation, shall terminate any liability of the Company under this policy as to that claim.

7. OPTIONS TO PAY OR OTHERWISE SETTLE CLAIMS; TERMINATION OF LIABILITY

In case of a claim under this policy, the Company shall have the following additional options:

(a) To Pay or Tender Payment of the Amount of Insurance or to Purchase the Indebtedness.

  (i) To pay or tender payment of the Amount of Insurance under this policy together with any costs, attorneys' fees, and expenses incurred by the Insured Claimant that were authorized by the Company up to the time of payment or tender of payment and that the Company is obligated to pay; or

  (ii) To purchase the Indebtedness for the amount of the Indebtedness on the date of purchase, together with any costs, attorneys' fees, and expenses incurred by the Insured Claimant that were authorized by the Company up to the time of purchase and that the Company is obligated to pay.

  When the Company purchases the Indebtedness, the Insured shall transfer, assign, and convey to the Company the Indebtedness and the Insured Mortgage, together with any collateral security.

Upon the exercise by the Company of either of the options provided for in subsections (a)(i) or (ii), all liability and obligations of the Company to the Insured under this policy, other than to make the payment required in those subsections, shall terminate, including any liability or obligation to defend, prosecute, or continue any litigation.

(b) To Pay or Otherwise Settle With Parties Other Than the Insured or With the Insured Claimant.

    (i) to pay or otherwise settle with other parties for or in the name of an Insured Claimant any claim insured against under this policy. In addition, the Company will pay any costs, attorneys' fees, and expenses incurred by the Insured Claimant that were authorized by the Company up to the time of payment and that the Company is obligated to pay; or

    (ii) to pay or otherwise settle with the Insured Claimant the loss or damage provided for under this policy, together with any costs, attorneys' fees, and expenses incurred by the Insured Claimant that were authorized by the Company up to the time of payment and that the Company is obligated to pay.

Upon the exercise by the Company of either of the options provided for in subsections (b)(i) or (ii), the Company's obligations to the Insured under this policy for the claimed loss or damage, other than the payments required to be made, shall terminate, including any liability or obligation to defend, prosecute, or continue any litigation.

8. DETERMINATION AND EXTENT OF LIABILITY

This policy is a contract of indemnity against actual monetary loss or damage sustained or incurred by the Insured Claimant who has suffered loss or damage by reason of matters insured against by this policy.

(a) The extent of liability of the Company for loss or damage under this policy shall not exceed the least of

    (i) the Amount of Insurance,

    (ii) the Indebtedness,

    (iii) the difference between the value of the Title as insured and the value of the Title subject to the risk insured against by this policy, or

    (iv) if a government agency or instrumentality is the Insured Claimant, the amount it paid in the acquisition of the Title or the Insured Mortgage in satisfaction of its insurance contract or guaranty.

(b) If the Company pursues its rights under Section 5 of these Conditions and is unsuccessful in establishing the Title or the lien of the Insured Mortgage, as insured,

    (i) the Amount of Insurance shall be increased by 10%, and

    (ii) the Insured Claimant shall have the right to have the loss or damage determined either as of the date the claim was made by the Insured Claimant or as of the date it is settled and paid.

(c) In the event the Insured has acquired the Title in the manner described in Section 2 of these Conditions or has conveyed the Title, then the extent of liability of the Company shall continue as set forth in Section 8(a) of these Conditions.

(d) In addition to the extent of liability under (a), (b), and (c), the Company will also pay those costs, attorneys' fees, and expenses incurred in accordance with Sections 5 and 7 of these Conditions.

9. LIMITATION OF LIABILITY

(a) If the Company establishes the Title, or removes the alleged defect, lien, or encumbrance, or cures the lack of a right of access to or from the Land, or cures the claim of Unmarketable Title, or establishes the lien of the Insured Mortgage, all as insured, in a reasonably diligent manner by any method, including litigation and the completion of any appeals, it shall have fully performed its obligations with respect to that matter and shall not be liable for any loss or damage caused to the Insured.

(b) In the event of any litigation, including litigation by the Company or with the Company's consent, the Company shall have no liability for loss or damage until there has been a final determination by a court of competent jurisdiction, and disposition of all appeals, adverse to the Title or to the lien of the Insured Mortgage, as insured.

(c) The Company shall not be liable for loss or damage to the Insured for liability voluntarily assumed by the Insured in settling any claim or suit without the prior written consent of the Company.

10. REDUCTION OF INSURANCE; REDUCTION OR TERMINATION OF LIABILITY

(a) All payments under this policy, except payments made for costs, attorneys' fees, and expenses, shall reduce the Amount of Insurance by the amount of the payment. However, any payments made prior to the acquisition of Title as provided in Section 2 of these Conditions shall not reduce the Amount of Insurance afforded under this policy except to the extent that the payments reduce the Indebtedness.

(b) The voluntary satisfaction or release of the Insured Mortgage shall terminate all liability of the Company except as provided in Section 2 of these Conditions.

11. PAYMENT OF LOSS

When liability and the extent of loss or damage have been definitely fixed in accordance with these Conditions, the payment shall be made within 30 days.

12. RIGHTS OF RECOVERY UPON PAYMENT OR SETTLEMENT

(a) The Company's Right to Recover

Whenever the Company shall have settled and paid a claim under this policy, it shall be subrogated and entitled to the rights of the Insured Claimant in the Title or Insured Mortgage and all other rights and remedies in respect to the claim that the Insured Claimant has against any person or property, to the extent of the amount of any loss, costs, attorneys' fees, and expenses paid by the Company. If requested by the Company, the Insured Claimant shall execute documents to evidence the transfer to the Company of these rights and remedies. The Insured Claimant shall permit the Company to sue, compromise, or settle in the name of the Insured Claimant and to use the name of the Insured Claimant in any transaction or litigation involving these rights and remedies.

If a payment on account of a claim does not fully cover the loss of the Insured Claimant, the Company shall defer the exercise of its right to recover until after the Insured Claimant shall have recovered its loss.

(b) The Insured's Rights and Limitations

(i) The owner of the Indebtedness may release or substitute the personal liability of any debtor or guarantor, extend or otherwise modify the terms of payment, release a portion of the Title from the lien of the Insured Mortgage, or release any collateral security for the Indebtedness, if it does not affect the enforceability or priority of the lien of the Insured Mortgage.

(ii) If the Insured exercises a right provided in (b)(i), but has Knowledge of any claim adverse to the Title or the lien of the Insured Mortgage insured against by this policy, the Company shall be required to pay only that part of any losses insured against by this policy that shall exceed the amount, if any, lost to the Company by reason of the impairment by the Insured Claimant of the Company's right of subrogation.

(c) The Company's Rights Against Noninsured Obligors

The Company's right of subrogation includes the Insured's rights against non-insured obligors including the rights of the Insured to indemnities, guaranties, other policies of insurance, or bonds, notwithstanding any terms or conditions contained in those instruments that address subrogation rights.

The Company's right of subrogation shall not be avoided by acquisition of the Insured Mortgage by an obligor (except an obligor described in Section 1(e)(i)(F) of these Conditions) who acquires the Insured Mortgage as a result of an indemnity, guarantee, other policy of insurance, or bond, and the obligor will not be an Insured under this policy.

13. ARBITRATION

Either the Company or the Insured may demand that the claim or controversy shall be submitted to arbitration pursuant to the Title Insurance Arbitration Rules of the American Land Title Association ("Rules"). Except as provided in the Rules, there shall be no joinder or consolidation with claims or controversies of other persons. Arbitrable matters may include, but are not limited to, any controversy or claim between the Company and the Insured arising out of or relating to this policy, any service in connection with its issuance or the breach of a policy provision, or to any other controversy or claim arising out of the transaction giving rise to this policy. All arbitrable matters when the Amount of Insurance is $2,000,000 or less shall be arbitrated at the option of either the Company or the Insured. All arbitrable matters when the Amount of Insurance is in excess of $2,000,000 shall be arbitrated only when agreed to by both the Company and the Insured. Arbitration pursuant to this policy and under the Rules shall be binding upon the parties. Judgment upon the award rendered by the Arbitrator(s) may be entered in any court of competent jurisdiction.

14. LIABILITY LIMITED TO THIS POLICY; POLICY ENTIRE CONTRACT

(a) This policy together with all endorsements, if any, attached to it by the Company is the entire policy and contract between the Insured and the Company. In interpreting any provision of this policy, this policy shall be construed as a whole.

(b) Any claim of loss or damage that arises out of the status of the Title or lien of the Insured Mortgage or by any action asserting such claim shall be restricted to this policy.

(c) Any amendment of or endorsement to this policy must be in writing and authenticated by an authorized person, or expressly incorporated by Schedule A of this policy.

(d) Each endorsement to this policy issued at any time is made a part of this policy and is subject to all of its terms and provisions. Except as the endorsement expressly states, it does not (i) modify any of the terms and provisions of the policy, (ii) modify any prior endorsement, (iii) extend the Date of Policy, or (iv) increase the Amount of Insurance.

15. SEVERABILITY

In the event any provision of this policy, in whole or in part, is held invalid or unenforceable under applicable law, the policy shall be deemed not to include that provision or such part held to be invalid, but all other provisions shall remain in full force and effect.

16. CHOICE OF LAW; FORUM

(a) Choice of Law: The Insured acknowledges the Company has underwritten the risks covered by this policy and determined the premium charged therefor in reliance upon the law affecting interests in real property and applicable to the interpretation, rights, remedies, or enforcement of policies of title insurance of the jurisdiction where the Land is located.

Therefore, the court or an arbitrator shall apply the law of the jurisdiction where the Land is located to determine the validity of claims against the Title or the lien of the Insured Mortgage that are adverse to the Insured and to interpret and enforce the terms of this policy. In neither case shall the court or arbitrator apply its conflicts of law principles to determine the applicable law.

(b) Choice of Forum: Any litigation or other proceeding brought by the Insured against the Company must be filed only in a state or federal court within the United States of America or its territories having appropriate jurisdiction.

17. NOTICES, WHERE SENT

Any notice of claim and any other notice or statement in writing required to be given to the Company under this policy must be given to the Company at [fill in].

NOTE: Bracketed [ ] material optional

APPENDIX I

ALTA Minimum Standard Detail Requirements for ALTA/ACSM Land Title Surveys

2005 MINIMUM STANDARD DETAIL REQUIREMENTS FOR
ALTA/ACSM LAND TITLE SURVEYS
as adopted by
American Land Title Association
and
National Society of Professional Surveyors
(a member organization of the American Congress on Surveying and Mapping)

It is recognized that members of the American Land Title Association (ALTA) have specific needs, peculiar to title insurance matters, which require particular information for acceptance by title insurance companies when said companies are asked to insure title to land without exception as to the many matters which might be discoverable from survey and inspection and not be evidenced by the public records. In the general interest of the public, the surveying profession, title insurers and abstracters, ALTA and the National Society of Professional Surveyors, Inc. (NSPS) jointly promulgate and set forth such details and criteria for standards. It is recognized and understood that local and state standards or standards of care, which surveyors in those respective jurisdictions are bound by, may augment, or even require variations to the standards outlined herein. Where conflicts between the standards outlined herein and any jurisdictional statutes or regulations occur, the more restrictive requirement shall apply. It is also recognized that title insurance companies are entitled to rely on the survey furnished to them to be of an appropriate professional quality, both as to completeness and as to accuracy. It is equally recognized that for the performance of a survey, the surveyor will be provided with appropriate data which can be relied upon in the preparation of the survey.

For a survey of real property and the plat or map of the survey to be acceptable to a title insurance company for purposes of insuring title to said real property free and clear of survey matters (except those matters disclosed by the survey and indicated on the plat or map), certain specific and pertinent information shall be presented for the distinct and clear understanding between the client (insured), the title insurance company (insurer), and the surveyor (the person professionally responsible for the survey). These requirements are:

1. The client shall request the survey or arrange for the survey to be requested and shall provide a written authorization to proceed with the survey from the person responsible for paying for the survey. Unless specifically authorized in writing by the insurer, the insurer shall not be responsible for any costs associated with the preparation of the survey. The request shall specify that an **"ALTA/ACSM LAND TITLE SURVEY"** is required and shall designate which of the optional items listed in Table A are to be incorporated. The request shall set forth the record description of the property to be surveyed or, in the case of an original survey, the record description of the parent parcel that contains the property to be surveyed. Complete copies of the record description of the property (or, in the case of an original survey, the parent parcel), any record easements benefiting the property, the record easements or servitudes and covenants burdening the property ("Record Documents"), documents of record referred to in the Record Documents, and any other documents containing desired appropriate information affecting the property being surveyed and to which the survey shall make reference shall be provided to the surveyor for notation on the plat or map of survey;

2. The plat or map of such survey shall bear the name, address, telephone number, and signature of the professional land surveyor who performed the survey, his or her official seal and registration number, the date the survey was completed, the dates of all of the surveyor's revisions and the caption "ALTA/ACSM Land Title Survey" with the certification set forth in paragraph 8;

3. An **"ALTA/ACSM LAND TITLE SURVEY"** shall be in accordance with the then-current "Accuracy Standards for Land Title Surveys" ("Accuracy Standards") as adopted, from time to time by the National Society of Professional Surveyors and the American Land Title Association and incorporated herein by reference;

1

4.   On the plat or map of an **"ALTA/ACSM LAND TITLE SURVEY,"** the survey boundary shall be drawn to a convenient scale, with that scale clearly indicated. A graphic scale, shown in feet or meters or both, shall be included. A north arrow shall be shown and when practicable, the plat or map of survey shall be oriented so that north is at the top of the drawing. Symbols or abbreviations used shall be identified on the face of the plat or map by use of a legend or other means. If necessary for clarity, supplementary or exaggerated diagrams shall be presented accurately on the plat or map. The plat or map shall be a minimum size of 8½ by 11 inches;

5.   The survey shall be performed on the ground and the plat or map of an **"ALTA/ACSM LAND TITLE SURVEY"** shall contain, in addition to the required items already specified above, the following applicable information:

(a)   All data necessary to indicate the mathematical dimensions and relationships of the boundary represented, with angles given directly or by bearings, and with the length and radius of each curve, together with elements necessary to mathematically define each curve. The point of beginning of the surveyor's description shall be shown as well as the remote point of beginning, if different. A bearing base shall refer to some well-fixed line, so that the bearings may be easily re-established. The North arrow shall be referenced to its bearing base and should that bearing base differ from record title, that difference shall be noted;

(b)   When record bearings or angles or distances differ from measured bearings, angles or distances, both the record and measured bearings, angles, and distances shall be clearly indicated. If the record description fails to form a mathematically closed figure, the surveyor shall so indicate;

(c)   Measured and record distances from corners of parcels surveyed to the nearest right-of-way lines of streets in urban or suburban areas, together with recovered lot corners and evidence of lot corners, shall be noted. For streets and highways abutting the property surveyed, the name, the width and location of pavement relative to the nearest boundary line of the surveyed tract, and the width of existing rights of way, where available from the controlling jurisdiction, shall be shown. Observable evidence of access (or lack thereof) to such abutting streets or highways shall be indicated. Observable evidence of private roads shall be so indicated. Streets abutting the premises, which have been described in Record Documents, but not physically opened, shall be shown and so noted;

(d)   The identifying titles of all recorded plats, filed maps, right of way maps, or similar documents which the survey represents, wholly or in part, shall be shown with their appropriate recording data, filing dates and map numbers, and the lot, block, and section numbers or letters of the surveyed premises. For non-platted adjoining land, names, and recording data identifying adjoining owners as they appear of record shall be shown. For platted adjoining land, the recording data of the subdivision plat shall be shown. The survey shall indicate platted setback or building restriction lines which have been recorded in subdivision plats or which appear in Record Documents which have been delivered to the surveyor. Contiguity, gores, and overlaps along the exterior boundaries of the surveyed premises, where ascertainable from field evidence or Record Documents, or interior to those exterior boundaries, shall be clearly indicated or noted. Where only a part of a recorded lot or parcel is included in the survey, the balance of the lot or parcel shall be indicated;

(e)   All evidence of monuments shall be shown and noted to indicate which were found and which were placed. All evidence of monuments found beyond the surveyed premises on which establishment of the corners of the surveyed premises are dependent, and their application related to the survey shall be indicated;

2

(f)   The character of any and all evidence of possession shall be stated and the location of such evidence carefully given in relation to both the measured boundary lines and those established by the record. An absence of notation on the survey shall be presumptive of no observable evidence of possession;

(g)   The location of all buildings upon the plot or parcel shall be shown and their locations defined by measurements perpendicular to the nearest perimeter boundaries. The precision of these measurements shall be commensurate with the Relative Positional Accuracy of the survey as specified in the current Accuracy Standards for ALTA/ACSM Land Title Surveys. If there are no buildings erected on the property being surveyed, the plat or map shall bear the statement, "No buildings." Proper street numbers shall be shown where available;

(h)   All easements evidenced by Record Documents which have been delivered to the surveyor shall be shown, both those burdening and those benefiting the property surveyed, indicating recording information. If such an easement cannot be located, a note to this effect shall be included. Observable evidence of easements and/or servitudes of all kinds, such as those created by roads, rights-of-way; water courses, drains, telephone, telegraph, or electric lines, water, sewer, oil or gas pipelines on or across the surveyed property and on adjoining properties if they appear to affect the surveyed property, shall be located and noted. If the surveyor has knowledge of any such easements and/or servitudes, not observable at the time the present survey is made, such lack of observable evidence shall be noted. Surface indications, if any, of underground easements and/or servitudes shall also be shown;

(i)   The character and location of all walls, buildings, fences, and other visible improvements within five feet of each side of the boundary lines shall be noted. Without expressing a legal opinion, physical evidence of all encroaching structural appurtenances and projections, such as fire escapes, bay windows, windows and doors that open out, flue pipes, stoops, eaves, cornices, areaways, steps, trim, etc., by or on adjoining property or on abutting streets, on any easement or over setback lines shown by Record Documents shall be indicated with the extent of such encroachment or projection. If the client wishes to have additional information with regard to appurtenances such as whether or not such appurtenances are independent, division, or party walls and are plumb, the client will assume the responsibility of obtaining such permissions as are necessary for the surveyor to enter upon the properties to make such determinations;

(j)   Driveways, alleys and other ways of access on or crossing the property must be shown. Where there is evidence of use by other than the occupants of the property, the surveyor must so indicate on the plat or map. Where driveways or alleys on adjoining properties encroach, in whole or in part, on the property being surveyed, the surveyor must so indicate on the plat or map with appropriate measurements;

(k)   As accurately as the evidence permits, the location of cemeteries and burial grounds: (i) disclosed in the Record Documents provided by clients; or (ii) observed in the process of performing the field work for the survey, shall be shown;

(l)   Ponds, lakes, springs, or rivers bordering on or running through the premises being surveyed shall be shown;

6.   As a minimum requirement, the surveyor shall furnish two sets of prints of the plat or map of survey to the title insurance company or the client. If the plat or map of survey consists of more than one sheet, the sheets shall be numbered, the total number of sheets indicated and match lines be shown on each sheet. The prints shall be on durable and dimensionally stable material of a quality standard acceptable to the title insurance company. The record title description of the surveyed tract, or the description provided by the client, and any new description prepared by the surveyor must appear on the face of the plat or map or otherwise accompany the

3

survey. When, in the opinion of the surveyor, the results of the survey differ significantly from the record, or if a fundamental decision related to the boundary resolution is not clearly reflected on the plat or map, the surveyor may explain this information with notes on the face of the plat or map or in accompanying attachments. If the relative positional accuracy of the survey exceeds that allowable, the surveyor shall explain the site conditions that resulted in that outcome with a note on the face of the map or plat;

7. Water boundaries necessarily are subject to change due to erosion or accretion by tidal action or the flow of rivers and streams. A realignment of water bodies may also occur due to many reasons such as deliberate cutting and filling of bordering lands or by avulsion. Recorded surveys of natural water boundaries are not relied upon by title insurers for location of title.

When a property to be surveyed for title insurance purposes contains a natural water boundary, the surveyor shall measure the location of the boundary according to appropriate surveying methods and note on the plat or map the date of the measurement and the caveat that the boundary is subject to change due to natural causes and that it may or may not represent the actual location of the limit of title. When the surveyor is aware of changes in such boundaries, the extent of those changes shall be identified;

8. When the surveyor has met all of the minimum standard detail requirements for an ALTA/ACSM Land Title Survey, the following certification shall be made on the plat:

To (name of client), (name of lender, if known), (name of title insurance company, if known), (name of others as instructed by client):

This is to certify that this map or plat and the survey on which it is based were made in accordance with the "Minimum Standard Detail Requirements for ALTA/ACSM Land Title Surveys," jointly established and adopted by ALTA and NSPS in 2005, and includes items _____ of Table A thereof. Pursuant to the Accuracy Standards as adopted by ALTA and NSPS and in effect on the date of this certification, undersigned further certifies that in my professional opinion, as a land surveyor registered in the State of _____, the Relative Positional Accuracy of this survey does not exceed that which is specified therein.

Date: (signed)   (seal)
                              Registration No.

NOTE: If, as otherwise allowed in the Accuracy Standards, the Relative Positional Accuracy exceeds that which is specified therein, the following certification shall be made on the plat:

To (name of client), (name of lender, if known), (name of title insurance company, if known), (name of others as instructed by client):

This is to certify that this map or plat and the survey on which it is based were made in accordance with the "Minimum Standard Detail Requirements for ALTA/ACSM Land Title Surveys," jointly established and adopted by ALTA and NSPS in 2005, and includes items _____ of Table A thereof. Pursuant to the Accuracy Standards as adopted by ALTA and NSPS and in effect on the date of this certification, undersigned further certifies that in my professional opinion, as a land surveyor registered in the State of _____, the maximum Relative Positional Accuracy is _____feet.

Date: (signed)   (seal)
                              Registration No.

The 2005 Minimum Standard Detail Requirements for ALTA/ACSM Land Title Surveys are

4

effective January 1, 2006. As of that date, all previous versions of the Minimum Standard Detail Requirements for ALTA/ACSM Land Title Surveys are superseded by these 2005 standards.

Adopted by the American Land Title Association on October 5, 2005.
Adopted by the Board of Directors, National Society of Professional Surveyors on October 24, 2005.
American Land Title Association, 1828 L St., N.W., Suite 705, Washington, D.C. 20036.
National Society of Professional Surveyors, Inc., 6 Montgomery Village Avenue, Suite 403, Gaithersburg, MD 20879

5

TABLE A

OPTIONAL SURVEY RESPONSIBILITIES AND SPECIFICATIONS

NOTE: The items of Table A must be negotiated between the surveyor and client. It may be necessary for the surveyor to qualify or expand upon the description of these items, e.g., in reference to item 6, there may be a need for an interpretation of a restriction. The surveyor cannot make a certification on the basis of an interpretation or opinion of another party. Items 16, 17 and 18 are only for use on projects for the U.S. Department of Housing and Urban Development (HUD).

If checked, the following optional items are to be included in the ALTA/ACSM LAND TITLE SURVEY, except as otherwise negotiated:

1. _____ *Monuments placed (or a reference monument or witness to the corner) at all major corners of the boundary of the property, unless already marked or referenced by an existing monument or witness to the corner;*

2. _____ *Vicinity map showing the property surveyed in reference to nearby highway(s) or major street intersection(s);*

3. _____ *Flood zone designation (with proper annotation based on federal Flood Insurance Rate Maps or the state or local equivalent, by scaled map location and graphic plotting onl.);*

4. _____ *Gross land area (and other areas if specified by the client;.*

5. _____ *Contours and the datum of the elevations;*

6. _____ *List setback, height, and floor space area restrictions disclosed by applicable zoning or building codes (beyond those required under paragraph 5d of these standards). If none, so state. The source of such information must be disclosed. See "Note" above;*

7. _____ *(a) Exterior dimensions of all buildings at ground level*

   (b) Square footage of:

   _____ *(1) exterior footprint of all buildings at ground level;*

   _____ *(2) gross floor area of all buildings; or*

   _____ *(3) other areas to be defined by the client.*

   _____ *(c) Measured height of all buildings above grade at a defined location. If no defined location is provided, the point of measurement shall be shown;*

8. _____ *Substantial, visible improvements (in addition to buildings) such as billboards, signs, parking structures, swimming pools, etc.;*

9. _____ *Parking areas and, if striped, the striping and the type (e.g. handicapped, motorcycle, regular, etc.) and number of parking spaces;*

10. _____ *Indication of access to a public way on land such as curb cuts and driveways, and to and from waters adjoining the surveyed tract, such as boat slips, launches, piers and docks;*

6

11.   *Location of utilities (representative examples of which are shown below) existing on or serving the surveyed property as determined by:*
_____ *(a) Observed evidence;*

_____ *(b) Observed evidence together with evidence from plans obtained from utility companies or provided by client, and markings by utility companies and other appropriate sources (with reference as to the source of information)*
- *railroad tracks and sidings;*
- *manholes, catch basins, valve vaults or other surface indications of subterranean uses;*
- *wires and cables (including their function, if readily identifiable) crossing the surveyed premises, all poles on or within ten feet of the surveyed premises, and the dimensions of all crossmembers or overhangs affecting the surveyed premises; and*
- *utility company installations on the surveyed premises.*

12. _____ *Governmental Agency survey-related requirements as specified by the client;*

13. _____ *Names of adjoining owners of platted lands;*

14. _____ *The distance to the nearest intersecting street as designated by the client;*

15. _____ *Rectified orthophotography, photogrammetric mapping, laser scanning and other similar products, tools or technologies may be utilized as the basis for the location of certain features (excluding boundaries) where ground measurements are not otherwise necessary to locate those features to an appropriate and acceptable accuracy relative to a nearby boundary. The surveyor shall: (a) discuss the ramifications of such methodologies (e.g. the potential accuracy and completeness of the data gathered thereby) with the title company, lender and client prior to the performance of the survey; and (b) place a note on the face of the survey explaining the source, date, relative accuracy and other relevant qualifications of any such data;*

16. _____ *Observable evidence of earth moving work, building construction or building additions within recent months;*

17. _____ *Any changes in street right of way lines either completed or proposed, and available from the controlling jurisdiction. Observable evidence of recent street or sidewalk construction or repairs;*

18. _____ *Observable evidence of site use as a solid waste dump, sump or sanitary landfill.*

19.   _____
_____

Accuracy Standards for ALTA/ACSM Land Title Surveys

Introduction

These Accuracy Standards address Relative Positional Accuracies for measurements that control land boundaries on ALTA/ACSM Land Title Surveys.

In order to meet these standards, the surveyor must assure and certify that the Relative Positional Accuracies resulting from the measurements made on the survey do not exceed that which is allowable.

If the size or configuration of the property to be surveyed, or the relief, vegetation or improvements on the property will result in survey measurements for which the allowable Relative Positional Accuracies will be exceeded, the surveyor must alternatively certify as to the Relative Positional Accuracy that was otherwise achieved on the survey.

Definition:

"Relative Positional Accuracy" means the value expressed in feet or meters that represents the uncertainty due to random errors in measurements in the location of any point on a survey relative to any other point on the same survey at the 95 percent confidence level.

Background

The lines and corners on any property survey have uncertainty in location which is the result of: (1) availability and condition of reference monuments; (2) occupation or possession lines as they may differ from record lines; (3) clarity or ambiguity of the record descriptions or plats of the surveyed tracts and its adjoiners; and (4) Relative Positional Accuracy.

The first three sources of uncertainty must be weighed as evidence in the determination of where, in the professional surveyor's opinion, the boundary lines and corners should be placed. Relative Positional Accuracy is related to how accurately the surveyor is able to monument or report those positions.

Of these four sources of uncertainty, only Relative Positional Accuracy is controllable, although due to the inherent error in any measurement, it cannot be eliminated. The first three can be estimated based on evidence; Relative Positional Accuracy can be estimated using statistical means.

The surveyor shall, to the extent necessary to achieve the standards contained herein: (1) compensate or correct for systematic errors, including those associated with instrument calibration; (2) select the appropriate equipment and methods, and use trained personnel; and (3) use appropriate error propagation and other measurement design theory to select the proper instruments, field procedures, geometric layouts, and computational procedures to control random errors.

If radial survey methods, GPS, or other acceptable technologies or procedures are used to locate or establish points on the survey, the surveyor shall apply appropriate procedures in order to assure that the allowable Relative Positional Accuracy of such points is not exceeded.

Computation of Relative Positional Accuracy

Relative Positional Accuracy may be tested by:
(1) comparing the relative location of points in a survey as measured by an independent survey of higher accuracy; or
(2) the results of a minimally constrained, correctly weighted least square adjustment of the survey.

Allowable Relative Positional Accuracy for Measurements Controlling Land Boundaries on ALTA/ACSM Land Title Surveys

0.07 feet (or 20 mm) + 50 ppm

8

APPENDIX J

ALTA Condominium Endorsement 4.1–06

American Land Title Association

Endorsement 4.1-06 (Condominium)
Adopted 6/17/06

ENDORSEMENT

Attached to Policy No. _____

Issued By

BLANK TITLE INSURANCE COMPANY

The Company insures against loss or damage sustained by the Insured by reason of:

1. The failure of the unit identified in Schedule A and its common elements to be part of a condominium within the meaning of the condominium statutes of the jurisdiction in which the unit and its common elements are located.

2. The failure of the documents required by the condominium statutes to comply with the requirements of the statutes to the extent that such failure affects the Title to the unit and its common elements.

3. Present violations of any restrictive covenants that restrict the use of the unit and its common elements and that are contained in the condominium documents. The restrictive covenants do not contain any provisions that will cause a forfeiture or reversion of the Title. As used in this paragraph 3, the words "restrictive covenants" do not refer to or include any covenant, condition, or restriction (a) relating to obligations of any type to perform maintenance, repair, or remediation on the Land, or (b) pertaining to environmental protection of any kind or nature, including hazardous or toxic matters, conditions, or substances, except to the extent that a notice of a violation or alleged violation affecting the Land has been recorded in the Public Records at Date of Policy and is not excepted in Schedule B.

4. Any charges or assessments provided for in the condominium statutes and condominium documents due and unpaid at Date of Policy.

5. The failure of the unit and its common elements to be entitled by law to be assessed for real property taxes as a separate parcel.

6. Any obligation to remove any improvements that exist at Date of Policy because of any present encroachments or because of any future unintentional encroachment of the common elements upon any unit or of any unit upon the common elements or another unit.

7. The failure of the Title by reason of a right of first refusal to purchase the unit and its common elements which was exercised or could have been exercised at Date of Policy.

This endorsement is issued as part of the policy. Except as it expressly states, it does not (i) modify any of the terms and provisions of the policy, (ii) modify any prior endorsements, (iii) extend the Date of Policy, or (iv) increase the Amount of Insurance. To the extent a provision of the policy or a previous endorsement is inconsistent with an express provision of this endorsement, this endorsement controls. Otherwise, this endorsement is subject to all of the terms and provisions of the policy and of any prior endorsements.

[Witness clause optional]

BLANK TITLE INSURANCE COMPANY

By:

APPENDIX K

ALTA Environmental Protection Lien 8.1–06

American Land Title Association

Endorsement 8.1-06 (Environmental Protection Lien)
Adopted 6/17/06

ENDORSEMENT

Attached to Policy No.

Issued by

BLANK TITLE INSURANCE COMPANY

The insurance afforded by this endorsement is only effective if the Land is used or is to be used primarily for residential purposes.

The Company insures against loss or damage sustained by the Insured by reason of lack of priority of the lien of the Insured Mortgage over

    (a) any environmental protection lien that, at Date of Policy, is recorded in those records established under state statutes at Date of Policy for the purpose of imparting constructive notice of matters relating to real property to purchasers for value and without Knowledge, or is filed in the records of the clerk of the United States district court for the district in which the Land is located, except as set forth in Schedule B; or

    (b) any environmental protection lien provided by any state statute in effect at Date of Policy, except environmental protection liens provided by the following state statutes:

This endorsement is issued as part of the policy. Except as it expressly states, it does not (i) modify any of the terms and provisions of the policy, (ii) modify any prior endorsements, (iii) extend the Date of Policy, or (iv) increase the Amount of Insurance. To the extent a provision of the policy or a previous endorsement is inconsistent with an express provision of this endorsement, this endorsement controls. Otherwise, this endorsement is subject to all of the terms and provisions of the policy and of any prior endorsements.

[Witness clause optional]

BLANK TITLE INSURANCE COMPANY

By: _____
    Authorized Signatory

APPENDIX L

Subdivision Approval with Covenant Contract

Know all men by these presents that whereas the undersigned has submitted an application dated _____ , 19 __, to the _____
Planning Board for approval of a definitive plan of a certain subdivision entitled _____

_____
and dated_____ , 19 __ and has requested the Board to approve such plan without requiring a performance bond,

NOW THEREFORE, THIS AGREEMENT WITNESSETH that in consideration of the
_____ Planning Board approving said plan without requiring a performance bond, and in consideration of one dollar in hand paid, receipt whereof is hereby acknowledged, the undersigned covenants and agrees with the (City/Town) of _____ as follows:

1. The undersigned will not sell any lot in the subdivision or erect or place any permanent building on any such lot until the construction of ways and municipal services necessary to serve adequately such lot has been completed in the manner specified in the aforesaid application, and in accordance with the covenants, conditions, agreements, terms and provisions thereof, excepting, however, as provided in paragraphs 4.A. and 4.B. hereof.

2. This agreement shall be binding upon the executors, administrators, devisees, heirs, successors and assigns of the undersigned.

   It is the intention of the undersigned and it is hereby understood and agreed that this contract shall constitute a covenant running with the land included in the aforesaid subdivision and shall operate as restrictions upon said land.

   It is understood and agreed that lots within the subdivision shall, respectively, be released from the foregoing conditions upon the recording of a certificate of performance executed by a majority of said Planning Board and enumerating the specific lots to be so released , such releases to be issued as provided in paragraphs 4.A. and 4.B. hereof.

3. The undersigned represents and covenants that undersigned is the owner* in fee simple of all the land included in the aforesaid subdivision and that there are no mortgages of record or otherwise on any of said land, except such as are described below and subordinated to this contract, and the present holders of said mortgages have assented to this contract prior to its execution by the undersigned.

4. A. In addition to, and notwithstanding anything to the contrary contained in the foregoing provisions, it is understood and agreed that, the Planning Board having agreed to release certain lots from the terms of the covenant prior to the completion of the required public improvements:

   (1)   lots, namely Lot   Lot
                                 and Lot
      all of which have lawful frontage on an existing public way, are excluded and released from the operation and effect of this covenant; and

   (2)   additional lots will be released from the operation and effect of this covenant upon application for such releases by the undersigned specifying the Lots to be released.

B. In addition to, and notwithstanding anything to the
    contrary contained in the foregoing provisions and/or
    in the Rules and Regulations Governing the Subdivision
    of Land of the Planning Board in the Town of
    in effect on   it is understood and
    agreed that:

    (1) The following roads shall be constructed to a
                    foot width to meet the Planning
        Board's specifications, subject to the modifications
        herein set forth, to wit: *   *   *

    (2) The Planning Board hereby waives the following
        requirements: *   *   *

        IN WITNESS WHEREOF the undersigned, applicant as aforesaid, does hereunto set his
hand and seal this_____ day of _____ , 19___.

Received by Town Clerk: Applicant's signature_____
                                Applicant's address_____

Date_____   _____
                                _____

Time _____   Owner's signature and address if not the
                                applicant   _____
Signature _____   _____
                                _____

Description of Mortgages: _____

_____
_____
        (Give complete names and Registry of Deeds reference.)

Agreed to:

_____   Assents of Mortgagees:

_____   _____

_____   By _____

_____   _____

    Planning Board

[acknowledgement]

APPENDIX M

Conservation Restriction

1. GRANT: MIDTOWN DEVELOPERS, LLC, a limited liability company organized under the laws of Massachusetts, having a principal address at _____ Street, in Midtown, _____ County, Massachusetts (the "Grantor"), acting pursuant to Sections 31, 32 and 33 of Chapter 184 of the General Laws, grants to MIDTOWN CONSERVATION TRUSTEES, INC., a Massachusetts non-profit corporation with a principal address at _____ Street, in said Midtown, and its successors and permitted assigns (the "Grantee") in perpetuity and exclusively for conservation purposes, the following described Conservation Restriction affecting certain portions, hereinafter specified, of certain parcels of land located on _____ Road in said Town of Midtown, containing in all approximately _____ acres, and being a part of the land intended by the Grantor to be included in the Suburban Acres Condominium (hereinafter referred to as the "Premises"), said parcels being shown on a plan entitled "Subdivision Plan in Midtown, MA," dated _____, 2007, by _____ Surveyors, recorded or to be recorded with _____ Registry of Deeds (hereinafter referred to as the "Plan").

2. PREMISES; RESTRICTED AREAS: The Premises comprise certain parcels of land described in a deed to the Grantor recorded with said Registry of Deeds (the "Registry") in Book _____ Page _____, and include Parcels 3 and 4, as shown on the Plan. Each of said Parcels 3 and 4 contains a "Restricted Area" as shown on the Plan. The portions of said Parcels 3 and 4 which are not included in such a Restricted Area are hereby excluded from and shall not be affected by this Conservation Restriction.

3. CONSERVATION VALUES: The Restricted Areas of the Premises, defined above, contain unusual, unique or outstanding qualities the protection of which in their predominantly natural, vegetated or open condition will be of benefit to the public. These qualities include:

    A. A combination of wooded upland, wooded swamp and ponds, all of which provide quality wildlife habitat;

    B. Midtown North Brook, which flows across the Premises into the Midtown River;

    C. Proximity to other permanently protected open space,

including the Town of Midtown North Brook Conservation Land and the Town of Midtown Wildlife Sanctuary Area;

D. Proximity to the dairy farm maintained by Brothers Farm, Inc. on a portion of which the Grantee holds a Conservation Restriction.

4. PROHIBITED ACTS AND USES: Subject to the exceptions herein set forth and specified in Section 4 hereof, the following acts and uses on or affecting the Restricted Areas are prohibited:

A. Construction or placing of any buildings or other structures on or above ground;

B. Dumping, placing or storing of refuse, trash, rubbish, debris, junk, waste, or unsightly, offensive or deleterious substances or materials of any kind or description;

C. Cutting, removal or destruction of trees, shrubs or other vegetation except for proper horticultural, forestry and landscape practices, as referred to in Section 4 hereof;

D. Excavation or removal of loam, soil, gravel, sand, rock or other mineral substance in such manner as to affect the surface of said land;

E. Activities detrimental to drainage, flood control, water or soil conservation or erosion control;

F. Commercial recreational activities; or

G. Other acts or uses detrimental to the preservation of said land in such open and natural condition.

5. RESERVED RIGHTS: The Premises within which the Restricted Areas are situated are, as indicated above, to be developed by the Grantor as the Suburban Acres Condominium, comprising residential buildings and various amenities, including club house, swimming pool, tennis courts, and other recreational and social facilities, and vehicular and pedestrian ways to serve the same, all together referred to herein as "the Project." In recognition thereof and in order to facilitate the development, occupancy and use of the Project, and to assure to the residents thereof the living amenities thereof, the Grantor shall have, and hereby reserves unto itself and its successors and assigns, the following rights and easements:

A. To develop and construct the Project pursuant to and in accordance with applicable law and permits issued and to be issued therefore, and for purposes of such development and construction, (i) to use and have access to such portions of the Restricted Areas as are necessary thereto, (ii) to install, construct, maintain, repair, replace, and use such underground utility lines, and underground drainage and sewage disposal facilities, and such fire lanes or emergency access ways, through the Restricted Areas as are necessary thereto, (iii) to grade and alter the grade of, and to landscape, plant and replant, those portions of the Restricted Areas as are presently open, unwooded fields and not affected by wetlands.

B. For the benefit and use of all residents of the Project, (i) to establish suitable parts of the Restricted Areas as sites for gardening and limited agricultural activities; (ii) to designate open fields as sites for outdoor sports and recreational purposes; (iii) to establish and maintain in suitable condition for such use, trails or paths over the Restricted Areas for passage on foot, horseback or cross-country skis; (iv) to prune, clear and trim damaged or decayed trees and brush for forest-fire prevention or management, (v) to place and maintain signs as duly permitted by law for the purposes of indicating the ownership, permitted uses and the restrictions on the use of the Restricted Areas, and (vi) to do all acts and things reasonably necessary or appropriate to accomplish the foregoing.

6. ACCESS LIMITATION: By hereby establishing this Conservation Restriction the Grantor does not hereby grant either to the Grantee, the Town of Midtown or the public any right to enter upon the Restricted Areas or any portion of the Premises. Notwithstanding that limitation, the Grantor hereby grants to the Grantee an easement of access, at reasonable times and after prior notice to the Grantor or its successors or assigns, by representatives of the Grantee for the purposes of inspecting the Restricted Areas in order to insure compliance with and fulfillment of the foregoing restrictions.

7. LEGAL REMEDIES OF THE GRANTEE:

A. Legal and Injunctive Relief: The rights hereby granted shall include the right to enforce this Conservation Restriction by appropriate legal proceedings and to obtain injunctive and other equitable relief against any violations, including, without limitation, relief requiring restoration of the Restricted Areas to the condition thereof prior to the time of the prohibited activity complained of.

B. Reimbursement of Costs of Enforcement: In the event that a court of competent jurisdiction shall determine that the Grantor, or its successors and assigns, shall have committed a violation of this Conservation Restriction, then the Grantor, or its successors and assigns, as the case may be, shall reimburse the Grantee for all reasonable costs and expenses (including without limitation counsel fees) incurred in enforcing this Conservation Restriction or in remedying or abating any violation thereof.

C. Liability Release: The Grantor hereby acknowledges and agrees that neither the Grantee nor any of its members, directors, officers, employees, agents or contractors, or its members, or the heirs, personal representatives, successors or assigns of any of them (collectively the "Released Parties"), shall have or be subject to any liabilities, penalties, fines, charges, costs, losses, damages, expenses, causes of action, claims, demands, orders, judgments, or administrative actions, arising from or in any way connected with: (1) injury to or death of any person, or physical damage to property, resulting from any act, omission, condition, or other matter related to or occurring on or about the Restricted Areas, regardless of cause, unless due solely to the negligence of any of the Released Parties; (2) the violation or alleged violation of, or other failure to comply with any state, federal, or local law, regulation, or requirement, by any person other than any of the Released Parties, in any way affecting, involving, or relating to the Premises; (3) the presence or release in, on, from, or about the Restricted Areas at any time, of any substance now or hereafter defined, listed or otherwise classified pursuant to any federal, state or local law, regulation, or requirement as hazardous, toxic, polluting, or otherwise contaminating to the air, water, or soil, or in any way harmful or threatening to human health or the environment, unless caused solely by any of the Released Parties. By its acceptance of this Conservation Restriction, the Grantee does not undertake any liability or obligation relating to the condition of the Restricted Areas including with respect to compliance with hazardous materials or other environmental laws and regulations.

D. Non-Waiver: Any election by the Grantee as to the manner and timing of its right to enforce this Conservation Restriction or otherwise exercise its rights hereunder shall not be deemed or construed to be a waiver of such rights.

E. Severability: If any provision of this Conservation Restriction shall to any extent be held invalid, the remainder shall not be affected.

8. PERMANENCE:

A. The Conservation Restriction hereby granted shall be permanent.

B. The Grantor and the Grantee agree that the grant of this Conservation Restriction gives rise to a real property right, presently vested in the Grantee, with a fair market value that is at least equal to the proportionate value that the Conservation Restriction, determined at the time of the grant, bears to the value of the land comprised in the Restricted Areas if unrestricted at that time, and represents the development rights associated with the Restricted Areas, except the development rights herein reserved to the Grantor.

C. In the event of a taking by eminent domain or any other event which has the effect of terminating, extinguishing or releasing this Conservation Restriction, then the Grantee, or its successors and assigns, shall be entitled to a portion of the proceeds of such taking or of the next occurring disposition of the Restricted Areas equal to such proportionate value, unless applicable law provides for other disposition of such proceeds.

9. DONATION: This Conservation Restriction is given as a voluntary donation by the Grantor to the Grantee.

Witness the execution hereof under seal this _____ day of _____, 2007.

[Signature; acknowledgement]

APPENDIX N

Condominium Master Deed

This MASTER DEED of SUBURBAN ACRES, a Condominium, made this _____ day of _____, 2007, Witnesseth That:

Midtown Developers, LLC, a Massachusetts limited liability company, having an usual place of business at _____ Midtown, Massachusetts (hereinafter called the Declarant), being the sole owner of certain premises in the Town of Midtown, _____ County, Massachusetts, hereinafter described, by duly executing and recording this Master Deed, does hereby submit said premises to the provisions of Chapter 183A; and to that end the Declarant hereby declares and provides as follows:

1. NAME. The name of the condominium shall be "Suburban Acres."

2. CONDOMINIUM PREMISES. The premises which constitute the condominium comprise the land situated on the northerly side of _____ Road in Midtown, _____ County, Massachusetts, described in Exhibit A attached hereto and made a part hereof, subject to and together with the benefit of the Special Permit Decision of the Midtown Planning Board (as specified in paragraph _____ of Exhibit A), and other rights, easements and provisions referred to in Exhibit A, and subject in part to the Condominium Phasing Lease hereinafter referred to, together with the buildings and improvements now situated on the portion of said land herein designated for condominium development purposes as Parcel A.

3. PRESENT AND FUTURE PHASES. The Condominium is to be established in several Phases. The Condominium is intended to comprise _____ buildings containing _____ Units, of which _____ buildings containing _____ Units, as hereinafter specified, constitute Phase 1. Each subsequent Phase of the Condominium will comprise one or more Buildings and will also include pertinent portions of the common areas and facilities. The land comprised in the Condominium is divided for such purposes into Parcels A, B and C, as shown on a plan attached to the Condominium Phasing Lease. Phase 1 of the Condominium consists of

Parcel A, which is not subject to the Condominium Phasing Lease, and the Buildings containing Units, and other improvements now thereon, as described in the following Sections 4 through 9. Subsequent Phases of the Condominium will consist of portions or subparcels of Parcel B or Parcel C, which are subject to the Condominium Phasing Lease, and the buildings and improvements hereafter to be erected thereon, to be included in the Condominium as Additions pursuant to provisions of Section 12 hereof. Subject to approval by boards of the Town of Midtown having jurisdiction with respect thereto, the Declarant reserves and shall have the right to add to the Condominium additional adjacent land, shown as Parcel D on said plan, and no more than _____ additional Units thereon.

4. DESCRIPTION OF BUILDINGS. The buildings containing Units comprised in Phase 1 of the Condominium consist of Buildings Nos. 1, 2, [etc.] _____ and _____, each of which is constructed principally of poured concrete foundations, basement walls and floor slabs, wood frame construction, wood siding and asphalt shingle roofing. Two of said Buildings each contains four Units, _____ of said Buildings each contain three Units, and _____ of said Buildings each contains two Units. The locations of said Buildings and of the access ways thereto on said premises are shown on the Site Plan hereinafter specified.

5. DESCRIPTION OF UNITS. The _____ Units in Phase I of the Condominium and the designations, locations, approximate floor areas, number of rooms, immediately accessible common areas and Unit Types thereof are as shown on the Floor Plans thereof, hereinafter specified, and as set forth in Exhibit B hereto annexed and incorporated herein. All Units in Phase I of the Condominium are of Unit Types A, B, C and D, as hereinafter defined. Future Phases of the Condominium will include Units of the same Types or other Types which are compatible therewith and have been approved by boards of the Town of Midtown having jurisdiction with respect thereto.

Each Unit of Type A is a two-bedroom residence which contains and includes: an entry porch, foyer, living room with fireplace, dining room, kitchen, laundry room, powder room, and outdoor deck/patio, on the first floor; master bedroom suite with full bath, a second bedroom with full bath, and a loft area on the second floor; an attached two-car garage; and a full basement.

Each Unit of Type B is a three-bedroom residence which contains and includes: * * *

Each Unit of Type C is a two-bedroom residence which contains and includes: * * *

Each Unit of Type D is a two-bedroom residence which contains and includes: * * *

Every Unit, of each of the Unit Types, also contains and includes closets, hallways, and an interior stairway connecting the floors of the Unit.

The elevations with respect to mean sea level of the floors of the Units are set forth in Exhibit D hereto annexed and incorporated herein.

6. BOUNDARIES OF UNITS. The boundaries of Units of Types A, B, C and D, with respect to the floors, ceilings and walls, and the doors and windows thereof, are as follows:

(i) Floors: The upper surfaces of the concrete basement or garage floors, and the planes of the upper and lower surfaces of the structural floor joists of other floors.

(ii) Ceilings: The planes of the lower surfaces of the ceiling joists.

(iii) Interior building walls between Units and bearing walls within Units: The planes of the surfaces facing such Unit of the wall studs.

(iv) Exterior building walls: The planes of the interior surface of the wall studs or of the concrete walls in the basement area.

(v) Doors and Windows, Screens: The exterior surfaces thereof; hereby designating as part of each Unit the entirety of all doors, windows and screens, including frames, jambs, mullions, thresholds, sills, flashing, molding, trim, hardware, glass and screens.

7. RIGHTS AND OBLIGATIONS APPURTENANT TO UNITS

A. The owner of any Unit may at any time and from time to time, subject always to the provisions of Section 10 and 11 hereof, and subject to the provisions of this paragraph A, (1) change the use and designation of any room or space within such Unit, (2) modify, remove and install non-bearing walls lying wholly within such Unit, (3) modify other features or facilities within such Unit, and (4) construct and install a screen porch on or adjacent to the original deck included with such Unit. It is provided, however, that (a) the number of bedrooms or rooms used as bedrooms in any Unit shall not at any time exceed two in Units of Types A, C and D, or three in Units of Type B, (b) any and all work with respect to installation, modification or removal of interior non-bearing walls or other improvements or modifications shall be done (i) by and at the sole and separate expense and responsibility of the Unit owners doing the same, (ii) in a good and workmanlike manner, in a fashion that will not impair the structural or architectural integrity of any part of the building in which the Unit is situated or any other part of the Condominium premise, or interfere with the use or enjoyment of any of the other Units or the common areas and facilities by others entitled thereto, (iii) pursuant to all applicable laws and regulations of governmental bodies having jurisdiction thereof, including without limitation, zoning, building, health, sanitation and fire protection laws and regulations, and pursuant to a building permit therefore, if required by law, and (iv) pursuant to plans and specifications therefore which have been submitted to and approved in advance of any work relating thereto (at the reasonable expense of the requesting Unit owner) by the Board of Trustees (and appropriate, professional consultants) of Suburban Acres Condominium Trust (said Trust being hereinafter referred to as the "Condominium Trust" or "Trust", and said Board of Trustees being sometimes hereinafter referred to as the "Trustees"), which approval shall not unreasonably be withheld or delayed. The Unit owner performing such work shall be responsible for any damage to other Units or common areas and facilities caused by or attributable to the same or any work relating thereto, and such Unit owner shall carry adequate and appropriate insurance relating to all such work (including any such insurance which may reasonably be required by the Trustees), and shall be liable for and pay any increase in common expenses directly caused by or attributable thereto, including, without limitation, any increase in insurance premium for the Condominium master policy or policies of insurance.

B. Each Unit shall have appurtenant thereto the exclusive rights and easements (the "Exclusive Unit Easements"), exercisable subject to and in accordance with the provisions and requirements of this Master Deed and the provisions of the By-Laws of the Condominium Trust and the rules and regulations promulgated pursuant thereto, to use (a) the deck or patio included with such Unit and the land area immediately beneath the deck, and such screen porch, if any, as has been installed, (b) the stoop adjacent to the front door of such Unit, (c) the chimney serving such Unit (but not the outside enclosure thereof), (d) the heating and air-conditioning unit serving the Unit, (e) if included with the Unit, such front and side or rear courtyard areas adjacent to such Unit as are shown on Sheet 1 of the Plans or the site plan of an Addition to the Condominium or are specified in a plan annexed to the deed of such Unit by the Declarant to a purchaser thereof, and the fences enclosing such courtyard, and (f) such driveway areas adjoining the garage of such Unit as are shown on Sheet 1 of the Plans or the site plan of an Addition to the Condominium, or are as specified in a plan annexed to the deed of such Unit by the Declarant to a purchaser thereof. The foregoing facilities or areas referred to in clauses (a), (b), (c), (d) and (e) of the preceding sentence shall be maintained, repaired and replaced as necessary, by and at the sole and separate expense and risk of the owners of such Units as hereinafter provided except that (i) the Trustees shall have the responsibility to have the fences referred to in clause (e) and the driveways referred to in clause (f) repaired, replaced, or maintained as necessary, and said driveways plowed and kept reasonably clean of snow and ice, the expense of which shall be treated as a common area expense hereunder and under the Declaration of Trust referred to in Section 11 hereof, and (ii) screen porches referred to in clause (a) shall be governed with respect to structural elements, and doors, windows and screens, by the provisions of Section 6 defining boundaries of Units. No modifications of or work on any of the facilities or areas referred to in said clauses (a), (b), (c), (d) and (e) shall be made or done except pursuant to plans and specifications therefore which have been submitted to and approved in advance by said Board of Trustees.

It shall be the responsibility of all Unit owners to maintain minimum temperatures in such Units sufficient to avoid the freezing of pipes, plumbing facilities, and the like, and to drain such facilities if heating is not so maintained. If any Unit owner fails to maintain a temperature as aforesaid, or to drain such facilities, said Trustees shall have the right of access to each Unit at any time to increase the heating in order to maintain the minimum temperature or in order to repair any damage caused by the failure to maintain the temperature aforesaid; and any heating bills thus incurred, or any repair bills thus incurred, shall be paid by the applicable Unit owners, and until so paid, shall constitute a lien against such Unit pursuant to Section 6 of said Chapter 183A.

C. All maintenance, repair and replacement required herein to be performed by and at the sole and separate expense of Unit owners shall be performed and conducted in accordance with the provisions and restrictions set forth herein, and in the Condominium Trust or the rules and regulations promulgated pursuant thereto. If the Owner of any Unit shall fail or neglect so to maintain, repair and replace any facility, area or item required herein in a proper manner, or if the Owner of any Unit shall fail to perform any other work or take any action required to be done or taken pursuant to this Master Deed, the Condominium Trust, or the rules and regulations promulgated pursuant thereto, the Trustees may, but shall not be required to, do so and charge such Unit owner for the costs thereof, for which such Unit owner shall be liable in addition to such Unit owner's share of the common expenses, and until such charges are paid by the such owner, the same shall constitute a lien against such Unit pursuant to the provisions of Section 6 of said Chapter 183A. Costs incurred by the Trustees in maintenance of screen porches shall also be assessed to the Unit owners having such porches in amounts reasonably determined by the Trustees, for which such Unit owners shall be liable in addition to such Unit owner's share of the common expense, and until such charges are paid by such owner, the same shall constitute a lien against such Unit as aforesaid.

D. The maintenance, repair and replacement obligations herein contained notwithstanding, the Trustees may, in the exercise of their discretion, require established levels of maintenance and upkeep by the various Unit owners with respect to those facilities, areas and items which Unit owners are required herein to so maintain, repair and replace and the Trustees may reasonably regulate and control and make rules relating to the appearance, painting, decorating and utilization of such facilities, areas and items.

8. DESCRIPTION OF COMMON AREAS AND FACILITIES

A. The common areas and facilities of the Condominium comprise and consist of: (a) the land described in Exhibit A, together with the benefit of and subject to the Special Permit Decision, the Order of Conditions, the Conservation Restriction, and the other rights, easements and provisions referred to herein and in Exhibit A, subject to the Condominium Phasing Lease affecting the portions of said land therein designated as Parcels B and C, and subject to the provisions of Section 12 hereof; (b) the foundations, structural columns, girders, beams, supports, exterior walls, interior structural or bearing walls, walls dividing Units from other Units or from common areas and facilities (but not including non-bearing walls within Units), and roofs of the Buildings; (c) all conduits, ducts, pipes, plumbing, sprinkler system facilities including timer controls, septic disposal tanks and equipment, leeching fields and related facilities, wastewater disposal facilities, wiring, chimneys, flues, fire protection systems, equipment and other facilities (including master television antenna and cable television systems, lines, and facilities, if any), all drainage swales, storm water management ponds and facilities, wells, and all facilities for the furnishing utilities and services which are contained in or serve portions of the buildings which contribute to the structure or support thereof, and all such facilities contained within any Unit which serve portions of the Condominium other than the Unit within which such facilities are contained; (d) the yards (including areas the exclusive use of which has been provided to Unit owners), lawns, roadways, plants, and walkways on the Condominium premises and the improvements thereon and thereof, including common mailbox facilities, and the open space and buffer areas; (e) the proposed clubhouse, swimming pool and all other existing or future recreational facilities on the Condominium premises (the right to construct and install the same being hereby reserved to the Declarant without the consent of any Unit owner); (f) the outside parking spaces (the "Guest Spaces") on the Condominium premises; and (g) all other elements and features of the Condominium property, however designated or described, excepting only the Units themselves as herein defined and described.

B. In addition to the Exclusive Unit Easements herein before provided, the Trustees may, from time to time in their discretion, with respect to each Unit grant an easement or license to a portion or portions of the common areas for the exclusive use of the Owner of such Unit for landscaping, gardening, parking and other purposes in accordance with plans approved by the Trustees. Each land area so designated shall be maintained properly by the Owner of such Unit at such owner's expense, subject to and in accordance with said By-Laws and rules and regulations, pursuant to which said Trustees may, if any of the same are not so properly maintained, undertake the maintenance thereof and charge such Unit owner the cost thereof for which such Unit owner shall be liable in addition to his share of the common expenses, and until such charges are paid by such Unit owner, the same shall constitute a lien against such Unit pursuant to the provisions of Section 6 of said Chapter 183A.

In addition to and not in limitation of the rights of Unit owners as elsewhere herein set forth and as provided in said Chapter 183A, the owner of each Unit shall have, as appurtenant to such Unit, the rights and easements, in common with the owners of all other Units and subject to like rights and easements appurtenant to such other Units, to use the common areas and facilities of the Condominium; provided. however, that the rights and easements in and to such common areas and facilities shall be subject always to (i) such exclusive rights, easements and limitations on use contained in other portions of this Master Deed or as may hereafter be established pursuant to the provisions of this Master Deed, the By-Laws of the Condominium Trust, and the Rules and Regulations of said Trust; (ii) provisions of Section 12 of this Master Deed; (iii) the easements, rights, and restrictions and provisions referred to in Exhibit A hereto; and (iv) provisions of the By-Laws of the Condominium Trust and to rules and regulations promulgated pursuant thereto.

C. The Trust and/or the Declarant shall have, and are hereby granted, the right of access to or through each Unit and any area or facility the exclusive use of which is provided to the Unit, for purposes of: (i) operation, inspection, protection, maintenance, and replacement of common areas and facilities or of other Units or any exclusive areas or facilities provided to such other Units; (ii) correction, termination and removal of things which interfere with the common areas and facilities or are otherwise contrary to or in violation of provisions hereof; and (iii) for such other purposes as the Trustees and/or the Declarant deem necessary, appropriate, or advisable. The Trustees and/or the Declarant may, for foregoing purposes, require each Unit owner to deposit a key to each Unit with the Trustees and/or the Declarant. The Trustees shall also have, and are hereby granted, the exclusive rights to maintain, repair, replace, add to and alter the roads, ways, paths, walks, utility and service lines and facilities and storm water management system, lawns, trees, plants and other landscaping comprised in the common areas and facilities, other than such common areas and facilities the exclusive benefit of which is for a particular Unit owner as herein elsewhere provided, and to make excavations for said purposes; and no Unit owner shall do any of the foregoing without the prior written permission of said Trustees in each instance. The Trustees shall have the right to use and to draw water from sillcocks belonging to Units; provided that the Trustees shall reimburse Unit owners for the reasonable costs, as determined by the Trustees, of water so drawn and charged to Unit owners.

D. If any portion of the common areas and facilities encroaches upon any Unit or any Unit encroaches upon any other Unit or upon any portion of the common areas and facilities as a result of settling or shifting of a Building or otherwise, an easement for the encroachment and for the maintenance of the same so long as the building stands, shall exist. If any Building, any Unit, and any adjoining Unit, or any adjoining part of the common areas and facilities shall be partially or totally destroyed as a result of fire or other casualty or as a result of eminent domain proceedings, and then rebuilt, encroachments of parts of the common areas and facilities upon any Unit or of any Unit upon any other Unit or upon any portion of the common areas and facilities, due to such rebuilding, shall be permitted, and valid easements for such encroachments and the maintenance thereof shall exist so long as the subject Building shall stand.

E. With respect to all wastewater disposal facilities, from and after the completion of construction thereof by the Declarant (hereinafter called the "wastewater facilities"), it is hereby provided that the Trustees shall operate, maintain and repair the wastewater facilities, and replace the same as necessary, in accordance with laws and governmental regulations applicable thereto. The wastewater facilities shall be common facilities of the condominium, and all costs of operation, maintenance, repair, and replacement as necessary, of the same, and provision of reserves for such purposes, shall be common charges, which the Trustees shall assess to the Unit owners proportionately to their respective percentages of interest in common areas and facilities of the Condominium.

9. PLANS. The Condominium Plans comprise a site plan entitled "Suburban Acres Phase 1 Site Plan," dated _____, 2007, prepared by _____ Surveyors, and floor plans entitled "Suburban Acres Phase 1 Floor Plans," dated _____, 2007, prepared by _____ Architects, (collectively, the "Plans"), recorded herewith. The site plan (Sheet 1 of the Plans), showing the Buildings in Phase 1 of the Condominium, and the floor plans of the Buildings and Units included in Phase 1 of the Condominium (Sheets 2 through _____ of the Plans), showing the layout, location, Unit designations and dimensions of the Units, and each bearing the verified statement of a registered professional land surveyor or architect stating that the Plans fully and accurately depict the same as built, are recorded herewith, and consist of the

following:

Sheet 1—Site Plan
Sheet 2—Building 1 Floor Plans
Sheet 3—Building 2 Floor Plans
Sheet 4—Building 3 Floor Plans
* * *

With respect to Buildings which may be added to the Condominium pursuant to Section 12 hereof, this Master Deed will be amended pursuant to said Section 12 at the time or times that such buildings are included in the Condominium, and each such amendment shall be recorded with _____ Registry of Deeds, together with a set of floor plans of each building in each such addition, showing the layout, location, Unit designations, and dimensions of the Units, and bearing the verified statement of a registered architect or engineer or land surveyor that said plans fully and accurately depict the same as built.

10. USE. The purposes for which the Buildings, the Units and other facilities (which terms shall include additional Buildings and facilities hereinafter added to the Condominium, and the Units and other facilities therein, as and when the same are included in the Condominium pursuant to Section 12 hereof), are intended to be used are as follows:

A. Each of the Units is intended to be used solely for owner-occupied single family residence purposes, subject to the restrictions set forth in the following Section 11; provided, however, that such Units may be used (a) by the Declarant hereof, for other purposes pursuant to provisions of the following paragraph D of this Section 10, and (b) for such other purposes as shall be approved in writing by the Trustees of the Condominium Trust.

B. Driveways and outside parking spaces adjacent to Units are intended to be used only for the parking of private passenger cars of occupants of Units in the Condominium or their guests and not for commercial trucks, campers, trailers, boats or other vehicles or storage except with the prior written permission of the Trustees of the Condominium Trust. Acres Drive shall not be used for parking and the parking turnouts thereon are for use by guests and not by Unit owners. No motorcycles or snowmobiles shall be operated on the condominium premises.

C. Any and all common recreational facilities from time to time included in the condominium are intended to be used for the private recreation and enjoyment of the Owners the Condominium Units and their families and guests, subject to provisions of the By-Laws of the Condominium Trust and to rules and regulations promulgated pursuant thereto, and subject to the provisions of the following Section 11; provided, however, that such common recreational facilities or portions thereof may be used for such other purposes as shall approved in writing by the Trustees of the Condominium Trust.

D. All portions of the premises of the Condominium that are subject to the Conservation Restriction referred to in Exhibit A shall be used for the purposes therein specified, and all of the Open Space comprised in the condominium shall be used for conservation, passive recreation or park purposes by residents of the Condominium, and shall be maintained by the Trustees of the Condominium Trust in its natural condition.

E. Notwithstanding the foregoing provisions of this Section 10, and the provisions of the following Section 11, the Declarant, any affiliate of the Declarant, or such other person or entity as is designated by the Declarant hereof may, for its own account:

(1) use any Units owned or leased by it as models, offices, and/or storage areas or otherwise, for purposes of construction, promotion, sale or resales of Units, or for other lawful purposes, and use any of the common areas and facilities, or portions thereof, for office and meeting purposes and for purposes of promotion, sale or leasing of Units;

(2) so long as Declarant or any affiliate of Declarant owns any Unit, including, without limitation, any model Units, in the Condominium, erect and maintain signs and on the common areas and facilities of the Condominium including, without limitation, for any of the purposes permitted in this Section 10;

(3) proceed, together with its contractors and other appropriate personnel, to complete any construction, landscaping or the like in or to the common areas and facilities and/or any renovations, finishing work or the like in or to any Units to be done by the Declarant, and exercise all rights reserved to or conferred upon the Declarant pursuant to and in accordance with the provisions of this Master Deed; and

(4) prior to transfer of title to a Unit by the Declarant to a qualified purchaser thereof under a duly executed purchase and sale agreement, grant the temporary right of occupancy of such Unit to such purchaser by

tenancy agreement or license.

11. RESTRICTIONS ON USE. The Units and the common areas and facilities of the Condominium shall be subject to the restrictions that, unless otherwise permitted by an instrument in writing duly executed by the Trustees of the Condominium Trust pursuant to provisions of the By-Laws thereof hereinafter referred to: (a) no such Unit shall be used for any purpose other than as a dwelling for one family, provided that nothing contained herein shall prohibit any Unit owner from having temporary guests, and (b) no business activities of any nature shall be conducted in any such Unit, except (i) as provided in Paragraph E of Section 10 hereof, and (ii) that a person residing in any such Unit may maintain therein an office for his or her personal professional use, but no employees or persons other than a resident of such Unit shall engage in any such activities and no such office shall be advertised, held out, or used as a place for service to customers, clients or patients.

The Units shall be subject to the further restrictions that, except as provided in Section 10, paragraph E(4), no such Unit shall be rented, let, leased or licensee for use or occupancy by others than the Owners thereof. The Units shall also be subject to the restrictions on use and modification contained in Section 7 hereof.

The architectural integrity of the Buildings and the Units shall be preserved without modification, and to that end, without limiting the generality of the foregoing, except as otherwise permitted by the Trustees in writing, no awning, screen, screen porch, antenna, sign, banner or other device, and no exterior change, addition, structure, projection, decoration or other feature shall be erected or placed upon, or attached to any such Unit, or any part thereof, no addition to or change or replacement of any exterior light fixture, door knocker or other exterior hardware shall be made, and no painting, attaching decalcomania, or other decoration shall be done on an exterior part or surface of any Unit, nor on the interior surface of any window. All windows, however, must have curtains, draperies, shades, or the like and no such curtains, draperies, shades, or the like shall be installed or maintained unless they are made of, or lined with, white, beige, natural or light grey material, or such other material as shall be approved by said Trustees. This paragraph shall not be applicable to the Declarant. No Unit owner (other than the Declarant) shall install or permit to be installed in any Unit any air conditioning system or device, or any heating system or device, without the prior written permission of the Trustees and unless the power therefore is separately metered or otherwise equitably apportioned in such manner as to be exclusively chargeable to the Unit owner installing such system or device. Any such installation which may be so permitted shall, in any event, be required to comply with code and to conform to and be subject to the provisions of this Master Deed and the Condominium Trust pertaining to alterations, modifications, installations, and changes in Units or any parts thereof. Wood or coal stoves, fireplaces or similar devices shall be permitted only in accordance with applicable law and fire regulations, only for occasional use and not for space heating use, and only upon the prior written approval of the Trustees, who shall as a condition of any such approval require (1) compliance with rules and regulations promulgated by them as to the installation, use, maintenance, repair and cleaning of any such device and the storage and handling of wood, coal or other fuels therefore, and (2) the right of the Trustees to enter any Unit in which such a device is installed and to correct any non-compliance with such rules and regulations, all at sole expense and risk of the owner of such Unit. No Unit owner shall install or permit the installation of any garbage disposal unit.

Said restrictions: (a) shall be for the benefit of the Owners of all the Units, and the Trustees of the Condominium Trust as the persons in charge of the common areas and facilities; (b) shall be enforceable solely by said Trustees; and (c) shall, insofar as permitted by law be perpetual, and to that end, may be extended by said Trustees at such time or times and in such manner as permitted or required by law for the continued enforceability thereof. No Unit owner shall be liable for any breach of the provisions of this Section 11 except such as occur during his or her ownership thereof.

12. ADDITIONS TO THE CONDOMINIUM

As referred to in Section 3 hereof, the Declarant reserves and shall have the right, without the consent of any Unit owner, pursuant to and in accordance with the provisions of this Section 12, to amend this Master Deed, at any time and from time to time, so as to include in the Condominium, as an Addition thereto, Parcel B, Parcel C, or any portions or subparcels thereof, together with Buildings containing Units and other improvements thereon. Each such Addition shall constitute Phase 2, Phase 3, Phase 4, or a subsequent phase thereof, comprising Units and common areas and facilities of the Condominium, as specified in such amendment. Upon the recording of each such amendment of this Master Deed the Units thereby included in the Condominium shall be owned by the Declarant, and as provided in the Condominium Phasing Lease, the land so included in the Condominium shall automatically and without necessity of any amendment of said Lease be released and excluded from the effect thereof.

In addition, as referred to in Section 3, subject to approval by boards of the Town of Midtown having jurisdiction with respect thereto, the Declarant reserves and shall have the right to add to the Condominium additional adjacent land and no more than _____ additional Units thereon.

Each Owner of a Unit in the Condominium, by acceptance of delivery of the deed of such Owner's Unit, shall thereby have (a) consented to (i) each such amendment of this Master Deed, (ii) the addition to the condominium of the Units of the Unit Types specified and described in such amendment, and (iii) the restatement of percentages of interest of the Units and the reduction of such Unit owner's percentage of interest as set forth in such amendment, all without the requirement or necessity of the Declarant's securing any further consent or execution of any further document by such Owner, and (b) authorized and empowered the Declarant as such Unit owner's attorney-in-fact to join in, execute, deliver and record such amendment.

With respect to all such Additions to the Condominium it is provided as follows:

A. The aggregate number of Units which may be included in the Condominium shall not exceed _____ and consequently the number of Units which may be added to the _____ Units in Phase 1 is _____, subject to the provisions in Section 3 and this Section 12 pursuant to which the number of Units may be increased by no more than _____.

B. Each Unit shall be of Unit Type A, B, C or D, or of other type, design, layout or size similar thereto or architecturally compatible therewith.

C. Regardless of the numbering or lettering of Parcels, Buildings, Units or Phases herein referred to, the Declarant may include the same in Additions in such order, and in such number of Buildings and Units, as the Declarant may elect in its own discretion.

D. The Declarant reserves and shall have the right, without the consent of any Unit owner, pursuant to and in accordance with the provisions of this Section 12, to develop and construct the Addition(s), including the buildings and Units to be included therein as hereinbefore set forth, and all roads, ways, utilities and other improvements and amenities pertaining thereto and to grant easements across, under, over and through the Condominium premises or any portion thereof which Declarant deems necessary or convenient in connection the development, construction or use of the Addition(s).

E. The Declarant shall not amend this Master Deed so as to include additional Units until the construction of the same have been completed sufficiently for the certification of plans provided for in Section 8(f) of said Chapter 183A.

F. The foregoing reserved rights to include Addition(s) in the Condominium shall terminate and be of no effect _____ years after the date hereof with respect to Addition(s) not theretofore included in the Condominium.

G. Nothing herein shall be deemed to obligate the Declarant to commence or complete construction of additional buildings containing Units or related improvements on Parcel B or Parcel C referred to herein and in Section 3 hereof.

H. The Declarant expressly reserves and shall have the right to make such use of the common areas and facilities of the Condominium as may reasonably be necessary or convenient to enable the Declarant and its contractors to complete construction of any buildings or other improvements on said Parcels B and C.

I. Upon completion and inclusion in the Condominium of the maximum number of Units permitted hereunder, or at such earlier time as the Declarant shall acknowledge in that it has waived any further right to add Units to the Condominium pursuant to this Section 12, the Declarant and the Trustees shall have the right (but not the obligation), without the consent of any Unit owner, pursuant to and in accordance with the provisions of this Section 12, to execute and record a Restated Master Deed of the Suburban Acres condominium comprising and consolidating Phase I and all such subsequent Addition(s), as were then and thereby established as a completed condominium upon and pursuant to the provisions applicable thereto as set forth in this Master Deed and in the amendments by which such subsequent Addition(s) are included, and in any other amendments hereto which have been duly made and recorded, which Restated Master Deed shall thereupon supersede this Master Deed and all such amendments and shall be and constitute the Master Deed of the Suburban Acres condominium as so completed.

13. PERCENTAGE INTERESTS OF UNITS IN COMMON AREAS AND FACILITIES

Each Unit in Phase I of the Condominium shall be entitled to an undivided interest in the common areas and facilities in the percentage specified therefore in Exhibit C annexed hereto and made a part hereof, for so long as the only Units in the Condominium are those comprised in said Phase 1.

From and after the inclusion in this Condominium of Addition(s) containing Units, pursuant to and in accordance with the provisions of Section 12 hereof, the percentages to which Units in Phase I are entitled shall be reduced accordingly, and the percentage to which Units in Phase I, and in each Addition to the Condominium subsequently included therein, shall at all times be in accordance with the provisions of said Chapter 183A and distributed among the Units then included in the Condominium in fair and equitable proportions. To that end, the percentages of undivided interest in the common areas and facilities to which a Unit of each of Types A, B, C and D, in Phase 1 and other Phases of the Condominium shall be entitled shall be a number (expressed as a percentage) equal to the Base for such Unit Type, specified herein or in an amendment of the Master Deed, divided by the number S, determined as herein specified. The Bases for the several present Unit Types shall be: _____ for Type A; _____ for Type B; _____ for Type C; and _____ for Type D. The bases for other Unit Types included in Addition(s) to the Condominium shall likewise be determined in accordance with the provisions of said Chapter 183A and in fair and equitable proportion to each other and to the Bases for present Unit Types, and shall be set forth in the amendment of this Master Deed by which such Addition(s) are included in the Condominium. The number S shall be the sum of the products of the then number of each Type of Unit included in the Condominium times the Base for such Unit Type. It is provided, however, that (a) the percentage figures so determined shall be rounded to the nearest one-thousandth (taking 5/10,000 as a major fraction), and further rounded to the least extent, if any, necessary, as determined by the Declarant in its reasonable discretion, to obtain a 100.000 percent total, and (b) the percentage figures so determined and so rounded shall be set forth in the amendment of this Master Deed by which the Addition resulting in such change of percentages is included in the Condominium.

14. AMENDMENT

This Master Deed may be amended by an instrument in writing: (a) signed by the owners of Units entitled to sixty-seven percent (67%) or more of the undivided interests in the common areas and facilities; and (b) signed and acknowledged by a majority of the Trustees of the Condominium Trust; and (c) duly recorded with said _____ Registry of

Deeds; Provided, However, that:

A. The date on which any such instrument is first signed by a Unit owner shall be indicated thereon as the date thereof and no such instrument shall be of any force or effect unless the same has been so recorded within six (6) months after such date.

B. No instrument of amendment which alters the dimensions of any Unit or adversely affects a Unit owner's exclusive right to use a common area and facility as provided herein shall be of any force or effect unless the same has been signed by the owner(s) of the Unit so altered or whose exclusive right is so affected.

C. Except as provided in, and in accordance with, provisions of Section 13 of this Master Deed, no instrument of amendment which alters the percentage of the undivided interest to which any Unit is entitled in the common areas and facilities shall be of any force or effect unless the same has been signed by the owners of all of the Units and said instrument is therein designated as an Amended Master Deed.

D. No instrument or amendment affecting any Unit in a manner which impairs the security of a first mortgage of record thereon shall be of any force or effect unless the same has been assented to by such holder, but an amendment of the Master Deed pursuant to Section 12 hereof reducing the undivided Unit percentages shall not be treated as an instrument impairing the security of any mortgage.

E. Nothing in this Section 14 contained, and no amendment adopted pursuant hereto shall be deemed or construed to vitiate or impair (a) the rights reserved to the Declarant in and by provisions of Section 12 of this Master Deed to amend this Master Deed without the consent of any Unit owner, so as to include Addition(s) in this Condominium in the manner provided in said Section 12; (b) the rights reserved to the Declarant in and by the provisions of paragraph 1 of Section 18 hereof to amend this Master Deed without the consent of any Unit owner so as to cause this Master Deed to comply in all material respects with the regulations of the Federal National Mortgage Association, its successors, or a similar institution; or (c) the rights conferred upon the Declarant in and by Section 17 and other provisions of this Master Deed.

F. No instrument or amendment which alters this Master Deed in any manner which would render it contrary to or inconsistent with any requirements or provisions of said Chapter183A of the General Laws of Massachusetts, the Special Permit Decision, or other applicable laws or governmental regulations, permits or approvals, shall be of any force or effect.

G. Notwithstanding the foregoing provisions of this Section 14 or any other provision to the contrary contained in this Master Deed, the Declarant reserves and shall have the right, at any time and from time to time until such time as neither the Declarant nor any affiliate of the Declarant any longer owns any Unit (including all Units currently contemplated to be added to the Condominium pursuant to Section 12 above, whether or not construction of such additional Units has yet commenced), to amend, alter, add to or change this Master Deed without the consent of any Trustee, Unit owner or Unit mortgage holder, by instrument in writing signed and acknowledged by the Declarant and duly recorded with said Registry of Deeds for (and only for) the specific purpose of making minor, clerical, or factual corrections to the provisions of this Master Deed, including, without limitation, the plans and provisions relating to the appurtenances to, or descriptions or undivided interests in the common areas and facilities of, any one or more Units.

15. THE SUBURBAN ACRES CONDOMINIUM TRUST

A trust through which the Unit owners will manage and regulate the Condominium established hereby is the Suburban Acres Condominium Trust under Declaration of Trust of even date and record herewith. Said Declaration of Trust establishes a membership organization of which all Unit owners shall be members and in which such Owners shall have beneficial ownership interests in proportion to the percentages of undivided interest in the common areas and facilities to which they are entitled hereunder pursuant to provisions of Section 13. The original and present sole Trustee thereof is Midtown Managers, LLC, a limited liability company organized under the laws of Massachusetts, and an affiliate of the Declarant. So long as said Midtown Managers, LLC, is the sole Trustee thereof, all references herein to "Trustees" and "Board of Trustees" shall be deemed to mean said Midtown Managers, LLC. Said Trustees have enacted By-Laws, which are set forth in said Declaration of Trust, pursuant to and in accordance with provisions of said Chapter 183A of the General Laws of Massachusetts.

16. RESERVATION OF RIGHTS AND EASEMENTS

Notwithstanding anything to the contrary hereinbefore contained, Midtown Developers, LLC, the Declarant hereof, hereby reserves to itself and its successors and assigns the right to grant or reserve in the future, without the consent of any Unit owner, such other easements or restrictions on, over, across, through, and/or under the land comprised in the Condominium premises which the Declarant deems necessary, appropriate or advisable in connection with the development of said land, provided only that such grants or reservations do not interfere unreasonably with the use of the Units for their intended purposes.

17. SENIOR RESIDENTIAL PROVISIONS

The Suburban Acres condominium is a development intended to provide housing accommodations to persons of age 55 or older, and this Master Deed and the Suburban Acres Condominium Trust are intended to comply with all provisions of law with respect thereto, [See § 15:19] and to provide for the continuing compliance by Unit owners and the Condominium Trust with all of such provisions which are applicable to this development. To that end it is hereby provided that:

A. At least one owner and occupant of each Unit shall be a person of age 55 or older.

B. The Trustees of Suburban Acres Condominium Trust shall on or before February 1 of each year prepare a report, and thereafter maintain a permanent record of such reports, specifying the Unit numbers of all Units having any occupants as of the preceding December 31 and with respect to each such Unit the name and age, as of the preceding December 31, of every person who is an owner and every person who is an occupant of such Unit and such other information as may reasonably be necessary to assure compliance with the requirements of applicable laws and regulations. Each owner of a Unit in Suburban Acres shall have the responsibility to provide to the Trustees upon request by them from time to time such information as the Trustees shall deem to be reasonably necessary for such compliance, including without limitation, a verified statement of the name and age of each person who resides in or is an occupant of such Unit, and in support of such statement a birth certificate, United States passport, Massachusetts driver's license or such other documentary evidence with respect to each such person as the Trustees shall in their own sole discretion deem to be sufficient.

C. In the event that any Unit ceases to be owned and occupied by at least one person of age 55 or older due to the death of such an owner/occupant or due to an involuntary termination of ownership or occupancy by virtue of foreclosure or otherwise, the ownership and occupancy of such Unit shall be revested in at least one person of age 55 or older within a period of two years after the occurrence of such event. During said two year period persons lawfully resident in said Unit at the time of such event may remain in occupancy, but no new occupancy or ownership shall be effected except so as to vest ownership and occupancy of such Unit in at least one person of age 55 or older. Notwithstanding the foregoing, the surviving spouse and dependent children of a deceased owner/occupant of age 55 or older may remain resident in the Unit for any period of time, regardless of the age of such surviving spouse or dependent children.

18. MISCELLANEOUS

A. The Units and the common areas and facilities, and the Unit owners and the Trustees of the Condominium Trust, shall have the benefit of and be subject to the provisions of said Chapter 183A of the Massachusetts General Laws, and in all respects not specified in this Master Deed or in said Declaration of Trust of the Condominium Trust and the By-Laws set forth therein, shall be governed by provisions of said Chapter 183A in their relation to each other, and to the Condominium established hereby, including, without limitation, provisions thereof with respect to common expenses, funds and profits, with respect to improvement and rebuilding of common areas and facilities, and with respect to removal of the Condominium premises or any portion thereof from the provisions of said Chapter 183A. In case any of the provisions of this Master Deed conflict with the provisions of said Chapter 183A, the provisions of said Chapter 183A shall control.

B. For so long as the Declarant has unsold Units, the Declarant shall have the same rights and obligations as owner of such unsold Units as any other Unit owner.

C. The captions herein are inserted only as a matter of convenience, and for reference, and in no way define, limit or describe the scope of this Master Deed nor the intent of any provision hereof.

D. Reference in this Master Deed to the Declarant shall mean Midtown Developers, LLC, a Massachusetts limited liability company, and its successors and assigns. The Declarant specifically reserves the right to transfer all of its right, title and interest hereunder, provided that any successor to the Declarant shall assume and agree to be bound by all of the obligations of the Declarant set forth in this Master Deed.

E. No provision contained in this Master Deed shall be deemed to have been abrogated or waived by reason of any failure to enforce the same, irrespective of the number of violations or breaches which may occur.

F. The invalidity of any provision of this Master Deed shall not be deemed to impair or affect the validity of the remainder of this Master Deed and, in such event, all of the provisions of this Master Deed shall continue in full force and effect as if such invalid provision had never been included herein.

G. It is the intent of this Master Deed that the provisions hereof shall comply in all material respects with the regulations of the Federal Home Loan Mortgage Corporation with respect to the purchase of residential condominium unit mortgage loans, and, except as otherwise required by applicable law, all questions with respect to such compliance shall be resolved consistently with such intention. Further, the Declarant may at some future time judge it desirable to amend this Master Deed so as to cause the provisions hereof to comply in all material respects with the regulations of the Federal National Mortgage Association, its successor, or any similar secondary market mortgagee, insurer or underwriter, and to that end, the Declarant reserves and shall have the right, without the consent of any Unit owner and notwithstanding the procedures set forth in Section 14 hereof, to amend this Master Deed form time so as to cause the provisions hereof so to comply with such regulations.

In Witness Whereof, Midtown Developers, LLC, has caused this Master Deed to be executed by _____ Manager thereof, as of the day and year first above written.

[Signature and acknowledgement]

EXHIBIT A

The land contained in Suburban Acres is shown on a plan entitled "Suburban Acres Condominium, Phase 1 Site Plan, Midtown, MA," dated _____, 2007, by _____, Surveyor, to be recorded herewith, and is bounded and described as follows:

[Metes and Bounds Description]

Being the premises conveyed to the Declarant by deed of _____, dated _____, 2007, recorded with _____ Registry of Deeds, Book _____ Page _____.

Said land is subject to and has the benefit of the following:

A. The provisions of Massachusetts General laws, Chapter 183A, and provisions of existing building, zoning, environmental and other laws and regulations of general applicability.

B. Rights, easements, restrictions and agreements hereafter established of record, provided that the same do not interfere unreasonably with the use and enjoyment of the Units and the common areas and facilities of the Condominium for their intended purposes.

C. The Suburban Acres Condominium Phasing Lease (pertaining to Parcels B and C therein designated) between Midtown Developers, LLC, as Lessor, and Midtown Phases, Inc., as Lessee, recorded with said Registry of Deeds prior hereto.

D. The provisions and effect of the following instruments recorded with said Registry of Deeds as herein specified, and the rights, easements, restrictions, agreements and requirements thereof, all insofar as the same are now in force and applicable, to wit:

[List of outstanding encumbrances]

EXHIBIT B

Bldg. Descrip.
No. Units
Unit Descrip.
No. Floors
Rooms
Sq.Ft.
Type
Features

EXHIBIT C

Unit No.
Percentage

EXHIBIT D

Elevations Above Mean Sea Level
Bldg. No.
Unit No.
First Floor
Second Floor

APPENDIX O

Condominium Trust

DECLARATION OF TRUST OF SUBURBAN ACRES CONDOMINIUM TRUST

THIS DECLARATION OF TRUST made this day of _____, 2007, at Midtown, in the County of _____ and Commonwealth of Massachusetts, by Midtown Managers, LLC, a limited liability company organized under the laws of Massachusetts (hereinafter referred to as the "Trustees", which term and any pronoun referring thereto shall be deemed to mean said Midtown Advisory LLC so long as it is the sole Trustee hereunder and shall be deemed to include its successors in trust hereunder and to mean the trustee or the trustees for the time being hereunder, wherever the context so permits).

ARTICLE I.—NAME OF TRUST

The Trust hereby created shall be known as the "Suburban Acres Condominium Trust" (sometimes hereinafter called the "Trust") and under that name, so far as legal, convenient and practicable, shall all business carried on by the Trustees be conducted and shall all instruments in writing by the Trustees be executed.

ARTICLE II.—THE TRUST AND ITS PURPOSE

Section 1. All of the rights and powers in and with respect to the common areas and facilities of Suburban Acres, a Condominium situated on _____ Road in Midtown, _____ County, Massachusetts, (the "Condominium"), established by a Master Deed of even date and recorded herewith, which are by virtue of provisions of Chapter 183A of the Massachusetts General Laws conferred upon or exercisable by the organization of unit owners of the Condominium, and all property, real and personal, tangible and intangible, conveyed to the Trustees hereunder shall vest in the Trustees, as joint tenants if more than one with right of survivorship as Trustees of this Trust, in trust to exercise, manage, administer and dispose of the same and to receive the income thereof for the benefit of the owners of record from time to time of the residence units (the "Units") of said Condominium, according to the percentages of beneficial interest referred to in Article IV, Section 1, hereof, and in accordance with provisions of said Chapter 183A, this Trust being the organization of the unit owners established pursuant to provisions of said Chapter 183A for the purposes therein set forth.

Section 2. It is hereby expressly declared that a trust and not a partnership has been created and that the Unit Owners are cestuis que trustent and not partners or associates nor in any other relation whatever between themselves with respect to the trust property, and hold no relation to the Trustees other than of cestuis que trustent, with only such rights as are conferred upon them as such cestuis que trustent hereunder and under and pursuant to provisions of said Chapter 183A of the General Laws.

ARTICLE III.—THE TRUSTEES

Section 1. There shall at all times be a Board of Trustees hereunder consisting of such number, not less than three nor more than seven, as shall be determined from time to time by a majority of the Unit Owners present in person or by proxy at the annual meeting of the Unit Owners (as provided in Article V, Section 78 hereof); provided, however, that until: (a) S Midtown Developers, LLC, the Declarant of said Master Deed (hereinafter the "Declarant", which term and any pronoun referring thereto herein shall be deemed to mean said Company and its successors and assigns) ceases to own any of the Units in the Condominium (including for these purposes Units in Part 1 of the Condominium and Model Units owned by Declarant or any affiliate of Declarant, as well as all Units currently contemplated or permitted to be added to the Condominium pursuant to Section 12 of the Master Deed, whether or not construction of such additional Units has yet commenced) or (b) the 2014 annual meeting of Unit Owners (the "annual meeting"), whichever of (a) or (b) shall first occur, Midtown Managers, LLC, or other entity designated by Declarant, shall be the sole Trustee hereunder, and thereupon the term of office of Midtown Managers, LLC, or such other entity so designated shall be deemed vacant, but shall not expire until such vacancy has been filled in the manner hereinafter set forth. Thereafter, the terms of office of the Trustees shall, except as hereinafter provided, be three (3) years. Such terms shall be staggered so that insofar as possible the terms of one-third (113) of the Trustees shall expire each year; provided, that in order to establish and maintain such staggering of terms, the terms of the persons first appointed as Trustees after the 2006 annual meeting shall be one (1) year, two (2) years and three (3) years, respectively, determined by lot, and thereafter upon any increase or decrease of the number of Trustees, the terms of any then newly appointed Trustee or Trustees shall be one (1) year, two (2) years, or three (3) years, determined insofar as necessary by lot, so as to maintain such staggering of terms insofar as possible.

Thereafter, if and whenever the number of such Trustees shall become less than three (3) or less than the number of Trustees last determined as aforesaid, a vacancy or vacancies in said office shall be deemed to exist. Each such vacancy shall be filled by an instrument in writing setting forth (a) the appointment of a natural person to act as such Trustee(s), signed (i) by a majority of the Trustees then in office, or the sole remaining Trustee, if only one, if the vacancy is in the office of a Trustee not chosen by the Declarant, certifying that such appointment was made by a majority of Unit Owners present in person or by proxy at a duly held meeting of Unit Owners (as provided in Article V, Section 78 hereof), or (ii) if the Declarant or such a majority of Unit Owners, as the case may be, has not within thirty (30) days after the occurrence of any such vacancy made such appointment, by a majority of the then remaining Trustees, or by the sale remaining Trustee if only one, and (b) the acceptance of such appointment signed and acknowledged by the person so appointed. If for any reason any vacancy in the office of Trustee shall continue for more than sixty (60) days and shall at the end of that time remain unfilled, a Trustee or Trustees to fill such vacancy or vacancies may be appointed by any court of competent jurisdiction upon the application of any Unit Owner and by notice to all Unit Owners and Trustees and to such other, if any, parties in interest to whom the court may direct that notice be given. With respect to each person appointed or elected as aforesaid to be a Trustee hereunder, there shall promptly be recorded with the _____ Registry of Deeds, a certificate of such appointment or election signed by anyone or more of the Trustees hereunder and an acceptance of such appointment signed by the person so appointed, and such appointment or election shall take effect upon such registration. The person so appointed or elected thereupon shall be and become such Trustee and shall be vested with the powers and titles of the Trustees, jointly with the remaining or surviving Trustees or Trustee without the necessity of any act of transfer or conveyance.

The foregoing provisions of this Section to the contrary notwithstanding, despite any vacancy in the office of Trustee, however caused and for whatever duration, the remaining or surviving Trustees, subject to the provisions of the immediately following Section, shall continue to exercise and discharge all of the powers, discretions and duties hereby conferred or imposed upon the Trustees.

Section 2. In any matters relating to the administration of the Trust hereunder and the exercise of the powers hereby conferred, the Trustees may act by a majority vote at any duly called meeting at which a quorum is present as provided in paragraph A of Section 7 of Article V; provided, however, that in no event shall a majority consist of less than two (2) Trustees hereunder, and, if and whenever the number of Trustees hereunder shall become less than two (2), the then remaining or surviving Trustees, if any, shall have no power or authority whatsoever to act with respect to the administration of the Trust hereunder or to exercise any of the powers hereby conferred except as otherwise provided in Section I of Article III. The Trustees may also act without a meeting by instrument signed by a majority of their number.

Section 3. Any Trustee may resign at any time by instrument in writing, signed and acknowledged in the manner required in Massachusetts for the acknowledgment of deeds and such resignation shall take effect upon the recording of such instrument with said Registry of Deeds. After reasonable notice and opportunity to be heard before the Board of Trustees, a Trustee (except a Trustee chosen by the Declarant) may be removed from office with or without cause by an instrument in writing signed by a majority of Unit Owners present in person or by proxy at a duly held meeting of Unit Owners (as provided in Article V, Section 7B hereof), such instrument to take effect upon the recording thereof with said Registry of Deeds.

Section 4. Except as otherwise provided in Article V, Section 3 hereof, no Trustee named or appointed as hereinbefore provided, whether as original Trustee or as successor to or as substitute for another, shall be obliged to give any bond or surety or other security for the performance of any of his duties hereunder, provided, however, that Unit Owners may at any time by instrument in writing signed by a majority of Unit Owners present in person or by proxy at a duly held meeting of Unit Owners (as provided in Article V, Section 7B hereof), and delivered to the Trustee or Trustees affected, require that anyone or more of the Trustees shall give bond in such amount and with such sureties as shall be specified in such instrument. All expenses incident to any such bond shall be charged as a common expense of the Condominium.

Section 5. No Trustee hereinbefore named or appointed as hereinbefore provided shall under any circumstances or in any event be held liable or accountable out of his personal assets or be deprived of compensation by reason of any action taken, suffered or omitted in good faith or be so liable or accountable for more money or other property than he actually receives, or for allowing one or more of the other Trustees to have possession of the Trust books or property, or be so liable, accountable or deprived by reason of honest errors of judgment or mistakes of fact or law, or by reason of the existence of any personal or adverse interest, or by reason of anything except his own personal and willful malfeasance and defaults.

Section 6. No Trustee shall be disqualified by holding such office from contracting or dealing with the Trustees or with one or more Unit Owners (whether directly or indirectly because of his interest individually or the Trustees' interest, or any Unit Owner's interest in any corporation, firm, trust or other organization connected with such contracting or dealing, or because of any other reason), as vendor, purchaser or otherwise, nor shall any such dealing, contract or arrangement entered into in respect of this Trust in which any Trustee so dealing or contracting or being so interested be liable to account for any profit realized by any such dealing, contract or arrangement by reason of such Trustee's holding office, or of the fiduciary relation hereby established, provided the Trustee shall act in good faith and shall disclose the nature of his interest before the dealing, contract or arrangement is entered into.

Section 7. The Trustees and each of them shall be entitled to indemnity both out of the Trust property and by the Unit Owners against any liability incurred by them or any of them in the execution hereof, including, without limiting the generality of the foregoing, liabilities in contract and in tort and liabilities for damages, penalties and fines. Each Unit Owner shall be personally liable for (i) all sums lawfully assessed for his share of the common expenses of the Condominium, and the same shall constitute a lien upon his Unit, (ii) all sums lawfully assessed for his share of the costs and expenses relating to exclusive common areas and facilities of the Condominium as to which he has been granted rights pursuant to Section 7 of said Master Deed, and the same shall constitute a lien upon his unit, and (iii) his proportionate share of any claim involving the Trust property in excess thereof, all as provided in Sections 6 and 13 of said Chapter 183A. Nothing contained in this paragraph shall be deemed, however, to limit in any respect the powers granted to the

Trustees in this instrument.

ARTICLE IV.—BENEFICIARIES AND THE BENEFICIAL INTEREST IN THE TRUST

Section 1. The cestuis que trustent or beneficiaries shall be the Unit Owners of the Condominium for the time being. The beneficial interest in the Trust hereunder shall be divided among the Unit Owners in the percentage of undivided beneficial interest appertaining to the Units of the Condominium as follows:

A. For so long as the only Units in the Condominium are those comprised in Phase I of the Condominium as defined in said Master Deed, the percentages set forth for such Units in Exhibit C annexed to the Master Deed, which is hereby incorporated herein and made a part hereof.

B. From and after the inclusion in the Condominium of other Phases, subphases or Addition(s) to the Condominium as defined in said Master Deed, the beneficial interest hereunder of each Unit then included in the Condominium shall be equal to the percentage of interest appertaining to such Unit as determined and specified pursuant to provisions of Section 13 of said Master Deed.

Section 2. The beneficial interest of each Unit of the Condominium shall be held and exercised as a unit and shall not be divided among several owners of any such Unit. To that end, whenever any of said Units is owned of record by more than one person, the several owners of such Unit shall (a) determine and designate which one of such owners shall be authorized and entitled to cast votes, execute instruments and otherwise exercise the rights appertaining to such Unit hereunder, and (b) notify the Trustees of such designation by a notice in writing signed by all of the record owners of such Unit. Any such designation shall take effect upon receipt by the Trustees and may be changed at any time and from time to time by notice as aforesaid. In the absence of any such notice of designation, the Trustees may, by majority vote, designate anyone such owner for such purposes.

ARTICLE V.—BY-LAWS

The provisions of this Article shall constitute the By-Laws of this Trust and the organization of Unit Owners established hereby, to wit:

Section 1. POWERS OF THE TRUSTEES.

The Trustees shall, subject to and in accordance with all applicable provisions of said Chapter 183A and said Master

Deed, have the absolute control, management and disposition of the Trust property (which term as herein used shall insofar as apt be deemed to include the common areas and facilities of the Condominium) as if they were the absolute owners thereof, free from the control of the Unit Owners and, without by the following enumeration limiting the generality of the foregoing or of any item in the enumeration, with full power and uncontrolled discretion, subject only to the limitations and conditions hereof and of provisions of said Chapter 183A and said Master Deed, at any time and from time to time, and without the necessity of applying to any court or to the Unit Owners for leave so to do:

(i) To retain the Trust property, or any part or parts thereof, in the same form or forms of investment in which received or acquired by them so far and so long as they shall think fit, without liability for any loss resulting therefrom;

(ii) To sell, assign, convey, transfer, exchange, and otherwise deal with or dispose of, the Trust property, or any part or parts thereof, free and discharged of any and all trusts, at public or private sale, to any person or persons, for cash or on credit, and in such manner, on such items and for such considerations and subject to such restrictions, stipulations, agreements and reservations as they shall deem proper, including the power to take back mortgages to secure the whole or any part of the purchase price of any of the Trust property sold or transferred by them, and to execute and deliver any deed or other instrument in connection with the foregoing;

(iii) To purchase or otherwise acquire title to, and to rent, lease or hire from others, for terms which may extend beyond the termination of this Trust, any property or rights to property, real or personal, and to own, manage, use and hold such property and such rights;

(iv) To borrow or in any other manner raise such sum or sums of money or other property as they shall deem advisable in any manner and on any terms, and to evidence the same by notes, bonds, securities or other evidence of indebtedness, which may mature at a time or times, even beyond the possible duration of this Trust, and to execute and deliver any mortgage, pledge, or other instrument to secure any such borrowing;

(v) To enter into any arrangement for the use or occupation of the Trust property, or any part or parts thereof, including, without thereby limiting the generality of the foregoing, leases, subleases, easements, licenses, or conces-

sions, upon such terms and conditions and with such stipulations and agreements as they shall deem desirable,
even if the same extend beyond the possible duration of
this Trust;

(vi) To invest and reinvest the Trust property, or any
part or parts thereof and from time to time and as often as
they shall see fit to change investments, including power
to invest in all types of securities and other property, of
whatsoever nature and however denominated, all to such
extent as to them shall seem proper, and without liability
for loss, even though such property or such investments
shall be of a character or in an amount not customarily
considered proper for the investment of trust funds, or
which does or may not produce income;

(vii) To obtain and maintain such casualty and liability
insurance on and with respect to the Trust property as
they shall deem necessary or proper;

(viii) To provide for payment by the Trust of real estate
taxes becoming due and payable after the date of recording of the master deed which are assessed upon all of the
land and/or improvements included within the Condominium, instead of upon individual Units and their proportionate interests in the common areas and facilities and to
levy, at the Trustees' election, an equitable assessment of
said tax payments among the individual Unit Owners;

(ix) To incur such liabilities, obligations and expenses,
and to pay from the principal or the income of the Trust
property in their hands all such sums, as they shall deem
necessary or proper for the furtherance of the purposes of
the Trust;

(x) To determine as to all sums of money and other
things of value received by them, whether and to what
extent the same shall be deemed to be and shall be accounted for as principal or as income, and as to all charges
or expenses paid by them, whether and to what extent the
same shall be charged against principal or against income,
including, without hereby limiting the generality of the
foregoing, power to apportion any receipt or expense between principal and income, and power to determine what
portion, if any, of the actual income received upon any asset purchased or acquired at a premium or any wasting
investment shall be added to principal to prevent a diminution thereof upon the maturity or exhaustion of such asset or investment;

(xi) To vote in such manner as they shall think fit any
or all shares in any corporation or trust which shall be

comprised in the Trust property, and for that purpose to give proxies, to any person or persons or to one or more of their number, to vote, waive any notice or otherwise act in respect of any such shares;

(xii) To guarantee performance of the obligations of others in any cases where they shall deem that it is to the advantage of this Trust that they give such guaranty;

(xiii) To maintain such offices and other places of business as they shall deem necessary or proper and to engage in business in Massachusetts or elsewhere;

(xiv) To provide and contract for maintenance, repair, cleaning and other services to owners of Units in the Condominium; provided if and to the extent that the Trust receives from a cable television company, or the like, compensation, payment or reimbursement for the acquisition or use of the cable television systems, wiring or facilities installed as common facilities of the Condominium, the Trust, from said funds, will reimburse the Declarant of the Master Deed for Declarant's cost of installation of said cable television systems, wiring or facilities;

(xv) To employ, appoint and remove such agents, managers, officers, board of managers, brokers, employees, servants, assistants and counsel (which counsel may be a firm of which one or more of the Trustees are members) as they shall deem proper, for the purchase, sale or management of the Trust property, or any part or parts thereof, or for conducting the business of the Trust and may define their respective duties and fix and pay their such designation by a notice in writing signed by all of the record owners of such Unit. Any such designation shall take effect upon receipt by the Trustees and may be changed at any time and from time to time by notice as aforesaid. In the absence of any such notice of designation, the Trustees may, by majority vote, designate anyone such owner for such purposes.

ARTICLE V.—BY-LAWS

The provisions of this Article shall constitute the By-Laws of this Trust and the organization of Unit Owners established hereby, to wit:

Section 1. POWERS OF THE TRUSTEES

The Trustees shall, subject to and in accordance with all applicable provisions of said Chapter 183A and said Master Deed, have the absolute control, management and disposition of the Trust property (which term as herein used shall insofar as apt be deemed to include the common areas and facilities of the Condominium) as if they were the absolute owners thereof, free from the control of the Unit Owners and, without by the following enumeration limiting the generality of the foregoing or of any item in the enumeration, with full power and uncontrolled discretion, subject only to the limitations and conditions hereof and of provisions of said Chapter 183A and said Master Deed, at any time and from time to time, and without the necessity of applying to any court or to the Unit Owners for leave so to do:

(i) To retain the Trust property, or any part or parts thereof, in the same form or forms of investment in which received or acquired by them so far and so long as they shall think fit, without liability for any loss resulting therefrom;

(ii) To sell, assign, convey, transfer, exchange, and otherwise deal with or dispose of, the Trust property, or any part or parts thereof, free and discharged of any and all trusts, at public or private sale, to any person or persons, for cash or on credit, and in such manner, on such items and for such considerations and subject to such restrictions, stipulations, agreements and reservations as they shall deem proper, including the power to take back mortgages to secure the whole or any part of the purchase price of any of the Trust property sold or transferred by them, and to execute and deliver any deed or other instrument in connection with the foregoing;

(iii) To purchase or otherwise acquire title to, and to rent, lease or hire from others, for terms which may extend beyond the termination of this Trust, any property or rights to property, real or personal, and to own, manage, use and hold such property and such rights;

(iv) To borrow or in any other manner raise such sum or sums of money or other property as they shall deem advisable in any manner and on any terms, and to evidence the same by notes, bonds, securities or other evidence of indebtedness, which may mature at a time or times, even beyond the possible duration of this Trust, and to execute and deliver any mortgage, pledge, or other instrument to secure any such borrowing;

(v) To enter into any arrangement for the use or occupation of the Trust property, or any part or parts thereof, including, without thereby limiting the generality of the foregoing, leases, subleases, easements, licenses, or concessions, upon such terms and conditions and with such stipulations and agreements as they shall deem desirable, even if the same extend beyond the possible duration of this Trust;

(vi) To invest and reinvest the Trust property, or any part or parts thereof and from time to time and as often as they shall see fit to change investments, including power to invest in all types of securities and other property, of whatsoever nature and however denominated, all to such extent as to them shall seem proper, and without liability for loss, even though such property or such investments shall be of a character or in an amount not customarily considered proper for the investment of trust funds, or which does or may not produce income;

(vii) To obtain and maintain such casualty and liability insurance on and with respect to the Trust property as they shall deem necessary or proper;

(viii) To provide for payment by the Trust of real estate taxes becoming due and payable after the date of recording of the master deed which are assessed upon all of the land and/or improvements included within the Condominium, instead of upon individual Units and their proportionate interests in the common areas and facilities and to levy, at the Trustees' election, an equitable assessment of said tax payments among the individual Unit Owners;

(ix) To incur such liabilities, obligations and expenses, and to pay from the principal or the income of the Trust property in their hands all such sums, as they shall deem necessary or proper for the furtherance of the purposes of the Trust;

(x) To determine as to all sums of money and other things of value received by them, whether and to what extent the same shall be deemed to be and shall be accounted for as principal or as income, and as to all charges or expenses paid by them, whether and to what extent the same shall be charged against principal or against income, including, without hereby limiting the generality of the foregoing, power to apportion any receipt or expense between principal and income, and power to determine what portion, if any, of the actual income received upon any asset purchased or acquired at a premium or any wasting investment shall be added to principal to prevent a diminution thereof upon the maturity or exhaustion of such asset or investment;

(xi) To vote in such manner as they shall think fit any or all shares in any corporation or trust which shall be comprised in the Trust property, and for that purpose to give proxies, to any person or persons or to one or more of their number, to vote, waive any notice or otherwise act in respect of any such shares;

(xii) To guarantee performance of the obligations of others in any cases where they shall deem that it is to the advantage of this Trust that they give such guaranty;

(xiii) To maintain such offices and other places of business as they shall deem necessary or proper and to engage in business in Massachusetts or elsewhere;

(xiv) To provide and contract for maintenance, repair, cleaning and other services to owners of Units in the Condominium; provided if and to the extent that the Trust receives from a cable television company, or the like, compensation, payment or reimbursement for the acquisition or use of the cable television systems, wiring or facilities installed as common facilities of the Condominium, the Trust, from said funds, will reimburse the Declarant of the Master Deed for Declarant's cost of installation of said cable television systems, wiring or facilities;

(xv) To employ, appoint and remove such agents, managers, officers, board of managers, brokers, employees, servants, assistants and counsel (which counsel may be a firm of which one or more of the Trustees are members) as they shall deem proper, for the purchase, sale or management of the Trust property, or any part or parts thereof, or for conducting the business of the Trust and may define their respective duties and fix and pay their compensation, and the Trustees shall not be answerable for the acts and defaults of any such person. Any agreement for professional management of the Condominium, or any other contract providing for services of the Declarant thereof, may not exceed three (3) years and any such agreement shall provide for termination by either party without cause and without payment of a termination fee on ninety (90) days or less written notice. The Trustees may delegate to any such agent, manager, officer, board, broker, employee, servant, assistant or counsel any or all of their powers (including discretionary power, except that the power to join in amending, altering, adding to, terminating or changing this Declaration of Trust and the trust hereby created shall not be delegated) all for such times and purposes as they shall deem proper. Without hereby limiting the generality of the foregoing, the Trustees shall, at least as often as annually, designate from their number a Chairman, a Treasurer, a Secretary, and such other officers of the Board of Trustees as the Trustees deem fit, and may from time to time designate one or more of their own number to be the Managing Trustee or Managing Trustees, for the management and administration of the Trust property and the business of the Trust, or any part or parts thereof;

(xvi) To effect the compliance of the Condominium premises and of the Units and Unit Owners with applicable provisions of law, governmental regulations, permits and approvals, restrictions and agreements of record, and other provisions affecting or applicable to the conduct of the Condominium Trust; and

(xvii) Generally, in all matters not herein otherwise specified, to control, manage and dispose of the Trust property as if the Trustees were the absolute owners thereof and to do any and all acts, including the execution of any instruments, which by their performance thereof shall be shown to be in their judgment for the best interest of the Unit Owners; and the Trustees shall have, without limitation, all of the rights and powers set forth in said Chapter 183A and the Trustees shall by the exercise and fulfillment of the powers and provisions set forth in this Article V provide for the necessary work of maintenance, repair and replacement of the common areas and facilities and payment therefore, including the approval of payment vouchers.

Section 2. COMMON EXPENSES, PROFITS AND FUNDS

A. The Unit Owners shall be liable for common expenses and entitled to common profits of the Condominium in proportion to their respective percentages of beneficial interest as described in Article IV hereof and as set forth in said Exhibit C, except that separate provision has been made in Section 6 of said Master Deed for the payment of or reimbursement for certain costs and expenses relating to those common areas and facilities of the Condominium the exclusive use of which is reserved to one or more (but not all) of the owners of Units pursuant to Section 6 of said Master Deed. The Trustees may at any time or times distribute common profits among the Unit Owners in such proportions. The Trustees may, to such extent as they deem advisable, set aside common funds of the Condominium as reserve or contingent funds, and may use the funds so set aside for reduction of indebtedness or other lawful capital purpose, or, subject to the provisions of the following Sections 3 and 4, for repair, rebuilding or restoration of the Trust property or for improvements thereto, and the funds so set aside shall not be deemed to be common profits available for distribution.

B. At least thirty (30) days prior to the commencement of

each fiscal year of this Trust, and within thirty (30) days after the execution hereof with respect to the portion of a fiscal year then remaining, the Trustees shall estimate the common expenses expected to be incurred during such fiscal year together with a reasonable provision for contingencies and reserves, and after taking into account any undistributed common profits from prior years, shall determine the assessment to be made for such fiscal year. The Trustees shall promptly render statements to the Unit Owners for their respective shares of such assessments, according to their percentages of interest in the common areas and facilities, and such statements shall, unless otherwise provided herein, be due and payable within thirty (30) days after the same are rendered. In the event that the Trustees shall determine during any fiscal year that the assessment so made is less than the common expenses actually incurred, or in the reasonable opinion of the Trustees likely to be incurred, the Trustees shall make a supplemental assessment or assessments and render statements therefore in the manner aforesaid, and such statements shall be payable and take effect as aforesaid. The Trustees may in their discretion provide for payments of statements in monthly or other installments. In the event any Unit Owner shall fail to make prompt payment of his common expenses, such Unit Owner shall be obligated to pay interest at a rate equal to eighteen percent (18%) (but in no event higher than the highest rate permitted by law) on such unpaid common expenses computed from the due date thereof, together with all expenses, including, without limitation, attorneys' fees, paid or incurred in any proceeding brought to collect such unpaid common expenses or in an action to enforce the lien on such Unit arising from such unpaid common expenses, and all of the foregoing shall constitute common expenses for such Unit and shall be secured by a lien on such Unit. The Trustees shall have the right to institute all proceedings deemed necessary or desirable by the Trustees to recover such unpaid common expenses, together with interest thereon computed as aforesaid and the expenses paid or incurred in connection with any such proceeding as aforesaid.

If, in any action brought by the Trustees to enforce a lien on a Unit because of unpaid common expenses, the lien shall be foreclosed, then for such period as the Unit Owner shall continue to use such Unit, the Unit Owner shall be required to pay a reasonable rental for the use of this Unit and the plaintiff in such action shall be entitled to the appointment of a receiver to collect the same. The Trustees, acting on behalf of all Unit Owners shall have the power to purchase such Unit at the foreclosure sale and to hold, lease, mortgage, conveyor otherwise deal with the same, except as otherwise provided in this Trust. A suit to recover a money judgment for unpaid common expenses shall be maintainable without enforcing or waiving the lien securing the same.

C. The Trustees shall expend common funds only for common expenses and lawful purposes permitted hereby and by provisions of said Chapter 183A.

Section 3. INSURANCE

A. The Trustees shall obtain and maintain, to the extent available, master policies of casualty and physical damage insurance for the benefit and protection of the Trustees and all of the Unit Owners, naming as the named insureds, and with loss proceeds payable to, the Trustees hereunder, or one or more of the Trustees hereunder designated by them, as Insurance Trustees for all of the Unit Owners collectively of the Condominium and their respective mortgagees, as their interests may appear, pursuant to such standard condominium property endorsement form as may from time to time be customarily used in Massachusetts, such insurance to cover the building and all other insurable improvements forming part of the common areas and facilities, including the heating equipment and other service machinery, apparatus, equipment and installations comprised in the common areas and facilities, and also all such portions and elements of the Units as are for insurance purposes normally deemed to constitute part of the Buildings and customarily covered by such insurance; but not including (i) the furniture, furnishings or other personal property of the Unit Owners, or (H) improvements within a Unit made by the Owners thereof, as to which it shall be the separate responsibility of the Unit Owners to insure.

Such insurance shall insofar as practicable be maintained in an amount equal to not less than one hundred percent (100%) of the full replacement value (exclusive of foundations), as determined by the Trustees (who shall review such value at least as often as annually), of the insured property, and shall insure against (a) loss or damage by fire and other hazards covered by the standard extended coverage endorsement, and (b) such other hazards or risks as the Trustees from time to time in their discretion shall determine to be appropriate, including, but not limited to, vandalism, malicious mischief, windstorm and water damage, and machinery explosion or damage. Such insurance may provide for a reasonable deductible amount from the coverage thereof, as determined by the Trustees in their reasonable discretion. In the event of any loss which related solely to the common areas and facilities, such deductible amount may be assessed to all Unit Owners as a special assessment of common expenses hereunder. In the event of any loss which relates in whole or in part to insurable improvements forming a part of a Unit, which loss is covered by such insurance, the Trustees may assess to the Owner of such Unit, as a special assessment, all or part of such deductible amount, such special assessment being in an amount directly proportional to the amount of such loss related to such Unit improvements and the amount of the loss related to the common areas and facilities. Unit Owners shall be liable for such special assessments in addition to their respective shares of the common expenses, and until such charges are paid by such Unit Owners, the same shall constitute a lien against their Units pursuant to the provisions of Section 6 of said Chapter 183A.

B. All policies of casualty or physical damage insurance shall insofar as practicable provide (a) that such policies may not be cancelled, terminated or substantially modified as to amount of coverage or risks covered without at least thirty (30) days' written notice to the insureds, (b) that, notwithstanding any provisions thereof which give the insurer the right to elect to restore damage in lieu of making a cash settlement, such election may not be exercisable without the approval of the Trustees and may not be exercisable if in conflict with the terms of said Chapter 183A, the Trust or these By-Laws, (c) for waiver of subrogation as to any claims (except claims involving arson or fraud) against the Trust, the Trustees, the manager, agents, employees, the Unit Owners and their respective employees, agents and guests, (d) for waivers of any defense based upon the conduct of any insured, and (e) in substance and effect that the insurer shall not be entitled to contribution as against any casualty insurance which may be purchased separately by Unit Owners.

C. The Trustee or Trustees hereunder designated as Insurance Trustee or Trustees as aforesaid shall collect and receive all casualty loss insurance proceeds and shall hold, use, apply and disburse the same in accordance with applicable provisions of the following Section 4 of this Article V. With respect to losses which affect portions or elements covered by such insurance of a Unit, or of more than one Unit to substantially the same or to different extents, the proceeds relating thereto shall be used, applied and disbursed by the Trustees in a fair and equitable manner.

D. The Trustees shall also so obtain and maintain, to the

extent available, master policies or insurance with respect to the common areas and facilities, for the benefit and protection of the Trustees and all of the Unit Owners, for:

(a) comprehensive public liability in such limits as the Trustees may, from time to time determine, but at least in the amount of $1,000,000.00 per occurrence for personal injury and/or property damage, cover the Trust, each Trustee, the managing agent, the manager and each Unit Owner with respect to liability arising out of ownership, maintenance or repair of those portions of the Condominium not reserved for exclusive use by the Owner or Owners of a single Unit, such insurance to provide for cross claims by the co-insureds. Such insurance policy shall contain a "severability of interest" endorsement which shall preclude the insurer from denying the claim of a Unit Owner because of negligent acts of the Trustees of other Unit Owners. The scope of coverage shall include all other coverage in the kinds and amounts required by private institutional mortgage investors for projects similar in construction, location and use;

(b) fidelity coverage against dishonest acts on the part of managers, Trustees, employees or volunteers responsible for handling funds belonging to or administered by the Trustees. The fidelity bond or insurance shall name the Trust as the named insured and shall be written in an amount sufficient to provide protection which is in no event less than one and one-half times the insured's estimated annual operating expenses including reserves. In connection with such coverage, an appropriate endorsement to the policy to cover any persons who serve without compensation shall be added if the policy would not otherwise cover volunteers;

(c) worker's compensation and employees' liability with respect to any manager, agent or employee of the Trust, but excluding any independent agent or manager;

(d) directors' and officers' liability with respect to the Trustees, in such amount as the Trustees may from time to time determine;

(e) non-owned automobile liability, in such amount as the Trustees may from time to time determine; and

(f) to insure such other risks as the Trustees in their discretion deem it appropriate to insure.

E. Subject to the requirements of applicable insurance and other law, all insurance maintained under this Section 3 shall be in such amounts and forms as the Trustees shall in their discretion deem appropriate (consistent, however, with the requirements set forth hereinabove), shall, insofar as practicable, be carried with reputable insurance companies (satisfying in all material respects applicable requirements of the Federal Unit Loan Mortgage Corporation), and shall, insofar as practicable, contain provisions as above set forth in this Section 3 with respect to non-cancellation, notice, waiver of subornation, waiver of defense based on conduct of any insured, and noncontribution. Certificates evidencing all or any portion of the insurance carried pursuant to the provisions of this Section 3, with such proper mortgagee endorsements as may be requested, shall be furnished to any Unit Owner or Unit mortgagee requesting to be furnished with the same.

F. The cost of all such insurance obtained and maintained by the Trustees pursuant to provisions of this Section 3 shall be a common expense of the Condominium.

Section 4. REBUILDING AND RESTORATION, IMPROVEMENTS

A. In the event of any casualty loss to the common areas and facilities, the Trustees shall determine in their reasonable discretion whether or not such loss exceeds ten percent (10%) of the value of the Condominium immediately prior to the casualty, and shall notify all Unit Owners of such determination. If such loss as so determined does not exceed ten percent (10%) of such value, the Trustees shall proceed with the necessary repairs, rebuilding or restoration in the manner provided in paragraph (a) of Section 17 of said Chapter 183A. If such loss as so determined does exceed ten percent (10%) of such value, the Trustees shall forthwith submit to all Unit Owners (a) a form of agreement (which may be in several counterparts) by the Unit Owners authorizing the Trustees to proceed with the necessary repair, rebuilding or restoration, and (b) a copy of the provisions of said Section 17; and the Trustees shall thereafter proceed in accordance with, and take such further action as they may in their discretion deem advisable in order to implement the provisions of Paragraph (b) of said Section 17. With respect to all rebuilding or restoration, it shall be the responsibility and obligation of each Unit Owner, as well as of the Trustees, to collect all such insurance proceeds as are applicable and to apply, contribute and pay over such proceeds to defer the costs of such rebuilding or restoration in a fair and equitable manner.

B. If and whenever the Trustees shall propose to make any improvement to the common areas and facilities of the Condominium, or shall be requested in writing by the Unit

Owners holding twenty-five percent (25%) or more of the beneficial interest in this Trust to make any such improvement, the Trustees shall submit to all Unit Owners (a) a form of agreement (which may be in several counterparts) specifying the improvement or improvements proposed to be made and the estimated cost thereof, and authorizing the Trustees to proceed to make the same, and (b) a copy of the provisions of Section 18 of said Chapter 183A. Upon the first to occur of (i) the receipt by the Trustees of such agreement signed by Unit Owners holding seventy-five percent (75%) or more of the beneficial interest, or (ii) the expiration of ninety (90) days after such agreement was first submitted to the Unit Owners, the Trustees shall notify all Unit Owners of the aggregate percentage of beneficial interest held by Unit Owners who have then signed such agreement. If such percentage exceeds seventy-five percent (75%), the Trustees shall proceed to make the improvement or improvements specified in such agreement, charging all Unit Owners in the same proportion as they contribute to the common expenses. If such percentage exceeds fifty percent (50%), but is less than seventy-five percent (75%), the Trustees shall resubmit the form agreement to those Unit Owners who originally assented thereto, and if the agreement is then signed by Unit Owners holding fifty percent (50%) or more of the beneficial interest, the Trustees shall proceed to make the improvement or improvements specified in such agreement, charging each Unit Owner who has so assented pro rata based upon such Unit Owner's beneficial interest in this Trust as a percentage of the aggregate percentage of beneficial interest in this Trust held by Unit Owners who have signed such agreement; for example, for purposes of illustration only, if such aggregate percentage is sixty percent (60%) and if an assenting Unit Owner has a beneficial interest in this Trust of 20%. such Unit Owner shall be charged with 30% of such improvement or improvements.

C. Notwithstanding anything in the preceding Paragraphs A and B contained, (a) in the event that any Unit Owner or Unit Owners shall by notice in writing to the Trustees dissent from any determination of the Trustees with respect to the value of the Condominium or any other determination or action of the Trustees under said Paragraphs A and B, and such dispute shall not be resolved within thirty (30) days after such notice, then either the Trustees or the dissenting Unit Owner or Unit Owners may submit the matter to arbitration, and for that purpose one arbitrator shall be designated by the Trustees, one by the dissenting Unit Owner or Unit Owners and a third by the two arbitrators so designated, and such arbitration shall be conducted in accordance with the rules and procedures of the American Arbitration Association, and (b) the Trustees shall not in any event be obliged to proceed with any repair, rebuilding or restoration, or any improvement, unless and until they have received funds in an amount equal to the estimate of the Trustees of all costs thereof.

D. If and whenever any Unit Owner (other than the Declarant) shall propose to make an improvement or alteration to or affecting the common areas and facilities of the Condominium at such Unit Owner's own expense, and the Trustees determine in their reasonable discretion that such improvement would be consistent and compatible with the provisions and intent of said Master Deed, the Trustees may, but shall not be obligated to, authorize such improvement or alteration to be made at the sole expense of the Unit Owner proposing such improvement or alteration as the Trustees in their reasonable discretion deem to be necessary or desirable in the circumstances.

Section 5. UNIT FIRST MORTGAGES

Notwithstanding anything to the contrary contained herein:

A. A Unit Owner who mortgages his or her Unit shall notify the Trustees of the name and address, and any changes therein, of the first mortgagee of such Unit. The Trustees shall maintain such information in a separate book. All provisions herein and in the Master Deed calling for notice to be given to (or for consent to be obtained from) mortgagees or mortgage holders shall relate to and require only the giving by United States mail (postage prepaid) of such notice to (and obtaining such consent from) the holders of Unit first mortgages of record for which such information has been provided to the Trustees. Upon written request from such a first mortgagee to the Trustees, a copy of any notice to be given by the Trustees to such first mortgagee also shall be given at the same time and in the same fashion to a suitably identified governmental insurer or guarantor of such mortgagee's mortgage and any suitably identified servicer thereof on behalf of the Federal Home Loan Mortgage Corporation. For the purposes of notices which may be given to the Trustees and other insureds by any insurance carrier, the Trustees shall notify the Trustees' insurance agent placing insurance for the benefit of Unit Owners at the Condominium of the names and addresses of such unit first mortgagees, insurers, guarantors, and servicers, which the Trustees have been requested to notify in accordance with the foregoing.

B. The Trustees, whenever so requested by the first mortgagee of a Unit, shall promptly provide to such mortgagee a written notification of any then unpaid common charges due from, or any other default by, the owner of the mortgaged Unit if any such default is not cured within sixty (60) days of notice of same to the Unit Owner.

C. Except as provided by said Chapter 183 of the General Laws in case of condemnation or substantial loss to the Units and/or common elements of the Condominium, unless at least sixty-six and two-thirds percent (66 2/3%) of the first mortgagees (based upon one vote for each first mortgage owned), or Owners of Units (other than Declarant) have given their prior written approval, said Trust shall not be entitled to:

(1) by act or omission, seek to abandon or terminate the Condominium regime;

(2) except as provided in said Master Deed in connection with Addition(s) (as defined in the Master Deed) to the Condominium, change the pro rata interest or obligations of any Unit for the purpose of (i) levying assessments or charges, (ii) allocating distributions of hazard insurance proceeds or condemnation awards, or (iii) determining the pro rata share of ownership of each Unit in the common areas and facilities;

(3) partition or subdivide any Unit;

(4) except as provided in said Master Deed, by act or omission, seek to abandon, partition, subdivide, encumber, sell, or transfer the common areas and facilities. The provisions of this subparagraph (4) shall not apply to such acts or omission in connection with Addition(s) to the Condominium (including, without limitation, the financing and construction thereof) or to the granting of easements for public utilities or for other public purposes consistent with the intended use of the common areas and facilities by the Condominium; or

(5) use hazard insurance proceeds for losses to any Condominium property (whether to Units or the common areas and facilities) for other than the repair, replacement or reconstruction of such Condominium property.

D. All taxes, assessments and charges which may become liens prior to a first mortgage on a Unit under Massachusetts laws shall relate only to the individual Units and not to the Condominium as a whole.

E. Any first mortgagee who obtains title to a Unit pursuant to the remedies provided in its mortgage or foreclosure of its mortgage will not be liable for more than six (6) months of such Unit's Condominium common expenses which accrue prior to such acquisition of title to such Unit by such mortgagee.

F. No Unit Owner, or any other party, shall have a priority over any rights of the first mortgagee of a Unit pursuant to its mortgage in the case of a distribution to such Unit Owner of insurance proceeds or condemnation awards for losses to or a taking of Units and/or common areas and facilities.

G. If the Federal Home Loan Mortgage Corporation ("FHLMC") shall own in whole or in part a mortgage of any Unit in the Condominium, the Trustees, on behalf of the Trust, shall give written notice to FHLMC (c/o its servicer at servicer's address) of any loss to or taking of common areas and facilities if such loss or taking exceeds $10,000.00 or of any damage to such Unit if such damage exceeds $1,000.00.

H. Unit assessments for common charges shall include an adequate reserve fund for maintenance, repairs and replacement of the common areas and facilities that must be replaced on a periodic basis and the Trustees shall so set aside and reserve such funds.

I. The Declarant reserves the right and power (but shall have no obligation) to record a special amendment to this Master Deed and the By-laws at any time and from time to time in order to conform the same to requirements of FHLMC, and also to insert herein and in the By-laws such provisions as may be required to qualify mortgages of Units in the Condominium for sale to the Federal Mortgage Association (FNMA), or to induce either FHLMC or FNMA to make, purchase, sell, insure, or guarantee first mortgages on Units. In furtherance of the foregoing, a power coupled with an interest is hereby reserved by and granted to the Declarant to vote in favor of, make, or consent to any such special amendment on behalf of each Unit Owner. Each deed, mortgage, or other instrument affecting a Unit and the acceptance thereof, shall be deemed to be a grant to, acknowledge of and consent to the reservation of, the power of Declarant to vote in favor of, make, execute and record any such special amendment. The right of the Declarant to act pursuant to rights reserved and granted under this subsection shall terminate when the Declarant no longer owns a Unit.

Section 6. RESTRICTIONS, REQUIREMENTS, RULES

AND REGULATIONS

The use of the Condominium and each Unit shall be restricted to and shall be in accordance with the provisions of said Master Deed, this Trust (including the By-Laws and, as to the common areas and facilities, such administrative rules and regulations as the Trustees may adopt pursuant to this Trust), all applicable laws, zoning ordinances, rules, regulations and requirements of all governmental bodies having jurisdiction over the Condominium or the use and occupancy thereof, and restrictions and agreements of record and other provisions affecting or applicable to the Condominium or the Units or the Unit Owners. The Trustees may eliminate any violation of any such provisions and the cost and expense of eliminating same shall constitute a common expense; except, however, that if a violation is caused in whole or in part by any Unit Owner, his family, servants, employees, agents, visitors, lessees, or licensees, the cost and expense of eliminating such violation, or such portion of such cost and expense as the Trustees may determine, shall be charged to the Unit of such Unit Owner, and shall constitute a portion of such Unit Owner's common expenses which shall be payable by the Unit Owner of such Unit upon demand and until same is paid by such Unit Owner, shall constitute a lien against such Unit pursuant to the provisions of this paragraph and section 6 of said Chapter 183A. The Trustees have adopted the Rules and Regulations (the "Rules and Regulations"), set forth in Schedule A annexed hereto, containing such restrictions on the requirements respecting the use and maintenance of the Units and the use of the common areas and facilities as are consistent with provisions of said Master Deed and are designed to prevent unreasonable interference with the use by Unit Owners of their Units and of the common areas and facilities. The Rules and Regulations are hereby expressly made a part of and incorporated by this reference into the By-Laws of this Trust.

The Trustees may at any time and from time to time amend, alter, add to or change the Rules and Regulations in accordance with the provisions of Section 1 of Article VII of this Trust. The Trustees shall have the non-delegable right at any time and from time to time to adopt, amend and rescind administrative rules and regulations governing the details of the operation and use of the common areas and facilities (including, without limitation, common areas and facilities the exclusive benefit of which is for one or more Units), provided same are not inconsistent with the Rules and Regulations set forth in Schedule A hereto. A majority of the Unit Owners present in person or by proxy at a duly held meeting of Unit Owners (as provided in Section 7B of this Article V) may overrule the Trustees. Copies of such administrative rules and regulations and any amendments thereof shall be furnished by the Trustees to each Unit Owner not less than fifteen (15) days prior to the effective date thereof.

The Rules and Regulations, as from time to time amended, and the administrative rules and regulations of the Trustees shall be enforced by the Trustees. The Trustees may eliminate any violation of any such Rules and Regulations and the cost and expense of eliminating same shall be chargeable to the Unit Owner who himself or whose family, servants, employees, agents, visitors, lessees, licensees, or pets are responsible for such violation and shall constitute a portion of such Unit Owner's common expenses which shall be payable by the Unit Owner of such Unit upon demand and until same is paid by such Unit Owner shall constitute a lien against such Unit pursuant to the provisions of this paragraph and Section of said Chapter 183A. The Trustees may also fine such Unit Owner for such violations and such fine shall constitute a portion of such Unit Owner's common expenses which shall be payable by the Unit Owner of such Unit upon demand and until same is paid by such Unit Owner shall constitute a lien against such Unit pursuant to the provisions of this paragraph and Section 6 of said Chapter 183A.

Section 7. MEETINGS

A. The Board of Trustees shall meet annually on the date of the annual meeting of the Unit Owners and at such meeting shall elect the Chairman, Treasurer, and Secretary hereinbefore provided for. Other meetings may be called by the Chairman and in such other manner as the Trustees may establish, provided, however, that written notice of each meeting stating the place, day and hour thereof shall be given at least four days before such meeting to each member of the Board of Trustees. One half (1/2) of the number of Trustees shall constitute a quorum at all meetings, and such meetings shall be conducted in accordance with such rules as the Trustees may adopt. Any action required or permitted to be taken at any meeting of the Board may be taken without a meeting if all Trustees consent to the action in writing and the written consents are filed with the records of the Board. Such consents shall be treated for all purposes as a vote at a meeting.

B. There shall be an annual meeting of the Unit Owners on the first Wednesday of December in each year at 7:30

P.M. at the Condominium premises or at such other reasonable place and time (not more than thirty (30) days before or after said date) as may be designated by the Trustees by written notice given to the Unit Owners at least fourteen (14) days prior to the date so designated. At the annual meeting of the Unit Owners, the Trustees shall submit reports of the management and finances of the Condominium.

Special meetings of the Unit Owners may be called at any time by the Trustees and shall be called by them upon the written request of Unit Owners entitled to thirty percent (30%) or more of the beneficial interest hereunder. Written notice of any such special meeting designating the place, day and hour thereof shall be given by the Trustees to the Unit Owners at least fourteen (14) days prior to the date so designated. Whenever at any meeting the Trustees propose to submit to the Unit Owners any matter with respect to which approval of or action by the Unit Owners is necessary or appropriate, the notice of such meeting shall so state and reasonably specify such matter.

Each Unit Owner, or a person designated by such Unit Owner to act as proxy on his behalf and who need not be a Unit Owner, shall be entitled to cast the votes appurtenant to the Unit. Designation of such proxy shall be made in writing to the Trustees and shall be revocable at any time prior to the meeting at which it is to be used by written notice to the Trustees by the Unit Owner so designating. Each Unit Owner shall be entitled to cast one vote for each of such Unit Owner's percentage beneficial interest hereunder at all meetings of the Unit Owners and for all other voting purposes hereunder. The vote of a majority of Unit Owners present in person or by proxy at a meeting at which a quorum shall be present shall be binding upon all Unit Owners for all purposes except where otherwise provided by law or by this Trust. Except as otherwise provided in this Trust, the presence in person or by proxy of Unit Owners with sixty percent (60%) or more of the beneficial interest under the Trust shall constitute a quorum at all meetings of the Unit Owners.

For purposes of this Trust, a majority of Unit Owners present in person or by proxy at a meeting of Unit Owners shall mean Unit Owners having more than fifty percent (50%) of the total number of votes entitled to be cast by the Unit Owners present in person or by proxy at such a meeting where a quorum is present.

Section 8. NOTICES TO UNIT OWNERS

Except as otherwise provided this Trust, every notice to

any Unit Owner required under the provisions hereof, or which may be deemed by the Trustees necessary or desirable in connection with the execution of trust created hereby or which may be ordered in any judicial proceeding shall be deemed sufficient and binding if a written or printed copy of such notice shall be given by one or more of the Trustees to such Unit Owner by leaving such notice with him at his residence in the Condominium or by mailing it, postage prepaid, and addressed to such Unit Owner at his address as it appears upon the records of the Trustees, at least seven (7) days prior to the date fixed for the happening of the matter, thing or event of which such notice is given.

Section 9. INSPECTION OF BOOKS, REPORT TO UNIT OWNERS

Books, accounts and records of the Trustees shall be open to inspection to anyone or more of the Trustees, the Unit Owners or the holder of a first mortgage on a Unit at all reasonable times. The Trustees shall, as soon as reasonably possible after the close of each fiscal year, or more often if convenient to them, submit to the Unit Owners a report of the operations of the Trustees for such year which shall include financial statements in such summary form and only in such detail as the Trustees shall deem proper. Any person who has been furnished with such report and shall have failed to object thereto by notice in writing to the Trustees given by registered mail within a period of six (6) months of the date of the receipt by him shall be deemed to have assented thereto.

Section 10. CHECKS, NOTES, DRAFTS AND OTHER INSTRUMENTS

Checks, notes, drafts and other instruments for the payment of money drawn or endorsed in the names of the Trustees or of the Trust may be signed by any two (2) Trustees, or by any person or persons, to whom such power may at any time or from time to time be delegated by not less than a majority of the Trustees.

Section 11. SEAL

The seal of the Trustees shall be circular in form, bearing the inscription "Suburban Acres Condominium Trust"—but such seal may be altered by the Trustees at pleasure and the Trustees may, at any time for from time to time, at their option, adopt a common or wafer seal which shall be valid for all purposes.

Section 12. FISCAL YEAR

The fiscal year of the Trust shall be the year ending with

the last day of December or such other date as may from time to time be determined by the Trustees.

ARTICLE VI.—RIGHTS AND OBLIGATIONS OF THIRD PARTIES DEALING WITH THE TRUSTEES

Section 1. No purchaser, mortgagee, lender or other person dealing with the Trustees as they then appear of record in said Registry of Deeds shall be bound to ascertain or inquire further as to the persons who are then Trustees hereunder or be affected with any notice, implied or actual, otherwise than by a certificate thereof, and such record or certificate shall be conclusive evidence of the personnel of said Trustees and of any changes therein. The receipts of the Trustees or any one or more of them for moneys or things paid or delivered to them or him shall be effectual discharges therefrom to the persons paying or delivering the same and no person from whom the Trustees or any one or more of them shall receive any money, property or other credit shall be required to see to the application thereof. No purchaser, mortgagee, lender or other person dealing with the Trustees or with any real or personal property which then is or formerly was Trust property shall be bound to ascertain or inquire as to the existence or occurrence of any event or purpose in or for which a sale, mortgage, pledge or charge is herein authorized or directed, or otherwise as to the purpose or regularity of any of the acts of the Trustees or anyone or ore of them purporting to be done in pursuance of any of the provisions or powers herein contained, or as to the regularity of the resignation or appointment of any Trustee, and any instrument of appointment of a new Trustee or of an old Trustee purporting to be executed by the Trustees, Unit Owners or other persons herein required to execute the same shall be conclusive evidence in favor of any such purchaser or other person dealing with the Trustees of the matters therein recited relating to such discharge, resignation or appointment or the occasion thereof.

Section 2. No recourse shall at any time be had under or upon any note, bond, contract order, instrument, certificate, undertaking, obligation, covenant, or agreement, whether oral or written, made, issued, or executed by the Trustees or by any agent or employee of the Trustees, or by reason of anything done or omitted to be done by or on behalf of them or any of them, against the Trustees individually, or against any such agent or employee or against any beneficiary either directly or indirectly, by legal or equitable proceeding, or by virtue of any suit or otherwise, and all persons extending credit to, contracting with or having any claim against the

Trustees, shall look only to the Trust property for payment under such contract or claim, or for the payment of any debt, damage, judgment or decree or of any money that may otherwise become due or payable to them from the Trustees, so that neither the Trustees nor the beneficiaries, present or future, shall be personally liable therefore; provided, however, that nothing herein contained shall be deemed to limit or impair the liability of Unit Owners under provisions of Section 7 of Article III hereof or under provisions of said Chapter 183A.

Section 3. Every note, bond, contract, order, instrument certificate, undertaking, obligation, covenant or agreement, whether oral or written, made, issued or executed by the Trustees, or by any agent or employee of the Trustees, shall be deemed to have been entered into subject to the terms, conditions, provisions and restrictions hereof, whether or not express references shall have been made to this instrument.

Section 4. This Declaration of Trust and any amendments hereto and any certificate herein required to be recorded an any other certificate or paper (including without limitation a certificate pursuant to General Laws, Chapter 183A, Section 6(d)) signed by said Trustees or any of them which it may be deemed desirable to record shall be recorded with _____ Registry of Deeds, and such recording shall be deemed conclusive evidence of the contents and effectiveness thereof according to the tenor thereof; and all persons dealing in any manner whatsoever with the Trustees, the Trust property or any beneficiary thereunder shall be held to have notice of any alteration or amendment of this Declaration of Trust, or change of Trustee or Trustees, when the same shall be recorded with said Registry of Deeds. Any certificate signed by two-thirds (2/3rds) of the Trustees in office at the time, setting forth as facts any matters affecting the Trust, including statements as to who are the beneficiaries, as to what action has been taken by the beneficiaries, and as to matters determining the authority of the Trustees to do any act, when duly acknowledged and recorded with said Registry of Deeds shall be conclusive evidence as to the existence of such alleged facts in favor of all third persons, including the Trustees, acting in reliance thereon. Any certificate executed by any Trustee hereunder, or by a majority of the Trustees hereunder, setting forth the existence of any facts, the existence of which is necessary to authorize the execution of any instrument or the taking of any action by such Trustee or majority, as the case may be, shall, as to all persons acting in good faith in reliance thereon be conclusive evidence of the truth of the statements made in such certificate and of the existence of the facts therein set forth.

ARTICLE VII.—AMENDMENTS AND TERMINATION

Section 1. The Trustees may at any time and from time to time amend, alter, add to, or change this Declaration of Trust in any manner or to any extent, provided such amendment, alteration, addition, or change is consented to in writing by a majority of the Unit Owners present in person or by proxy at a duly held meeting of Unit Owners (as provided in Article V, Section 78 hereof), or if such amendment, alteration, addition or change affects a provision then requiring more than a majority, then by such larger percentage, with the Trustees first, however, being duly indemnified to their reasonable satisfaction against outstanding obligations and liabilities; provided always, however, that no such amendment, alteration, addition or change (a) made without the consent of the Declarant of said Master Deed during the time period specified in the first paragraph of Section 1, Article 11 hereof; (b) according to the purport of which the Declarant's rights under Section I of Article III hereof are changed in any way; (c) according to the purport of which the percentage of the beneficial interest hereunder of any Unit Owner would be altered, or in any manner or to any extent whatsoever modified or affected so as to be different than the percentage of the individual interest of such Unit Owner in the common areas and facilities as set forth in said Master Deed, other than by consent of all the Unit Owners; or (d) which would render this Trust contrary to or inconsistent with any requirements or provisions of said Chapter 183A, the Special Permit Decision as referred to in the Master Deed, or other applicable laws or governmental regulations, permits or approvals shall be valid or effective, provided further, however, that nothing herein contained shall be deemed or construed to vitiate or impair the rights reserved to the Declarant of the Master Deed in and by provisions of Section 12 thereof without the consent of any Unit Owner to amend said Master Deed so as to include Additions to the Condominium as therein defined and thereby to alter the percentages of beneficial interest as set forth in Article IV, Section 1, hereof.

Any amendment, alteration, addition, or change pursuant to the foregoing provisions of this section shall become effective upon the recording with said Registry of Deeds of an instrument of amendment, alteration, addition, or change, as the case may be, signed, sealed and acknowledged in the manner required in Massachusetts for the acknowledgement of deeds, by the Trustees, setting forth in full the amendment, alteration, addition, or change, and reciting the consent of the Unit Owners herein required to consent thereto. Such recitation of consent may be in the form of a certificate of the Trustees, signed, sealed and acknowledged in the manner required in Massachusetts for the acknowledgment of deeds, stating that the amendment, alteration, addition, or change was consented to in writing by a majority of the Unit Owners present in person or by proxy at a duly held meeting of Unit Owners (as provided in Article V, Section 7B hereof). Such instrument and certificate, so executed and registered, shall be conclusive evidence of the existence of all facts and of compliance with all prerequisites to the validity of such amendment, alteration, addition, or change, whether stated in such instrument or not, upon all questions as to title or affecting the rights of third persons and for all other purposes.

Section 2. The Trust hereby created shall terminate only upon the removal of the Condominium from the provisions of Chapter 183A in accordance with the procedure therefore set forth in Section 19 of said Chapter.

Section 3. Upon the termination of this Trust, the Trustees may, subject to and in accordance with provisions of said Chapter 183A, sell and convert into money the whole of the trust property, or any part or parts thereof, and, after paying or retiring all known liabilities and obligations of the Trustees and providing for indemnity against any other outstanding liabilities and obligations, shall divide the proceeds thereof among, and distribute in kind, at valuations made by them which shall be conclusive, all other property then held by them in trust hereunder to the Unit Owners according to their respective percentages of beneficial interest hereunder. And in making any sale under this provision the Trustees shall have power to sell or vary any contract of sale and to resell without being answerable for loss and, for said purposes, to do all things, including the execution and delivery of instruments, as may by their performance thereof be shown to be in their judgment necessary or desirable in connection therewith. The powers of sale and all other powers herein given to the Trustees shall continue as to all property at any time remaining in their hands or ownership, even though all times herein fixed for distribution of trust property may have passed.

ARTICLE VIII.—CONSTRUCTION AND INTERPRETATION SEVERABILITY

A. In the construction hereof, whether or not so expressed, words used in the singular or in the plural, respectively, include both the plural and the singular, words denoting males include females, and words denoting persons include individuals, firms, associations, companies (joint stock or otherwise), trusts and corporations unless a contrary intention is to be inferred from or required by the subject matter or context. The cover, title, headings of different parts hereof, the table of contents and the marginal notes, if any, are inserted only for the convenience of reference and are not to be take to be any part hereof, or to control or affect the meaning, construction, interpretation or effect hereof. All the trusts, powers and provisions herein contained shall take effect and be construed according to the laws of the Commonwealth of Massachusetts.

B. The invalidity of any provision of this Trust shall not be deemed to impair or affect the validity of the remainder of this Trust; and, in such event, all of the provisions of this Trust shall continue in full force and effect, as if such invalid provision had never been included herein.

IN WITNESS WHEREOF, the said Midtown Management, LLC, has executed this instrument under seal as of the day and year first hereinabove set forth.

[signature; acknowledgement]

APPENDIX P

Condominium Phasing Lease

SUBURBAN ACRES CONDOMINIUM PHASING LEASE

THIS LEASE executed this _____ day of _____, 2007, by and between MIDTOWN DEVELOPERS, LLC, a Massachusetts limited liability company, having an usual place of business in Midtown, Massachusetts, hereinafter referred to as "LESSOR", and MIDTOWN PHASING, INC., a Massachusetts corporation having an usual place of business in said Midtown, hereinafter referred to as "LESSEE",

WITNESSETH THAT, in consideration of the rents herein reserved and the covenants and agreements herein contained, Lessor hereby rents and demises to Lessee, and Lessee hereby rents from Lessor, those certain parcels of land in Midtown, _____ County, Massachusetts, shown as Parcel B and Parcel C on a plan entitled "Suburban Acres—Phase 1 Site Plan," dated _____, 2007, by _____ Surveyors, recorded or to be recorded with _____ Registry of Deeds with the Master Deed of Suburban Acres, a Condominium, together with the buildings and improvements from time to time erected and situated on said land and all appurtenances and easements thereto belonging or appertaining, situated in said Midtown, and hereinafter referred to as the "Leased Premises";

TO HAVE AND TO HOLD the Leased Premises for the term and upon the conditions hereinafter set forth:

ARTICLE I.—Term

The term of the lease shall be for a period of seven (7) years commencing _____, 2007.

ARTICLE II.—Rent

Lessee covenants and agrees to pay to Lessor a net rental ("net rent") of Ten (10) dollars per year for each year of the term of this lease, payable annually.

ARTICLE III.—Taxes

Lessor covenants and agrees to pay all taxes and assessments, both real and personal, of every nature and description which is levied against the Leased Premises during or applicable to said lease term and all other expenses incident to the ownership of the land and the buildings and improvements thereon.

ARTICLE IV.—Condominium

A. Lessee and Lessor acknowledge and agree that Lessor intends to create and establish a condominium, pursuant to provisions of Massachusetts General Laws, Chapter 183A, and in accordance with provisions of a Special Permit issued by the Midtown Planning Board, as the same may be modified and supplemented, of the premises shown on said Suburban Acres—Phase 1 Site Plan, including Parcel A thereof, not subject to this lease, and the Leased Premises, comprising and being Parcel B and Parcel C thereof, and to provide in the Master Deed of said condominium (the "Master Deed") for the subsequent inclusion therein at any one time or from time to time by suitable amendments to the Master Deed, of additional condominium units and/or recreational or other common facilities as and when the construction thereof is completed on said Parcel B or said Parcel C, or on portions or subparcels of either thereof, with which suitable elements of and on said Parcel B or said Parcel C, or such portions or subparcels thereof will then, by such amendments, be included in the common areas and facilities of said condominium.

B. Lessee hereby consents to the creation and establishment of such condominium and to such subsequent amendments, and to such modification and supplement to said special permit, and agrees with Lessor to execute and deliver to Lessor, or to join with Lessor in the execution and delivery of, such instruments as Lessor may at any time and from time to time reasonably request in order to effect or facilitate the creation and establishment of said condominium and the subsequent inclusion therein from time to time of such additional units and common areas and facilities on said Parcel B or said Parcel C, or portions or subparcels of either thereof, including, without limitation, amendments to this lease to reflect changes in the area of the Leased Premises resulting from such amendments of the Master Deed, and such modification and supplement to said special permit.

C. Lessor hereby grants to and confers upon Lessee the right and authority to proceed with the construction of such additional units or facilities on said Parcel B and Said Parcel C, or on portions or subparcels of either or both thereof, in accordance with applicable provisions, requirements, plans, and specifications of the Master Deed, the architectural plans and specifications thereof, of which copies have been delivered by Lessor to Lessee, and the architectural and construction contracts with respect to portions thereof which have been entered by Lessor, of which copies have been delivered by Lessor to Lessee; provided, however, that Lessee covenants and, agrees with Lessor not to exercise the right and authority hereby granted so long as, in the reasonable opinion of Lessee, lessor is itself proceeding with construction in accordance with all such provisions, requirements, plans and specifications in a manner and with a rate of progress which, in the reasonable opinion of Lessee as aforesaid, will result in the completion of such construction and inclusion of such additional units and common areas and facilities in said condominium within the time periods allowed therefore in said Master Deed. So long as this lease remains outstanding and in effect on or with respect to any Parcel or portion or subparcel thereof, all buildings, structures and improvements in construction on such Parcel or portion or subparcel thereof, shall remain the separate property of the Lessor and/or Lessee and shall not pass with the reversionary estate. Upon the expiration or termination of this lease with respect to any parcel or a portion thereof, all buildings, structures and improvements on such parcel or a portion thereof shall become the property of the Lessor.

ARTICLE V.—Use

The Leased Premises may be used for any lawful purpose consistent with the provisions of the foregoing Article IV and with the provisions of the Master Deed.

ARTICLE VI.—Indemnification

Lessee agrees to indemnify Lessor from and against any and all claims and demands, except such as result from the negligence of Lessor or its agents, servants and/or employees, for or in connection with any accident, injury or damage whatsoever caused to any person or to any personal property arising directly or indirectly out of the possession or use of the Leased Premises of any part thereof by the Lessee.

ARTICLE VII.—Defaults

If any default be made in the payment of rent and if Lessee fails to cure such default within thirty (30) days after receipt of written notice to Lessee, or if default be made in the performance of any other condition, covenant or agreement herein, and if lessee fails to cure such default within thirty (30) days after written notice thereof to Lessee, or commence to cure such default within said thirty (30) day period and thereafter diligently proceed to completion, then. Lessor may immediately take legal action on account of such default for such relief at law or in equity as may be appropriate except for termination of this lease or recovery of possession of Leased Premises, but Lessor shall not have any right, except as provided in Article IX hereof, to terminate this lease, or to re-enter or take possession, or in any manner interrupt or disturb Lessee's peaceful possession, or enjoyment, of the Leased Premises.

ARTICLE VIII.—Quiet Enjoyment

Lessor hereby covenants and agrees that Lessee and its successors and assigns, upon paying the rents and performing and fulfilling the conditions and provisions herein upon Lessee's part to be paid or fulfilled, shall and may peaceably and quietly hold, occupy and enjoy the Leased Premises during the term of this lease, subject to provisions of Article IX hereof, free from any hindrance or molestation by Lessor, or any personal or persons rightfully claiming through or under lessor. Lessor hereby warrants that it has good record and title to the Leased Premises in fee simple, free of encumbrances, and that it has the unrestricted right to enter into this lease upon the terms herein contained.

ARTICLE IX.—Termination

With respect to each of Parcel B and Parcel C, or portions or subparcels of either thereof, comprising the Leased Premises, the leasehold hereunder shall terminate and this lease shall cease and be void with respect to such Parcel B or Parcel C, or a portion or subparcel of either thereof, together with the buildings and improvements thereon, upon the recording with _____ Registry of Deeds of an Amendment of the Master Deed of the condominium referred to in Article IV hereof by which Amendment condominium units then constructed on such Parcel B or Parcel C, or any such portion or subparcel thereof, together with the buildings and condominium Units and the common facilities thereon, are included in the condominium established by the Master Deed. Each such partial termination hereof shall be effected by the recording of each of such Amendments, ipso facto, without the execution or recording of any instrument other than such Amendment of said Master Deed. It is provided, however, that Lessee shall, and hereby agrees to, execute and deliver to Lessor such instruments as Lessor shall reasonably request in order to confirm and establish each such termination. If and when all of said Parcel B and all of said Parcel C are so removed from the operation and effect of this Lease, then and thereupon this Lease shall terminate in its entirety and be void without recourse to the parties hereto.

ARTICLE X.—Encumbrance of Leasehold

Lessee shall have the right and authority to mortgage, pledge, assign or otherwise encumber the leasehold hereunder, and the holder of any such mortgage, pledge, assignment or other encumbrance shall have and may exercise all of the rights and authorities of the Lessee hereunder.

ARTICLE XI.—Binding on Successors

This lease shall inure to the benefit of and be binding upon the parties hereto and their successors and assigns.

IN WITNESS WHEREOF, the parties hereto have executed this Lease under seal the day and year first above-written.

[Signatures; acknowledgements]

APPENDIX Q

Condominium Phasing Amendment

SUBURBAN ACRES AMENDMENT OF MASTER DEED ADDING PHASE 2

This first AMENDMENT of the MASTER DEED of SUB-URBAN ACRES, dated _____, 2008, recorded with _____ Registry of Deeds, Book _____ Page _____, Witnesseth That:

WHEREAS, Midtown Developers, LLC, a Massachusetts limited liability company, did by said Master Deed, as the Declarant thereof, create Suburban Acres, a Condominium, situated in _____ County, Massachusetts, pursuant to provisions of Massachusetts General Laws, Chapter 183A; and

WHEREAS, it is provided in Sections 3 and 12 of said Master Deed that the Declarant reserves and shall have the right, without the consent of any Unit Owner, upon the completion of construction sufficiently for the certification of plans provided for in Section 8(f) of said Chapter 183A, of certain buildings as therein specified on land therein referred to, to amend said Master Deed so as to include in said Condominium, as a Phase thereof, additional buildings containing Units, together with other improvements and together with the land and other facilities constituting common areas and facilities of the Condominium; and

WHEREAS, it is provided in Section 13 of said Master Deed that, from and after the inclusion of any such subsequent Phase in said Condominium, the percentage of undivided interest in the common areas and facilities of the Condominium of Units in Phase 1 and in each such subsequent Phase of the Condominium shall be determined and specified as provided in said Section 13, and the percentage of interest of each Unit shall be set forth in the Amendment of the Master Deed by which such subsequent Phase is included in the Condominium; and

WHEREAS, the construction of Buildings containing Units, and related facilities, on Parcel B-1, being a subparcel of Parcel B, shown on the Site Plan, intended to constitute Phase 2 of the Condominium, has now been so completed;

NOW, THEREFORE, Midtown Developers, LLC, being the Declarant as aforesaid, by duly executing and recording this Amendment of Master Deed, does hereby submit to the provisions of Chapter 183A of the General Laws of Massachusetts and does hereby include in Suburban Acres as Phase 2 thereof, the Units hereinafter specified, owned by the Declarant, and the common areas and facilities relating thereto, as hereinafter specified, and the possessory estate, free and discharged of the Condominium Phasing Lease, in and to said Parcel B-1, subject to and with the benefit of the provisions set forth in Exhibit A to the Master Deed, and to that end, Midtown Developers, LLC, does hereby declare and provide as follows:

1. Description of Buildings. The buildings comprised in Phase 2 of the Condominium are Building _____, containing _____ Units, Building _____, containing _____ Units, and Building _____, containing _____ Units. The buildings are constructed principally of poured concrete foundations, basement walls and floor slabs, wood frame construction, wood siding and asphalt shingle roofing. The location of said buildings and of the access ways thereto on said premises are shown on the Site Plan hereinafter specified.

2. Description of Units. The Units included in Phase 2 of the Condominium are designated as Units Nos. _____ and _____. The designation, location, approximate floor area, number of rooms, immediately accessible common areas, and other descriptive specifications thereof are as shown on the Floor Plans thereof, hereinafter specified, and as set forth in Exhibit B hereto annexed and incorporated herein.

Each Unit also contains and includes closets, hallways, and where there is more than one floor, an interior stairway connecting the floors of the Unit. The elevations of the floors of the Units in said Buildings with respect to mean sea level are as set forth in Exhibit D hereto annexed and incorporated herein.

The provisions and limitations of the Master Deed with respect to rights and obligations appurtenant and applicable to Units, as set forth in Section 7 of the Master Deed, shall apply to the Units in said Phase 2 as well as to Units in Phase 1, all of the provisions of said Section 7 being hereby incorporated herein by reference. Each Unit shall be subject to the restrictions, requirements, rules and regulations set forth in Section 7 of Article V of the Suburban Acres Condominium Trust.

The Units in Phase 2 shall include, as a part of such Unit or as a limited common area and facility hereby allocated for the exclusive use of such Unit, all and the same structures, facilities and areas as are set forth and defined in paragraph B of Section 7 the Master Deed. The rights of the Unit Owners with respect thereto shall be exercisable subject to and in accordance with the provisions, requirements and limitations of Section 7 of the Master Deed, and of Sections 10 and 11 of the Master Deed, and the provisions of the By-Laws of the Suburban Acres Condominium Trust and the rules and regulations promulgated pursuant thereto.

3. Description of Common Areas and Facilities. The common areas and facilities of the Condominium, including Phases 1 and 2, comprise and consist of all and the same lands, elements, features and facilities of the buildings and grounds which are described, defined and referred to in Section 8 of the Master Deed as common areas and facilities. As provided in Section 8 of the Master Deed, said common areas and facilities shall be subject to provisions set forth therein, in the By-Laws of the Suburban Acres Condominium Trust, and in rules and regulations promulgated pursuant thereto, with respect to the use and maintenance thereof; it being hereby expressly provided that all of the provisions of said Section 8 of the Master Deed are and shall be applicable to Phase 2 as well as Phase 1 of the Condominium. It is also hereby expressly provided that all of the provisions of Section 16, Section 17 and of Section 18 of the Master Deed are and shall be applicable to Phase 2 as well as Phase 1 of the Condominium.

4. Plans. The plans for Phase 2 comprise a site plan entitled "Suburban Acres—Phase 2 Site Plan," dated _____, 2008, by _____, Surveyors, and floor plans entitled "Suburban Acres—Phase 2 Floor Plans", dated _____, 2003, prepared by Architects (collectively, the "Plans"), recorded herewith. The Plans, showing the layout, location, Unit designations and dimensions of the Units, and bearing the verified statements of a registered professional land surveyor or registered architect that said plans fully and accurately depict the same, as built, are recorded herewith, and consist of the following:

Sheet 1—Phase 2 Site Plan
Sheet 2—Building _____—Floor Plans
Sheet 3—Building _____—Floor Plans

Sheet 4—Building _____—Floor Plans

5. Percentage Interests of Units in Common Areas and Facilities. Pursuant to provisions of Section 13 of the Master Deed, each Unit in Phases 1 and 2 of the Condominium shall henceforth be entitled to an undivided interest in the common areas and facilities in the percentage specified therefore in Exhibit C annexed hereto and made a part hereof, the only Units in the Condominium being those comprised in said Phases 1 and 2, the same having been determined in accordance with provisions of said Section 13.

6. Applicability of Master Deed. Except as herein expressly amended, all terms and provisions of the Master Deed shall remain in full force and effect and shall be applicable to govern all Units, the Unit Owners thereof, and all common areas and facilities in Phases 1 and 2 of the Condominium, and all rights therein reserved to the Declarant shall remain in full force and effect.

WITNESS the execution hereof under seal this _____ day of _____, 2008.

Midtown Developers, LLC

By:_____ Manager

EXHIBIT B, EXHIBIT C, EXHIBIT D *[Like those in Master Deed]*

APPENDIX R

Nominee Trust

THIS DECLARATION OF TRUST made this _____ day of _____, 2007, by _____, of _____, Massachusetts, and _____ of _____, Massachusetts (hereinafter called the Trustees, which term and any pronoun referring thereto shall be deemed to include their successors in trust hereunder and to mean the Trustee or the Trustees for the time being hereunder. wherever the context so permits), WITNESSETH THAT:

ARTICLE I

The trust hereby created shall be known as the _____ REALTY TRUST and under that name so far as legal, convenient and practicable, shall all acts of the Trustee be made and all instruments in writing by the Trustee be executed.

ARTICLE II

All property, real and personal, tangible and intangible. conveyed to the Trustees hereunder (hereinafter called the "trust property") shall vest in the Trustees as trustees of this trust, in trust to manage, administer and dispose of the same for the sole benefit of the beneficiary or beneficiaries from time to time hereof with the powers and subject to the limitations hereinafter contained concerning the same.

ARTICLE III

Section 1. Any Trustee may resign at any time by instrument in writing signed and acknowledged in the manner required in Massachusetts for the acknowledgment of deeds and such resignation shall take effect upon the recording of such instrument with _____ Registry of Deeds. If and whenever (a) there shall be no trustee in office hereunder, or (b) the beneficiary or beneficiaries hereof desire to appoint additional trustees hereunder, a succeeding and/or additional trustee or trustees shall be appointed by (a) an instrument in writing signed and acknowledged (in the manner required for the recording of deeds in Massachusetts) by the beneficiary or all of the beneficiaries, if more than one, hereunder, and delivered to the then trustee or trustees, if any, hereunder, and (b) an acceptance of such appointment, signed and so acknowledged by the person or persons so appointed. Any such appointment and acceptance shall become effective upon the recording thereof with said Registry of Deeds, and the person or persons so accepting shall then be and become such Trustee or Trustees and shall be vested with title to the trust property, jointly with the remaining or surviving Trustee or Trustees, if any, without the necessity of any act of transfer or conveyance. The foregoing provisions of this Section to the contrary notwithstanding, despite any vacancy in the office of Trustee, however caused and for whatever duration, the remaining or surviving Trustee or Trustees, if any, shall continue to exercise and discharge all of the powers, discretions and duties hereby conferred or imposed upon the Trustee.

Section 2. No Trustee named or appointed as hereinbefore provided, whether as original Trustee or as successor to or as substitute for another, shall be obliged to give any bond or surety or other security for the performance of any of his or her duties hereunder, provided, however, that the beneficiary or all of the beneficiaries hereof may at any time by instrument in writing signed by such beneficiary or beneficiaries, and delivered to the Trustee or Trustees affected, require that any one or more of the Trustees shall give bond in such amount and with such sureties as shall be specified in such instrument. All expenses incident to any such bond shall be charged as an expense of the trust. No Trustee hereinbefore named or appointed as hereinbefore provided shall under any circumstances or in any event be held liable or accountable out of his or her personal assets by reason of any action taken, suffered or omitted in good faith or be so liable or accountable for more money or other property than he or she actually receives, or by reason of anything except his or her own personal and willful malfeasance and defaults.

ARTICLE IV

The Trustees shall have no power whatsoever to control, manage, dispose of, or deal in or with the trust property or any part thereof except when, as and in the manner and to the extent specifically directed in writing by the beneficiary or beneficiaries hereof, being the owner or owners for the time being of all of the beneficial interest hereunder. When, as and in the manner and to the extent so specifically directed, the Trustees shall have full power and authority, at any time and from time to time and without the necessity of applying to any court for leave so to do:

(i) To retain the trust property, or any part or parts thereof, in the same form or forms in which received or acquired by them so far and so long as they shall think fit;

(ii) To sell, assign, convey, transfer, exchange, and otherwise deal with or dispose of, the trust property, or any part or parts thereof, free and discharged of any and all trusts, at public or private sale, to any person or persons, for cash or on credit, and in such manner, on such terms and for such considerations and subject to such restrictions, stipulations, agreements and reservations, if any, as shall have been so specified by the beneficiary or beneficiaries hereof, including the power to take back mortgages to secure the whole or any part of the purchase price of any of the trust property sold or transferred by him, and to execute and deliver any deed or other instrument in connection with the foregoing;

(iii) To purchase or otherwise acquire title to, and to rent, lease or hire from others for terms which may extend beyond the termination of this trust any property or rights to property, real or personal, and to own and hold such property and such rights;

(iv) To borrow or in any other manner raise such sum or sums of money or other property and to evidence the same by notes or other evidences of indebtedness, which may mature at a time or times even beyond the possible duration of this trust, and to execute and deliver any mortgage, pledge, or other instrument to secure any such borrowing;

(v) To enter into any arrangement for the use or occupation of the trust property, or any part or parts thereof, including, without thereby limiting the generality of the foregoing, leases, subleases, easements, licenses, or concessions, even if the same extend beyond the possible duration of this trust;

(vi) To invest and reinvest the trust property, or any part or parts thereof and from time to time and to change investments, including power to invest in all types of securities and other property of whatsoever nature and however denominated, even though such property or such investments shall be of a character or in an amount not customarily considered proper for the investment of trust funds or which does or may not produce income; and

(vii) To declare a condominium or condominiums of the trust property or any part or parts thereof;

PROVIDED ALWAYS, that the trustees shall have no power or authority, by virtue of any provision anywhere in this instrument contained or otherwise, either:

A. To borrow money on the credit, or on behalf of the beneficiary or beneficiaries hereof or any of them personally or to make any contract on behalf of, or binding, the beneficiary or beneficiaries hereof, or any of them personally or to incur any liability whatever on behalf of, or binding, the beneficiary or beneficiaries hereof or any of them personally or otherwise to bind the beneficiary or beneficiaries or any of them personally; or

B. To maintain a bank account, collect or receive rent or other payments, make disbursements or pay bills, distribute income or other property, maintain books, own other assets other than as a nominee, or to engage in any activity which would subject this trust to Massachusetts taxation; it being hereby expressly provided that any provision anywhere in this instrument contained which may be construed as contrary to this clause shall be null and void and of no effect.

ARTICLE V

The original cestuis que trustent or beneficiaries hereof are the persons designated as beneficiaries of this trust in an instrument captioned "Designation of Beneficiary of the _____ Realty Trust," dated this day, executed by said beneficiary and the Trustees. The original beneficiary and/or any subsequent beneficiary shall have the right to assign and transfer the beneficial interest of such beneficiary hereunder in whole or in part, by instrument in writing and under seal, executed by the beneficiary so assigning and transferring, designating the beneficial interest so assigned and transferred (whether all or any part of the beneficial interest of such beneficiary) and the person to whom the same is so assigned and transferred, and any such instrument shall for all purposes take effect upon the receipt thereof by the Trustee or Trustees then in office hereunder. The beneficiary or beneficiaries hereof at any time and from time to time shall be entitled to receive and collect all of the income and profits of the trust and/or the trust property and assets then held by the Trustee or Trustees. Any such distribution of or from the trust property among the beneficiaries hereof, if more than one, shall be according to the percentage of beneficial interest held by them respectively.

ARTICLE VI

Section 1. No purchaser, mortgagee, lender or other person dealing with the Trustee or Trustees (as then appears of record with said Deeds) shall be bound to ascertain or inquire further as to the person or persons who are or is then Trustee or Trustees hereunder. The receipts of the Trustee (or anyone or more of them, if more than one) for money or things paid or delivered to them or him, or to the beneficiaries or beneficiary hereof, shall be effectual discharges therefrom to the persons paying or delivering the same and no person from whom such Trustee or beneficiaries shall receive any money, property or other credit shall be required to see to the application thereof. No purchaser, mortgagee; lender or other person dealing with such Trustee or with any real or personal property which then is or formerly was trust property shall be bound to ascertain or inquire as to the existence or occurrence of any event or purpose in or for which a sale, mortgage, pledge or charge is herein authorized or directed, or otherwise as to the purpose or regularity of any of the acts of such Trustee purporting to be done in pursuance of any of the provisions or powers herein contained, or as to the regularity of the resignation or appointment of any Trustee, and any instrument of acceptance of appointment by a new Trustee shall be conclusive evidence in favor of any such purchaser or other person dealing with the Trustee of the matters therein recited relating to such discharge, resignation or appointment or the occasion thereof.

Section 2. This Declaration of Trust and any amendments hereto and any certificate herein required to be recorded and any other certificate or paper signed by the Trustee or Trustees hereunder or any of them which it may be deemed desirable to record shall be recorded with said Registry of Deeds and such record shall be deemed conclusive evidence of the contents and effectiveness thereof according to the tenor thereof; and all persons dealing in any manner whatsoever with the Trustee or the trust property shall be held to have notice of any alteration or amendment of this Declaration of Trust, or change of Trustee or Trustees, when the same shall be recorded with said Registry of Deeds. Any certificate signed by the Trustee or Trustees in office at the time, setting forth as facts any matters affecting the trust, including statements as to what action has been taken by the beneficiary or beneficiaries hereof, and as to matters determining the authority of the Trustee to do any act, when duly acknowledged and recorded with said Registry of Deeds shall be conclusive evidence as to the existence of such alleged facts in favor of all third persons, including the Trustees, acting in reliance thereon.

ARTICLE VII

Section 1. This trust may at any time and from time to time be amended in any manner or to any extent, or may be terminated by instrument in writing signed and acknowledged by the beneficiary or all of the beneficiaries, if more than one, hereunder, and delivered to the Trustee or Trustees hereunder. Any such amendment or termination shall become effective upon the recording with said Registry of Deeds of an instrument of amendment or termination, as the case may be, signed and acknowledged in the manner required in Massachusetts for the acknowledgment of deeds, by the Trustee or Trustees hereunder, setting forth in full the amendment or termination and reciting the receipt of an instrument making such amendment or termination signed and so acknowledged by the beneficiary or all of the beneficiaries hereof. Such instrument, so executed and recorded, shall be conclusive evidence of the existence of all facts and of compliance with all prerequisites to the validity of such amendment or termination upon all questions as to title or affecting the rights of third persons and for all other purposes.

Section 2. The trust hereby created shall, unless sooner terminated pursuant to other provisions hereof, terminate at the expiration of the period of twenty (20) years from this date.

Section 3. Upon the termination of this trust, the Trustees may, if so directed by the beneficiary or all of the beneficiaries hereof, sell and convert into money the whole of the trust property, or any part or parts thereof, and, after the payment or retirement of all known liabilities and obligations of the Trustees, the proceeds thereof, and all other property then held by the Trustees in trust hereunder, shall be distributed and paid over to the beneficiary or beneficiaries hereof, according to their respective beneficial interests if more than one. And in making any sale under this provision the Trustee shall have the power, subject to such direction by the beneficiary or beneficiaries hereof, to sell by public auction or private contract and to buy in or rescind or vary any contract of sale and to resell without being answerable for loss and, for said purposes to do all things, including the execution and delivery of instruments as may be necessary or desirable in connection therewith. The powers of sale and all other powers herein given to the Trustees shall, subject to such direction by the beneficiary or beneficiaries hereof, continue as to all property at any time remaining in the hands or ownership of the Trustees, even though all times herein fixed for distribution of trust property may have passed.

ARTICLE VIII

In the construction hereof, whether or not so expressed, words used in the singular or in the plural respectively include both the plural and singular, words denoting males include females and words denoting persons include individuals, firms, associations, companies, trusts and corporations unless a contrary intention is to be inferred from or required by the subject matter or context. All the trusts, powers and provisions herein contained shall take effect and be construed according to the laws of the Commonwealth of Massachusetts.

IN WITNESS WHEREOF said _____ and _____ have hereunto set their hands and seals on the day and year first hereinabove set forth.

[Signatures and acknowledgement]

APPENDIX S

Mortgage Covenants

Including as part of the realty all portable or sectional buildings, partitions, heating apparatus, plumbing, electrical and electronic wiring, fixtures and installed equipment, oil burners, gas, oil and electric fixtures, air conditioning apparatus, storm doors and windows, screens, screen doors, window shades, awnings, stoves, ranges, mantels, and other fixtures of whatever kind and nature, on said premises, or hereafter placed thereon prior to the full payment and discharge of this mortgage, insofar as the same are or can by agreement of the parties be made a part of the realty.

The mortgagor covenants and agrees as follows:

1. To perform and observe all of the terms and conditions of the mortgage note secured by this mortgage.

2. If requested by the mortgagee, to pay the mortgagee, in addition to the payments of principal and interest therein required, a monthly apportionment of the sum estimated by the mortgagee to be sufficient to make all payments of all taxes, charges and assessments upon the mortgaged property as they become due and any balance due for any of said payments shall be paid by the mortgagor to the mortgagee on demand. The mortgagee is hereby specifically authorized to pay when due or at any time thereafter all of said payments and to charge the same to the account of the mortgagor.

3. To pay on demand to the mortgagee sums equivalent to the same percentage on the debt secured hereby as the mortgagee shall from time to time be required to pay as a State tax on its funds invested in loans secured by mortgages of real estate.

4. To insure in sums satisfactory to the mortgagee and for its benefit the buildings now or hereafter standing on said land against fire, and such other hazards, casualties and contingencies as the mortgagee may from time to time direct, and to deposit all such insurance policies with the mortgagee.

5. That a foreclosure of this mortgage shall forever bar the mortgagor and all persons claiming under the mortgagor from all right, title and interest in and to any and

all of the fire or other hazard insurance policies on the buildings upon the land covered by this mortgage at the time of such foreclosure, including all rights to return premiums on cancellations, whether at law or in equity.

6. To keep all and singular the said premises in such repair and condition as the same are now or may be put in while this mortgage is outstanding.

7. Not to use or permit the premises to be used in violation of any law or municipal ordinance or regulation or for any unlawful or improper purpose.

8. Not to commit, permit or suffer any waste, impairment, or deterioration of the property or any part thereof.

9. Not to create or permit any encumbrance upon, or security interest in, said premises or any fixture or article of personal property now or hereafter subject to this mortgage, or purporting by the terms hereof to be made so subject, which would take priority over this mortgage, whether under the provisions of the Uniform Commercial Code, so called, or otherwise.

10. That upon default in any condition of this mortgage or the note secured hereby, the mortgagee may apply any sums credited by or due from the mortgagee to the mortgagor to cure such default without first enforcing any of the other rights of the mortgage; against the mortgagor or the mortgaged premises.

11. That the mortgagor will pay on demand to the mortgagee, or the mortgagee may at its option add to the principal balance then due, any sums advanced or paid by the mortgagee on account of any default, of whatever nature, by the mortgagor, or to secure the release or discharge of any encumbrance or security interest of the character described in the foregoing Clause 9 hereof, any sums advanced or paid by the mortgagee, whether before or after default, for taxes, repairs, improvements or insurance, and any sums paid by the mortgagee, including reasonable attorney's fees, in prosecuting, defending, or intervening in any legal or equitable proceeding wherein the mortgagee deems any of the rights created by this mortgage are jeopardized or in issue.

12. That this mortgage shall also secure the repayment of such future advances as the mortgagee may, from time to time for any purpose, make to the mortgagor, and the same may be added to the mortgage debt.

13. That upon default in any condition of the mortgage or the note secured hereby, or in the event that the mortgagor shall convey or transfer the mortgaged pre-

mises, or any part thereof, or in the event that the owner-ship of the mortgaged premises, or any part thereof shall become vested in any other person or persons, the entire mortgage debt shall become due and payable on demand at the option of the mortgagee.

14. That in the event the ownership of the mortgaged premises, or any part thereof, becomes vested in a person other than the mortgagor, the mortgagee may, without no-tice to the mortgagor, deal with such successor or succes-sors in interest with reference to the mortgage and the debt hereby secured, and in the same manner as with the mortgagor, without in any way vitiating or discharging the mortgagor's liability hereunder or upon the debt hereby secured. Except as hereinabove provided, no sale of the premises hereby mortgaged and no forbearance on the part of the mortgagee and no extension whether oral or in writing of the time for the payment of the debt hereby secured given by the mortgagee shall operate to release, discharge, modify, change or affect the original liability of the mortgagor herein, either in whole or in part.

15. At any time upon notice from the mortgagee to submit for examination all leases of the mortgaged premises or any part thereof then in force and on demand to assign and deliver to the mortgagee any or all of such leases (hereby granting to the mortgagee full authority as attorney irrevocable of the mortgagor to make, execute, ac-knowledge and deliver such assignments), such assign-ments to be in form satisfactory to the mortgagee, to empower the mortgagee to assign any or all leases so as-signed to it to any subsequent holder hereof or to any person or persons claiming title to the mortgaged premises or any part thereof by virtue of foreclosure proceedings and to provide that after foreclosure no assignee of any lease so assigned shall be liable to account to the mortgagor or the mortgagor's successors in title either for rents or profits thereafter accruing or otherwise.

16. That wherever the words "mortgagor" and "mort-gagee" are used herein they shall include their several heirs, executors, administrators, successors, grantees and assigns subject to the limitations of law and of this instru-ment, and if the context requires, the words "mortgagor" and "mortgagee" and the pronouns referring to them shall be construed as plural, neuter or feminine.

Table of Laws and Rules

INTERNAL REVENUE CODE

UNITED STATES CODE ANNOTATED

UNITED STATES PUBLIC LAWS

CODE OF FEDERAL REGULATIONS

INTERNAL REVENUE SERVICE PUBLICATION

INTERNAL REVENUE SERVICE REVENUE RULINGS

MASSACHUSETTS CONSTITUTION

MASSACHUSETTS GENERAL LAWS

MASSACHUSETTS GENERAL LAWS—Continued

Ch	Sec.
21J	13:19, 14:1
22, § 13A	14:11
23A	14:1
23B	14:1
23B, § 16	11:6
23D	14:1
23F	14:1
23G	14:1
28A, § 9	11:6, 11:20
30, § 61 to 62H	13:3
30, § 62H	13:3
30A	2:9
30B	2:8
34, § 14	2:3
34, § 25	2:3
34A	2:3
34B	2:3
34B, § 6	2:3
36	6:2
36, § 12A	19:17
36, § 13A	6:21
36, § 13B	6:21
36, § 14	6:4
36, § 15	19:15
36, § 18A	19:17
36, § 24B	19:17
36, § 31A	19:17
39	2:9
40	2:4, 2:9
40, § 3A	2:4
40, § 6N	15:11
40, § 8C	2:9, 14:16
40, § 15	2:4
40, § 15A	2:4
40, § 15C	13:22
40, § 21	13:22
40, § 22E	17:27
40, § 32	11:9
40, § 54A	13:22, 14:5
40A	10:8, 11:1, 11:2, 11:5
40A, § 3	11:6
40A, § 4	11:5
40A, § 5	11:9
40A, § 6	11:10, 11:12, 11:14, 11:15, 11:16, 12:4, 12:10, 12:16
40A, § 7	10:17, 11:10
40A, § 9	11:5, 14:13, 14:16
40A, § 9	11:6
40A, § 9A	11:5
40A, § 9B	11:6, 14:11
40A, § 9C	11:6
40A, § 10	11:18
40A, § 11	6:27, 11:19
40A, § 13	11:19
40A, § 15	11:19
40B	11:4, 14:13
40B, § 20 to 23	11:7
40B, § 21	11:7, 14:16
40B, § 23	11:7
40B, § 30	11:20
40C	11:20, 13:22, 15:23
40C, § 1 to 17	14:7
40E	14:1
40F	15:14
40G	14:1
40H	14:1
40J	14:1
40L	14:1, 14:4
40O	14:1
40P	17:25
40Q	14:1
40R	11:4, 14:1
41, § 81-P	11:17
41, § 81-W	12:7
41, § 81GG	12:1
41, § 81K to 81GG	12:1
41, § 81L	11:13, 12:4
41, § 81Q	14:11
41, § 81U	14:13
42, § 12	10:9
43D	14:18
44, § 53G	12:11, 14:16
44, § 63A	2:4
44B	11:7, 14:17
59, § 5C	18:4
59, § 11	18:5
59, § 57C	1:22
60	2:5, 10:9
60, § 23	6:30, 8:11, 12:14
60, § 37 et seq.	2:5
60, § 37	6:30
60, § 37A	6:30
60, § 60	7:5
60, § 69A	2:5
60, § 79 et seq.	2:5
60, § 80B	2:5

MASSACHUSETTS GENERAL LAWS—Continued

MASSACHUSETTS GENERAL LAWS—Continued

MASSACHUSETTS GENERAL LAWS—Continued

MASSACHUSETTS GENERAL LAWS—Continued

CODE OF MASSACHUSETTS REGULATIONS

MASSACHUSETTS STATE BAR ASSOCIATION COMMITTEE ON PROFESSIONAL ETHICS

UNIFORM COMMERCIAL CODE

Table of Cases

App. Ct. 249, 861 N.E.2d
491 (2007)—1:39

Allen v. Batchelder, 17 Mass.
App. Ct. 453, 459 N.E.2d
129 (1984)—16:3

Alliance to Protect Nantucket
Sound, Inc. v. Energy Facilities Siting Bd., 448 Mass.
45, 858 N.E.2d 294 (2006)—
13:22

Aloha Foundation v. Zoning Bd.
of Appeals of Norwell, 4
L.C.R. 199 (1996)—11:18

Alroy v. Zoning Bd. of Appeals
of Newton, 5 L.C.R. 245
(1998)—11:19

Altobelli v. Montesi, 300 Mass.
396, 15 N.E.2d 463 (1938)—
16:3

Amberwood Development Corp.
v. Board of Appeals of Boxford, 65 Mass. App. Ct. 205,
837 N.E.2d 1161 (2005)—
11:3

Amerada Hess Corp. v. Garabedian, 416 Mass. 149, 617
N.E.2d 630 (1993)—3:2, 5:1

American Mechanical Corp. v.
Union Mach. Co. of Lynn,
Inc., 21 Mass. App. Ct. 97,
485 N.E.2d 680 (1985)—5:4

American Min. Congress v. U.S.
Army Corps of Engineers,
951 F. Supp. 267 (D.D.C.
1997)—13:5

American Unitarian Ass'n v.
Minot, 185 Mass. 589, 71
N.E. 551 (1904)—10:7

Anderson v. Healy, 36 Mass.
App. Ct. 131, 629 N.E.2d
312 (1994)—6:29

Anderson v. Monaghan, 7 L.C.R.
224 (1999)—17:15

Anderson v. Old King's Highway
Regional Historic Dist.
Com'n, 397 Mass. 609, 493
N.E.2d 188 (1986)—14:7

Anderson v. Town of Wilmington, 347 Mass. 302, 197
N.E.2d 682 (1964)—10:8

Anderson Insulation Co., Inc. v.
Department Of Public
Health, 61 Mass. App. Ct.
913, 814 N.E.2d 1100
(2004)—14:11

Anderson Insulation Co., Inc. v.
Department of Public
Health, 48 Mass. App. Ct.
80, 717 N.E.2d 662 (1999)—
14:11

Anderson Street Associates v.
City Of Boston, 442 Mass.
812, 817 N.E.2d 759
(2004)—2:6, 14:2

Andover, Town of v. State Fi-
nancial Services, Inc., 48
Mass. App. Ct. 536, 723
N.E.2d 531 (2000)—2:5

Andover Housing Authority v.
Shkolnik, 443 Mass. 300,
820 N.E.2d 815 (2005)—
15:19

Andre v. Ellison, 324 Mass. 665,
88 N.E.2d 340 (1949)—4:5

Andrews v. Town of Amherst,
13 L.C.R. 528 (2005)—11:5

Andrews v. Charon, 289 Mass.
1, 193 N.E. 737 (1935)—4:7

Angelus v. Board of Appeals of
Canton, 25 Mass. App. Ct.
994, 521 N.E.2d 1373
(1988)—11:21

Anthony's Pier Four, Inc. v.
HBC Associates, 411 Mass.
451, 583 N.E.2d 806
(1991)—5:4

Antonelli v. Planning Bd. of
North Andover, 4 L.C.R. 67
(1996)—11:17, 12:8

Anzalone v. Strand, 14 Mass.
App. Ct. 45, 436 N.E.2d 960
(1982)—1:16

Apahouser Lock and Sec. Corp.
v. Carvelli, 26 Mass. App.
Ct. 385, 528 N.E.2d 133
(1988)—16:15

APT Asset Management, Inc. v.
Board of Appeals of Mel-
rose, 50 Mass. App. Ct. 133,
735 N.E.2d 872 (2000)—
11:21

Baker v. Planning Bd. of Framingham, 353 Mass. 141, 228 N.E.2d 831 (1967)—12:7

Baker v. Seneca, 329 Mass. 736, 110 N.E.2d 325 (1953)—15:13

Baldiga v. Board of Appeals of Uxbridge, 395 Mass. 829, 482 N.E.2d 809 (1985)—11:13

Ball v. Planning Bd. of Leverett, 58 Mass. App. Ct. 513, 790 N.E.2d 1138 (2003)—12:2

Ballarino, In re, 180 B.R. 343 (D. Mass. 1995)—20:6

Ballentine v. Eaton, 297 Mass. 389, 8 N.E.2d 808 (1937)—5:6

BankBoston, N.A. v. Yodice, 54 Mass. App. Ct. 901, 763 N.E.2d 80 (2002)—20:41

Bankers Trust Company of California, N.A. v. Halliday, 6 L.C.R. 122 (1998)—17:21

Barber v. Fox, 36 Mass. App. Ct. 525, 632 N.E.2d 1246 (1994)—5:6

Barclay v. DeVeau, 384 Mass. 676, 429 N.E.2d 323 (1981)—17:1

Bardon Trimount, Inc. v. Guyott, 49 Mass. App. Ct. 764, 732 N.E.2d 916 (2000)—13:15

Barlow v. Chongris & Sons, Inc., 38 Mass. App. Ct. 297, 647 N.E.2d 437 (1995)—15:3, 15:5, 15:8

Barney & Casey Co. v. Town of Milton, 324 Mass. 440, 87 N.E.2d 9 (1949)—11:5

Barrell v. Britton, 252 Mass. 504, 148 N.E. 134 (1925)—1:33

Barrett v. Building Inspector of Peabody, 354 Mass. 38, 234 N.E.2d 884 (1968)—11:5

Barrett v. Lyons, 4 L.C.R. 235 (1996)—15:3, 15:9

BarryGeneral Mortg. & Loan Corp., 254 Mass. 282, 150 N.E. 293 (1926)—20:7

Bartlett v. Bartlett, 86 Mass. 440, 4 Allen 440, 1862 WL 3771 (1862)—19:4

Bartlett v. Board of Appeals of Lakeville, 23 Mass. App. Ct. 664, 505 N.E.2d 193 (1987)—11:10

Barton Properties, Inc. v. Planning Bd. of Concord, 4 L.C.R. 293 (1996)—12:2

Barvenik v. Board of Aldermen of Newton, 33 Mass. App. Ct. 129, 597 N.E.2d 48 (1992)—11:23

Baseball Pub. Co. v. Bruton, 302 Mass. 54, 18 N.E.2d 362, 119 A.L.R. 1518 (1938)—4:3

Bateman v. Board of Appeals of Georgetown, 56 Mass. App. Ct. 236, 775 N.E.2d 1276 (2002)—15:9

Bay State Harness Horse Racing & Breeding Ass'n, Inc. v. PPG Industries, Inc., 365 F. Supp. 1299 (D. Mass. 1973)—6:24, 10:15

BDS Realty, LLC v. Broutsas, 11 L.C.R. 94 (2003)—15:7

Beaconsfield Towne House Condominium Trust v. Zussman, 416 Mass. 505, 623 N.E.2d 1115 (1993)—17:17

Beaconsfield Towne House Condominium Trust v. Zussman, 401 Mass. 480, 517 N.E.2d 816 (1988)—17:17

Beaconsfield Townhouse Condominium Trust v. Zussman, 49 Mass. App. Ct. 757, 733 N.E.2d 141 (2000)—17:22

Bead Portfolio, LLC v. Follayttar, 47 Mass. App. Ct. 533, 714 N.E.2d 372 (1999)—20:41

Beal v. Building Commissioner of Springfield, 353 Mass. 640, 234 N.E.2d 299 (1968)—11:5

685, 52 A.L.R. 886 (1927)—
16:4, 16:5

Bernstein v. Chief Building Inspector, 52 Mass. App. Ct. 422, 754 N.E.2d 133 (2001)—17:16

Bernstein v. Planning Bd. of Stockbridge, 14 L.C.R. 266 (2006)—12:7

BFP v. Resolution Trust Corp., 511 U.S. 531, 114 S. Ct. 1757, 128 L. Ed. 2d 556 (1994)—20:38

Bible Speaks v. Board of Appeals of Lenox, 8 Mass. App. Ct. 19, 391 N.E.2d 279 (1979)—11:6

Bickford v. Dillon, 321 Mass. 82, 71 N.E.2d 611 (1947)—1:33

Bicknell Realty Co. v. Board of Appeal of Boston, 330 Mass. 676, 116 N.E.2d 570 (1953)—11:18

Billerica, Town of v. Card, 11 L.C.R. 195 (2002)—14:4

Bills v. Nunno, 4 Mass. App. Ct. 279, 346 N.E.2d 718 (1976)—7:18

Bingham v. City Council of Fitchburg, 52 Mass. App. Ct. 566, 754 N.E.2d 1078 (2001)—11:22

Bisson v. Eck, 40 Mass. App. Ct. 942, 667 N.E.2d 276 (1996)—13:18

Bisson v. Planning Bd. of Dover, 43 Mass. App. Ct. 504, 684 N.E.2d 7 (1997)—12:3

Bissonnette v. Keyes, 319 Mass. 134, 64 N.E.2d 926 (1946)—1:34

Bjorklund v. Bd. of Appeals of Scituate, 3 L.C.R. 141 (1995)—11:10

Bjornlund v. Zoning Bd. of Appeals of Marshfield, 353 Mass. 757, 231 N.E.2d 365 (1967)—11:22

Black v. Coastal Oil New England, Inc., 45 Mass. App. Ct. 461, 699 N.E.2d 353 (1998)—13:18

Blackstone, Town of v. Town of Millville, 59 Mass. App. Ct. 565, 797 N.E.2d 390 (2003)—6:16

Blakeley v. Gorin, 365 Mass. 590, 313 N.E.2d 903 (1974)—10:6, 15:12, 15:15

Block v. Zoning Bd. of Appeals of Otis, 3 L.C.R. 1 (1994)—11:11

Blomendale v. Imbrescia, 25 Mass. App. Ct. 144, 516 N.E.2d 177 (1987)—3:1

Blood v. Blood, 40 Mass. 80, 23 Pick. 80, 1839 WL 3019 (1839)—6:9

Blood v. Edgar's, Inc., 36 Mass. App. Ct. 402, 632 N.E.2d 419 (1994)—17:21

Bloom v. Planning Bd. of Brookline, 346 Mass. 278, 191 N.E.2d 684 (1963)—12:2

Blum v. Kenyon, 29 Mass. App. Ct. 417, 560 N.E.2d 742 (1990)—3:2, 5:1, 18:3

Board of Aldermen of Newton v. Maniace, 429 Mass. 726, 711 N.E.2d 565 (1999)—11:21

Board of Appeals of Hanover v. Housing Appeals Committee in Dept. of Community Affairs, 363 Mass. 339, 294 N.E.2d 393 (1973)—11:7, 11:20

Board of Appeals of Maynard v. Housing Appeals Committee in Dept. of Community Affairs, 370 Mass. 64, 345 N.E.2d 382 (1976)—11:7

Board of Appeals of North Andover v. Housing Appeals Committee, 4 Mass. App. Ct. 676, 357 N.E.2d 936 (1976)—11:7

Board of Appeals of Southampton v. Boyle, 4 Mass. App. Ct. 824, 349 N.E.2d 373 (1976)—11:21

Boulter Bros. Const. Co., Inc. v. Zoning Bd. of Appeals of Norfolk, 45 Mass. App. Ct. 283, 697 N.E.2d 997 (1998)—11:11

Boutin v. Perreault, 343 Mass. 329, 178 N.E.2d 482 (1961)—7:8

Bouvier v. L'Eveque, 324 Mass. 476, 86 N.E.2d 915 (1949)—4:5

Bova v. Clemente, 278 Mass. 585, 180 N.E. 611 (1932)—16:8

Bowditch v. Attorney General, 241 Mass. 168, 134 N.E. 796, 28 A.L.R. 713 (1922)—16:4

Boyajian v. Hart, 292 Mass. 447, 198 N.E. 764 (1935)—20:36

Boylston, Town of v. Dovetail Homes, Inc., 11 L.C.R. 132 (2003)—14:4

Boynton v. Rees, 25 Mass. 329, 8 Pick. 329, 1829 WL 1869 (1829)—19:4

Brady v. City Council of Gloucester, 59 Mass. App. Ct. 691, 797 N.E.2d 479 (2003)—11:21

Brady v. Zimmerman, 7 L.C.R. 101 (1999)—17:17

Bransford v. Zoning Bd. of Appeals of Edgartown, 444 Mass. 852, 832 N.E.2d 639 (2005)—11:11

Brassard v. Flynn, 352 Mass. 185, 224 N.E.2d 221 (1967)—15:7, 15:9

Brear v. Fagan, 447 Mass. 68, 849 N.E.2d 211 (2006)—15:14

Brennan v. DeCosta, 24 Mass. App. Ct. 968, 511 N.E.2d 1110 (1987)—15:4

Bresnick v. Lautenberg, 8 L.C.R. 127 (2000)—15:15

Bressel v. Jolicoeur, 34 Mass. App. Ct. 205, 609 N.E.2d 94 (1993)—19:4

Breuing v. Callahan, 50 Mass. App. Ct. 359, 737 N.E.2d 507 (2000)—13:20

Brewster, Town of v. Sherwood Forest Realty, Inc., 7 L.C.R. 141 (1999)—2:5

Brewton v. Spiegel, 14 L.C.R. 468 (2006)—11:6, 11:20

Bridgewater, Town of v. Chuckran, 351 Mass. 20, 217 N.E.2d 726 (1966)—11:11

Briggs v. Stevens, 224 Mass. 46, 112 N.E. 487 (1916)—8:15

Bringhurst v. Planning Bd. of Walpole, 1 L.C.R. 12 (1993)—12:15

Brintnall v. Graves, 168 Mass. 384, 47 N.E. 119 (1897)—10:5

Britton v. Zoning Bd. of Appeals of Gloucester, 59 Mass. App. Ct. 68, 794 N.E.2d 1198 (2003)—11:11

Broderick v. Board of Appeal of Boston, 361 Mass. 472, 280 N.E.2d 670 (1972)—11:18

Brodeur v. Lamb, 22 Mass. App. Ct. 502, 495 N.E.2d 324 (1986)—15:7, 15:10

Brogle v. Martin, 20 Mass. App. Ct. 901, 477 N.E.2d 605 (1985)—11:18

Bronstein v. Prudential Ins. Co. of America, 390 Mass. 701, 459 N.E.2d 772 (1984)—2:6, 14:2

Brooker v. Motiva Enterprises, LLC, 11 L.C.R. 102 (2003)—15:10

Brook House Condominium Trust v. Automatic Sprinkler Appeals Bd., 414 Mass. 303, 607 N.E.2d 744 (1993)—14:11

Brookings v. Cooper, 256 Mass. 121, 152 N.E. 243, 46 A.L.R. 745 (1926)—1:37

Brookline, Town of v. Carey, 355 Mass. 424, 245 N.E.2d 446 (1969)—10:3

Mass. App. Ct. 435, 827 N.E.2d 216 (2005)—11:23

Buttaro v. Bd. of Appeals of Woburn, 4 L.C.R. 111 (1996)—11:19

Butts v. Zoning Bd. of Appeals of Falmouth, 18 Mass. App. Ct. 249, 464 N.E.2d 108 (1984)—11:22

C

Caires v. Building Com'r of Hingham, 323 Mass. 589, 83 N.E.2d 550 (1949)—11:5

Caldeira v. Zoning Bd. of Appeals of Taunton, 3 L.C.R. 195 (1995)—11:6

Calnan v. Planning Bd. of Lynn, 63 Mass. App. Ct. 384, 826 N.E.2d 258 (2005)—12:15

Cambridgeport Sav. Bank v. Boersner, 413 Mass. 432, 597 N.E.2d 1017 (1992)—5:4

Cameron v. Board of Appeals of Yarmouth, 23 Mass. App. Ct. 144, 499 N.E.2d 847 (1986)—11:21, 11:24

Campbell v. Boston Housing Authority, 443 Mass. 574, 823 N.E.2d 363 (2005)—14:11

Campbell v. City Council of Lynn, 32 Mass. App. Ct. 152, 586 N.E.2d 1009 (1992)—11:6

Campbell v. Olender, 27 Mass. App. Ct. 1197, 543 N.E.2d 708 (1989)—1:7

Campbell v. Town of Weymouth, 6 L.C.R. 276 (1998)—11:6

Campos v. Chelsea Zoning Bd. of Appeals, 5 L.C.R. 128 (1997)—11:10

Canteen Corp. v. City of Pittsfield, 4 Mass. App. Ct. 289, 346 N.E.2d 732 (1976)—11:5

Canter v. Planning Bd. of Westborough, 7 Mass. App. Ct. 805, 390 N.E.2d 1128 (1979)—12:11, 12:12

Canter v. Planning Bd. of Westborough, 4 Mass. App. Ct. 306, 347 N.E.2d 691 (1976)—12:7

Cape Ann Land Development Corp. v. City of Gloucester, 371 Mass. 19, 353 N.E.2d 645 (1976)—11:17

Cape Cod Conservatory of Music and Arts, Inc., 8 L.C.R. 472 (2001)—15:15

Cape Resort Hotels, Inc. v. Alcoholic Licensing Bd. of Falmouth, 385 Mass. 205, 431 N.E.2d 213 (1982)—11:24

Capodilupo v. Vozzella, 46 Mass. App. Ct. 224, 704 N.E.2d 534 (1999)—8:3, 15:7

Capone v. Zoning Bd. of Appeals of Fitchburg, 389 Mass. 617, 451 N.E.2d 1141 (1983)—11:21

Cappa v. Murray, 13 L.C.R. 67 (2005)—15:3

Cappuccio v. Zoning Bd. of Appeals of Spencer, 398 Mass. 304, 496 N.E.2d 646 (1986)—11:22

Capus Developments v. R. (No. 2), 1975 WL 155925 (Fed. T.D. 1975)—11:6

Caputo v. Board of Appeals of Somerville, 331 Mass. 547, 120 N.E.2d 753 (1954)—11:5

Carbone v. Planning Bd. of Beverly, 33 Mass. App. Ct. 909, 596 N.E.2d 1031 (1992)—12:12

Cardwell v. Board of Appeals of Woburn, 61 Mass. App. Ct. 118, 807 N.E.2d 207 (2004)—11:7

Carey v. Planning Bd. of Revere, 335 Mass. 740, 139 N.E.2d 920 (1957)—12:15

Carlisle Land Trust v. Pannell, 8 L.C.R. 101 (2000)—14:4

Carlson v. Czerpak, 3 L.C.R. 58 (1995)—15:12

Carlson v. Czerpik, 3 L.C.R. 58 (1995)—10:16

Daly Dry Wall, Inc. v. Board of Appeals of Easton, 3 Mass. App. Ct. 706, 322 N.E.2d 780 (1975)—11:9

Danca v. Taunton Sav. Bank, 385 Mass. 1, 429 N.E.2d 1129 (1982)—5:4, 21:9

Dane v. Delaney, 125 F. Supp. 594 (D. Mass. 1954)—16:4

Daniel v. Shaw, 166 Mass. 582, 44 N.E. 991 (1896)—10:2

D'Annolfo v. D'Annolfo Const. Co., Inc., 39 Mass. App. Ct. 189, 654 N.E.2d 82, 27 U.C.C. Rep. Serv. 2d 493 (1995)—5:6, 20:11

Danusis v. Longo, 48 Mass. App. Ct. 254, 720 N.E.2d 470 (1999)—5:4, 14:12

Darley v. Halifax, 5 L.C.R. 121 (1997)—11:6

Dawson v. Board of Appeals of Bourne, 18 Mass. App. Ct. 962, 469 N.E.2d 509 (1984)—11:10

DDRC Gateway, LLC v. Massachusetts Bay Transportation Authority, 8 L.C.R. 177 (2000)—8:9

De Blois v. Boylston & Tremont Corp., 281 Mass. 498, 183 N.E. 823 (1933)—1:38

DeGrace v. Conservation Com'n of Harwich, 31 Mass. App. Ct. 132, 575 N.E.2d 373 (1991)—13:10

Deignan v. Harwich Bd. of Appeals, 13 L.C.R. 244 (2005)—11:10

Delconte v. Salloum, 336 Mass. 184, 143 N.E.2d 210 (1957)—15:10

Dellert v. Geryk, 13 L.C.R. 37 (2005)—15:4

DeLuca v. Bd. of Appeals of Bedford, 5 L.C.R. 51 (1997)—11:22

Denneny v. Zoning Bd. of Appeals of Seekonk, 59 Mass. App. Ct. 208, 794 N.E.2d 1269 (2003)—11:23

Dennis Housing Corp. v. Zoning Bd. of Appeals of Dennis, 439 Mass. 71, 785 N.E.2d 682 (2003)—11:7

Dennis Seashores, Inc., 7 L.C.R. 369 (1999)—18:4

Den Norske Bank v. First Nat. Bank of Boston, 1993 WL 773796 (D. Mass. 1995)—20:1

Department of Environmental Quality Engineering v. Cumberland Farms of Connecticut, Inc., 18 Mass. App. Ct. 672, 469 N.E.2d 1286 (1984)—13:9

Department of Environmental Quality Engineering v. Town of Hingham, 15 Mass. App. Ct. 409, 446 N.E.2d 406 (1983)—13:9

Derby Refining Co. v. Board of Aldermen of Chelsea, 407 Mass. 718, 555 N.E.2d 584 (1990)—13:19

Derby Refining Co. v. City of Chelsea, 407 Mass. 703, 555 N.E.2d 534 (1990)—11:11

DeSanctis v. Planning Board of Saugus, 2 L.C.R. 12 (1994)—12:11

Des Brisay v. Foss, 264 Mass. 102, 162 N.E. 4 (1928)—4:5, 4:6, 4:7

Design Housing, Inc. v. Town of Stoughton, 6 L.C.R. 51 (1998)—12:12

DesLauries v. Shea, 300 Mass. 30, 13 N.E.2d 932 (1938)—20:36

Devine v. Town of Nantucket, 16 Mass. App. Ct. 548, 452 N.E.2d 1167 (1983)—2:5

Dewey v. Bulkley, 67 Mass. 416, 1 Gray 416, 1854 WL 4957 (1854)—10:4

Dial Away Co., Inc. v. Zoning Bd. of Appeals of Auburn, 41 Mass. App. Ct. 165, 669 N.E.2d 446 (1996)—11:13

Diamond Crystal Brands, Inc.

Farms, Inc., 4 L.C.R. 75 (1996)—17:16

Dufault v. Millennium Power Partners, L.P., 49 Mass. App. Ct. 137, 727 N.E.2d 87 (2000)—11:20

Duff v. U. S. Trust Co., 327 Mass. 17, 97 N.E.2d 189 (1951)—4:3

Dugan v. Wellock, 348 Mass. 778, 202 N.E.2d 921 (1964)—8:4

Duncan v. DiFranco, 2 L.C.R. 85 (1994)—16:3

Dunham v. Ware Sav. Bank, 384 Mass. 63, 423 N.E.2d 998 (1981)—20:18

Dunham's Corner Residents Association, Inc. v. Edgartown Planning Bd., 12 L.C.R. 163 (2004)—12:15

Dunphy v. Com., 368 Mass. 376, 331 N.E.2d 883 (1975)—15:14

Durand v. IDC Bellingham LLC, 10 L.C.R. 36 (2002)—11:5

Durkin v. Board of Appeals of Falmouth, 21 Mass. App. Ct. 450, 488 N.E.2d 6 (1986)—11:10

Dwyer v. Cempellin, 424 Mass. 26, 673 N.E.2d 863 (1996)—16:2, 16:4

Dyer v. Key, 4 L.C.R. 205 (1996)—15:10

Dzog Chen Community of America v. Town of Buckland, 10 L.C.R. 198 (2002)—11:6

E

East Boston Savings Bank v. Ogan, 5 L.C.R. 186 (1997)—20:31

Eastern Elec. Co. v. Taylor Woodrow Blitman Const. Corp., 11 Mass. App. Ct. 192, 414 N.E.2d 1023 (1981)—16:8

Edwards v. City of Boston, 408 Mass. 643, 562 N.E.2d 834,

63 Ed. Law Rep. 998 (1990)—2:8

Egbert v. Freedom Federal Sav. and Loan Ass'n, 14 Mass. App. Ct. 383, 440 N.E.2d 22 (1982)—20:18

Eisenberg v. Phoenix Ass'n Management, Inc., 56 Mass. App. Ct. 910, 777 N.E.2d 1265 (2002)—17:18

Elder Care Services, Inc. v. Zoning Bd. of Appeals of Hingham, 17 Mass. App. Ct. 480, 459 N.E.2d 832 (1984)—11:21

Electronics Corp. of America v. City Council of Cambridge, 348 Mass. 563, 204 N.E.2d 707 (1965)—2:6, 14:2

Eliades v. Callahan, 13 L.C.R. 225 (2005)—12:7, 12:9

Ellen M. Gifford Sheltering Home Corp. v. Board of Appeals of Wayland, 349 Mass. 292, 208 N.E.2d 207 (1965)—12:11

Ellis v. Wingate, 338 Mass. 481, 155 N.E.2d 783 (1959)—6:16

Elm Farm Foods Co. v. Cifrino, 328 Mass. 549, 105 N.E.2d 366 (1952)—1:8

Emerson College v. City of Boston, 393 Mass. 303, 471 N.E.2d 336, 21 Ed. Law Rep. 672 (1984)—11:27

Emerson College v. City of Boston, 391 Mass. 415, 462 N.E.2d 1098 (1984)—11:27

Emond v. Board of Appeals of Uxbridge, 27 Mass. App. Ct. 630, 541 N.E.2d 380 (1989)—11:20

Englander v. Department of Environmental Management, 16 Mass. App. Ct. 943, 450 N.E.2d 1120 (1983)—13:11

Enos v. City of Brockton, 354 Mass. 278, 236 N.E.2d 919 (1968)—11:6

Friends and Fishers of Edgartown Great Pond, Inc. v. Department of Environmental Protection, 446 Mass. 830, 848 N.E.2d 393 (2006)—13:8

Fulton v. Katsowney, 342 Mass. 503, 174 N.E.2d 366 (1961)—16:4

Fuss v. Fuss, 373 Mass. 445, 368 N.E.2d 276 (1977)—16:4

G

Gadreault v. Hillman, 317 Mass. 656, 59 N.E.2d 477 (1945)—7:2, 7:9, 7:18

Gage v. Town of Egremont, 409 Mass. 345, 566 N.E.2d 597 (1991)—11:20

Gagne v. City of Chicopee, 278 Mass. 121, 179 N.E. 680 (1932)—8:4

Gagnon v. Coombs, 39 Mass. App. Ct. 144, 654 N.E.2d 54 (1995)—6:11

Gallagher v. Board of Appeals of Acton, 44 Mass. App. Ct. 906, 687 N.E.2d 1277 (1997)—11:3

Gallitano v. Board of Survey and Planning of Waltham, 10 Mass. App. Ct. 269, 407 N.E.2d 359 (1980)—12:2

Gamsey v. Building Inspector of Chatham, 28 Mass. App. Ct. 614, 553 N.E.2d 1311 (1990)—17:25

Garabedian v. Water and Sewerage Bd. of Medfield, 359 Mass. 404, 269 N.E.2d 275 (1971)—12:12

Garabedian v. Westland, 59 Mass. App. Ct. 427, 796 N.E.2d 439 (2003)—11:21

Gardner-Athol Area Mental Health Ass'n, Inc. v. Zoning Bd. of Appeals of Gardner, 401 Mass. 12, 513 N.E.2d 1272, 42 Ed. Law Rep. 381 (1987)—11:6

Gardner v. Governor Apartments Associates, 396 Mass. 661, 488 N.E.2d 3 (1986)—2:6, 14:2

Garfield v. Board of Appeals of Rockport, 356 Mass. 37, 247 N.E.2d 720 (1969)—11:18, 11:22

Garland v. Rosenschein, 2 L.C.R. 52 (1994)—10:6

Garland v. Rosenshein, 420 Mass. 319, 649 N.E.2d 756 (1995)—15:9, 15:15

Garvey v. Board of Appeals of Amherst, 9 Mass. App. Ct. 856, 400 N.E.2d 880 (1980)—11:21

Gates v. Planning Bd. of Dighton, 48 Mass. App. Ct. 394, 722 N.E.2d 477 (2000)—12:2

Gattozzi v. Director of Inspection Services of Melrose, 6 Mass. App. Ct. 889, 376 N.E.2d 1266 (1978)—12:2, 12:4

General Chemical Corp. v. Department of Environmental Quality Engineering, 19 Mass. App. Ct. 287, 474 N.E.2d 183 (1985)—13:17

Gennari v. City of Revere, 23 Mass. App. Ct. 979, 503 N.E.2d 1331 (1987)—2:4

Geoffrion v. Lucier, 336 Mass. 532, 146 N.E.2d 654 (1957)—1:39

George v. Thornton, 6 L.C.R. 127 (1998)—20:33

Germagian v. Berrini, 60 Mass. App. Ct. 456, 803 N.E.2d 354 (2004)—3:1

Giarrizzo, In re, 128 B.R. 321 (Bankr. D. Mass. 1991)—16:2

Gifford v. Otis, 14 L.C.R. 197 (2006)—8:3

Gifford v. Planning Bd. of Nantucket, 376 Mass. 801, 383 N.E.2d 1123 (1978)—12:2

Gilman v. Gilman, 171 Mass. 46, 50 N.E. 452 (1898)—10:4

H

Hawkins v. Jamaicaway Place Condominium Trust, 409 Mass. 1005, 568 N.E.2d 1126 (1991)—17:22

Hawthorne's, Inc. v. Warrenton Realty, Inc., 414 Mass. 200, 606 N.E.2d 908 (1993)—3:2, 5:1

Hazen Paper Co. v. U.S. Fidelity and Guar. Co., 407 Mass. 689, 555 N.E.2d 576 (1990)—13:18

Heavey v. Board of Appeals of Chatham, 58 Mass. App. Ct. 401, 792 N.E.2d 651 (2003)—11:13

Heller v. Silverbranch Const. Corp., 376 Mass. 621, 382 N.E.2d 1065 (1978)—5:4

Heller v. Turner Bros. Const., Inc., 40 Mass. App. Ct. 363, 663 N.E.2d 1243 (1996)—6:25

Hendrickson v. Sears, 365 Mass. 83, 310 N.E.2d 131 (1974)—5:6, 21:9

Henry v. Board of Appeals of Dunstable, 418 Mass. 841, 641 N.E.2d 1334 (1994)—11:6

Heritage Park Dev. Corp. v. Town of Southbridge, 3 L.C.R. 93 (1995)—11:17

Hess v. Gilson, 4 L.C.R. 98 (1996)—15:15

Hickey v. Green, 14 Mass. App. Ct. 671, 442 N.E.2d 37 (1982)—4:7

Higgins v. Department of Environmental Protection, 64 Mass. App. Ct. 754, 835 N.E.2d 610 (2005)—13:12

Highlands Ins. Co. v. Aerovox Inc., 424 Mass. 226, 676 N.E.2d 801 (1997)—13:18

Highland Tap of Boston, Inc. v. Commissioner of Consumer Affairs and Licensing of Boston, 33 Mass. App. Ct. 559, 602 N.E.2d 1095 (1992)—11:5

Hill v. Levine, 252 Mass. 513, 147 N.E. 837 (1925)—15:14

Hill v. Metropolitan Dist. Com'n, 439 Mass. 266, 787 N.E.2d 526 (2003)—13:18

Hill v. Upton Zoning Bd. of Appeals, 12 L.C.R. 46 (2004)—11:8

Hillis v. Lake, 38 Mass. App. Ct. 221, 646 N.E.2d 1081 (1995)—3:4

Hillman v. Roman Catholic Bishop of Fall River, 24 Mass. App. Ct. 241, 508 N.E.2d 118, 39 Ed. Law Rep. 776 (1987)—6:16

Hobbs Brook Farm Property Co. Ltd. Partnership v. Conservation Com'n Of Lincoln, 65 Mass. App. Ct. 142, 838 N.E.2d 578 (2005)—13:10

Hobbs Brook Farm Property Co. Ltd. Partnership v. Planning Bd. of Lincoln, 48 Mass. App. Ct. 403, 721 N.E.2d 398 (2000)—12:2

Hodgkins v. Bianchini, 323 Mass. 169, 80 N.E.2d 464 (1948)—7:19, 15:9

Hogan v. Hayes, 19 Mass. App. Ct. 399, 474 N.E.2d 1158 (1985)—11:19, 11:24

Holmes v. Johnson, 324 Mass. 450, 86 N.E.2d 924 (1949)—7:2, 7:8, 7:9

Home-Like Apartments, Inc. v. Architectural Access Bd., 27 Mass. App. Ct. 851, 545 N.E.2d 58 (1989)—14:11

Home Builders Ass'n Of Cape Cod, Inc. v. Cape Cod Com'n, 441 Mass. 724, 808 N.E.2d 315 (2004)—14:14

Homer v. Town of Yarmouth, 40 Mass. App. Ct. 916, 662 N.E.2d 1056 (1996)—2:5

Homeside Lending, Inv. v. Hurley, 6 L.C.R. 104 (1998)—20:33

Hopengarten v. Board of Ap-

Kirkwood v. Board of Appeals of Rockport, 17 Mass. App. Ct. 423, 458 N.E.2d 1213 (1984)—11:18, 11:22

Klein v. Planning Bd. of Wrentham, 31 Mass. App. Ct. 777, 583 N.E.2d 892 (1992)—11:21

Kline v. Gutzler, 18 Mass. App. Ct. 915, 464 N.E.2d 399 (1984)—5:1

Knight v. Travell, 13 Mass. App. Ct. 1008, 433 N.E.2d 464 (1982)—10:18, 16:4

Knott v. Racicot, 442 Mass. 314, 812 N.E.2d 1207 (2004)—3:3

Knott v. Zoning Bd. of Appeals of Natick, 12 Mass. App. Ct. 1002, 429 N.E.2d 353 (1981)—11:21

Konover Management Corp. v. Planning Bd. of Auburn, 32 Mass. App. Ct. 319, 588 N.E.2d 1365 (1992)—11:22

Kostigen v. Leone, 4 L.C.R. 89 (1996)—20:38

Kostorizos v. Samia, 9 L.C.R. 117 (2001)—15:7

Kozdras v. Land/Vest Properties, Inc., 382 Mass. 34, 413 N.E.2d 1105 (1980)—8:3, 8:13, 8:14

Krikorian v. Grafton Co-op. Bank, 312 Mass. 272, 44 N.E.2d 665 (1942)—20:1

Kupperstein v. Planning Bd. of Cohasset, 66 Mass. App. Ct. 905, 845 N.E.2d 1141 (2006)—12:3

Kurker v. Shoestring Properties Ltd. Partnership, 68 Mass. App. Ct. 644, 864 N.E.2d 24 (2007)—3:1

Kurtz v. Salter, 8 L.C.R. 113 (2000)—15:10

Kurz v. Board of Appeals of North Reading, 341 Mass. 110, 167 N.E.2d 627 (1960)—11:6

L

Laberis v. Building Inspector of Peabody, 2 L.C.R. 99 (1994)—11:19

Labounty v. Vickers, 352 Mass. 337, 225 N.E.2d 333 (1967)—7:18, 7:19, 10:21, 15:3, 15:13, 15:14

La Chance v. Rubashe, 301 Mass. 488, 17 N.E.2d 685 (1938)—7:5

Ladd v. Swanson, 24 Mass. App. Ct. 644, 511 N.E.2d 1112 (1987)—16:2

LaFond v. Frame, 327 Mass. 364, 99 N.E.2d 51 (1951)—1:37

Lakeside Builders, Inc. v. Planning Bd. of Franklin, 56 Mass. App. Ct. 842, 780 N.E.2d 944 (2002)—12:12, 12:13

Lamarre v. Commissioner of Public Works of Fall River, 324 Mass. 542, 87 N.E.2d 211 (1949)—11:5

Lamontagne v. Knightly, 30 Mass. App. Ct. 647, 572 N.E.2d 1375 (1991)—2:5

Landers v. Board of Appeals of Falmouth, 31 Mass. App. Ct. 939, 579 N.E.2d 1375 (1991)—11:7

Landgraf Associates, Inc. v. Building Commissioner of Springfield, 4 Mass. App. Ct. 840, 354 N.E.2d 887 (1976)—12:8

Lane v. Provost, 9 L.C.R. 324 (2001)—17:13

Lane v. Zoning Bd. of Appeals of Falmouth, 65 Mass. App. Ct. 434, 841 N.E.2d 260 (2006)—11:7, 15:3, 15:5, 15:8

Langton v. LaBrecque, 25 Mass. App. Ct. 463, 519 N.E.2d 1361 (1988)—17:17

Lantner v. Carson, 374 Mass. 606, 373 N.E.2d 973 (1978)—5:4

Levy v. Reardon, 43 Mass. App. Ct. 431, 683 N.E.2d 713 (1997)—17:15

Lewis v. Crowell, 205 Mass. 497, 91 N.E. 910 (1910)—10:5

Lewis v. Emerson, 391 Mass. 517, 462 N.E.2d 295 (1984)—3:4

Lewis v. Town of Leverett, 5 L.C.R. 116 (1997)—10:8

Libby v. Gaughan, 14 L.C.R. 214 (2006)—12:2

Liberty Mut. Ins. Co. v. SCA Services, Inc., 412 Mass. 330, 588 N.E.2d 1346 (1992)—13:18

Libman v. Zuckerman, 33 Mass. App. Ct. 341, 599 N.E.2d 642 (1992)—5:6, 17:22

Licker v. Gluskin, 265 Mass. 403, 164 N.E. 613 (1929)—16:5

Lilley v. Rich, 27 Mass. App. Ct. 1212, 545 N.E.2d 622 (1989)—17:20

Lima v. Lima, 30 Mass. App. Ct. 479, 570 N.E.2d 158 (1991)—6:12

Linhares v. Medeiros, 14 Mass. App. Ct. 927, 436 N.E.2d 1233 (1982)—12:2, 12:4

Linse v. O'Meara, 338 Mass. 338, 155 N.E.2d 448 (1959)—5:1

Locke v. Spaulding, 24 Mass. App. Ct. 977, 512 N.E.2d 1145 (1987)—17:17

Lombard v. Board of Appeal of Wellesley, 348 Mass. 788, 204 N.E.2d 471 (1965)—11:21

Lomelis v. Board of Appeals of Marblehead, 17 Mass. App. Ct. 962, 458 N.E.2d 740 (1983)—11:11, 11:22

Long v. Board of Appeals of Falmouth, 32 Mass. App. Ct. 232, 588 N.E.2d 692 (1992)—11:17

Long v. Lowrey, 243 Mass. 414, 137 N.E. 634 (1923)—6:12

Long Pond Estates, Ltd. v. Planning Bd. of Sturbridge, 406 Mass. 253, 547 N.E.2d 914 (1989)—12:2

Lopes v. Board of Appeals of Fairhaven, 27 Mass. App. Ct. 754, 543 N.E.2d 421 (1989)—11:19

Lopes v. City of Peabody, 3 L.C.R. 78 (1995)—11:22

Lopes v. City of Peabody, 417 Mass. 299, 629 N.E.2d 1312 (1994)—11:5

Lord v. Zoning Bd. of Appeals of Somerset, 30 Mass. App. Ct. 226, 567 N.E.2d 954 (1991)—10:17, 11:25

Lordan v. Town of Pepperell, 11 L.C.R. 252 (2003)—11:5

Lorden v. Town of Templeton, 13 L.C.R. 319 (2005)—11:4

Loring Hills Developers Trust v. Planning Bd. of Salem, 5 Mass. App. Ct. 813, 361 N.E.2d 417 (1977)—12:7

Loud v. Pendergast, 206 Mass. 122, 92 N.E. 40 (1910)—15:13

Lovequist v. Conservation Commission of Town of Dennis, 379 Mass. 7, 393 N.E.2d 858 (1979)—11:20, 13:10

Lowell Inst. v. City of Lowell, 153 Mass. 530, 27 N.E. 518 (1891)—15:14

Lucas v. South Carolina Coastal Council, 505 U.S. 1003, 112 S. Ct. 2886, 120 L. Ed. 2d 798 (1992)—11:5

Lumbermens Mut. Cas. Co. v. Belleville Industries, Inc., 407 Mass. 675, 555 N.E.2d 568 (1990)—13:18

Lussier v. Zoning Bd. of Appeals of Peabody, 447 Mass. 531, 854 N.E.2d 1236 (2006)—11:18

Lynch v. Andrew, 20 Mass. App.

Marblehead, Town of v. Deery, 356 Mass. 532, 254 N.E.2d 234 (1969)—11:24

Marblehead, Town of v. Rosenthal, 316 Mass. 124, 55 N.E.2d 13 (1944)—11:5

Marco Realty Trust v. Commissioner of Revenue, 385 Mass. 798, 434 N.E.2d 200 (1982)—16:13

Margolis v. Tarutz, 265 Mass. 540, 164 N.E. 451 (1929)—1:37, 5:1

Marinelli v. Board of Appeal of Bldg. Dept. of City of Boston, 275 Mass. 169, 175 N.E. 479 (1931)—11:21

Marinelli v. Board Of Appeals Of Stoughton, 65 Mass. App. Ct. 902, 840 N.E.2d 61 (2005)—11:13

Marinelli v. Board of Appeals of Stoughton, 440 Mass. 255, 797 N.E.2d 893 (2003)—11:13, 12:4

Marlborough Sav. Bank v. City of Marlborough, 45 Mass. App. Ct. 250, 697 N.E.2d 143 (1998)—12:8

Marr v. Back Bay Architectural Com'n, 32 Mass. App. Ct. 962, 592 N.E.2d 756 (1992)—11:27

Marr v. Back Bay Architectural Com'n, 23 Mass. App. Ct. 679, 505 N.E.2d 534 (1987)—11:27

Marshall v. Francis, 327 Mass. 702, 100 N.E.2d 840 (1951)—8:3, 8:4, 10:4

Martignetti v. Haigh-Farr Inc., 425 Mass. 294, 680 N.E.2d 1131 (1997)—13:18

Martin v. Building Inspector of Freetown, 38 Mass. App. Ct. 509, 649 N.E.2d 779 (1995)—6:29, 15:11

Martin v. Corporation of Presiding Bishop of Church of Jesus Christ of Latter-Day Saints, 434 Mass. 141, 747 N.E.2d 131 (2001)—11:6

Martin v. Town of Rockland, 1 Mass. App. Ct. 167, 294 N.E.2d 469 (1973)—11:5

Masa Builders, Inc. v. Hanson, 30 Mass. App. Ct. 930, 568 N.E.2d 636 (1991)—7:5

Maselbas v. Zoning Bd. of Appeals of North Attleborough, 45 Mass. App. Ct. 54, 694 N.E.2d 1314 (1998)—11:11

Mass., Com. of v. Pace, 616 F. Supp. 815 (D. Mass. 1985)—13:18

Massachusetts Broken Stone Co. v. Town of Weston, 430 Mass. 637, 723 N.E.2d 7 (2000)—11:17

Massachusetts Company, The v. Midura, 3 L.C.R. 138 (1995)—20:35

Massachusetts Rental Housing Ass'n, Inc. v. Lead Poisoning Control Director, 49 Mass. App. Ct. 359, 729 N.E.2d 673 (2000)—14:11

Massey v. Cloutier, 26 Mass. App. Ct. 1003, 530 N.E.2d 359 (1988)—20:33

Massidda v. Lurvey, 12 L.C.R. 95 (2004)—6:12

Mastriani v. Building Inspector of Monson, 19 Mass. App. Ct. 989, 475 N.E.2d 408 (1985)—11:5

Matulewicz v. Planning Bd. of Norfolk, 438 Mass. 37, 777 N.E.2d 153 (2002)—12:2

Maurice Callahan & Sons, Inc. v. Board of Appeals of Lenox, 30 Mass. App. Ct. 36, 565 N.E.2d 813 (1991)—11:18

Mavro v. CKA, LLC, 11 L.C.R. 46 (2003)—11:7

Mavro v. DKA, LLC, 11 L.C.R. 46 (2003)—14:13

May v. New England R. Co., 171

McLaughlin v. Town of Marblehead, 68 Mass. App. Ct.
490, 863 N.E.2d 61 (2007)—
7:4, 8:4

McLaughlin v. Rockland Zoning
Bd. of Appeals, 351 Mass.
678, 223 N.E.2d 521
(1967)—11:18

McLean Hospital Corporation v.
Town of Belmont, 8 L.C.R.
155 (2000)—11:5

McLendon v. Town of Stockbridge, 13 L.C.R. 241
(2005)—11:3

McMahan v. McMahan, 205
Mass. 99, 91 N.E. 298
(1910)—10:5

McManus v. City of Boston, 171
Mass. 152, 50 N.E. 607
(1898)—4:5

McMullen v. Porch, 286 Mass.
383, 190 N.E. 835 (1934)—
8:3

McOuatt v. McOuatt, 320 Mass.
410, 69 N.E.2d 806 (1946)—
6:9, 19:11

M. DeMatteo Const. Co. v.
Board of Appeals of Hing-
ham, 3 Mass. App. Ct. 446,
334 N.E.2d 51 (1975)—
11:17, 12:13

Meachen v. Selectmen of Sudbury, 6 L.C.R. 235 (1998)—
14:4

Meadowbrooks Development
Corp. v. Medway, 6 L.C.R.
110 (1998)—11:6

Mechanics Nat. Bank of Worcester v. Killeen, 377 Mass.
100, 384 N.E.2d 1231, 25
U.C.C. Rep. Serv. 891
(1979)—5:4

Melrose Housing Authority v.
New Hampshire Ins. Co.,
402 Mass. 27, 520 N.E.2d
493 (1988)—5:6

Menard v. Courchaine, 278
Mass. 7, 179 N.E. 167
(1931)—20:1

Mendes v. Board of Appeals of
Barnstable, 28 Mass. App.

Ct. 527, 552 N.E.2d 604
(1990)—11:10

Mendonca v. Cities Service Oil
Co. of Pa., 354 Mass. 323,
237 N.E.2d 16 (1968)—7:1,
7:2, 7:9

Merry v. A.W. Perry, Inc., 18
Mass. App. Ct. 628, 469
N.E.2d 73 (1984)—5:1

Merry v. White, 13 L.C.R. 339
(2005)—15:10

Metropolitan Credit Union v.
Matthes, 46 Mass. App. Ct.
326, 706 N.E.2d 296
(1999)—4:3

Meyer v. Planning Bd. of Westport, 29 Mass. App. Ct. 167,
558 N.E.2d 994 (1990)—
12:13

Michaelson v. Silver Beach Imp.
Ass'n, Inc., 342 Mass. 251,
173 N.E.2d 273, 91
A.L.R.2d 846 (1961)—8:7

Michelson v. Sherman, 310
Mass. 774, 39 N.E.2d 633,
139 A.L.R. 960 (1942)—4:5

Middleborough, Town of v.
Housing Appeals Commit-
tee, 66 Mass. App. Ct. 39,
845 N.E.2d 1143 (2006)—
11:7

Middlesex & Boston St. Ry. Co.
v. Board of Aldermen of
Newton, 371 Mass. 849, 359
N.E.2d 1279 (1977)—11:21

Mierzwa v. Planning Bd. of Haverhill, 7 L.C.R. 240 (1999)—
12:9

Miles v. Planning Bd. of Millbury, 404 Mass. 489, 536
N.E.2d 328 (1989)—12:11,
12:12

Milford, Town of v. Boyd, 434
Mass. 754, 752 N.E.2d 732
(2001)—17:21

Milford Common J.V. Trust, In
re, 117 B.R. 15 (Bankr. D.
Mass. 1990)—20:10

Miller v. Board of Appeals of
Canton, 8 Mass. App. Ct.
923, 396 N.E.2d 180
(1979)—11:17

Moskow v. Commissioner of Dept. of Environmental Management, 384 Mass. 530, 427 N.E.2d 750 (1981)—13:11

M.P.M. Builders, LLC v. Dwyer, 442 Mass. 87, 809 N.E.2d 1053 (2004)—15:6

Mt. Washington Co-op. Bank v. Benard, 289 Mass. 498, 194 N.E. 839 (1935)—6:4

Mucci v. Brockton Bocce Club, Inc., 19 Mass. App. Ct. 155, 472 N.E.2d 966 (1985)—3:3, 10:2

Muir v. City of Leominster, 2 Mass. App. Ct. 587, 317 N.E.2d 212 (1974)—2:4

Mullen Lumber Co., Inc. v. Board of Appeals of Marshfield, 7 Mass. App. Ct. 917, 389 N.E.2d 736 (1979)—11:17

Mullett v. Peltier, 31 Mass. App. Ct. 445, 579 N.E.2d 174 (1991)—3:2

Mulvanity v. Pelletier, 40 Mass. App. Ct. 106, 661 N.E.2d 952 (1996)—4:7

Murley v. Murley, 334 Mass. 627, 137 N.E.2d 909 (1956)—20:5

Murphy v. Board of Selectmen of Manchester, 1 Mass. App. Ct. 407, 298 N.E.2d 885 (1973)—11:15

Murphy v. Charlestown Sav. Bank, 380 Mass. 738, 405 N.E.2d 954 (1980)—5:4

Murphy v. Kotlik, 34 Mass. App. Ct. 410, 611 N.E.2d 741 (1993)—11:10, 11:11

Murphy v. Mart Realty of Brockton, Inc., 348 Mass. 675, 205 N.E.2d 222 (1965)—15:3, 15:9

Murphy v. Olsen, 63 Mass. App. Ct. 417, 826 N.E.2d 249 (2005)—15:3

Murphy v. Planning Bd. of Hopkinton, 14 L.C.R. 143 (2006)—15:14

Murphy v. Planning Board of Pembroke, 3 L.C.R. 200 (1995)—12:2

Murphy v. Smith, 411 Mass. 133, 579 N.E.2d 165 (1991)—21:9

Murray v. Board of Appeals of Barnstable, 22 Mass. App. Ct. 473, 494 N.E.2d 1364 (1986)—11:11

Murray v. Sullivan, 13 L.C.R. 193 (2005)—15:10

Musto v. Planning Bd. of Medfield, 54 Mass. App. Ct. 831, 768 N.E.2d 588 (2002)—12:12, 12:13

Muto v. City of Springfield, 349 Mass. 479, 209 N.E.2d 319 (1965)—11:5

Myers v. Salin, 13 Mass. App. Ct. 127, 431 N.E.2d 233 (1982)—15:13

N

Nab's Corner Realty Trust v. Martha's Vineyard Com'n, 9 L.C.R. 444 (2001)—14:13

NAB Asset Venture III, L.P. v. Brockton Credit Union, 62 Mass. App. Ct. 181, 815 N.E.2d 606 (2004)—20:6, 20:27, 20:39

Nab Asset Venture III, L.P. v. Gillespie, 7 L.C.R. 375 (1999)—15:2

Nahigian v. Lexington, 1 L.C.R. 1 (1993)—12:12

Nahigian v. Town of Lexington, 32 Mass. App. Ct. 517, 591 N.E.2d 1095 (1992)—12:11, 12:12

Nantucket Conservation Foundation, Inc. v. Russell Management, Inc., 2 Mass. App. Ct. 868, 316 N.E.2d 625 (1974)—15:5

Nantucket Land Council, Inc. v. Planning Bd. of Nantucket,

v. Watertown Zoning Bd. of Appeals, 12 L.C.R. 301 (2004)—11:7

State St. Bank & Trust Co. v. Beale, 353 Mass. 103, 227 N.E.2d 924 (1967)—8:9

St. Botolph Citizens Committee, Inc. v. Boston Redevelopment Authority, 429 Mass. 1, 705 N.E.2d 617 (1999)—2:6, 11:27, 14:2

Steege v. Board of Appeals of Stow, 26 Mass. App. Ct. 970, 527 N.E.2d 1176 (1988)—11:6

Stefanick v. Planning Bd. of Uxbridge, 39 Mass. App. Ct. 418, 657 N.E.2d 475 (1995)—12:15

Stenmark Realty Trust v. Finn, 1 L.C.R. 163 (1993)—6:16

Sterling, Town of v. Poulin, 2 Mass. App. Ct. 562, 316 N.E.2d 737 (1974)—11:24

Stivaletta v. Zoning Bd. of Appeals of Medfield, 12 Mass. App. Ct. 994, 429 N.E.2d 66 (1981)—11:21

Stone v. Perkins, 59 Mass. App. Ct. 265, 795 N.E.2d 583 (2003)—7:18

Stone v. W.E. Aubuchon Co., Inc., 29 Mass. App. Ct. 523, 562 N.E.2d 852 (1990)—3:2

Stonehedge Farm Condominium Associates v. American Stonehenge, Inc., 6 L.C.R. 286 (1998)—17:15

Stonehedge Farm Condominium Trust v. American Stonehenge, Inc., 13 L.C.R. 176 (2005)—17:15

Stop & Shop Supermarket Co. v. Urstadt Biddle Properties, Inc., 433 Mass. 285, 740 N.E.2d 1286 (2001)—15:14

Strauss v. Oyster River Condominium Trust, 417 Mass. 442, 631 N.E.2d 979 (1994)—17:13

Strazzulla v. Building Inspector of Wellesley, 357 Mass. 694, 260 N.E.2d 163 (1970)—11:21

Striar v. Cape Cod Com'n, 4 L.C.R. 221 (1996)—14:14

Sturbridge, Town of v. McDowell, 35 Mass. App. Ct. 924, 624 N.E.2d 114 (1993)—11:6

Sturdy v. Planning Bd. of Hingham, 32 Mass. App. Ct. 72, 586 N.E.2d 11 (1992)—12:2

Sturges v. Town of Chilmark, 380 Mass. 246, 402 N.E.2d 1346 (1980)—11:4, 11:13

Sturnick v. Watson, 336 Mass. 139, 142 N.E.2d 896 (1957)—15:2

Subaru of New England, Inc. v. Board of Appeals of Canton, 8 Mass. App. Ct. 483, 395 N.E.2d 880 (1979)—11:21

Sudbury, Town of v. Mahoney, 9 L.C.R. 297 (2001)—14:4

Sudbury, Town of v. Scott, 439 Mass. 288, 787 N.E.2d 536 (2003)—14:4

Suga v. Maum, 29 Mass. App. Ct. 733, 565 N.E.2d 793 (1991)—6:16

Sullivan v. Town of Acton, 38 Mass. App. Ct. 113, 645 N.E.2d 700 (1995)—11:5

Sullivan v. Board of Appeals of Belmont, 346 Mass. 81, 190 N.E.2d 83 (1963)—11:18

Sullivan v. Board of Appeals of Harwich, 15 Mass. App. Ct. 286, 445 N.E.2d 174 (1983)—11:11

Sullivan v. Burkin, 390 Mass. 864, 460 N.E.2d 572 (1984)—6:32

Sullivan v. F.E. Atteaux & Co., 284 Mass. 515, 187 N.E. 906 (1933)—10:1

Sullivan v. Leonard, 13 L.C.R. 482 (2005)—15:10

Sullivan v. Planning Bd. of Acton, 38 Mass. App. Ct. 918,

Ass'n v. Board of Appeal of Boston, 426 Mass. 485, 688 N.E.2d 1363 (1998)—17:20

Tiffany v. Sturbridge Camping Club, Inc., 32 Mass. App. Ct. 173, 587 N.E.2d 238 (1992)—18:10

Tindley v. Department of Environmental Quality Engineering, 10 Mass. App. Ct. 623, 411 N.E.2d 187 (1980)—15:8

Tisbury, Town of v. Martha's Vineyard Com'n, 27 Mass. App. Ct. 1204, 544 N.E.2d 230 (1989)—11:6

Tisbury Fuel Service, Inc. v. Martha's Vineyard Com'n, 68 Mass. App. Ct. 773, 864 N.E.2d 1229 (2007)—14:13

Tisdale v. Brabrook, 102 Mass. 374, 1869 WL 5754 (1869)—10:4

Titcomb v. Board of Appeals of Sandwich, 64 Mass. App. Ct. 725, 835 N.E.2d 295 (2005)—11:11

Toda v. Board of Appeals of Manchester, 18 Mass. App. Ct. 317, 465 N.E.2d 277 (1984)—11:3

Tofias v. Butler, 26 Mass. App. Ct. 89, 523 N.E.2d 796 (1988)—11:6

Toothaker v. Planning Bd. of Billerica, 346 Mass. 436, 193 N.E.2d 582 (1963)—12:12

Tortorella v. Board of Health of Bourne, 39 Mass. App. Ct. 277, 655 N.E.2d 633 (1995)—14:7

Tosney v. Chelmsford Village Condominium Ass'n, 397 Mass. 683, 493 N.E.2d 488 (1986)—17:3, 17:6

Totman v. Malloy, 431 Mass. 143, 725 N.E.2d 1045 (2000)—7:8, 7:11

Town Council of Franklin v.

Zoning Bd. of Appeals of Bellingham, 6 L.C.R. 334 (1998)—11:23

Trager v. Peabody Redevelopment Authority, 367 F. Supp. 1000 (D. Mass. 1973)—2:6, 14:2

Tremblay v. Tewksbury Bd. of Appeals, 11 L.C.R. 206 (2003)—11:19

Tremont Tower Condominium, LLC v. George B.H. Macomber Co., 436 Mass. 677, 767 N.E.2d 20 (2002)—6:22

Trenz v. Town of Norwell, 68 Mass. App. Ct. 271, 861 N.E.2d 777 (2007)—7:19, 15:6

Trial v. Rodrigues, 3 L.C.R. 232 (1995)—19:16

Triangle Center, Inc. v. Department of Public Works, 386 Mass. 858, 438 N.E.2d 798 (1982)—8:3, 8:14

Trifiro v. New York Life Ins. Co., 845 F.2d 30 (1st Cir. 1988)—3:1

Trio Algarvio, Inc. v. Commissioner of Dept. of Environmental Protection, 440 Mass. 94, 795 N.E.2d 1148 (2003)—13:12

Tristram's Landing, Inc. v. Wait, 367 Mass. 622, 327 N.E.2d 727 (1975)—3:4

True v. Wisniowski, 13 Mass. App. Ct. 501, 434 N.E.2d 686 (1982)—6:25

Trust for Public Land, The v. Farmer, 4 L.C.R. 90 (1996)—14:4

Tsagronis v. Board of Appeals of Wareham, 415 Mass. 329, 613 N.E.2d 893 (1993)—11:23

Tsagronis v. Board of Appeals of Wareham, 33 Mass. App. Ct. 55, 596 N.E.2d 369 (1992)—11:18

Tucker v. Poch, 321 Mass. 321, 73 N.E.2d 595 (1947)—7:18

571, 132 N.E. 348 (1921)—
7:8

Van Renselaar v. City of Springfield, 58 Mass. App. Ct. 104,
787 N.E.2d 1148 (2003)—
11:5

Vazza Properties, Inc. v. City
Council of Woburn, 1 Mass.
App. Ct. 308, 296 N.E.2d
220 (1973)—11:21

Veterans' Agent of Randolph v.
Rinaldi, 21 Mass. App. Ct.
901, 483 N.E.2d 829
(1985)—16:7

Vickery v. Walton, 26 Mass.
App. Ct. 1030, 533 N.E.2d
1381 (1989)—3:1

Viera v. Zoning Bd. Of Appeals
of Basrnstable, 4 L.C.R. 285
(1996)—11:6

Villages Development Co., Inc.
v. Secretary of Executive
Office of Environmental Affairs, 410 Mass. 100, 571
N.E.2d 361 (1991)—13:3

Viola v. Millbank II Associates,
44 Mass. App. Ct. 82, 688
N.E.2d 996 (1997)—17:13

Vitale v. Hanson Zoning Bd. of
Appeals, 9 L.C.R. 189
(2001)—11:21

Vitale v. Planning Bd. of Newburyport, 10 Mass. App. Ct.
483, 409 N.E.2d 237
(1980)—12:7

Vokes v. Avery W. Lovell, Inc.,
18 Mass. App. Ct. 471, 468
N.E.2d 271 (1984)—11:11

Volandre v. Bd. of Appeals of
Norwell, 13 L.C.R. 465
(2005)—11:6

Volandre v. Opdyke, 14 L.C.R.
384 (2006)—11:22

Von Jess v. Bd. of Appeals of
Littleton, 1 L.C.R. 170
(1993)—11:6

V.S.H. Realty, Inc. v. Texaco,
Inc., 757 F.2d 411 (1st Cir.
1985)—13:18

V.S.H. Realty, Inc. v. Zoning Bd.

of Appeals of Plymouth, 30
Mass. App. Ct. 530, 570
N.E.2d 1044 (1991)—11:21

W

Wagley v. Danforth, 46 Mass.
App. Ct. 15, 702 N.E.2d 822
(1998)—16:9

Wagner v. Bd. of Appeals of
Acton, 2 L.C.R. 141 (1994)—
10:17

Waldron v. Planning Bd. of
Dartmouth, 2 L.C.R. 3
(1994)—12:15

Walker v. Board of Appeals of
Harwich, 388 Mass. 42, 445
N.E.2d 141 (1983)—11:21

Walker v. Gross, 362 Mass. 703,
290 N.E.2d 543 (1972)—10:6

Walker v. Sanderson, 348 Mass.
409, 204 N.E.2d 108
(1965)—10:6, 15:15

Walker Development Corp. v.
Gore, 14 L.C.R. 280
(2006)—12:2

Walker Realty, LLC v. Planning
Bd. of Hopkinton, 10 L.C.R.
63 (2002)—11:6

Wallace v. Building Inspector of
Woburn, 5 Mass. App. Ct.
786, 360 N.E.2d 664
(1977)—11:9

Walorz v. Town of Braintree, 2
L.C.R. 53 (1994)—10:16

Walpole, Town of v. Secretary of
the Executive Office of Environmental Affairs, 405
Mass. 67, 537 N.E.2d 1244
(1989)—13:3

Walters v. Voicestream Wireless, 11 L.C.R. 147 (2003)—
11:8

Warcewicz v. Department of
Environmental Protection,
410 Mass. 548, 574 N.E.2d
364 (1991)—13:9

Wareham, Town of v. Onset Bay
Corporation, 10 L.C.R. 131
(2002)—2:5

Wareham Land Trust v. A.D.

Index